The

WAR & PEACE

Of A New

METAPHYSICAL PERCEPTION

Volume I

Daniel J. Shepard

&

Stephen Moore

Editing & Layout

Global Publications, Binghamton University
Binghamton, New York
2002

Copyright © 2002 by Daniel J. Shepard

All rights reserved. No portion of this publication may be duplicated in any way without the expressed written consent of the publisher or author, except in the form of brief excerpts or quotations for purpose of review or scholarly research.

Published and distributed by Global Publications

LNG 99, Binghamton University
State University of New York at Binghamton
Binghamton, New York, 13902-6000
(607) 777-4495. Fax (607) 777-6132
e-mail: pmorewed@binghamton.edu
http://ssips.binghamton.edu

Library of Congress Cataloging-in-Publication Data

Shepard, Daniel J., 1945-
 The war and peace of a new metaphysical perception / Daniel J. Shepard.
     p. cm.
Includes bibliographical references and index.
 ISBN 1-58684-168-8 (pbk. : alk. paper)
 1. Metaphysics. 2. Panentheism. I. Title.
BD111 .S49 2002
110--dc21

2002002686

Please visit our companion websites:

www.panentheism.com
   A New Metaphysical Perception
www.wehope.com
   A Competition for a Universal Philosophy
www.e-philosophyonline.com
   Online Philosophy Resource

Universal Ethics Emerging from Metaphysical Perceptions
Metaphysical Systems

About the Author:

Daniel J. Shepard was born 1945. He graduated with a Bachelor of Science Degree from the University of Michigan in 1967 and obtained his Master of Science Degree from Eastern Michigan University in 1975. He taught mathematics and science for thirty years and is presently retired.

Abstract:

'being' *being* 'Being' – Symbiotic Panentheism
A Perceptual Shift for Humankind

'being' *being* 'Being' - symbiotic panentheism establishes a metaphysical model that accepts, while at the same time dismantles, the paradoxes of omnipresence, omniscience, and omnipotence. In addition, it is a model that circumvents the state of permanent equilibrium we have assigned to 'Being', a state we often refer to as stagnation. The foundation of panentheism, defining the location of reality in terms of 'Being's' location, doesn't seem to be immensely significant, but the subtlety leads to the initiation of enormous perceptual and behavioral shifts for our specie, society, the environment, and the individual. Panentheism addresses the paradox of omnipresence, omnipotence, and omniscience through accepting the concepts of omnipotence, omnipresence, and omniscience while at the same time acknowledging the full significance of these concepts by recognizing 'Being's' ability to become even more so. Under the symbiotic portion of symbiotic panentheism, the significance of the human specie - the significance of the individual - is placed at the level of 'Being' and given an importance to 'Being'; thus emerges the rationality for the respect due to the individual. Symbiotic panentheism places the soul, 'being', in a symbiotic relationship with 'Being'. Under the model of 'being' being 'Being', nothing, not even annihilation of our reality's physical mechanism, can diminish our purpose for existence. Nothing, not even total annihilation of our reality itself, can destroy our accomplishments as souls, for they transcend reality itself and embrace - fuse - with the very essence of God. Symbiotic panentheism displays its full impact by placing the responsibility for individual actions where it belongs - with the individual. Symbiotic panentheism also provides the logic needed to dismantle all hierarchical systems and perceptions of relative worth. 'being' *being* 'Being' eliminates the most fundamental hierarchical system created by humankind for humankind - the hierarchy system between God and humans. It eliminates status levels between beings. 'being' *being* 'Being' does not destroy what humanity has; it adds to what humanity has. 'being' *being* 'Being' accepts the significance of 'Being' to the individual and to the species. At the same time, it adds the significance of the individual and of the species to 'Being'. God is significant to humanity. Humanity has significance to God.

**To Err is
Human**

**To Forgive
Divine**

•

Alexander Pope

The Distant Past

500 BC – 1804 AD

❖

On

'being'

Passive Observation

Introduction

In the history of Western philosophy we have established two fundamental metaphysically unique and opposing systems: Aristotelian Cartesianism and Hegelian non-Cartesianism.

The War and Peace of a New Metaphysical Perception introduces a third fundamental metaphysical system.

The work is intent upon establishing the understanding of a new metaphysical system which combines the Aristotelian metaphysical system of Cartesianism and the Hegelian metaphysical system of non-Cartesianism into one system.

The new metaphysical system being put forward is a metaphysical system composed of three elements: singularity, multiplicity, and nothingness. The element of singularity is characterized as being non-Cartesian in nature. The element of multiplicity is characterized as being Cartesian in nature. Within the system as a whole, the Cartesian portion of the system powers the non-Cartesian portion of the system. A third element, nothingness, plays an important - but not necessarily essential - role within the system.

All three elements begin in the passive state of being and proceed to the active state of being through *being – action/process/reality*.

There are four states of being within the system:

1. 'being'/knowing n.: Individuality – existence of multiplicity
2. 'Being'/Knowing n.: The whole/summation in the form of singularity – existence of singularity
3. *being/knowing vb.*: The universe – action/process/reality – the active state of existence
4. being/unknowing vb.: The passive state of existence

The understanding of the four states of being can philosophically be described as 'knowing' *knowing* 'Knowing' or 'being' *being* 'Being'. Cosmologically and Ontologically the description might best be described as 'symbiotic panentheism'.

This new metaphysical system incorporates both a Cartesian and non-Cartesian system where the Cartesian lies within the non-Cartesian. Within the non-Cartesian aspect of the system, 'Being' and 'being' are abstractions and the Cartesian aspect of the system is not 'something' rather the Cartesian aspect of the system, the universe, is a 'process' providing the means by which 'being' and 'Being' interact and thus the Cartesian aspect of the system is perceived as 'something'

The work demonstrates what 'being', 'Being', *being*, and being are and how it is they interact.

The work generates an understanding of 'being' *being* 'Being'.

The work begins in complexity and ends in simplicity. The reason the work begins in complexity and moves toward simplicity originates from the understanding that we live in a complex world and it is from the point in time within which we find ourselves that we must begin, since it is reality with which this work deals.

The new metaphysical perception being presented suggests potentially new perceptions capable of resolving long-time paradoxes we face. The work does not suggest the philosophical works being examined were short sighted. Paradoxes are paradoxes because the limits of knowledge allow them to remain irresolvable in nature.

The metaphysical system is composed of two subset systems existing simultaneously. Each system simultaneously operates both independently and dependently one upon the other. The two systems are singularity and multiplicity.

Cartesian system/multiplicity generates a unique perception of 'one follows the other'. This Cartesian perception, existing in a vacuum void non-Cartesianism, establishes the perception of 'relative worth', relative value, which in turn leads to the perception of transcendence, which in turn leads to the perception of human purpose being the glorification of… So it was, 'being', individuality/multiplicity, became subservient to 'Being'/singularity.

A non-Cartesian system/singularity generates its own unique perception. The non-Cartesian perception, existing in a vacuum void Cartesianism, establishes the perception of nihilism, lack of purpose, and finally: "God is Dead" – Nietzsche.

The new metaphysical system reverses the negativity generated by the Cartesianism metaphysical system and the negativity generated by the non-Cartesian metaphysical system.

In addition, the new metaphysical system generates perceptions rationalizing actions steeped in pluralism as opposed to the presently existing metaphysical systems, which generate perceptions rationalizing actions steeped in exclusivism or inclusivism. Much is being said about perception. Why is perception important?

- Perception generates actions
- Actions generate reactions
- Reactions generate social ambiance
- And it is social ambiance which washes over each and every one of us day in and day out

The work adds a new metaphysical perception to humanities short list of two metaphysical systems: Aristotle – Cartesianism and Kant/Hegel – non-Cartesianism.

Table of Contents

Volume I - The Distant Past

On 'being': Cartesianism - Passive Observation

Introduction: Metaphysical system number three

#1:	The Error of Zeno	Resolving the problem of Abstraction	1
#2:	The Error of Aristotle	Resolving the problem of Cartesianism	75
#3:	The Error of Boethius	Resolving the problem of Free Will	147
#4:	The Error of Copernicus	Resolving the problem of Centricism	233
$5:	The Error of Leibniz	Resolving the problem of Theodicy	331
#6:	The Error of Kant	Resolving the problem of Universal Ethics	367

Volume II - The Recent Past

On 'being' *being:* Non-Cartesianism - Active Observation

Preface: A New Tool for Conflict Resolution

#7:	The Error of Hegel	Resolving the problem of non-Cartesianism
$8:	The Error of Einstein	Resolving the problem of 'i'
#9:	The Error of Russell	Resolving the problem of Non-Members
#10:	The Error of Heidegger	Resolving the problem of The Void of a Void
#11:	The Error of Philosophy	Resolving the problem of Either/Or
#12:	The Error of 'being' *being*	Resolving the problem of Nihilism

Volume III - The Future

On 'being' *being* 'Being': Cartesianism 'within' Non-Cartesianism:
Active Observation within Passive Observation

Preface: How to Regain the Love of Wisdom

#13:	Metaphysical System 28	Introducing the problem of Metaphysical Systems 7 & 9
#14:	Principle Three	Introducing the problem of Principles One and Two
#15:	Ockham's Razor	Introducing the problem of Reductionism
#16:	Wrong Again	Introducing the problem of Being Right
#17:	The Beginning	Introducing the problem of The End
#18:	Why Now?	Introducing the problem of History's Vector

Conclusion: The Peer Review

Table of Contents - Expanded

Volume I: 500 BC – 1804 AD The Distant Past
On 'being': Cartesianism - Passive Observation

Introduction: Metaphysical System Number Three

Tractate 1: 500 BC The Error of Zeno: Resolving the problem of Abstraction

Part I: The Paradox of seamlessness and multiplicity / Introduction / Zeno's paradoxes / The scholarly confusion regarding Zeon's Paradoxes / Zeno's paradox of space/distance

Part II: Resolving the issue with a new metaphysical perception / Zeno: The appearance of the 'real' and the 'real illusion' / A 'New Metaphysical Perception' regarding Zeno's paradox: / Reversing perceptions – counter view / The point – individuality / The 'real' and the 'real illusion' illustrated / Working backward to Zeno / Zeno's Paradox of Motion revisited / The Greek concept of increments / Calculus is but a tool – it does not eliminate what is / Incrementalism and the Individual / Concrete/Physical Functionality / Removing the physical while leaving the abstract intact / The truth 'I exist.' vs. the truth 'You exist.' / Abstract Functionality / Being a Part of 'Being' is not a new idea / Zeno Himself Says It / The multiplicity of individuality

Tractate 2: 322 BC The Error of Aristotle: Resolving the problem of Cartesian Systems

Part I: The Paradox of Cartesian Systems and non-Cartesian Systems / Introduction / Incremental concentric circles / The intricacies of concentric circles / Confinement is confinement / The concept of Cartesian / Cartesian Systems / The paradox of Cartesian Systems

Part II: Resolving the issue with a new metaphysical perception / Introduction /Relativistic 1st Principles /The dance of the angels / The 'Land of Limited Abstracts: Infinite Finites' / The 'Land of Unlimited Abstracts: Finite Infinities' / Understanding how 'a' 'whole' can be greater than the sum of its parts / The equality of 'relativistic 1st principle' / Resolving the paradox of 'a' Cartesian System composed of Infinite Finites / Reopening the walls of confinement / What it all means to humanity/all forms of virgin consciousness universally

Tractate 3: 525 AD The Error of Boethius: Resolving the problem of Free Will

Part I: The Paradox of free will and divine foreknowledge / Introduction / A misconception of determinism / Three forms of action / Limits placed upon Boethius / Some thoughts expounded by Boethius / Boethius' metaphysical system / Boethius' metaphysical system and social acceptance / Boethius' metaphysical system and perpetual historical acceptance / Boethius' metaphysical system and why it is we have not presently discarded such a system

Part II: Resolving the issue with a new metaphysical perception / 'The wall' of perception / Rationalizing the irrational / The limits of language / Oil and Water / The four forms of action / What 'will be': Free will - A location for 'being' – individuality / What 'has been': Divine foreknowledge - A location for 'Being' – the whole / What 'is being': Determinism - A location for *being* – action, process/reality – the universe / What 'is':Pre-destination/predestination - A location for being – existence of existence / Functionality of action / Locations for actions / Divine foreknowledge, predestination, pre-destination, and determinism versus free will / Internationality: the need 'for' a location of determinism / Potentiality: the need 'for' a location of free will / Nothing: the need 'for' a location of nothing / The Book of Divine Foreknowledge/ The Location of Free Will / The Location of Determinism / The misnomer of 'free will' / Letting go

Tractate 4: 1543 AD The Error of Copernicus: Resolving the problem of Centricism

Part I: Part I: The Paradox of Centricism and non-Centricism / Introduction I / Introduction II / Pre-Copernican / Post-Copernican / Copernicus' paradoxes

Part II: Resolving the paradox with a new metaphysical perception / Centricism / A location of Centricism / A location of non-Centricism / The dynamics of Centricism / Stepping 'out': into Centricism: Independence / Stepping 'in': 'beyond' Centricism: Independence / The dynamics of non Centricism / The law of inverse proportionality / The 'location' of 'nothingness' / Virgin physicality/'virgin physical life' / Virgin consciousness/'virgin abstract knowing' / Stepping 'in' beyond Centricism: Dependency / Stepping 'into' Centricism: Independence / The significance of insignificance: Random Sequencing / The explosive nature of the potentiality of knowing / Removing a piece of Randomness / Boethius' metaphysical system and why we can now file it away as a part of the annals of history / Archimedean Points / Philosophical infinities / A bag of marbles is not dependent upon sequential time / A unit of knowing is not a marble

Tractate 5: 1716 AD The Error of Leibniz: Resolving the problem of Theodicy

Part I: The Paradox of omni benevolence / Introduction / Errors created through the passive process of definition / 'Defining' theodicy / First / Second / Third / Error through the active process of extrapolation as opposed to the passive process of definition

Part II: Resolving the issue with a new metaphysical perception / The Core: Omniscience / The first shell: Omnipotence and Omnipresence / Leibniz and the error of addition / The Second Shell: Answers to three questions / The location of 'imperfection' / The Location of 'perfection' / Conclusion

Tractate 6: 1804 AD The Error of Kant: Resolving the problem of Universal Ethics

Part I: The Paradox of the 'unknowable' / Introduction / Cartesian / So, do we need a 'system'? / 'The' Missing Foundation / Boredom and knowledge / 'Everything' / Passive observing / Active observing / Raising metaphysics up from the dead

Part II: Resolving the issue with a new metaphysical perception / Metaphysics and Cartesianism revisited / 'a' Foundation / The need for 'a' whole / The whole does not change / A new meaning of the term 'everything' / How something, which is unchangeable, can change and remain unchangeable / The death of God / Analytic versus Synthetic 'a priori' / The causal / The non-causal / The boundary separating the causal and the non-causal / The 'Absolute Zero' point of abstraction / The fusion of: 0 / ∞ and ∞ / 0 / God does not change / The future does not exist / The past does not exist / What is exists / Resolving Kant's four antinomies / The prioritized natural emergence of the first two categorical imperatives / Morality versus categorical imperatives

Volume II: 1831 – 1998 The Recent Past
On 'being' *being:* Non-Cartesianism - Active Observation

Preface: A New Tool for Conflict Resolution

Tractate 7: 1831 AD The Error of Hegel: Resolving the problem of Non-Cartesian Systems

Part I: The Paradox of the death of 'knowing' / Introduction / The land without the concepts 'before' and 'after' / Non-Cartesainism / The lack of a Foundation / The need for 'a' whole remains / The whole/ first cause becomes a redundancy / The idea leads to the concept that 'first cause' is not necessary but the whole is necessary / The whole versus the sub-element/the individual / Hegel: Metaphysics is dead / Nietzsche: God is dead / The death of God leads to the death of Metaphysics / God: Nietzsche is dead and for that matter Hegel is also dead.

Part II: Resolving the issue with a new metaphysical perception / Introduction / Thesis, antithesis, synthesis / Hegel, Nietzsche and God are all wrong / You are that of which you are a part / The whole does change / What happens to potentiality? / What happens to nothingness? / Expanding knowing / Conclusion

Tractate 8: 1955 AD The Error of Einstein – Resolving the problem of Physical Time

Part I: The paradox of 'i' / Introduction / Dimensions / Goodbye concrete, Hello abstract / Real Numbers / The Tunnel of Abstraction / Imaginary Numbers / The Constancy of time verses the Variability of time: /

Part II: Resolving the issue with a new metaphysical perception / Part IIa: The Newtonian 'i' - Velocity Equals Distance Divided by Time / Introduction: / Expanding knowing revisited / The constant (k) variable / The 'constant' factor of variability / The 'constant' variable of physicality / Hegel introduces the first mirror: Inverse physicality / Einstein introduces the second mirror: The 'i' inversion / $d = t$ / 1 / 0 / Introduction to ∞ / 1 and $1/\infty$ / $\infty/1$ / $1/\infty$ / $1 = 0/0$ / $1 = \infty/\infty$ / $0/\infty$ versus $\infty/0$ / $0 = 0$ / Time and distance both divided by 1 / Knowledge: The universal building block / The tunnel of perception / Part IIb: The Einsteinian 'i' – The Constant Variable Equals the Square Root of the Distance Divided by the Square Root of the Time / Introduction / The square root of Einstein's equations: 'i' / Einstein's mirror revisited / Illusion / The 'real' and the 'real' illusion / The real / Coherency of time / Variability of time / The 'real illusion' / Incoherency of time / Constancy of time / The 'Taser' / What does it mean

Tractate 9: 1970 AD The Error of Russell: Resolving the problem of Separation Through Exclusion

Part I: The Paradox of seamlessness and multiplicity / Introduction: 'Nothingness' is an integral part of it all / The Wittgensteining of Russell / Understanding Russell's paradox

Part II: Resolving the issue with a new metaphysical perception / An alternative solution to Russell's Paradox / The significance of Russell's paradox as discussed in a simulated conversation between Russell and Wittgenstein / Simplicity itself: The end of the beginning / Caution #1: This section is intended only for the mathematically and scientifically inclined / Caution #2: This section is intended only for the religiously inclined / Caution #3: This section is intended only for the philosophically inclined

Tractate 10: 1976 AD The Error of Heidegger: Resolving the problem of The Void of the Void

Part I: The Paradox of 'the void' / Introduction / Creating the paradox of a Physical System / What is a void / What is a lack of a void / Zero / Infinity / Matter/energy / Space and time / The influence of fear / The paradox of nothing having no function

Part II: Resolving the issue of a void with a new metaphysical perception / The function of something / The function of 'nothing' / Where one can find a void of a void / Where one can find a void / Symmetry emerges out of a void / Where one can find a void of time / What the void of time 'means' / Where one can find a void of space / What the void of space 'means' / The void of infinity / The size of an infinite void / 'Something' reducing to a void / Abstraction and the void / Where a void cannot be found (and why it cannot be found there) / The multiplicity of individuality: / 'knowing' *knowing* 'Knowing' / 'being' *being* 'Being' / 'Nothing' is not a 'thing' / Theoretical metaphysics now evolves into: 'Being' *being* 'being' versus 'being' *being* 'Being'

Tractate 11: 1996 AD The Error of Philosophy: Resolving the problem of Monism and Dualism

Part I: The Paradox of Either/Or / Introduction / Singularity of Multiplicity / The quagmire of diversity / Either/Or / The desire for Homogeneity / The role of guilt / Being right / Homogeneity / The historical conflicted expanded / The sins of the father in regards to the son / The right 'to be' versus submission / Diversity and the right to be who you are – freedom / The advantage of diversity / The monist is wrong but the monist is right / The dualist is right but the dualist is wrong:

Part II: Resolving the issue regarding the conflict between homogeneity and diversity / Introduction / Examination of Contemporary thought / Who owns the body / Diversity and the disadvantaged / What society 'owes' entities of knowing / Our point of departure lies in the heart of metaphysics itself / Let me buy you a beer / Reversing perceptions – counter view / The Point – Individuality / Conclusion:

Tractate 12: 1998 AD: Resolving the problem of Nihilism

Introduction / The Whole and Panentheism / The Soul and Symbiosis / Human Significance / Social Ramifications / Omniscience / Omnipotence / Omnipresence / The Whole / Three Ultimate Paradoxes

Volume III: 2003 -   The Future
On 'being' *being* 'Being': Cartesianism 'within' Non-Cartesianism:
Active Observation within Passive Observation

Preface: How to Regain the Love of Wisdom

Tractate 13: Metaphysical System #28: Introducing the problem of Metaphysical Systems 7 & 9

Metaphysical Engineering

Tractate 14: Principle Three: Introducing the problem of Principles One and Two

Responsibility

Tractate 15: Ockham's Razor: Introducing the problem of Reductionism

Understanding

Tractate 16: Wrong Again: Introducing the problem of Being Right

Purpose

Tractate 17: The Beginning: Introducing the problem of The End

Infinite infinities

Tractate 18: Why Now: Introducing the problem of History's Vector

History's Vector

Conclusion: The Peer Review

Tractate 1

The Error
Of
Zeno

❖

The Paradox of:

Multiplicity or Seamlessness

•

The Need for:

Either the Physical or the Abstract

The War & Peace of a New Metaphysical Perception

1.   500 BC Zeno – The Error of:
       Physical Distance – a new perception 2000 AD

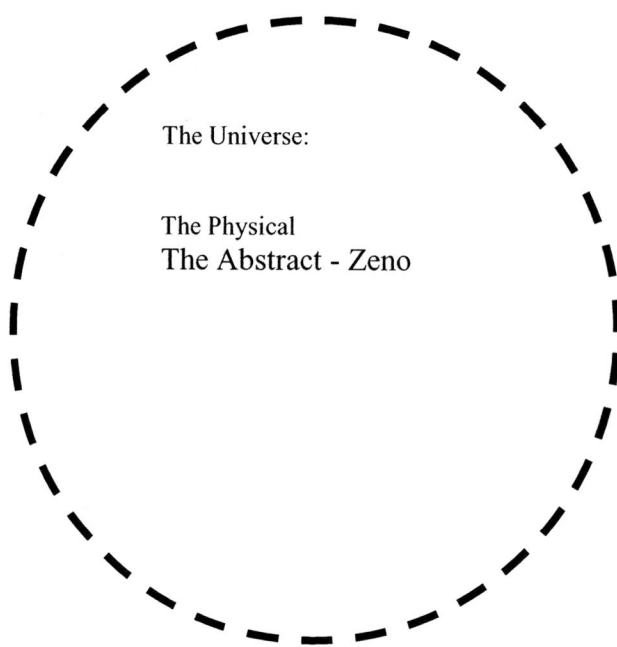

The error: The paradox of Distance: The System is filled with increments of distance

The perception: Zeno moves our perceptual understanding of the system into that of being a system filled with both multiplicity and seamlessness. As such, multiplicity and seamlessness, with the help of Zeno, now have a location within which they can be found. However, the understanding regarding the role of multiplicity and seamlessness as well as the understanding regarding the interrelationship between multiplicity and seamlessness not only remain in a state of confusion but even more disconcerting, the existence of such an interrelationship is not recognized as a significant aspect of the 'larger' system.

It is this state of confusion which will be specifically addressed within this tractate.

Contents

Part I: The Paradox of seamlessness and multiplicity

Introduction
Zeno's paradoxes
The scholarly confusion regarding Zeon's Paradoxes
Zeno's paradox of space/distance

Part II: Resolving the issue with a new metaphysical perception

Zeno: The appearance of the 'real' and the 'real illusion'
A 'New Metaphysical Perception' regarding Zeno's paradox
Reversing perceptions – counter view
The point – individuality
The 'real' and the 'real illusion' illustrated
Working backward to Zeno
Zeno's Paradox of Motion revisited
The Greek concept of increments
Calculus is but a tool – it does not eliminate what is
Incrementalism and the Individual
Concrete/Physical Functionality
Removing the physical while leaving the abstract intact
The truth 'I exist.' vs. the truth 'You exist.'
Abstract Functionality
Being a Part of 'Being' is not a new idea
Zeno Himself Says It
The multiplicity of individuality

Terms/concepts

Abstract
Abstract Functionality
Concrete
Concrete Functionality
Incrementalism
Illusion
Multiplicity
Real
Real Illusion
Seamlessness
Silent conspiracy of collusion
Singularity of location
Totality/Whole

Tractate 1
Zeno – The Error of
Physical Distance

Part I: Creating the paradox of a Physical System

Introduction

Zeno: So near and yet so far
           Faltering on the brink of understanding the nature of man

Zeno is where the perception of physical distance[1] split from abstract distance[2]. Zeno, and for that matter philosophers throughout the past two thousand five hundred years, were not aware of what it was they were on the verge of understanding. The understanding eluding philosophers was not to reveal itself until after Einstein and his concept of 'relative' time was verbalized. Even then, even with the concept of 'relative' time being verbalized, the potential understanding regarding the relationship of 'being', 'Being', and being (vb)[3] was not to be immediately understood.

And why would understanding the relationship of 'being', 'Being', and being (vb) not be understood when Einstein revealed the concept of relative time? It was not understood because philosophers had proclaimed the demise of Metaphysics and having done so, buried Metaphysics deep within the most inaccessible realms of the philosophical subconscious. As such, the tool needed to understand the concept of individuality/'being', the whole/'Being', and action, process/reality/being (vb) was to languish until the time when Metaphysics was once again brought forth from the dark sub-sub conscious realm of philosophy. After all Metaphysics is by its most primal definition, the understanding of fundamental, universal, truths and their interrelationship in the active sense[4] of their coexisting as opposed to the previously perceived passive sense[5] of their coexisting.

And where does all this 'being', 'Being', being (vb), active, passive, demise of Metaphysics, Metaphysics resurrection, incrementalism, abstract functionality, concrete functionality, ad infinitum begin? It begins with Zeno because Zeno expressed 'a' good point from which we can begin the discussion. Zeno verbalized the long and arduous task of understanding the development regarding the technicality of a radically new metaphysical perception. Zeno initiated a discussion regarding the multiplicity of distance vs. the seamlessness of distance, which, after twenty-five hundred years of philosophical debate, has lead us to the development of a new metaphysical perception.

It was Zeno who established an excellent 'beginning' point from which the most primal understanding of the universe, our home, could begin. It is through the paradoxes of Zeno that we were to learn the difference between the abstract and the physical, the concrete.

So who is this solitary man standing at this point we call 'a' beginning rather than 'the' beginning of the journey traveled by this thing we call humanity, this thing we call 'a' human?

There were many Zeno's in Greek history. This Zeno is Zeno of Elea. This man is like you and I, a simple human with a simple idea which when added to ideas, perceptions, emerging over the next twenty-five hundred years would create a metaphysical picture capable of answering three questions which were to trouble our specie since time began: 'Where am I?' 'What am I?' And, 'Why do I exist?'

In order to begin we must know what this man called Zeno had to say.

Zeno's paradoxes describe a puzzle regarding the concept of 'actually' passing 'through' distance as opposed to 'being unable' to pass through distance. We might better describe the paradox as simply a means of illustrating the difference between the concrete and the abstract.

How does one make the leap from a second, a third, a fourth, and finally infinitesimally small quantities of distance to another quantity of distance? Science and mathematics, through Calculus, believe they have answered the question to the satisfaction of humankind. In truth, however, science and mathematics have not addressed Zeno's paradox. Science and mathematics have just covered up[6] the paradox in order to ward off the annoying ramifications of the paradox regarding actuality vs. perception. This was not a negative action[7] on the part of science or mathematics for it has allowed science to do what it is science is intended to do and that is expand our understanding of the physical.

The paradox of space and time is not solved by the limits of Calculus. Calculus simply becomes a tool, which allows us to move on with out lives and leave the paradox behind, unsolved.

Zeno was on the verge of understanding the nature of man and incremental aspects of reality. Zeno, however, fell short of his goal. Zeno did not make the necessary leap needed to solve his paradox. Science through mathematics thought it made the leap but in fact it did not. Science using the language of mathematics only swept Zeno's paradox under the rug. As such, Zeno's paradox remains and until it is rationally understood, we, humanity, will continue to remain as we are mentally and spiritually confused, perplexed, mystified, empty… Until we resolve Zeno's paradox, we, humanity, will continue to act as we do, saying one thing and doing another.

To place such a heavy emphasis upon the correlation of the solution to Zeno's paradox and the change in human nature would seem to be a ludicrous parallel. But resolving Zeno's paradox holds the key to understanding our reality, understanding a new metaphysical perception, understanding why we exist.

One cannot ignore the impact ideas, perceptions, have had, do have upon actions we as individual, we as a specie initiate towards our own selves, our environment, our specie. This past history of action is not to be taken lightly for we are about to venture into space and this in turn means we will not only continue to impact our own selves, our own environment, and our own specie, but we are about to impact environments that are not our own. We are about to affect other species throughout space, a region we presently call 'our' universe.

The concept of 'falling short' is not a failing of Zeno; rather it is a part of our make-up as specie. We have a difficult time being what we are not and one thing we, as a specie, are not, is being capable of perceiving what lies beyond our ability to perceive.

This inability, this limitation, is the very reason one must never accept any model we develop of a universal philosophy as a fact, as an absolute, as 'the' model. Whatever universal philosophy we decide or decide not to develop must always have a label attached to it reading:

> 'A Universal Philosophy' - as best we are able to determine based upon our perceptions 'today.' A universal philosophy must never be taken to be an absolute for there are no such things as absolutes. There are only perceived absolutes, which we, humankind, attempt to define based upon perceptions we develop through our limited means of observation, faith, and reason – science, religion, and philosophy.

Zeno's paradoxes

Zeno presents us with our first graphic glimpse of the philosophical paradox regarding 'a' location of the abstract and its functionality as opposed to 'a' location of the physical and its functionality.

We always assume the two, the physical and the abstract, are one in the same or if not one in the same, then, at the least, located within the same region, namely the universe. But why is it we consider this to be the case? We assume it is the case because we assume there is 'one' location of existence. As such, we do not, cannot, look beyond our assumption that the solution to Zeno's paradox lies in singularity of location. This concept regarding singularity of location historically leads us to resolving Zeno's paradox in a paradoxically manner. We have resolved Zeno's paradox through the process of avoiding the paradox rather than solving the paradox. In essence, we attempt to solve the paradox of motion and distance through the process of denial rather than pragmatism. A pragmatic solution to Zeno's paradox is the essence of this article. The means by which we find a solution to Zeno's paradox is through the development of a new metaphysical perception.

With this said let's begin reevaluating Zeno's paradoxes by first examining Zeno's paradoxes.

Zeno

The abstract concept of Distance:

What is it Zeno had to say about distance that leads to the concept of distance being an abstract concept and being a physical concept simultaneously yet independently of each other?

In order to begin we must know a little about what it is this man called Zeno had to say, was thinking.

> *Zeno's paradoxes, four paradoxes relating to space and motion attributed to Zeno of Elea (fifth century B.C.): the racetrack, Achilles and the tortoise, the stadium, and the arrow. Zeno's work is known to us through secondary sources, in particular Aristotle*
>
> *The racetrack paradox:*
>
> *If a runner is to reach the end of the track, he must first complete an infinite number of different journeys: getting to the midpoint, then to the point midway between the midpoint and the end, then to the point midway between this one and the end, and so on. But it is logically impossible for someone to com- plate an infinite series of journeys. Therefore, the runner cannot reach the end of the track. Since it is irrelevant to the argument how far the end of the track is- it could be a foot or an inch or a Micron Lotion is impossible. Moving to any point will involve an infinite number of journeys, and an infinite number of journeys cannot be completed.*
>
> *The paradox of Achilles and the tortoise:*
>
> *Achilles can run much faster than the tortoise, so when a race is arranged between them the tortoise is given a lead. Zeno argued that Achilles can never catch up with the tortoise no matter how fast he runs and no matter how long the race goes on. For the first thing Achilles has to do is to get to the place from which the tortoise started. But the tortoise, though slow, is unflagging: while Achilles was occupied in making up his handicap, the tortoise has advanced a little farther, So the next thing Achilles has to do is to get to the new place the tortoise occupies. While he is doing this, the tortoise will have*

gone a little farther still. However small the gap that remains, it will take Achilles some time to cross it, and in that time the tortoise will have created another gap. So however fast Achilles runs, all that the tortoise has to do, in order not to be beaten, is not to stop.

The stadium paradox:

Imagine three equal cubes, A, B, and C, with sides all of length I, arranged in a line stretching away from one. A is moved perpendicularly out of line to the right by a distance equal to l. At the same time, and at the same rate, C is moved perpendicularly out of line to the left by a distance equal to I. The time it takes A to travel l/2 (relative to B) equals the time it takes A to travel to I (relative to C). So, in Aristotle's words, "it follows, he [Zeno] thinks, that half the time equals its double" (Physics 259b35b)

The arrow paradox:

At any instant of time, the flying arrow "occupies a space equal to itself." That is, the arrow at an instant cannot be moving, for motion takes a period of time, and a temporal instant is conceived as a point, not itself having duration. It follows that the arrow is at rest at every instant, and so does not move. What goes for arrows goes for everything: nothing moves. (Cambridge Dictionary of Philosophy, Robert Audi, Cambridge University Press, 1995)[8]

The scholarly confusion regarding Zeon's Paradoxes

Scholars disagree about what Zeno himself took his paradoxes to show. There is no evidence that he offered any absolutions" to them. One view is that they were part of a program to establish that multiplicity is an illusion, and that reality is a seamless whole. The argument could be reconstructed like this: if you allow that reality can be successively divided into parts, you find yourself with these insupportable paradoxes; so you must think of Reality as a single indivisible One. (Cambridge Dictionary of Philosophy, Robert Audi, Cambridge University Press, 1995)[9]

Why is it Scholars disagree about what Zeno himself understood his paradoxes to show? Could it be that Zeno lived in a time void of an understanding, void of a perception, void of the concept regarding a limit to the very size of the physical universe itself? As such Zeno may not have been certain regarding what it was he was trying to say other than wanting to say what he did simply because he felt it had to be said, so he said it. If such is the case, without his knowing it, he may have initiated the process of understanding, initiated a truly exciting journey for our specie.

So why list these particular paradoxes of Zeno when it is thought he may have outlined as many as forty or more paradoxes. They are listed because they give us a flavor regarding what it was Zeno was attempting to resolve.

This then leads us to the more interesting of Zeno's paradoxes, the paradox of distance 'through' space and the paradox of time 'through' space:

Space/distance:

Space is a contradictory notion and reality is indivisible, for the opposite claim leads to absurdity. Suppose that reality is divisible. It will be composed either of a finite or of an infinite number of parts. Reality could have a finite number of parts only if the magnitude of the parts disappeared in a finite number of divisions; but this would lose the finite space with which we began, since a finite number of parts without magnitude cannot produce a magnitude. If, on the other hand, reality has a infinite number of parts, the parts will have magnitude or else they will not. If they do not have magnitude, once again we have lost the space with which we began. If they do have magnitude, and we have an infinite number of them, we can construct a space as much larger than the initial space as we please. Hence, we must give up the idea of space, and of a divisible reality.

Space/time:

Time, likewise, is contradictory. Let us suppose three rows of bodies, one row ("A") at rest, and the other tow ("B" and "C") moving in opposite directions. Beginning from the positions indicated in figure one, by the time they are in the same part of the course (figure two), the B's will have passed twice as many C's as A's. (Consider the matter from the standpoint of the B on the right by way of illustration.) hence, it would take twice as long to pass the A's as it takes to pass the C's; but it takes B and C exactly the same time t reach the position of A. Hence, double the time is equal to half.

A A A A	*A A A A*
B B B B	*B B B B*
C C C C	*C C C C*
(fig. One)	*(fig. Two)*

Dictionary of Philosophy and Religion, William L. Reese, Humanities Press, 1996.

It is these two paradoxes we will examine in detail. It is the unraveling of these two paradoxes which will leads us to the understanding regarding why our present metaphysical system creates concepts such as inclusion vs. exclusion, either/or. It is the unraveling of these two paradoxes, which will leads us to the understanding regarding a new metaphysical system, a non-Cartesian system powered by a Cartesian system. The resolution of Zeno's paradoxes will lead us to an understanding regarding the new metaphysical system of 'being' *being* 'Being' better known as symbiotic panentheism as opposed to our old metaphysical system of either a Cartesian system or a non-Cartesian system.

To understand Zeno's paradoxes, however, will require us to take the paradox of space/distance and space/time as they come. Since the paradox of space/distance is presented first, we will begin with Zeno's paradox of space and distance. We will leave the latter, the paradox of space/time until later, much later. In fact, we will not visit the concept regarding the paradox of space and time until we reach the point of Einstein unknowingly making his contributions to our understanding regarding how a Cartesian system drives a non-Cartesian system: Chapter 9, Einstein: The Error of Abstract Time.

Zeno's paradox of space/distance

There are, in essence, two types of distances to which Zeno is unwittingly referring. There is Conceptual/abstract Distance and Concrete/Physical Distance. Zeno referred to them as:

'...part of a program to establish that multiplicity is an illusion, and that reality is a seamless whole. The argument could be reconstructed like this: if you allow that reality can be successively divided into parts, you find yourself with these insupportable paradoxes; so you must think of Reality as a single indivisible One.

In essence Zeno is implying 'multiplicity is an illusion...', physical reality is an illusion, '...that the 'location' where the physical, 'multiplicity', lies is not the real but rather the real is where 'multiplicity' does not lie. In short, Zeno is implying the 'real' reality lies in the realm, the 'location', of the abstract, the abstract world, the 'larger' reality ('Larger', 'smaller', relative size will be addressed elsewhere.)

If Zeno is implying the realm of multiplicity is not what is real, why didn't he simply state this as his perception? Let's answer that question with a question. How could Zeno directly come out and state the concept of the physical, the realm of multiplicity, is an illusion unless he had something else with which to replace this illusion, the realm of multiplicity, the realm of the physical? This illusional realm, the physical universe is the location 'within' which we find ourselves existing

Zeno had no other alternative to offer as to what is real if the universe is an illusion and therefore Zeno could not rationally declare the universe, the realm of multiplicity, to be an illusion.

So has anything changed? Absolutely, and that is exactly the point of this work

Functional distance lies in the concrete. It is where 'multiplicity' lies. Functional, multiplicity of distance is where we see ourselves existing. Incremental distance is found in the reality of our universe, in the concrete, in the physical, where Kant goes with his concept of a Cartesian metaphysical system known as 'reality'. Functional distance is just that, functional. (More of that in Chapter 6: Kant: The Error of Cartesian Systems.)

Conceptual distance lies in the abstract. Abstraction is where a 'seamless whole' lies. Seamlessness is found in the reality of abstract understanding, a place where Hegel goes with his concept of a foundationless metaphysical system, a non-Cartesian system, the 'greater' Reality. (More of that in Chapter 7, Hegel: The Error of Non-Cartesian Systems.)

In this chapter, the focus is upon Zeno and the concept of functional distance/incremental distance/ physical versus conceptual distance/seamless distance/abstract distance. These two concepts, multiplicity and seamlessness, will lead us to an understanding regarding conceptual time and functional time as addressed within the chapter reserved for Newton and Einstein, Chapter 9. The four Kant, Hegel, Newton, and Einstein developed independent perceptions of Cartesian systems and non-Cartesian systems or to put it another way: Kant, Hegel, Newton, and Einstein developed independent perceptions of abstract time - constant distance and constant time - abstract distance.

It must also be noted here, in order to avoid the perception that this discussion of Zeno implies the physical is not 'real' - is an illusion, that Zeno may have been alluding to an incorrect perception. One does not necessarily need to make a choice between the physical being what is 'real' or the abstract being what is real. Physical existence and abstractual existence could both be 'real' simultaneously while only appearing to be alternately real and illusional. For the purposes of this chapter, we will remove the concept of 'time' in order to remove the complexity time adds to the equation. We will replace the concept of time when we move into Chapter 9.

When time is removed, both realms, that of the 'real' and that of the 'real illusion', find themselves to be 'real' and 'real illusions' alternately, depending upon where one 'stands' when referring to each. In short, the 'real' and the 'real illusion' could both be what is 'real' depending upon where one stands as one discusses the 'realness' of one to the other.

With the concept of the physical existing 'within' the abstract:

> When one stands within the perception of the physical, the existence of 'multiplicity', it is the physical, 'multiplicity', that becomes 'real' and the abstract, 'seamlessness', becomes a 'real illusion'.
>
> When one stands within the perception of the abstract, the existence of 'seamlessness', it is the abstract, 'seamlessness', that becomes 'real' and the physical, 'multiplicity', becomes a 'real illusion'.

Now what is the difference between an 'illusion' and a 'real illusion'? An illusion is just that: an illusion. It is not real. A 'real illusion', on the other hand, is likewise an illusion but it is more than an illusion. It is 'real', and as such becomes a 'place', an existence, within which one can literally, not figuratively, 'go'. A real illusion becomes an actuality of which one can literally become a part. A 'real illusion' becomes as much a viable entity as that which is 'real'. In fact, a 'real illusion' is what makes what is 'real' real.

On the other hand, if something is an 'illusion' it is not 'real'; it is not an alternative 'location' of existence.

Zeno had no idea 'how' to convert the illusion from the state of being 'just' an illusion into that of being a 'real illusion' and it is only by performing this conversion that a 'real illusion' becomes a viable location for existence. It is only through the process of understanding how 'seamlessness' can exist independent of 'multiplicity' that we can logically, rationally, begin a discussion regarding the solution to the paradox of 'seamless' motion versus motion of 'multiplicity'. In essence, we must understand Reality as opposed to reality before we can resolve Zeno's paradoxes of space/distance and space/time.

Because the distinction regarding independent locations of the abstract and the physical has not yet been undertaken, our understanding of Zeno's paradoxes, our understanding of life remains as it had been for two thousand five hundred years. Until we resolve the paradoxes of space/distance and space/time so aptly expressed by Zeno we will not advance our metaphysical perceptions and metaphysics will remain a mystery.

Are Zeno's paradoxes relevant topics of philosophical discussion in our modern day era? Absolutely, for we have yet to resolve them as opposed to having glossed over them through the development of mathematical tools.

So how do we begin the process of philosophically resolving Zeno's paradoxes? We initiate the process through a rational discussion. We begin a rational discussion addressing the relationship between the 'real' and the 'real illusion'.

Part II: Resolving the issue with a new metaphysical perception

Zeno: The appearance of the 'real' and the 'real illusion'

Pre-Zeno:

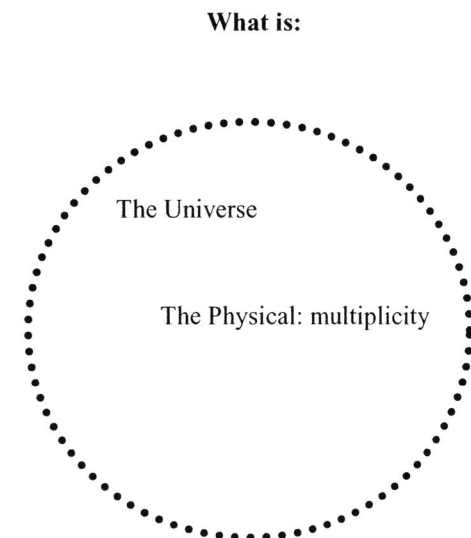

What is:

But why the 'dotted' line? The line is dotted to represent the lack of understanding regarding 'a' universe, 'a' system, existence being existence whatever that means in the metaphysical sense. The picture will change as the chapters evolve and will be summarized in Chapter 16: Summation: A New Slant on the Old.

Zeno begins the process of expanding upon our perceptual understanding of 'what is' through the identification of paradoxes, which arise when we maintain the perception of 'a' single location of existence:

The War & Peace of a New Metaphysical Perception

Zeno's perception of 'what is':

What is:

Physical Distance - Multiplicity
&
Abstract Distance – 'seamlessness'

The Universe **Grows:**

The Physical: multiplicity

The Abstract: seamlessness

Zeno expands upon the perception of existence: Existence now becomes a new but elusive concept of the physical – 'multiplicity' 'containing' abstraction – 'seamlessness'

What is:

Physical Distance – 'multiplicity'
&
Abstract Distance – 'seamlessness'

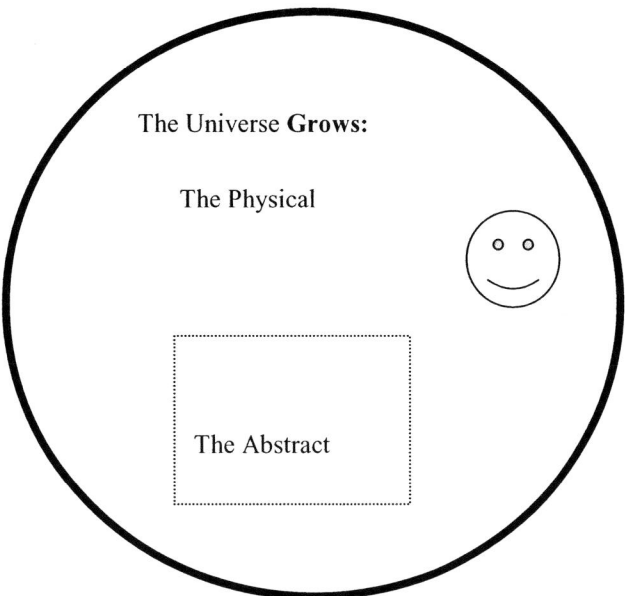

As such, the 'size' of the universe grows to accommodate, make room for the abstract. The concept of 'growth' at this stage of understanding was not growth in actuality, for 'what is' is. Rather 'growth' was growth in 'our' perception of 'what is'.

Zeno's concept of the abstract 'seamlessness' inadvertently begins an emergence of a perceptual concept of location (see previous diagram). Zeno's work causes us to contemplate questions regarding ourselves and just what it is we are and why it is we exist.

The next sequence of drawings regarding the existence of abstraction, 'seamlessness', verses the existence of the concrete, the physical, 'multiplicity' is not as simple as first glance may imply.

Depending upon where one stands as one addresses the issue, the drawing can reverse itself and become perceptually something altogether different.

The War & Peace of a New Metaphysical Perception

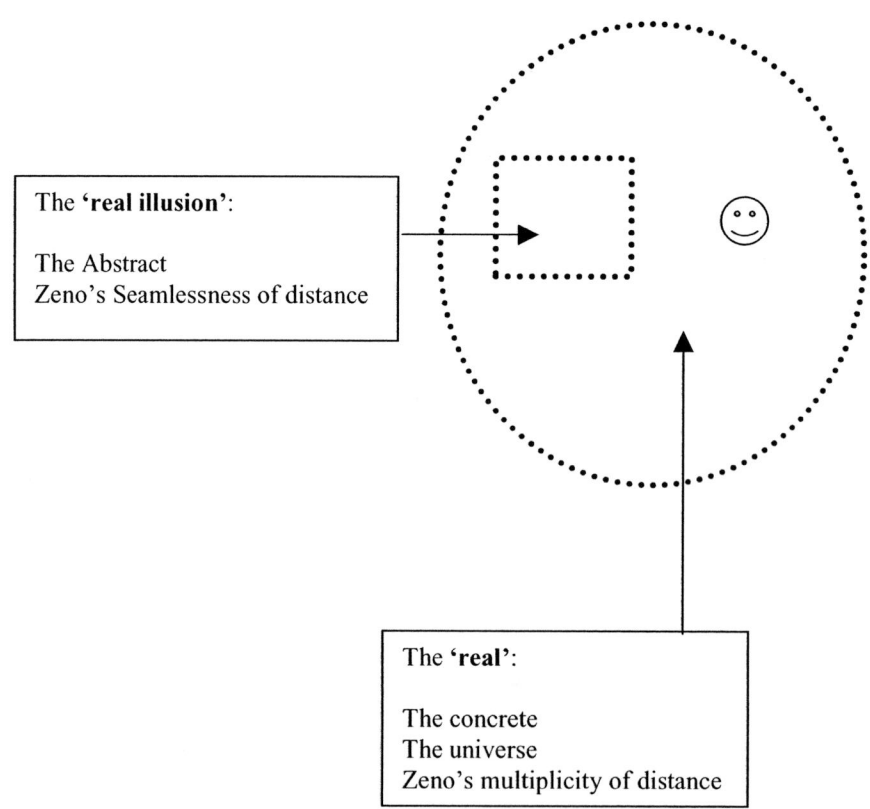

The Error of Zeno

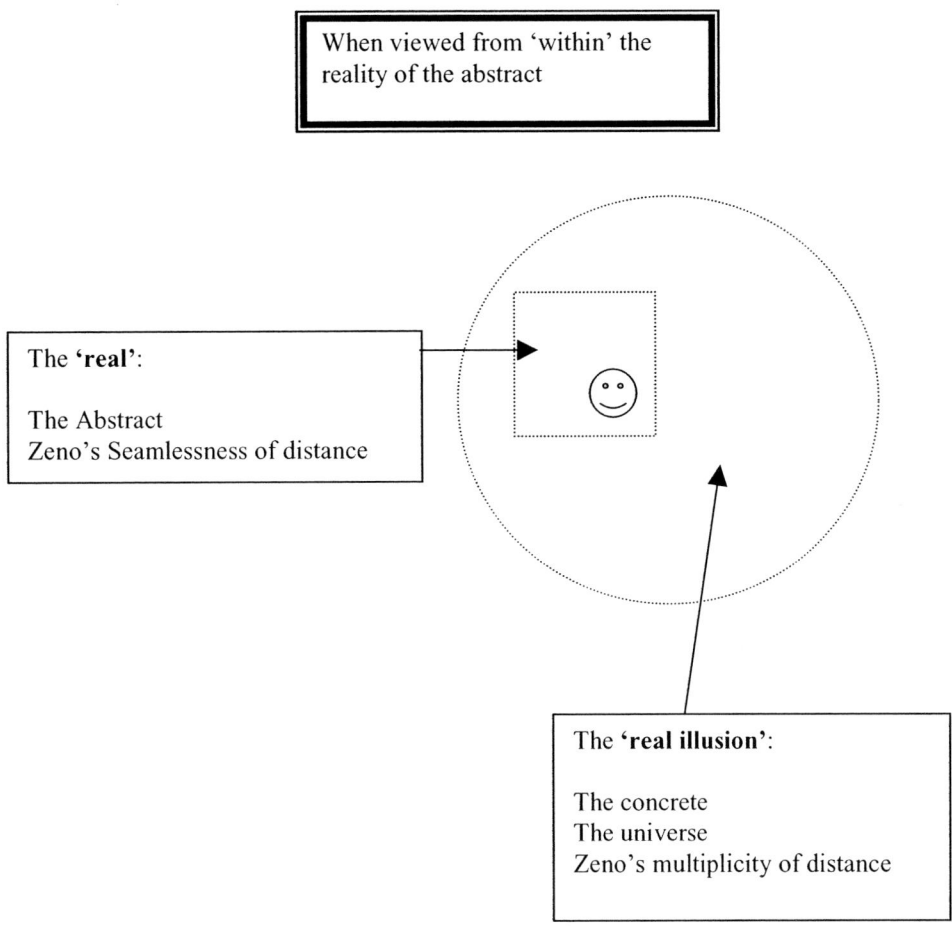

Therefore, it is the 'real' and the 'real illusion', which become the 'real illusion' and the 'real' as one moves from one position to another. Rapid motion often causes us to become disoriented and confused. So it is we become perplexed with the introduction of independent locations for 'seamlessness' and 'multiplicity' or what might better be called the abstract and the physical.

Now what does all this flip-flopping of position have to do with Zeno and his famous paradoxes? What does this have to do with Zeno's inference regarding an existence of 'multiplicity' and 'seamlessness'? Zeno implies two existences, the abstract ('seamlessness') and the physical ('multiplicity'). But Zeno is unable to visualize such a concept. Part of Zeno's problem regarding the concept of two locations of existence lies in the fact that zero, infinity, nothingness, relative time, Cartesian systems, non-Cartesian systems, ... had not yet evolved. As such, Zeno was lacking many of the tools modern metaphysicians have at their disposal.

This being the case, Zeno was perplexed by his thoughts and as such, Zeno was unable to perceive of the possibility vis-à-vis the process of establishing two separate locations, one for the abstract and one for the physical, to then introducing the concept of oscillating what is the 'real' with what is the 'real illusion' was next to impossible. In short, Zeno was unable to perceptualize potential reversal roles for 'locations' of the abstract and the physical.

A 'New Metaphysical Perception' regarding Zeno's paradox

In the case of a new metaphysical perspective, the process of reversing perceptions involves two systems of reality, one within the other. Both systems are 'real'. Both systems are 'real illusions'; neither system corresponds directly to being 'real' while the other is 'real', nor a 'real illusion' while the other is a 'real illusion'. Rather one is 'real' when the other is a 'real illusion' and becomes a 'real illusion' when the other is 'real'. Both have a function. The first grows through the action of the second. The second 'is' because of the action of the first.

The innermost system involves a Kantian system, a Cartesian system, a physical system based upon 'a' foundation. In this case, 'the' foundation's 'first truth' is: consciousness exists. This Kantian system finds itself immersed within the larger system, the Hegelian system, a non-Cartesian system - a foundationless system of abstraction. In short, both Kant and Hegel were correct: there is such a thing as 'a' system.

On the other hand both Kant and Hegel were incorrect. The system is not a singular system but a complex system composed of two systems in one: a Cartesian system fueling a non-Cartesian system and a non-Cartesian system initiating a Cartesian system in order to fuel its own non-Cartesian self. In short the existence of a perpetual motion machine of abstraction vs. the theoretically impossible existence of a physical perpetual motion machine.

Now we all know perpetual motion machines do not, cannot, exist, but that understanding applies only to the laws of thermodynamics, laws found 'within' the physical, laws found 'within' the universe, laws found 'within' a Cartesian System. The system being proposed here is not a Cartesian system but rather a non-Cartesian System fueled by a Cartesian System. But more of this in future chapters. Our function regarding Zeno is to begin our understanding regarding a new perception, which Zeno inadvertently and unknowingly initiated.

Reversing perceptions – counter view

It is possible, metaphysically, to reverse the perceptual 'locations' of the physical and the abstract.

Zeno was only able to perceive of the abstract being 'located' 'within' the physical for the physical was what was.

However, it is possible today to understand the concept of the physical being 'located' 'within' the abstract. This possibility has emerged as a possibility because we now understand the universe may be limited. The limits may exist in terms of time. They may exist in terms of implosion, infinite expansion, vacuum collapse, ad infinitem. Regardless of the type of speculation regarding the demise of the universe the result is the same, the concept of the universe being limited exists.

The very existence of the potential demise of the universe allows us to view the previous diagram from a different perspective, from the perspective of the physical universe being 'inside' the abstract. When viewed as such, one obtains an entirely different sequence of drawings from what

Zeno had at his disposal. (Note the reversal of the abstract – the square and the physical – the circle.)

The appearance of the 'real' and the 'real illusion' now becomes:

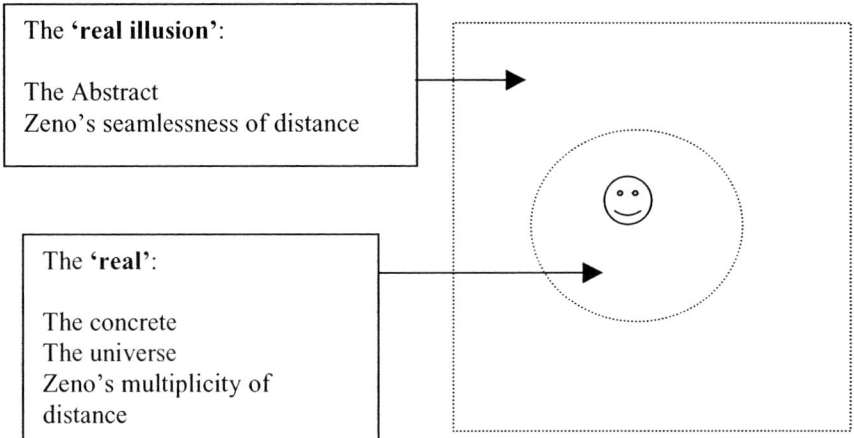

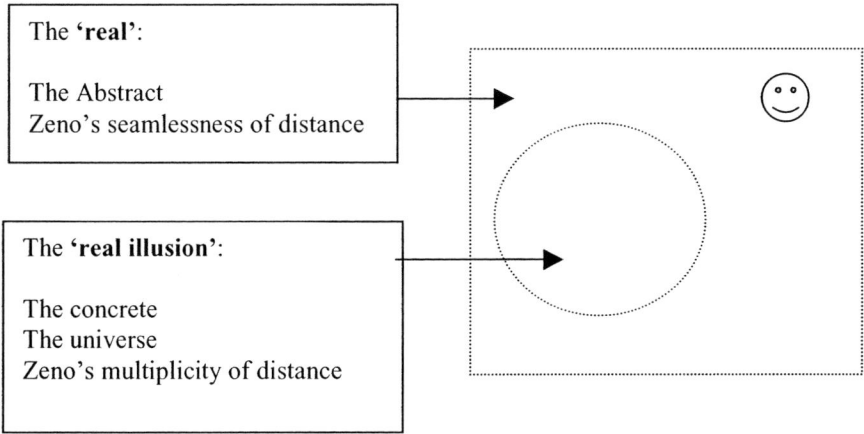

The War & Peace of a New Metaphysical Perception

Once again, we see the 'real' and the 'real illusion' become the 'real illusion' and the 'real' as one moves from one position to another.

What is different regarding this sequence of drawing as opposed to the previous sequence of drawings? In this sequence of drawings, the abstract 'contains' the physical. Multiplicity finds itself to be 'within', a part of seamlessness 'as opposed to' 'seamlessness' being 'within', a part of, multiplicity.

This brings us back to the twentieth century concept regarding 'innate characteristics of…' Is multiplicity, the physical, the concrete, a part … an innate characteristic of the abstract – seamlessness or is the abstract, seamlessness, an innate characteristic of the concrete, the physical, multiplicity.

When viewed from 'within' the physical, it would appear the abstract is an innate characteristic of the physical.

When viewed from 'within' the abstract, it would appear the physical is an innate characteristic of the abstract.

In essence, the understanding of what is 'real' was the concept being put before us, before humanity, by Zeno. In essence, the answer to 'What is real?' provides the answer to:

> 'The scholarly confusion regarding Zeon's Paradoxes:
>
> *Scholars disagree about what Zeno himself took his paradoxes to show. There is no evidence that he offered any absolutions" to them. One view is that they were part of a program to establish that multiplicity is an illusion, and that reality is a seamless whole. The argument could be reconstructed like this: if you allow that reality can be successively divided into parts, you find yourself with these insupportable paradoxes; so you must I think of Reality as a single indivisible One. (Cambridge Dictionary of Philosophy, Robert Audi, Cambridge University Press, 1995)* [10]

What does this have to do with Zeno's inference of an existence of 'multiplicity' and an existence of 'seamlessness'? The concept of location, the concept of 'one' located 'within' 'the other' expands upon Zeno's perception of 'one' location of existence. Zeno, however, could not speculate regarding two 'realities', upon two realities dependent upon each other for existence itself. As such, the most Zeno could do was expand upon what was:

What Was:

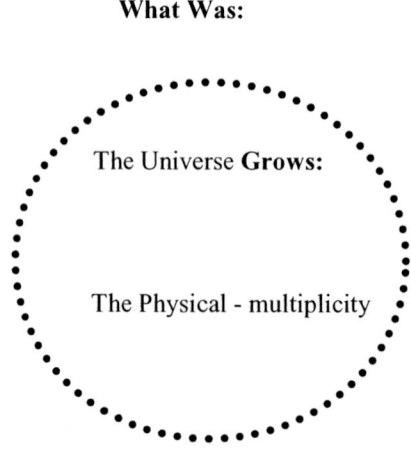

The Error of Zeno

…and turn it into what is (Zeno's point in history)

What is:

Physical Distance - Multiplicity
&
Abstract Distance – 'seamlessness'

The Universe **Grows:**

The Physical - multiplicity

The Abstract – seamlessness

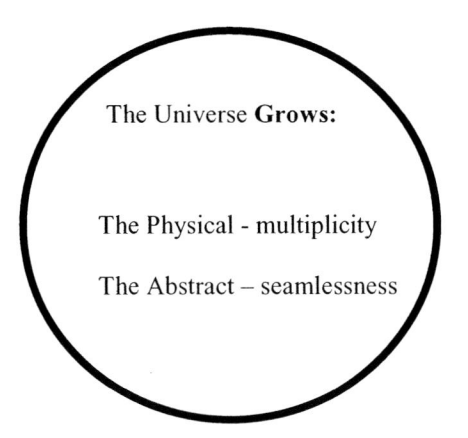

… which in turn moves to becoming (over the next twenty-five hundred years): a new perception 2000 AD

Physical Distance – 'multiplicity'
&
Abstract Distance – 'seamlessness'

The Universe **Grows:**

The Physical: multiplicity
The 'real illusion'

The Abstract: seamlessness
The 'real'

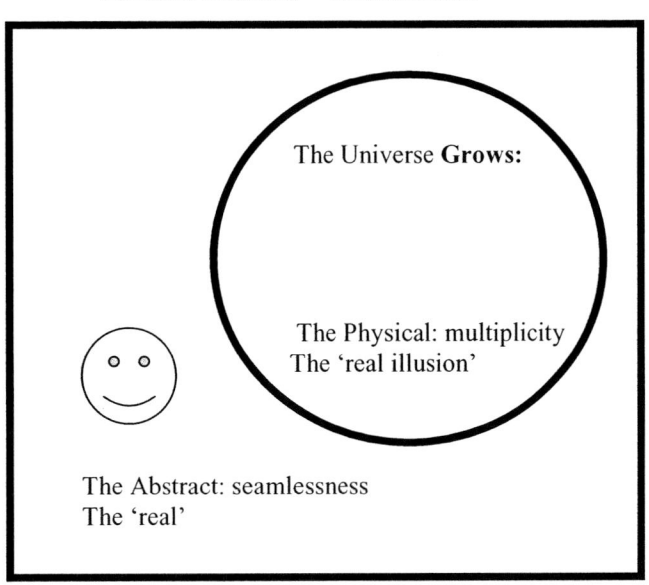

The War & Peace of a New Metaphysical Perception

Or:

Physical Distance – 'multiplicity'
&
Abstract Distance – 'seamlessness'

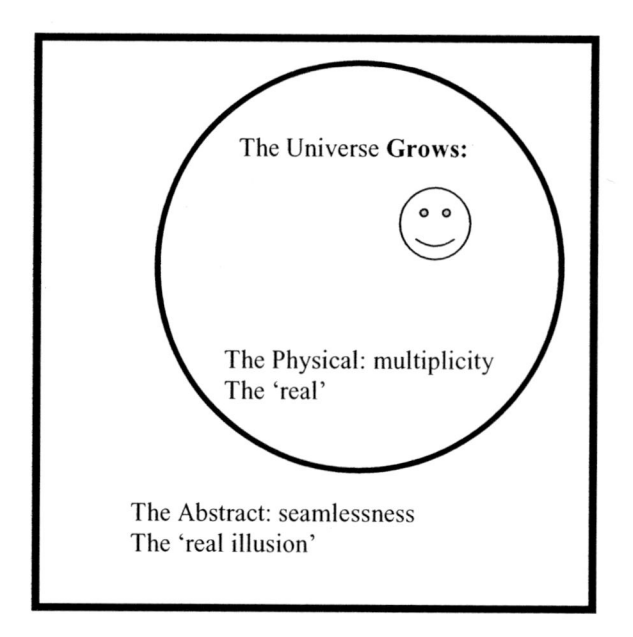

```
┌─────────────────────────────────────┐
│            ╱⎯⎯⎯⎯⎯⎯⎯⎯⎯⎯⎯╲            │
│          ╱                ╲          │
│         │  The Universe Grows:       │
│         │         ◔ ◔               │
│         │          ‿                │
│         │                            │
│         │  The Physical: multiplicity│
│         │  The 'real'                │
│          ╲                ╱          │
│            ╲⎯⎯⎯⎯⎯⎯⎯⎯⎯⎯⎯╱            │
│                                     │
│     The Abstract: seamlessness      │
│     The 'real illusion'             │
└─────────────────────────────────────┘
```

…depending upon where one stands as one addresses the issue.

The movement from Zeno's dotted boundaries to present day solid lines is nothing less than an understanding regarding the rational possibility of the two existences co-existing.

The process of moving from one location of existence to another, the seeming process of reversion, is in essence not reversion but inversion.

All this theory seems so inconsequential when one views a small child starving in Uganda, but is it?

The Point - Individuality

As we will see throughout this work, it is the very concept of points in history, the small child starving in Uganda, which is being accentuated in this discussion. It is distinct points, the uniqueness of 'a' point itself, which represents transformational events in the life of 'a' unique entity that will stand out in this work.

However, more of this in future chapters.

Once again, what of Zeno? Zeno had something to tell us, which even he did not understand. What Zeno had to tell us, without understanding how to verbalize the concept, picture the concept, even

perceive the concept, dealt with the very concept of a point. The point is a particular point, be it a geometric point, a point of history, a point of action, a point of abstraction, a point of individuality, or for that matter any point of awareness of its own awareness be it terrestrial or extraterrestrial.
To better understand the lesson Zeno initiated, we need to understand a few things about points of space and points of abstraction…

As such, lets look at the concept of 'a' geometric point and then look at the concept of 'an' individual. We will then expand our view to include the concept of individual points of abstraction as it relates to the concept of individual points of space. This understanding is what will reveal some very interesting points indeed.

Geometry
Metaphysics:

'a' Virgin Point of Geometry
'a' Virgin Consciousness of Metaphysics::

> Beginning at the beginning: definitions - Geometry:
> Beginning at the beginning: perceptions - Metaphysics:
>
> The first step: a systematic examination of the first definition put forward by Euclid begins with the word 'a'. This is a critical step. It implies existence. It implies singularity. Mathematics could not move forward unless it was willing to accept this most Husserlian of all steps. The process of beginning not from the 'whole' and moving inward to the least of all elements but rather beginning with the least of all elements and moving outward to describe the 'whole' was crucial to Mathematics.
>
> Mathematics made tremendous strides by not begging the question: 'Why begin with the least and move outward to the 'totality' of space.' By moving from the least outward, Mathematics left the 'size' of 'what is' open and as such we, humanity, were able to expand upon the outer limits we perceived to exist.
>
> Metaphysics may find it to can make tremendous strides if it would be willing to humble itself and follow the lead of Mathematics, if it would be willing to not 'beg the question' of why start with the least as opposed to the 'whole'. If the process of starting with the least of the elements and moving outward to the 'whole' is successful, then, just as in geometry, once we get to the 'whole' we should be able to move in either of two directions. If successful, we should be able to continue to expand upon our perception of what is or we should be able to reverse the process and reduce everything down to the most fundamental element. However, some philosophers are not inclined to forgo the debate regarding, 'Why start with the least and move outward'. Lets begin with the 'least' and move 'outward' despite their objections. Lets do so assuming this process will do for Metaphysicians what this process did for Mathematicians and Scientists. Lets assume this process will provide for an unlimited growth of 'what is' as opposed to confining 'what is' to 'what it is' and then moving inward to the least.
>
> As such, we will begin with the concept of the 'least' and move outward to the 'totality' of knowing, to the totality of knowledge. Once having reached the perceived end, we will judge our success through two means:
>
>> First: 'looking' 'outward': Does the result of our building perception 'outward' from the least element of 'what is' lead us to the furthest boundaries of our

ability to speculate. Does our building upon our least element of perception leads us to 'reality' as we know it just as moving from 'a' point outward leads us to the concept of three dimensional space as we know it. Does the process of building upon the least of 'what is', leave our perception of 'what is out there' open, able to be expanded even further, leave our perceptions of 'what else there is' beckoning to our natural instinct of curiosity. Once having reached the outer boundaries of our perceptual abilities do we find ourselves wrapped in a state of excitable agitation regarding what else there is to discover 'beyond' what we 'know'.

Second: 'looking' 'inward': Having reached the furthest limits of our perceptual ability for any particular point in time can we logically reduce our most expansive perception of 'what is' back once again to the least of the elements. Using Husserl's process of reduction, do we find ourselves once again examining the primal element with which we started?

❖

Geometry: 'a' point
Metaphysics: 'a' consciousness

    Geometry's second critical step is to determine 'a' what. Euclid did not decide to start with a 'point' but rather Euclid decided to start with a 'location', the smallest location of which he could conceive. He named this location 'a' 'point'.

    For metaphysics to follow suit, it must decide to start with 'a' something. Now metaphysics could begin with 'a' 'first cause' but this would not be following in the steps of Euclid. For Euclid to forge such a path, he would have had to start with the concept of 'a' 'space'. In other words Euclid would have had to start with the 'largest' rather than the 'least' element.

    So what is it with which metaphysics must begin. Since metaphysics is the study of knowledge and since the process of knowledge is 'knowing' then it would appear metaphysics would have to begin with awareness of knowledge. In other words, it would appear Metaphysics would need to begin with the least element of awareness or 'a' 'consciousness'.

❖

Geometry: 'a' point is ...
Metaphysics: 'a' consciousness is.

    Geometry acknowledges the concept of existence

    How can Metaphysics begin by doing anything less than the same?

❖

Geometry: 'a' point is that ...
Metaphysics: 'a' consciousness is that.

    Geometry begins to define

    Metaphysics following suit

❖

Geometry: 'a' point is that which
Metaphysics: 'a' consciousness is that which

    Geometry does not just define but defines specifically.

    Metaphysics: following suit

❖

Geometry: 'a' point is that which has ...
Metaphysics: 'a' consciousness is that which has...

    Geometry moves from recognizing we 'can' 'define specifically' into accepting its ability to do so. Not only does geometry recognize its ability to do so but Geometry proceeds to do so with no thought of it being arrogant in doing so. Geometry proceeds to do so with no apology. Geometry proceeds to define its field of study without looking back to see who is lying in wait ready to spring upon each and every word it utters.

    Metaphysics: following suit

❖

Geometry: 'a' point is that which has no ...
Metaphysics: 'a' consciousness is that which has no.

    An interesting step for geometry, for Euclid at this stage decides to define the point through a 'lack of' rather than define the point in a substantive form. Euclid recognized one cannot get to the 'least' through a process of acknowledging the least having substance. He understood 'having substance' implied an existence capable of being divided again and again and again and....

    Metaphysics: follows suit

❖

Geometry: 'a' point is that which has no part.
Metaphysics: 'a' consciousness is that which has no knowledge.

    Metaphysics takes its second diversion from geometry.

    The first diversion:

    The first diversion deals with what it is which distinguishes the two, geometry and metaphysics. Geometry deals with existence of location and metaphysics deals with existence of awareness. This is not to say metaphysics has no concern regarding location for, as we shall see, location plays a vital part in the more advanced stages of metaphysics. But for know, in terms of the most primary of primary steps regarding metaphysics, we have little choice but to begin at the beginning, to begin with the 'least element' of metaphysics and that is 'a', 'the' concept of 'a' consciousness void of location.

The second diversion:

The second diversion describes the 'substance' with which each deals. Geometry deals with space and metaphysics deals with awareness. Geometry deals with the 'least element' of location, a location so small it has no size. Metaphysics deals with the 'least element' of awareness, awareness so small it has no awareness.

Now just what is the defining characteristic of this awareness, this consciousness? It is the same as the defining characteristic of 'a' point. Just as 'a' point has no part, has a lack of physical location, 'a' consciousness has no knowledge, has a lack of abstraction. In short, 'a' consciousness is so small it has no consciousness, no awareness, no experience, no knowing, and no knowledge. We will refer to such a consciousness as 'a' 'virgin consciousness'

The question becomes: Why should Metaphysics and Geometry take any diversions from each other at all? Geometry is geometry and metaphysics is metaphysics. If metaphysics took no diversion at all from geometry, it would be geometry not metaphysics.

Understanding Geometry in order to deal with the perception of location, space, multiplicity takes an understanding regarding the 'least' of space, 'where' no location, begins.

Understanding Metaphysics in order to deal with the perception of awareness, knowing, seamlessness takes an understanding regarding the 'least' of knowledge, 'where' no knowing, begins. The concept of a quantity of knowledge, a 'beginning' for knowledge, and the concept of a location, a 'place' for knowledge, assists us in understanding a new perception regarding what is 'real' and what is 'kind of real'.

The 'real' and the 'real illusion' illustrated

Inverted views: Both real, one the inversion of the other

Diagram #1:

The elements:

1. The perceived 'real' – the physical
2. The perceived 'real' illusion - abstraction

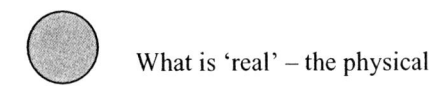

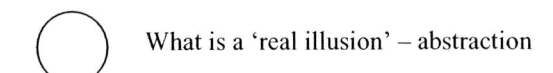

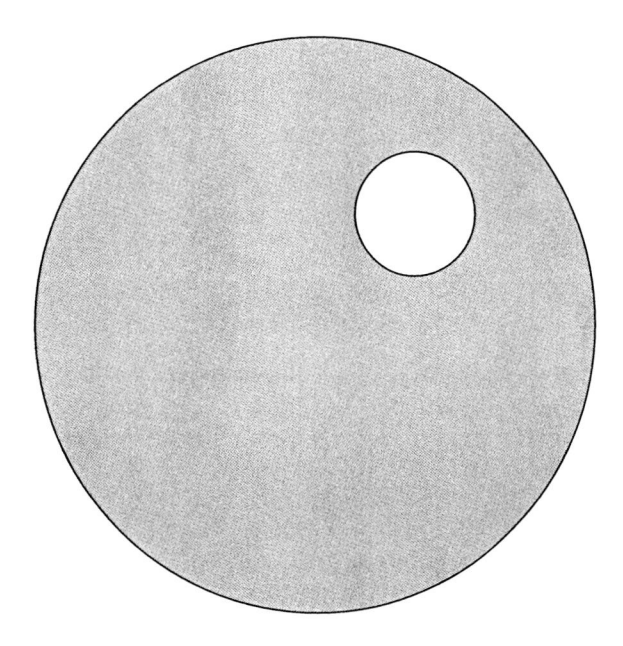

○ What is 'real' – the physical

○ What is a 'real illusion' – abstraction

We know abstractions exist in physical reality. Few of us can deny non-physical concepts such as love, hate, jealousy, happiness, curiosity, hope, …These concepts do not seem to be composed of any form of matter or energy. They appear to be forms of abstraction.

Zeno recognized this concept and in fact verbalized it mathematically with his various paradoxes of space, time, and distance. Space, time, and distance also appear to be as much abstractions as hope, joy, love, and hate.

Zeno focused upon the concept of distance for distance was an abstraction scholars of his time could most readily manipulate mathematically. Zeno then lead scholars into a debate regarding the abstractual world, illusional concepts of seamless distance vs. the physical world's, realities, concepts of multiplicity of distance. As we know, illusional seamless distance is just that: illusional. The concept of a seamless distance does not appear to exist in the physical world.

We might better use the term for 'being illusionary but 'kind of' real' as being a 'real illusion' of existence.

This is similar to what we, from the point of view of being 'within' the concrete, functioning 'within' the physical, perceive to be.

If we expanded upon the view of Diagram #1, we would obtain the negative of the print or the inversion of Zeno's perception of the world as we shrink the size of the abstract found 'within' the physical.

Diagram #2:

    The elements:

        1. The perceived 'real' – the physical
        2. The perceived 'real' illusion - abstraction

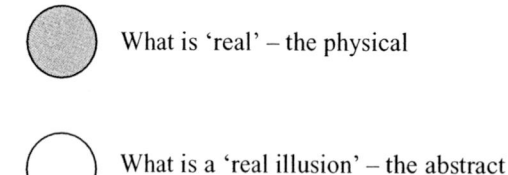

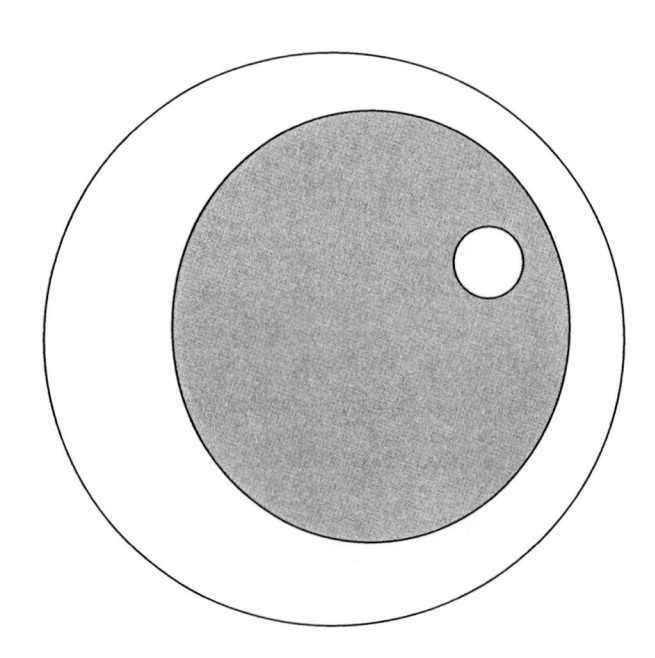

● What is 'real' – the physical

○ What is a 'real illusion' – the abstract

Continuing to shrink the abstraction within the physical we get:

Diagram #2a:

The elements:

3. The perceived 'real' – the physical
4. The perceived 'real' illusion - abstraction

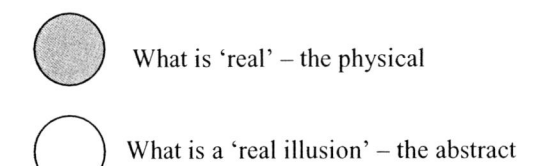

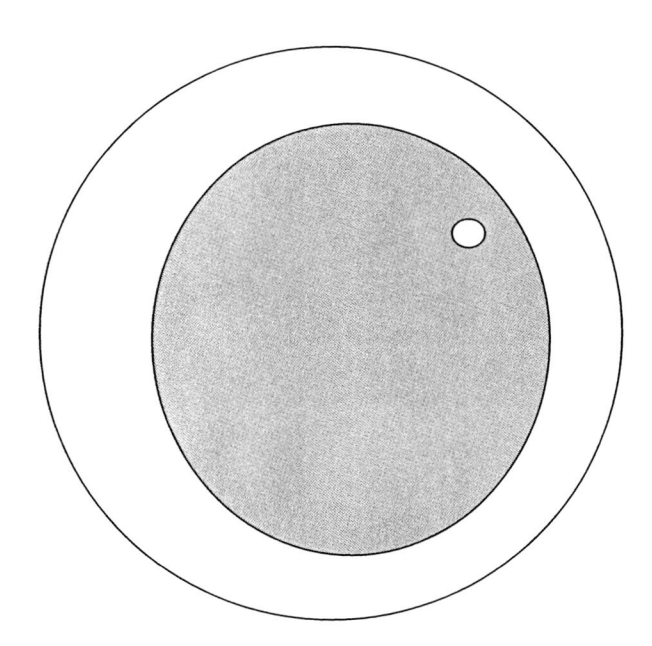

○ What is 'real' – the physical

○ What is a 'real illusion' – the abstract

The War & Peace of a New Metaphysical Perception

And then, if we add multiplicity to abstraction found 'within the physical we get:

Diagram #2b:

The elements:

    5. The perceived 'real' – the physical
    6. The perceived 'real' illusion - abstraction

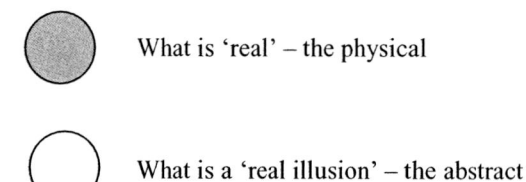

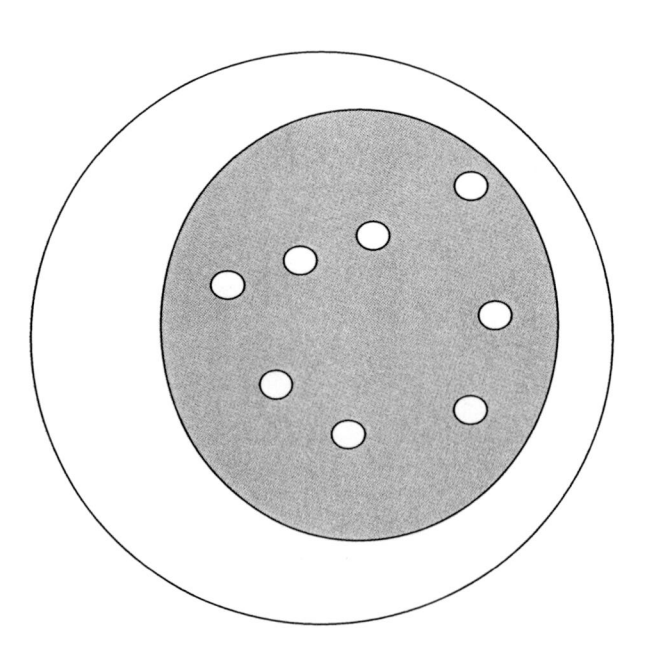

⬤ What is 'real' – the physical

◯ What is a 'real illusion' – the abstract

How is it we are able to 'arbitrarily enclose the physical with abstraction? How are we logically able to draw such a perception? If the physical should cease to exist, it would appear the only item left would be the abstract:

The Error of Zeno

Diagram #3 with the physical removed:

The elements:

    1. The 'real' - erased
    2. The 'real' illusion

○ What is 'real' - erased

○ What is a 'real illusion'?

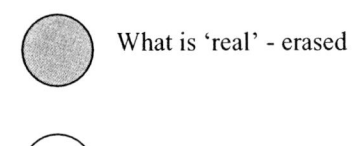

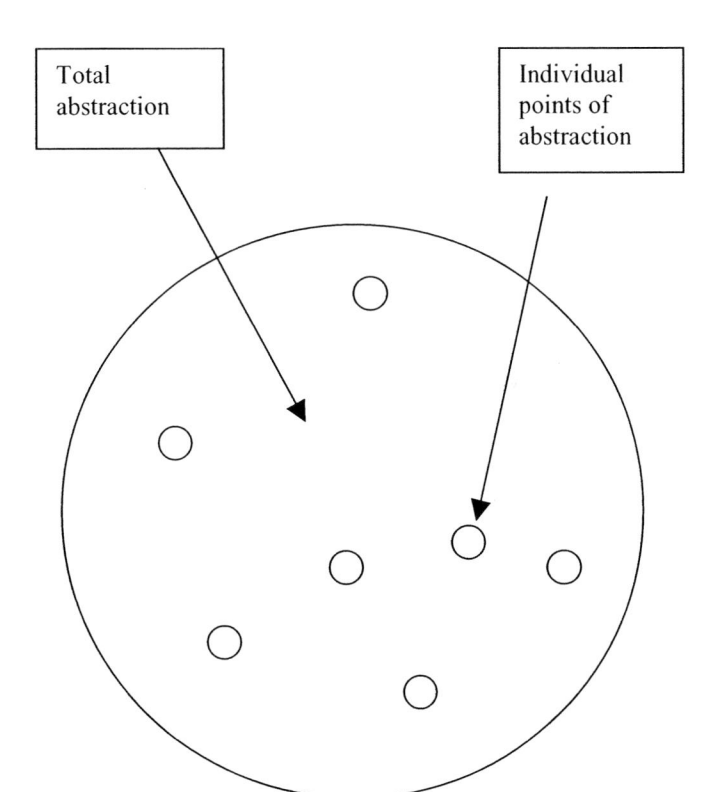

Total abstraction

Individual points of abstraction

Now it appears the abstract is all that is left. But if there is no physical, only consciousness does the 'real illusion', does abstraction really exist and even if it did would it matter? Of course it would matter for awareness is all that appears to matter in the final analysis. Awareness is the only logical existence we can tie to timelessness. Awareness is the only existence we can rationally perceive as having significance.

The War & Peace of a New Metaphysical Perception

It is abstraction, knowledge, knowing, awareness of… that would remain should we remove the physical, should the physical be removed. As such, it is the physical that would appear to be immersed 'within' the abstract even if the physical in actuality is not there, is nowhere, for there is nowhere else to 'put' the 'real', the physical but 'within' the abstract.

But couldn't we follow this same process and end up with the physical and thus find ourselves with the same logic, find ourselves confronting the concept of the only place to 'put' the abstract is 'within' the physical? The way to find out is to try it.

To understand what happens in such a scenario we must begin once again with diagram #1.

Diagram #1:

    The elements:

        3.   The perceived 'real' – the physical
        4.   The perceived 'real' illusion - abstraction

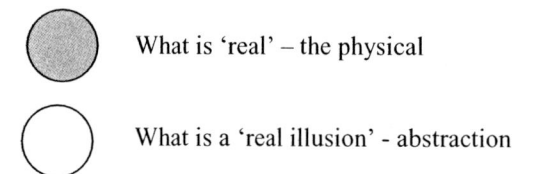

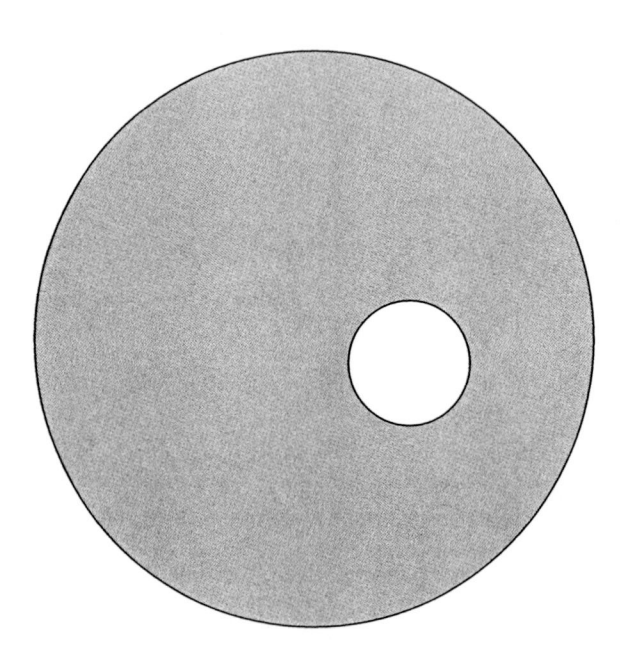

⬤   What is 'real' – the physical

◯   What is a 'real illusion' - abstraction

The Error of Zeno

This time we will place the physical 'within' a larger view of the physical and rather than obtain diagram #2 we find we have a different diagram which we shall label diagram #3.

Diagram #3:

    The elements:

        7.   The perceived 'real' – the physical
        8.   The perceived 'real' illusion - abstraction

●   What is 'real' – the physical

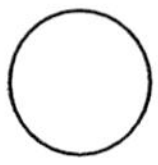

○   What is a 'real illusion' – the abstract

The War & Peace of a New Metaphysical Perception

Continuing to shrink the abstraction within the physical we get:

Diagram #3a:

    The elements:

        9.   The perceived 'real' – the physical
        10. The perceived 'real' illusion - abstraction

⬤   What is 'real' – the physical

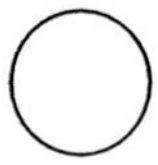

◯   What is a 'real illusion' – the abstract

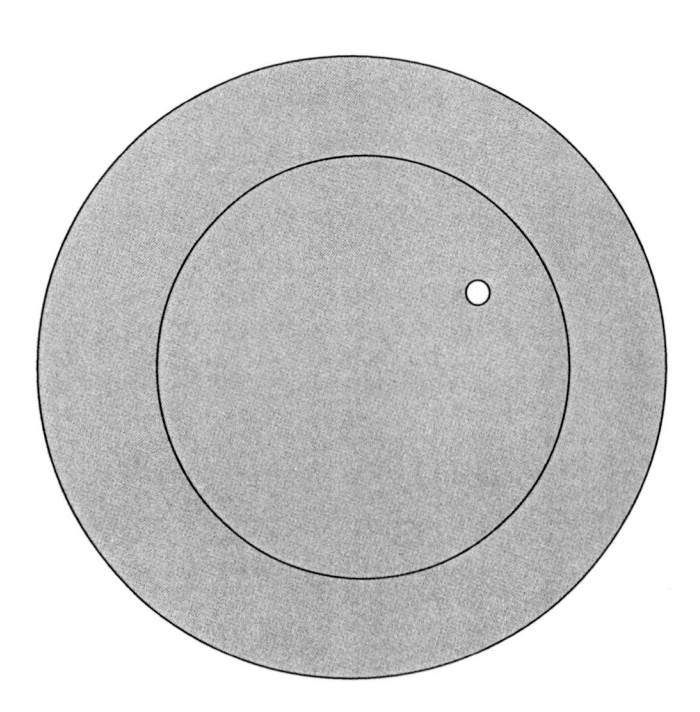

And then, if we add multiplicity to abstraction found 'within the physical we get:

Diagram #3b:

The elements:

> 11. The perceived 'real' – the physical
> 12. The perceived 'real' illusion - abstraction

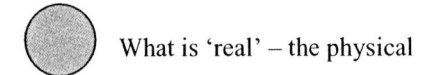

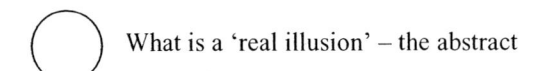

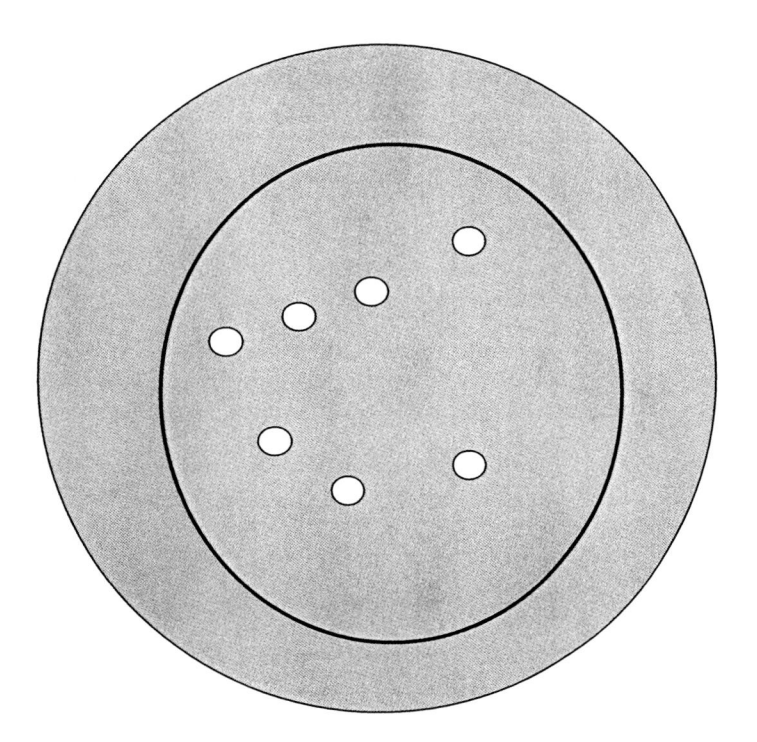

⬤ What is 'real' – the physical

◯ What is a 'real illusion' – the abstract

How is it we are able to 'arbitrarily enclose the physical with more of the physical? How are we logically able to draw such a perception? One might better ask the experts. One might want to ask the astrophysicists who argue for the 'Big Bang Theory'. One might inquire of the cosmologists supporting the theory of various vacuum level potentialities. One might even approach the experts in quantum mechanics, thermodynamics, or string theory. If one were to ask the metaphysician, which after all is a logical starting point since this discussion is being conducted by a metaphysician, one would receive the answer: we can increase the perceived 'size' by simply expanding our perception of the physical.

The War & Peace of a New Metaphysical Perception

What happens, now, if the physical remains and the abstract is removed which is the opposite of our previous scenario? If the abstract should cease to exist, it would appear the only item left would be the physical.

Diagram #3c with the abstract removed:

    The elements:

        3.   The 'real'
        4.   The 'real' illusion - erased

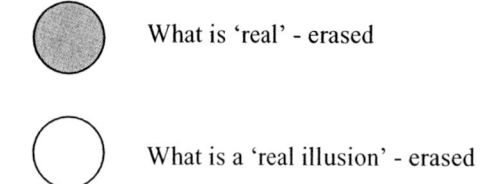

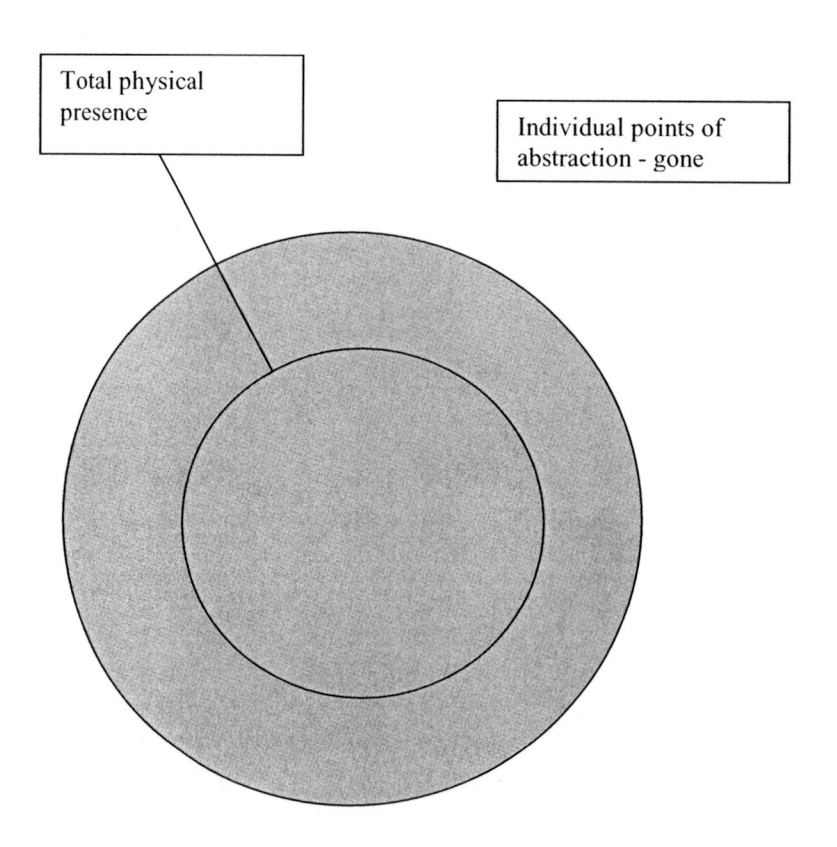

●   What is 'real' - erased

○   What is a 'real illusion' - erased

Total physical presence

Individual points of abstraction - gone

Now it appears the physical is all that is left. But if there is no awareness, no consciousness, does the 'real' really exist and even if it did would it matter? Regarding the existence of the physical void awareness, there is no rational argument we can present demonstrating an existence of the concept we refer to as 'significance of'.

This inverted view of what is 'real' and what is a 'real illusion', diagram #2, cannot be shown to be 'what is 'for in fact it 'isn't' anymore than diagram #1 'is'.

During Zeno's time, diagram #1 was 'real' only from the point of view of the concrete, the physical, when one was 'inside' the physical 'looking' 'into' the abstract. With the advent of today's ability to remove one's perception 'outside' of the 'real' we are able to move into a perception better illustrated by diagram #2.

The perception of diagram #2 is real from the point of perspective of being inside the inner form of abstraction looking 'out' into the physical as well as from the point of perspective of being inside the outer form of abstraction looking 'into' the physical. In addition, the perception created by diagram #2 is logical from the point of perception of being inside the physical looking either 'inward' into abstraction or looking 'outward' into abstraction. In short, regardless of where one stands within the system of diagram #2, the view is rational. This fact reinforces the concept of Diagram #2 being a logical perspective of totality. (The concept of standing in the 'outer' abstraction and looking 'outward' into (?) will be address in Chapter 18: Theoretical Metaphysics.)

Zeno's perception, Diagram #1, on the other hand has many problems regarding rational thinking. If one is standing within the physical and the abstract is erased, what of significance remains? It is rational to add an increment of awareness, abstraction, into the physical of diagram #2 but is it rational to add an increment of the physical into an abstraction of diagram #1? Etc.

Now what does all this have to do with Zeno and the paradox of motion? It leads to understanding Zeno's paradox as not being what it is perceived to be, namely a paradox.

To resolve Zeno's paradox we need a metaphysical perception, which would acknowledge and maintain the legitimacy regarding Zeno's perception of the multiplicity of distance existing simultaneously with the seamlessness of distance. Such a metaphysical perception would establish why Zeno's paradoxes are not paradoxes but rather only perceived paradoxes. In essence, such a perception may well assist both religion and science in better understanding what we call 'reality'. In fact, a new perspective may well be a necessity for our travels within the new frontiers of space and what better means of establishing a new perspective than metaphysics itself.

Working backward to Zeno

In order to better understand Zeno, we must understand Zeno's perspective of what was.
Let's begin with Diagram #1:

The War & Peace of a New Metaphysical Perception

Diagram #1:

    The elements:

        1. The 'real'
        2. The 'real' illusion

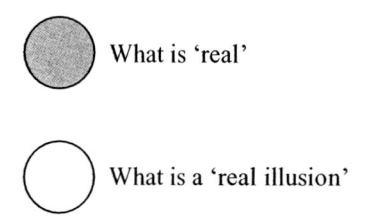

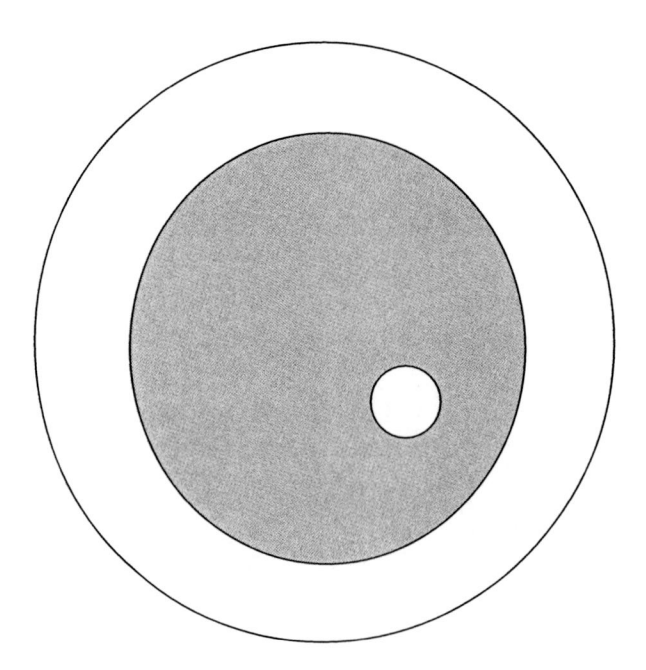

⬤ What is 'real'

○ What is a 'real illusion'

To get to Zeno's perception we will begin by extracting the outer circle composed of a 'real illusion' and discarding it.

Diagram #1a:

    The elements:

        1. The 'real'
        2. The 'real' illusion

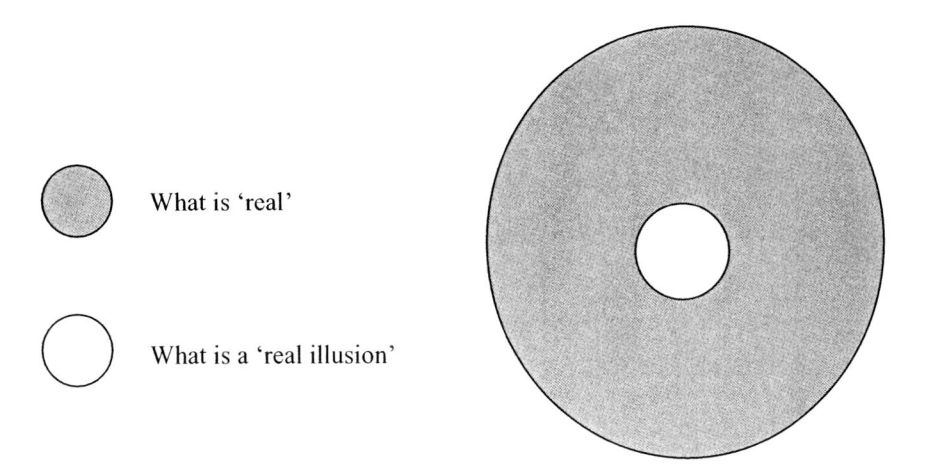

        ● What is 'real'

        ○ What is a 'real illusion'

This process gives us a much better understanding of where it was Zeno stood while perceiving 'things'. The next step is to shrink the size of the 'real illusion' and duplicate the locations of the 'real illusion' many times over.

Diagram #3:

    The elements:

        3. The 'real'
        4. The 'real' illusion

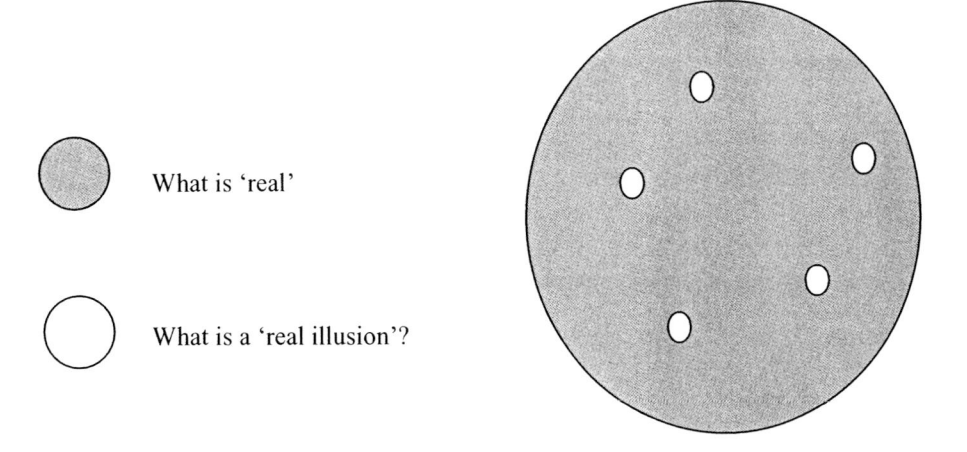

        ● What is 'real'

        ○ What is a 'real illusion'?

The War & Peace of a New Metaphysical Perception

The multiple circles of 'real illusions' represents illusions maintained, formed by multiple locations of individuality found within reality, found within a reality we call the 'real' world.

This Diagram comes closer to Zeno's perception than 'a' single location, a single perception of one and only one 'real illusion'. This may seem strange but in fact, it was a major leap for society and in particular for philosophy. In essence, not only was the real world of distance, the real world itself, subject to the laws of multiplicity but so too were abstractions subject to the laws of multiplicity.

Before this perception philosophy, society, basically looked at existence as:

Diagram #1:

>The elements:
>
>>1. The 'real'
>>2. The 'real' illusion

○ What is 'real'

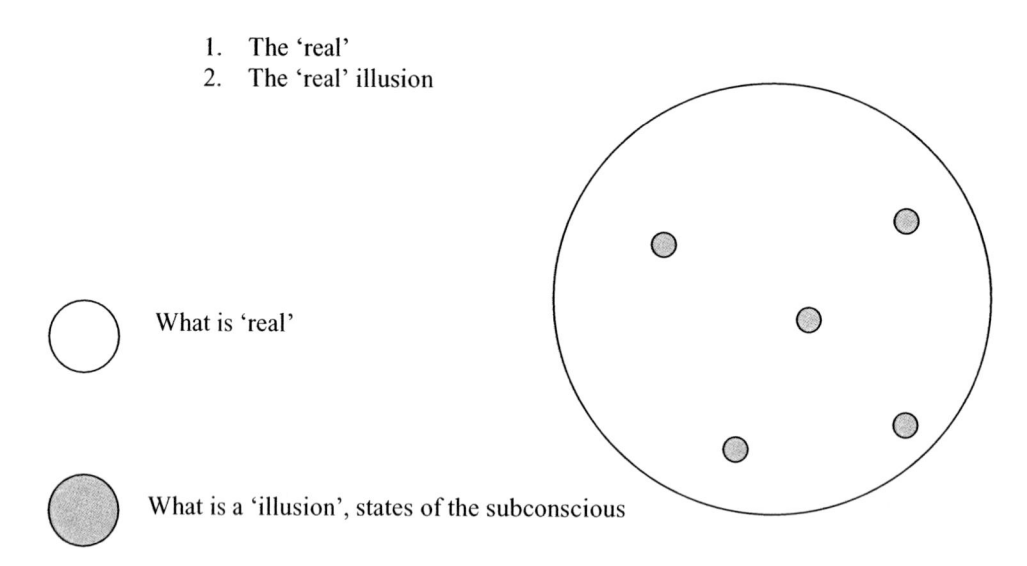

● What is a 'illusion', states of the subconscious

In essence, there were no 'real illusions'; rather there were simply illusion, abstractions that terminated with the death of the individual, and abstractions, which terminated with the death of the universe.

Zeno was unwittingly taking the first step in establishing the concepts 'being' *being* 'Being'.

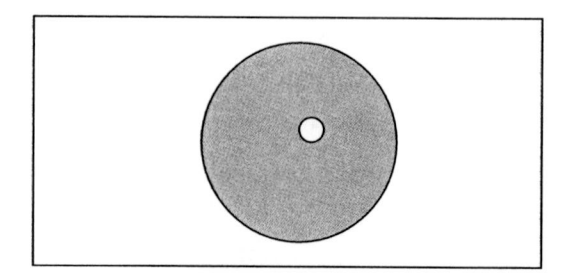

It would be another twenty-five hundred years before we could understand this evolving perception. It would take Boethius, Aristotle, Copernicus, Leibniz, Kant, Hegel, Russell,

Heidegger, Einstein, Dennett, Searle, Husserl, and Hawking before the picture of the 'real' existing simultaneously with a 'real illusion' would or for that matter could be painted. A new perception regarding what is 'real', what is a 'real illusion', and how the two were related would not emerge until the end of the second millennium and the beginning of the third millennium. This new perception would present itself within the mind of an unknown theoretical Metaphysician.

But what of Zeno? Zeno, himself, was not implying indirectly let alone directly that there were such things as 'real illusions'. Nevertheless, the simultaneous existence of the 'real' and of a 'real illusion', which became the 'real illusion' and the 'real' depending upon one's 'location' as one examined the two, is in fact what Zeno was unwittingly establishing. In all fairness to Zeno, we must acknowledge Zeno lived in another time and Zeno lacked many of the perceptual tools we have at our disposal today. As such, we must acknowledge Zeno could not logically have participated in, let alone initiated, the details required for this discussion as it presently transpires today.

Zeno's Paradoxes of Motion Revisited

Zeno initiated the concept of incrementalization, which in essence was the recognition of individuality. This individuality is not individuality only in terms of a living entity. Rather this individuality extends far beyond our universe and into the realm of unique individual universes themselves, universes infinite in terms of the dimensions length, width, depth, and time. Strangely enough, this 'infiniteness' of space is confined within a boundary bounding what we commonly call the universe or universes.

However, a boundary implies a 'region', which in turn takes up 'space', takes up 'distance', and as we shall see, takes up 'time', takes in time, and incorporates time. This 'bounded' 'region' 'contains' an infinite 'quantity' of time. But infinity is not always what it seems to be, as we shall see.

There is another alternative to concrete distance. There is a concept of abstract distance, which in effect takes up no 'space' for it is abstraction. Zeno showed us distance has two aspects to it. Distance has the aspect of physicalness and the aspect of abstraction. Both are real.

One is reality when one is immersed within it. From this viewpoint, from the viewpoint one perceives when one is immersed within the physical, the other, abstract distance, becomes a real illusion. One must not loose track of the fact, however, that abstractional distance does not 'go away' just because one is immersed 'within' the concrete functionality of distance, just because one is immersed within physical reality. Abstraction does not become unimportant, does not become 'just' an illusion when one is immersed 'within' the physical, the concrete, multiplicity.

One can erase the picture of a flower but the flower remains and the concept of the flower remains as well. Both the flower and the concept of the flower are real and both remain even after one erases the picture of the flower. Whether the flower itself or the concept of the flower itself, is 'real' is not the question for they are both 'real'. When one is 'real', the other appears to be a 'real illusion'. They oscillate back and forth from being 'real' to being a 'real illusion' depending upon where it is one 'stands' as one examines the flower, experiences the flower, finds oneself immersed 'with' the flower be it in an abstract sense or a physical/concrete sense.

Once 'within' the concrete, it is the reality of abstraction which takes on the appearance of being an illusion but which in fact is a 'real illusion', a 'functional' illusion. Once 'within' the abstract, it is the reality of the concrete, which takes on the appearance of being an illusion but which in fact is a 'real illusion', a 'functional' illusion. Neither the 'real' nor the 'real illusion' become

The War & Peace of a New Metaphysical Perception

unimportant to the whole for the whole cannot exist without the two for the two are integrated as one, and are in fact the 'whole'. Each is dependent upon the other. The one, the Cartesian, the physical/concrete, is the engine of the other, the non-Cartesian, the abstract. And the other, the non-Cartesian, the abstract is the 'creator' of the other, the physical/concrete, of its own engine, of its means to 'grow' as opposed to stagnating or decaying away.

So which is the innate characteristic of which? Is the abstract – seamlessness the innate characteristic of the physical – multiplicity or is the physical - multiplicity the innate characteristic of the abstract – seamlessness. The complex answer is: It all depends upon where one is standing when one asks the question. Since we perceive ourselves to be 'within' the physical when we ask the question, the answer surprisingly becomes: the physical is the innate characteristic of the abstract. The physical is simply a 'real illusion'. The physical has something inherently related to it. The physical is connected with time and time, by its very property of having infinity and zero attached to it, is limited.

And how can this be so? It is so because zero and infinity are one in the same, meet in the same place.

To better understand this concept one only need examine a simple number line:

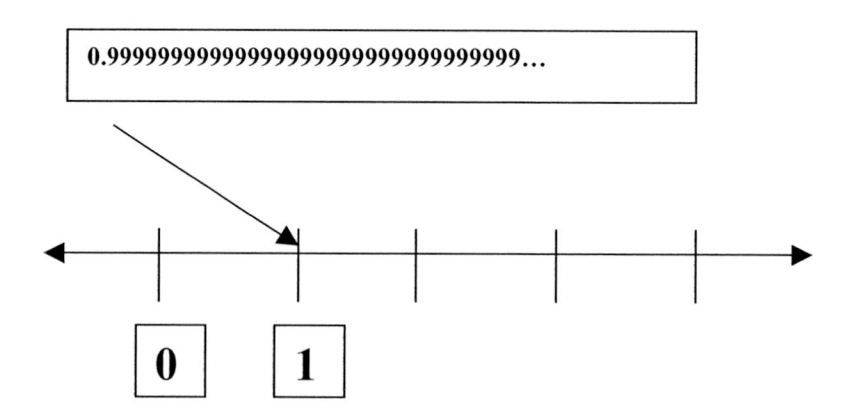

> 0.9999999999999999999999999999999...

| 0 | 1 |

Now it would appear the next step is:

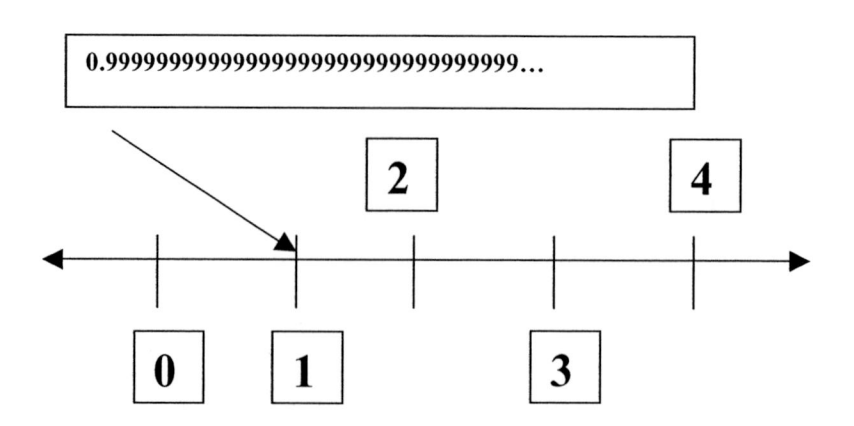

> 0.9999999999999999999999999999999...

| 0 | 1 | | 2 | | 3 | | 4 |

40

The Error of Zeno

But this is not so. It is only the case if one ignores the concept of individuality. If one retains the concept of individuality, then the graph becomes:

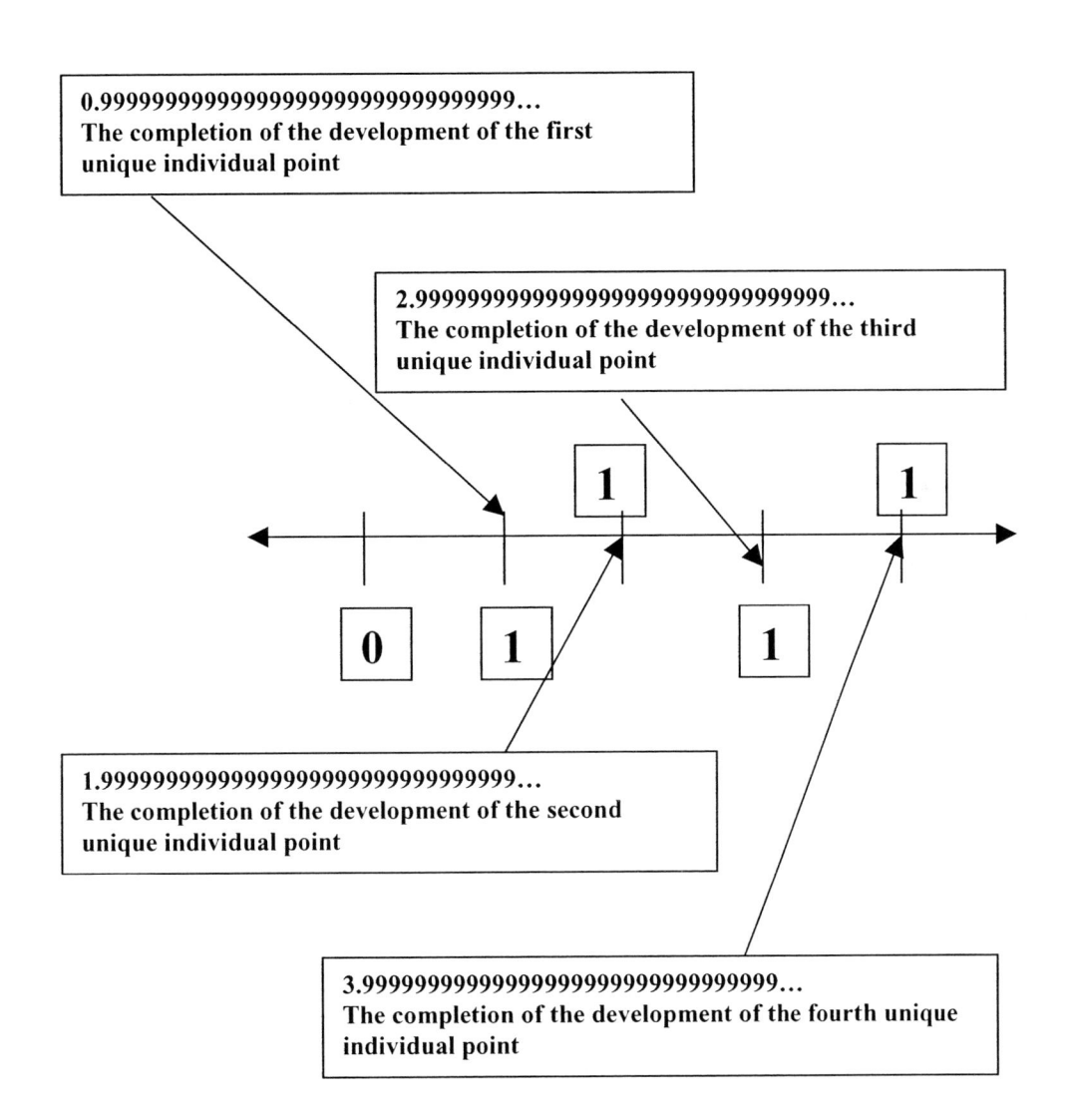

0.999999999999999999999999999999...
The completion of the development of the first unique individual point

2.999999999999999999999999999999...
The completion of the development of the third unique individual point

1.999999999999999999999999999999...
The completion of the development of the second unique individual point

3.999999999999999999999999999999...
The completion of the development of the fourth unique individual point

The War & Peace of a New Metaphysical Perception

And what then is zero? Why zero is the beginning of the development of the unique individual point. But if that is so then the graph is once again incomplete and should in actuality become:

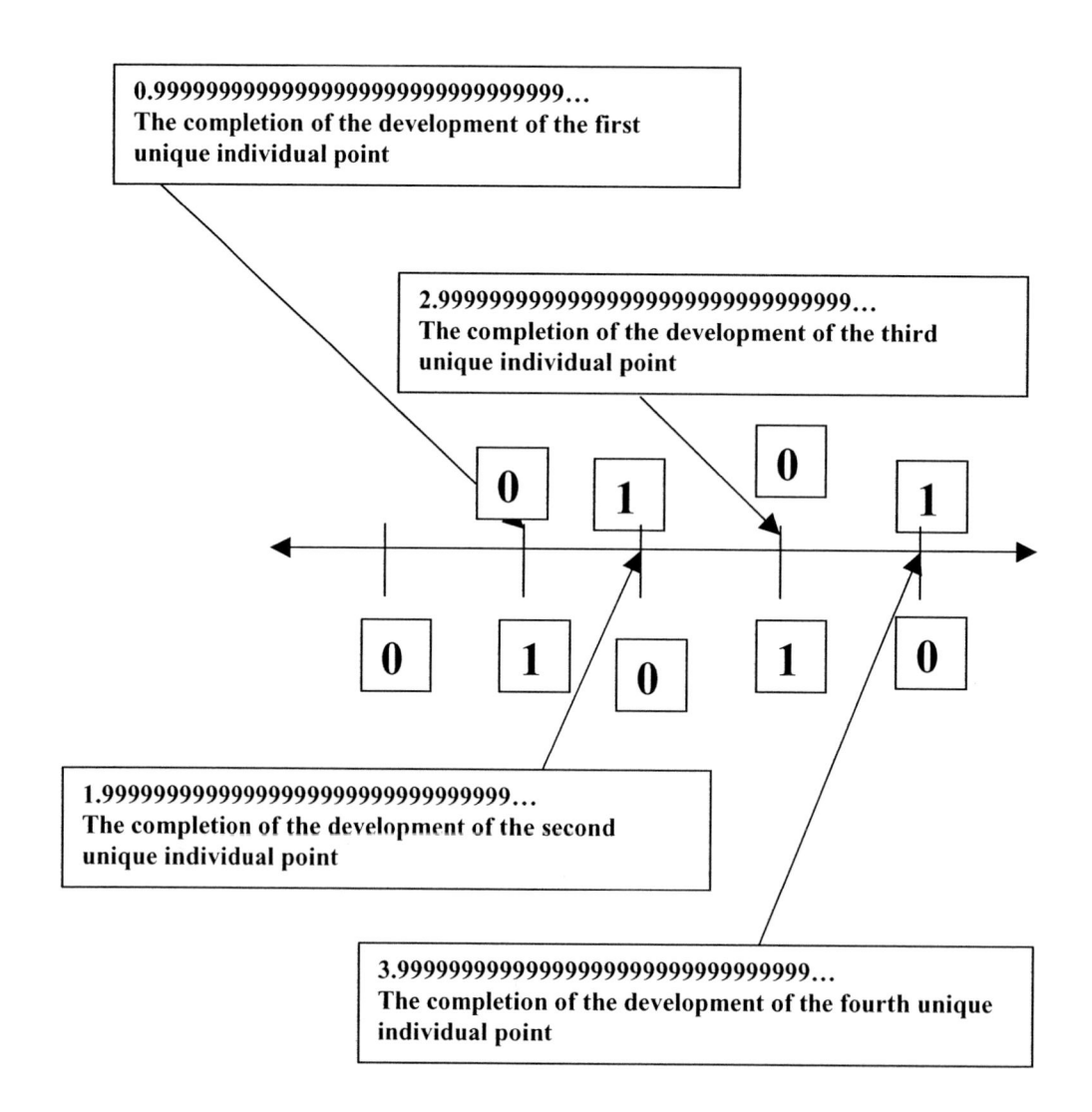

0.999999999999999999999999999999...
The completion of the development of the first unique individual point

2.999999999999999999999999999999...
The completion of the development of the third unique individual point

1.999999999999999999999999999999...
The completion of the development of the second unique individual point

3.999999999999999999999999999999...
The completion of the development of the fourth unique individual point

Or more simply put:

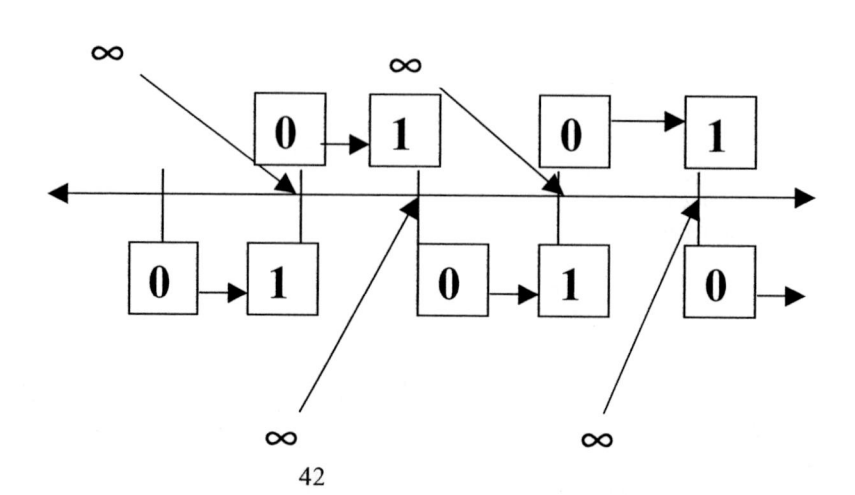

As we can see, individual units of mathematics, in fact individual points themselves, albeit they are incrementally so small they do not exist in terms of dimensions, begin with zero and expand to the point of infiniteness itself. Now this may be the case with mathematical points but what of individuality?

The individuality of each unique 'piece' of awareness also begins with zero, zero awareness, and expands into being itself, unique, through Zeno's concept of infinite 'multiplicity' or as is the case of individuals, infinite numbers of events an individual experiences. Regardless of the number of years, months, days, hours, minutes, seconds... the individual, once put into action of being, having 'become', experiences infinitely.

Who is to deny, once having gone from point A to point B the individual has experienced infinitely. After all, one experiences while having gone half the distance and one experiences while going half the remaining half, etc. On the other hand one has experienced differently if one views the summation of one's experience in terms of the summation of experience incurred when having gone two thirds the distance as opposed to the summation of experience incurred having gone one half the distance. The two summations of experiences provide the individual with an entirely different and unique perception of its existence. The very establishment of the zero point of becoming, what may better be referred to as virgin consciousness, one's very existence, is in a sense an establishment of infinite existence for the individual in terms of multiplicity of being.

For example, lets us say the life existed for a nanosecond, Zeno's paradox shows that in fact the life lived for half of a nanosecond and half of the remaining half, and half of the remaining half. But that deals with time, what about motion? In that nanosecond the form moved however little it moved and as such it moved half the distance from it original position its final position, and then half that half then half that half etc.

The individual's perception of its total summation of half experiences is different from that same individual's perception of its total summation of two thirds of its whole experience plus two thirds of the remainder plus two thirds of the remainder of the remainder etc.

Perceptions differ by increments of fourths, fifths, sixths,

Now mathematicians would step in at this point and say: No, it was just one continual flow from point 'A' to point 'B'. But they are wrong. Calculus may allow us to understand, see, a continual flow of motion but Zeno is still correct, during each step of the way, at each point existing between point 'A' and point 'B', the life, awareness, was aware of, experienced, and as such an infinite series of experiences occurred, multiplicity occurred and Calculus cannot negate this fact.

Now it is true Calculus can provide us with a means of moving on and leaving this point of confusion behind but it cannot eradicate the fact that incrementalization does in fact occur.

'So what?', one may ask. So it is up to us, philosophers, to answer Zeno's paradox, bring forth a rational resolution to this paradox. It is up to us, philosophers, to bring forth a rational resolution regarding Zeno's paradox. Such a resolution takes a detailed understanding of this paradox. Understanding Zeno's paradox assists us in understanding ourselves, understanding where we are, understanding what we are, and most interestingly of all, understanding why we exist, understanding what our function for existing is.

With this in mind lets once again look at the number line and think of it in terms of the abstract concept of awareness rather than the impersonal cold concept of points on a line.

The War & Peace of a New Metaphysical Perception

The end of each unit on the number line can be thought of as the end of one increment of individuality and the beginning of another increment of individuality, a form of individualistic seamlessness. But seamlessness of distance can only be seamlessness when viewed in the abstract. The same applies to individuality. In the abstract then the diagram would look more like:

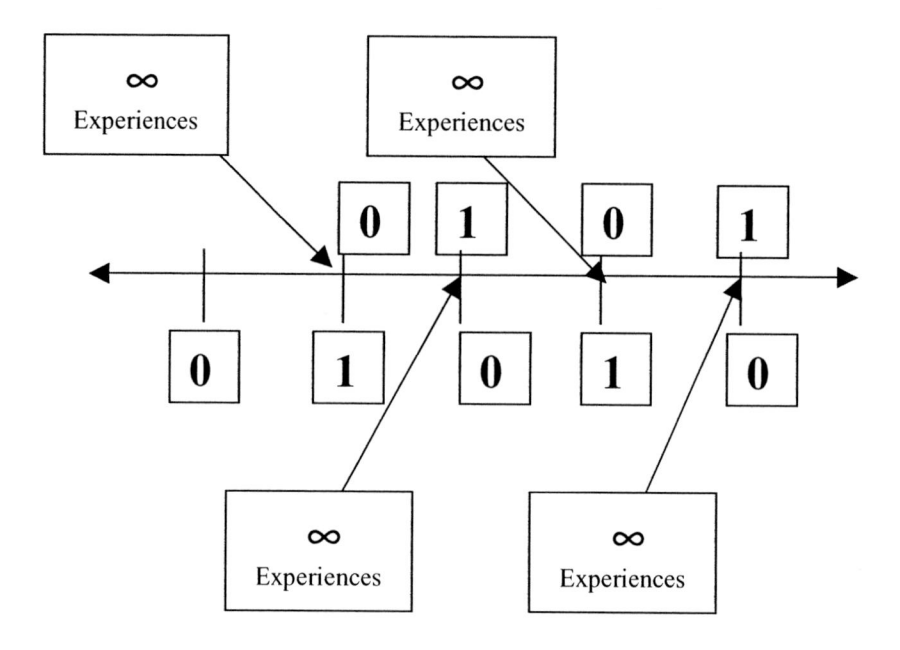

Now if we break this diagram up into its unique pieces of individuality we obtain:

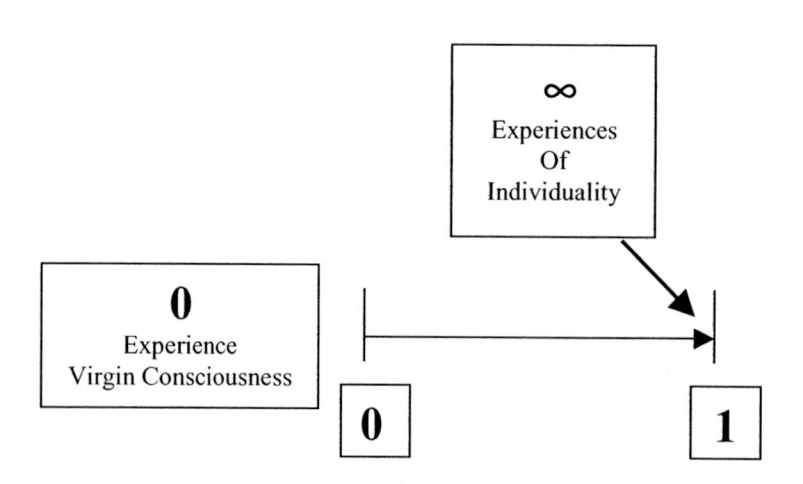

Now where is time in all this? Time is a part of experience and so we obtain:

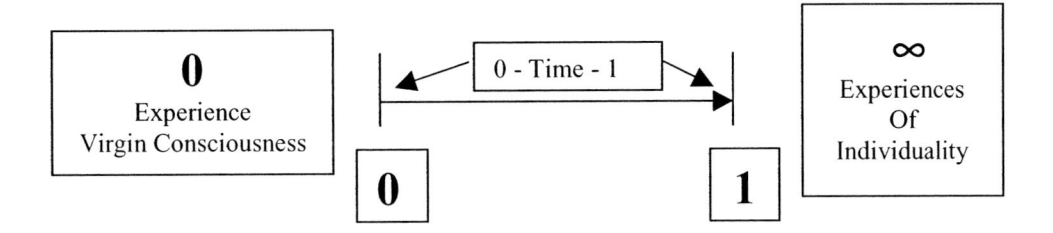

```
┌──────────────────┐                                    ┌──────────────────┐
│        0         │         ┌─ 0 - Time - 1 ─┐         │        ∞         │
│    Experience    │      ←──┤                ├──→      │    Experiences   │
│ Virgin Consciousness│     └────────────────┘          │        Of        │
│                  │                                    │   Individuality  │
└──────────────────┘      ┌───┐            ┌───┐        └──────────────────┘
                          │ 0 │            │ 1 │
                          └───┘            └───┘
```

Therefore, it is the individual who moves through time. It is the individual who gains experience beginning with no experience, beginning with virgin consciousness and ends with the end of consciousness, the end of the individual traveling through time. So it is the individual leaves the concrete, the physical, multiplicity and moves into the abstract, seamlessness.

We can examine the concept regarding the meaning of Zeno's implied concept of abstractional existence – seamlessness existing within the physical – multiplicity but first we need to examine the concept regarding Greek 'incrementals' a little further.

Or

One could say: Before we can go there, before we examine the concept of the meaning of Zeno's implied concept of an existence, of the physical – multiplicity within which abstraction – seamlessness can be found, we need to examine the concept of Greek 'incrementals' a little further.

Now what is the difference between these two statements? The difference can be more clearly understood through diagrams rather than words.

The War & Peace of a New Metaphysical Perception

The appearance of the 'real' and the 'real illusion':

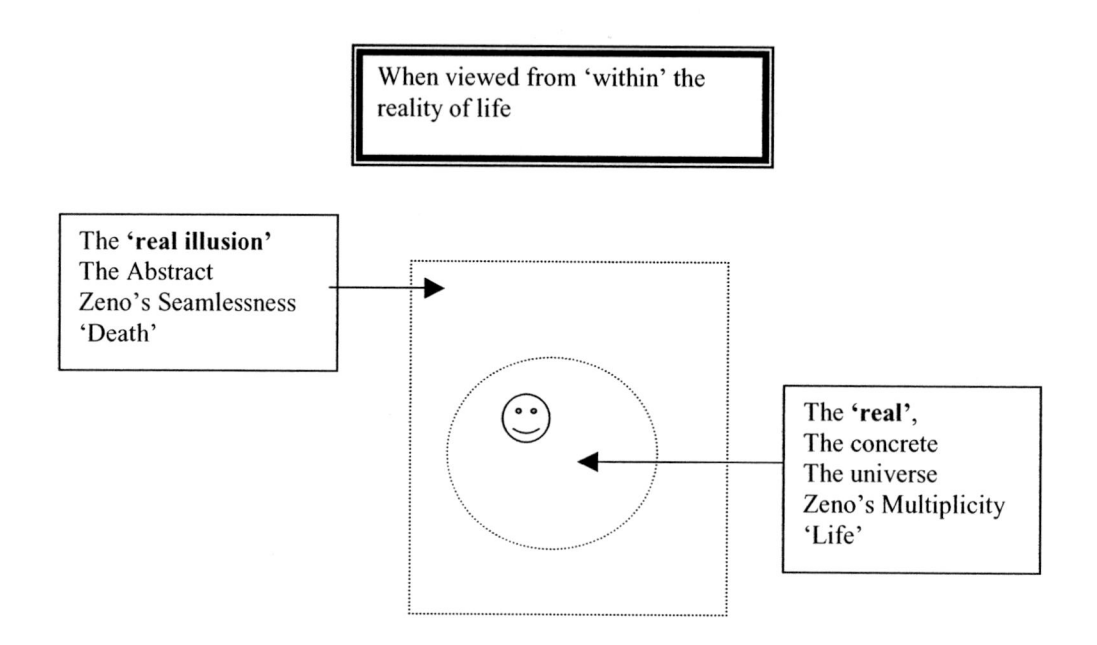

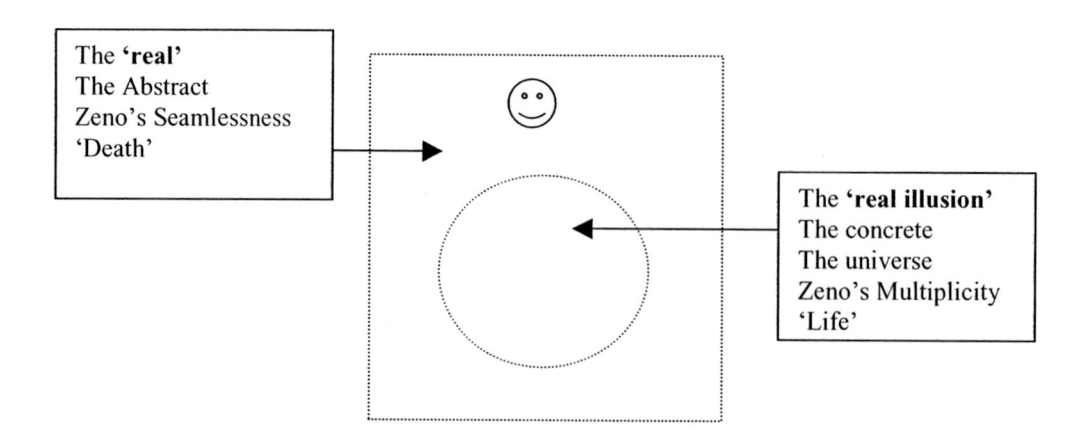

When viewed from 'within' the reality of life

The **real illusion**
The Abstract
Zeno's Seamlessness
'Death'

The **real**,
The concrete
The universe
Zeno's Multiplicity
'Life'

When viewed from 'within' the reality of Death

The **real**
The Abstract
Zeno's Seamlessness
'Death'

The **real illusion**
The concrete
The universe
Zeno's Multiplicity
'Life'

Look familiar?

Now what does one view from the point of view of being 'within' death? One views experiences that are. One views all experiences that 'are' but none that 'are yet to be'. One would think this concept of 'to be' implies the existence of time and that is true but not in the traditional sense for time is not a part of what the incremental pieces of awareness, find themselves located 'within' abstraction. Rather time is a part of the experiences individuality has created for itself, created for the whole while being a part of, 'within' the physical.

Thus time is not something 'within' which the whole, the abstract – seamlessness, finds itself immersed but rather time is something immersed within the pieces of individuality, tied to the physical, concrete multiplicity of the individual's awareness. Time is but a process by which the chaos of the Brownian motion of time itself becomes orderly.

The implications of this will be fully addressed within Chapter 9: 'Einstein and i'. At this stage of the examination of a new philosophical perception, we have all we can do to remain focused upon the concept of the individual in terms of abstraction – seamlessness and the physical – multiplicity.

So what of life and death? We view life as existing and death as the state of non-existence. As such we view life as not only being sacred but we view life as something to be protected at all costs. Some would say we should allow one individual to take the life of another rather than perform the ultimate act of finality ourselves, the act of taking the life of a third party threatening to take the life of an innocent second party.

From the point of view of 'death', or might we better say, from the point of view of purely abstract existence, it is the journey itself which must be protected. It is the journey, through the process of living life that has significance.

It must be noted here, that to perform capital punishment is not protecting life, protecting a journey. Once incarceration of the guilty party has occurred, the journey of others has already been protected. To electrocute the incarcerated life form, to electrocute the guilty party, is nothing short of needlessly terminating a journey, which has already been restrained from harming other journeys. In short, capital punishment is nothing less than 'murder'.

The Greek concept of 'the incremental'

So where does this bring us in terms of the Greek concept of incrementals? It brings us to the concept that it is the individual which must be protected, for the individual is 'the' increment of awareness.

We naturally fall into the argument that it is life, which we must protect but that in fact is only one perception that can be derived from this line of thought. Perhaps a more rational argument is that it is not life which must be raised to the level of the ultimate significance but rather the journey of life itself, the 'right' to travel in one's own unique manner, uninhibited by the desire of others to dominate, subjugate, dictate how others are to journey, which must be raised to the level of the ultimate significance.

The validity of each argument, whether it is life or the journey of life that is to be protected, is dependent upon the location from which one views the argument. There is, however, no denying that now, at this point in time, that the second point - the point that it is the journey - which must be protected, and not life as such, becomes a potentially viable alternative.

The War & Peace of a New Metaphysical Perception

So lets look at the concept of life, the beginning of an individual, the initiation of the individual, the beginning of existence in the physical/concrete - multiplicity, and lets look at the concept of death, the end of the individual, the end of existence in the physical/concrete – multiplicity.

Just what does this have to do with 'incremental' concepts? The individual is in essence 'an' incremental piece of 'the whole'. The individual is in essence a piece of the 'whole' of awareness.

Zeno's Perspective

When viewed from 'within' the reality of 'life'

The **'real illusion'**
The Abstract
Zeno's seamlessness
Death

The **'real'**,
The concrete
The universe
Zeno's multiplicity
Life

Zeno's perception generates a paradox for there is no 'whole' of perception. The perception becomes even more muddled when we move awareness from consciousness of its own awareness into what we perceive to be nonawareness of its own awareness:

The Error of Zeno

> When viewed from 'within' the reality of 'death'

The 'real'
The Abstract
Zeno's Seamlessness
'Death'

The 'real illusion'
The concrete
The universe
Zeno's Multiplicity
'Life'

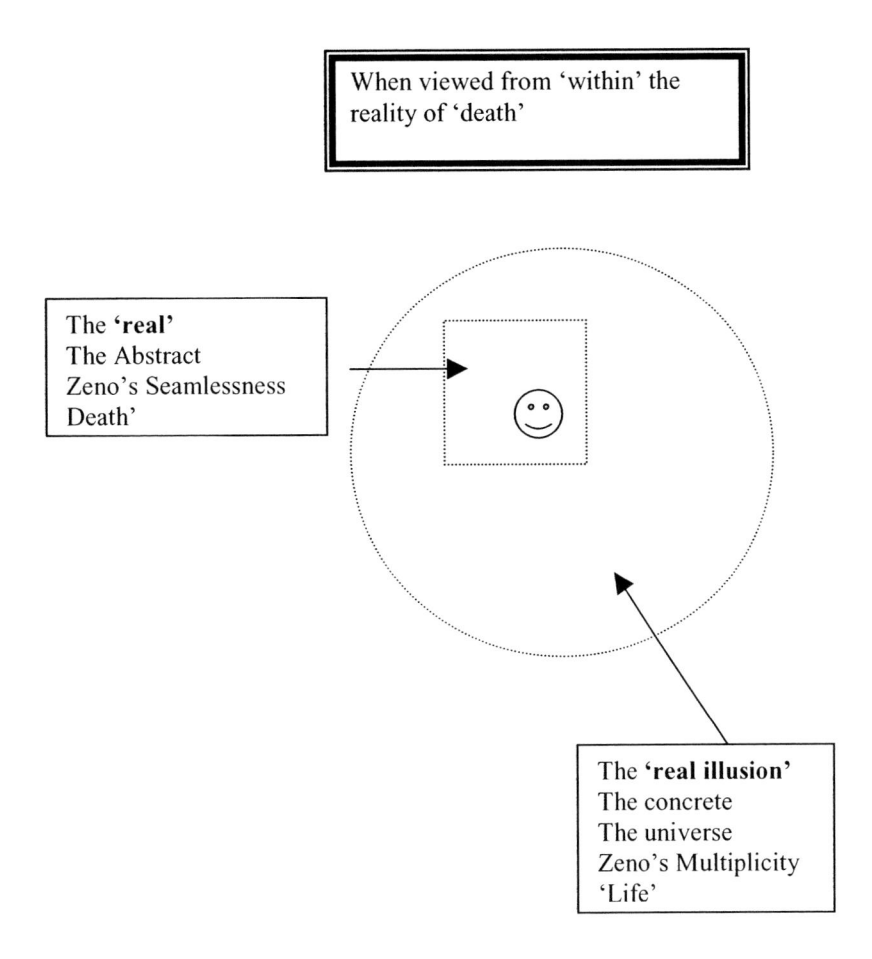

So it is the 'real' and the 'real illusion' become the 'real illusion' and the 'real'. The 'real' and the 'real illusion' alternate back and forth as one moves from one to the other. We do not, however, view it as such. Instead, we view it as life being the state of existing and death being the state of not existing, death being the end of it all….

In the case of life and death, the perceptual 'size' of the universe did not grow to accommodate, make room for the abstract. Zeno's perception of an abstractual existence did not interpret into an understanding of death being simply a movement into a form of abstractual existence. Instead, we discard death because we view it as the end. As such, death did not expand upon our perception of what is but rather death simply became a non-existence taking up no space in reality and thus reality remained what it was: small, limited, a permanent location for temporary existence.

In spite of our faith in life after death, we have not been able to rationalize such a concept. Science has been unable to observe such an existence and philosophy has been unable to rationalize such an existence. As such, existence after death remains only a matter of faith.

We are an entity capable of forming perceptions using three basic means of action: believing, observing, and reasoning. As of yesterday, only one means of forming perceptions existed. This perceptual process for reinforcing the concept of eternity existing for the individual was a matter of faith, believing.

Zeno, with his paradox of motion, put into play the philosophical and scientific debate regarding an understanding of timelessness, of eternal existence. It was only a matter of time as to which, science or philosophy, was to reach an understanding of timelessness second.

That point has now been reached by philosophy. It could be argued philosophy has not reached a point of rationally understanding the existence of seamlessness, rationally understanding an existence without time being the ether within which existence is immersed.

It could be argued that philosophy has not reached an understanding regarding an eternal existence independent of time resting upon the understanding of mathematics and science, resting upon the understanding regarding the primitive concept of nothingness being the spark for the explosion separating the symmetrical concepts of matter, anti-matter, energy, and anti-energy.

Such arguments however, are not the point. The point is philosophy, as of the end of the twentieth century and the beginning of the third millennium, has reached this point and science has not. No, actually the point is the vote for an existence of a timeless awareness is now two to one in favor of the concept rather than two to one against the concept of timeless awareness. The tide has turned. The significance in this turning of the tide lies in the fact that an overwhelming majority, two to one, the two, religion and philosophy, verses the one, science, means we now have the votes necessary to move toward the acceptance of the individual as 'the' increment of timeless awareness. Thus the necessary votes to treat the individual treat all individuals, as 'the' significant entity because it is eternal.

This in turn brings us back to the question that had been previously asked: This seems so inconsequential when one views a small child starving in Uganda, but is it?

We can now return to the concept regarding the significance of such a child. No longer is the child simply a child, dies, and is no more. Two out of three means we have for developing perceptions, religion and philosophy, now both agree the child is not simply a child, dies, and is no more. Two out of three means we have for developing perceptions, religion and philosophy, now both agree the child is a child, leaves the temporariness of the physical, and enters the timelessness of the abstract.

(The function of this piece of awareness, of this child, to the Whole is intuitively obvious. Despite this fact, however, the concept will be dealt with in detail in many of the following chapters and in particular in Chapter 10: Heidegger and Chapter 14: Metaphysical Systems.)

Repeatedly we come back to Zeno. Zeno leads us from what was before he began thinking...

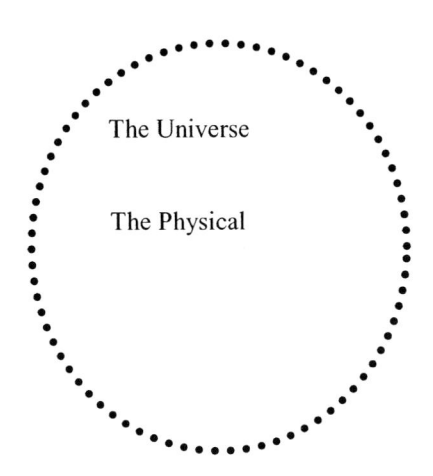

Physical Distance

The Universe

The Physical

...to what was after he began thinking...

Physical Distance - 'Multiplicity'
&
Abstract Distance – 'Seamlessness'

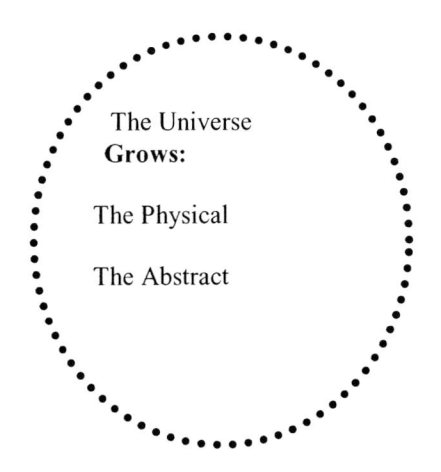

The Universe
Grows:

The Physical

The Abstract

The War & Peace of a New Metaphysical Perception

…which in turn became a new but elusive concept of the physical – 'multiplicity' 'containing' abstraction – 'seamlessness'. Zeno initiated the debate within which religion, philosophy, and science became embroiled. Zeno in essence defined the debate.

Zeno initiated the perceptual growth of what we understood to be true. Zeno forced us into debating the concept of multiplicity existing separate from the concept of seamlessness verses multiplicity existing simultaneously with seamlessness. This in turn forced us into examining multiplicity and seamlessness, examining where such concepts were 'located' with respect to each other, examining how such concepts interacted, and examining what our role was in such an interaction

Zeno began this long-term (twenty five hundred years) speculation through the process of expanding upon what we perceived to be with the simple introduction of his paradoxes of space/distance and space/time. Zeno lead to the growth of what it was we perceived to be. Zeno expanded upon our perception of the universe. Zeno added the concept of seamlessness to our perceptual understanding as to what was to be 'found' within the universe.

But the increase in perception did not resolve Zeno's paradox for it did not explain why the paradox was a paradox when viewed from Zeno's perception as seen from his 'location' 'within' the physical/concrete. The resolution of Zeno's paradox would take a greater expansion than that proposed by Zeno – the inclusion of seamlessness/abstraction, within the concrete/multiplicity.

In essence, Zeno was standing on the departure platform he built and waving goodbye to us, humanity, as we boarded the train for the long trip which would lead us to our present destination, an understanding of a 'location', a definition, and a significance of what is.

The Error of Zeno

After twenty-five hundred years we would find ourselves expanding Zeno's perception of what is. After twenty-five hundred years, we would find ourselves looking at a simple diagram of a new perception of what is.

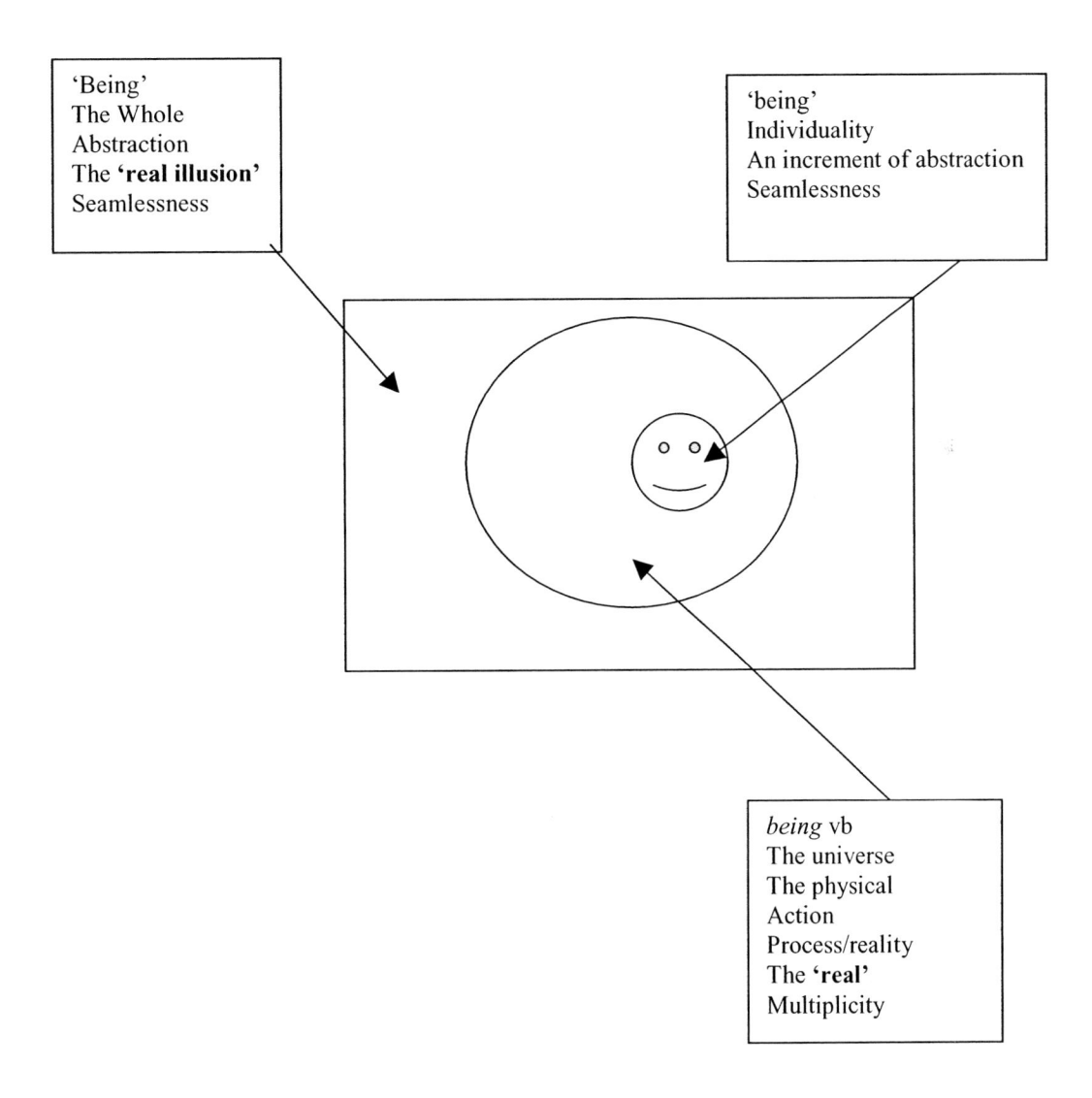

'Being'
The Whole
Abstraction
The **'real illusion'**
Seamlessness

'being'
Individuality
An increment of abstraction
Seamlessness

being vb
The universe
The physical
Action
Process/reality
The **'real'**
Multiplicity

Or what one might call:

    Philosophically speaking: **'being'** *being* **'Being'**
    Religiously speaking: symbiotic **panentheism**
    Scientifically speaking: ? (**symbiotic** panentheism)

Before we leave Zeno, lets examine a few more aspects regarding the logic of Symbiotic Panentheism

It all lies in the details: Regarding 'being' *being* 'Being'

Why place a question mark following scientifically speaking in the previous paragraph? We place a question mark following science for science has yet to agree to the concept of existence without time.

But, one may protest, neither has philosophy confirmed its agreement regarding an existence without time. The difference is the philosophical argument has been put forward in detail, via this work, and as such it exists. Until an overwhelming rationale such as this work has been logically torn apart and its demise confirmed by the majority of philosophers, it remains what it is:

> A new metaphysical perception incorporating the simultaneous existence of a non-Cartesian and Cartesian where the non-Cartesian system is 'powered' by the Cartesian system.

Lets examine how this new perception would deal with such a complex statement. In essence, we are about to delve deeper into Zeno's concepts of multiplicity and seamlessness.

Calculus is but a tool – it does not eliminate what is

Calculus helps us mentally move from point A to point B in a smooth transitional manner but it does not eliminate the concept of multiplicity. How is it we can assume the Greek concept of the incremental 'is' rather than the new perception of no incremental segments of existence?

We can be fairly certain the existence of the incremental of multiplicity, exists. Not only does the concept of the incremental, multiplicity appear all around us but the incremental, multiplicity, lies at the heart of individuality. The individual is an incremental slice of total awareness, knowing. If the individual is not a packet in and of itself interacting with other independent packets of individuality, than the individual becomes sliding pieces of experience fusing with other packets which all in the end loose their property of being independent of, distinct from, each other. The process, the concept of seamless individualism, leads to the loss of individuality itself through the process of universal fusion with the whole.

The process of the individual fusing with other individuals is the process the establishment, the leaders of our specie, want individuals to accept. The loss of individuality is the driving force within our specie, which generates perceptions of superiority of one over another. The fusion of individuals into a single entity, into singularity, generates the concept of our specie being superior to other species of the universe, generates the concept of the ends justifies the means, generates the concept of 'let's get 'em boys'. The concept 'we are one', 'there is an end to it all', 'there is no individuality', all gain their coherency and strength through the concept 'death is the end of it all', the end of your existence.

It is only through the concept of 'don't think for yourself let me do it for you' that 'the' leader and thus 'the' 'special' individual gains power while the masses lose their individuality through being just that, the masses. It is through the concept of fusion, seamlessness, as opposed to the acceptance of individuality, multiplicity, that individuality loses all its uniqueness upon death. It is only through the perceptual establishment of the concept 'seamlessness prevails' which reinforces the faith we have in letting others think for us rather than thinking for ourselves that we find the individual looses its significance and thus is rationally treated as it is: positively/supportively and negatively/abusively.

How does calculus fit into all this? Calculus is a tool needed to help us move beyond the concept of incrementalism, move on with our process of functioning 'within' the universe, functioning 'within' the real illusion. As much as Mathematicians yearn for the elimination of the paradoxes

The Error of Zeno

multiplicity generates, Calculus does not eliminate the individual points, does not eliminate the concept of distance, does not eliminate the concept of dividing 'it all' into smaller parts, does not eliminate the simple concept of the incremental.

As far as we are aware, the smallest part of the Whole that affects ourselves directly, is the individual packet of the abstract, the increment of knowing, from which the very concept of knowledge comes.

The basic unit of the whole of knowing is not the quark nor the 'string particle' but the individual. As such, lets look at the individual more closely in terms of its symbolic representation through our continued use of the mathematical concept - a number line.

Incrementalism and the Individual

We can now take:

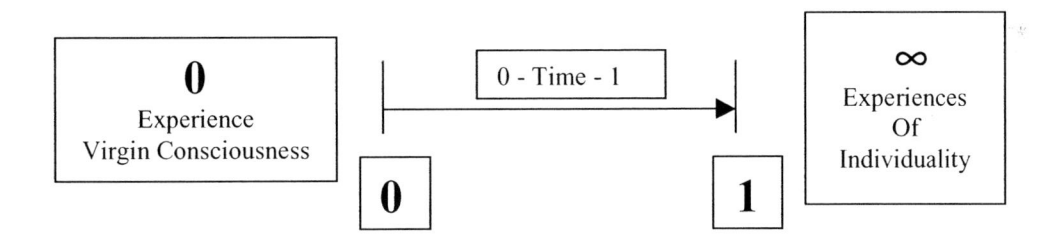

```
┌─────────────────┐                                    ┌─────────────────┐
│        0        │      ┌──── 0 - Time - 1 ────┐      │        ∞        │
│   Experience    │      ├──────────────────────▶│      │   Experiences   │
│Virgin Conscious-│      │                       │      │       Of        │
│     ness        │    ┌─┴─┐                   ┌─┴─┐    │  Individuality  │
└─────────────────┘    │ 0 │                   │ 1 │    └─────────────────┘
                       └───┘                   └───┘
```

And simplify its representation in order to expand upon our understanding of it.

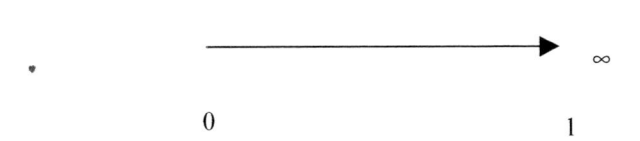

```
            •      ─────────────────▶  ∞
                   0                1
```

In spite of having simplified matters, we understand this to be a representation of the individual. We also understand the individual to be an entity existing within more than 'one' dimension when it comes to existing within our particular universe. As such, our understanding of the individual grows to become two dimensional:

The War & Peace of a New Metaphysical Perception

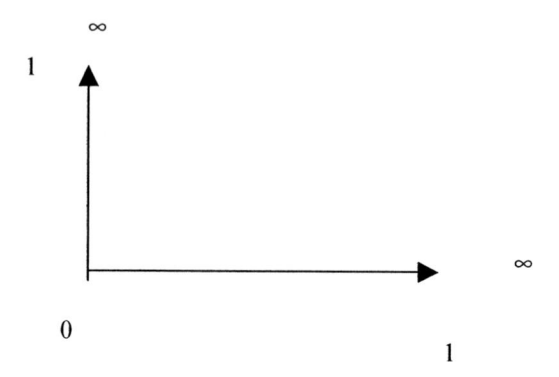

And grows again to become three dimensional:

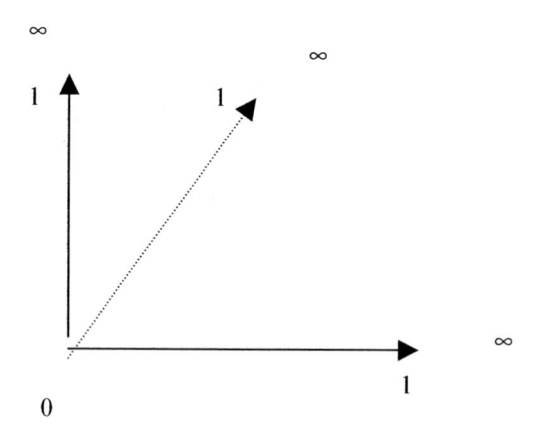

And we must not forget time in all this:

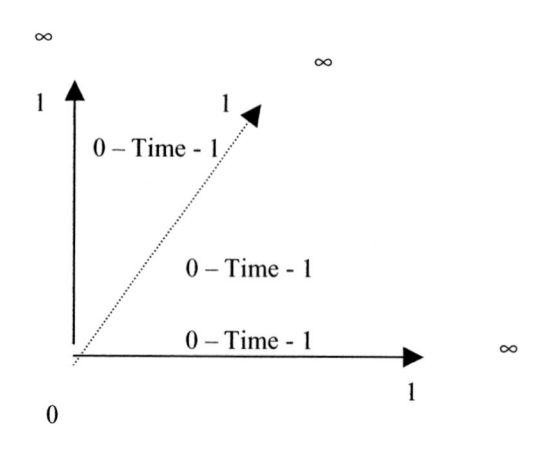

The Error of Zeno

This then becomes:

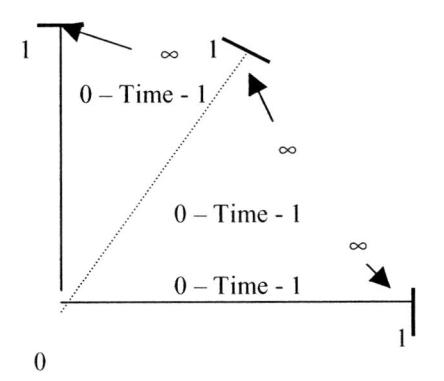

Which becomes:

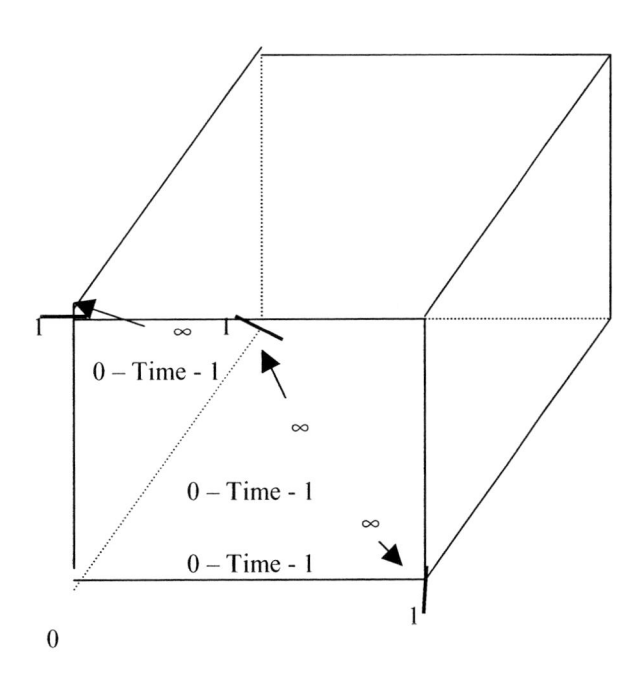

The War & Peace of a New Metaphysical Perception

Or to simplify matters

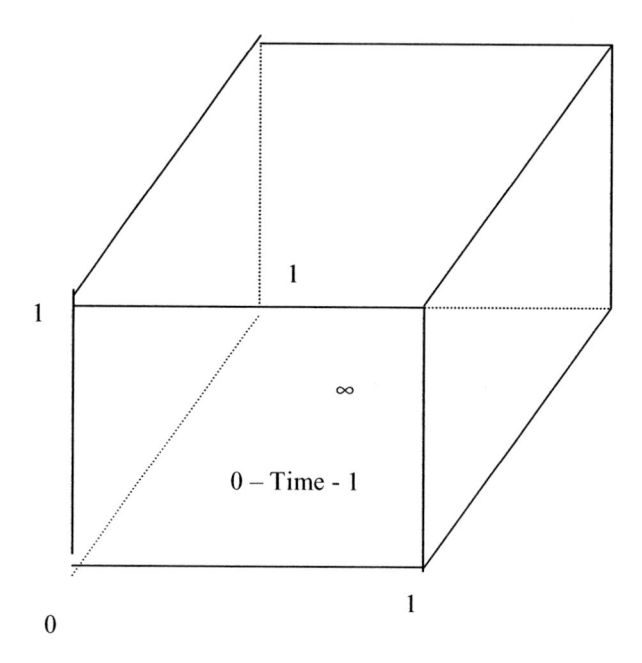

[Diagram: a rectangular box with labels "1" on top edge, "1" on left edge, "1" on right edge, "0" at bottom left, "1" at bottom right, "∞" inside, and "0 – Time - 1" labeled across the middle]

In essence, we begin to understand that time is found 'within' an increment of an individual rather than an increment of an individual found 'within' time.

In short, we begin to see time as a function of the individual increment rather than the reverse. From this point forward in this discussion, it is imperative not to lose track of the concept that time is not being referred to as simply a characteristic of 'an' 'aware' 'being'. We assume we have awareness but all existences, be they 'aware' or otherwise (rocks, trees, rivers…), would 'contain' time. Thus time is an innate characteristic of simply 'existing' 'within' reality, existing 'within' the universe, existing 'within' the 'real illusion' of the universe, if viewed from 'within' the relative position of the abstract.

If we reduce the apparent size of the diagram above representing the individual, we obtain:

[small cube diagram]

The Error of Zeno

And further reduction gives us:

and again:

If we place this increment within the new perception, into the perception of 'being' *being* 'Being', symbiotic panentheism, we obtain:

When viewed from 'within' the reality of perceived Death

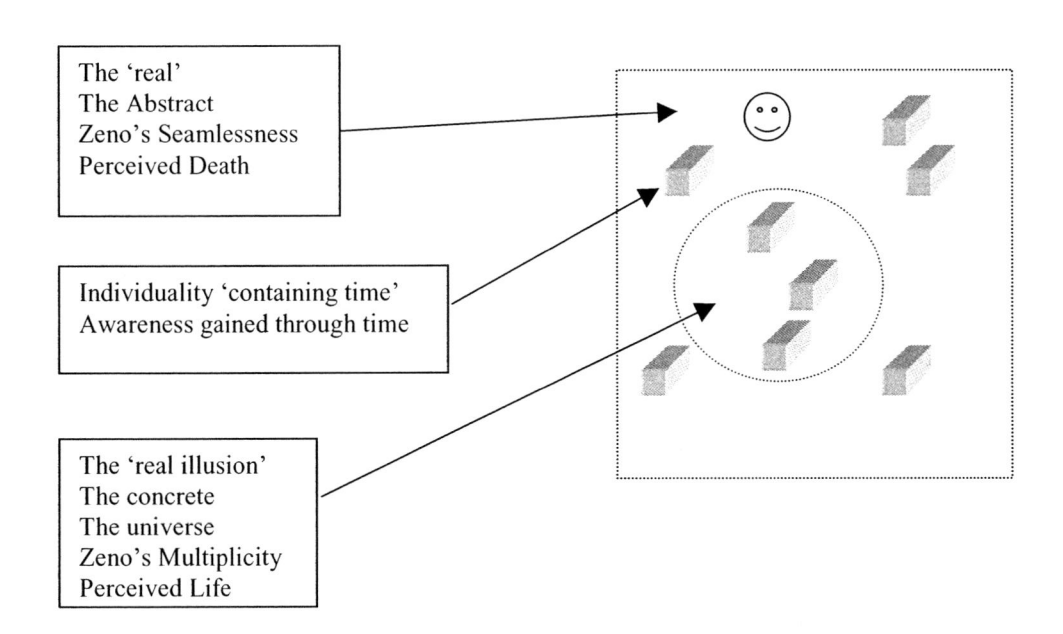

The 'real'
The Abstract
Zeno's Seamlessness
Perceived Death

Individuality 'containing time'
Awareness gained through time

The 'real illusion'
The concrete
The universe
Zeno's Multiplicity
Perceived Life

The War & Peace of a New Metaphysical Perception

With such a perception, time becomes a factor of the entity rather than the entity a factor of time. (The ramifications of this perception and its potential emergent significance when related to Einstein and his perception of relativistic time will be discussed in Chapter 9: Einstein and i.)

So what exactly is it we have developed with this series of thoughts? We have developed an understanding of the Greek concept regarding incrementalization as it pertains to the individual. The individual begins with 'virgin consciousness' and moves on to gain experience, an infinite amount of experience, as we now understand.

So it is we understand…

… when magnified appears as:

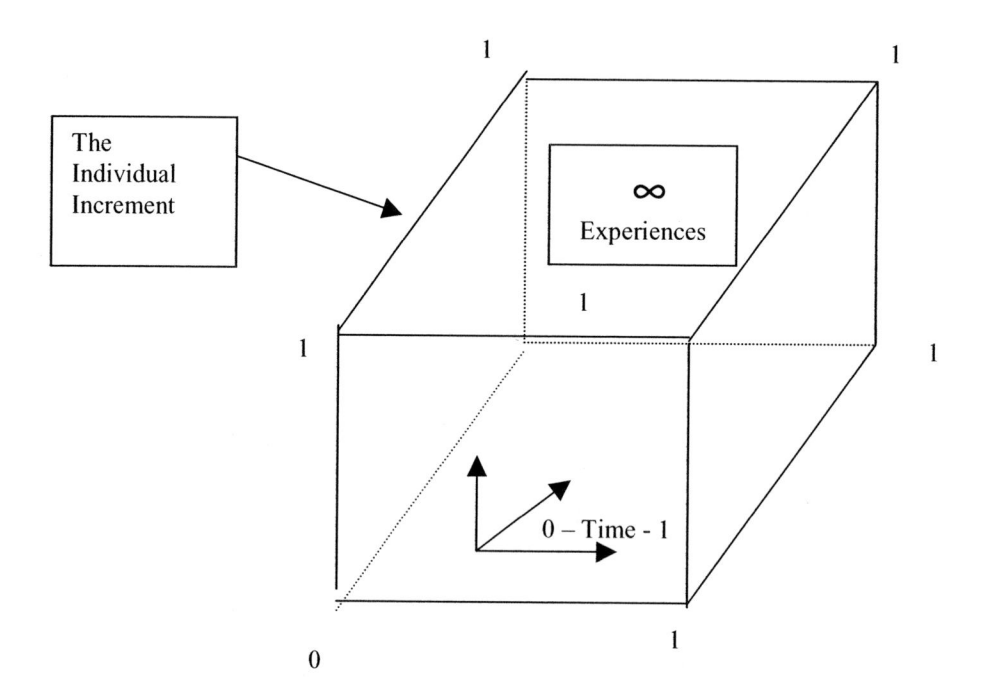

This perception leads to our understanding that it is not time which gives infiniteness to life experience but rather existence itself, which gives infiniteness to life experiences. It is the concept of concrete, physical, functionality as implied by Zeno's multiplicity found within the concrete, the physical, the universe itself that imparts a sense of the beginning, zero, and infiniteness, the end, upon each and every incremental piece of awareness.

Now that we have a perception of the individual, having its own identity separate from other identities, now what? Now we can put them together in a simplistic format and we get a simplistic understanding of a new perception of time in regards to the individual and the individual, be it an individual with or without awareness, to the physical.

So it is that not only does incremental motion through the concept of space/distance become an aspect of our physical reality but also likewise individuality becomes an aspect of incrementalization, multiplicity as Zeno would say.

Concrete/Physical Functionality

During Zeno's time in history, it was thought the universe existed and the universe was thought to be the 'only' 'container' for both the concrete/physical – multiplicity and abstraction - seamlessness.

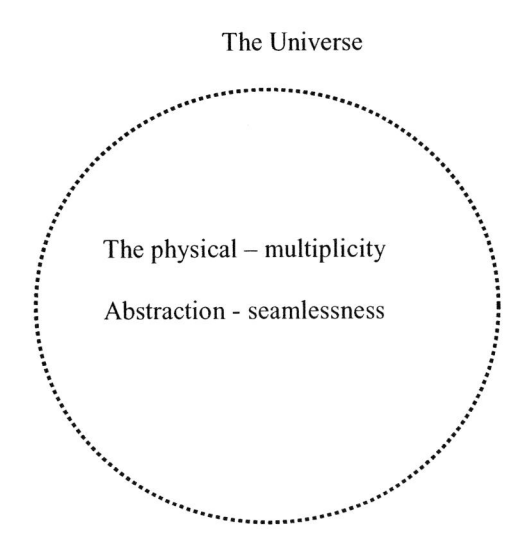

The Universe

The physical – multiplicity

Abstraction - seamlessness

As such, abstract functionality becomes confused with concrete/physical functionality not because it became so but because there was no other perception available to those living at the time of Zeno.

Because abstraction and the concrete were viewed as being all within one container, those of that period became not only confused but remain confused. This confusion continued to remain in place for the next twenty-five hundred years and in fact, remains in place today. In fact, this perceptual confusion has had no potential alternative replacement until the development of the metaphysical concept of 'being' *being* 'Being' or generically speaking, symbiotic panentheism.

Removing the physical while leaving the abstract intact

Three factors are involved with 'being' *being* 'Being': 1. you, individuality/seamlessness, exists, 2. the universe – the physical/multiplicity, exists, and 3. causation, seamlessness/totality, exists. This needs some clarification for these are stated, as we would perceive them to be, from the point of reference of our being located within the universe itself.

The War & Peace of a New Metaphysical Perception

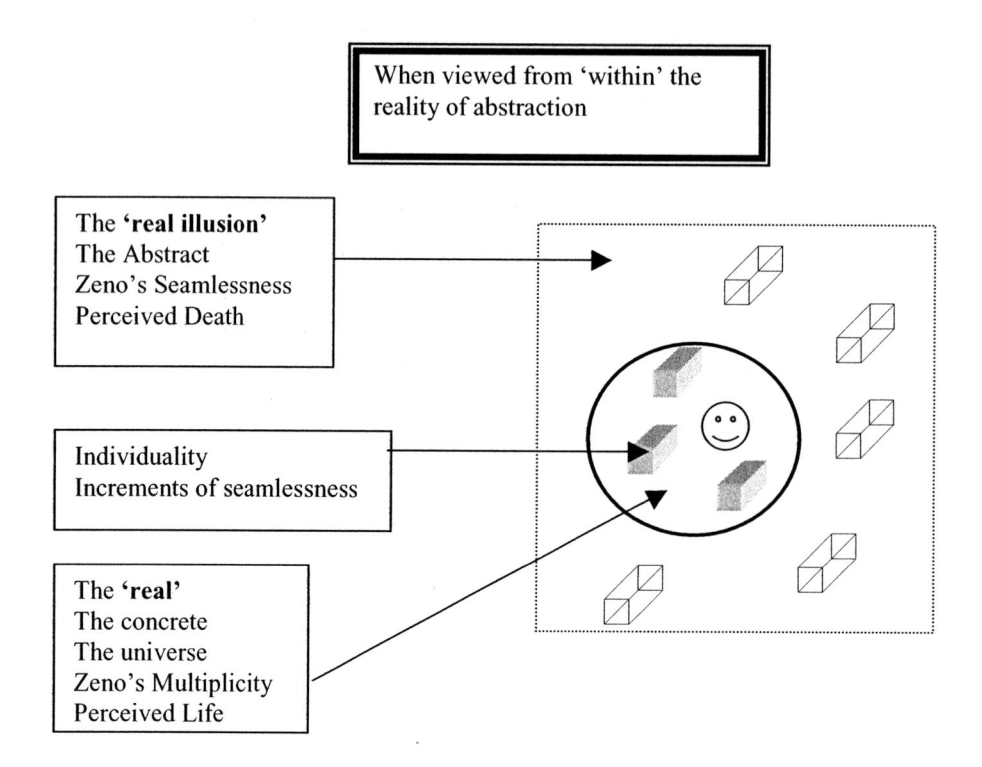

When viewed from 'within' the reality of abstraction

The 'real illusion'
The Abstract
Zeno's Seamlessness
Perceived Death

Individuality
Increments of seamlessness

The 'real'
The concrete
The universe
Zeno's Multiplicity
Perceived Life

There is no outside to the universe from this point of view, from the point of view of our being within the concrete/physical, being where it is that no abstract seamlessness exists.

The Error of Zeno

If we leave the concrete, the physical, multiplicity, behind by stepping out of the realm of the physical and into the realm of the abstract we obtain …

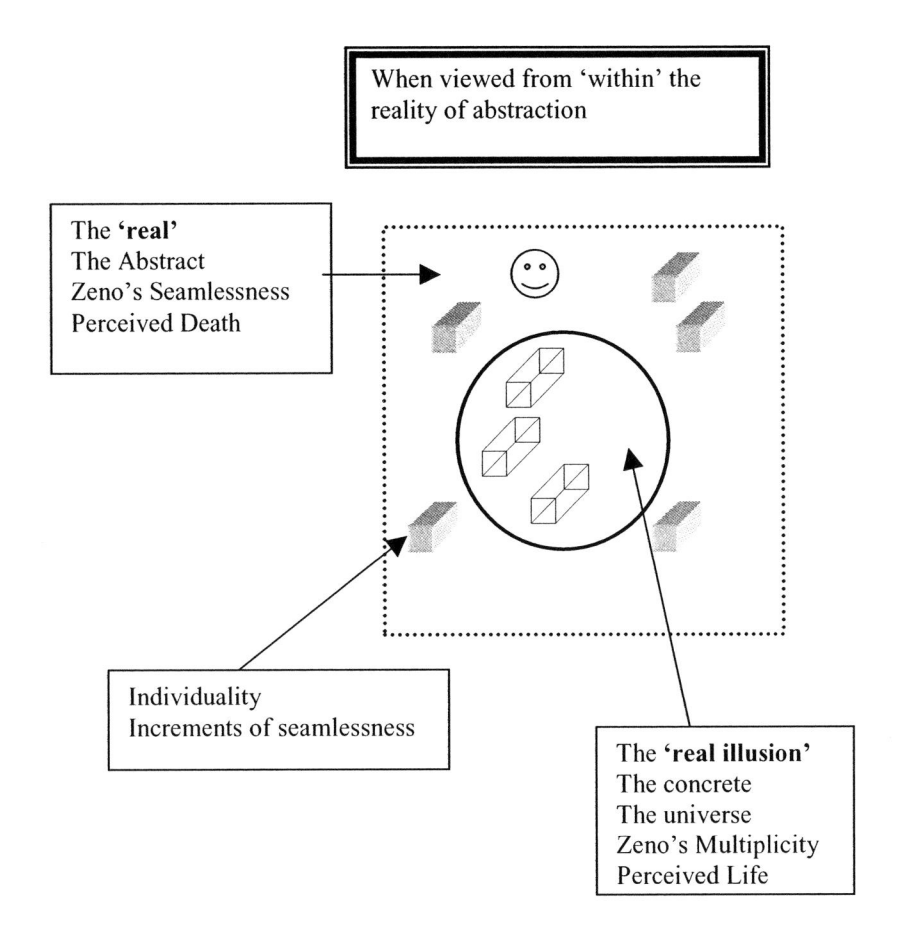

When viewed from 'within' the reality of abstraction

The **'real'**
The Abstract
Zeno's Seamlessness
Perceived Death

Individuality
Increments of seamlessness

The **'real illusion'**
The concrete
The universe
Zeno's Multiplicity
Perceived Life

There is no universe from this point of view, from the point of view of our being within abstraction, being where it is that no concreteness exists.

So now, what are the three factors, the truths, which remain? The three truths remain but now they become: 1. I exist, 2. process exists, and 3. totality exists. This could perhaps better be expressed as totality being the summation of its three parts: individuality, action – process/reality, and totality minus the specific individually of 'I'. Action – process/reality in this case is experiences, which have occurred as opposed to action – process/reality that could occur.

To shorten this up we might better express it as 1. Individuality – 'being', the noun, 2. process – being, the verb of action, and 3. 'Being', the noun, which in this case is the summation of individuality and process, or Being and Nothingness as Sartre would say. But Sartre had it wrong. First nothingness does not evolve out of individuality, out of 'being', as he implied. Rather nothingness evolves out of totality, Being. Secondly, nothingness is not the summation of negation for negation is as much an abstract as the positive. Nothingness rather is something and it is from this something of nothingness that process evolves, action's potentiality emerges, physicalness literally 'pops', multiplicity springs forth as a 'reality' in and of itself, yet all become an interactive part of seamlessness.

Nothingness is not negation; rather nothingness is just that nothing, the lack of all things and non-things, the lack of, becomes literally nothing at all. As such, is it something? No, it is nothing. It is only a noun when viewed from 'within' nothingness itself, when viewed from 'within' the physical itself, the universe itself. Nothingness on the other hand becomes a verb, an abstraction when viewed from 'within' abstraction, seamlessness. Nothingness is process when viewed from 'outside' the physical universe.

The truth 'I exist.' vs. the truth 'You exist.'

What is the difference between the two, between 'I exist' And 'You exist'? From your point of view, there is a significant difference. From my point of view, there is a significant difference. From the point of view of Being – totality – 'all is one', there is a significant difference. From the point of view within a physical realm, there is a significant difference. From the point of view separated from 'all is one', there is basically no difference, for, from the point of view removed from it all, from the point of view of being outside it all, although there is no such place, there is specifically a difference but, fundamentally, there is no difference.

And just what does all this mean? It means that the 'I' and 'you' specifically are just that but on the other hand, fundamentally represent 'a' commonality in multiplicity, in particular, individuality as well as representing simultaneously a commonality in seamlessness, in particular, totality – 'oneness'.

Now it is crucial to keep in mind, that if there is no free will, there is no individuality for the whole becomes the whole and that is the end of it. On the other hand, if there is free will of individuality the whole now becomes the whole, seamlessness, by means of the summation of individuality, by means of incrementalism, by means of multiplicity.

The existence of free will or no free will, determinism, are two entirely different scenarios and each perception germinates its own unique actions, reactions, and ambience, in both the abstract sense of reality and the physical sense of reality.

When one 'steps out' of both the physical and the abstract, it becomes understandable, that it is not 'you exist', nor 'I exist', which becomes the first truth but rather individuality becomes the first truth.

Within the concept of the metaphysical system of symbiotic panentheism, a Cartesian system lying 'within' and 'driving' a non-Cartesian system, the first truth of physical reality would be 'you exist', the individual exists, multiplicity exists. It is the vast majority of 'you's', which came before the 'I'. In the realm of the abstract, however, it is the 'I exist', which becomes the 'first' truth. It is in the abstract where your existence could have no meaning to me until after my consciousness became just that consciousness. In short the, my, virgin consciousness had to swell, expand, develop before you became an entity. Without the 'me', the 'I', you could not exist to me.

Thus, we have removed the physical, the concrete, in order to understand Zeno from a slightly different point of view. Thus we removed the physical, we removed the concrete immersed 'within' time and moved time to be a factor of the individual in order to better understand seamlessness. The process of removing the physical allows us to view ourselves from outside the physical itself. In fact, the process of removing the physical not only allows us to view ourselves from outside the physical but to view ourselves with the physical dissolved. Thus it is we are able

The Error of Zeno

to step beyond this physical thing called the concrete, the physical, or what we would call 'process' when viewed from the abstract perspective.

We are going to take one more step. We are going to step out of the abstract. We as a single piece of individuality will do so by regressing back to the point at which our consciousness was 'virgin', had potential to be but had not yet become.

Having regressed back to this point of 'nothingness', we will step 'outside' abstraction itself. This process of stepping 'outside' abstraction itself places us 'within' a place that does not exist. Even though it is impossible to limit the unlimitable, to limit abstraction we will do so anyway. Having removed the physical we find abstraction, we have no concept with which to replace this abstraction should we then remove it. To speculate where we would be once the physical is removed and then speculate what remains if the abstract is removed next provides no rational base for us to stand 'within'. Having acknowledged this dilemma, we will now proceed to ignore the dilemma and step above totality in order to view totality.

This process of stepping 'above' totality in order to view totality is made partially possible through having left an individual intact while hypothetically regressing that individual to the point of being a 'virgin consciousness', to the point of being finally 'nothing'. This allowed us to place this nonexistent existence outside of abstraction itself, a location that does not exist. In essence, we have done nothing and placed it nowhere.

It is from here we will begin to understand the non-understandable.

And what is the first thing we see when viewing totality from the point of view 'above' totality? We see summation is just that, summation. We see the 'I' from the point of view of the abstract, immersed within the abstract. We see 'you' from the point of view of process, immersed within the physical, the universe. We see individuality from the point of view of it all. The point is we see 'individuality' as a part of it all.

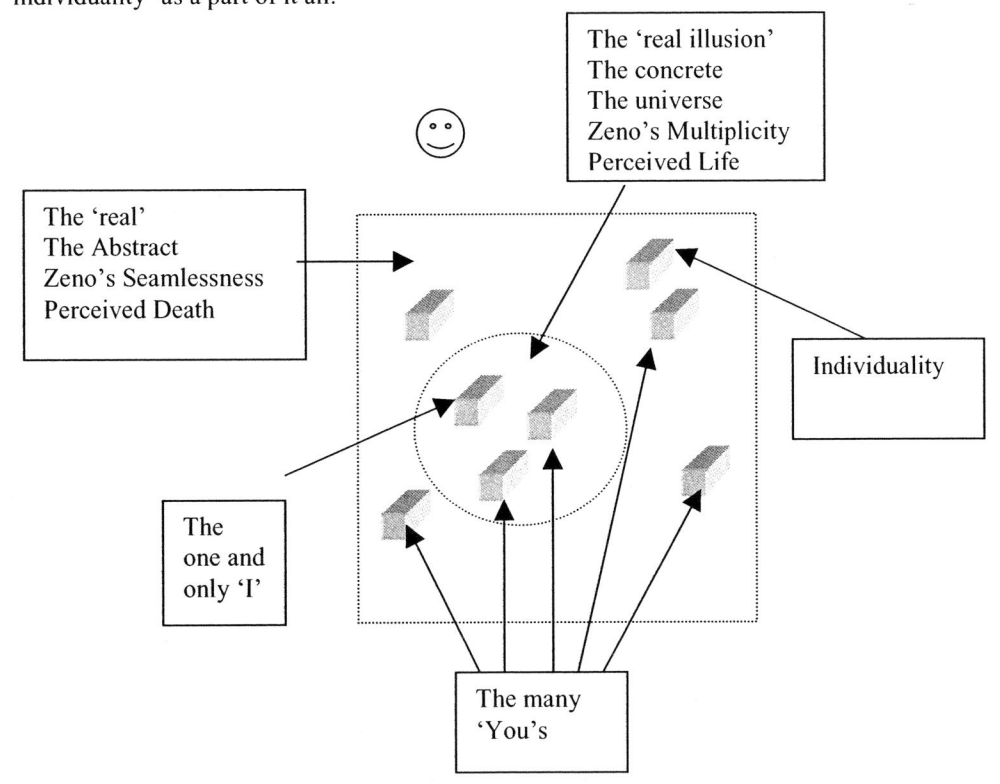

The 'real illusion'
The concrete
The universe
Zeno's Multiplicity
Perceived Life

The 'real'
The Abstract
Zeno's Seamlessness
Perceived Death

Individuality

The one and only 'I'

The many 'You's

Abstract Functionality

Our understanding of abstraction emerges as we gain an understanding of the interrelationship between multiplicity and seamlessness.

As the increments of individuality move from points of virgin consciousness and experience through the process of existing within the physical universe, they become unique. These pieces of unique 'knowing', these pieces of unique awareness, pick up time as a part of their existence.

When these pieces, increments of multiplicity, emerge out of the physical (die) they enter the totality of abstraction, enter an existence void of time, enter a 'location' where time is found 'within' the increments of individuality rather than individuality found 'within' time. It is the process of the virgin consciousnesses having grown into incremental pieces of knowing and then moving from the concrete into the abstract that we find abstractual existence itself growing. Thus abstraction grows, expands its very self.

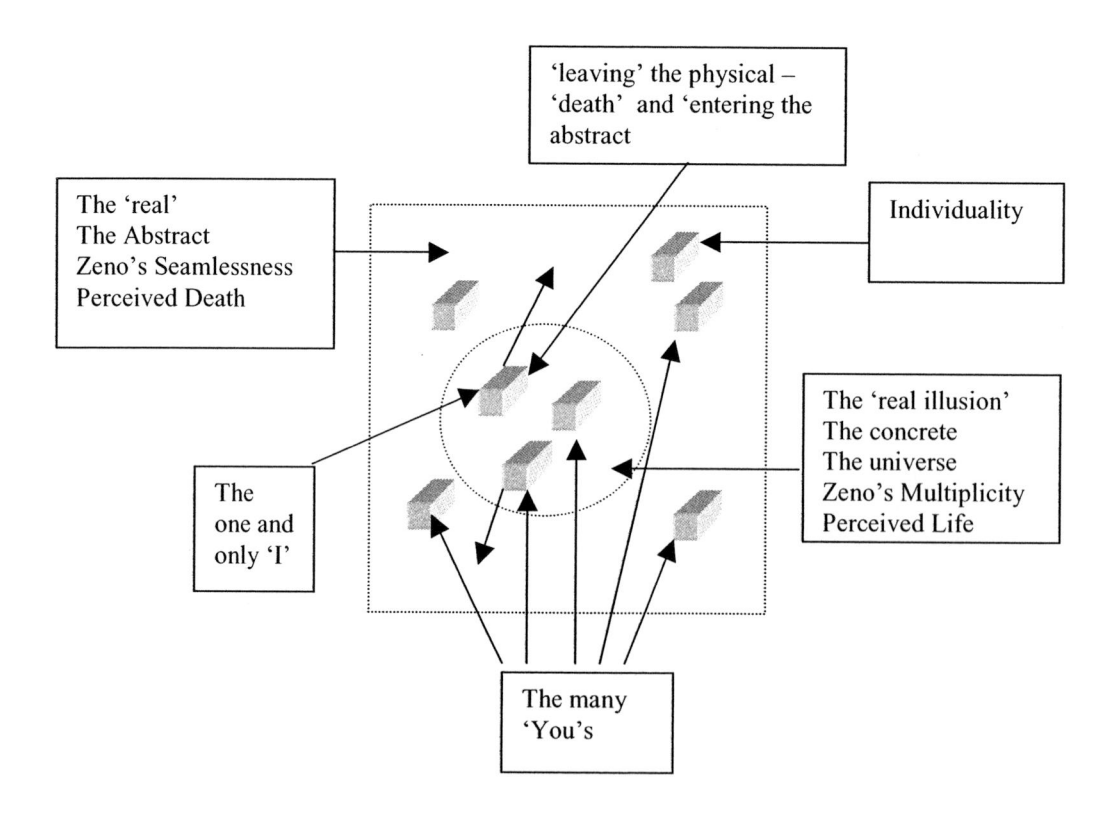

'leaving' the physical – 'death' and 'entering the abstract

The 'real'
The Abstract
Zeno's Seamlessness
Perceived Death

Individuality

The 'real illusion'
The concrete
The universe
Zeno's Multiplicity
Perceived Life

The one and only 'I'

The many 'You's

New virgin consciousness are continually emerging 'in' the physical to find themselves expanding evolving into increments of awareness of awareness itself.

This concept would appear to imply we are all a part of totality. In fact, it does nothing of the sort. Rather it goes beyond implying such a concept and instead outright and pointedly states that to be the case. Its very philosophical name: 'being' *being* 'Being' states this to be the case.

Being a part of God is not a new idea

The concept, our being a part of, a piece of Causation, a part of Being, an increment of God is considered to be a blasphemous perception in the eyes of today's western religions, today's western society. The concept our being a part of the whole, being a piece of Causation, being a part of 'Being', and being an increment of God is a basic principle, which emerges out of the metaphysical system of 'being' *being* 'Being' or what could generically be termed symbiotic panentheism.

Is such a perception new to western thought?

>Epictetus, philosopher, first century A.D.

>'The Golden Sayings of Epictetus:

>IX:

>… *Whereas if Caesar were to adopt you, your haughty looks would be intolerable: will you not be elated at knowing that you are the son of God? Now however it is not so with us: but seeing that in our birth these two things are commingled-the body which we share with animals, and the Reason and Thought which we share with the Gods, many decline towards this unhappy kinship with the dead, few rise to the blessed kinship with the Divine.*

>XV:

>*If what philosophers say of the kinship of God and Men be true, what remains for men to do but as Socrates did:-never, when asked one's country, to answer, 'I am an Athenian or a Corinthian,' but 'I am a citizen of the world.'*

>XVI:

>… *but to all things that are born and grow upon the earth, and in an especial manner to those endowed with Reason (for those only are by their nature fitted to hold communion with God, being by means of Reason conjoined with Him)-why should not such an one call himself a citizen of the world? Why not a son of God:…*

>… *while to have God for our Maker and Father, and Kinsman, shall not this set us free from sorrows and fears?*

>XVII:

>… *after recognizing their kindred to the Gods, and their bondage in these chains of the body…*

>… *Are we not in a manner kinsmen of the Gods, and have we not come from them?*

>XVIII:

>… *Friends, wait for God. When He gives the signal, and releases you from this service, then depart to Him. But for the present, endure to dwell in the place wherein He hath assigned you your post. Short indeed is the time of your habitation therein, and easy to those that are thus minded.…*

...Stay: depart not rashly hence!

XXI:

How did Socrates bear himself in this regard? How else than as became one who was fully assured that he was the kinsman of the Gods?

XXII:

If God had made that part of His own nature, which He severed from Himself and gave to us, liable to be hindered or constrained either by Himself or any other, He would not have been God, nor would He have been taking care of us as He ought...

XXIII:

... Most of us dread mortification of the body, and would spare no pains to escape anything of that end. But of mortification of the soul we are utterly heedless.

XXXIII:

Knowest thou what a speck thou art in comparison with the universe?-That is, with respect to the body; since with respect to Reason, thou art not inferior to the Gods, nor less than they. For the greatness of Reason is not measured by length or height, but by the resolves of the mind. Place then they happiness in that wherein thou art equal to the Gods.

XXXIV:

... And if you are stationed in a high position, are you therefore forthwith to set up for a tyrant? Remember who you are, and whom you rule, that they are by nature your kinsmen, your brothere, the offspring of God.

But I paid a price for them, not they for me.

Do you seee whether you are looking-down to the earth, to the pit, to those despicable laws of the dead? But to the laws of the Gods you do not look.

XXXVI:

... If then all things that grow, nay, our own bodies, are thus bound up with the whole, is not this still truer of the soul? And if our souls are bound up and in contact with God, as being very parts and fragments plucked from Himself,...

LXI:

... Were an image of God present, thou wouldst not dare to act as thou dost, yet, when God Himself is present within thee, beholding and hearing all, thou dost not blush to think such thought or do such deeds, O thou that are insensible of thine own nature and liest under the wrath of God!

It appears the concept of our being a part of totality, a piece of the Whole, a part of First Cause, a part of God is more universal in terms of human history than we have previously been lead to believe.

We in the twentieth century think we have advanced the cause of humankind by cutting ourselves off from the perception of our being a part of something other than matter and energy.

Who is it then that really is the blasphemer? Is the one who elevates the nature of being and thus irrationalizes the actions of abuse a blasphemer or is the one who debases the nature of being and thus rationalizes the actions of abuse a blasphemer?

Epictetus may not have concluded you are 'inside' God, as does symbiotic panentheism. Epictetus may not have deduced you 'impact' God, as does symbiotic panentheism, but there is no denying he did, as is shown from his aphorisms, rationalize you are the 'son' of God, a piece of the divine, as does symbiotic panentheism.

Now is such a perception just an old dilapidated relic of the ancient Greek philosophers? We will explore this question in great detail when we discuss Einstein and time, Chapter 9: Einstein – The error of:

Zeno himself says it

> *Scholars disagree about what Zeno himself took his paradoxes to show. There is no evidence that he offered any absolutions" to them. One view is that they were part of a program to establish that multiplicity is an illusion, and that reality is a seamless whole. The argument could be reconstructed like this: if you allow that reality can be successively divided into parts, you find yourself with these insupportable paradoxes; so you must think of Reality as a single indivisible One. (Cambridge Dictionary of Philosophy, Robert Audi, Cambridge University Press, 1995)*[11]

The War & Peace of a New Metaphysical Perception

In short:

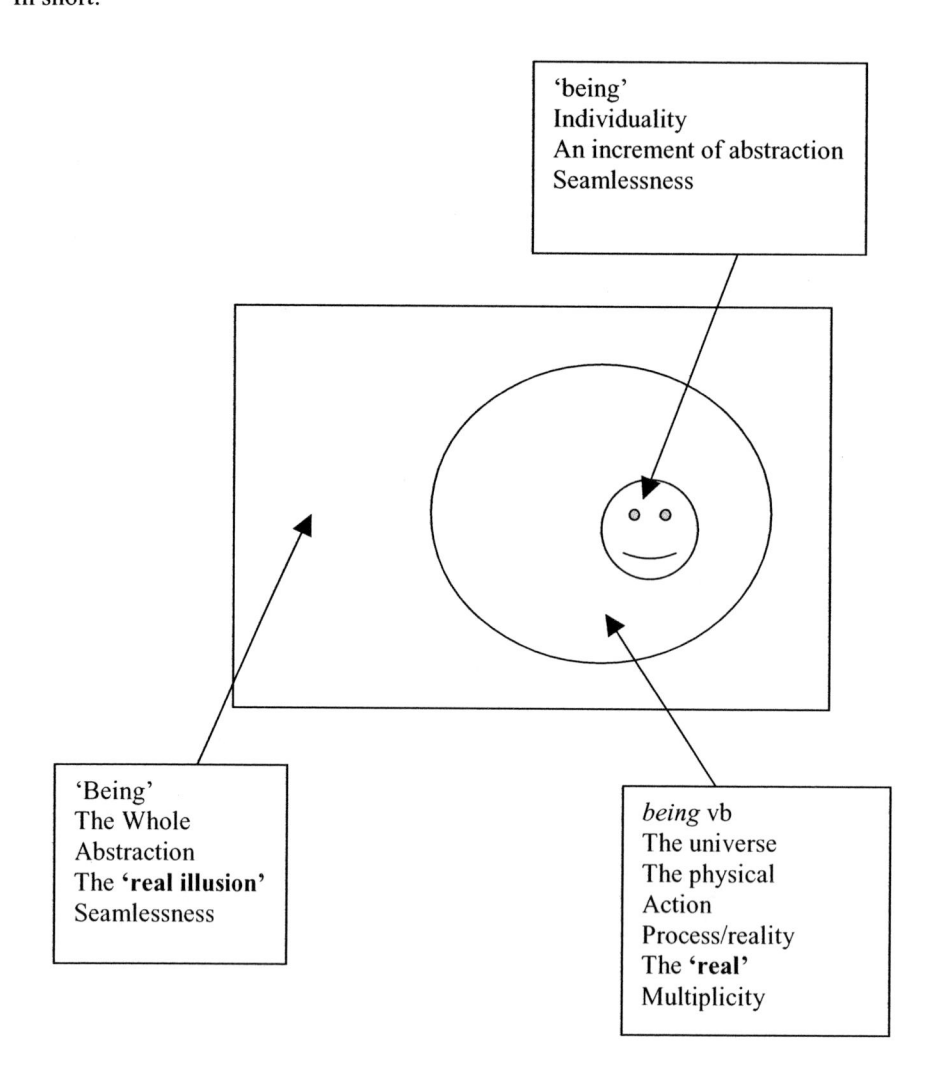

'being'
Individuality
An increment of abstraction
Seamlessness

'Being'
The Whole
Abstraction
The **'real illusion'**
Seamlessness

being vb
The universe
The physical
Action
Process/reality
The **'real'**
Multiplicity

Or what one might call:

        Religiously speaking: symbiotic **panentheism**
        Scientifically speaking: **symbiotic** panentheism
        Philosophically speaking: **symbiotic panentheism**

    Or

'being' *being* **'Being'**

But what does this have to do with seamlessness and multiplicity?

Seamlessness exists in the abstract, outside the physical. Seamlessness is also found 'within' the physical. The seamlessness found 'within' the physical is bounded within packets, increments of

The Error of Zeno

individuality as established through experiencing the physical as individuality moves through space, through distance. The seamlessness of abstraction found 'within' the physical is found immersed within time, seamless time.

The multiplicity of individuality

The packet of individuality gains experience, knowledge of its own existence through experience. This experiencing, gaining of existence, acquiring of knowledge, occurred merely by passing through the physical, passing through the universe within which time stretches from boundary to boundary. What then happens to time? Time is, in essence, attached to the very experiences the packet of individuality accumulates.

This packet of individuality then moves into seamlessness, abstraction, and adds its abstraction, adds the awareness of its experiences, adds knowledge to total abstraction.

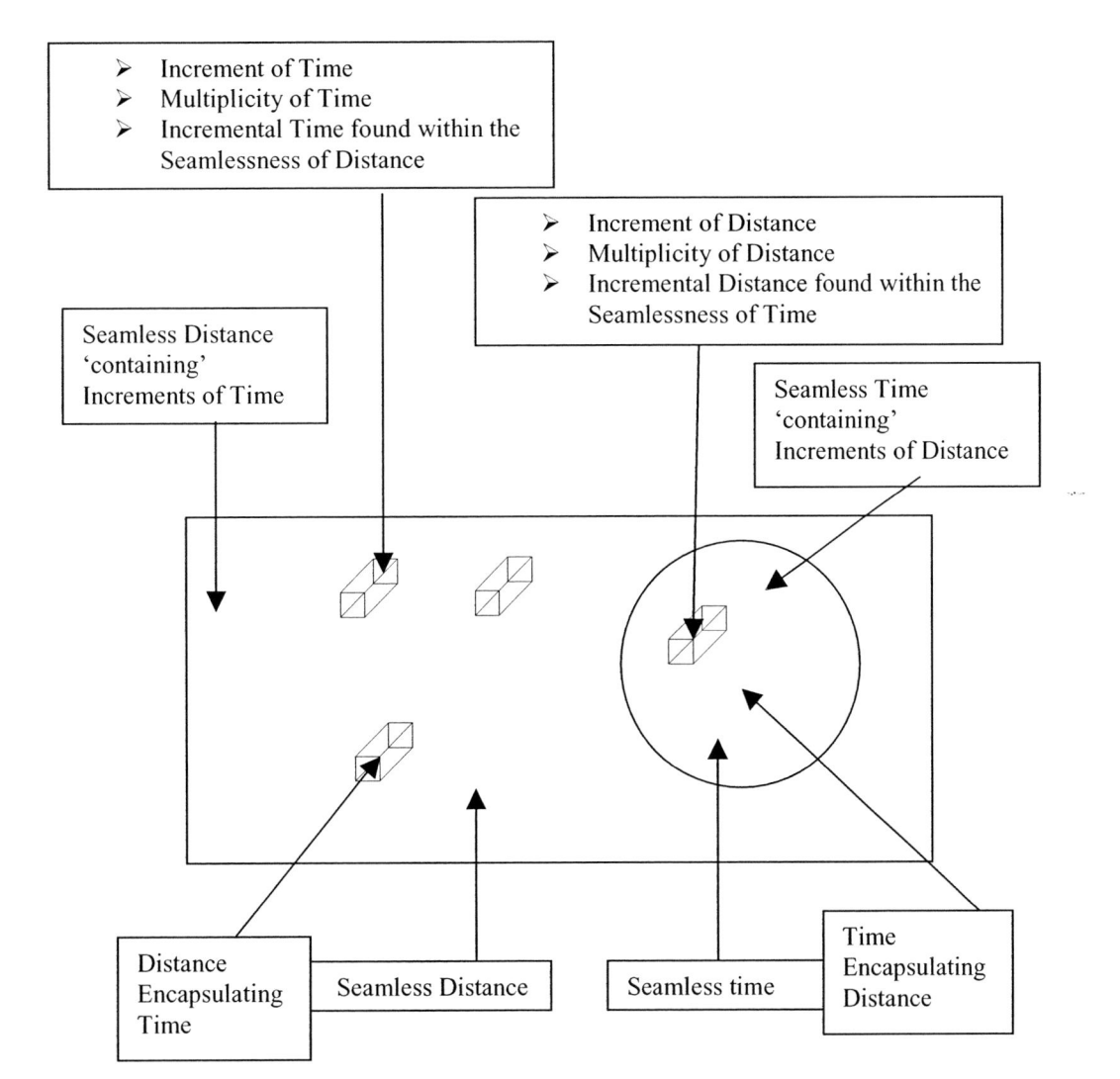

- ➢ Increment of Time
- ➢ Multiplicity of Time
- ➢ Incremental Time found within the Seamlessness of Distance

- ➢ Increment of Distance
- ➢ Multiplicity of Distance
- ➢ Incremental Distance found within the Seamlessness of Time

Seamless Distance 'containing' Increments of Time

Seamless Time 'containing' Increments of Distance

Distance Encapsulating Time

Seamless Distance

Seamless time

Time Encapsulating Distance

71

Now how is it distance can be seamless, undivided, when located 'within' abstraction?

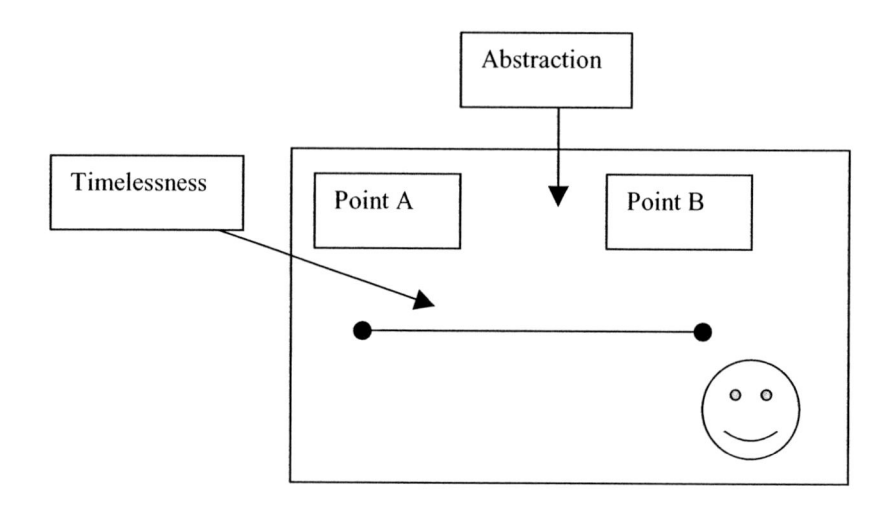

```
                              ┌──────────────┐
                              │ Abstraction  │
                              └──────┬───────┘
    ┌──────────────┐  ┌───────────┐  │  ┌───────────┐
    │ Timelessness │  │  Point A  │  ▼  │  Point B  │
    └──────────────┘  └───────────┘     └───────────┘
              ●────────────────────●
                                      ☺
```

Time permeates every part of the physical universe. In abstraction, there is no time existing between point A and point B. as such it is possible to go from A to B instantaneously. Now is this logical? Actually, yes it is logical. To go from one point of thought to another, be it thoughts of location or thoughts of concepts, is an instantaneous process. As an example, one can be sitting in a chair in one city and instantaneously move one's thoughts, move one's abstractual presence, to another city, planet, galaxy or even another universe. In fact one could move one's self beyond the very boundary of the whole itself..

This is in essence the realm of theoretical metaphysics.

Therefore, in answer to the question: Is it possible to move instantaneously from point A to point B? The answer is yes. In fact we do it all the time.

What does this all imply? This complete treatise involving Zeno implies, directly demonstrates, the logic regarding two locations of existence: abstractual location separate from physical location, seamlessness separate from multiplicity. This is not to say seamlessness does not exist within multiplicity nor does it suggest multiplicity does not exist within seamlessness. Rather, the two exist, one 'within' the other simultaneously.

It is only through this new perception, through the perception generated by the metaphysical system of 'being' *being* 'Being', symbiotic panentheism, that we can rationally, reasonably resolve Zeno's paradox.

We now understand that

Zeno is a vital link in moving our perceptual understanding forward regarding the 'system' being filled with multiplicity, into that of being 'the' system filled with both multiplicity and seamlessness. As such, both multiplicity and seamlessness, with the help of Zeno, now have a location within which each dominates. As such, the understanding regarding the role of multiplicity and seamlessness as well as the understanding regarding the interrelationship between multiplicity and seamlessness no longer remain in a state of confusion. Even more interestingly, the existence of such an interrelationship is not only recognized as a significant aspect of the 'larger' system but it is now understood how seamlessness and multiplicity interact one with the other.

---

[1] **Definition**: Physical distance: 1. distance found 'within' the physical, 2. distance subject to the characteristics of multiplicity, 3. distance subject to the parameters of time and space

[2] **Definition**: Abstract distance: 1. distance found 'within' the abstract, 2. distance subject to the characteristics of seamlessness, 3. distance subject to the parameters of timelessness and the absence of space

[3] **Clarification**: of 'being' 'Being' and being
    i. 'being': individuality, individual knowing
    ii. 'Being': the whole
    iii. being (vb): action, process/reality

[4] **Question**: What is 'active' sense? **Answer**: The 'active' sense refers to how the agreed upon universal truths interact with each other, affect each other

[5] **Question**: What is 'passive' sense? **Answer**: The 'passive' sense refers to the simple existence of the universal truth without regard to the actions they 'affect' upon each other.

[6] **Clarification**. Science found the concept of increments of distance to be very disturbing. In fact science was unable to resolve Zeno's paradoxes. When mathematics developed the concept of taking distance and reducing it to a summation of infinitely small increments taken over time, Calculus, science grasped the tool of Calculus and universally declared it to be the answer to Zeno's paradoxes of motion. This universal acceptance of Calculus as the solution to Zeno's paradoxes in fact did not resolve Zeno's paradoxes. It simply reduced Zeno's paradoxes to the incremental realm of infinitely small segments but segments nonetheless.

[7] **Clarification**. The universal acceptance on the part of science regarding Calculus being the resolution to Zeno's paradox, allowed science the means of 'moving on' with its intended function, which is to observer the physical universe, observe multiplicity itself. It was philosophy's function to examine seamlessness but because philosophy could not resolve Zeno's paradoxes of motion, philosophy followed the lead of science and mathematics and declared Calculus to be the solution to Zeno's paradoxes. This was philosophy's error not the error of science and mathematics.

[8] Cambridge Dictionary of Philosophy, Robert Audi, Cambridge University Press, 1995
[9] Cambridge Dictionary of Philosophy, Robert Audi, Cambridge University Press, 1995
[10] Cambridge Dictionary of Philosophy, Robert Audi, Cambridge University Press, 1995
[11] Cambridge Dictionary of Philosophy, Robert Audi, Cambridge University Press, 1995

Tractate 2

The Error

Of

Aristotle

❖

The Paradox of:

Cartesian Systems

•

The Need for:

A Beginning Leading to an End

The War & Peace of a New Metaphysical Perception

1.   322 BC Aristotle – The Error of:
            A Cartesian System – a new perception 2000 AD

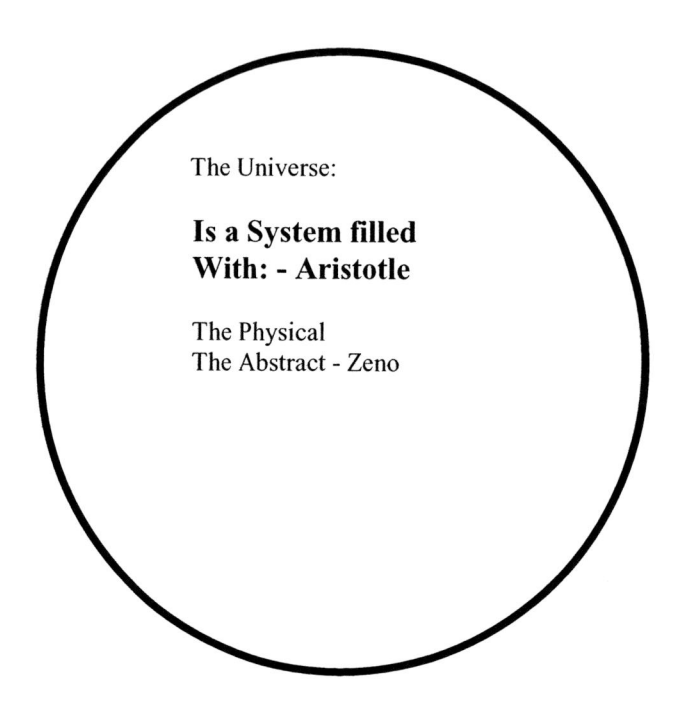

> The Universe:
>
> **Is a System filled With: - Aristotle**
>
> The Physical
> The Abstract - Zeno

The error: The paradox of systems: The Universe is 'the' system.

The perception: Aristotle moves our perceptual understanding regarding the system into that of being 'the' system filled with both abstract and concrete/physical functionality. As such, abstract and concrete/physical functionality, with the help of Aristotle, now have a location within which they can be found. However, the understanding regarding the role of both abstractual functionality and concrete/physical functionality as well as the understanding regarding the interrelationship between abstract and concrete/physical functionality not only remain in a state of confusion but even more disconcerting, the existence of such an interrelationship is not recognized as a significant aspect of the 'larger' system.

It is this state of confusion which will be specifically addressed within this tractate.

Contents

Part I: The Paradox of Cartesian Systems and non-Cartesian Systems

Introduction
Incremental concentric circles
The intricacies of concentric circles
Confinement is confinement
The concept of Cartesian
Cartesian Systems
The paradox of Cartesian Systems

Part II: Resolving the issue with a new metaphysical perception

Introduction
Relativistic 1st Principles
The dance of the angels
The 'Land of Limited Abstracts: Infinite Finites'
The 'Land of Unlimited Abstracts: Finite Infinities'
Understanding how 'a' 'whole' can be greater than the sum of its parts
The equality of 'relativistic 1st principle'
Resolving the paradox of 'a' Cartesian System composed of Infinite Finites
Reopening the walls of confinement
What it all means to humanity/all forms of virgin consciousness universally

Terms/concepts

Abstractual hedonism
Cartesian
Cartesian system
'Equality of principle'
Finite infinities
Finite finites
Infinite finites
Infinite infinities
Limited abstracts
Mimesis
Perceptual confinement
Physical hedonism
'reality'
'Reality'
Relativistic 1st principles
Unlimited abstracts
Virgin consciousness

Tractate 2
Aristotle – The Error of
Cartesian Systems

Part I: Creating the paradox of a Cartesian System

Introduction

Aristotle divided the universe into incremental layers of distance heading outward from a center. As such humankind became confined to the limits of 'a' system

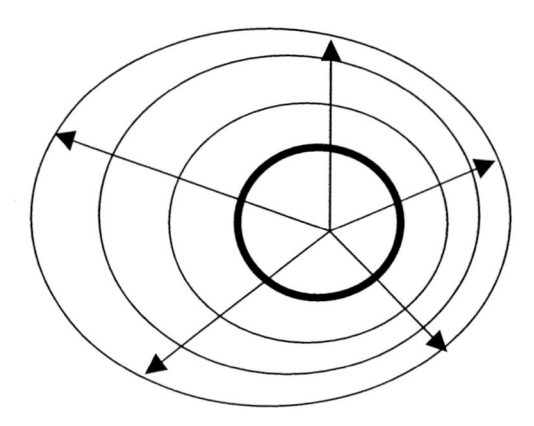

We are an amazing specie. Confining humanity to the restrictions of a closed space does something to humanity's psyche. It does not matter if the confines are physical or abstract, the results are the same. Confinement generates an overpowering need to 'escape', to once again 'breath' the air of expansiveness, to 'breath' the air of freedom, to 'breath' the air of the 'open spaces', to journey unimpeded.

Confinement can be physical or abstract. Examples of both types of confinement are exemplified as: a jail cell, an elevator, solitary, a domineering spouse, a religion, stress, and social labels. Whatever the form of confinement, humankind has always attempted to throw off the oppressive weight, throw off the yoke of confinement. The desire to be free becomes our obsession, our driving force.

Perhaps the most significant, the most visible, means we have of throwing off the yoke of confinement is characterized through active vs. passive action. Genocide, spousal abuse, infanticide, obscene language, ostracism, proselytizing, abortion, incarceration, etc. in essence come down to a fundamental primitive instinct. Humanity appears to have an innate desire not to be 'cornered', not to be 'boxed in', not to be 'placed under', not to be confined 'by' someone or something.

So, what does this have to do with Aristotle?

Aristotle – 384 BC followed Zeno of Elea – 500 BC. Zeno moved the concept Zeno alluded to:

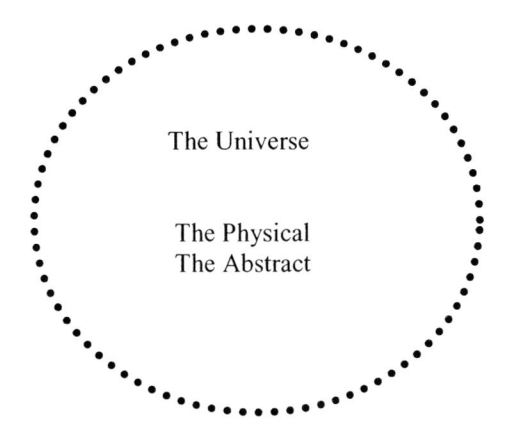

```
            The Universe

          The Physical
          The Abstract
```

and imposed a new perception upon the system:

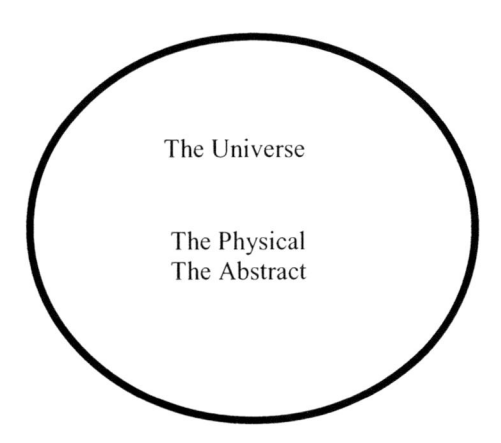

```
            The Universe

          The Physical
          The Abstract
```

Isn't this the same perception Zeno developed? No, it is not. Understanding the perception Aristotle put into play for humanity and understanding the resultant effect upon us as a specie as well as understanding the resultant effect Aristotle's system 'placed upon' us as individuals is what the first section of this article will address. The second section of this tractate will address an alternative perception. In addition, the second half of this article will examine how such a new perception could and would retain the basic components of Aristotle's system while simultaneously retaining the basic components of Zeno's perception.

So, once again, what exactly did Aristotle do to change Zeno's 'system'? Aristotle closed the system:

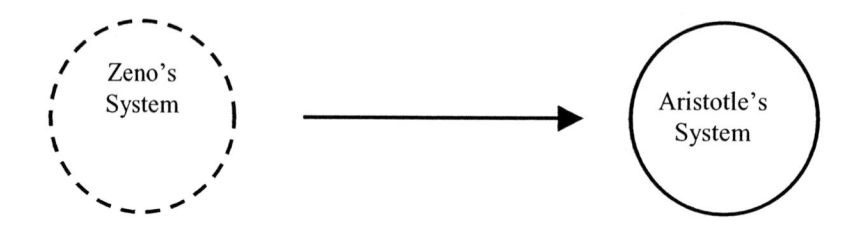

The closure of the system was not necessarily a 'negative' development. Aristotle moved humanity in the direction of understanding our universe as a physical entity. Aristotle's perceptions allowed science to evolve as just that, science. The development of science provided the means by which we could understand what lies within 'the system'.

Our problem as a specie, however, does not exist with understanding what lies 'inside' Aristotle's system but rather understanding what lies 'outside' Aristotle's system. Our problems evolved through our decision to pay no heed to what 'existed' 'outside' 'the system'. Multiple philosophical paradoxes emerged through our decision to diminish the significance of the abstract. Ethical issues developed through our decision to disregard the interrelationship between the abstract and the physical, between seamlessness and multiplicity.

'Aristotle's system' leads us to the perception that 'the whole' is the universe and the universe is 'the whole'. 'Aristotle's system' leads to the philosophical perception that 'God is dead', metaphysics is dead, and philosophy reached its end with the development of the 'Hegelian non-Cartesian system'.[1]

It may have taken thousands of years, but philosophy, through 'Aristotle's system' reached the same point science reached in the mid-twentieth century: Philosophy reached the point of 'believing' there is nothing 'new' to learn. Philosophically much of society believes the only 'new' perceptions left to explore are simply variations of what we already 'know'. In regards to science, how wrong we were, as the second half of the twentieth century so dramatically pointed out. In regards to philosophy, philosophy is about to discover it is no different than science in this regard.

We cannot blame Aristotle for our having given up our pursuits regarding the essence of the whole, individuality, and the universe. Aristotle did not force us to take the limited approach we took. We, humanity, made that decision.

In order to resolve our socially conflicting views and actions, we need to step back in time and begin to examine the entities of individuality, the universe, and the whole from a fresh perspective. Philosophical paradoxes will remain paradoxes until we integrate all three entities into 'a' system we can understand

Science is probing the universe aimlessly. The overall picture of the universe remains invisible to science because philosophy has failed to provide the vision of a 'larger' picture of the universe. Philosophy is responsible for providing a model explaining the purpose of the universe itself. Such a model is needed by science in order for science to establish a 'directed' effort attempting to prove or disprove purpose, significance of the universe and the elements found within the universe, namely ourselves.

Such a model is the task of philosophy to develop. The model of the 'whole' is what philosophy/reason must develop. Science measures, probes, and observes the universe. Mathematics formulates the universe. Religion stabilizes actions of free will within the universe. Philosophy – and metaphysics in particular - expands our perception of the whole and defines the role the universe and the individual play within such a system.

Science has been making phenomenal progress in terms of measurement and observation. Science, however, does not understand what it is it is measuring and has been given no direction as to the models it should be testing regarding the whole. As such, science measures the 'infinitely' large and the 'infinitely' small, but science does not test these forms of measurement against a 'model' of the whole other than the model provided by Aristotle two thousand four hundred years ago. The model: The whole system is the physical universe and the physical universe is the whole system.

Is there an alternative? Absolutely, symbiotic panentheism, 'being' *being* 'Being, is a new metaphysical perception.

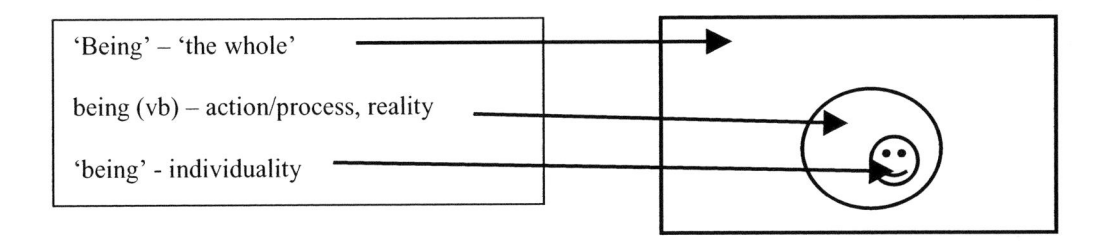

```
┌─────────────────────────────────────┐     ┌──────────────────────────┐
│ 'Being' – 'the whole' ──────────────┼────▶│                          │
│                                     │     │         ╭───╮            │
│ being (vb) – action/process, reality┼─────┼────────▶│ ☺ │            │
│                                     │     │         ╰───╯            │
│ 'being' - individuality ────────────┼─────┼──────────┘               │
└─────────────────────────────────────┘     └──────────────────────────┘
```

Now science may say: 'There is nothing 'outside' the universe.' If this is the case, then we must begin to understand just what this means to being (vb) and 'being'. If there is 'nothing' 'outside' the universe,

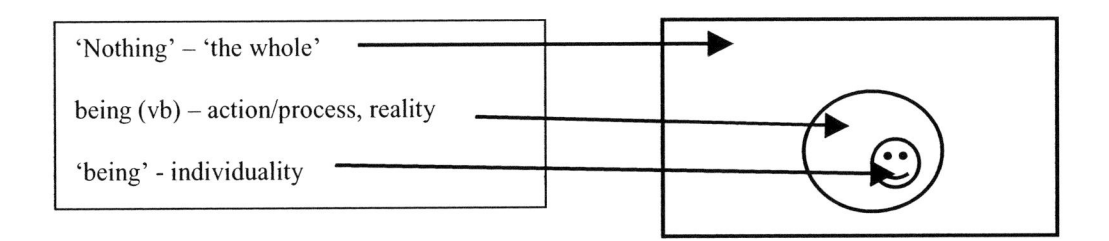

```
┌─────────────────────────────────────┐     ┌──────────────────────────┐
│ 'Nothing' – 'the whole' ────────────┼────▶│                          │
│                                     │     │         ╭───╮            │
│ being (vb) – action/process, reality┼─────┼────────▶│ ☺ │            │
│                                     │     │         ╰───╯            │
│ 'being' - individuality ────────────┼─────┼──────────┘               │
└─────────────────────────────────────┘     └──────────────────────────┘
```

The War & Peace of a New Metaphysical Perception

then we must begin to understand just what this 'nothingness' is which is 'outside' the universe.

The scientific statement, 'There is nothing 'outside' the universe', does not put an end to the debate regarding an 'outside' to the universe. The statement does not put an end to the debate regarding the three concepts: 'Being', being (vb), and 'being'.

However, if this work in essence is about resolving paradoxes, just what do the concepts of metaphysics; violence, and confinement have to do with Aristotle? That is exactly what we are about to discover.

Incremental concentric circles

Aristotle's perception of the universe began with Zeno:

Aristotle added to Zeno's perception. Aristotle added the concept of 'a' system to Zeno's perception by taking a potentially open and/or closed system and converted it to 'a' closed system. As such, Aristotle's system looked as follows:

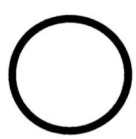

which expanded to become:

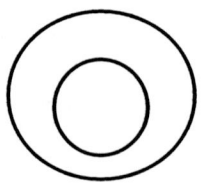

and then:

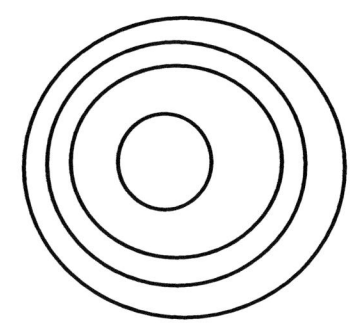

ad infinitum.

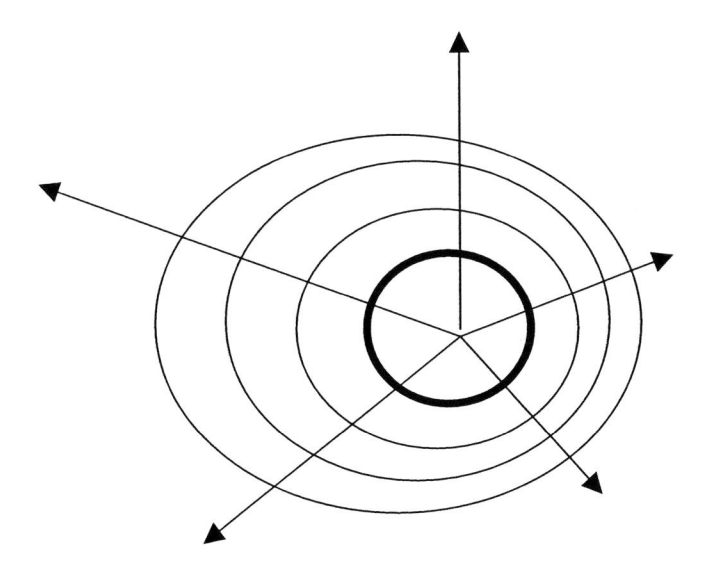

Now 'ad infinitum' does not apply only to an infinite number of additional circles expanding outward. 'Ad infinitum' applies to circles 'branching off from', levels of vacuum potentials, strings 'within', strings throughout, 'holes' 'within' going from place to place, creating additional physical ness 'within', reaching points of universal heat level equilibrium, etc....

Aristotle's system, a closed system, a Cartesian system, 'created' a perception of 'reality' as opposed to creating a perception of a larger 'Reality'. Limits were placed upon the whole, upon 'Reality'. The limits became defined as physicality, multiplicity, and incrementalism.

As we shall see, the two words, the two perceptions – 'reality' and 'Reality', have a phenomenally different implication for us as individuals and for us as a specie.

The lower case 'reality' applies to the physical universe, which may or may not be the 'whole'. The upper case 'Reality' applies to the 'whole', recognizes the 'whole' may be 'greater' than the physical, greater than the concrete, greater than our universe, 'greater' than various aspects found 'within' time, greater then various aspects found immersed 'within' time, greater than various aspects found to have time 'attached' to them.

Aristotle moved Zeno's concept of an open system represented by a dotted line, to a closed system represented by a closed circle. The 'closed system did not characterize its outer boundary by how far one moved outward, nor was the 'closed' system limited to a degree of complexity imposed upon the 'closed system. Regardless of the complexity and regardless of the expanse of distance found within the system, the fact remained the system was closed.

The perception of a 'closed system' philosophically, scientifically, and religiously generated a fundamental principle which was and is found permeating all original perceptions to emerge since the time of Aristotle. The underlying principle, the foundation, the first and foremost principle of action operating within this closed system was a principle one might refer to as 'Cartesian perceptions'.

What is meant by 'Cartesian'? When we speak of Cartesian, we are not referring so much to Descartes and his perception of metaphysics as we are referring to the metaphysical concept of what is. In short, we are referring to the concept of total reality as opposed to a portion of reality. Condensing this thought even further: When we refer to Cartesian, we are referring to a closed system as opposed to an open system or one might say: Kantian system as opposed to Hegelian system.

The intricacies of concentric circles

Aristotle 'advanced' Zeno's concepts of 'a' system. Zeno had not meant to imply his system was 'a' system. It could be argued Zeno left in place his perception of just what 'a' system of multiplicity and seamlessness was and how the two interacted. It could be argued: Instead of leaving us with 'a' system, Zeno left us simply with an elementary understanding that 'seamlessness' and 'multiplicity', the abstract and the physical, exist.

Zeno left us with the impression we could expand our perceptions to include the abstract with our concepts of the physical. Zeno, not knowing how to build such a model, left us with a perception of 'a' system of reality, which 'was' but at the same time, 'was not' enclosed. Zeno was uncertain if the two, seamlessness and multiplicity, could exist separate from each other. He was uncertain if multiplicity and seamlessness could exist one 'within' the other or instead if the two existed side by side. In fact, Zeno was uncertain if both multiplicity and seamlessness existed or if just one or the other existed.

Zeno was overwhelmed with uncertainty regarding not only the existence of multiplicity and seamlessness but also with the interrelationship between the two. Because Zeno could not resolve the issue of modeling the interrelationship of multiplicity and seamlessness, Zeno left his system 'open'.

Out of respect, Zeno's system is drawn as being enclosed in a dotted line.

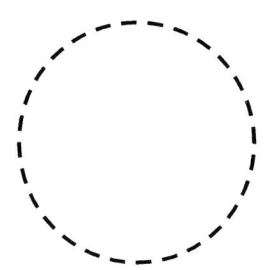

Such a depiction embraces the concept of a potentially 'physical universe' with a 'way out' for its occupants. What one was to go 'into', as one left the physical confines of the universe, was questionable. That is not the point however. The point is, Zeno 'left' a 'way out' of his system. Recognizing his limitations for his particular point in time, Zeno conceded the perceptual development of what lay 'outside' 'the' system to future philosophers and in particular, to metaphysicians.

Again, we come back to the question: What did Aristotle do to advance the system Zeno put into place? Aristotle took Zeno's system, which was enclosed by a dotted line and filled with the physical and the abstract, and 'advanced' it through the process of converting the dotted line to a solid closed circle.

Suddenly, with this simple action, humanity found itself enclosed, confined. Aristotle did not intentionally imprison humanity within the metaphysical confines of limited 'location' nor was Aristotle intending to subjugate humanity to the unavoidable repercussions,[2] which were naturally to follow such confinement. Regardless of what Aristotle intended, however, the results remained the same, humanity became confined and as such, humanity became an animal caged. The result, the repercussions of being caged manifested itself as it does with all animals. Humanity, sensing itself caged, began to pace back and forth within its cage.[3] Humanity found itself embracing its past acts of violence. Humanity found itself 'improving' upon its past actions of 'mimesis' as Renee Gerard fully explains in his various works.

Abstractions cannot be 'bound', caged. The physical can be 'bound', caged. Having found ourselves 'bound' we began to 'see' ourselves as physical 'beings' rather than abstractual 'beings'. As time moved forward, what we observed, scientific theories of the universe supported by measurement, did nothing but reinforce such a perception.

Aristotle's perception of 'a closed system', the development of a model, and of 'a' Cartesian system of reality was to remain with humanity for thousands of years. Humankind is a very innovative specie. As we developed, we encountered religious, philosophical, and scientific perceptions, which were to challenge and shake the very foundations of Aristotle's 'closed system' perceptions.

Aristotle, however, had verbalized a principle, which was so fundamental it was inconceivable to deny. As such, each scientific principle, philosophical principle, and religious principle was modified, shape-shifted to fit the one fundamental concept of Aristotle's: All things must fit some place within the parameters of our universe. Since we have never remained stagnant as a specie in terms of perceptual developments, faith, observation, and reason, we have advanced Aristotle's perception to the point of creating a very complex 'closed system' indeed. Were it possible, Ockham would be absolutely turning over in his grave.

So it is, the concentric circles created by Aristotle became all manners of circles, convolutions, involutions, bubbling up, bubbling down, levels of potentiality, and inclusions of strings from one end of reality to another. Never a word was spoken regarding what lies 'outside' it all, what lies 'outside' matter/energy/time. Only whispers were heard regarding what the concept of 'outside' means, what Reality/Totality vs. reality/the universe is. The concept eventually did evolve that we should be 'appreciative', 'beholden' for our existence. We, over time, began to understand we were not 'needed' by Totality. However, the questions did not arise as to just how we as individuals and how we as a specie fit into such a concept as Reality vs. reality. Nor did the question arise as to how we as individuals and how we as a specie fit into the mechanism of Totality. The question did not arise as to what reasonable, observable, and believable part we play in such a 'system'.

As things evolved over time, the complexity of Aristotle's system became enormous. As such, philosophy/reason had little option but to take a stand. Philosophy had to stand with or against the religious and scientific developments built over the two and a half millennium following Aristotle. Philosophy, after centuries of debate, moved in the direction of protecting Aristotle's idea of a closed system. Over time, philosophy, having nothing else to offer, embraced Aristotle's system, a 'Cartesian' system.

For a long time, philosophy stood alone and isolated from the debates both science and religion were initiating regarding the whole being a 'closed system'. Isolation, however, is a lonely and unnatural state not only for individuals but for academic studies as well. The process of belonging took one simple act. Recognizing this, philosophy acted. Philosophy acceded to its desire to belong.

As is the case with most initiation rites, the act of becoming a part of the group, required one basic act: The initiation rite required the act of 'compromising' one's principles. Philosophy compromised its principles with one simple statement. Philosophy declared: We cannot 'know' truth to be truth. With that statement, philosophy relegated metaphysics to the ash heaps of the mythical, the supernatural, the occult. Philosophy announced metaphysics to be dead, to be an outmoded perceptual tool.

With that simple statement, philosophy became conformist and humanity became confined to limits. With that simple statement, humanity became subjected to the acceleration of all the negatives, which go hand in hand with confinement.

Some would regard philosophy declaring, 'We cannot 'know' truth to be truth.', is simply an honest statement. In terms of absolutisms, that may be the case. One must not forget however, that the same applies to everything we state to be a 'fact'. 'We cannot 'know' truth to be truth' applies to all 'absolute' scientific observations and principles and to all 'absolute' religious fundamentals and cornerstones. 'We cannot 'know'…' applies to all statements of 'fact' made not just be philosophy but to all statements of fact made by science and religion as well.

It was not the statement, 'We cannot 'know' truth to be truth.' which caused philosophy to have compromised itself. What caused philosophy to compromise itself was the acceptance of philosophy to place such a perceptual principle upon itself while not applying this same perceptual principle to science/observation and religion/faith. In short, philosophy not only accepted but initiated a double standard. Philosophy set one standard for itself and another for science and religion.

Should philosophy have expected science and religion to 'apply' the principle, 'We cannot 'know' truth to be truth', to themselves? Actually, no, it had no right to apply such a standard upon these two means of perceptual development. Philosophy rather should have done what science and religion had done. Philosophy should have accepted the concept, 'We cannot 'know' truth to be truth.' and moved on from there. Philosophy should have accepted the 'fact' of the statement: 'We cannot 'know' truth to be truth.' and proceeded to say: That may be the case but we can define 'truth' to be 'truth' as best we can and proceed from there.

That is hindsight. The point is we can learn from the past and having done so, change the future.

There is no denying the past is the past and there is no denying humanity became a 'caged animal'. As such, 'mimesis' became our driving force, our fundamental behavioral motivator. Mimesis, the process of patterning behavior using a template of existing behavior, animalistic behavior, became the rational 'thing to do'.

Irrational, contradictory, intolerant actions of fear and desperation became a major characteristic of humankind. Now this is not to say such actions did not exist 'before' Aristotle. Rather it simply says we had two options open to us after Aristotle established his works.

Option 1 was to pursue our understanding of Zeno's 'seamlessness', the understanding of abstraction, the understanding of knowledge, knowing, awareness of one's very awareness.

Option 2 was to pursue our understanding of Zeno's 'multiplicity', the understanding of the physical, the understanding of matter, energy, thermodynamics, entropy, innate characteristics of atoms, molecules, and physical forces/laws.

Option 1 would lead to the rejection of mimesis. Option 1 would establish the rational understanding of 'altruistic' behavior, 'spiritual hedonism'

Option 2 would lead to the acceptance of mimesis. Option 2 would establish the rational understanding regarding 'physical' behavior, 'physical hedonism' .

Aristotle took one step down the path of 'multiplicity' and we, humanity, followed him and never looked back. Thus, it is that mimesis, physical hedonism, became the rationale for the next two and a half millennium. Physical hedonism and mimesis did not become humanity's main behavioral thrust due to historical trends, nor did physical hedonism and mimesis become humanity's main behavioral thrust because Aristotle suggested this path was the path to follow. Physical hedonism and mimesis simply became the extension of Aristotle's work because we, humanity, decided it should be so.

Zeno left an infinite number of doors open for understanding the potential significance of abstraction/seamlessness.

The War & Peace of a New Metaphysical Perception

Aristotle: We can understand the 'inside' through measurement and observation.

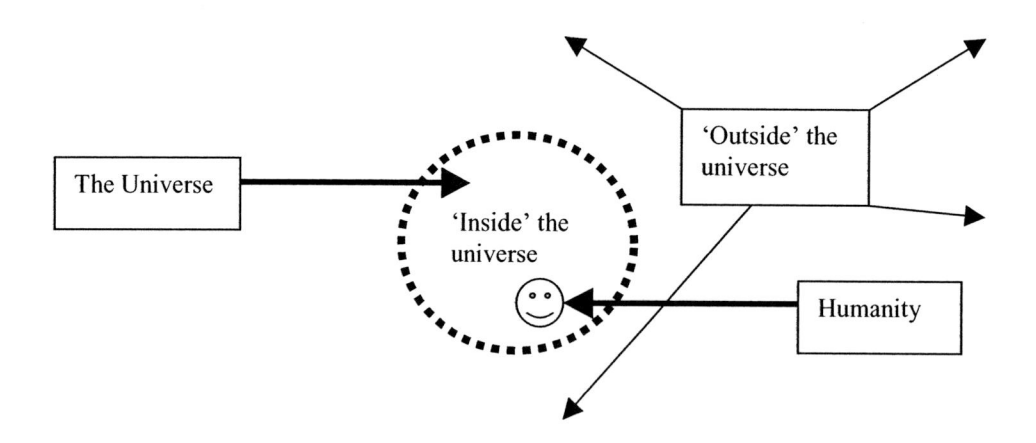

Aristotle closed all the doors but one. Aristotle left the concept of metaphysics in place. It was, therefore, not Aristotle but philosophy itself, which came along and slammed shut the last remaining open door, giving us:

Philosophy: We cannot understand what it is we cannot measure or observe.

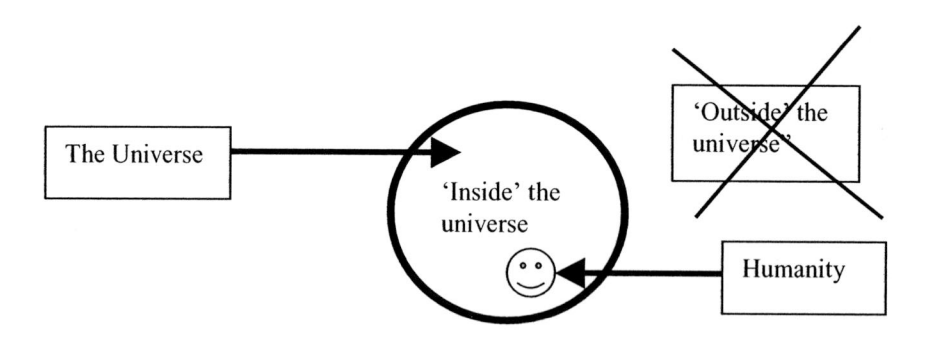

Philosophy drove the final nail in coffin of metaphysics. Philosophy closed all options regarding an outside to the universe. Philosophy isolated humanity from the 'outside' and thus limited us to a form of perceptual confinement.

Now we cannot 'blame' Aristotle for limiting us. We did not have to go exclusively down the path upon which Aristotle stepped. That was our choice. We had the free will to retrace our steps at any point in history.

We chose, however, to go down the path of 'seeing is believing'. We, you and I, chose to go exclusively down the path of measurement, the path of hypothesizing and testing. We, you and I together, chose to go exclusively down the path of 'the physical is what is', the path of 'the abstract is simply an innate characteristic of intelligence which in turn is created through specific molecular formations.

It was our choice and we made it. We are still making it today. The doors leading to the understanding regarding the interrelationship of the abstract and the physical remain shut not because we cannot open them but rather they remain shut because we choose not to open them.

Confinement is confinement

The most basic, the most fundamental driving force we have permeating our specie's essence is not the desire for sex, nor is it the need for food, nor the want of shelter. The most basic, the most fundamental driving force we have as individuals and as a specie is the need for 'open' space, the need for freedom. If we cannot find physical space, we create it in our minds. Now many biologists would disagree. Biologists would argue that a man would crawl into the confinement of a small box to obtain food, to seek shelter, or to engage in sexual acts. That may be true but they speak of the physical and ignore the workings of the mind. To be enclosed physically is one thing to be enclosed mentally is quite another and to be enclosed perceptually is still another. The most confining of all these forms of confinement is perceptual confinement. Perceptual confinement becomes a process of 'enclosing' our knowing, enclosing our very souls, enclosing our very essence.

We chose to go down the path of 'seeing is believing'. We choose to go down the path of 'seeing is believing'. There is no denying such a choice is perhaps the most obvious choice. This path is 'something' we can 'see'. This path is 'something' we can measure. We can see we are in the universe. We can see we are surrounded by the physical. We can see we are surrounded by time. We can 'see' we are immersed in time.

Regardless of 'how rational' such a choice may be, the point remains: 'Aristotle's system encloses us within the confines of the obvious, encloses us within the confines of the physical.

The concept of Cartesian

Let's look at the concept of confinement and 'see' if we can understand how it is we got into this predicament.

The concept of the essence being separate from the body evolved religiously long before it emerged philosophically, rationally, and long before it emerged through the process of reason.

Since Aristotle, we have scientifically reduced the concept regarding the simultaneous independent existence of the physical and the abstract to that of being simply an interesting anomaly. At the same time we have elevated the concept of the abstract being an innate characteristic of the physical to the level of being what is rational.

The rationality regarding the abstract emerging 'out of' the physical in essence is a process of embracing Cartesian reality and rejecting non-Cartesian Reality. The concept of Cartesian perception is credited to Descartes although the philosophical debate raged long before Descartes emerged upon the scene.

The War & Peace of a New Metaphysical Perception

An interesting process of looking at the concept of Cartesian rationality is through the use of mathematics:

●

A point
The origin
A beginning

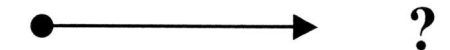

●——————▶   ?

A beginning exists and leads to '?'
A beginning exists and leads to perhaps an end, perhaps not
Beginning/end emerges in a simplistic fashion
A question emerges: How long does it take one to get to the end if one can ever in fact get to the end?

The concept of mortality vs. immortality enters the realm of mathematics

? ◀——————●——————▶ ?

A beginning exists and leads to '?' in two vs. one direction.
A beginning exists and leads to perhaps an end, perhaps not.
Beginning/end emerges in a complex fashion
Three new questions emerge:
1. If one travels backward through time can one change what 'was' and would this change what 'will be'?
2. If one travels backward through time can one change what 'was' and would this change what 'is'?
3. If one travels backward through time can one change what 'was' and if so what became of the 'old' 'what was'?

The concept of 'negative time' enters the realm of mathematics and philosophy becomes confused.

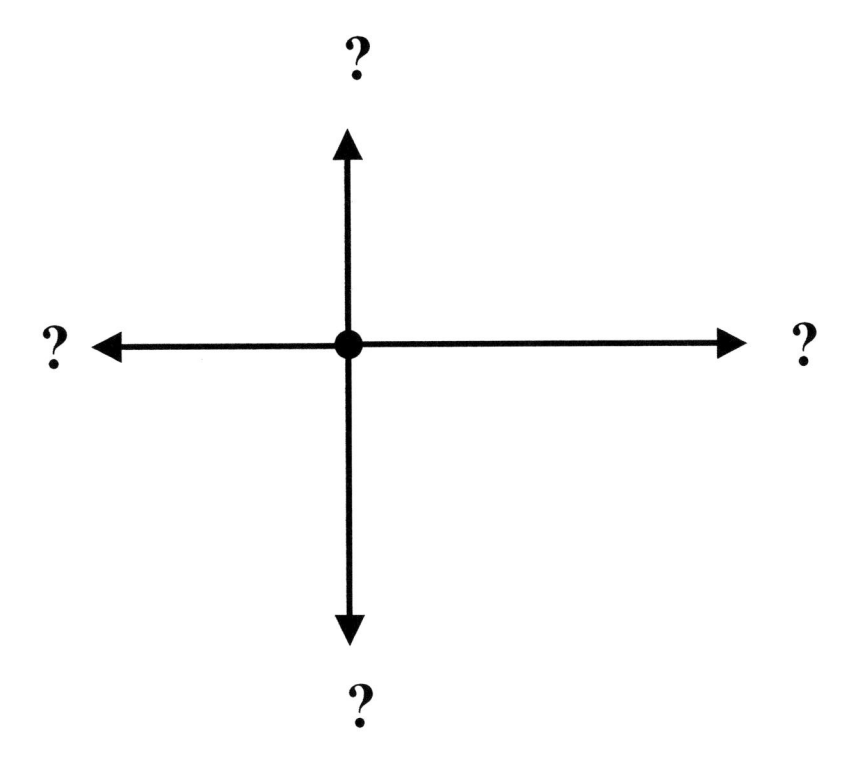

```
            ?
            ↑
            |
   ? ←──────●──────→ ?
            |
            ↓
            ?
```

The War & Peace of a New Metaphysical Perception

Beginning/end remains and its complexity accelerates geometrically.
A fifth question emerges: If one can travel forward and backward in time, how does one travel 'up' and 'down' in time?

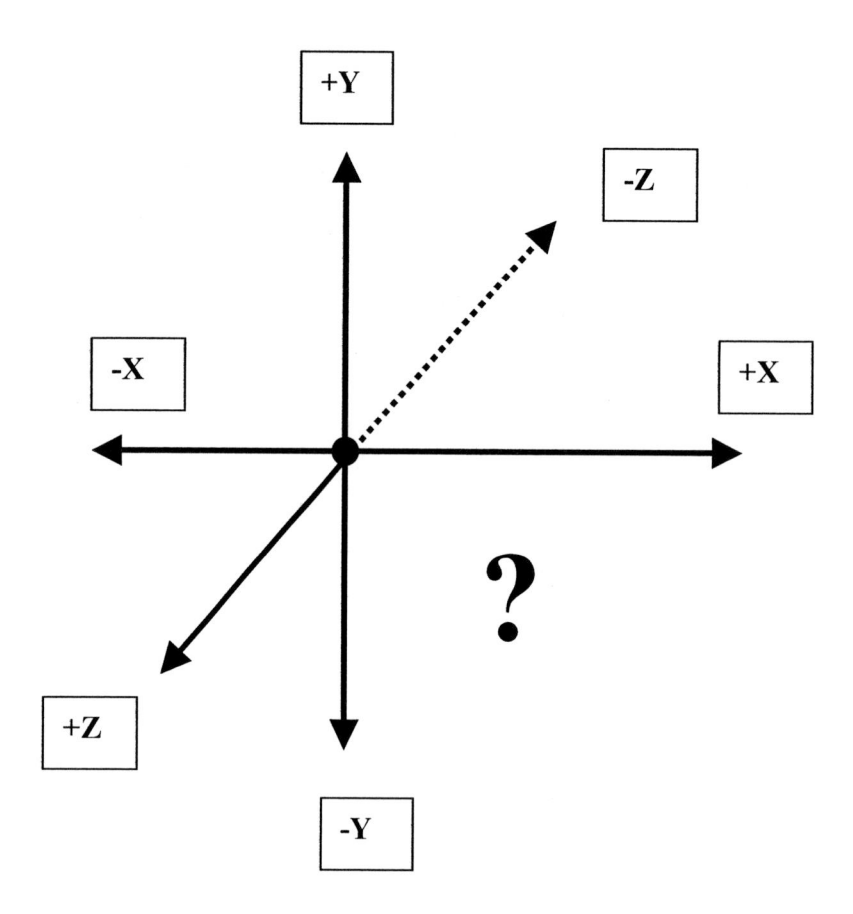

Beginning/end not only gain an additional dimension but gain the characteristic of expanding in a geometrically complex fashion. Beginning/end become a three dimensionally 'Cartesian' form of complexity.

A sixth question emerges: If one can travel 'forward', 'backward', 'up', and 'down', in time, can one slide sideways through time?

Now it is not being argued that the concept of a Cartesian existence, an emergence of the essence of the individual as an innate characteristic of the very the physical ness of the body, evolved from the examination of Cartesian mathematical depiction of physical space itself.

What is being suggested is that Aristotle, through the process of 'closing' our universe, initiated the process of pointing humanity in the direction of examining what we 'see'. Aristotle pointed humanity in the direction of accepting the principle, 'Seeing is believing.' and rejecting all else.

Aristotle pointed humanity in the 'scientific direction'. Humanity, following Aristotle's lead, drew 'legitimate' conclusions from these observations, 'laid' 'legitimate' foundations based upon a

The Error of Aristotle

Cartesian system. Humanity, emulating Aristotle, proceeded down a path it would find almost irrefutable. The direction of 'seeing' is 'believing' evolved into 'seeing' 'is' what 'in fact' is.

Humanity began the process of accepting science/observation, as not only it's main form of perception but its only 'believable' form of perception.[4] Humanity's other forms of perception, the perception of faith and the perception of reason were to take on new meaning. The perception of 'faith', believing in what one cannot see, was to become questionable and the perception of 'reason', attempting to rationalize the function of 'knowing', was to ironically become an irrational exercise.

As time passed, our perception of 'reality' became increasingly complicated. With each new scientific observation regarding the laws of our universe, philosophy found the concept of 'truth' and the understanding of metaphysics became exponentially more complex.

Philosophy made a stand and declared: 'Cogito ergo sum.' 'I think therefore I am.'

This simple statement led to the understanding that from the point of view of others, I may not be, but from my point of view, I am. The universe exists in my mind but it may not exist. Totality greater than myself may not exist but if I exist and totality 'outside' myself does not exist, than there is still the sum total of myself. Strangely enough, this 'truth' did not arise as the 'first' truth but rather became established after the establishment of two other truths.

Aristotle moved 'truth' from existing as one basic truth, one first principle, to existing as two basic truths, two first principles from which all other truths, first principles sprung. Before Aristotle, religions held to the concept that God/Totality exists. Aristotle brought forth the concept of science, which produced the basic 'truth': the universe exists.

Religion thus had its first principle, first truth and science now had its first principle, first truth.

Descartes would introduce philosophical, metaphysical first 'truth', first principle. Thus two basic truths, two firsts principles would now become three basic truths, three first principles. Now truths, vying for the position of being truths, became: for religion - God/Totality exists, for science - the universe exists, and for philosophy – I, the individual, exists.

Through it all, the concept of beginning/end remained intact for it permeates every 'observable' region of our universe. Through it all, the concept of Cartesianism remains. Through it all, the quest to find the 'beginning' point, to find the 'beginning' cause remains. Through it all, the quest to establish which of the three 'truths' was the first truth, was the 'true' first principle. Finding 'first' truth became the holy grail of science, philosophy, and religion. The concept of seeking 'the' 'first' truth, which in turn leads to the development of other truths, created a quest for which of the three, totality, the universe, or individuality, is 'in fact' 'the' first truth.

So it is Cartesianism, the concept of beginning/end, became a critical factor in the quest for truth. Cartesianism, beginning/end concepts, being the primary perceptual principle of science, grew in importance as the influence of science grew in importance.

To better understand the concept of Cartesianism, lets examine a few characteristics of 'a' Cartesian system.

A Cartesian system has an 'origin', has a 'zero' point, has a 'location' from which one begins. All systems found 'within' such a system, found 'within' a Cartesian system, also have an 'origin', have a 'zero' point, have a 'location' from which they begin. So it is metaphysics originating from 'within' a Cartesian system, exploring 'truths' found 'within' a Cartesian system, perceive truths to have an 'origin'. This is why metaphysics yearns to find, attempts to define its beginning point, its 'first truth', its fundamental principle.

A Cartesian system of spatial depiction has a point of origin. The point of origin within a spatially oriented Cartesian system is the intersection of the 'x', 'y', and 'z' axis. When one first studies this point of origin, the point of origin is presumed to be 'fixed'. As one becomes familiar with the system, one begins to realize the point of origin is not 'fixed' but can be shifted in space. This shift of the origin does not destroy the Cartesian system, nor does it change the actual location of permanently fixed points. The shift of the origin does not change the perception we have of the 'locations' in space but simply changes what appears to be the 'origin'. The shift of the origin changes the name, the coordinates we give to the permanently fixed points but this does not change what the point is nor does it change the characteristics of the point nor does it change the relative location, the relative abstractual function of one point to another.

Now all this sounds complicated and confusing. Perhaps putting a name to the concept would help. We could call the concept an existence of 'relativistic perception'. Relativistic perception does not change what 'is' but simply changes one's perception of what is.

Now what does this have to do with Aristotle? What does this have to do with philosophy? What does this have to do with metaphysics? What does this have to do with 'first truth'?

Aristotle closed Zeno's open universal system. Aristotle 'created' a system 'within' which both the physical and the abstract could be found but 'from' which neither the physical nor the abstract nor both the physical and the abstract could rationally 'escape'. Under Aristotle's direction, confinement became true confinement. Thus, Aristotle directed us to examine first truth from 'within' the confines of 'the' universe. Aristotle directed us to 'find', 'look for' first truth 'within' the universe. Aristotle directed us to look for first cause within the confines of the universe having forms such as 'a' primal atom from which the big bang 'originated', such as the source of 'Om', such as the source of the our very essence, and such as the origin of the soul 'within' physicality.

It is important to reemphasize over and over again that Aristotle did not 'force' us to move primarily in the direction of 'closing' the system upon ourselves. We closed the system upon ourselves through our desire to find answers to the questions, Where am I?, What am I?, and Why do I exist? It was the desperate desire to find the answers to these questions which motivated us to 'close' the system. And it was the closing of the self-imposed closing of the outer boundaries of our perception, which caused the concept of 'knowing' 'truth' to become a perceived unsolvable paradox.

The process of 'closing' the system led to the concept of 'physical reality' becoming 'the' 1st principle, first truth. The 1st principle, the 1st truth began to emerge as: The universe exists. As this 'truth' emerged, the concept of 'seeing is believing' initiated the acceleration of the acceptance of this truth as being the 'first truth'.

In Zeno's open system, the individual becomes 'knowing' and the physical body becomes just that, the physical. Such a statement appears to reinforce the concept of dualism, the perception of the physical and knowing being separate

In a 'closed' Cartesian system being examined from 'within' itself, perceptions emerge such as: If the physical is 1st truth, then 'knowing' evolves out of the physical. As such 'knowing' becomes an innate characteristic of the physical. The conclusion: Knowing is the 2nd truth and evolves out of the 1st truth: The universe exists.

Again: What does this have to do with Aristotle? Aristotle closed the semi-open system of Zeno. Aristotle established the perceived 'undeniable' 1st truth: the universe along with its observable features are 'the' system'. The individual evolves out of the physical and there was no place to put the abstract other than label it, perceive it as nothing other than an innate characteristic of the physical. In short, Aristotle in essence established the concept of monism from which philosophy; try as it might over the next twenty-five hundred years, never recovered.

Zeno had established the initial understanding of dualism, the physical body and abstract 'knowing' are separate entities. Both seamlessness and multiplicity exist simultaneously. Both the physical and the abstract exist independently of each other while existing dependent upon each other. Both the abstract and the physical are 'real' yet 'real illusions'. Zeno was not sure how such a system would appear perceptually. Zeno was not sure how such a system could be understood. Nevertheless, Zeno took the first philosophical step towards understanding such a system by stating the obvious: Seamlessness and multiplicity exist. In order to accommodate such a perception, Zeno left the system semi-closed or semi-open depending upon one's point of view.

Aristotle, who was to follow Zeno, closed the system. Aristotle established a linear perception of truth. Aristotle established the '1st truth': The universe exists. There is no 'denying' the fact, the universe exists, for it is 'obvious', we can see it. Aristotle established: Individual 'knowing' and 'summation of knowing'/the whole are not 'facts' for they are not 'observable'. The result: The universe exists is 'the' '1st truth, and all other truths evolve from this 1st truth and as such all other truths take second place to the most basic of truths, take second place to the 'holy grail': The universe exists. The result: Not only is a solid foundation for monism established, but monism gains an edge over dualism.

Cartesian Systems

A Cartesian system is:
1. a closed system: 'what is 'is".
2. a system with a beginning
3. a system leading to a state of permanent equilibrium

Now who is to deny such things as obvious as these and that is exactly the point of view from which Aristotle came. The genius of Aristotle was in the stating of the obvious. However, the obvious was the obvious because the perceptions of the day were just that, perceptions of 'the' day. A broader perception, a more intuitive perception was not conceivable by men of science or religion for they saw what they saw and believed what they believed. Philosophy, reason, was not the issue. Faith and observation, believing and seeing superceded reason. Neither the concept of an existence with no physical substance, nor an existence of the physical immersed 'within' the non-physical nor the concept of a 'nonphysical' immersed 'within' the physical was inconceivable. Such discussions were unreasonable to people in the 500s and 300s BC. What was obvious for the time was that the perceived physical was immersed within itself. Such an existence was verifiable while the concept of 'knowing'; the concept of abstraction was unverifiable by anything we could see or believe and for that matter by anything we could reason. Zeno alluded to an existence of seamlessness, abstraction, but Zeno could not verify its 'existence'.

It may have been Aristotle who was to 'close' Zeno's system, who was to close the open border surrounding the physical. However, it was science and religion, which were to take their advancements over the next two thousand years and mold them to Aristotle's closed system.

Now this was not a 'necessary' movement on the part of science and religion. Science and religion could have just as well have molded their advancements to Zeno's suggestions regarding a possible abstractual existence. However, science and religion examined Aristotle's perceptions and agreed they were logical. They then molded their initial perceptual developments to Aristotle's system, a closed system. As time passed, religion and science found themselves increasingly entrenched, increasingly committed to 'a' closed system. Their traditions, perceptions, principles, laws, cultures, fundamentals became so entangled with the concept of a closed system, they could not turn back. To turn back took on the appearance of having to scuttle their most cherished ceremonies and establishments.

Science and religion could have just as well molded their observations and beliefs to the open system Zeno had initiated. Philosophy could have reinforced the alternative action on the part of science and religion by offering a more expansive view of what existed 'outside' the system. Philosophy could have moved the concept of an exclusively closed system into being a closed system located 'within' an open system. Such a perception would have established the concept of a Cartesian system, the physical, being located 'within' an open system. In essence, this would have established a Cartesian system within a non-Cartesian system. This would have established a Cartesian system powering a non-Cartesian system. This would have established a system where all the parts make up the whole but the whole is not equal to the sum of its parts, rather the whole is greater than the sum of its parts.

Before we can understand such concepts, we must further examine the paradox created by a closed system.

The paradox of Cartesian Systems

A Cartesian System is: 1. a closed system 2. a system with a beginning 3. a system leading to a state of permanent equilibrium

1. A closed system: The only conceivable perception of reality during the time of Aristotle was that
   'reality' existed as it was as opposed to 'reality' existing as a potentially expanding entity. Eventually the constancy of the physical moved to being potentially expanding but in essence, due to its closed nature, remained static for there was no 'outside' within which to 'expand'. Such a system produced the perception: If the universe, the physical, dissolved into nothingness, nothingness would be all that remained. This led to the concept that the 'creator' of the universe was 'within' the universe, 'was' the universe. This is a pantheistic approach vs. a panentheistic approach. Panentheism as opposed to pantheism takes the approach: If the universe, the physical, dissolved into nothingness, nothingness may remain but this nothingness would be 'located' 'within' the creator, which in turn would remain part of the creator.

2. A system with a beginning: Aristotle's system conceived of a beginning to all that existed within the universe and ignored the concept of: What if the physical dissolved? What would remain? This was a senseless question to Aristotle for the concept of nothing did not exist. The concept of 'nothing' had been suppressed[5] by the Greeks. In essence, Aristotle's system had no end and no beginning. The universe, the physical, always existed and always would exist. (see: Zero: 'The Biography of a Dangerous Idea', Charles Seife, 2000)

3. A system leading to a state of permanent equilibrium: Aristotle's system found itself constantly under attack. The concept of an expanding and shrinking universe – the Big Bang, the concept of an origin to the universe – Om, the concept of energy seeking to

The Error of Aristotle

reach a state of equilibrium – entropy, etc. evolved over time only to find themselves being shape-shifted to 'fit' the Aristotelian 'closed', Cartesian system.

The concept of reverting to Zeno's perception of 'reality',

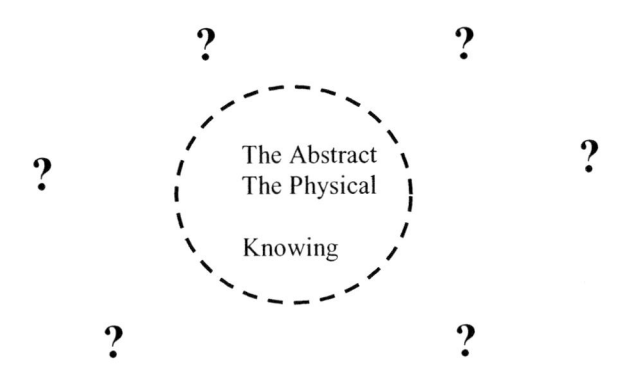

$$? \quad ?$$

$$? \quad \left(\begin{array}{c}\text{The Abstract} \\ \text{The Physical} \\ \text{Knowing}\end{array}\right) \quad ?$$

$$? \quad ?$$

never became a realistic option for humanity. Humanity had too many unanswered questions regarding such a system. When removing dotted line, removing the boundaries confining humankind, removing the boundaries confining all beings with consciousness of consciousness, what becomes of 'knowing'? What becomes of self-remembering? What becomes of an ending to matter, energy, time, and mortality? What becomes of the concept of growth? What becomes of the concept of immortality? What becomes of the concept regarding the existence of three minutes 'before' creation? What becomes of the very concept of 'a' 'significance' of the individual, of 'a' significance of our specie, of 'a' significance of the essence of Totality itself. Just what is '?', and how does '?' interact with the 'substance' 'within' the visible system?

Even more unsettling was the lack of understanding of,

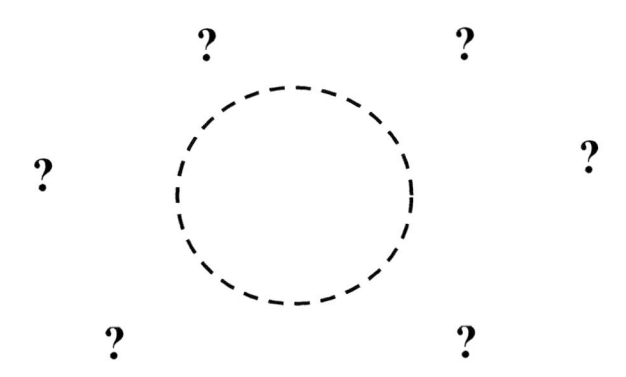

The War & Peace of a New Metaphysical Perception

should the universe be removed for then one only has,

?   ?

?   ?

?   ?

and just what does that imply?!!!

Just as surely as Aristotle closed the exits Zeno left open at the very outer edges of his system, Aristotle slammed shut the discussion regarding questions pertaining to an 'outside'. Aristotle took the first step in the direction of confining humanity to the limits of the physical and pushing humanity into the void regarding the lack of understanding the reasonableness of anything lying 'outside' what we see or believe. A sense of hopelessness and despair became the insidious hidden ambiance of humankind, for humankind found itself confined perceptually and unable to rationalize any other alternative.

However, in truth, the blame for the confinement of humanity was neither that of Aristotle nor that of religion nor that of science but rather that of philosophy. Philosophy was the one to declare metaphysics, declare the search for the ultimate truth, to be dead, to be unreasonable. Philosophy was the one to sell 'humanity out' in order to 'belong'[6]

Part II: Resolving the paradox

Introduction

Resolving the paradox of our individuality, 'being's', existing 'within' the physical while remaining an abstraction, does not require our discarding Aristotle's perception of the physical being a 'closed' system, a Cartesian system. To discard Aristotle's system in its entirety would generate as many problems as does accepting Aristotle's system as 'the' one and only system.

If we do not discard Aristotle's Cartesian system, if we do not discard the concept of the universe being all there is, with what do we 'replace' it? First, we need only concede the physical as being 'the' system 'within' which we find ourselves 'located' and as such, we are able to study it scientifically.

The Error of Aristotle

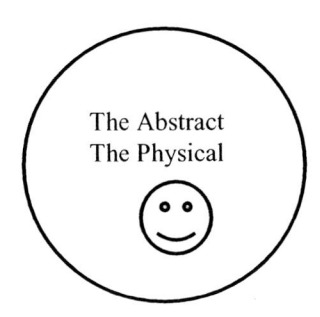

```
    ┌─────────┐
    │ The Abstract │
    │ The Physical │
    │    ◡     │
    └─────────┘
```

This may have the appearance of accepting Aristotle's Cartesian system as being 'the' system while professing not to regard it as such. How can this be? Is such a statement simply a process of substituting one paradox with another?

If we follow up the concept of our abstractual 'form' existing 'within' the physical with the concept of the physical existing 'within' abstraction we obtain a different system than the one Aristotle put into place.

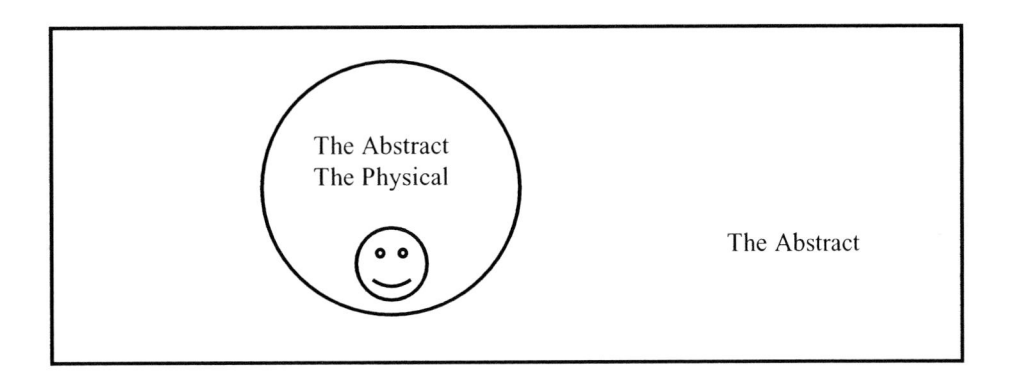

```
┌──────────────────────────────────┐
│   ┌─────────┐                     │
│   │ The Abstract │                │
│   │ The Physical │    The Abstract│
│   │    ◡     │                    │
│   └─────────┘                     │
└──────────────────────────────────┘
```

In essence, such a perceptual development allows us to retain Aristotle's perception while simultaneously retaining Zeno's basic theories regarding seamlessness and multiplicity.

This process allows us the luxury of speculating upon the existence of parallel 'unattached' realities existing 'within' the larger 'Reality'. The process allows us the luxury of speculating upon the existence of a region where 'things' move through time, allows the luxury of speculating upon 'things' being immersed within time, and allows us the luxury of speculating upon a region 'within' which time is found to be immersed while simultaneously being a region independent of time.

But such a discussion cannot be fully addressed in an 'introductory section'. This fact necessitates the need to establish the remainder of this tractate.

Before we jump into the effort of resolving the paradoxes Aristotle's Cartesian system creates, a few more generalities are appropriate.

The War & Peace of a New Metaphysical Perception

Aristotle established the concept of 'a' system,

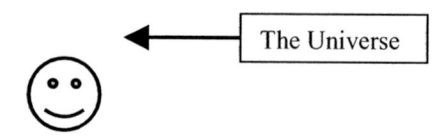

[diagram: a smiley face with an arrow pointing to it from a box labeled "The Universe"]

which leads to the perception of a universal philosophy based upon 'a' 1st principle, based upon the concept that 'a' 1st truth exists: The universe exists. Now there is nothing 'wrong' with this 1st principle. It does, however, affect its occupants if accepted as 'first' truth. Aristotle's Cartesian system leads, generally speaking, to a concept we call materialism. To put it another way, a Cartesian system leads to physical hedonism. This is not a statement of negativity any more than stating that objects fall 'down'. The concept of a 'closed' system, a Cartesian system leading, generally speaking, to materialism is simply a statement of observation.

The metaphysical system of

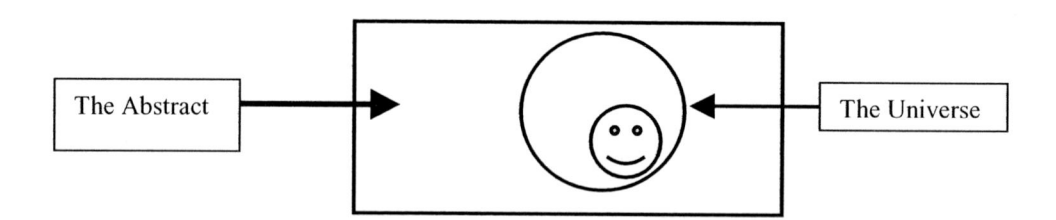

[diagram: a rectangle containing a circle with a smiley face inside; arrows point into the rectangle from boxes labeled "The Abstract" (left) and "The Universe" (right)]

on the other hand leads to the concept of 'spiritual' hedonism, abstractual hedonism. This is not to say 'spiritual' hedonism is 'better' than 'physical' hedonism, rather it simply states that the two perceptions of 1st truth, a first truth based upon a constancy of physical 'location'/a Cartesian system vs. a first truth based upon the relativity of 'location'/a non-Cartesian system, develop different perceptions regarding the 'purpose of life'. This well become clearer as we move further along in this tractate.

Aristotle's system moves 'outward' to incorporate various developing scientific perceptions.

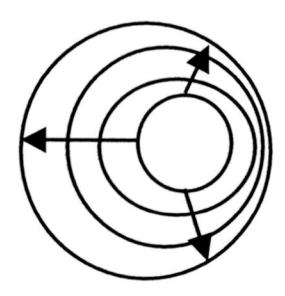

[diagram: concentric circles with arrows pointing outward]

The Error of Aristotle

The concentric circles begin filling up with concepts of solar systems, galaxies, vacuum potential levels, entropy, thermodynamics, etc. However, regardless of the complexity, which arises, the 'fact' remains: There is 'a' 1st truth and the 1st truth is: The universe exists. From this most basic of basic understandings arises a specific perception: There is 'nothing' that exists 'outside' the physical. Such a statement, such a perception, gains more and more credibility over time because we 'look' for an alternative 'location' but can never seem to 'find' it because we never 'see' it regardless of how hard we try to 'see' it.

Each new scientific development further reinforces the argument: If we cannot see it or measure it, it does not exist. This very statement of principle reinforces the 1st truth which underlies the very nature of science: The universe exists. Science takes the lead regarding this 1st truth. It is science to which we look when attempting to understand the abstract. However, is science the logical place to look when science itself is limited to 'seeing/measuring' the physical if the abstract is not physical, has no physical properties?

We found ourselves embroiled for the next several millenniums within this debate. Such a perception appeared to have resolution. If we revert back to Zeno and reestablish the open boundaries Zeno places upon the universe as opposed to the closed boundaries Aristotle placed upon the universe we find we have:

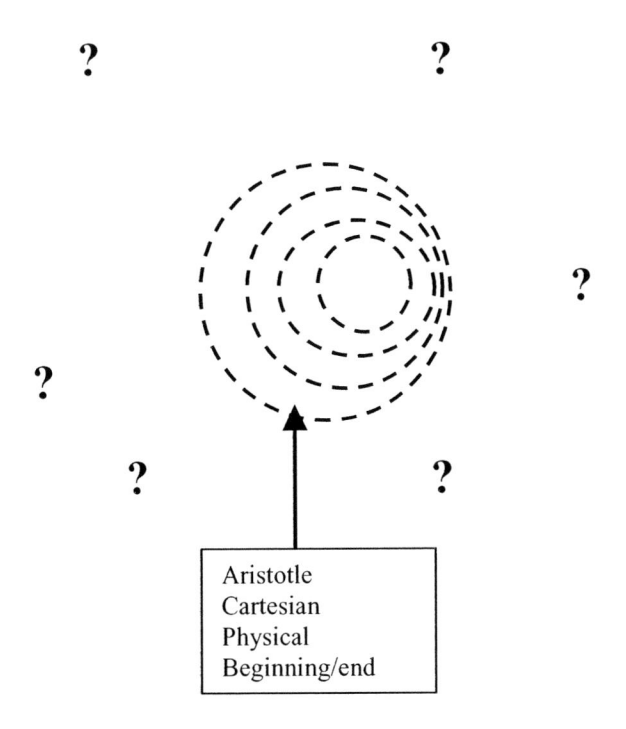

? ?

?

?

? ?

Aristotle
Cartesian
Physical
Beginning/end

This becomes:

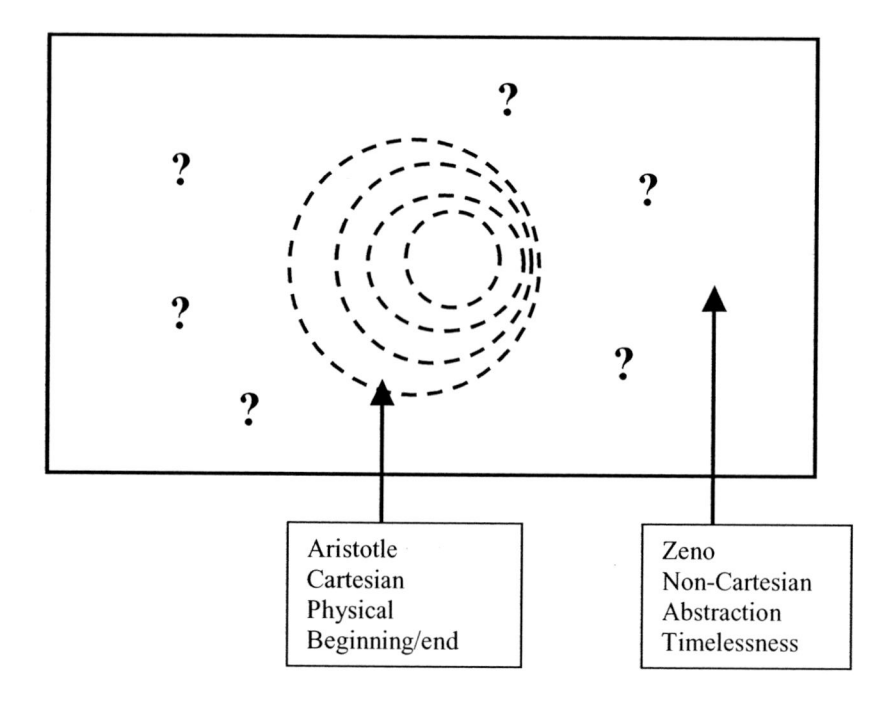

[Diagram: A rectangle containing question marks scattered around a series of dashed concentric circles. Two arrows point upward from labeled boxes below:
- Left box (pointing to circles): Aristotle / Cartesian / Physical / Beginning/end
- Right box (pointing into the rectangle): Zeno / Non-Cartesian / Abstraction / Timelessness]

if we establish the whole to be a 'system'.

With this potential 'system' modeled, it is time to examine what the above perception would do to the concept of '1st' principle or what some call '1st' truth.

Relativistic 1st Principles

First principle based upon 1st truth:

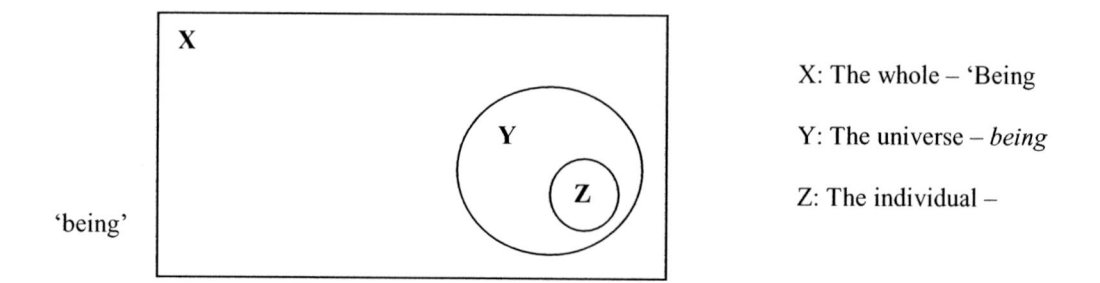

[Diagram: A rectangle labeled X in the top-left, with 'being' at the lower left outside. Inside the rectangle is a circle labeled Y, which contains a smaller circle labeled Z.]

X: The whole – 'Being

Y: The universe – *being*

Z: The individual –

1st principle:

    a. Region 'X' 'viewing' region 'Y' and region 'Z'

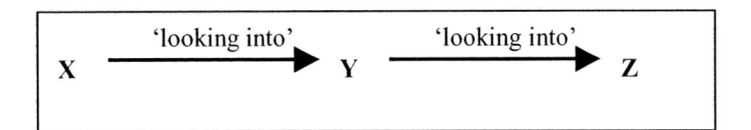

```
X ---'looking into'---> Y ---'looking into'---> Z
```

        1st principle exists and becomes region 'X'
        2nd principle exists and becomes region 'Y'
        3rd principle exists and becomes region 'Z'

    b. Region 'Y' 'viewing ' region 'Z' and region 'X'

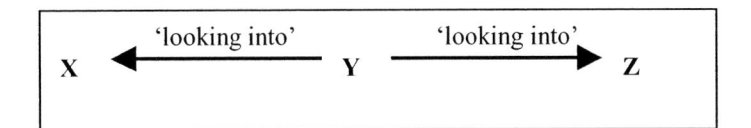

```
X <---'looking into'--- Y ---'looking into'---> Z
```

        1st principle exists and becomes region 'Y'
        2nd principle exists and becomes either region 'X' or region 'Z'
        3rd principle exists and becomes region 'Z' or region 'X' depending upon the perception of '2nd principle

    c. Region 'Z' 'viewing' region 'X' and region 'Y'

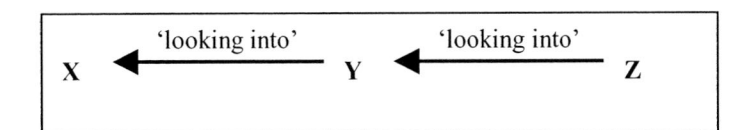

```
X <---'looking into'--- Y <---'looking into'--- Z
```

        1st principle exists and becomes region 'Z'
        2nd principle exists and becomes region 'Y'
        3rd principle exists and becomes region 'X'

Because the regions 'X', 'Y', and 'Z' exist, be it as the 'real' or a 'real illusion', from the 'point of view' of regions 'X', 'Y', or 'Z', first principle always begins with itself. Without the region making the observation, the other two, 2nd and 3rd principles would not exist to '1st principle' thus the 2nd and 3rd principles would not be a topic of discussion for 1st principle.

The War & Peace of a New Metaphysical Perception

Strangely enough, such a perception changes when 'viewed' not from the point of view of the 'region' but when viewed from the point of view of the 'object' found 'within' the regions 'X', 'Y', or 'Z'. The region and the object 'found within' the region have different perception regarding 1st truth, 1st principle. We can examine this concept by 'looking' at the issue of 1st principle from the point of view of the 'object' found within the region. To do so we will find if helpful to examine such perceptions of the object through using the perceptual tools available to the object, the tools of 'believing'/religion, 'observing'/science, and 'reasoning'/philosophy.

1st principle from the point of view of the object/individuality found 'within' 'X':

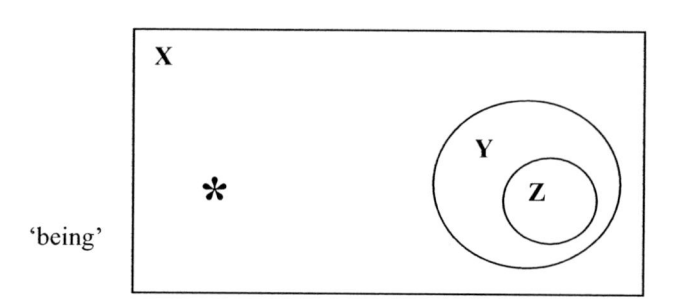

✱ The object/individuality doing the observing

X: The whole – 'Being

Y: The universe – *being*

Z: The individual –

'being'

    a.   When inside 'X' 'viewing' 'Y' and 'Z'

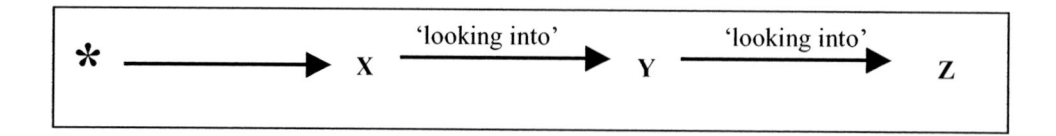

✱ ⟶ X ⟶ 'looking into' ⟶ Y ⟶ 'looking into' ⟶ Z

Religiously/believability:

    1st principle begins with the object/individuality
    2nd principle becomes region 'X'/the whole
    3rd principle becomes region 'Y'/the universe
    4th principle becomes region 'Z'/other individualities

Scientifically/observability:

    1st principle begins with the object/individuality
    2nd principle becomes region 'X'/the whole
    3rd principle becomes region 'Y'/the universe
    4th principle becomes region 'Z'/other individualities

Philosophically/reasonablity:

    1st principle begins with the object/individuality
    2nd principle becomes region 'X'/the whole
    3rd principle becomes region 'Y'/the universe
    4th principle becomes region 'Z'/other individualities

1st principle from the point of view of the object/individuality found 'within' 'Y':

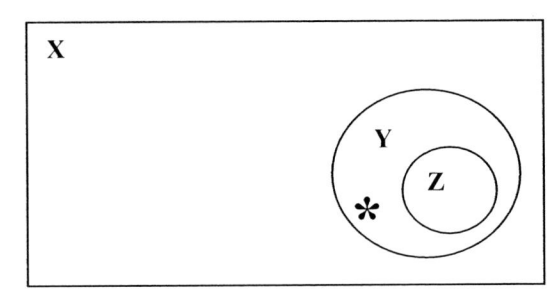

✱ The object/individuality doing the observing

X: The whole – 'Being'

Y: The universe – *being*

Z: The individual –

'being'

    b.   When at 'Y' 'viewing' 'Z' and 'X'

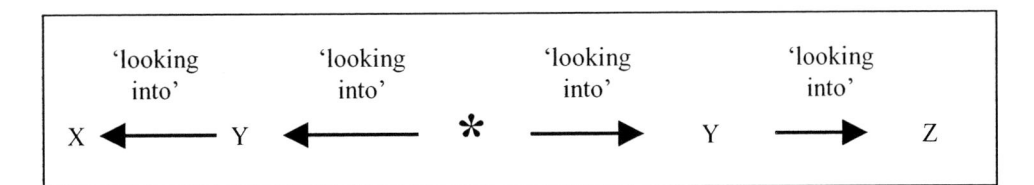

'looking into'   'looking into'   'looking into'   'looking into'

X ← Y ← ✱ → Y → Z

Religiously/believability:

1st principle begins with the object/individuality
2nd principle becomes region 'Y'/the universe
3rd principle becomes either region 'X'/the whole or region 'Z'/other individualities
4th principle becomes region 'Z'/other individualities or region 'X'/the whole

Scientifically/observability:

1st principle begins with the object/individuality
2nd principle becomes region 'Y'/the universe
3rd principle becomes either region 'X'/the whole or region 'Z'/other individualities
4th principle becomes region 'Z'/other individualities or region 'X'/the whole

Philosophically/reasonablity:

1st principle begins with the object/individuality
2nd principle becomes region 'Y'/the universe
3rd principle becomes either region 'X'/individuality or region 'Z'/the whole
4th principle becomes region 'Z'/the whole or region 'X'/individuality

The War & Peace of a New Metaphysical Perception

1st principle from the point of view of an object/individuality found 'within' 'Z':

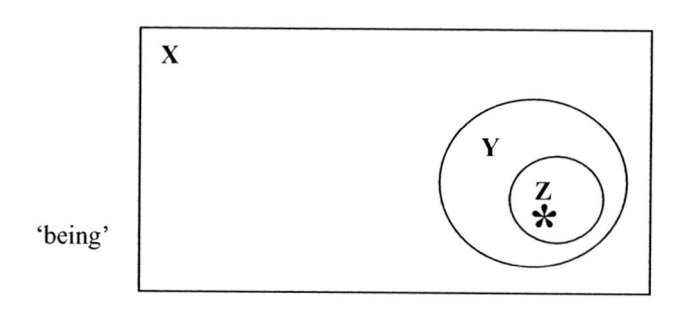

✱ The object/individuality doing the observing

X: The whole – 'Being

Y: The universe – *being*

Z: The individual –

'being'

c. When at 'Z' 'viewing' 'X' and 'Y'

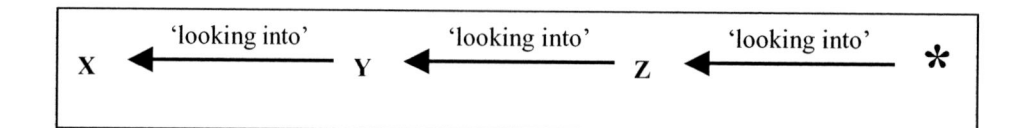

X ← 'looking into' ← Y ← 'looking into' ← Z ← 'looking into' ← ✱

Religiously/believability:

    1st principle begins with the object/individuality
    2nd principle becomes region 'Z'/other individualities
    3rd principle becomes the region 'Y'/the universe
    4th principle becomes region 'X'/the whole

Scientifically/observability:

    1st principle begins with the object/individuality
    2nd principle becomes region 'Z'/other individualities
    3rd principle becomes the region 'Y'/the universe
    4th principle becomes region 'X'/the whole

Philosophically/reasonablity:

    1st principle begins with the object/individuality
    2nd principle becomes region 'Z'/other individualities
    3rd principle becomes the region 'Y'/the universe
    4th principle becomes region 'X'/the whole

So what does all this analysis demonstrate? It demonstrates that 1st principle/1st truth, when viewed from the point of view of the 1st truth itself, remains constant. 1st truth, 1st principle, when viewed from the point of view of 1st truth, 1st principle itself is itself.

On the other hand, when 1st truth is viewed from the point of view of the object/individuality, 1st truth is always the object/individuality. The reason individuality has difficulty seeing 1st truth as anything other than individuality is because we view it from our point of view, we view it from the point of view of individuality because we are entities of individuality. We are individuals.

In short, if one removes the bias of individuality from the mix, 1st principle 'shifts'. To remove the perception of 1st truth being illusive, one must view 1st truth from the point of the perspective of the three first truths themselves rather than from the point of view of the object of individuality alone. The three regions, the three 1st truths being: the whole exists– 'X', the universe exists – 'Y', and individuality exists – 'Z'.

We have been debating 1st truth from our point of view, from the point of view of individuality, for the last two thousand years. This explains why we have not resolved the issue of 'first' principle. This explains why we are confused. It explains why we have appeared to make little progress in philosophical, scientific, and religious fundamental, primal, perceptions regarding the issue of monism and dualism. We have been unable to resolve the issue of 1st truth because we have been debating the issue from our/individualities point of view rather than the point of view of 1st truth itself.

After thousands of years debating, we find ourselves seeking 'a' 1st principle. We find ourselves seeking what we perceive to be a 1st truth. We believe 1st truth, 1st principle must be a constant. We believe 1st principle/1st truth must always be 'the' 1st truth. Each of our three means of perception, belief/religion, observation/science, and reason/philosophy, refuse to acknowledge the validity of the other's 1st principle.

The three, science, religion, and philosophy, view 1st principle differently. Since we are a visual creature, we might better understand the concept of a shifting 1st principle, a shifting 1st truth through the use of graphics:

The War & Peace of a New Metaphysical Perception

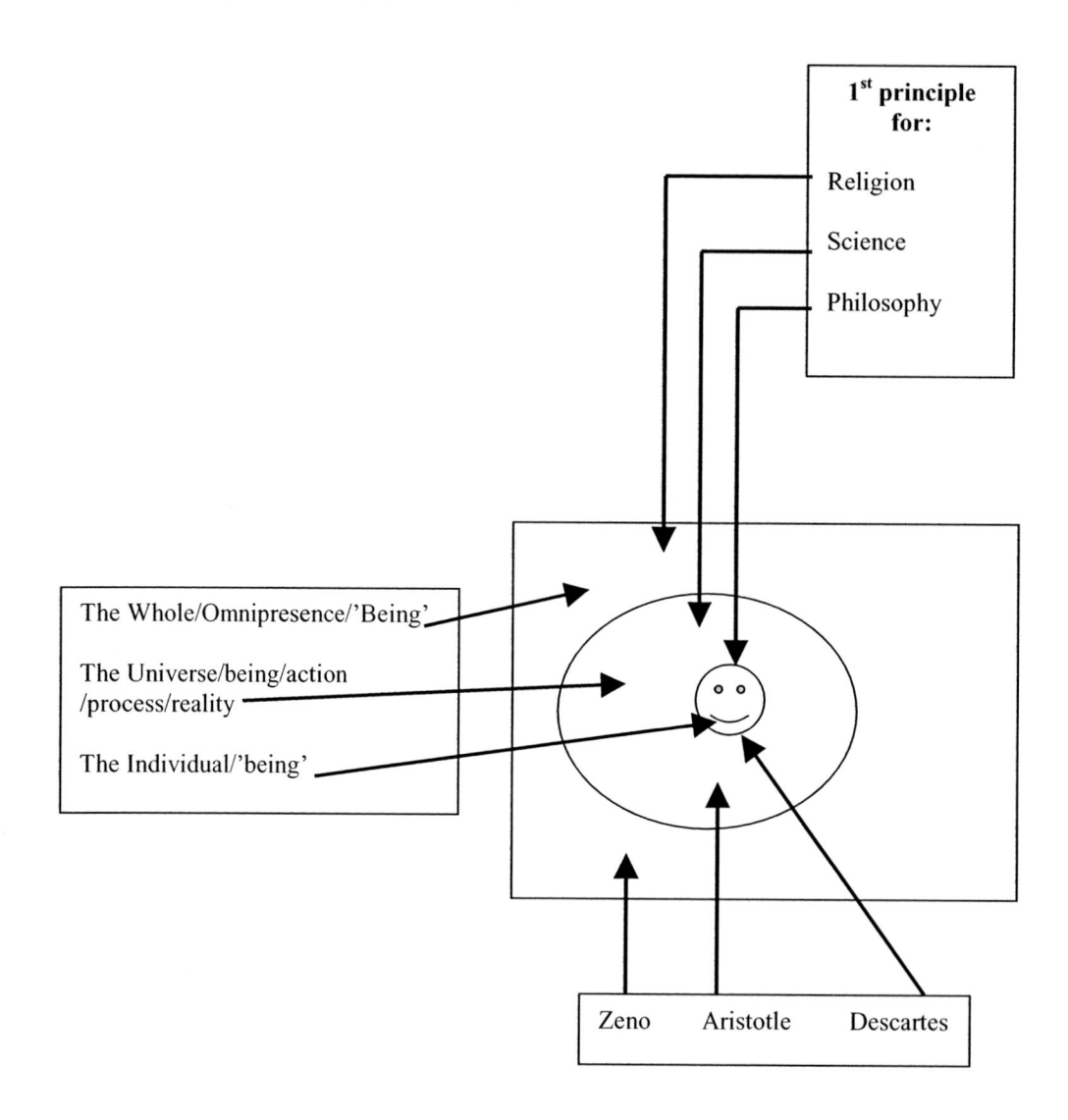

```
                                    ┌─────────────────┐
                                    │  1st principle  │
                                    │      for:       │
                                    │                 │
                                    │   Religion      │
                                    │                 │
                                    │   Science       │
                                    │                 │
                                    │   Philosophy    │
                                    └─────────────────┘
```

- The Whole/Omnipresence/'Being'
- The Universe/being/action /process/reality
- The Individual/'being'

Zeno   Aristotle   Descartes

The three, science, religion, and philosophy, have not been able to find a means of 'accepting', acceding to the 1st principle of the others. With a concept of 'relativistic 1st principle', this problem dissipates. With the concept of 'relativistic 1st principle', none of our three means of developing perceptions find themselves 'needing' to compromise their perception of 1st principle. Each maintains their perception of just what 1st principle is when viewed from their particular point of region, when viewed from their particular point of reference, when viewed from the recognition that 1st principle exists but varies with ones 'location' of perception.

Why look at 1st truth from the point of view of the 'region' itself rather than from our personal point of view, from the point of view of the object found 'within' the region? To put the question another way: Why should we discontinue looking at 1st truth from the point of view of ourselves, from the point of view of the individual doing the perceiving?

From our point of view, from the point of view of the individual, from the point of view of the entity of knowing, there would appear to be nothing left 'after' we are gone. We like to think it is not ourselves, which dies when we die but rather it is our physical presence which 'dies'. We like

The Error of Aristotle

to think we 'go to heaven or hell' and it is the physical no longer has relevance for us. We like to think we 'enter nirvana' and it is the universe which then is gone and out of our lives for good.

It is for this reason, we subconsciously think of 1st truth, 1st principle from 'our' point of view rather than from a 'relativistic' point of view of the region.

This concept of 'a region' making the observation is such a new perspective, it might be beneficial to once again review just what happens when it is the region making the observation rather than the object 'within' the region. As such, we obtain:

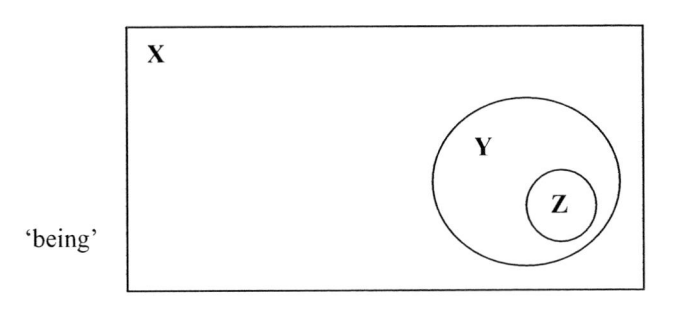

X: The whole – 'Being

Y: The universe – *being*

Z: The individual –

'being'

First principle based upon 1st truth:

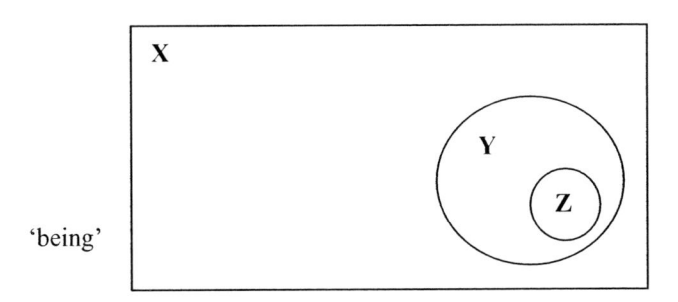

X: The whole – 'Being

Y: The universe – *being*

Z: The individual –

'being'

1st principle:

    a.   Region 'X' 'viewing' region 'Y' and region 'Z'

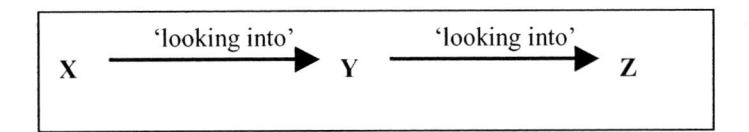

$$X \xrightarrow{\text{'looking into'}} Y \xrightarrow{\text{'looking into'}} Z$$

1st principle exists and becomes region 'X'
2nd principle exists and becomes region 'Y'
3rd principle exists and becomes region 'Z'

b.   Region 'Y' 'viewing ' region 'Z' and region 'X'

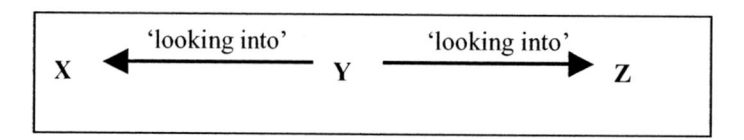

```
X  ←── 'looking into' ──  Y  ── 'looking into' ──→  Z
```

1st principle exists and becomes region 'Y'
2nd principle exists and becomes either region 'X' or region 'Z'
3rd principle exists and becomes region 'Z' or region 'X' depending upon the perception of '2nd principle

c.   Region 'Z' 'viewing' region 'X' and region 'Y'

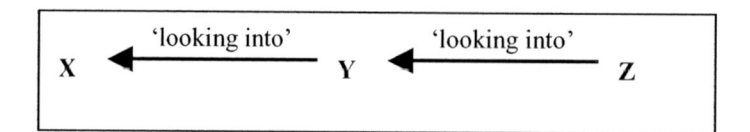

```
X  ←── 'looking into' ──  Y  ←── 'looking into' ──  Z
```

1st principle exists and becomes region 'Z'
2nd principle exists and becomes region 'Y'
3rd principle exists and becomes region 'X'

The shifting of first truths, the shifting of 1st principles, is not an illusion. The model allows us to 'see' that 1st truth 'shifts' relative to which 1st truth 'region' is making the observation. In short, we obtain what one might call 'relativistic 1st principle' based upon what 'is' rather than based upon one of the 1st truths making or developing 'all' the conjectures, axioms, and principles.

The dance of the angels

So where does all this relativistic shifting of 1st principle lead us? It leads us back to the historic question regarding: How many angels can dance on the head of a pin? Now obviously this does not literally become the question, however, it does become the question in the figurative sense.

The Error of Aristotle

The age-old question regarding how many angels can dance on the head of a pin, now becomes:

> If there are three 1st principles, you/'being' exist, the universe/being (vb), action, process reality exists, and 'Being'/the whole exists, then how many universes can fit into the whole? How many universes can fit into 'Being'?

This is not to imply angels are universes nor does it imply universes are angels.

To better understand the question, let's examine the basic model shifting 1st principles, shifting 1st truths, implies exists regarding, the whole, the universe, and individuality.

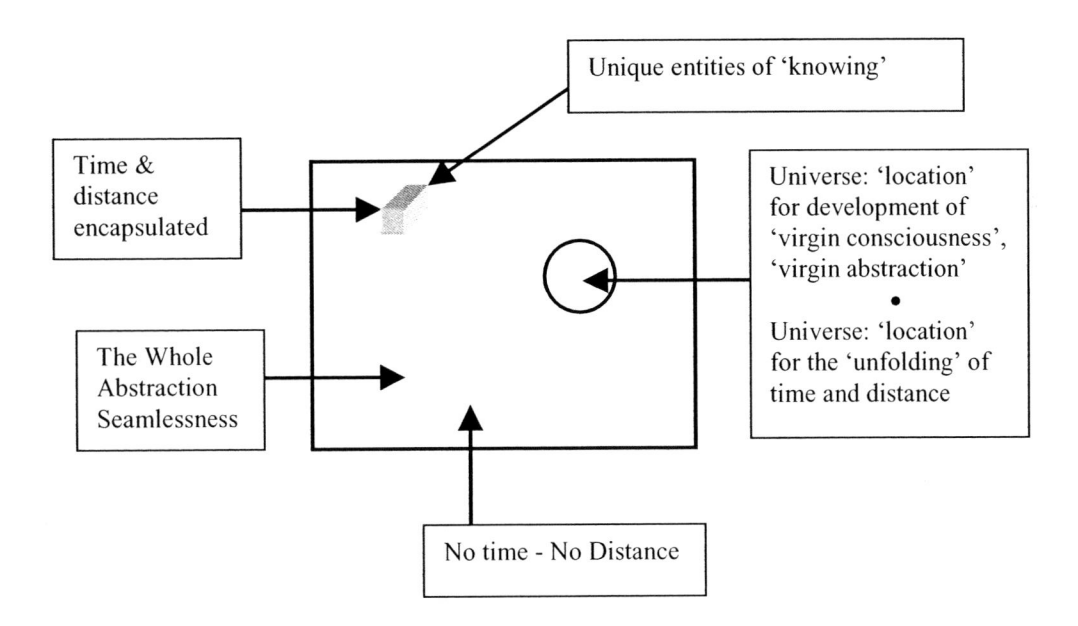

```
                        Unique entities of 'knowing'

  Time &                                          Universe: 'location'
  distance  ──▶                                   for development of
  encapsulated                                    'virgin consciousness',
                                                  'virgin abstraction'
                              ○  ◀──
  The Whole                                       Universe: 'location'
  Abstraction  ──▶                                for the 'unfolding' of
  Seamlessness                                    time and distance

                              ▲
                        No time - No Distance
```

The question regarding how many universes can exist within the model, suggests: If a universe exists 'within' a region void the universal presence of time and distance (see diagram), then how many other universes could exist simultaneously within that same region we find our own universe existing. The question suggests: If there is a region within which time/distance relationships are present as unique entities, if there is a region where time/distance relationships find themselves immersed rather than finding themselves, time/distance relationships, being 'the' abstractions 'within' which all 'things' are immersed then how many such relationships can exist within the 'whole'?

The question becomes: How many of these 'things' we call physical universes, these 'things' we call 'realities' can be fit 'into' this abstraction, this 'region' of seamlessness, we call the whole? The question becomes: How many of these 'things' we call the 'lesser' 'realities' (lower case 'r'), would 'fit into' what could be called the 'greater' Reality (upper case 'R')?

This 'region' of timelessness, this 'region' of what some might call eternity, finds itself void the all-embracing concept of distance and time. As can be seen from the preceding diagram, time and distance are found within the whole but not as an all – embracing characteristic but rather time and distance are found 'within' elements of the whole. Examples of such elements are units of 'knowing' such as an individual, and units of universes.

As such, the issue of 'how many' universes can fit into the totality of abstraction arises just as the question regarding how many angels can dance on the head of a pin arose over a thousand years ago. Hopefully we will not find ourselves distracted by such an issue. Hopefully we will recognize the irrelevance of such an issue and stick to the task at hand: The task is to understand what the components of a 'universal system' are and how we, you and I, you and I together, fit into such a system? To put it in slightly different terms, the task is to answer questions such as: Where are we? What are we? And why do we exist?

Just how many universes could potentially exist within a 'region' we call abstraction? How many universes could potentially exist within a region void the characteristic of universal time and universal distance or could exist within a region void the characteristic of multiplicity? Such questions are, in essence, irrelevant. What becomes relevant is understanding the concept of a universe existing immersed 'within' abstraction rather than immersed 'within' time and distance.

Now granted time and distance are abstractions but they appear to be abstractions emerging out of 'nothingness'. Time and distance appear to be distractions emerging from the innate paradoxical characteristic of 'nothingness' itself rather than emerging from the abstraction of 'knowing', 'knowledge'.
Time and distance appear to be innate characteristics of what we call the physical, what we call a universe, what we call reality (lower case 'r').

Time and distance become the tools we use to understand and comprehend 'nothingness'. Time and distance do not appear to be the tools we use to understand, observe/measure abstractions.

Distance and time become the means by which the lack of physical characteristics found within 'nothingness' itself. Distance and time do not appear to be the means by which the lack of abstractual characteristics found within 'nothingness' itself.

Time and distance are characteristics of 'nothingness' 'within' which 'new' knowing, 'new' knowledge, 'new' consciousness, 'new' unique experiences can emerge and become a part of abstraction.

There is no denying the concept of a region immersed 'within' time and distance as opposed to a region 'within' which time and distance are immersed is of immense interest. It is the utterance of this apparent paradoxical statement which in fact is not paradoxical which leads us to two concepts: the concept of 'finite infinites and the concept of infinite finites.

The land of Limited Abstracts: finite infinites

To 'go' to the land of Limited Abstracts, we need a player, a traveler. In the previous section, The dance of the angels, we have seen the development of two lands and one player:

The Error of Aristotle

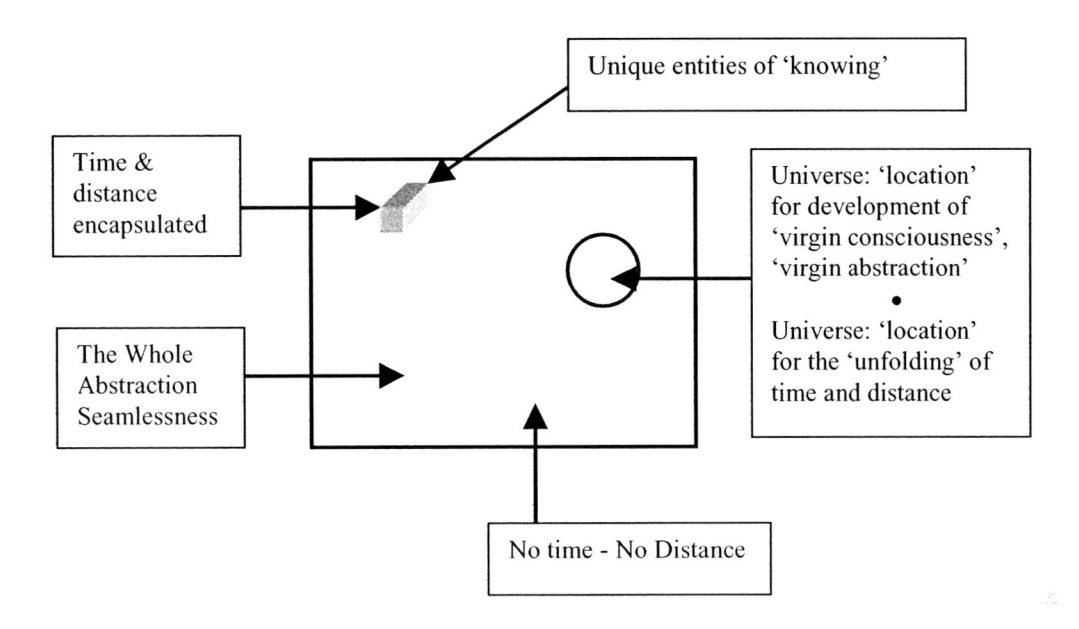

[Diagram: A rectangle with arrows pointing in from labeled boxes.
- "Time & distance encapsulated" → points into the rectangle
- "Unique entities of 'knowing'" → points to a shape in upper-left of rectangle
- "Universe: 'location' for development of 'virgin consciousness', 'virgin abstraction'" and "Universe: 'location' for the 'unfolding' of time and distance" → points to a circle inside rectangle
- "The Whole Abstraction Seamlessness" → points into the rectangle
- "No time - No Distance" → points up into the rectangle from below]

which now becomes:

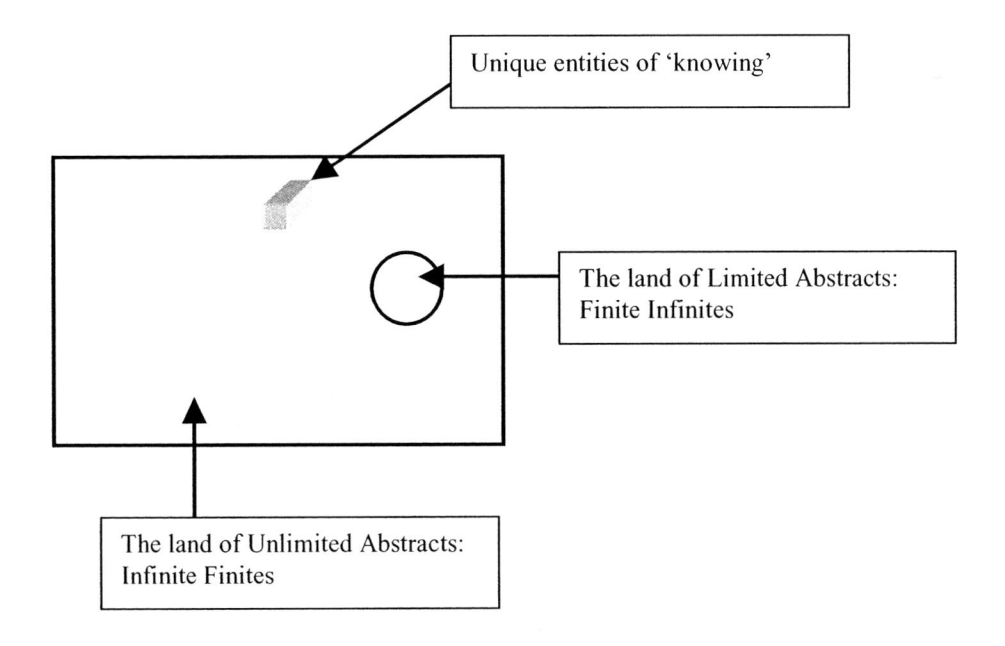

[Diagram: A rectangle with arrows pointing in from labeled boxes.
- "Unique entities of 'knowing'" → points to shape in upper-left
- "The land of Limited Abstracts: Finite Infinites" → points to circle inside rectangle
- "The land of Unlimited Abstracts: Infinite Finites" → points up into rectangle from below]

From the diagram, it now becomes obvious we have only three choices as to who will be the traveler. We can choose one of many unique entities of 'knowing' to be the traveler. We can choose the whole to be the traveler. Or we can choose the universe to be the traveler.

113

The War & Peace of a New Metaphysical Perception

Perhaps the most comfortable choice to use as the 'traveler' is a 'unique entity of 'knowing' since it most closely approximates ourselves, since it most closely approximates what we are capable of 'relating' to.

Since we are to examine the Land of Limited Abstracts, we will need to go there. As such we shall graphically depict the 'move' as:

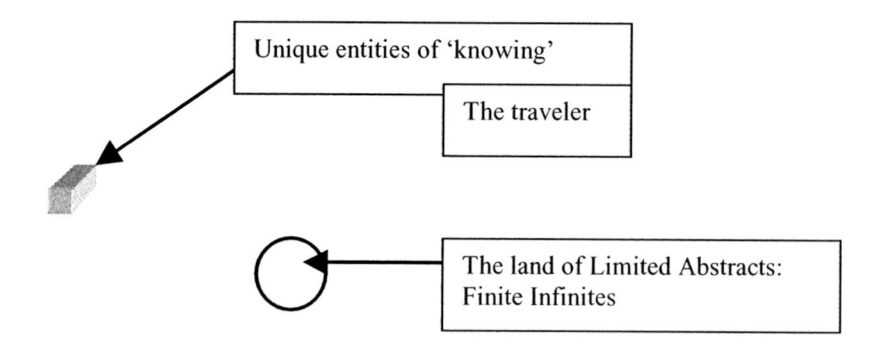

Unique entities of 'knowing'
The traveler

The land of Limited Abstracts: Finite Infinites

Now, rather than 'move' the 'traveler', we shall simple expand the universe, the Land of Limited Abstracts. As such, we will obtain:

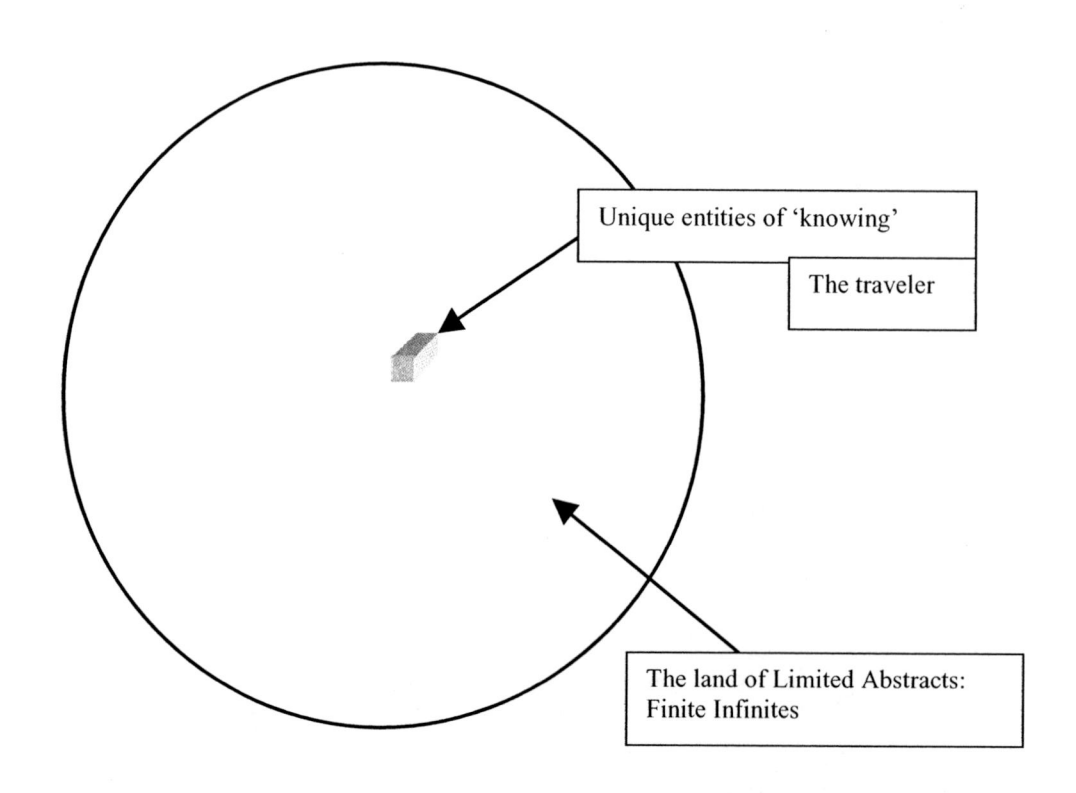

Unique entities of 'knowing'
The traveler

The land of Limited Abstracts: Finite Infinites

Immediately we see we have recreated Aristotle's Cartesian System. We have recreated Aristotle's 'closed' system. We recognize it for what it is. The land of Limited Abstracts is the universe. We recognize the system for what it 'contains'. The land of Limited Abstracts contains ourselves, contains individuals, contains unique entities of 'knowing'.

The universe, the land of Limited Abstracts appears to encapsulate individuality. Surprisingly the medium, which, through our direct observations, appears to be found in every nook and cranny throughout the land is time and distance. One may recall that time and distance were the concepts Zeno was unable to place into 'a' system in a manner acceptable to himself,

In the system, which emerged, time and distance appear to stretch from 'border' to 'border' 'within' the universe. All the while, time and distance appear to be embracing the most microcosmic as well as embracing the most macrocosmic aspect found within this land, found within the universe.

The traveler observes an obvious innate characteristic of this place of physicality 'within' which the traveler, a unique entity of 'knowing', a unique entity of abstraction finds itself traveling. The traveler observes a constancy of time and distance. However, one may say, time and distance are not constants 'within' this place called the universe. Aren't they? Einstein did not say time and distance 'change'. Einstein said time and distance 'change' 'relative' to other points of perceiving. Einstein said time and distance change 'relative' to other observers, when 'compared' to other observers, when 'compared' to other points of reference.

Upon further examination, the traveler observes time and distance seeming to incorporate the very characteristics of infinite dimensions itself. To the traveler, time appears to 'go' on forever and distance appears to do likewise. On the other hand, to the traveler, the development of individual pieces, the development of unique entities of 'knowing' appears to begin and end. Each piece of awareness, each piece of 'knowing' appears to be unique because each interaction is experienced uniquely yet it's knowing and its experiencing appears to 'end', appears to terminate.

To the traveler, each piece of experiencing appears to start from 'an' existence of virgin-ness and expand from there. Each unique entity appears to be shaped by interactions, which in turn emerge from not only observable action but out of each atomic and subatomic movement itself. The very motion of each atom found 'within' each unique entity 'located' 'within' the land of Limited Abstracts, found 'within' the traveler itself, finds itself 'contained' not only 'within' the 'boundaries' of the Aristotelian 'closed system' but 'contained' 'within' the 'knowing' emerging from the 'virgin-ness' of each unique entity.

Each motion of each atom, each motion of each sub-atomic particle in effect impacts the very perceptions the 'growing' 'knowing' formulates. The very motion of each atom coming into contact with the 'outside' boundaries of the traveling vehicle 'within' which the unique entity of knowing finds itself, affects, impacts the very perceptions the expanding 'knowing' formulates.

To further impact the unique entities of knowing are the aspects of the seemingly infinite subtle varieties of visible and invisible energy forms, which add to the individual unique motions of atoms and molecules. The interactions affecting the development of each unique entity's perception regarding 'knowing' does not stop with atoms, molecules, and energy but moves on to interactions of free will components. The free will components involve not just 'the' unique entity of emerging 'knowing' but involves the myriad other pieces of unique entities of knowing interacting with each other and each other's environment. The process of unique entities developing unique 'knowing', 'growing' seems to the traveler to be infinite in scope. As infinite as the scope of expanding 'knowing' 'appears' to be, the traveler senses finiteness to the process for an end 'appears' in sight.

The unique piece of knowing ends its growth within the realm of the universe, within physicalness or so it appears to the traveler. The traveler recognizes itself involved in the process, recognizes each unique entity having developed, having 'become' its own unique self.

In actuality, does the process ever end? That is another topic much too complex to address at this time. However, one thing the traveler notices is that the piece of 'knowing' representing itself, representing the traveler, appears to be unique. It appears the entity, which creates its own unique identity, is different from other entities of knowing.

The traveler perceives itself to be the primary point of interest, the primary 1st truth. Surprisingly, however, it is not the uniqueness of 'a' particular individual traveler that is the primary point of significance but rather the primary point of significance lies in the concept that individuality itself exists as an entity.

From the point of view of the traveler 'located' within the land of Limited Abstracts, each unique piece of 'knowing' appears to have infinite influences affecting its development regardless of 'when' it ends or the length of time it traveled.

To the traveler, the whole, the Land of Limited Abstracts appears to be comprised of finite numbers of individual entities and each entity in turn appears to have infinite 'knowing' potential while 'within' the land of Limited Abstracts. The appearance of a potentially infinite 'knowing' arises from the assumption that each unique entity of 'knowing' will end its travel through time but this is not known to be an 'absolute' until after the fact. As such, the entity of knowing to have a sense of absolute uniqueness due to the myriad, almost infinite, if not infinite, internal and external interactions of free will interactions, molecular Brownian movement, atomic vibrations, subatomic motions, etc.

In essence the land of Limited Abstracts becomes a location of both infinite finites and finite finites. This would appear to be a contradictory statement but in fact it is not. The contradiction simply emerges from a lack of fully comprehending the concept of 'relativistic 1st truth'.

The Error of Aristotle

Perhaps a graphically examination of the land of Limited Abstracts would help:

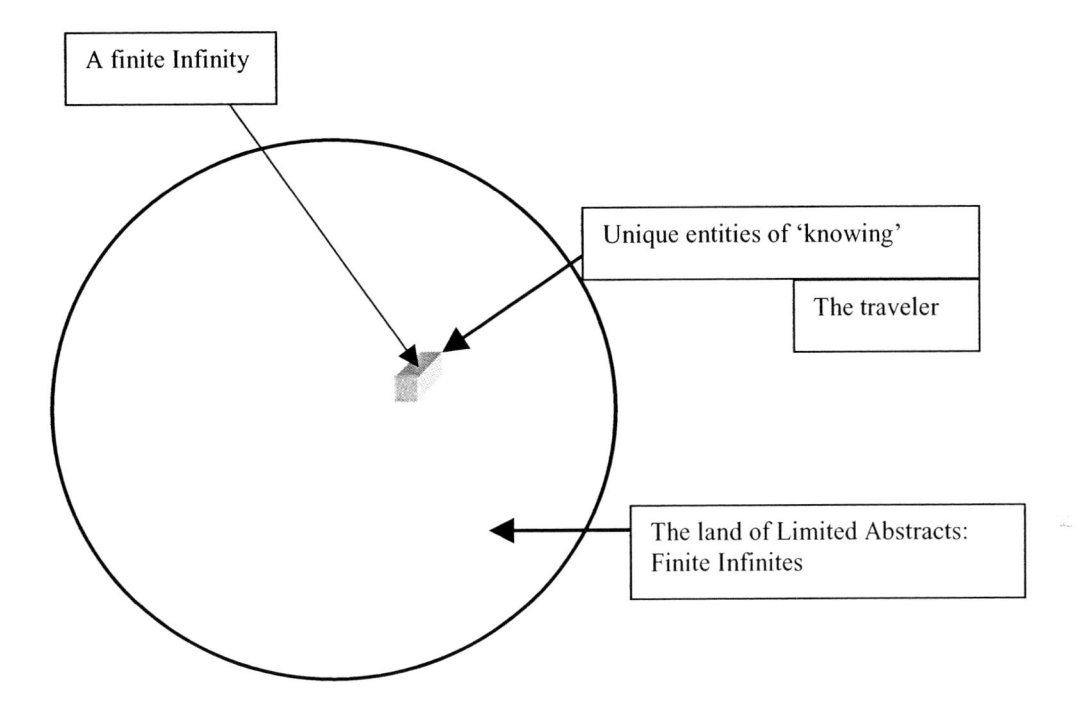

A finite Infinity

Unique entities of 'knowing'

The traveler

The land of Limited Abstracts: Finite Infinites

to the traveler, becomes:

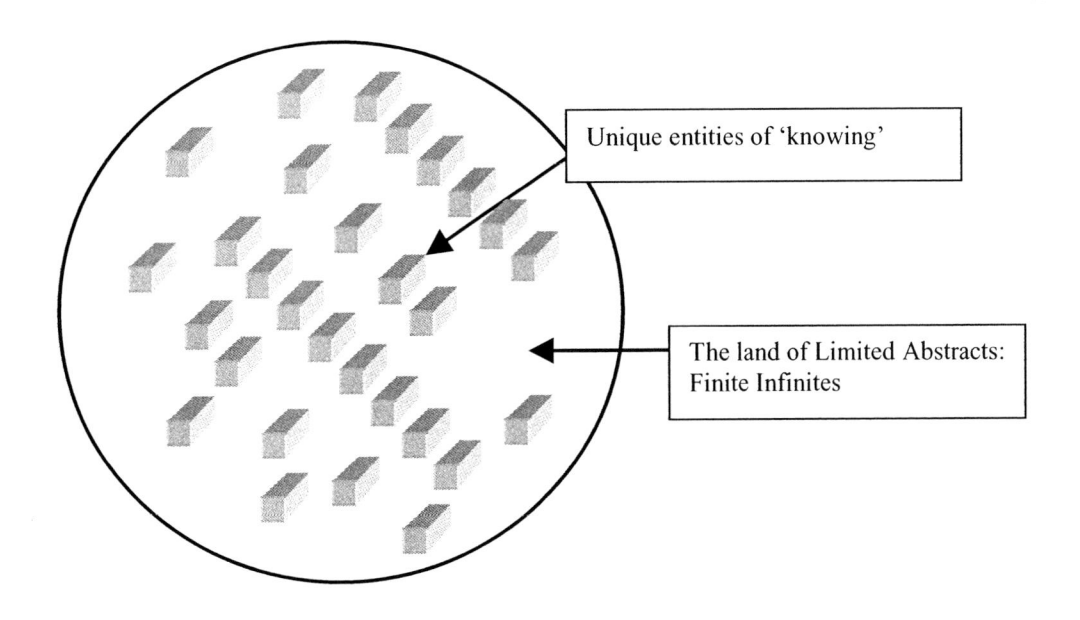

Unique entities of 'knowing'

The land of Limited Abstracts: Finite Infinites

For the traveler, the perception becomes:

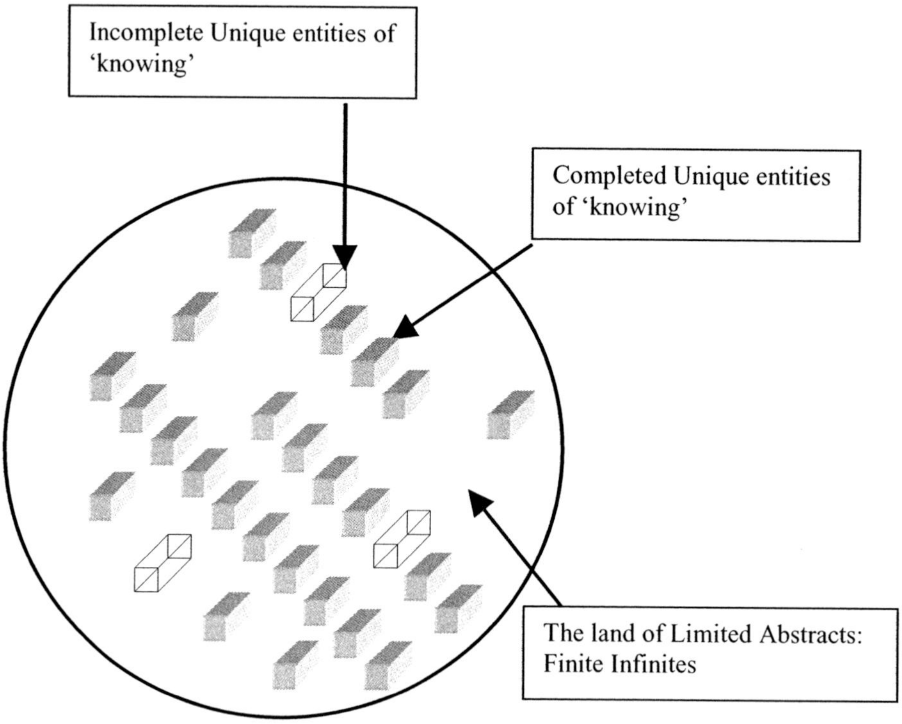
Incomplete Unique entities of 'knowing'
Completed Unique entities of 'knowing'
The land of Limited Abstracts: Finite Infinites

The concept of 'Finite Infinites' emerges out of a sense that 'knowing' continually evolves through time and time is sensed to be endless.

The concept of 'Infinite finites' emerges out of the sense that because time appears to be endless, the land of Limited Abstracts is endless and thus appears to produce 'finite 'potential' infinites' infinitely thus.

The land of Limited Abstracts appears to be filled with finite numbers of limited Abstracts of infinite experiencing, knowing being produced infinitely. The land of Limited Abstracts, the universe, appears to be filled with abstractions 'floating' within the physical, appears to be a suspension of the abstract within the physical. However, the very nature of matter and energy give us a sense that the universe itself will end and if so had a beginning. The very concept of a beginning implies an end.

Upon closer examination and observation, however, it appears time and distance themselves are located within the universe, located 'within' our 'reality'. As such it appears time and distance may not be endless after all. Upon very close scrutiny, it appears time and distance may have had a beginning and thus may, at some point, come to an end.

The question arises: Is it possible for time and distance to be endless yet end? That also is a question unto itself and takes far too much space to discuss in this tractate.

The land of Unlimited Abstracts: Infinite Finites

To get to the land of Unlimited Abstracts we must begin 'somewhere'. As such we will begin where we ended in the last section. We will begin 'within' the walls of Aristotle:

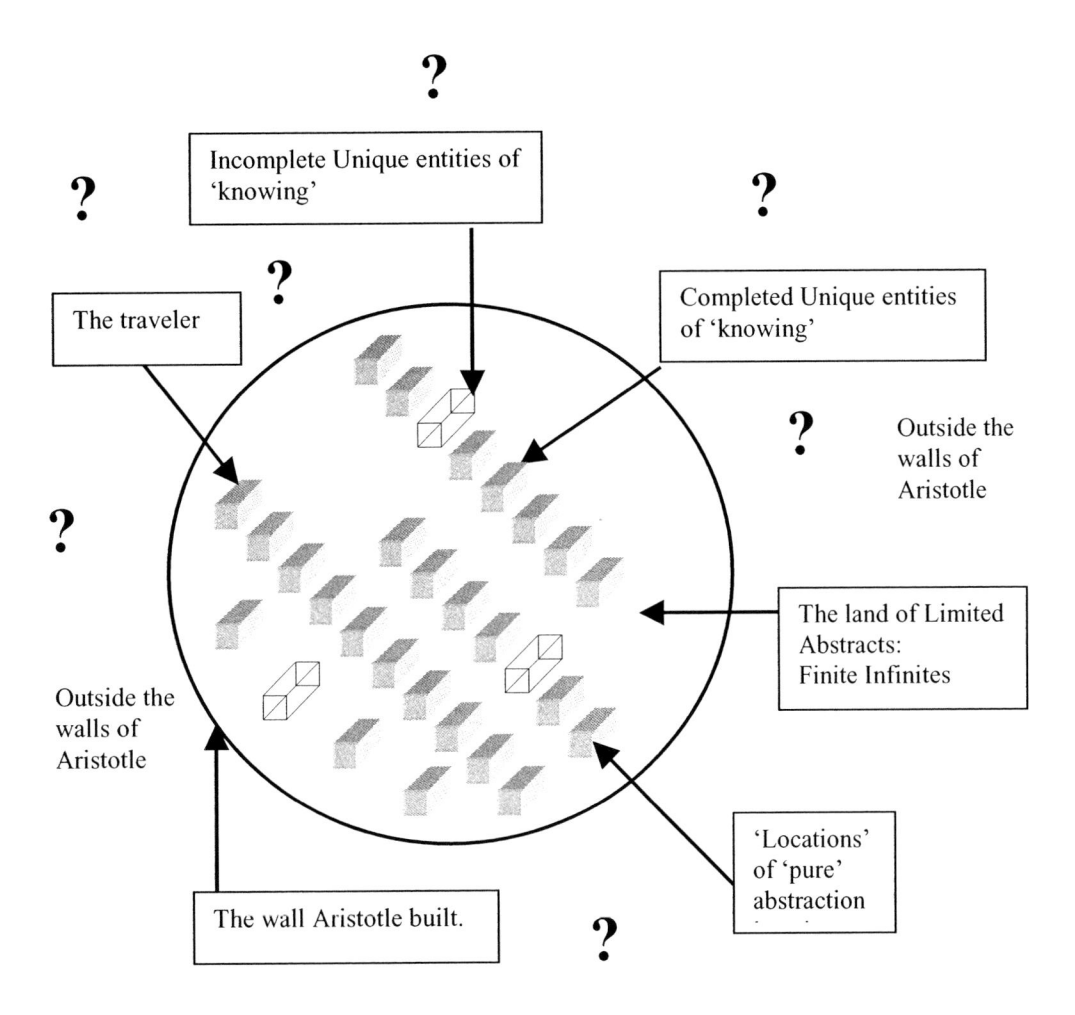

[Diagram: A circle containing arrow-like shapes and cube outlines, surrounded by question marks. Labels point to various elements:
- Incomplete Unique entities of 'knowing'
- Completed Unique entities of 'knowing'
- The traveler
- Outside the walls of Aristotle
- The land of Limited Abstracts: Finite Infinites
- Outside the walls of Aristotle
- The wall Aristotle built.
- 'Locations' of 'pure' abstraction]

Now to get to the land of Unlimited Abstracts we must leave the land of Limited Abstracts. To do so we again will not move the traveler but rather we will move the land of Limited Abstracts. However there apparently is 'nowhere' to move this land. Moving the land of Limited Abstracts appears to be an impossible task.

Religions state there was a beginning to the land of Limited Abstracts, a beginning to the universe as such there may be an end. Science advocates an expanding universe, which could conceivable produce a contracting universe. Philosophy implies: For each beginning there appears to be an end.

Therefore, with this in mind, we will not 'move' the land of Limited Abstracts for there appears to be 'nowhere' to move it. Instead of 'moving' the land of Limited Abstracts, we will erase it. You may object to this process. However, did you object to our erasing the Land of Unlimited

The War & Peace of a New Metaphysical Perception

Abstracts when we proceeded to focus upon the land of Limited Abstracts? Since we found it acceptable to erase the Land of Unlimited Abstracts in order to study the Land of Limited Abstracts, our universe, we should not object to extending the same process to the second region of 'possible' location.

By erasing the land of Limited Abstracts we obtain:

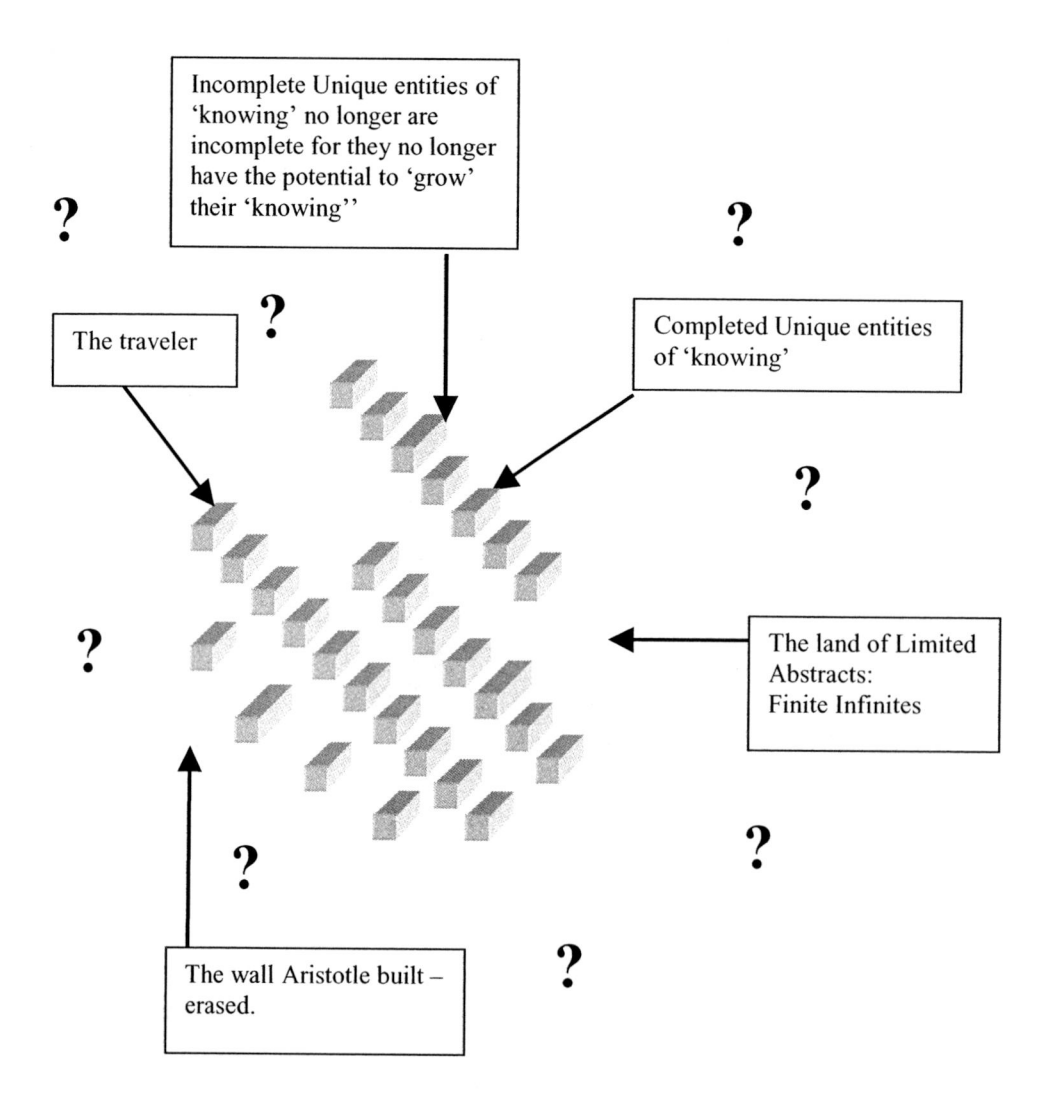

- Incomplete Unique entities of 'knowing' no longer are incomplete for they no longer have the potential to 'grow' their 'knowing''
- The traveler
- Completed Unique entities of 'knowing'
- The land of Limited Abstracts: Finite Infinites
- The wall Aristotle built – erased.

Immediately one notices that although we erased the location, erased the land of Limited Abstracts, we did not erase the non-physical entities of knowing.

The Error of Aristotle

The graphic is getting very complicate. To simplify things we will perform a few strokes of simplification:

1. We will 'enclose' the diagram in order to focus upon its 'location'
2. We will remove the '?' marks for now we understand the '?' indicates the land of Unlimited Abstracts
3. We will remove the captions now that we understand what the objects represent
4. We will reduce the number of unique entities since we understand that the 'quantity' of unique entities appear to be defined as limited in the sense that they exist as entities. Be prepared, however, to observe our perception expand in its magnitude in terms of what is 'defined' to be.

With these four steps of simplification, our graphical depiction becomes manageable.

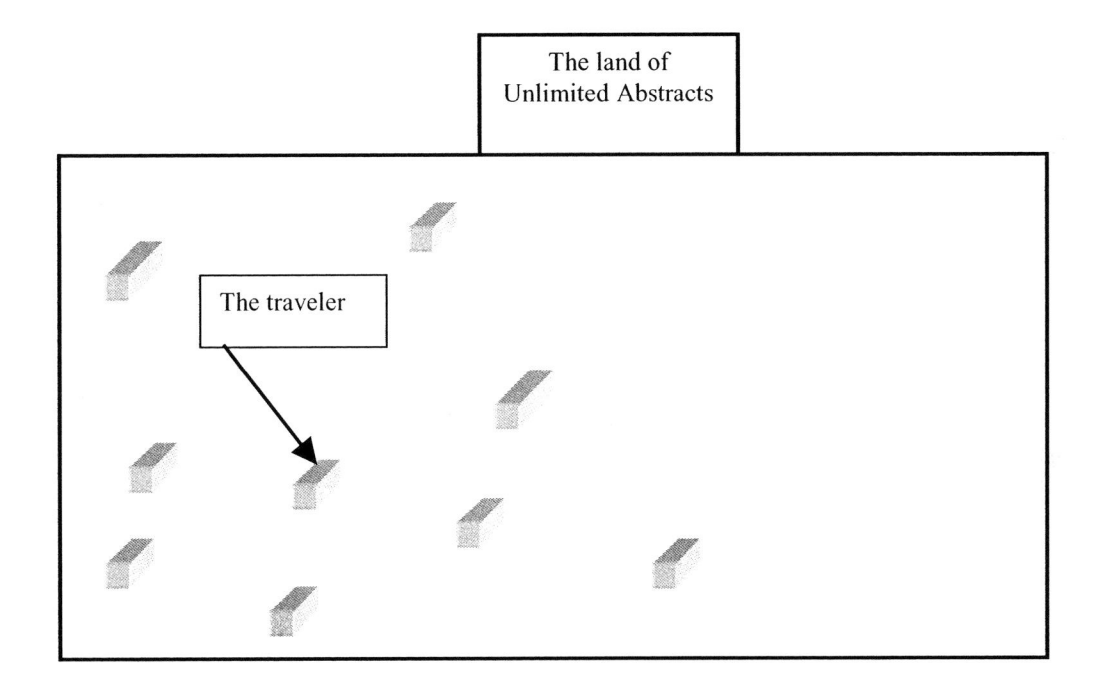

This land obtains the characteristic of 'finite infinites' in the sense that each entity appears to be composed of infinite interactions as was discussed in the previous section: The land of Limited Abstracts. In fact, however, the land of Unlimited Abstracts gains the characteristic of Infinite finites for as we shall see there is no 'limit' to the development of these unique entities of 'knowing', We are about to 'see' that Infinite finites are not the same as finite infinites.

The concept of the Land of Unlimited Abstracts being composed of infinite entities which in turn are composed of infinite numbers of finite infinities, , evolves out of the concept initiated in the section: The dance of the angels. To understand this we must take the above diagram and reintroduce the universe: The Land of Limited Abstracts.

The War & Peace of a New Metaphysical Perception

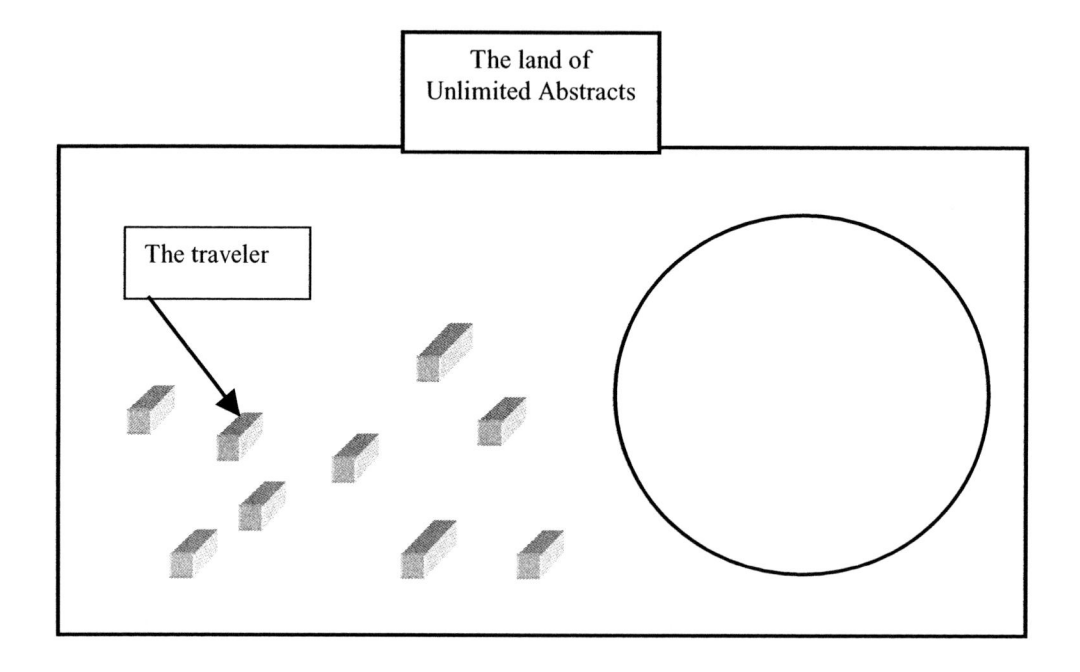

The universe, being the 'location' for the production of unique pieces of knowing, takes on the following appearance:

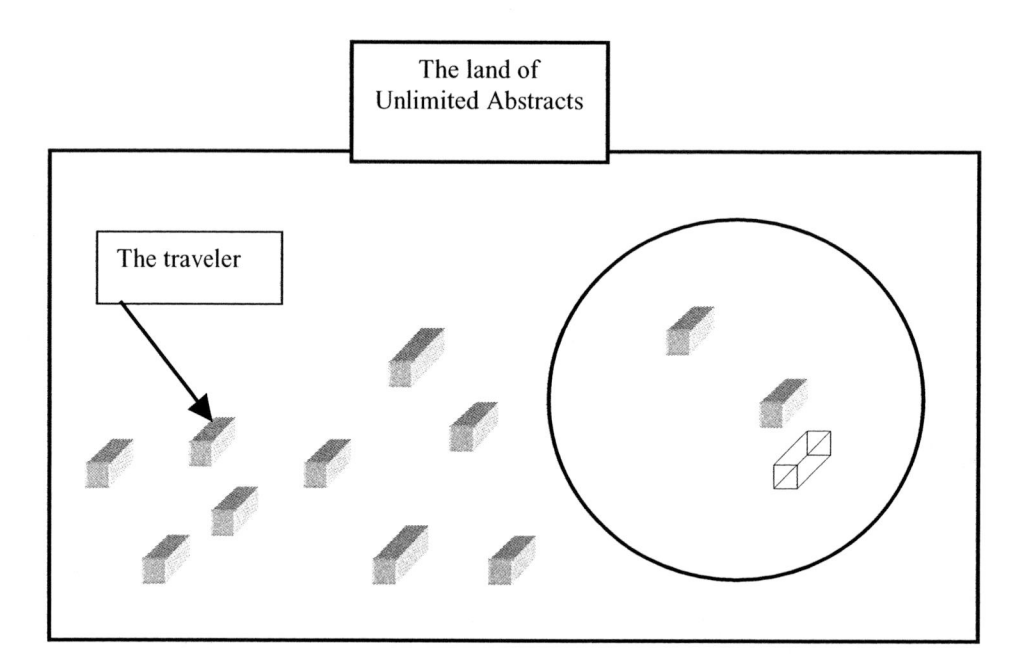

where the unique entities of 'knowing' become a part of the total abstraction. If we remove all the unique entities of 'knowing' we obtain:

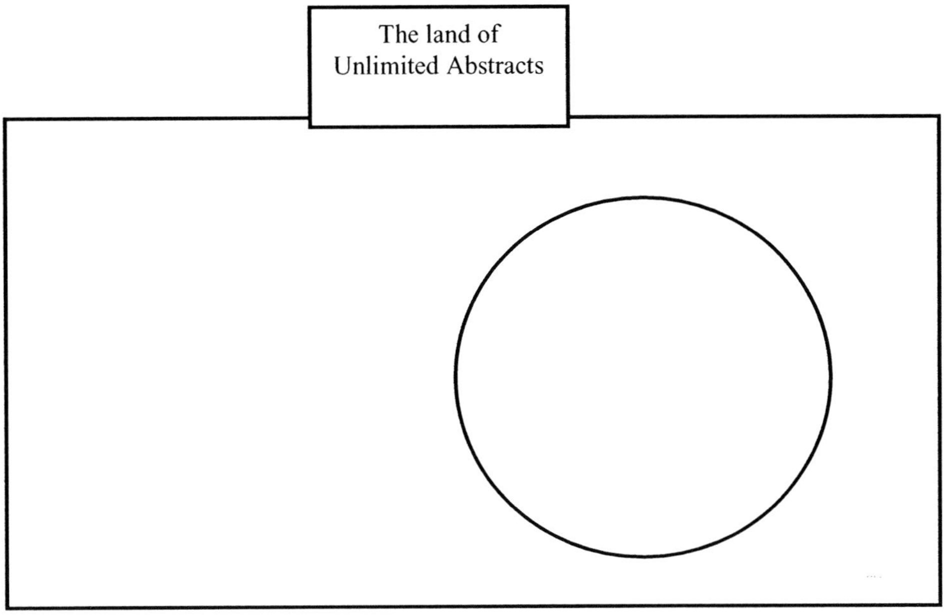
The land of
Unlimited Abstracts

which becomes:

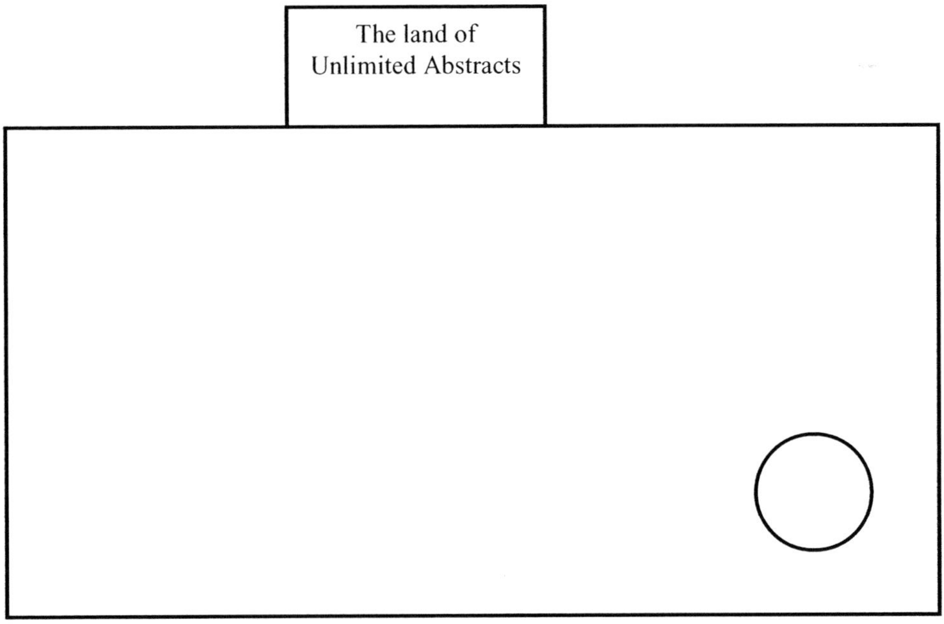
The land of
Unlimited Abstracts

Now the dance of the angels begins. The question: How many universes can fit into the Land of the Abstract?

The War & Peace of a New Metaphysical Perception

[The land of Unlimited Abstracts]

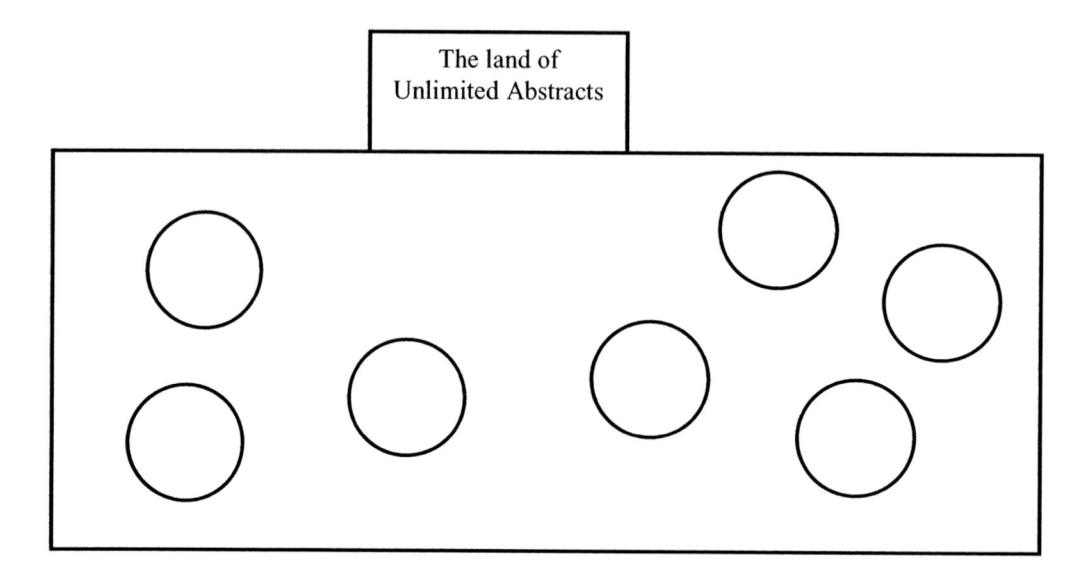

Keeping in mind the 'number' of universes, the number of 'regions' of physicalness 'located' 'within' abstraction only becomes a question of numbers if the universes are immersed 'within' time and distance as opposed to universes be the location within which time and distance are 'located'. As such, we can graphically label the location where time and distance, as universally uniformly distributed abstraction,. are 'found' and where also graphically label where it is time an distance are not 'found'

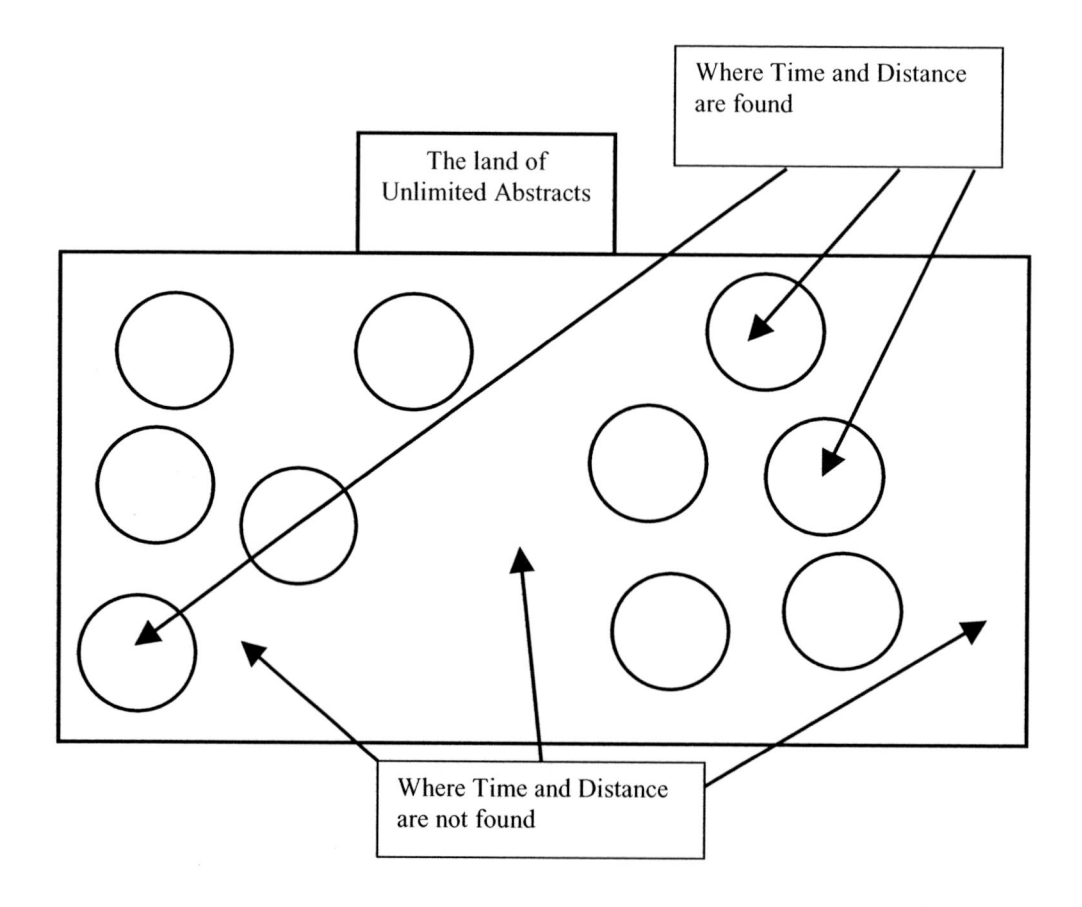

Diagramming in this manner, initiates the understanding regarding how it is infinite universes could exist in a region void the all encompassing characteristic of time and distance.

In addition, this diagram demonstrates how it is that the 'number' of 'regions' 'within' which virgin consciousness develops and 'within' which universes themselves develop. As such, the 'number' of entities of unique 'knowing' has no meaning from the perspective of the region void the concepts of universal time and distance.

The concept of 'number' only takes on a sense of meaning in terms of the whole if the 'things', which the numbers represent, are related in some form through the process of sequencing connected to time or distance. The number 'five' for instance only has meaning if it represents what it implies and that is one more than four items. This concept of 'cardinality' both in terms of sequencing and in terms of representation loses its meaning in a 'region' void time and distance. Sequencing implies 'coming before' or 'coming after'. Both the concept of 'coming before' and 'coming after' only have meaning to 'things' be they physical or abstractual, if the 'things' are located 'within' time or distance or both time and distance. 'Things 'containing' time but 'located' 'within' the lack of time lose the meaning implied by the term 'number'. This too is a complex topic worthy of future examination.

It appears an extraordinary number of concepts will be examined 'later'. Unfortunately, this is a correct observation. Space and time are both limited by the concept known as 'a' 'tractate'. It is time itself, which confines us to the parameter of limited discussions. It is the concept of 'tractate', which limits us to staying on task rather than chaotically diverting our attention away from the discussion at hand. The task is to develop understanding regarding how it is we became confined, regarding how it is we became caged in the first place. It is only through understanding the concept of how it is we are 'caged', that we can begin to explore the means of unlocking the door of our cage and stepping 'out' in to the realm of free space once again.

Entities of 'knowing' found 'within' the Land of Unlimited Abstracts cannot be compared to each other through the process of 'relative' sequencing. The concept of which came first and which came second is a concept of time and therefore a region void time and distance lacks such a concept as a innate characteristic of itself. The concept of sequencing, however, can be found as an element of a subset found within such region, i.e. a universe. This type of time and distance is better known as physical time and physical distance, physical multiplicity and multiplicity of distance.

It is also appropriate to note that abstractual time and abstractual distance, seamless time and seamless distance, may be found 'within' the unique piece of 'knowing' located 'within' the whole in the form of either an entity located 'within' universes or found 'within' the location void physical time and physical distance. As such, the concept of travel 'within' the universe is different than the concept of travel 'outside' the universe. 'Outside' the universe travel is not a situation of traveling from here to there for there is no distance found within Zeno's 'seamless' abstraction

These two concepts also deserve further examination. Again, we must pull ourselves away from the temptation to digress. Again, we must rely on self-discipline and return to the task at hand.

Understanding how 'a' 'whole' can be greater than the sum of its parts

When discussing a metaphysical concept of 'relativistic 1st truth' or what could be called 'relativistic 1st principle', we must gain an elementary understanding of what we refer to as 'summation'. In our present society, we embrace the concept: The whole is equal to the sum of its parts. The mathematical perception of the whole being equal to the sum of its parts, lies at the very core of scientific perceptions generated by observation.

Just because the statement, The whole is equal to the sum of its parts, lies at the heart of observation, does not make it the heart of philosophy nor does such a statement become the heart of religion. In fact, as we have seen, the statement does not even surface as a factor when we discuss the most basic understanding regarding the three shifting 1st truths. One may ask: How could it be that the whole may not be the sum of its parts?

In the situation of 'relativistic 1st principle', there is 'Being'/the whole, being/action, process/reality – the universe, and 'being'/individuality.

These shifting 1st truths, these shifting 1st principles create the situation where there are the unique pieces of 'knowing'/individuality, there is the summation of the parts - unique pieces of 'knowing', and then there is the sum itself.

In short there is not just the sum of 'knowing' but there is the sum being aware of itself rather than being simply a sum.

The concept of the whole being aware of itself as well as aware of its parts is significantly different to the sum of numbers being simply a sum the individual number values. The sum of numbers is the sum of numbers and exists having no awareness of itself.

The concept of a sum of knowing entities being its own unit of knowing is also different than we find to be the case of ourselves as individuals. Although we do appear to have awareness of ourselves and awareness of our parts as humans we do not appear to have parts of ourselves which themselves are independent entities of individualistic entities of 'knowing'.

With this understanding, we can now revisit the Land of Unlimited Abstracts. The whole, the Land of Unlimited Abstracts, now gains the following graphical appearance:

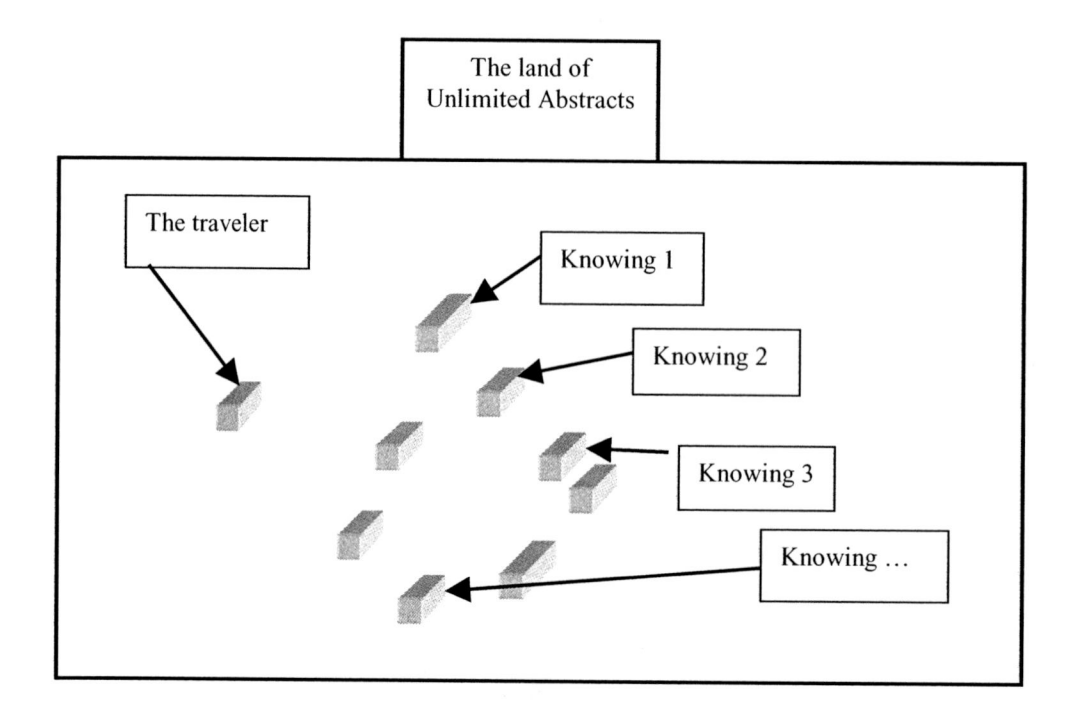

The Error of Aristotle

In such a situation, total knowing does not equal the sum of all knowing but rather total knowing 'knows' of itself as the total. As such, total knowing is an entity itself rather than simply the composite of individual entities of 'knowing'. The result: The whole is greater than the sum of its parts.

The simplicity of such a statement takes on a form of complexity when one factors into the concept of total 'knowing', being a 'Being'. The complexity expands when one adds the component of 'Being' not only having a conscious awareness of summation, but having its own uniqueness in that it has the ability to expand upon itself.

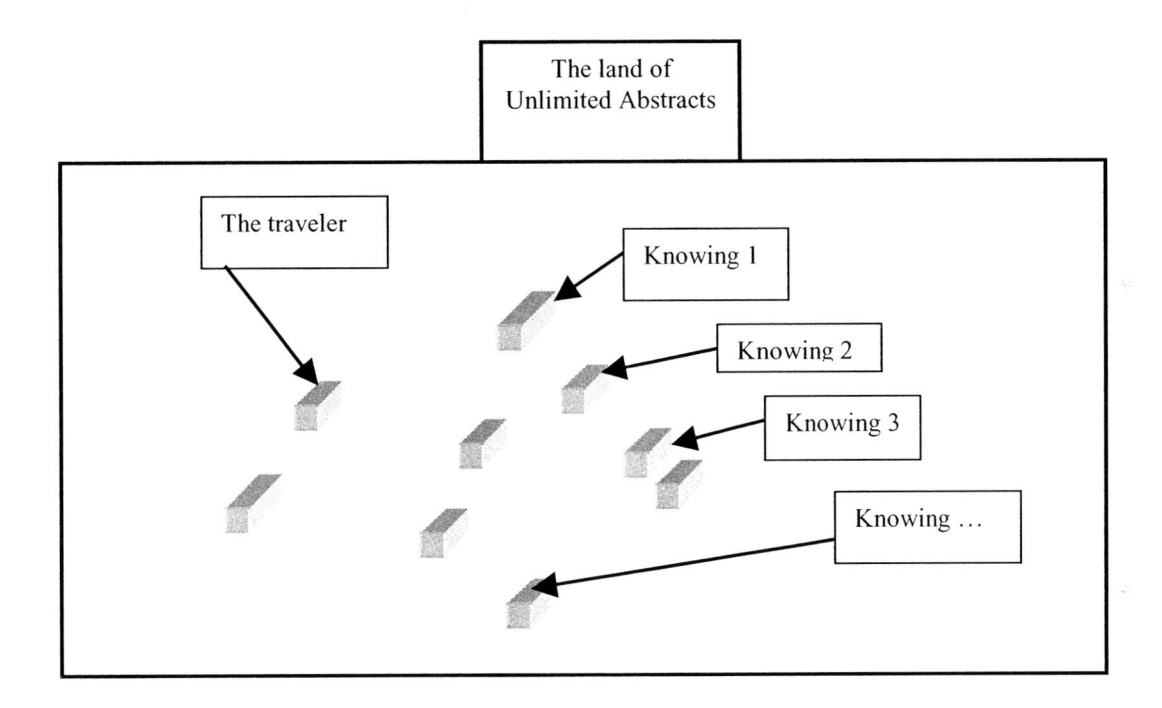

```
                    ┌─────────────────┐
                    │  The land of    │
                    │ Unlimited Abstracts │
                    └─────────────────┘
┌──────────────────────────────────────────────────┐
│                                                  │
│   ┌──────────────┐                               │
│   │ The traveler │         ┌───────────┐         │
│   └──────┬───────┘         │ Knowing 1 │         │
│          ▼                 └─────┬─────┘         │
│                                  ▼               │
│                          ┌───────────┐           │
│                          │ Knowing 2 │           │
│                          └─────┬─────┘           │
│                                ▼                 │
│                        ┌───────────┐             │
│                        │ Knowing 3 │             │
│                        └─────┬─────┘             │
│                              ▼                   │
│                         ┌───────────┐            │
│                         │ Knowing … │            │
│                         └─────┬─────┘            │
│                               ▼                  │
└──────────────────────────────────────────────────┘
```

The War & Peace of a New Metaphysical Perception

Combined with:

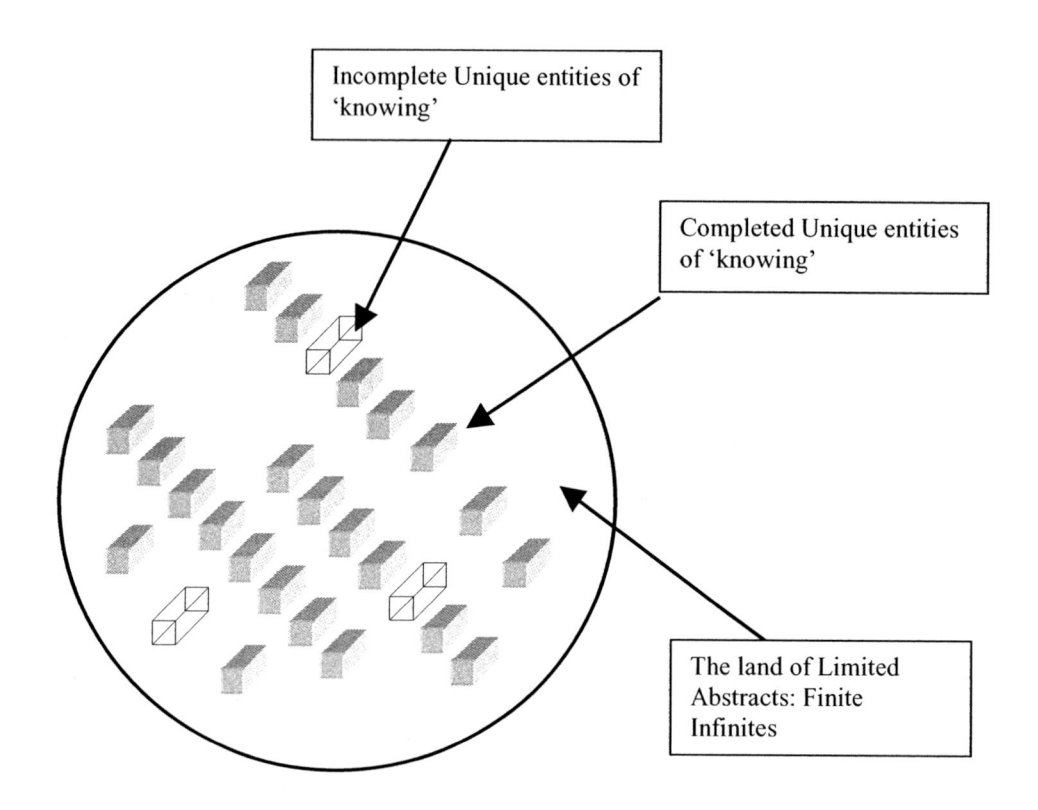

Incomplete Unique entities of 'knowing'

Completed Unique entities of 'knowing'

The land of Limited Abstracts: Finite Infinites

produces:

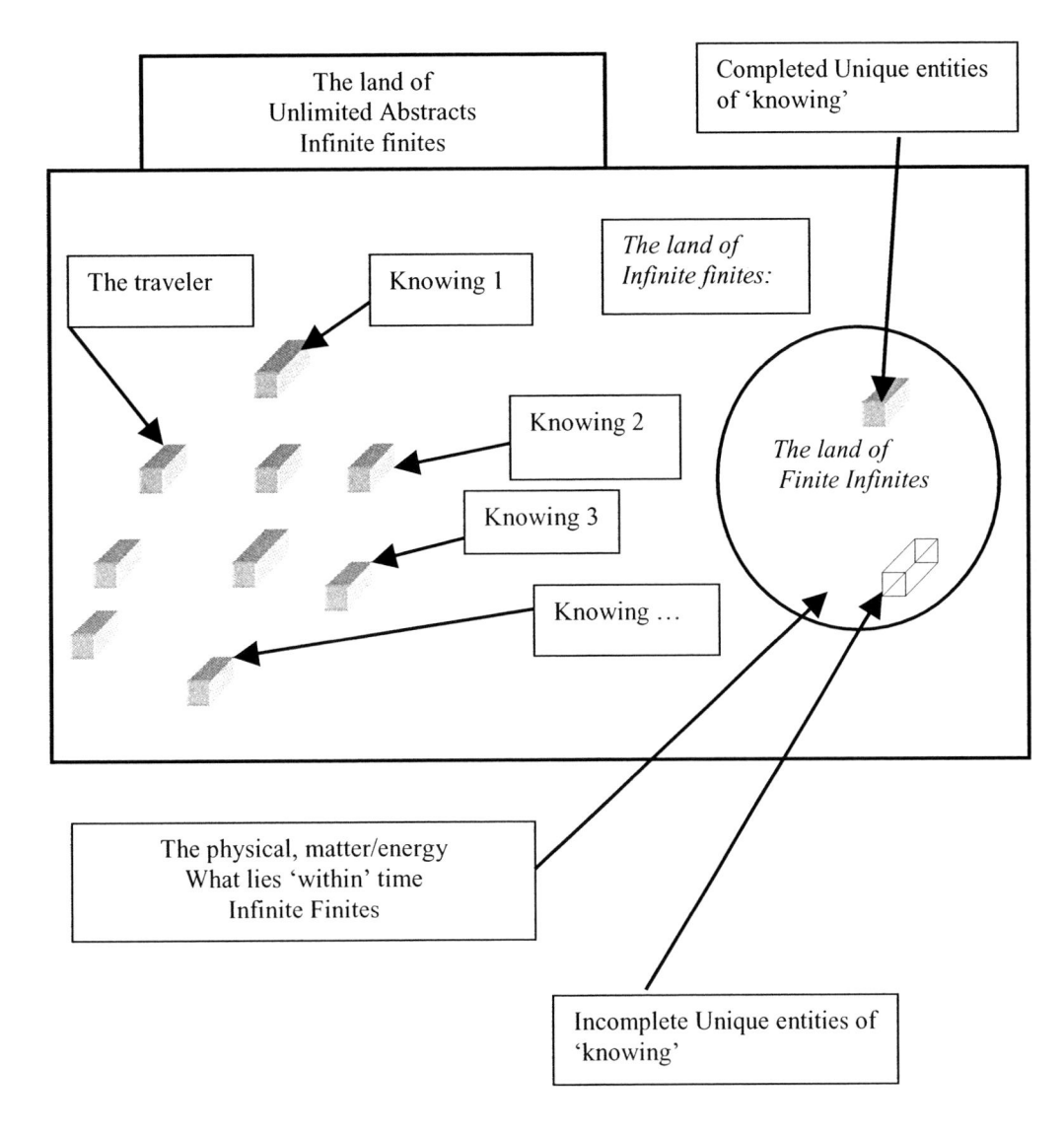

The land of Unlimited Abstracts — Infinite finites

The land of Infinite finites:

- The traveler
- Knowing 1
- Knowing 2
- Knowing 3
- Knowing …

The land of Finite Infinites

Completed Unique entities of 'knowing'

Incomplete Unique entities of 'knowing'

The physical, matter/energy
What lies 'within' time
Infinite Finites

Oddly enough the abstracts 'outside' time, outside the physical, are limited, have no means of 'growth'. They are just what they are. Interestingly enough, since these entities of abstractions are located 'outside' time and distance, they have no association with the concepts of 'past', 'present', or 'future'. This very lack of association demonstrates the significance of 'knowing' being added to the land of Unlimited Abstracts via the Land of Limited Abstracts.

However, wouldn't the land of Unlimited Abstracts be taking on an aspect of time if items are 'added' to it? The aspect of time, which would be implied, would be the concept of chronological order.

In fact no such order would be infused 'into' the land of Unlimited Abstracts, for the land of Unlimited Abstraction is void both time and distance for time and distance are found encapsulated 'within' the entities of 'knowing'

How can this be? Time and distance become a function of mass and energy, which in turn are found 'within' the land of Limited Abstracts. Thus, it is time and distance become aspects unique to entities of knowing developing 'within' the concept of the physical, developing 'within' the region of what is 'perceived' to be the real.

It appears we come back to complexity again and again. Ockham would not be pleased. But the whole point of the two lands is that we have various potentials for developing answers to the quest for the holy grail philosophers have been seeking, religion has been seeking, and science has been seeking. It appears, depending upon the 'point of view' of the 'region' determining 1st truth/1st principle, the issue of 1st principle/1st truth is irresolvable. Such a perception emerges out of the lack of understanding rather than emerging out of understanding what has been said.

What has been stated is simply that 1st principle is relative. Each 1st principle is as much 1st principle as another. Each 1st principle is 1st principle if stating from 'within' the region of its emergence. Each 1st principle gains equal rights to the status of being 1st principle and as such each 1st principle gains the potentiality of being just that, being 1st principle. As such, each 1st principle gains the equality of potentiality regarding being not just 1st principle but even more importantly, being 1st truth. Once again, the three 1st principles are: The individual exists, The universe exists, The whole exists. In essence, we are establishing a concept known as 'relativistic 1st principle'. The concept of 'relativistic 1st principle' does something 'for' the concept of 1st truth, which the concept of 'constancy of 1st principle' cannot.

The equality of 'relativistic 1st principle'

'Relativistic 1st principle' leads to 'equality of a floating 1st principle'. The existence of three 1st principles, three 1st truths simultaneously may not seem important but it is the only way to establish the equality of our three means of perception: faith/religion, observation/science, and reason/philosophy. After twenty-five hundred years of debate, it appears it is only through the process of recognizing the equally of each 1st truth that we can recognize the significant each truth has to ourselves, has to all of humanity, has to perhaps all forms of 'knowing' universally. It appears it is only through the process of recognizing the equality of each 1st truth that the potential to perceive 'knowledge', perceive abstraction, form unique abstractual perceptions, will emerge. It appears it is only through the process of recognizing the equality of each 1st truth that we will ever be able to resolve the conflict existing, to resolve the conflict perpetually erupting, to resolve the conflict which keeps us divided as a specie, as individuals.

Let's examine just how it is that the concept of 'relativistic 1st principle' equates into the concept of equality for all three 1st truths, 1st principle.

The equality of 'relativistic 1st principle		
Aristotle: Observation Cosmology	Descartes Reason Metaphysics	Zeno Belief Ontology
1st Principal: *being* (vb) exists The universe exists reality exists The physical exists	1st Principle: 'being' exists Individuality exists 'Knowing' exists The soul exists Distinct/unique Multiplicity of 'Being' exists	1st Principle: 'Being' exists Summation exists The whole exist 'God' exists
2nd Principle: 'being' exists	2nd Principle: 'Being' exists	2nd Principle: *being* (vb) exists
3rd Principle: 'Being' exists	3rd Principle: *being* (vb) exists	3rd Principle: 'being' exists

The result of such a system, of a shifting relative 1st principle based upon relative 'location':
1. Each 1st principle, each 1st truth appears once as 1st truth, 1st principle
2. Each 2nd principle, each 2nd truth appears once as 2nd truth, 2nd principle
3. Each 3rd principle, each 3rd truth appears once as 3rd truth, 3rd principle

The result: the emergence of a concept which could be call: the Equality of Principle

Resolving the paradox of 'a' Cartesian System

Relativistic 1st principle: The process of 1st principle changing as one changes the 'location of reference moves us from a Cartesian system built upon 'a' 1st principle to a system of 'multiple' 1st principles. Such a perceptual shift moves us towards what one might term a non-Cartesian system.

The War & Peace of a New Metaphysical Perception

This process can better be understood using graphics. The process becomes:

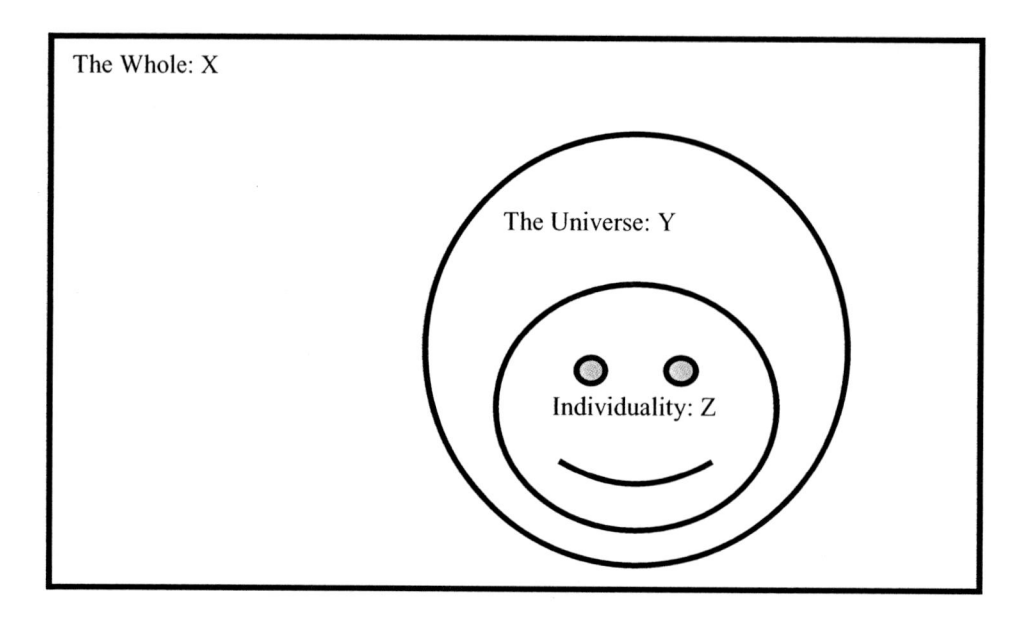

[Diagram: A rectangle labeled "The Whole: X" containing a large circle labeled "The Universe: Y", which contains a smaller circle labeled "Individuality: Z" drawn as a smiley face.]

Regions 'X', 'Y', and 'Z' look familiar because they are the regions from which we initiated the resolution to the Paradox Aristotle established through the natural extension of Zeno's paradox.

With the perspective of the graphic established, we will shrink the size of individuality to better represent the relative size of individuality, 'being', knowing, unique entities with awareness of awareness. Obviously, the true scale cannot be depicted in graphics compatible to this word processing program but we can at least begin to make the effort.

As such, the diagram might better be portrayed as:

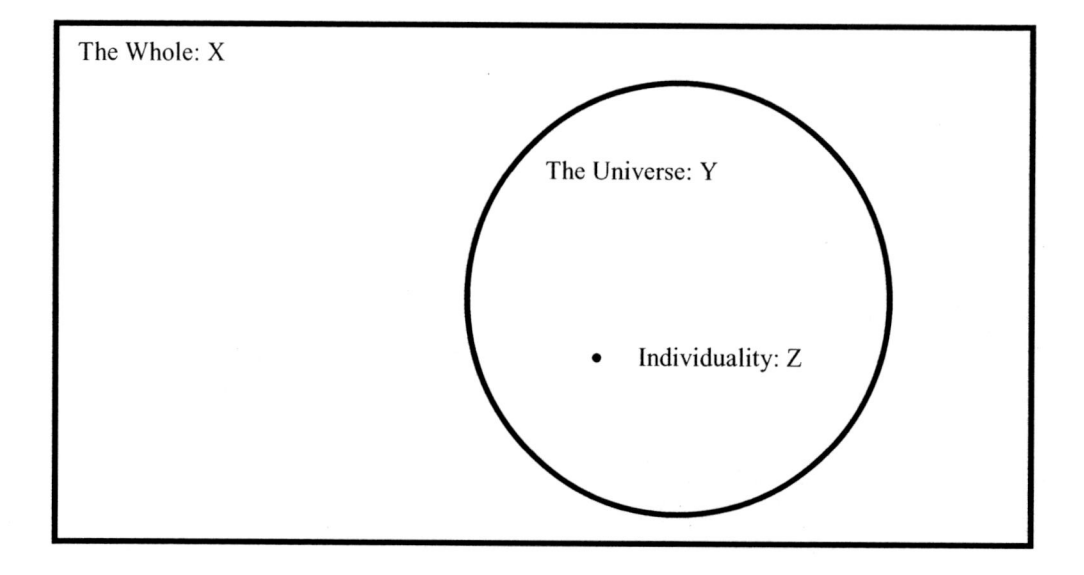

[Diagram: A rectangle labeled "The Whole: X" containing a large circle labeled "The Universe: Y", which contains a small dot labeled "Individuality: Z".]

The Error of Aristotle

Having made the effort to more closely approximate the three 'locations', we will now proceed to reintroduce our concept of Cartesian space, a Cartesian concept embracing the principle of a 'beginning' having a point of 'origin', of a beginning point having an origin. With the establishment of an origin we can expand the graphic if we 'move outward' from the point we designate as the 'origin', 'move outward' from the point whose coordinates are (o,o,o), 'move outward' from the 'beginning point'. If we implement the process we obtain:

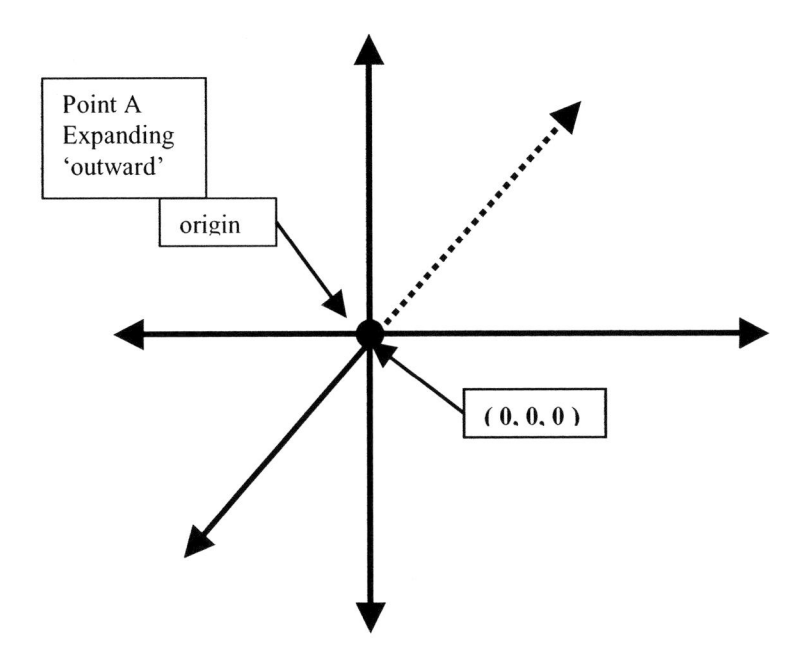

We will shrink this Cartesian concept we obtain:

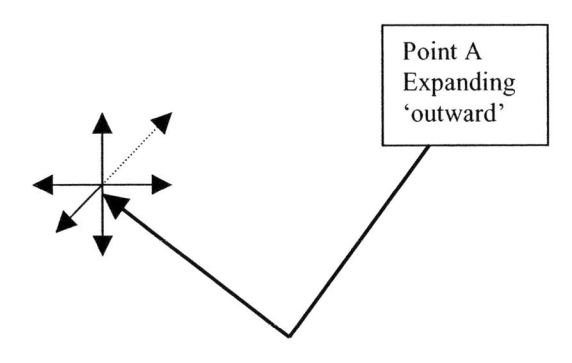

Having done this we will place this point of origin 'within' each of the three points of 'location': first within the universe, then within the whole, and finally within the individual. We will further examine each unique situation separately. We will examine each unique situation in terms of why we obtain three different 1st principles. Due to the fact this tractate deals in particular with Aristotle, we will begin by first placing the point of reference, the origin of a Cartesian physical system inside the universe but 'outside' the individual, outside the unique perception of one's individuality, outside of the 'location' of one's consciousness.

Following, these guidelines we obtain:

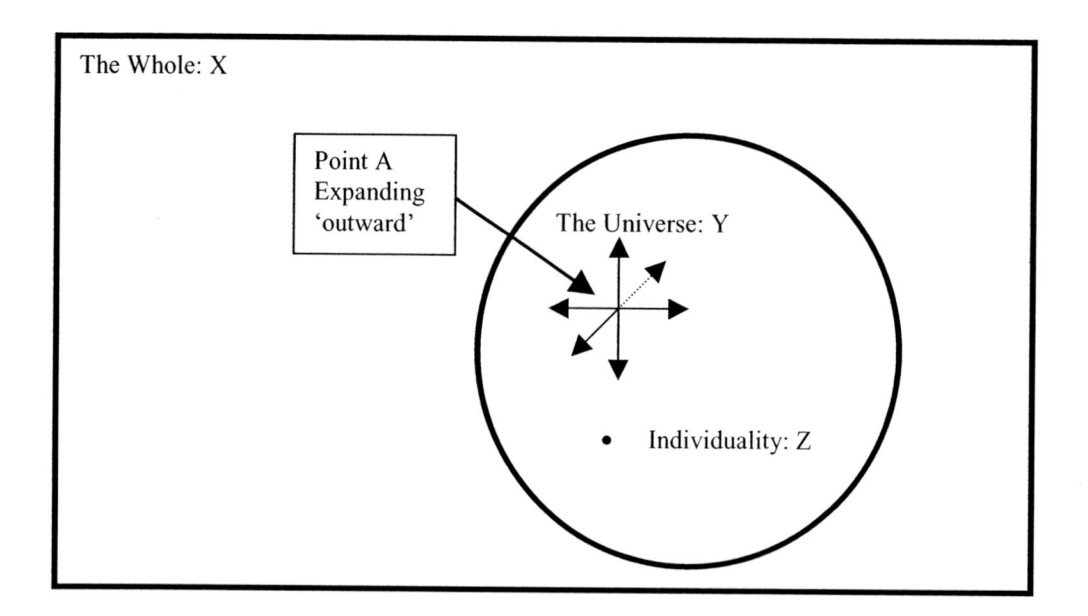

The Whole: X

Point A Expanding 'outward'

The Universe: Y

• Individuality: Z

Now we will call this point of origin located within a spatial universe permeated with time, point 'A'. Keep in mind that point 'A' is just that, a point. Point 'A' is not an awareness nor does it itself have awareness of awareness. Point 'A' does not have consciousness of its own consciousness for it has no consciousness to begin with. Point 'A' is a point and a point by definition has no length, depth, or height. In essence, point 'A' is nonexistent in the sense of what we perceive existence to be from the point of view of the universe. Point 'A' is nonexistent in the sense of what 'things' are which are from the perspective a physical universe perceives existence to be. Point 'A' is, in essence, an abstraction. Point 'A' is.

From 'A's' point of reference:

1. The physical exists
2. The physical is observable, measurable
3. Individual Z, is physical in nature
4. Individual Z, if in fact Individual Z does have the ability to perceive abstraction, understands abstraction because of its unique assembly of atoms and molecules.
5. Abstraction does not exist.
6. Abstraction is simply an understanding of 'perfection' (i.e. a perfect circle)
7. Abstraction, perfection, is simply a natural extrapolation of physical states
8. Abstractions of love, hate, jealousy, desire, etc. exist

The Error of Aristotle

9. Abstractions of love, hate, jealousy, desire, etc. are attempts to understand perfect abstraction towards which imperfect abstractions lead.
10. Imperfect abstractions do not exist as abstractions any more than abstractions exist.
11. Imperfect abstractions, as with perfect abstractions such as the perfect, do not exist.
12. Imperfect abstractions can be found in the physical only in the imperfect form found in the reality of the physical
13. The 'outside' to the universe is not physical
14. The 'outside' to the universe is simply an idea and thus an abstraction
15. 'The' 'outside' to the universe, being simply an idea, being an abstraction, does not exist.
16. The net result:
    a. 'Being', totality, the whole, only exists as the physical, the universe.
    b. The universe is the ultimate form of reality.
    c. God is an abstraction
    d. God is 'dead'
    e. God does not exist
    f. The individual only lives while its physical form functions
    g. The 'knowing' of the individual exists only as long as the individual exists
    h. Immortality is a myth
    i. God is nature itself
    j. While Atheism may not be completely accurate, pantheism, as opposed to panentheism, is completely accurate
    k. Man can conceive of things which do not exist
    l. Free will only applies to an infinitesimal period of time for any one individual
    m. Concepts such as: 'Prey we are wrong.' 'Hope we are wrong.' 'Follow the rules of faith and you may get lucky.' begin to emerge.
    n. Hopelessness emerges from the understanding: 'A' span of time is 'relatively' insignificant to the 'whole'
    o. All things emerge from the physical
    p. All 'things' emerge from Mother Nature including ideas themselves.
    q. Etc.

Transferring the Cartesian system to the location representing the individual entity of continuously emerging 'knowing', we obtain:

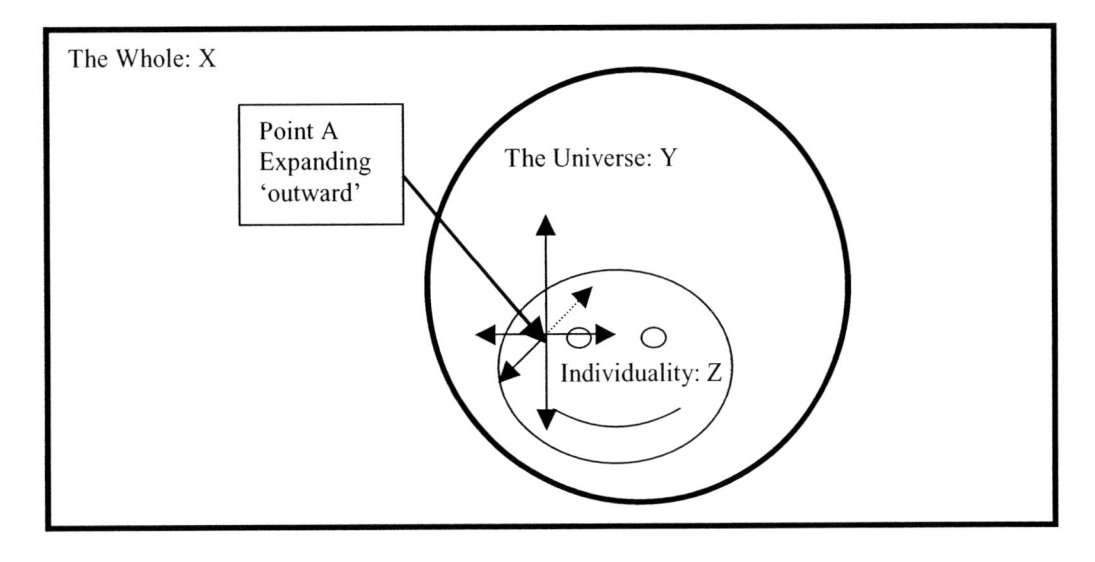

The Whole: X

Point A Expanding 'outward'

The Universe: Y

Individuality: Z

The War & Peace of a New Metaphysical Perception

The point of origin now finds itself located within an entity of 'knowing' which in turn is located within a spatial universe permeated with time. The point of origin, however, is itself located within abstractual knowing. We call this point of origin, point A. Point 'A' finds itself immersed within and surrounded by the universe. Point 'A' finds itself immersed within and surrounded by a biological sensory vehicle of physical ness. Being the origin of 'knowing', point 'A' has a sense there may be a limit to physicalness. Point 'A' has intuitive sense there may lie an 'outside' to the universe. However, Point 'A' is so far removed from what lies 'outside' the universe it is only able to make one observation. Point 'A' observes that it is immersed within the physical. As such:

From 'A's' 'new' point of reference we now obtain:

1. The physical exists
2. The physical is observable, measurable
3. Individual Z, is physical in nature
4. Individual Z, if in fact Individual Z does have the ability to perceive abstraction, understands abstraction because of its unique assembly of atoms and molecules.
5. Abstraction does not exist.
6. Abstraction is simply an understanding of 'perfection' (i.e. a perfect circle)
7. Abstraction, perfection, is simply an 'idea'
8. Abstractions of love, hate, jealousy, desire, etc. exist
9. Abstractions of love, hate, jealously, desire, etc. are attempts to understand perfect abstraction towards which imperfect abstractions lead.
10. Imperfect abstractions do not exist as abstractions any more than abstractions exist.
11. Imperfect abstractions, as with perfect abstractions such as the perfect, do not exist.
12. Imperfect abstractions can be found in the physical only in the imperfect form found in the reality of the physical
13. The 'outside' to the universe is not physical
14. The 'outside' to the universe is simply an idea and thus an abstraction
15. 'The' 'outside' to the universe, being simply an idea, being an abstraction, does not exist.
16. The net result:
    a. 'Being', totality, the whole, only exists as the physical, the universe.
    b. The universe is the ultimate form of reality.
    c. God is an abstraction
    d. God is 'dead'
    e. God does not exist
    f. The individual only lives while its physical form functions
    g. The 'knowing' of the individual exists only as long as the individual exists
    h. Immortality is a myth
    i. God is nature itself
    j. While Atheism may not be completely accurate, pantheism, as opposed to panentheism, is completely accurate
    k. Man can conceive of things which do not exist
    l. Free will only applies to an infinitesimal period of time for any one individual
    m. Concepts such as: 'Prey we are wrong.' 'Hope we are wrong.' 'Follow the rules of faith and you may get lucky.' begin to emerge.
    n. Hopelessness emerges from the understanding of 'a' span of time being 'relatively' insignificant to the 'whole'
    o. All things emerge from the physical
    p. All 'things' emerge from Mother Nature including ideas themselves.
    q. Etc.

Transferring the Cartesian system to the location of the 'whole' of continuously emerging 'knowing', we obtain:

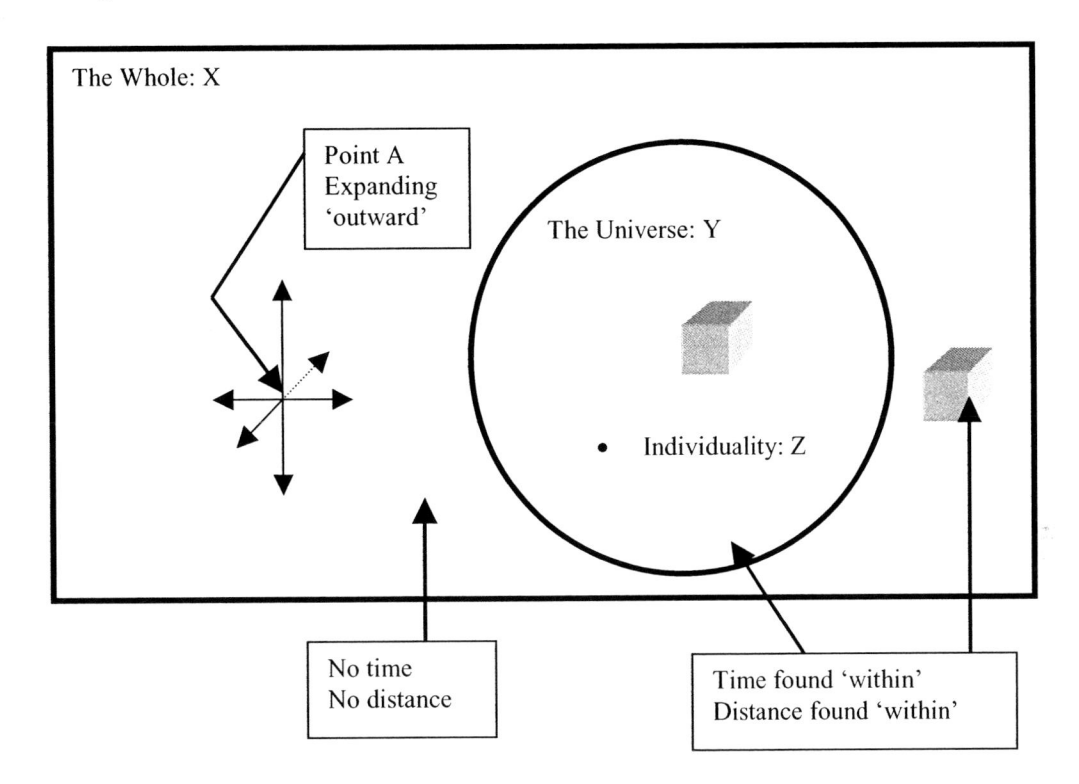

[Diagram: A large rectangle labeled "The Whole: X" contains a circle labeled "The Universe: Y" with a cube inside and a point labeled "Individuality: Z". Outside the circle but inside the rectangle are arrows expanding outward labeled "Point A Expanding 'outward'". Another cube is outside the circle. Labels below: "No time / No distance" (pointing inside rectangle, outside circle) and "Time found 'within' / Distance found 'within'" (pointing inside circle).]

Now we once again will call this point of origin located within timelessness, point 'A'. In a sense, it is inaccurate to depict a Cartesian system lying 'within' such a location for the location is void of time and distance existing as universal abstractions. Time and distance only find themselves 'encapsulated' 'within' the unique entities of consciousness which have uniquely 'moved' through both time and distance while 'traveling' 'within' the physical, 'traveling' 'within' the universe 'within' which time and distance are found to exist as 'universal' entities (universal in terms of the limits of the physical universe itself).

From 'A's' 'new' point of reference we now obtain:

1. The physical exists
2. The physical is observable, measurable
3. The physical of individual Z, is physical in nature
4. The abstract of individual Z is abstract in nature
5. Individual Z, if in fact Individual Z does have the ability to perceive abstraction, understands abstraction because its unique assembly of atoms and molecules allows the abstract as an entity to 'observe' the physical.
6. Abstraction does exist.
7. Abstraction understands 'perfection' (i.e. a perfect circle)
8. Abstraction, perfection, is separate from, yet found both 'inside' and 'outside', the physical
9. Abstractions of love, hate, jealousy, desire, etc. exist
10. Abstractions of love, hate, jealously, desire, etc. are not attempts to understand perfect abstraction but exist as unique entities, exist as 'perfect' variations of 'perfection'.

11. Imperfect abstractions do not exist as 'imperfections' but rather exists as 'perfect' entities of themselves.
12. Perceived imperfect abstractions, as with perfect abstractions such as the perfect, exist.
13. Perceived imperfect abstractions can be found in the whole only in the imperfect form found encapsulated 'within' a unique entity which developed from 'virgin consciousness' having experiences 'within' the reality of the physical
14. The 'outside' to the universe is not physical
15. The 'outside' to the universe an abstraction
16. 'The' 'outside' to the universe, being an abstraction, exists.
17. The net result:
    a. 'Being', totality, the whole, exists as the whole.
    b. The whole and its parts, the universe and the individual, are the ultimate form of Reality.
    c. The whole is.
    d. The whole exists.
    e. The physical individual lives while its physical form functions
    f. The 'knowing' of the individual exists 'eternally' not because the 'knowing' moves through time endlessly but because the 'knowing' of the individual exists in a region of timelessness, exists in a region where time is a function found 'within' the 'knowing' of the individual.
    g. Immortality exists because unique entities find themselves immersed in a 'region' void the universal presence of both time and distance.
    h. The whole is a unique entity itself.
    i. The whole has its own 'understanding' of what 'is' through it's understanding of what it is the sum of all its parts 'creates'.
    j. While Atheism may not be completely accurate, panentheism, as opposed to pantheism, is accurate in terms of what we are 'able' to perceive at this point in time
    k. Man and other forms of 'knowing' can conceive of things which do not exist
    l. Free will only applies to an infinitesimal period of time for any one individual
    m. Concepts such as: 'You are unique.' 'I am unique.' 'Our physical needs and appearances are not what we have in common. What we have in common is our need to develop uniquely as abstractual knowing.' 'We, you and I, you and I together, add to the emergence of the very uniqueness of the whole itself.' begin to emerge.
    n. Hope emerges from the understanding of 'a' span of time being 'relatively' significant to the 'whole' for the whole cannot be uniquely the whole without all of its parts, including your unique 'knowing'
    o. Virgin consciousness 'develops into unique 'knowing' and emerges from the physical
    p. One means by which unique 'knowing evolves is through 'traveling' and 'emerging' from Mother Nature. This applies to the concept of unique ideas themselves.
    q. To the 'whole' one 'span of time' has no more significance than another 'span of time' located within unique entities of 'knowing' because 'spans of time' have no significance to the whole for time is not found as 'an' element of the whole but rather is 'an' element of individual entities.
    r. Etc.

The Error of Aristotle

Things emerge from the physical, emerge from Mother Nature and 'enter' the abstract. The physical emerges from 'within' the abstract and unique experiencing, creating, 'knowing' can develop from experiencing 'within' this 'region'. Newness emerges through the process of being separated from totality through a process called 'exclusion through inclusion' versus the more commonly understood concept of 'exclusion through separation'.

Reopening the walls of confinement

A Cartesian system implies a 'beginning' and an 'end' even though the 'end' may not be perceivable. A Cartesian system 'going' from here to there, going from infinite 'smallness' to infinite 'largeness' suggests all 'things' lie somewhere between the two. This in turn suggests totality is the summation of all 'things'.

'From' beginning towards the end is the perceptual direction Aristotle initiated. This does not imply only 'one' direction of perceptual observation. Such a perceptual observation has a seemingly infinite number of possibilities:

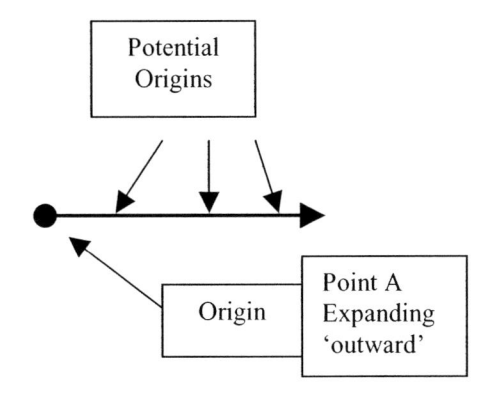

And

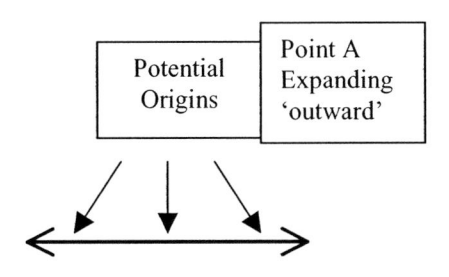

The War & Peace of a New Metaphysical Perception

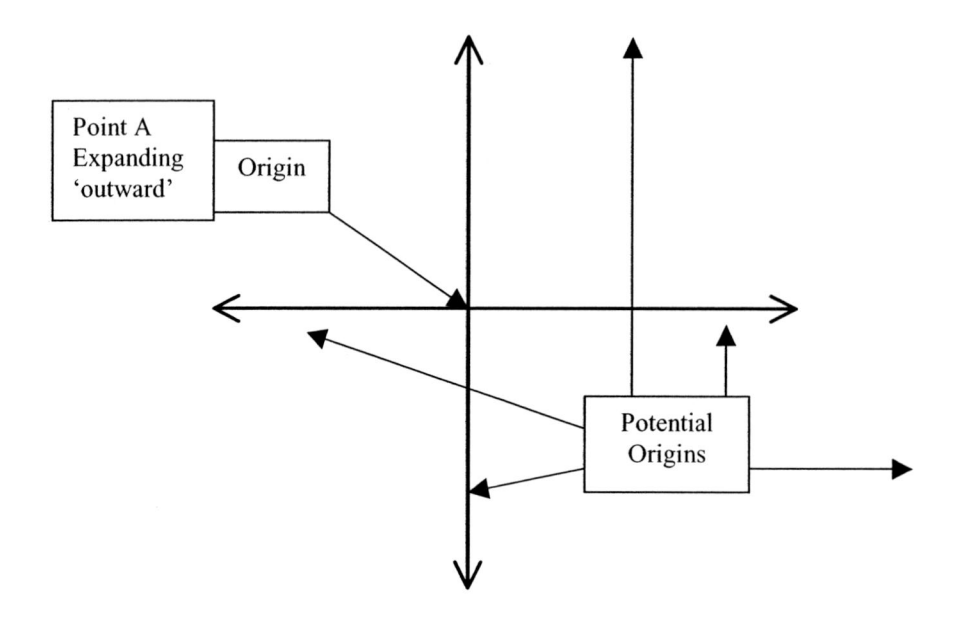

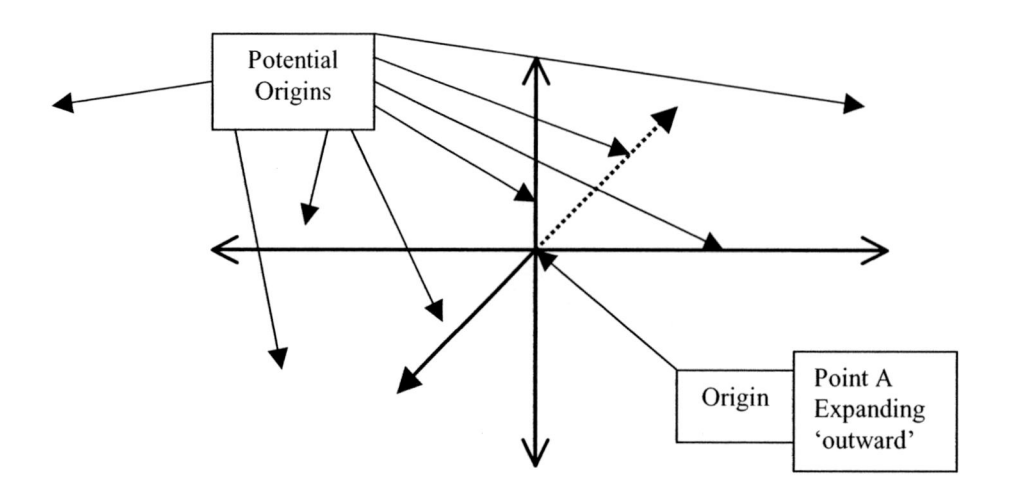

and

And

The Error of Aristotle

By no means did Aristotle 'limit' us in our ability to perceive. Aristotle did not have the 'power' to 'control' us. Aristotle simply took the step towards examining the universe, examining Zeno's concept of multiplicity. Aristotle took the step towards examining all 'things' found 'within' the universe. In essence, Aristotle began an examination of the region of Limited Abstracts.

Unfortunately, we, humanity, took this to be 'the' way and the only way to go. We ignored abstraction. We ignored going back to Zeno. We ignored taking 'a' step towards understanding seamlessness, abstraction.

When one maps humanities perceptual historical path beginning with Zeno, one obtains:

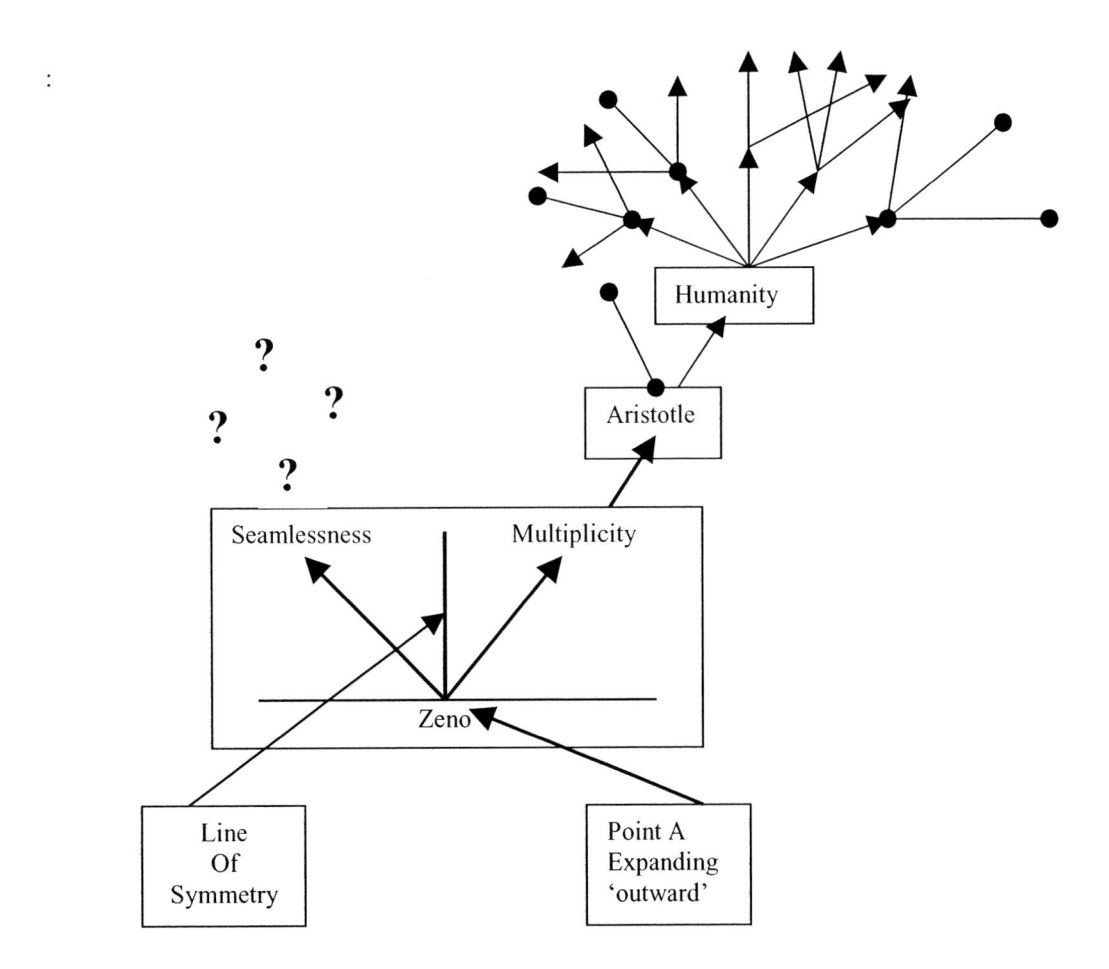

The question becomes: What happened? Why did we ignore the other half of Zeno's implied system.?

We forgot the second half of Zeno's implied system because it is easier to 'believe' what one sees than to believe one's rationality. The last perceptual means of development to succumb to the principle, 'Seeing is believing.' was philosophy. As we discussed earlier in this tractate, philosophy held out admirably for almost two thousand years before it joined the ranks of science and religion in embracing this principle.

The War & Peace of a New Metaphysical Perception

As the last graphic suggests, we moved collectively towards the concept of 'The universe exists and we are in the universe.' As such, we accepted an inside to the universe. We accepted a Cartesian perception of 'beginning/end' and rejected the concept of multiplicity/physicality and seamlessness/abstraction existing simultaneously in an independent yet dependent manner. For that matter we even left behind the concept of abstraction being 'the' form of existence and the physical being simply an illusion. With the acceptance of an 'inside' but not an 'outside' to the universe we moved towards the concept of monism verses pluralism.

Now why mention it as monism verses pluralism rather than as monism verses dualism? The reason might better be depicted graphically than verbally:

Monism verses dualism:

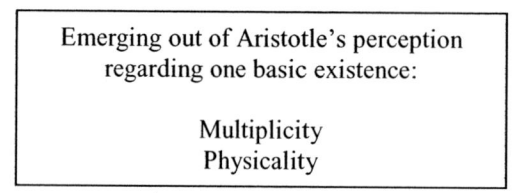

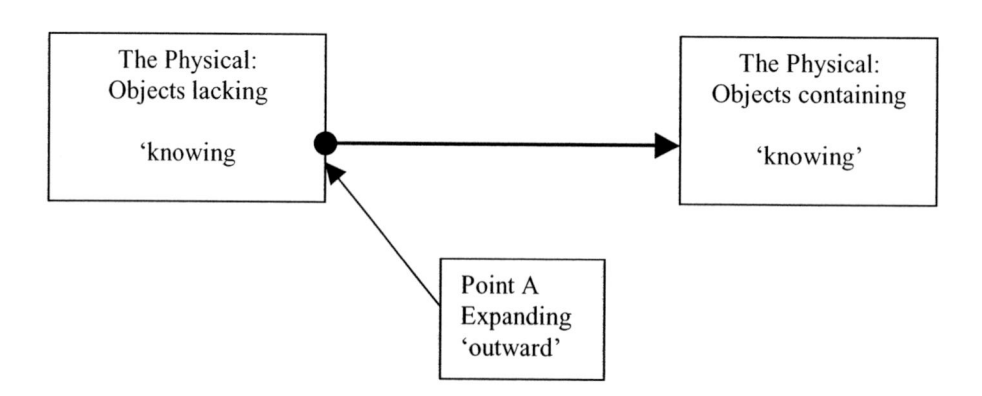

```
        ┌─────────────────────────────────────┐
        │  Emerging out of Aristotle's        │
        │  perception regarding one basic     │
        │  existence:                         │
        │                                     │
        │          Multiplicity               │
        │          Physicality                │
        └─────────────────────────────────────┘


┌──────────────────┐                    ┌──────────────────┐
│  The Physical:   │                    │  The Physical:   │
│  Objects lacking │●──────────────────▶│  Objects containing│
│                  │▲                   │                  │
│  'knowing        │ \                  │  'knowing'       │
└──────────────────┘  \                 └──────────────────┘
                       \
                    ┌─────────────┐
                    │  Point A    │
                    │  Expanding  │
                    │  'outward'  │
                    └─────────────┘
```

In a sense, the above is simply a line of continuum representing monism. Such a continuum develops through the perception of consciousness being an innate characteristic of unique physical structure.

The Error of Aristotle

Monism verses pluralism:

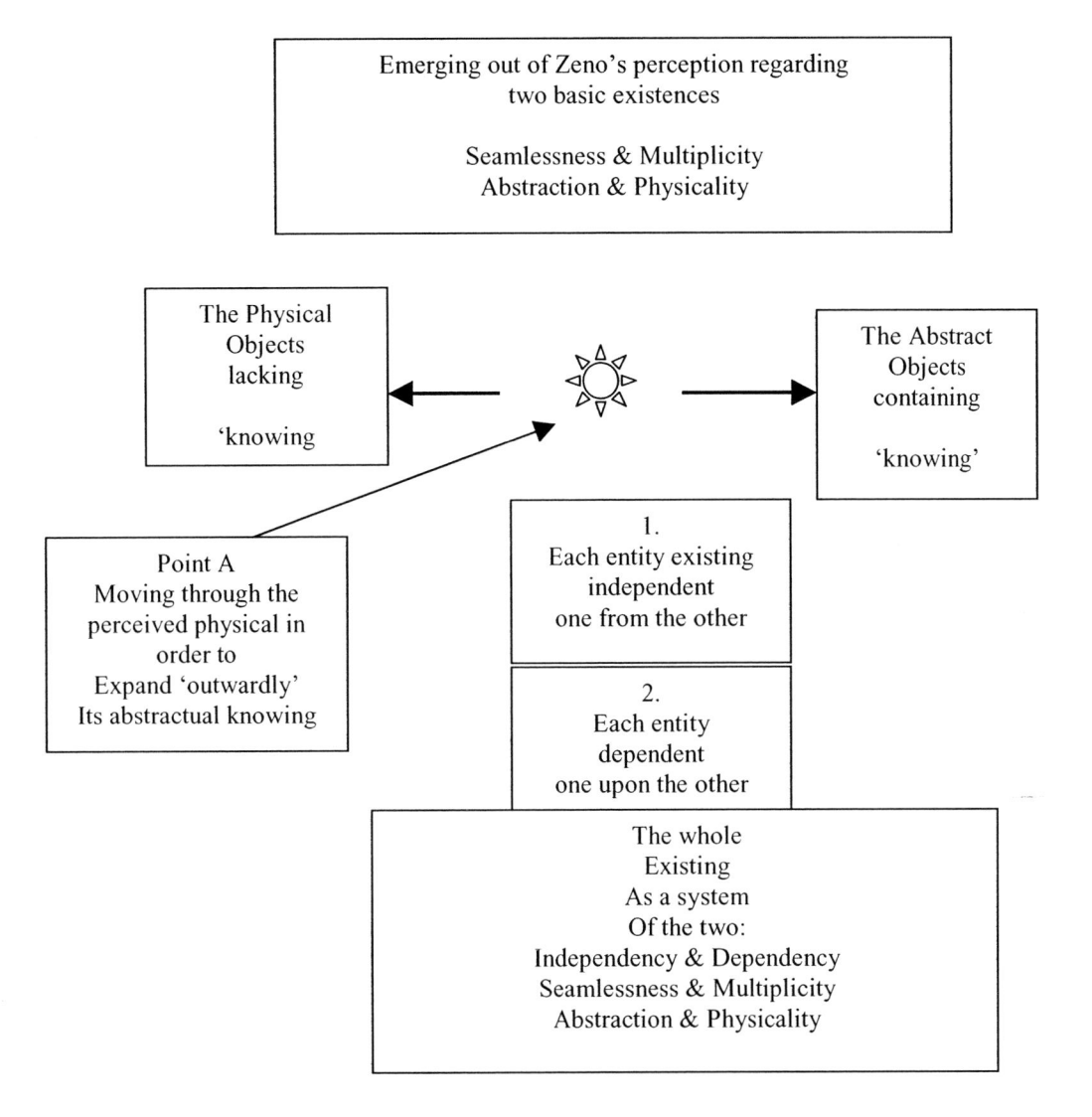

```
┌─────────────────────────────────────────┐
│   Emerging out of Zeno's perception     │
│         regarding two basic existences  │
│                                         │
│      Seamlessness & Multiplicity        │
│      Abstraction & Physicality          │
└─────────────────────────────────────────┘
```

┌──────────────┐   ┌──────────────┐
│ The Physical │   ☀   │ The Abstract │
│   Objects   │ ←─────   ─────→   │   Objects   │
│   lacking   │   │ containing │
│   'knowing   │   │   'knowing' │
└──────────────┘   └──────────────┘

┌────────────────────┐   ┌─────────────────────┐
│   Point A   │   │   1.   │
│ Moving through the │   │ Each entity existing│
│ perceived physical │   │   independent   │
│   in order to   │   │ one from the other │
│ Expand 'outwardly' │   └─────────────────────┘
│ Its abstractual   │   ┌─────────────────────┐
│   knowing   │   │   2.   │
└────────────────────┘   │   Each entity   │
                          │   dependent   │
                          │ one upon the other │
                          └─────────────────────┘
                     ┌──────────────────────────────┐
                     │   The whole   │
                     │   Existing   │
                     │   As a system   │
                     │   Of the two: │
                     │ Independency & Dependency   │
                     │ Seamlessness & Multiplicity │
                     │ Abstraction & Physicality   │
                     └──────────────────────────────┘

You may notice there is a lack of a 'connecting' line. The lack of such a line implies the two are separate entities. It does not imply one does not affect the other, nor does it imply the two are not interconnected, interwoven.

Within 'a' system of symbiotic panentheism, the growth of abstract concepts evolves and is 'created' through growth of 'virgin consciousness'. Virgin knowing expands uniquely through the parameters of free will choosing in an uninfluenced manner how it will do so. Free will choosing to grow uninfluenced by stability and perceived of what 'is' 'outside' the physical.

What it means to Humanity specifically and all forms of virgin consciousness universally generally

The result generated by the new metaphysical perception of symbiotic panentheism, 'being' *being* 'Being", leads to a concept of infinite expansion of abstraction through growth. To put it another way, the result leads to opening the door to Humanity's prison.

This may not seem like such a significant concept until one begins to reflect upon the question: Does confining humanity, does encaging humanity, lead to an increase in violence? If such is the case, then 'opining the 'walls' Aristotle built around the physical, may lead to a reduction of human violence universally…

If such is the case then perhaps the detail given to the re-examination of Aristotle's system may not be insignificant after all.

Aristotle's 'closed system' closed us off from the abstractual and 'placed' us 'within' the physical. Aristotle's system imprisoned us and as such we moved forward with our mimicry of the physical as opposed to our option of moving toward the perception of being abstractual. Physical hedonism became rational behavior and abstractual hedonism became irrational.

Mimesis, as described by Renee Girard, grew out of the closed system initiated by Aristotle. Mimeses is the act of learning behavior through the act of mimicry. Mimesis is the act of mimicking the physical animalistic behavior we find all around us. Mimesis becomes what we embrace since it is what we 'see'. The concept of 'altruistic' behavior becomes just that 'altruistic' since we cannot 'see' it's abstractual rationality. Altruistic behavior therefore appears to be baseless thus 'altruistic'.

By opening up Aristotle's system and establishing the rationale of abstractual existence we move 'altruistic' behavior to the level of simply being reasonable and we move animalistic behavior to the level of being irrational behavior for an entity encapsulating abstractually perceptual abilities. Physical hedonism thus gives way to abstractual hedonism and becomes rational only if one 'wishes' to perceive oneself as being simply a physical 'thing', perceive oneself as being simply temporary.

The result:

Responsibilities emerge:

1. The first responsibility: to universally protect the 'right' of virgin consciousness (one's self and others equally) to journey unimpeded
2. The second responsibility: to journey unimpeded

The understanding of 'a' solution to the paradox Aristotle initiated can be graphically depicted. Using Ockham's razor to the maximum, we obtain the graphic:

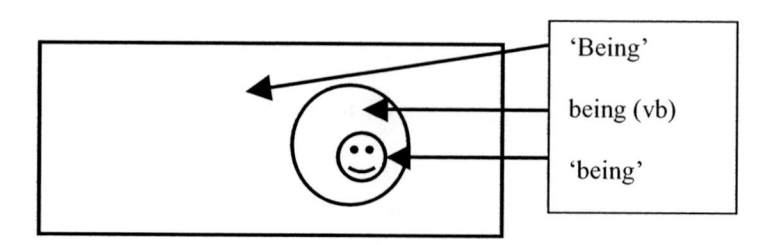

Generically speaking: we obtain symbiotic panentheism or more simply put: 'being' *being* 'Being'.

As such, should the universe 'dissolve', 'implode', 'die', we will remain 'within' abstraction, we will remain a part of the whole and nobody can take that away from you regardless of any denials on your part.

But doesn't this do just what Aristotle did to Zeno's 'system'? Isn't enclosing abstraction in a 'box' in essence the same as enclosing humankind in a circle? Surprisingly, no it is not the same thing but that also is another topic found outside the scope of this tractate

If we must wait to understand the true nature of freedom, then where are we to go from here? We are about to examine perhaps one of the most treasured dreams of humankind. We are about to examine the potential reasonableness of freedom existing 'within' the confines of time. We are going to move forward in time itself. We are going to leave Zeno – 500 BC and Aristotle – 384 BC and visit Boethius – 480 AD.

We now understand that

Aristotle is a vital link in moving our perceptual understanding forward regarding the 'system' being filled Cartesianism, into that of being 'the' system filled with both Cartesianism and non-Cartesianism. As such, systems with a beginning end format and systems without a beginning end format, with the help of Aristotle, now have a location within which each dominates. As such, the understanding regarding the role of the Cartesianism and non-Cartesianism as well as the understanding regarding the interrelationship between Cartesianism and non-Cartesianism no longer remain in a state of confusion. Even more interestingly, the existence of such an interrelationship is not only recognized as a significant aspect of the 'larger' system but it is now understood how Cartesianism and non-Cartesianism interact one with the other.

---

[1] **Question**: What was Aristotle's own views on the existence of God? The sentence implies that he was an atheist. **Answer**: This is not to imply that Aristotle was an Atheist, rather it is to imply that the perception of reality being 'what is' leads to historical development of the 'lack' of 'a' causative force of the universe, leads to the historical development of a Hegelian foundationless system lacking the concept of 'beginning'/'end' as Eastern philosophy suggests.

[2] **Question**: Why were those repercussions unavoidable? Answer: Certain types of 'action' leads to what we perceive to be 'unavoidable' reactions. An example: If one steps off a cliff, one will fall. Now this not need be the case for one may step off a cliff and find one is held up by an invisible floor, however, the most likely result, the most assured result of stepping off a cliff is that one will fall. Confining, placing a person within a sensory deprivation chamber can eventually lead one to forms of violent actions while within the chamber in order to find a means of gaining sensory input once again. Now granted the universe is 'quite' large, but it becomes confining nevertheless when one establishes a 'boundary' to the universe. The 'boundary Aristotle established is the limit of matter, energy, time, and distance.

[3] **Question**: Why use the "caged animal" metaphor? **Answer**: Renee Gerard suggests humanity learns behavior through mimicry. The 'caged animal' metaphor simply uses the concept of mimicry and applies a natural understanding of what happens to 'free animals' being 'caged' to that of humanity being 'caged through the limiting of knowledge itself.

[4] **Question**: Would people of religious faith agree with you on this point? **Answer**: In spite of the fact that people of faith often wish to dismiss science, it science finds enough factual evidence to support their claims, for the most part, even people of faith eventually accept the findings of

science. As such they either learn to the scientific concept around their religion or they mold their religion around the scientific concept. i.e. the earth is spherical, the sun is the center of the solar system, man can fly, ...

[5] **Question**: The word "suppressed" implies conspiracy and intent. Are you sure it was intentional, or simply a consequence or by-product? **Answer**: It was intentional – see Zero – The Biography of a Dangerous Idea, by Charles Seife, Viking Penguin, 2000

[6] **Question**: Are you being fair in stating that Philosophy sold out humanity? **Answer**: Absolutely! Philosophy has become 'a' toy of the academics and as such has shut itself off from the public. The only philosophers recognized as having any form of authenticity are those whose credentials include: Professor, Dr., affiliated with..., from the University of..., etc. It is not the idea, which has merit with 'philosophers' but the source.

Tractate 3

The Error

Of

Boethius

❖

The Paradox of:

Free Will

•

The Need for:

God, Free Will, and Immortality

The War & Peace of a New Metaphysical Perception

1.   525 AD Boethius – The Error of:
            Free Will – a new perception 2000 AD

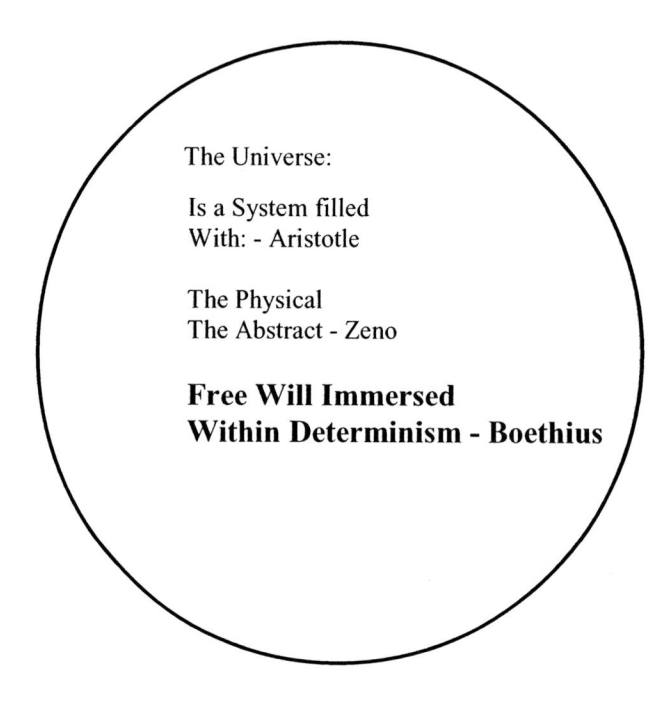

The Universe:

Is a System filled
With: - Aristotle

The Physical
The Abstract - Zeno

**Free Will Immersed
Within Determinism - Boethius**

The error: The paradox of free will and divine foreknowledge

The perception: Boethius moves our perceptual understanding regarding the system being filled with free will into that of being 'the' system filled with both free will and divine foreknowledge. As such, free will and divine foreknowledge, with the help of Boethius, now have a location within which they can be found. However, the understanding regarding the role of both free will and divine foreknowledge as well as the understanding regarding the interrelationship between free will and divine foreknowledge not only remain in a state of confusion but even more disconcerting, the existence of such an interrelationship is not recognized as a significant aspect of the 'larger' system.

It is this state of confusion which will be specifically addressed within this tractate.

Contents

Part I: The Paradox of free will and divine foreknowledge

Introduction
A misconception of determinism
Three forms of action
Limits placed upon Boethius
Some thoughts expounded by Boethius
Boethius' metaphysical system
Boethius' metaphysical system and social acceptance
Boethius' metaphysical system and perpetual historical acceptance
Boethius' metaphysical system and why it is we have not presently discarded such a system

Part II: Resolving the issue with a new metaphysical perception:

'The wall' of perception
Rationalizing the irrational
The limits of language
Oil and Water
The four forms of action
    What 'will be': Free will - A location for 'being' – individuality
    What 'has been': Divine foreknowledge - A location for 'Being' – the whole
    What 'is being': Determinism - A location for *being* – action, process/reality – the universe
    What 'is': Pre-destination/predestination - A location for being – existence of existence
Functionality of action
Locations for actions
Divine foreknowledge, predestination, pre-destination, and determinism versus free will
Internationality: the need 'for' a location of determinism
Potentiality: the need 'for' a location of free will
Nothing: the need 'for' a location of nothing
The Book of Divine Foreknowledge
The Location of Free Will
The Location of Determinism
The misnomer of 'free will'
Letting go

Terms/concepts

Adjacent actions of multiplicity
Determinism
Divine Foreknowledge
Formulation
Free will
Individuality
Pre-destination
Predestination
Cardinal Sequencing
Random Sequencing/factorial
Removing a piece of Randomness

The War & Peace of a New Metaphysical Perception

Tractate 3
Boethius – The Error of
Free Will Confined within the Boundaries of Determinism

Part I: Creating the paradox of 'the' System 'containing' free will

Introduction

Free will confined within the boundaries of determinism is simply an illusion of free will.

> 'There can be little question that Boethius, more than any other philosophic author, helped the great Schoolmen to retain a general comprehensive view of the world as a whole, in spite of the distractions of their minute inquiries.'[1]

Boethius presented humanity with a model of a metaphysical system, which led to an understanding regarding how it is men retain free will within the parameters of an all-knowing entity. Boethius' metaphysical system describes an omniscient God and It's interrelationship to free will. Examination of Boethius' metaphysical system becomes the point of the first part of this tractate. The second part of this tractate is an examination of a means by which we can embrace such a system while freeing ourselves of the contradiction divine foreknowledge, determinism, pre-destination, or predestination impose upon the very concept of 'free' will.

Paradoxically, the process of freeing ourselves of the confines of determinism is accomplished through a process of removing free will from the realm of determinism and then reinserting free will back into determinism through a process of 'separation through inclusion' versus 'separation through exclusion'. The exploration of 'separation through inclusion' versus 'separation through exclusion' is itself fully explored in Tractate 8: Russell. Although the in depth understanding regarding the concept of 'separation through inclusion' must wait for the Russell Tractate, we will initiate the understanding regarding such a concept within this tractate.

Boethius argued we must accept free will as being recessive, submissive to divine foreknowledge, determinism, pre-destination, and predestination. Now if submissive independence is not an error, what is?

Is Boethius to blame for our having been able to resolve the paradox regarding free will and divine foreknowledge?

The answer is no. We are now the ones responsible for not resolving the issue regarding the paradox of the simultaneous independent existence of free will and determinism. Philosophers have expanded our understanding of abstraction and scientists have expanded our understanding of the physical. Now it is up to us to merge the two sets of knowledge. We have the knowledge. Therefore, it is up to present day metaphysicians to assemble these pieces of the puzzle and create a new metaphysical model.

An alternative metaphysical perception, metaphysical model, to Boethius' metaphysical perception exists. The problem is to gain the attention of religion, philosophy, and science, all of whom have rejected the very validity of metaphysics itself.

With this in mind, let's examine what it was Boethius laid out for us as a metaphysical perception. Let us then proceed to examine why this metaphysical system was accepted as a logical argument. We will then examine why such a metaphysical model advanced intact through history followed by an examination as to why it is we have not yet discarded this metaphysical system. Finally, let us examine why it is we can now file Boethius' system away as an interesting perception found within the annals of philosophical history as opposed to its status of being an unresolved perplexing paradox of philosophical perception.

A misconception of determinism

Determinism and free will are perceived to be the two states of being/action found only 'within' process - reality (vb). This is a limited perception. It is a perception of 'confinement'. In order to expand our perception regarding free will and determinism, it will help to examine the types of action, which appear to exist.

There appear to be three types of action correlating to the three regions of truth, the existence of 'relativistic truth' as explored in the previous tractate: Tractate 2: Aristotle and Cartesian Systems.

Action can be categorized as either active or passive.

In terms of action, there is being/action in the active sense and being/action in the passive sense. This statement suggests only two forms of action rather than three forms of action. Upon closer examination, however, one finds each of these two forms of action, these two forms of being/action are themselves subdivided into two subgroups.

Doesn't such a statement imply there are in fact only two forms of action? No, there are four forms of action, which emerge from the two primary sets of action. Each of these four forms of action are not themselves relegated to a lesser significance than the two sets from which they emerge. It is the action itself, which 'is' as opposed to the two sets within which they can be categorized.

Understanding Boethius requires only the examination of three of the four forms of action. It is for this reason Part I: The Introduction of this tractate suggests there are three forms of action. Understanding the resolution to the paradoxical independent existence of free will and determinism requires the examination of all four forms of action. It is for this reason Part II: Resolving Boethius' Paradox deals with four versus three forms of action.

Part I deals with three regions within which 'a' unique truth can be found to exist.

Part II expands upon this understanding to include not three but four regions, not three unique truths but four unique truths. In fact, it might better be said: Each of the four action forms dominates a particular 'region' of 'location and that 'a' unique truth exists as 'a' unique dominate form of action, which 'gives' the 'region' its unique innate characteristics.

Such a statement, however, is misleading for it would better be said that each region of first truth evolves an innate characteristic through the primary action found to dominate the region itself.

To begin understanding the means of resolving Boethius' paradox, we must first examine Boethius' metaphysical system in terms of three action forms.

The War & Peace of a New Metaphysical Perception

Three forms of action

Before naming the three forms of action, it will help to briefly examine the three 'regions', which contain their own unique 1st truth. The in-depth examination of such an understanding was explored in Tractate 2: Aristotle and Cartesian Systems.

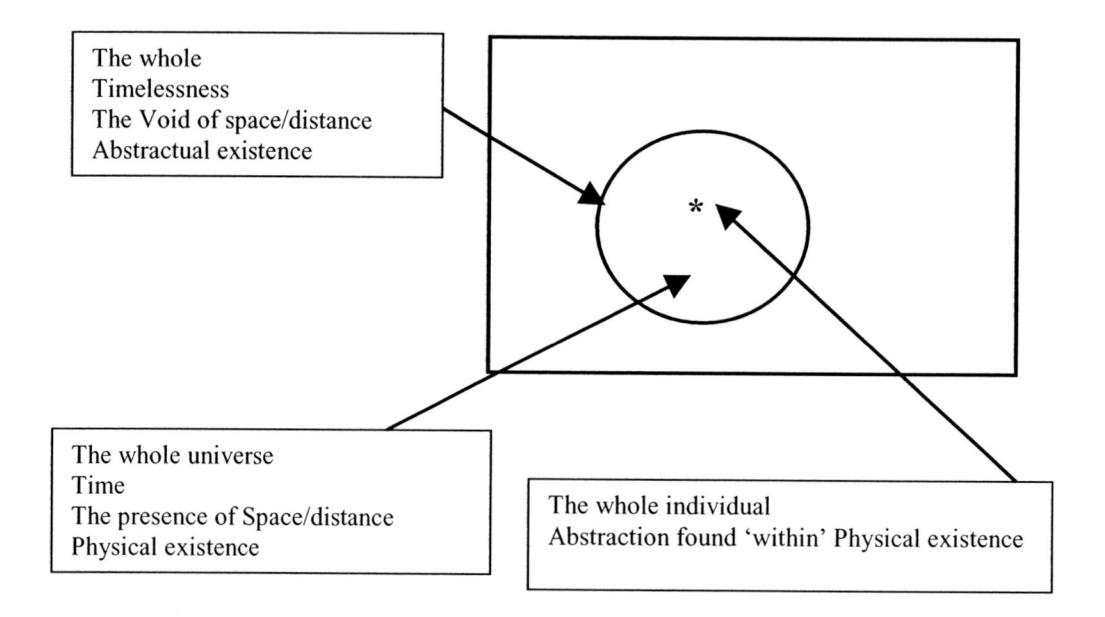

The whole
Timelessness
The Void of space/distance
Abstractual existence

The whole universe
Time
The presence of Space/distance
Physical existence

The whole individual
Abstraction found 'within' Physical existence

Having identified three 'locations', we can list three action forms. We can then demonstrate why it is we find such action existing as an innate characteristic of the region. We can demonstrate how it is first truth is first truth while being first truth only from the point of view of the region itself. In short, we will both demonstrate what is meant by the term 'relativistic first truth' examined in Tractate 2: Aristotle and Cartesian Systems and demonstrate how 'relativistic first truth' can resolve the paradox of the independent existence of free will and determinism.

Action:

    I.   Passive action

        1. Action bound by the laws of nature
        2. Action bound by the laws of determinism

    II.   Active action

        3. Action bound by the laws of free will

The Error of Boethius

Expanding upon our diagram through the placement of action, we obtain:

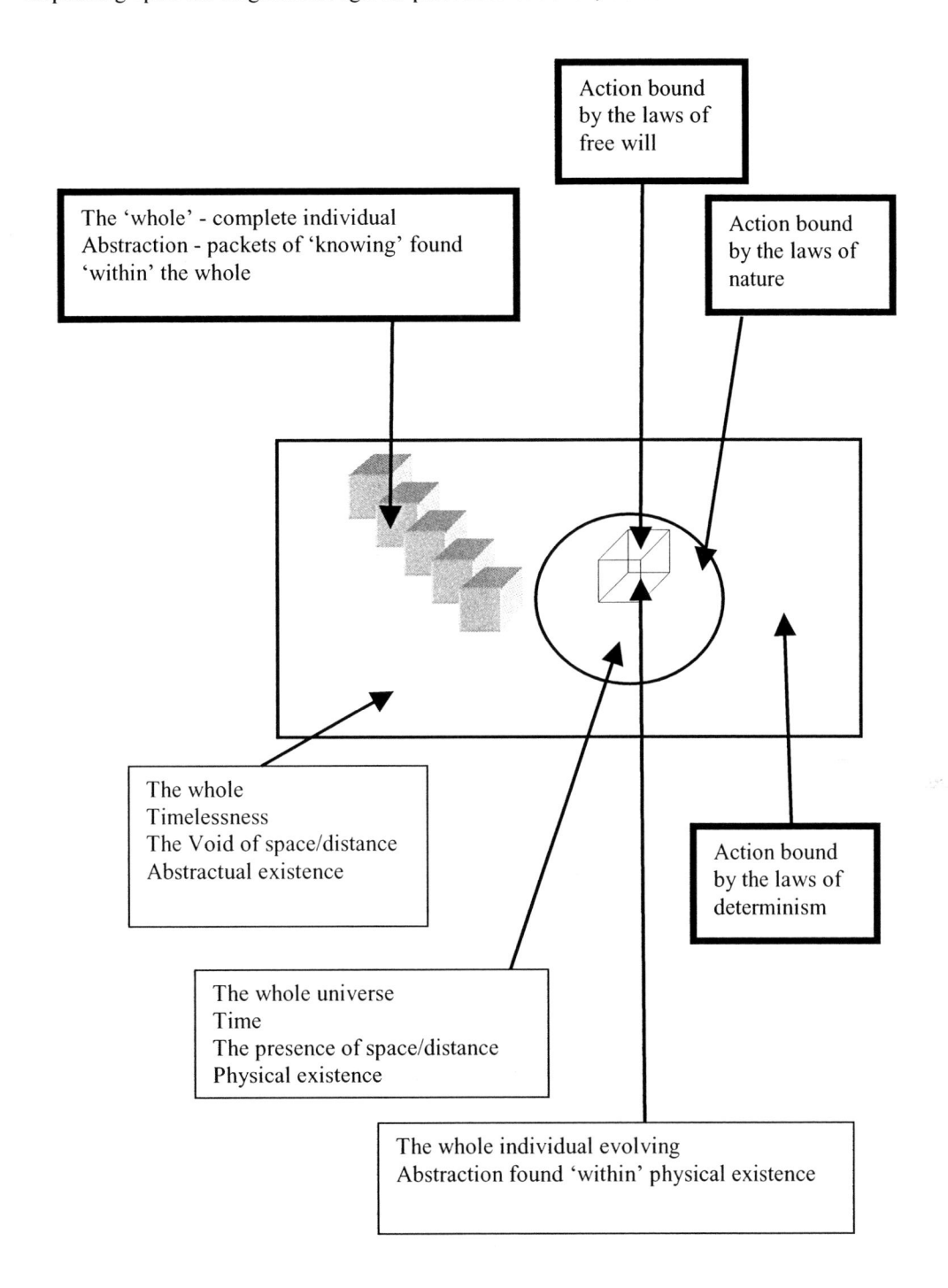

Action bound by the laws of free will

The 'whole' - complete individual
Abstraction - packets of 'knowing' found 'within' the whole

Action bound by the laws of nature

The whole
Timelessness
The Void of space/distance
Abstractual existence

The whole universe
Time
The presence of space/distance
Physical existence

Action bound by the laws of determinism

The whole individual evolving
Abstraction found 'within' physical existence

And why is it actions found bound by the laws of nature and actions bound by the laws of determinism are both considered to be 'passive' forms of action? Action bound by the laws of nature and actions bound by the laws of determinism are both 'predetermined' and as such, they are not 'free' but 'bound' to be what they are.

This is not to imply actions bound by the laws of nature are each proceeded by conscious 'intent' to have the action be what it is. Rather it implies that the laws of nature determine action naturally.

Within a system of divine foreknowledge, it could be said: Actions bound by the laws of free will are also 'bound'. Such a perception, however, evolves out of a perception that being 'bounded' by the lack of control of one's action is a form of control itself. Such a perception is correct. However, it is not correct in the sense one may first think. Actions bounded by the laws of nature and actions bounded by the laws of determinism are forms of 'controlled actions', which lie 'outside' the realm of one's control. Actions bound by the laws of free will are by definition 'controlled' in the sense that they are not controlled by a source 'outside' one's control but rather controlled by one's self.

The question then arises: What do we call states of 'being'? Such existence is said to simple 'be' without action. In essence, there is no action to such forms of existence found within the physical universe. A rock exists, an atom exists, a star exists. These are forms of simply 'being' often referred to as states of being as opposed to states of action.

One may object and point out that a star is a dynamic object. It is in essence a summation of many states of action. Fusion is but one such process taking place 'within' the star. This form of action does not apply just to the star however. The rock is composed of its own unique forms of action. Atomic vibration, subatomic particle movement, heat exchange, electromagnetic interactions, etc. 'fill' the rock with action no less than the star is 'filled' with action, states of active being.

These states of action are not forms of determinism. These forms of actions are actions bound by the 'laws' of nature. Such actions are discoverable through observation and measurement. We call such action, actions bound by the laws of nature. Laws of nature are not only predictable but lend themselves to a concept known as formulation. Formulation is simply a predictable pattern capable of being expressed through a mathematical equation. We may not have the mathematical sophistication capable of predicting all such actions but there is no denying we are working diligently on developing just such a level of sophistication. We may not have the time to develop this level of mathematical sophistication. The concept of limited time, however, is not stopping us from exploring such mathematical formulations.

Such states of being/action, process – reality are not examples of determinism. They are instead actions generated by the laws of nature, which are inherent in our universe. Such actions are universal to our universe because they exist within a universe where such laws 'rule'. It is very possible such laws of nature may not exist in another universe. It is possible other universes abide by different 'laws' or lack of 'laws' as we might perceive an existence lacking 'rules' to be.

We are not, however, here to discuss unique possibilities regarding a variety of existences potentially found within unique universes. We are here to understand our personal universe. Part of understanding our universe, understanding ourselves, understanding the whole, understanding the interactions of the three lies in understanding action.

Actions bound by the 'laws' of nature are not forms of determinism nor are they forms of free will, they are rather just what they were stated to be, actions bound by the 'laws' of nature.

What are actions classified as forms of determinism and what are actions classified as forms of free will? Actions of determinism and actions of free will are actions, which are not bound by the 'laws' of nature.

Newton identified three basic laws of action, as well as inaction. Inaction is an extreme form of action. Inaction is the purest form of minimalistic action found on the extreme end of the action continuum.

Newton's laws[2] of motion/action existing 'within' nature:

1. A body continues in a state of rest or uniform motion in a straight line unless it is acted upon by external forces.
2. The rate of change of momentum of a moving body is proportional to and in the same direction as the force action on it, *ie*. F=d(mv)/dt, where F is the applied force, 'v' is the velocity of the body, and 'm' its mass. If the mass remains constant, F = mdv/dt or F= ma, where 'a' is the acceleration.
3. If one body exerts a force on another, there is an equal and opposite force, called a reaction, exerted on the first body by the second.

Actions of determinism and actions of free will are distinguishable from forms of action or inaction bound by the laws of nature. If one jumps off a cliff, they will fall. The process of falling, the action of falling is bound by the 'law of nature'. The decision to jump is a case of personal choice. One decides to jump or not to jump.

It is the issue of choice being an option or not being an option, which is to be addressed in this article. It is the issue of whether the book of life 'is already written' or whether the book of life 'is in the process of being written' which is to be examined in this tractate. It is the development of a new means of 'looking' at, of perceiving the function of determinism existing simultaneously with, yet independently from, free will. It is the intent of this article to demonstrate that not only do the two, free will and determinism, exist uniquely and simultaneously but they do so in a critically interdependent fashion.

The concept regarding a critical interdependence of free will and determinism establishes a metaphysical system wherein determinism and free will are dependent upon each other for their very existence as unique forms of action.

But what of actions bound by the 'laws of nature'? Actions bound by the laws of nature will find themselves addressed in detail throughout this work. One need but revert to Tractate 1: Zeno and Seamlessness to find such an example. Within Tractate 1, one can find a detailed discussion regarding a region where an understanding emerges regarding the 'real' being simultaneously a 'real illusion' and the 'real illusion' being simultaneously the 'real'.

Limits placed upon Boethius

To understand Boethius' metaphysical system one must understands the place in history Boethius occupied. Boethius followed Aristotle. It was Aristotle who, as we discussed in Tractate 2, closed the 'region' we call reality.

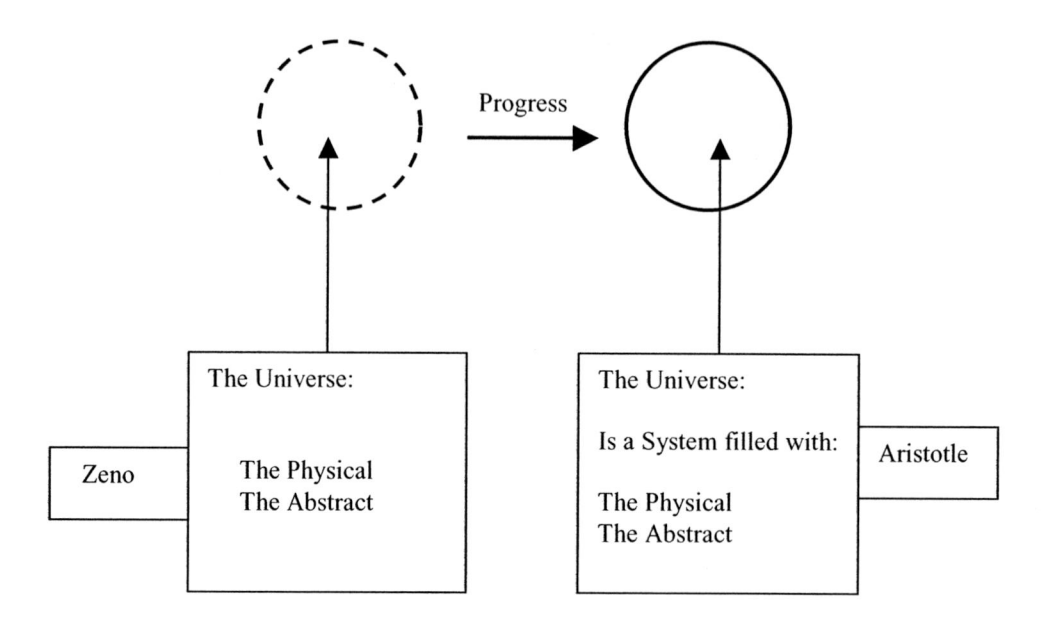

The War & Peace of a New Metaphysical Perception

Progress →

Zeno — The Universe: The Physical / The Abstract

Aristotle — The Universe: Is a System filled with: The Physical / The Abstract

Boethius was therefore faced with one and only one choice in terms of where to place all action, be they actions bound by the laws of free will or actions bound by the laws of determinism.

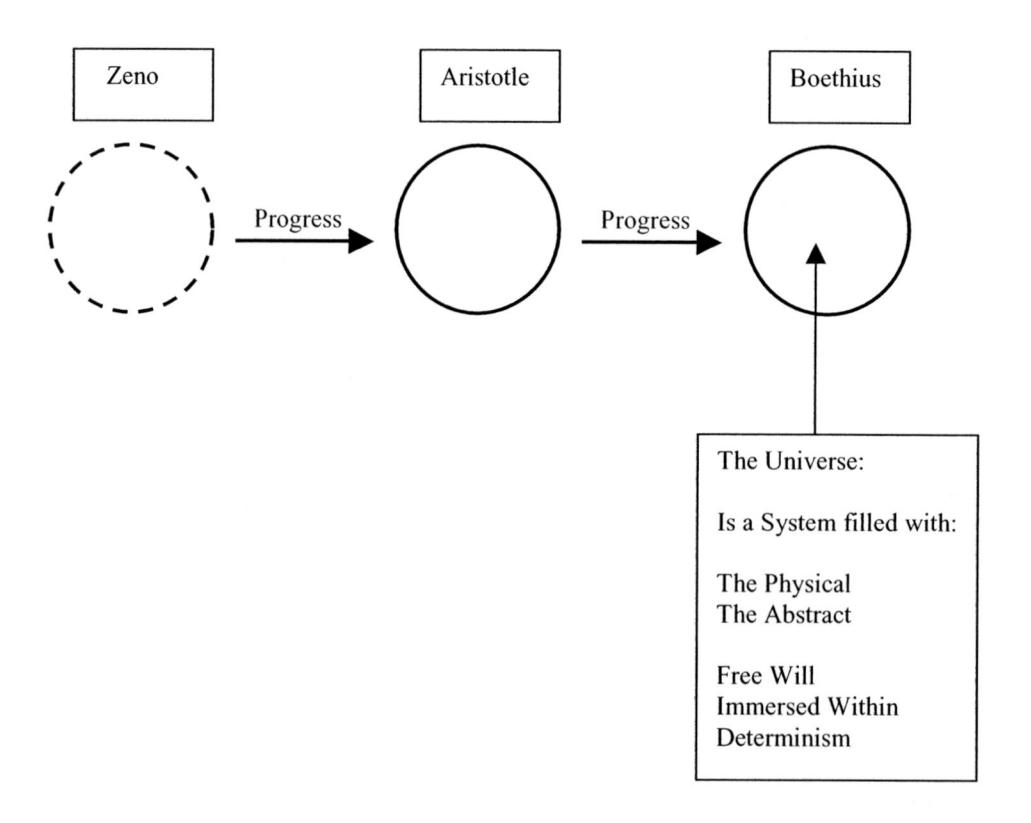

Zeno → Progress → Aristotle → Progress → Boethius

The Universe:

Is a System filled with:

The Physical
The Abstract

Free Will
Immersed Within
Determinism

156

This is better understood if we diagram it as:

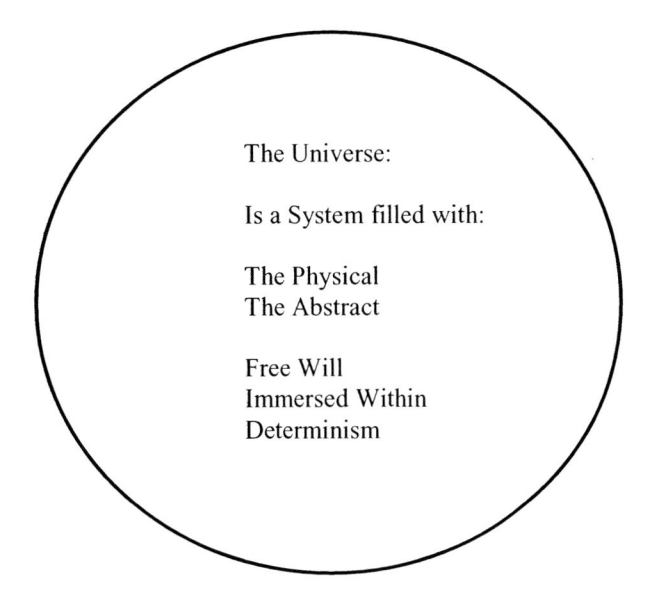

> The Universe:
>
> Is a System filled with:
>
> The Physical
> The Abstract
>
> Free Will
> Immersed Within
> Determinism

The diagram demonstrates there being no 'outside' to 'reality'. Why is there no 'outside' to Boethius' 'observable' reality? There is no outside to physical reality because Aristotle closed it off from rational perceptual examination through the process of establishing a subconscious acceptance of the concept: 'Seeing is believing.'

The result of Aristotle's action: Free will and determinism found themselves immersed 'within' the universe and only the universe. As such, humanity had no choice but to reconcile the apparently contradictory actions classified as free will and determinism.

The process of finding a solution to the apparent paradoxical coexistence of free will and determinism existing simultaneously within the same location was the fundamental objective Boethius attempted to establish in his work: Boethius – The Consolation of Philosophy. The problem Boethius confronted, however, emerged from the limits within which Boethius found himself. Boethius found himself limited to 'a' reality comprised of the physical. As such, Boethius found himself limited to developing a means of reconciling the existence of free will and determinism 'within' the limits of a 'physical system'.

An in depth examination of the paradox Boethius generated regarding the coexistence of free will and determinism can better be understood after having refreshed oneself with a few of Boethius' thoughts extracted from his tractate: The Consolation of Philosophy.

Some thoughts expounded by Boethius

Boethius: The Consolation of Philosophy

> Book V, section III:
>
> 'Look,' I said, 'there is something even more difficult I find perplexing and confusing.

The War & Peace of a New Metaphysical Perception

> 'Tell me,' she said, 'though I can guess what is troubling you.'
>
> 'Well, the two seem clean contrary and opposite, God's universal foreknowledge and freedom of the will. If God foresees all things and cannot be mistaken in any way, what Providence has foreseen as a future event must happen. So that if from eternity Providence foreknows not only men's actions but also their thoughts and desires, there will be no freedom of will. No action or desire will be able to exist other than that which God's infallible Providence has foreseen. For if they can be changed and made different from how thy were foreseen, there will be no sure foreknowledge of the future, only an uncertain opinion; and this I do not think can be believed of God….

Book V, section IV:

Then Philosophy spoke. 'This is an old complaint about Providence.

> 'It cannot be that what is foreseen as a future event does not come to pass. It would be as if we believed that what Providence foreknows as future events are not going to happen, instead of believing that although they happen, they were not predestined in their own nature. You will easily be able to see it in this way; we see many things before our eyes as they happen, like the actions we see charioteers performing in order to control and drive their chariots, and other things of this sort. But no necessity forces any of them to happen in this way, does it?
>
> …'Therefore, all those things which happen without happening of necessity are, before they happen, future events about to happen, but not about to happen of necessity. For just as the knowledge of present things imposes no necessity on what is happening, so foreknowledge imposes no necessity on what is going to happen.
>
> 'The cause of this mistake is that people think that the totality of their knowledge depends on the nature and capacity to be known of the objects of knowledge. But this is all wrong.'…
>
> 'The point of greatest importance here is this: the superior manner of knowledge includes the inferior, but it is quite impossible for the inferior to rise to the superior.'…
>
> 'In the same way, human reason refuses to believe that divine intelligence can see the future in any other way except that in which human reason has knowledge.'…

Herein lies the crux of Boethius' argument, we, humans must accept his argument for it supposedly rises above human rationality and flows into the rationality of God, approximates God's rationality which is and forever will be unknowable to us.

In short, Boethius is saying: It is so even if we cannot comprehend it. And just what is 'it'? 'It' is the perception: 'In the same way, human reason refuses to believe that divine intelligence can see the future in any other way except that in which human reason has knowledge…For just as the knowledge of present things imposes no necessity on what is happening, so foreknowledge imposes no necessity on what is going to happen.'

According to Boethius, divine foreknowledge, existing simultaneously with legitimate free will, is what it is. Such a concept reduces free will to a state of irrationality. The simultaneous existence of free will existing as free will even though the actions are pre-known is to be accepted as free will because Boethius has decided that such a state of existence is a primary theorem. As we can see from the previous quotes, Boethius tells us such a basic premise is to be accepted as a non-debatable theorem. Why is it Boethius claims we must accept, without debate, such a theorem? We must accept such a theorem because the theorem resolves the paradox of free will existing simultaneously with divine foreknowledge.

Such a perception is proposed as an ironclad theorem of metaphysics because it establishes a means of creating a rational understanding of an irrational position. In essence, Boethius attempted to rationalize an irrational metaphysical position. We cannot completely fault Boethius. There is no denying that Aristotle's perception of the physical universe existing as 'the' system is a very tempting metaphysical system to embrace.

Aristotle established the scientific perception of there being 'a' singular location of existence. Aristotle established the scientific perception of there being 'a' location bound 'within' the physical, bound by the limits of the physical, confined by the limits of the physical. There is little doubt that such a metaphysical system is very difficult to refute since we can 'see'/observe this metaphysical system.

Only an observable system, a physical system, is 'provable' through observation/measurement, an action of the physical itself. Abstraction is not measurable. Abstraction itself is not observable. What is observable in terms of abstraction is the affect abstraction has upon the awareness found within the physical. Free will and determinism are not the action itself but rather intent, which initiates action found within the physical. This is what is meant by: Free will being confined within the same boundaries, as determinism.

Boethius' metaphysical system

Boethius' metaphysical system displays free will as being confined within the same boundaries as determinism.

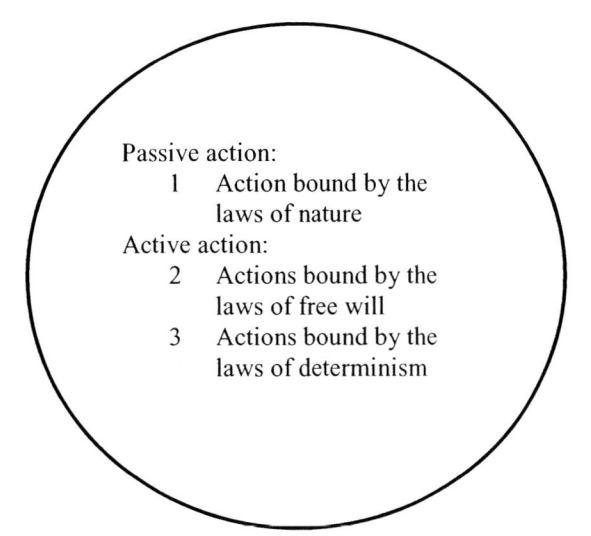

Passive action:
1   Action bound by the laws of nature

Active action:
2   Actions bound by the laws of free will
3   Actions bound by the laws of determinism

It is obvious from the metaphysical system diagramed that the three forms of action must be reconciled metaphysically in terms of their interrelationships 'within' such a system.

The War & Peace of a New Metaphysical Perception

To assist us in understanding the three forms of action we will examine the three forms of action through a series of diagrams:

Key:

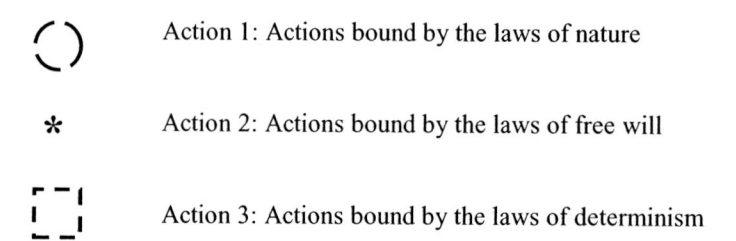

◯ Action 1: Actions bound by the laws of nature

* Action 2: Actions bound by the laws of free will

▭ Action 3: Actions bound by the laws of determinism

Boethius' metaphysical system placed all three forms of action 'within' the same container and shook up the three forms of action until they were completely emulsified. As such, the appearance of equality of action emerged. As with all emulsions, however, if one 'waits' long enough, the emulsion of action will eventually separate into layers of relative value.

Such a process would take on the following initial appearance:

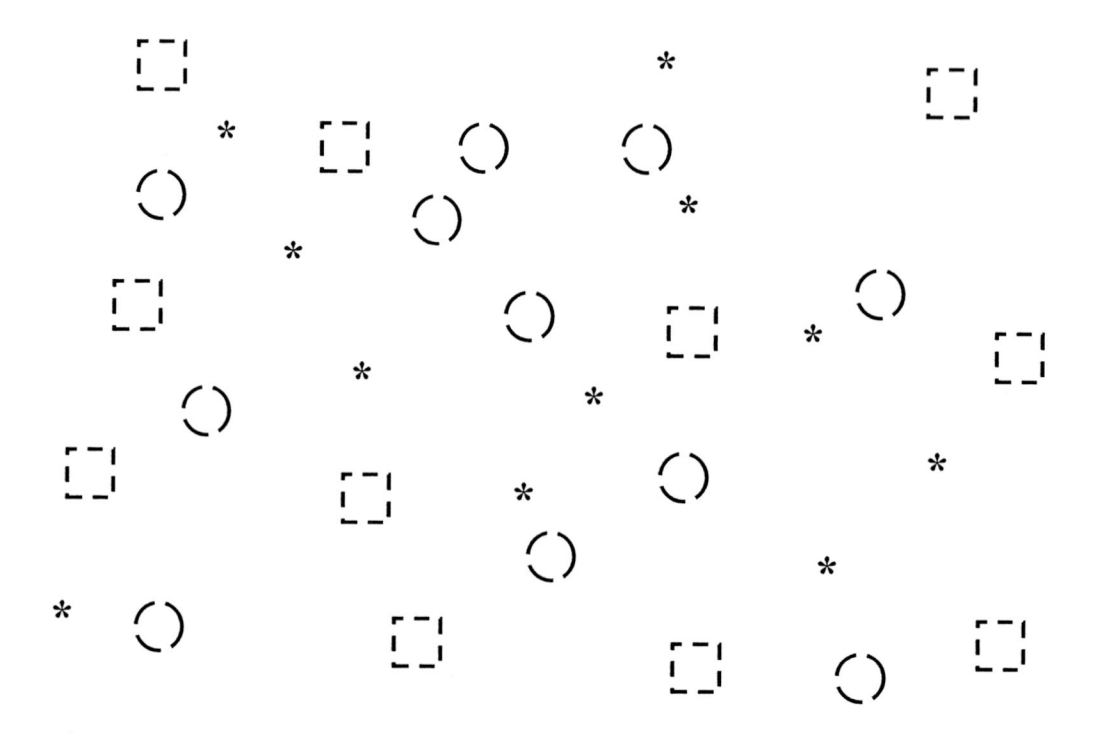

The Error of Boethius

This, over time, settles into its various layers of value and becomes:

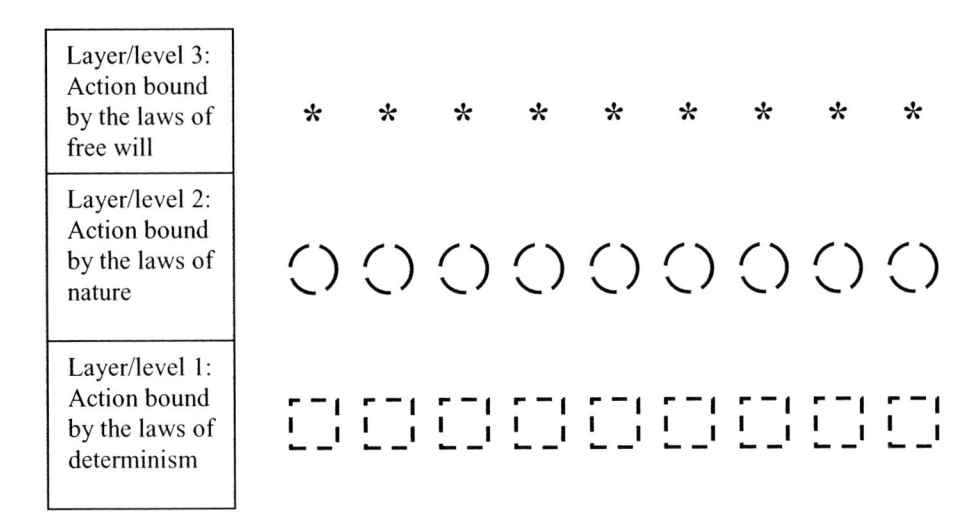

Layer/level 3: Action bound by the laws of free will	* * * * * * * * *
Layer/level 2: Action bound by the laws of nature	○ ○ ○ ○ ○ ○ ○ ○ ○
Layer/level 1: Action bound by the laws of determinism	▢ ▢ ▢ ▢ ▢ ▢ ▢ ▢ ▢

Within Boethius' metaphysical system, determinism becomes level one for without levels, two and three being predetermined by level one levels two and three could not exist. Level two, a location for level three, becomes level two for without level two level three has no 'place' to be and as such could not exist.

The graphic of Boethius' metaphysical system, when viewed from the point of perception regarding higher levels of value, higher levels of dominance of one over the other, becomes:

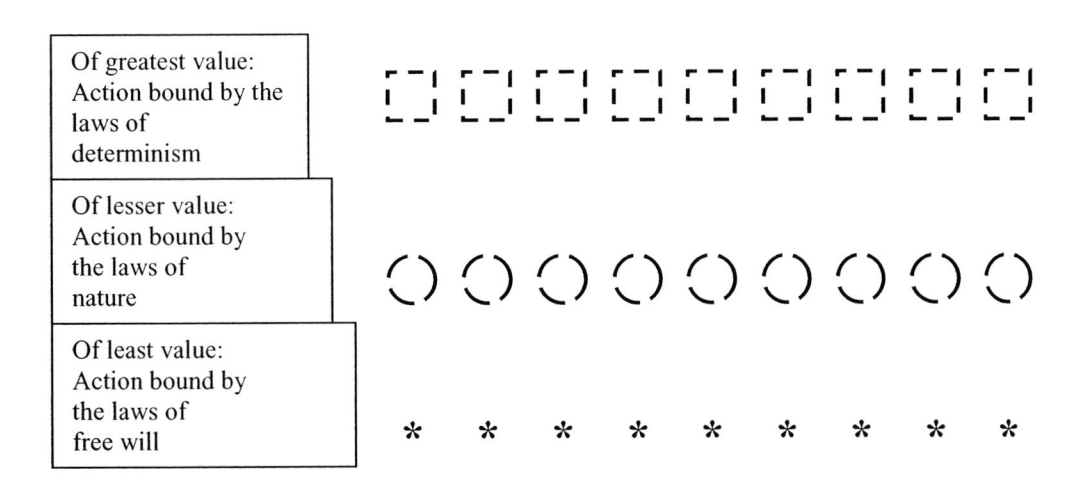

Of greatest value: Action bound by the laws of determinism	▢ ▢ ▢ ▢ ▢ ▢ ▢ ▢ ▢
Of lesser value: Action bound by the laws of nature	○ ○ ○ ○ ○ ○ ○ ○ ○
Of least value: Action bound by the laws of free will	* * * * * * * * *

This form of categorizing action provides the logic of accepting, as well as provides the means of understanding how it is determinism could exist 'within' a region of free will. This form of categorizing action provides an understanding as to how it is possible for one form of action, free will, to fall 'under' the influence of determinism through the action of determinism superceding

The War & Peace of a New Metaphysical Perception

free will. An example of just such a situation would be one forcefully holding the hand of another on a hot stove. This action supercedes the desired action of the victim and thus the concept of 'victim itself emerges.

Within Boethius' metaphysical system, what happens to the concept of 1st truth? First truth precedes the 'levels' generated by such a system:

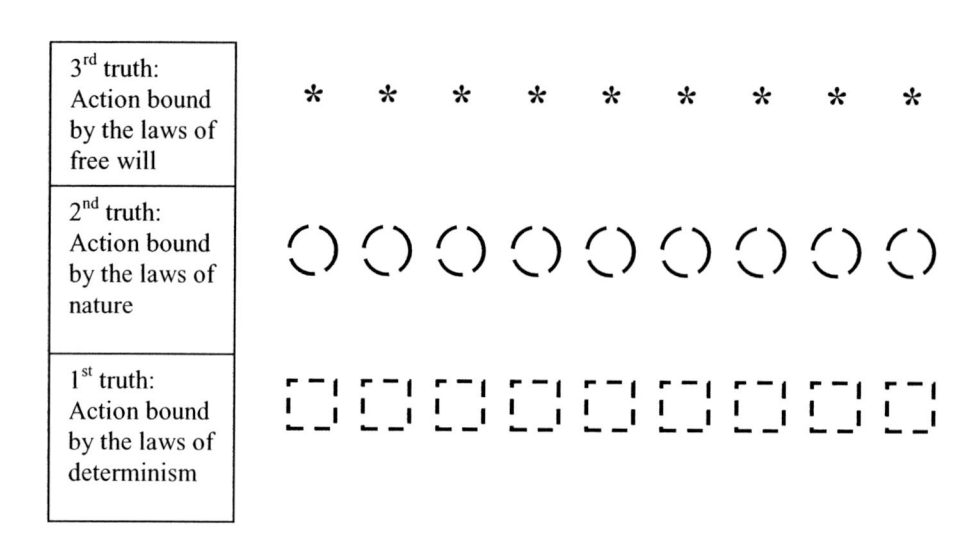

3rd truth: Action bound by the laws of free will	* * * * * * * * *
2nd truth: Action bound by the laws of nature	( ) ( ) ( ) ( ) ( ) ( ) ( ) ( ) ( )
1st truth: Action bound by the laws of determinism	[ ] [ ] [ ] [ ] [ ] [ ] [ ] [ ] [ ]

But, one may say: How could it be that first truth does not correlate to anything other than what Boethius suggests? Boethius used the metaphysical system Aristotle suggested: The physical is real and the physical is 'the' system. Isn't that in fact why 1st truth is called 1st truth? Doesn't the concept of there being 'a' single location of existence itself suggest there is 'a' singular 1st truth to which this system can be reduced?

As we shall see in the next few sections, the answer to both questions is 'Yes' if we apply Boethius' 'layers' of truth to the Aristotelian metaphysical system of 'a' location of existence being the universe itself, being physical existence itself.

As we shall see in Part II, the answer to both questions is 'No' if we apply an independent location for each form of action for there are not three 'locations' of existence equating to three forms of action but rather there are four locations independent of each other equating to four forms of action.

Boethius' metaphysical system and social acceptance

Boethius' metaphysical system appears to provide the understanding necessary regarding the paradox of omniscience and free will existing simultaneously. Boethius' system provides the rational explanation regarding the contradictory simultaneous existence of an 'all knowing' whole and men having 'control' of their lives. Boethius appears to provide an understanding regarding why men are responsible for their actions in the presence of divine foreknowledge.

However, does Boethius' metaphysical system really provide answers regarding the contradictory simultaneous existence of free will and divine foreknowledge – predestined results, or is Boethius' metaphysical system simply a system which attempts to do so while falling short of the mark?

Is there any other choice? Is there any other metaphysical system, which solves the paradox? Is there any metaphysical system which would remain standing once we applied Ockham's Razor to an alternative solution regarding 'free will' and divine foreknowledge, omniscience', existing simultaneously?

Presently there is no other alternative metaphysical system other than Aristotle's metaphysical system of there being only one location of existence. As such, even today, we still perceive Boethius' solution to be 'the' solution to the paradox of free will and divine foreknowledge existing simultaneously. Thus:

> 'There can be little question that Boethius, more than any other philosophic author, helped the great Schoolmen to retain a general comprehensive view of the world as a whole, in spite of the distractions of their minute inquiries.'[3]

remains the order of the day.

And so it is we continue to accept Boethius' solution:

> 'In the same way, human reason refuses to believe that divine intelligence can see the future in any other way except that in which human reason has knowledge.'…

Boethius' metaphysical system and perpetual historical acceptance

Historically we had little choice but to accept Boethius' metaphysical system for we had no 'place' else to place either 'free will' or 'determinism' or 'free will and determinism' for that matter.

Until we understand the concept of multiple locations of existence, we 'will' continued to accept Boethius' solution:

> 'In the same way, human reason refuses to believe that divine intelligence can see the future in any other way except that in which human reason has knowledge.'…

Boethius' metaphysical system and why it is we have not presently discarded

We presently have no choice but to accept Boethius' metaphysical argument regarding the contradictory simultaneous existence of free will and determinism existing 'within' the confines of a physical universe for the very confines of the physical is 'the' location Aristotle recognized as being 'existence', 'the' existence.

We remain 'boxed in'. We insist upon following the primary principle of science that if one cannot measure it, it has no validity in terms of 'existing'.[4] As such, we relegate faith and reason, two means we have of developing truth, understanding truth, to the level of being second-rate perceptual tools. Because we perceive faith and reason to be second-class perceptual tools, we submit to the perception of observation/science being 'the' only 'true' perceptual tool we have in our arsenal of perceptual weapons. We 'believe', have faith in, and we think it is 'rational',

The War & Peace of a New Metaphysical Perception

reasonable, that our understanding of the whole and of our, individualities' relationship to the whole is comprehensible only through what it is we 'see', what it is we can measure.

Where does this leave us in terms of our present perceptions regarding the contradictory simultaneous existence of the individual's free will and the whole's divine foreknowledge? It leaves us in the same state of confusion regarding the interrelationship of determinism and free will as we experienced over fifteen hundred years ago:

> 'In the same way, human reason refuses to believe that divine intelligence can see the future in any other way except that in which human reason has knowledge.'…

In short, we remain frustrated. We continue to fall back upon the argument: 'Get used to it, because that's just the way it is.'

Part II: Resolving the issue with a new metaphysical perception

The wall of perception

'It is not allowed to man to comprehend in thought all the ways of the divine work.'[5]

So it is our debates, regarding religion, begins. So it is our predisposition regarding ontological rationality emerges. All our debates regarding ontological, cosmological, and metaphysical discussions begin with a conscious or subconscious foundation that: 'It is not allowed to man to comprehend in thought all the ways of the divine work.'

This is no way to begin a discussion regarding the concept of 1st truth. This is no way to begin a discussion of 1st principle. Who would dispute the concept that we 'cannot 'know' truth to be 'truth'. However, just as surely as no one would deny we may not be able to 'know' truth to be truth, no one would profess we are incapable of defining 1st truth, 1st principle, as best we can. Having defined 1st truth, we are then capable of proceeding with the dialectic regarding the defined truth and the impact such a defined truth has upon ourselves, our universe, and the whole.

Without the acknowledgement of our being able to define 'truth' as best we can and moving on from that point, all science collapses. Without the acknowledgement of our being able to define 'truth' as best we can and moving on from there, all faiths evaporate. Without the acknowledgement of our being able to define 'truth' as best we can and moving on with life itself, all reason becomes sheer irrationality itself.

Time after time our religious, scientific, and philosophical opinions fall back upon the ultimate point of view we throw in the path of arguments persistently eroding away at our bastions of reason, faith, and observation: 'It is not allowed to man to comprehend in thought all the ways of the divine work.'

If we have in fact reached the limits of metaphysical philosophical arguments, it is not because there is no infinitely expansive realm of metaphysics left to be explored. If a metaphysical limit has been reached it is because we have defined the further limits of metaphysics to be nonexistent through the proclamation that: 'It is not allowed to man to comprehend in thought all the ways of the divine work.'

Boethius' words: 'It is not allowed to man to comprehend in thought all the ways of the divine work.' Are repeated over and over because they themselves are the words describing the barrier which keeps us separated from the great expanse of creativity regarding our further understanding the interactions and interrelationships between 'being'/individuality, being/action, process – reality, and 'Being'/the whole.

As such, within this tractate, within this work, we are going to reject the concept of: 'It is not allowed to man to comprehend in thought all the ways of the divine work.' while at the same time accepting its basic premise. This may sound contradictory but it is not. In essence, what we are going to do is accept that while the statement, '…man may not be able to comprehend in thought 'all' the ways of divine work.', we are going to presume that any questions man is capable of initiating, man is capable of resolving. The only limits man is incapable of understanding are limits man is incapable of defining.

This is an exciting principle. It is the very principle that establishes as well as accepts humanity's purpose in terms of leaning and humanity's purpose in terms of gaining knowledge will never come to an end as long as 'the' universe exists. Such a principle establishes: If one loves the pursuit of knowledge, as it appears our specie does, then one need never agonize as regards potentially approaching the end of the learning process.

With this in mind, we have little choice but to accept the concept that free will may in fact exist independent of determinism and vice versa, determinism may in fact exist independent of free will. In fact, we may have little choice but to accept the fact that both statements exist as 'truths' simultaneously.

How can we make such a statement when it appears we have apparently rejected just such a statement through our initial rejection of Boethius' metaphysical perception regarding the simultaneous existence of free will and divine foreknowledge?

The very perception of the simultaneous existence of:

       1. Free will existing independent of determinism
                  while
       2. Determinism exists independent of free will

is where the essence of this tractate lies. How can this be the essence of this tractate if the point of this tractate is to dismantle the issue of determinism and free will existing simultaneously as Boethius professes them to be? It is not the concept regarding the very existence of free will, divine foreknowledge, and the universe, which are being questioned. Rather what is being questioned, is the limited confinement itself, the limits we place upon such concepts that are being challenged within this tractate.

Boethius asserted that we can create a solution regarding the two concepts: free will and determinism, through the process of mixing the two. Try as we might over the last 1500 years, we have been unable to create a 'solution' regarding the two. We have only been able to create a mixture of the two.

A true solution of free will and determinism would create a system where each is independent of the other yet a system where each is dependent upon what the other has to offer. More contradictions? The statement is only a contradiction if one retains our present philosophical orientation of being 'enclosed' within 'a' system rather than being 'enclosed' within a system, which finds itself in turn enclosed within a system.

We have a perception regarding a metaphysical system in place. One aspect of the perception we have in place was alluded to via Zeno. Aristotle identified a second aspect of the perception. Boethius then began the process of introducing a contradictory perception, which confused the issue regarding the simultaneous existence of free will and determinism. Boethius embraces Zeno's self-stated assertions of uncertainty as well as Aristotle's arguments regarding the universe being the only 'location' of the action.

In order to embrace both Zeno and Aristotle, Boethius strongly suggests that free will and 'divine foreknowledge' are compatible in the form of adjacent actions of multiplicity found 'within' a region of multiplicity itself.

The complexity of such a statement requires the application of Ockham's razor in order to reduce the statement to a more intelligible form. If the statement is unintelligible as it is, why make the statement in the first place? The statement is made because it accurately represents where we as philosophers presently find ourselves. Boethius led us into such depths of confusion. Boethius led us into the blind alley. However, can we really lay the blame upon Boethius for our being mired in the perpetual cyclical argument:.

'It is not allowed to man to comprehend in thought all the ways of the divine work.'

We cannot, in good conscious, 'blame' Boethius for our previous inability to break out of the catch 22 within which we find our present metaphysical thought

We, you and I and you and I together, willingly, through the process of free will, accept Boethius' presumptions. We embrace such a perception under the assumption that we are limited creatures not just in terms time but also in terms of timelessness itself. We embrace such a perception in the name of being humble before the majestic awesome presence of an 'all knowing' entity.

False modesty leads to the entrapment of the mind within the confines of prison walls impossible to break through. The only way we have of breaking through our self-created wall of confinement is to break down the wall of humility we have built around ourselves. Boethius may have built the wall of limits within which we find ourselves entrapped, but we are the ones who have passively accepted their perceived impenetrability.

To free ourselves of these prison walls, we must rely upon ourselves. The method of breaking through this wall of perception is to replace the perception itself with a new perception.

Having said this, let's begin an examination of 'the wall'

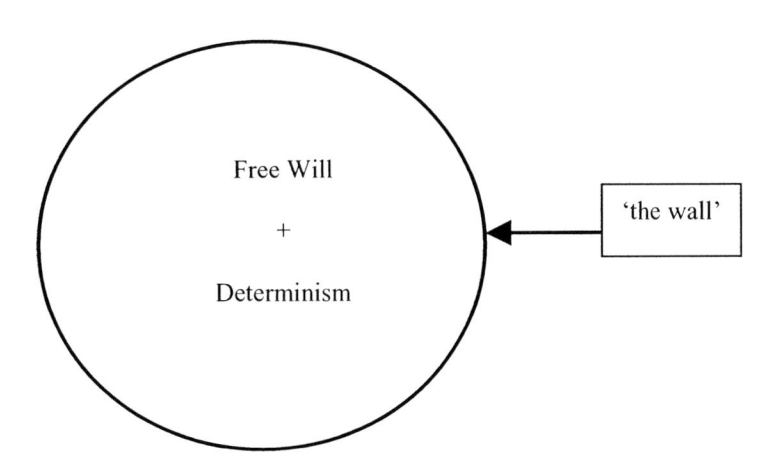

We perceive free will and determinism to coexist not as a mixture but as a solution in and of itself. Try as we might, oil and water do not naturally create a solution. They are incompatible and that is just the point. Free will and determinism do not create a solution and as such, we cannot comprehend an alternative potential solution unless we are willing to remove the walls of Aristotle and begin looking for a different perception regarding how to incorporate the two, free will and determinism, into a different metaphysical model than the one Boethius suggested.

Boethius asserted the two, determinism – 'divine foreknowledge' as he puts it, and free will exist side by side, exist as companions forever tied to the very substantive travels of all individuals be they human or other forms of existence which have the distinctive mark of free will stamped upon their brows.

The only means we have of throwing off the yoke of determinism is through a new means of perception regarding just where it is we perceive ourselves to be. Such a perception would have

The War & Peace of a New Metaphysical Perception

the effect of allowing ourselves to redefine what it is we understand ourselves to be. Such a redefinition would have the impact of allowing us to establish an understanding of just why it is we may exist as individuals and why it is we may exist as the sole remaining member of the specie, Homo sapiens.

It is possible to model an understanding demonstrating how pure free will can exist uncompromised by 'divine foreknowledge'. In the process of building such an understanding, we will establish a model where free will and determinism may not only be independent of each other but may simultaneously be interdependent of each other's existence. The final result: We will see how it is metaphysics is alive rather than being 'dead' as we presently 'believe'.

Even more excitingly, we will begin to gain an insight as to how it is metaphysics retains an ever-moving horizon, which may well extend infinitely beyond our reach just as finality to the extent of knowledge itself may extend infinitely beyond our reach.

This tractate, however, is not the tractate within which this last statement will be specifically examined. The detailed examination of such a statement will have to wait for tractate 18: The End of the Beginning. For the time being, we must stay on track and return to our understanding regarding a new solution to the long-standing paradox regarding the simultaneous presence of free will and divine foreknowledge.

Rationalizing the irrational

'I must be right because you don't 'know' that what you are telling me is an absolute.'

What is this argument that because we have perceptual limitations, there are things we cannot 'know' and therefore it must be accurate to assume 'divine foreknowledge' exists yet 'divine foreknowledge' is not determinism.

Is a metaphysical system, which embraces the simultaneous existence of free will and determinism co-existing in the form of adjacent actions of multiplicity, found 'within' a region of multiplicity itself, a logical point of metaphysical perception? In terms of a metaphysical system of the past, yes it is. In terms of the new knowledge we have gleaned over the last millennium and a half, no it isn't.

It is time to update our perception of rational metaphysical perceptions. In order to do so, lets examine a new metaphysical system to understand just how free will and determinism may coexist without contradicting one another as is the case with Boethius' metaphysical system.

The limits of language

We live 'within' the limits of what it is we are able to communicate to each other. We live 'within' this thing we call language. The implication is we will never 'know' truth.

Regardless of whether or not one agrees with such a statement, one cannot ignore the fact that we are confined by language. Likewise it must be remembered that we are immersed 'within language and thus must either find a means to break out of the limits language places upon us or we must expand language to meet our expanded perceptions.

We presently embrace concepts such as:

> Free will has been predetermined yet predestined acts remain acts of free will.
> Predestined free will is free will.
> Free will immersed within divine foreknowledge is free will

We accept such contradictions because we 'believe'

> 'In the same way, human reason refuses to believe that divine intelligence can see the future in any other way except that in which human reason has knowledge.'...

We hide behind the perception that it is 'too difficult' a paradox to understand the whole and as such we submit to arguments that we should not 'waste' our energies upon such impossible tasks as understanding the relationship between free will and determinism.

Until we refuse to end our actions of hiding behind the conceptual perception that it is too complicated to revise language so as to elevate language to the level capable of describing advanced metaphysical perceptions, we will never understand how it is:

> Free will that has been predetermined is not free will.
> Predestined free will is not free will.
> Free will immersed within 'divine' foreknowledge might very well be free will

It is understandable why we hesitate to release the concept of determinism and begin to embrace the full ramifications of free will. Free will places a yoke of responsibility upon each and every one of us. Determinism, on the other hand:

1. Provides the rational for our not being responsible for our actions
2. Accepts our actions as a matter of fact, actions which we cannot avoid
3. Excuses our need to take responsibility for our action

Who would be so irrational as to accept one's responsibility for one's own action when there is a way to avoid such responsibility? That may be a fair statement, but to ignore 'what is' in favor of 'what is not' does not nullify 'what is' being 'what is'.

Should we be afraid of exploring a rational understanding of the whole and our relationship to the whole? Perhaps, on the other hand, perhaps Churchill provided some insightful perspective we can apply to such a situation when he said: 'We have nothing to fear but fear itself.'

Oil and Water

Free will and determinism are like oil and water – you cannot put them together and obtain a solution. You may put them together but what you obtain is simply a mixture.

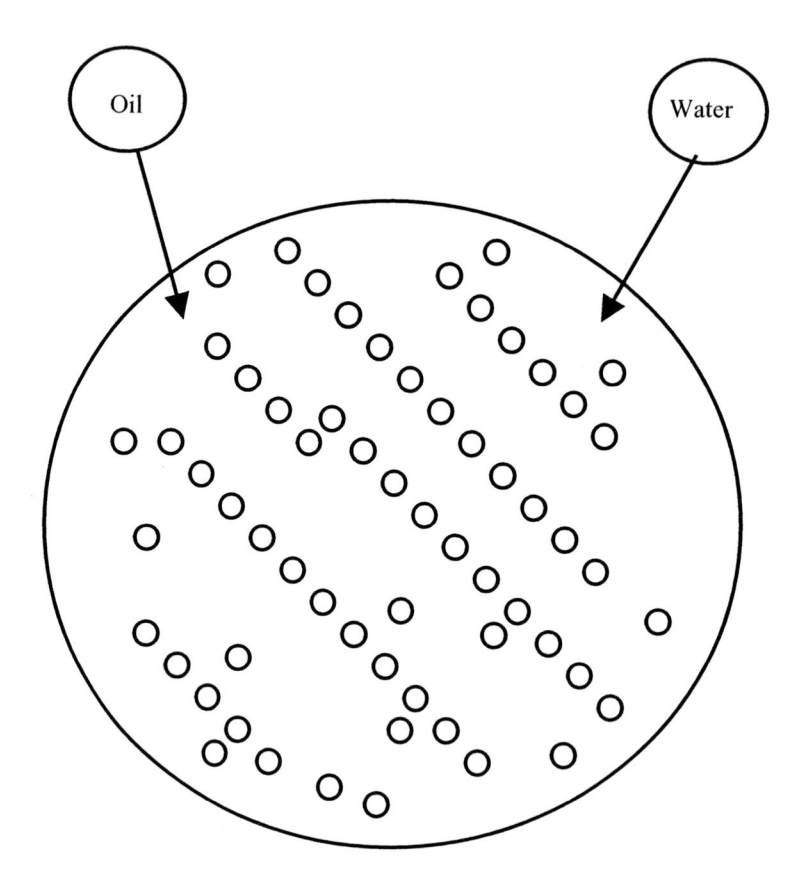

So, which is the water and which is the oil? Is free will oil or water? Is determinism oil or water? If one is oil is the other water?

When one performs the operation of mixing oil and water one obtains oil being contained within water unless one factors in the container itself. If one factors in the container itself, one may obtain a layer of oil coating the inside of the container within which water is found to contain the droplets of oil. This is not to be ignored for the analogy itself exists. For the time being however, we have little choice but to ignore this aspect of the analogy and move on with our discussion. The more complex analogy will be addressed later.

As such, lets examine the two possibilities:

The Error of Boethius

Possibility 1:

Oil/free will
Water/determinism

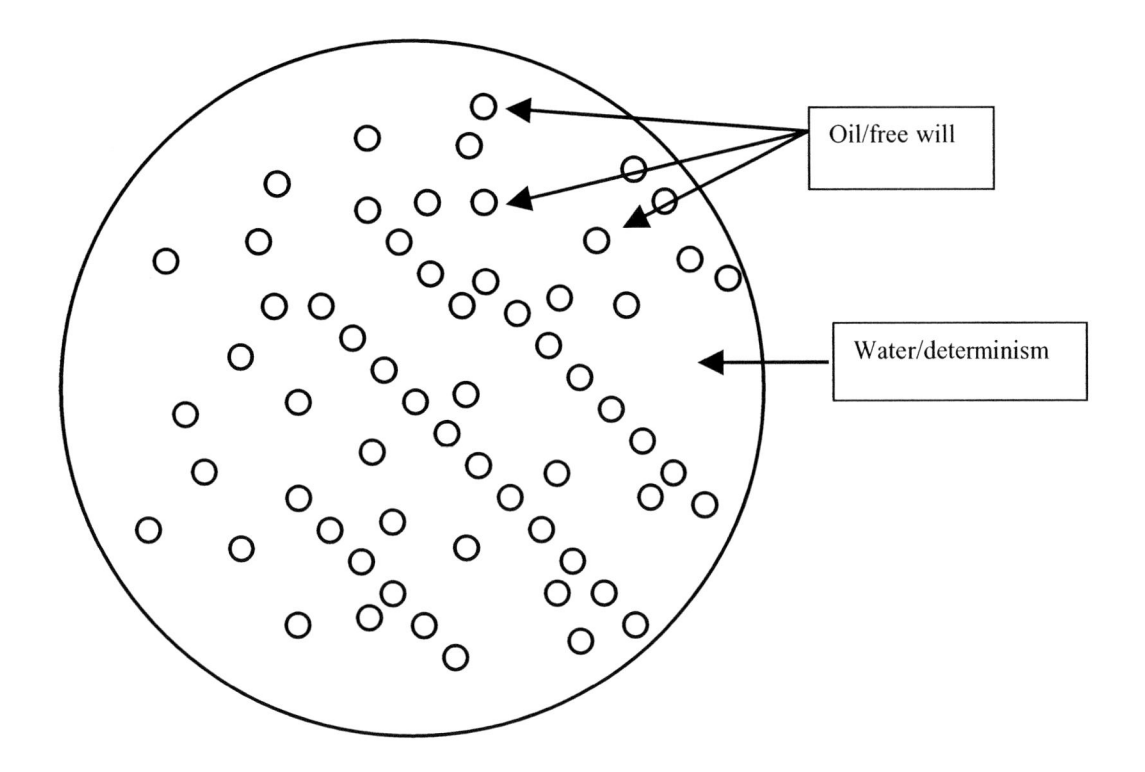

Possibility 2:

Oil/determinism
Water/free will

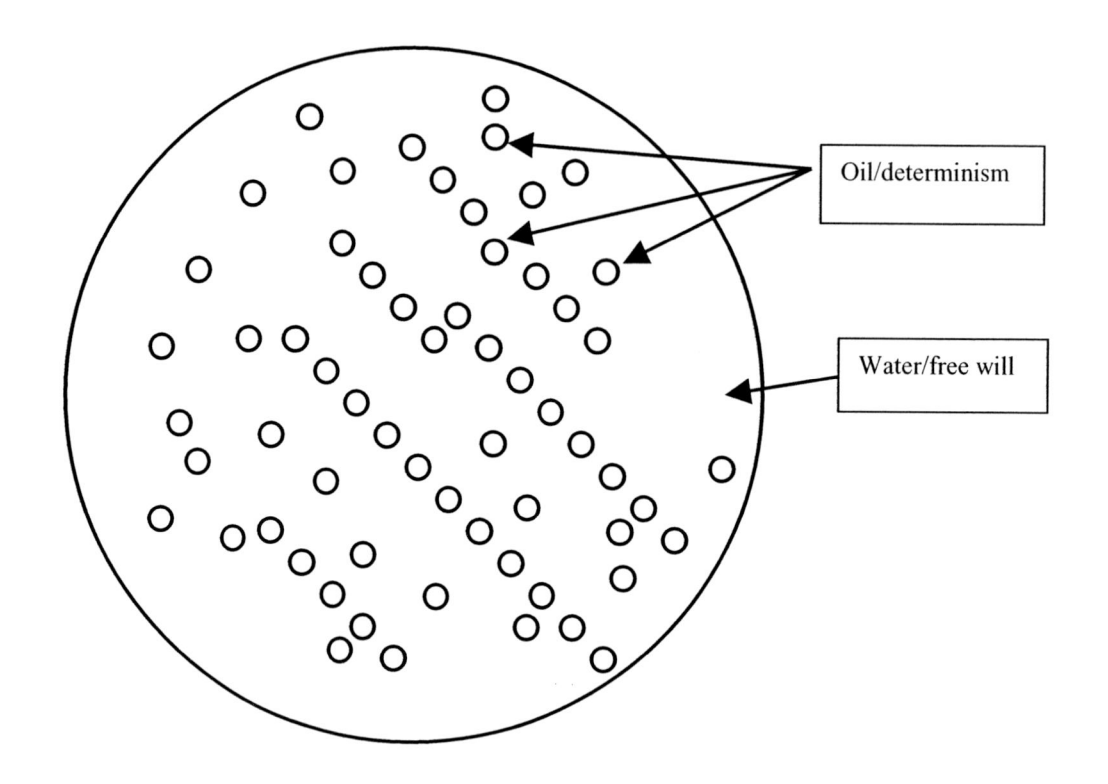

Possibility #1 suggests free will is found immersed 'within determinism. Possibility # 2 suggests determinism is found immersed 'within' free will. Which is the 'correct' perspective?

Let's examine the two possibilities and see where it gets us. As we do so, lets change the shape of the container for the purposes of making them more user friendly:

The Error of Boethius

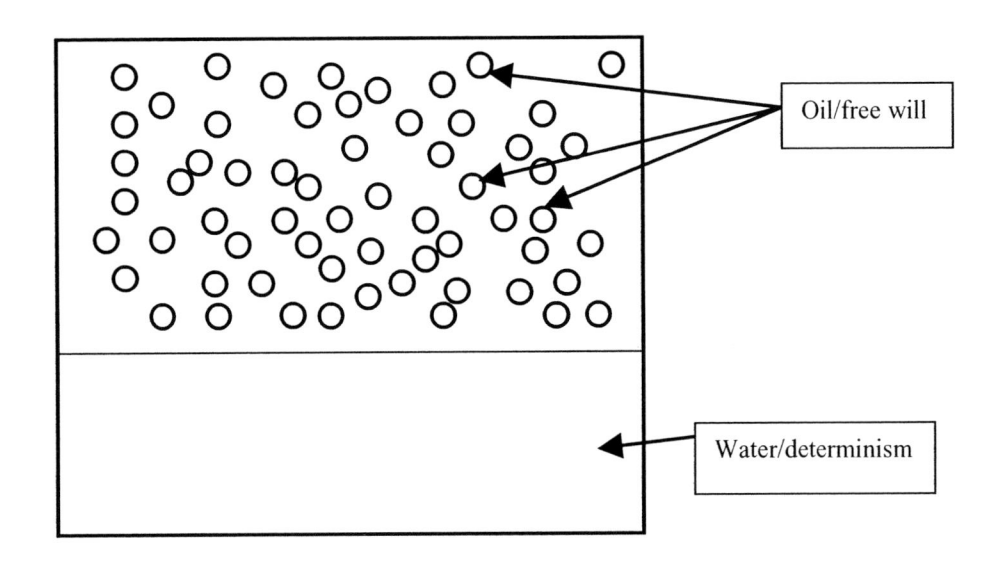

Possibility 1:

Oil/free will
Water/determinism

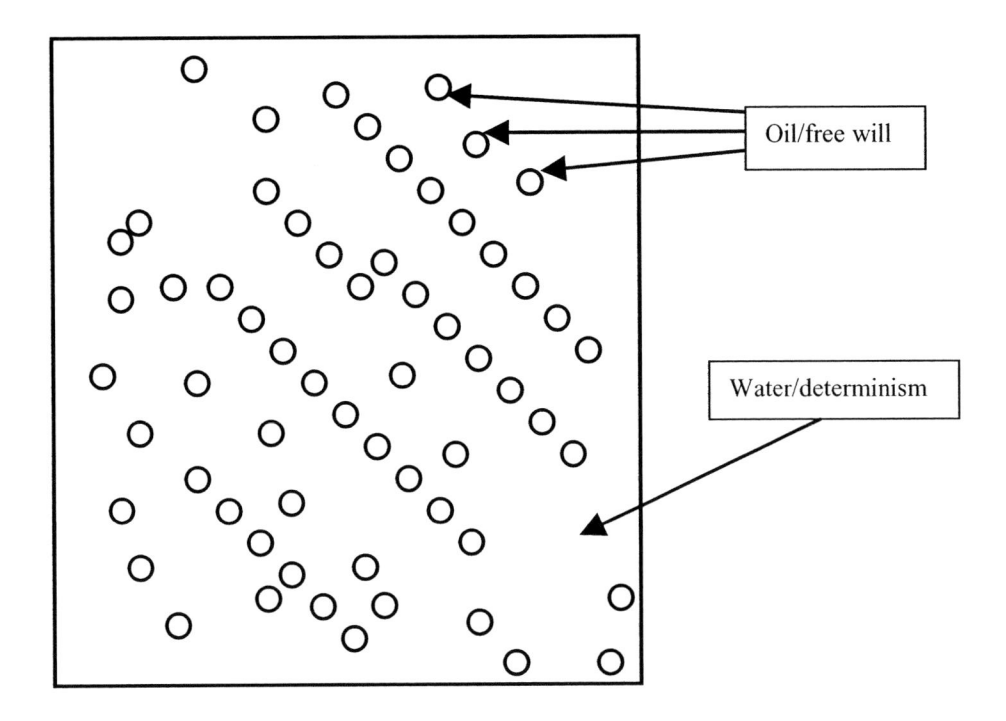

becomes:

Oil/free will
Water/determinism

The War & Peace of a New Metaphysical Perception

Possibility 2:

Oil/free will
Water/determinism

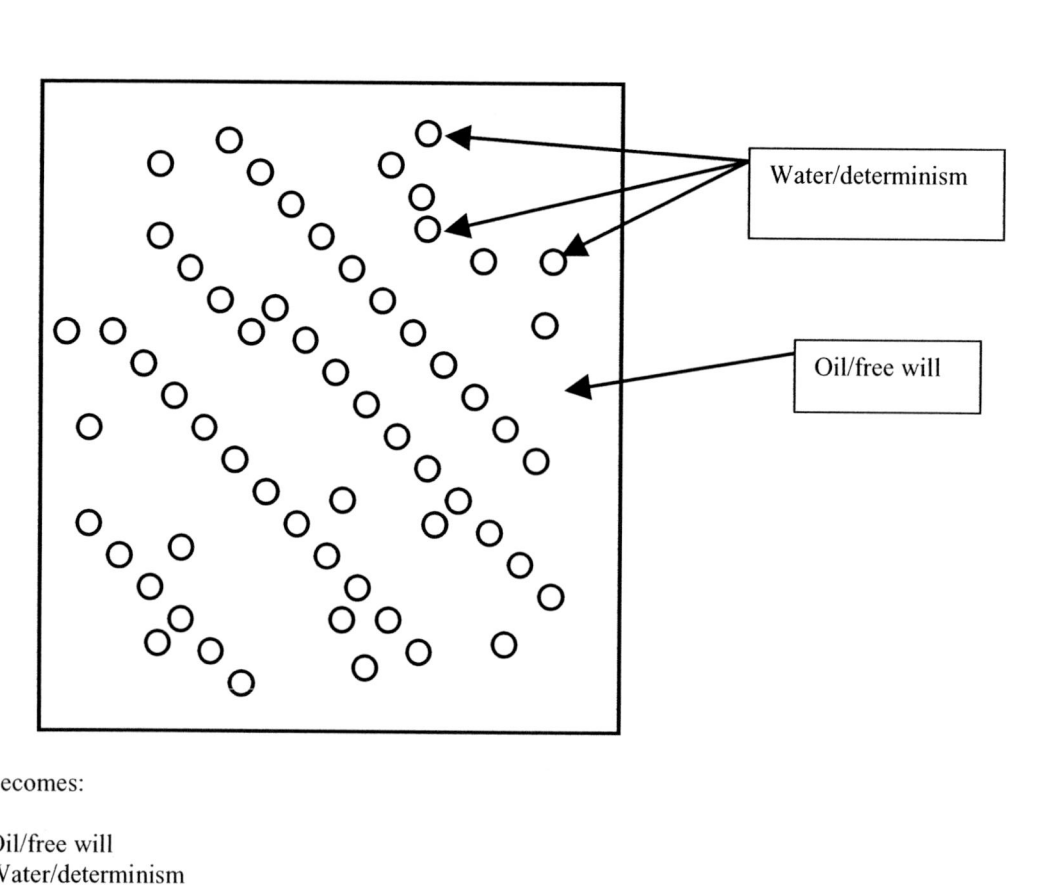

becomes:

Oil/free will
Water/determinism

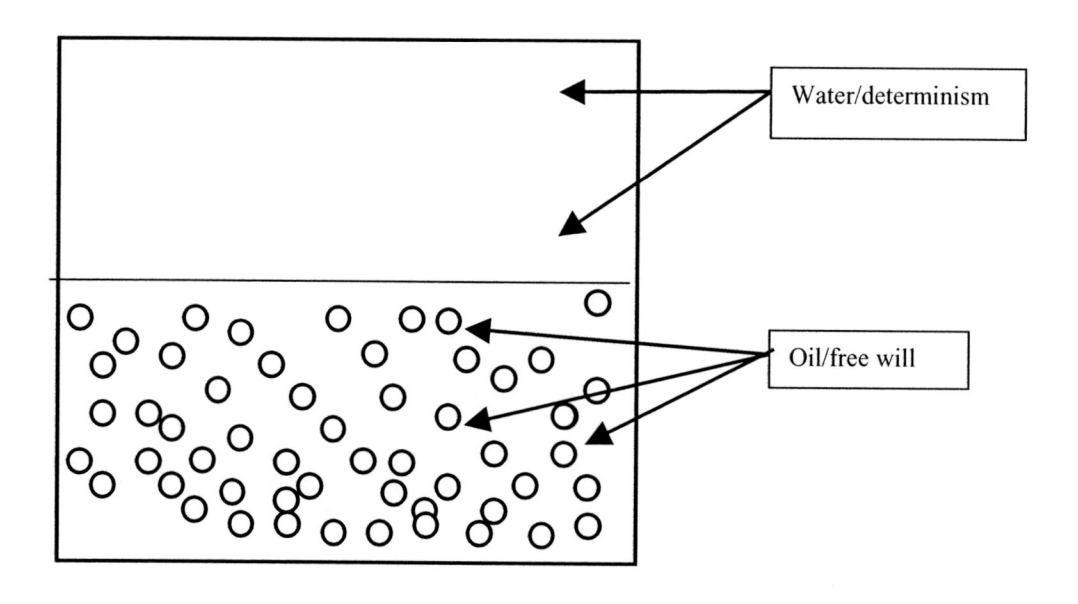

Now one will object to possibility #2 due to the general perception that oil is less dense than water. The objection evaporates, however, when one acknowledges that it is not oil and water we are examining but free will and determinism. Neither free will nor determinism can be measured in terms of density but the two are recognized as incompatible and thus the only rational we have been able to apply to our understanding regarding the existence of both existing simultaneously lies in Boethius' argument that the two can coexist if we accept:

>...'Therefore, all those things which happen without happening of necessity are, before they happen, future events about to happen, but not about to happen of necessity. For just as the knowledge of present things imposes no necessity on what is happening, so foreknowledge imposes no necessity on what is going to happen.
>
>'The cause of this mistake is that people think that the totality of their knowledge depends on the nature and capacity to be known of the objects of knowledge. But this is all wrong.'...
>
>'The point of greatest importance here is this: the superior manner of knowledge includes the inferior, but it is quite impossible for the inferior to rise to the superior.'...
>
>'In the same way, human reason refuses to believe that divine intelligence can see the future in any other way except that in which human reason has knowledge.'...

Boethius argues we must accept what we cannot possible understand as being what it is men say it is. Boethius argues we must accept our limits and stop trying to gain an understanding since we will never be able to understand. Boethius implies we have the ability to outline the problem but not the ability to understand the solution.

So it is we have remained mired in the lack of understanding.

Boethius states that free will finds itself subordinate to determinism, finds itself subordinate to divine foreknowledge yet remains free will and we must accept this in spite of the contradictory position such a statement forces us to assume.

In spite of the historic acceptance of such a position, the question remains: Is 'free will' free or is free will subordinate to determinism? The true existence of free will as opposed to the subordination of free will to determinism is what we must rationally examine and examine in detail.

The analogy of oil and water lies at the heart of the debate regarding: a) the independent – oil above water, b) the independent – an oil and water emulsion, or c) the interdependence - simultaneous existence of free will and determinism existing as a solution.

Why all the concern regarding the two simple concepts of free will and determinism? If our actions are 'controlled' by the forces of determinism, we, each one of us, is 'controlled'. If our actions are 'controlled' by a 'higher' force - we are controlled. If our actions are controlled by ourselves – we are free. 'Being's' puppets or 'being free' that is the issue.

This dialectic does not immerse itself only within past arguments, but rather this dialectic suggests a new solution to the debate. This dialectic suggests we reexamine the paradox from a new metaphysical perception. The new metaphysical perception is known:

    a. Metaphysically as 'being' *being* 'Being'
    b. Generically as 'symbiotic panentheism'

Let's begin to examine a new solution to this age old question regarding the simultaneous independent existence of free will and determinism by dividing action into four categories found 'within' this thing we call existence.

The four forms of action:

Four forms of action:

    Passive action:

1. Action as a state of being:

   The passive action of being is action in the form of the primal state of existence as opposed to other forms of action emerging from the primal state of existence

2. Actions bound by the laws of nature

   Actions bound by the laws of nature are passive actions taken by inanimate objects as well as actions that simulate the action of inanimate objects – a rock falls, you fall, a rock exists, you exist

    Active action:

3. Free will

   Active actions of free will are actions taken by a 'knowing' object, action which could go various ways and whose action was directed by the 'knowing' object of it own accord.

4. Determinism

   Active actions of free will taken by a 'knowing' object whose intended actions have been overridden by actions of free will generated by a dominating second 'knowing' object

This form of categorizing action provides the logic of accepting, as well as provides the means of understanding how determinism could exist 'within' a region of free will. This form of categorizing action provides an understanding how free will can fall under the influence of determinism through the action of determinism superceding free will. An example of just such a situation would be one forcefully holding the hand of another on a hot stove. The action of holding someone's hand in the fire supercedes the desired action of the victim to remove their hand and thus the concept of 'victim itself emerges.

Passive action:

1. The state of being: What 'is'

   The state of being is a form of action requiring no 'knowing'. The state of being is:

       a. The most basic form of action.
       b. The most elementary form of all forms of action.
       c. The primal state of existence.

All other forms of action emerge from this most basic form of action.

Examples of states of being: I exist. A rock exists.

2. Actions bound by the laws of nature: What 'is being'

Actions bound by the laws of nature are action requiring no 'knowing'. Since these actions require no 'knowing' they are classified as forms of passive actions. These are actions taken by inanimate objects. Such actions also include the actions of animate entities that simulate the action of inanimate objects.

Examples of actions bound by the laws of nature: When dropped from a cliff, a rock falls. When dropped from a cliff, you fall.

Active action:

3. Actions bound by the laws of free will: What 'will be'

Actions bound by the laws of free will are 'knowing' actions taken by a 'knowing' entity and are independent of the laws of nature and independent of the laws of determinism. These actions are actions directed by the 'knowing' entity.

Examples of actions bound by the laws of free will are: I will step off the cliff.

4. Actions bound by the laws of determinism: What 'has been'

Actions bound by the laws of determinism are active 'knowing' actions taken by a 'knowing' object and are independent of the laws of nature. These actions are actions taken by a 'knowing' entity whose intended actions have been over-ridden by actions of free will generated by a dominating second 'knowing' entity.

Examples of actions bound by the laws of determinism are: I am, against my will, pushed off the cliff by an entity itself bound by the laws of free will.

Having classified action in this manner, it is now possible to find a unique location for these four forms of action. The process of 'finding' a unique location for the four forms of action, provides us the means of examining the unique function of each action to the whole.

The unique location of:

1. What 'will be': A location for 'being' – individuality
2. What 'is being': A location for *being* – action, process/reality – the universe
3. What 'has been': A location for 'Being' – the whole
4. What 'is': A location for being – existence of existence

The order listed is different from the order originally listed. There is a reason for this. The order was intentionally reordered to emphasize the concept:

The individual value related to the four action forms have no relative greater significance or lesser significance to the metaphysical system within which they are found. The metaphysical system within which the four actions forms are found could not be 'the' unique metaphysical system it is if any of the four forms of action were to be eliminated. The value of each form of action is not a value of relativeness but rather the value of each

The War & Peace of a New Metaphysical Perception

of the four action forms have not only equal value for its own self but have equal value for each of the remaining three.

It must be emphasized repeatedly that the order is unimportant due to the lack of relative value existing within the system itself. What is important is the existence the four action forms. Without the existence of any of the four action forms, the system of 'being' *being* 'Being' becomes something it is not, which is a dynamic system.

What 'will be':   Free will - A location for 'being' – individuality

A location for Free Will: The existence of 'the potential to be'
A location of: What 'will be'

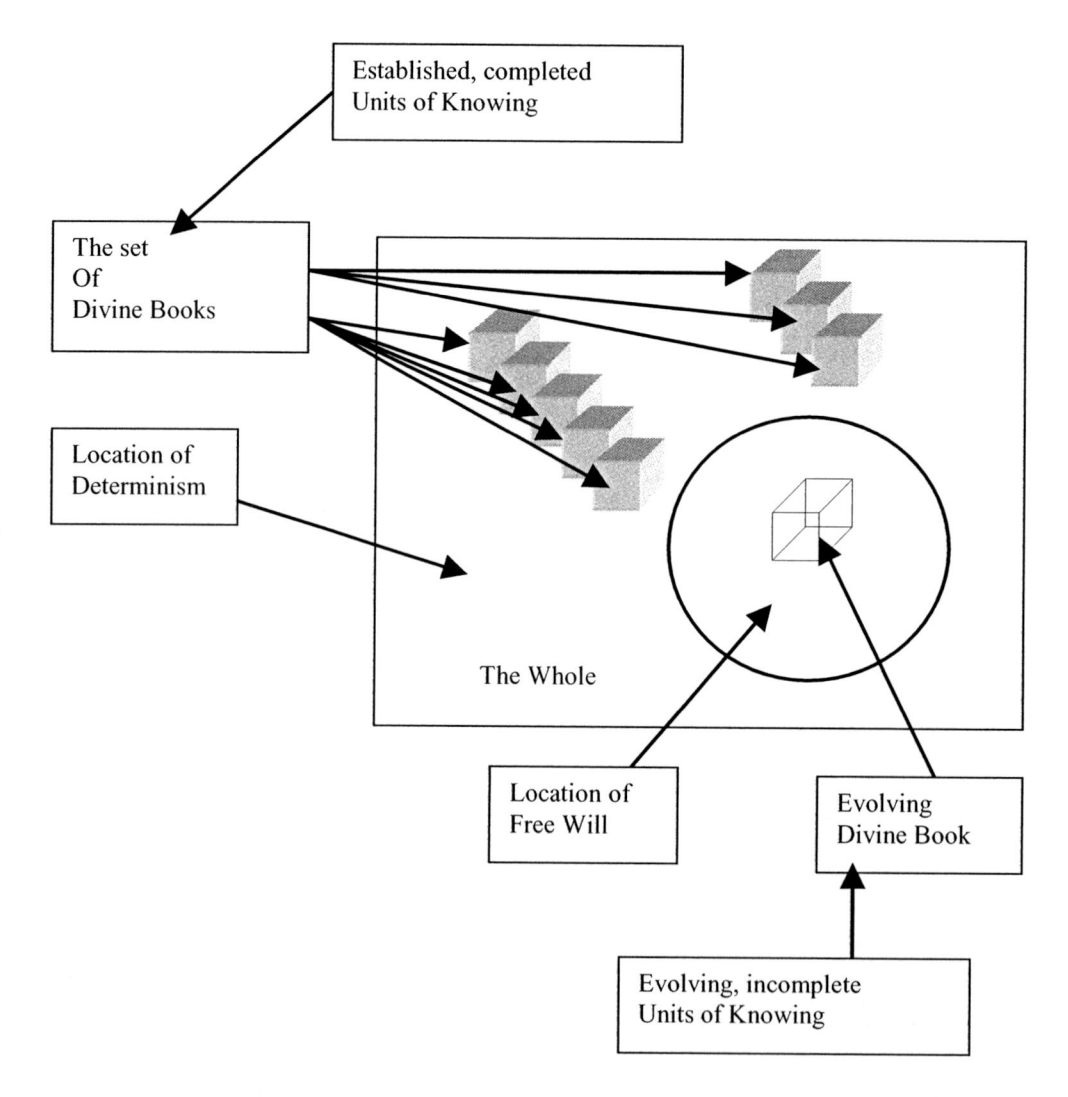

[Diagram with the following labeled elements:
- Established, completed Units of Knowing
- The set Of Divine Books
- Location of Determinism
- The Whole
- Location of Free Will
- Evolving Divine Book
- Evolving, incomplete Units of Knowing]

The 'location' of free will is a location where 'knowing' develops. The location of free will is itself a process. The location of free will, the 'location' of the process of what will be, provides the 'location' for the development of 'becoming'. As such, under free will, 'becoming' develops itself

The Error of Boethius

as a unique point of knowledge. It may even be possible that this 'location', the 'location' for the action of pure free will, itself grows as the entities of knowing gain a more in depth understanding of the 'location' itself. In essence, the very growth of knowledge, the very growth of the 'location' where 'becoming' becomes, may influence further development of that very location.

Such a statement strongly implies: Complex abstractual perceptions developed through 'knowing' evolving 'within' a location where free will exists, may lend themselves to shifts of the location itself which in turn could conceivable alter the very perceptual potential of its very 'occupants'. This could lead to an infinite number of qualitative and quantitative variations of evolution of the location of free will, thus expanding the 'location of free will's' very ability to influence the development of new units of knowing.

As complex as this may all appear, the simple point remains: It becomes obvious why 'location' becomes a necessary component of a metaphysical system such as 'symbiotic panentheism.' The whole has the characteristic of not only *being* but the whole is dependent upon the existence of free will to 'produce', evolve, establish unique units of knowing which expand the very knowing of the whole.

The reason determinism, as an aspect of the whole, is found 'outside' free will is because the knowledge, which has been established, the knowledge, which 'is', is. Each unit of knowing is a part of the whole. Each unit of 'knowing' can be 'examined' as infinite variations of partial units of itself, yet each unit of knowing can be 'examined' as a whole unit in and of itself found within the greater Whole.

Since there is a seemingly endless, infinite number of units of 'knowing', units of knowledge, units of perceptions gained through the process of acquiring knowledge while evolving within a location for free will, there emerges a sense of omniscience of the whole. In fact, there would be what one would call omniscience of the whole.

The question then becomes: Does free will exist as a part of the whole? Within a metaphysical system of 'being' *being* 'Being', free will does exist as a part of the whole for there is a location of free will located 'within', and therefore is a part of, the whole.

The question then becomes refined: Does free will exist as a part of the whole void the 'locations' of free will? In essence the question becomes: Does the whole as itself have free will?

Well now, this is a question, which goes to the understanding of the whole as the whole as opposed to the interrelationship of individual units of knowing and the whole. This is a question philosophy has never asked before because philosophy did not understand the concept of the whole having its own knowing separate from its knowing as the sum of individual packets of knowing which was thought to equal the whole. It was never considered how it was possible for the whole to be greater than the sum of its parts.

So again: Does the whole have free will other than that found within the physical universe within which knowing itself grows?

The question leads us back to the concept: Which came first, the chicken or the egg?

In terms of the whole: Could the whole have developed free will as a mechanism of growth or did the whole exist initially as the whole whose primal characteristics included the innate characteristic of free will? Alternatively, did the whole become the whole because it in fact used its preexisting free will to develop itself in the manner with which it does so?

This is not a typical question asked of metaphysics. Rather the question is a more theoretical problem requiring a theoretical solution. In essence, metaphysics, with the aid of these tractates, is becoming specialized into a field of theoretical metaphysics as opposed to the more practical metaphysics we find within our perception regarding reality of the physical universe, as we perceive it today. Again, another field of metaphysics arises, practical metaphysics. Once we begin to ask the more theoretical question we find ourselves being able to do so only 'after' we have accepted the more basic premises of metaphysics. The very acceptance of basic metaphysics premises produces what we call Practical Metaphysics. And with the establishment of practical metaphysics comes a natural out cropping, Metaphysical Engineering, the process of shaping society based upon what our most acceptable metaphysical system implies. The emergence of Metaphysical Engineering suggests Plato may have been more correct than he ever dreamed when he stated: It is the philosopher who should head government.

What is: Divine foreknowledge - A location for 'Being' – the whole

A location for divine foreknowledge: the existence of 'what is'
A location of: What 'has been'

Near the beginning of the book: Boethius: The Consolation of Philosophy, Penguin Classics, 1969, one finds the statement:

> 'It is not allowed to man to comprehend in thought all the ways of the divine work.'
> (Boethius: The Consolation of Philosophy, IV, 6)

Boethius then ends his work with the statement:

> 'What does it matter, then, if they are not necessary, when because of the condition of divine foreknowledge it will turn out exactly as if they were necessary? The answer is this. It is impossible for the two events I mentioned just now – the rising of the sun and the man walking – not to be happening when they do happen: and yet it was necessary for one of them to happen before it did happen, but not so for the other. And so, those things, which are present to God, will without doubt happen: but some of them result from the necessity of things, and some of them from the power of those who do them. We are not wrong, therefore, to say that if these things are considered with reference to divine foreknowledge, they are necessary, but if they are considered by themselves, they are free of the bonds of necessity: just as everything that the senses perceive is universal if considered with reference to the reason, but individual if considered in itself.

> 'But, you will reply, if it lies in my power to change a proposed course of action, I will be able to evade Providence, for I will perhaps have altered things which providence foreknows. My answer will be that you can alter your plan, but that since this is possible, and since whether you do so or in what way you change it is visible to Providence the ever present and true, you cannot escape divine foreknowledge, just as you cannot escape the sight of an eye that is present to watch, though of your own free will you may turn to a variety of actions.

> 'Well, you may ask, isn't divine knowledge changed as a result of my rearrangement, so that as I change my wishes it, too, seems to change its knowledge? The answer is no. Each future thing is anticipated by the gaze of God which bends it back and recalls it to the presence of its own manner of knowledge: it does not change… but with one glance anticipates and embraces your changes in its constancy… So that the difficulty you put forward a short time ago, that it was unfitting if our future is said to provide a cause of

God's knowledge, is solved. The power of this knowledge, which embraces all things in present understanding, has itself set a limit upon things and owes nothing to events, which come after. And since this is so, man's freedom of will remains inviolate and the law does not impose reward and punishment unfairly, because the will is free from all necessity. God has foreknowledge and rests a spectator from on high of all things: and as the ever present eternity of His vision dispenses reward to the good and punishment to the bad, it adapts itself to the future quality of our actions. Hope is not placed in God in vain and prayers are not made in vain, for if they are the right kind they cannot but be efficacious. Avoid vice, therefore, and cultivate virtue: lift up your mind to the right kind of hope and put forth humble prayers on high. A great necessity is laid upon you, if you will be honest with yourself, a great necessity to be good, since you live in the sight of a judge who sees all things.' [6]

In essence, Boethius stipulates the book is already written. 'To which book are we referring?' one may ask. We are referring to the book, which has more significance to ourselves than any other book. We are referring to the book, which outlines life itself. We are referring to what one might call the 'Divine Book'.

The Divine Book includes the chapters: Divine Foreknowledge, Pre-destination, Predestination, and Determinism.

The book to which Boethius refers is not an ongoing book but rather a closed book, a completed book. The closed book – the fallacy of the argument regarding a 'closed' book and God opening the book does not mean the ending is not 'known' just because the players themselves do not know the ending until they get to the end.

We speak of 'a' book because Divine Foreknowledge suggests all is 'known'. As such, the 'book' has been written. So where is it one finds the 'divine book'? One finds the divine book located in a region of established abstraction void actions bound by the laws of nature:

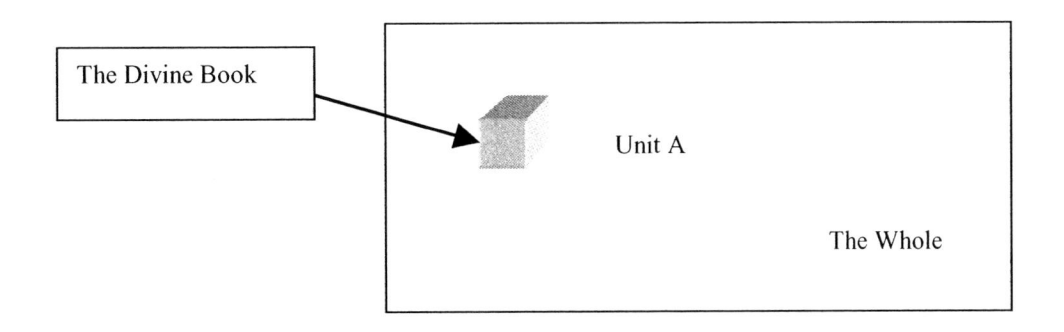

The Divine Book	→	Unit A
		The Whole

Perhaps one could say: The book is not 'a' book but rather 'a' set of books.

The War & Peace of a New Metaphysical Perception

Such a perceptions could be represented as follows:

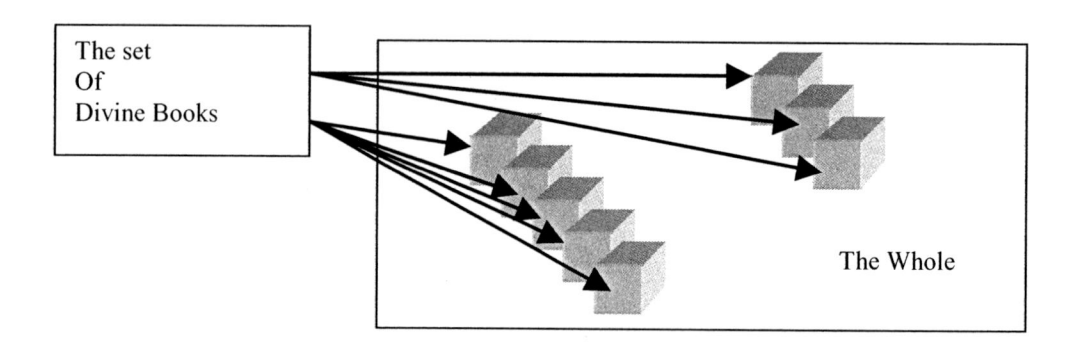

[Diagram: "The set Of Divine Books" with arrows pointing to multiple cubes within a box labeled "The Whole"]

This representation demonstrates the concept Boethius suggested regarding Divine Foreknowledge. So, what is the difference between the first and second diagram? The difference lies in the different perception, which emerges from each perception.

The first diagram suggests the existence of 'a' book and thus suggests 'all is known' to the whole.

The second diagram suggests a series of books, which in turn suggests a production of books. The second diagram suggests there is a 'source' of these books. As such, the question arises: Is there a 'location' from which the books evolve?

The first diagram suggests the existence of 'a' book:

[Diagram: "The Divine Book" with an arrow pointing to a single cube labeled "Unit A" within a box labeled "The Whole"]

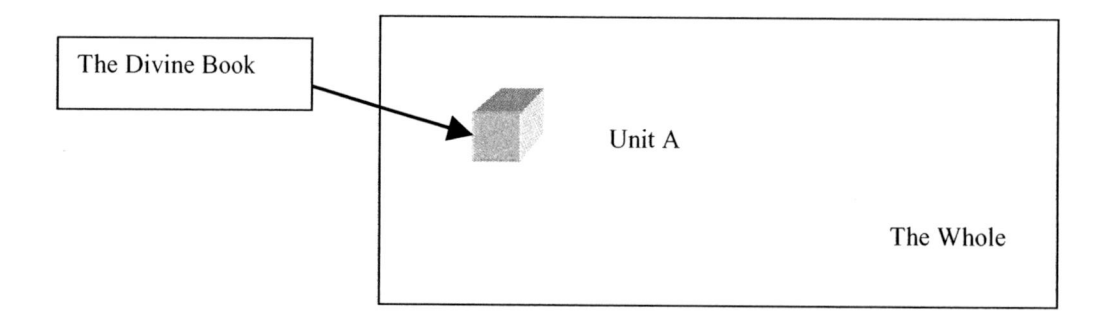

The Error of Boethius

Upon further examination, 'The Divine Book' becomes:

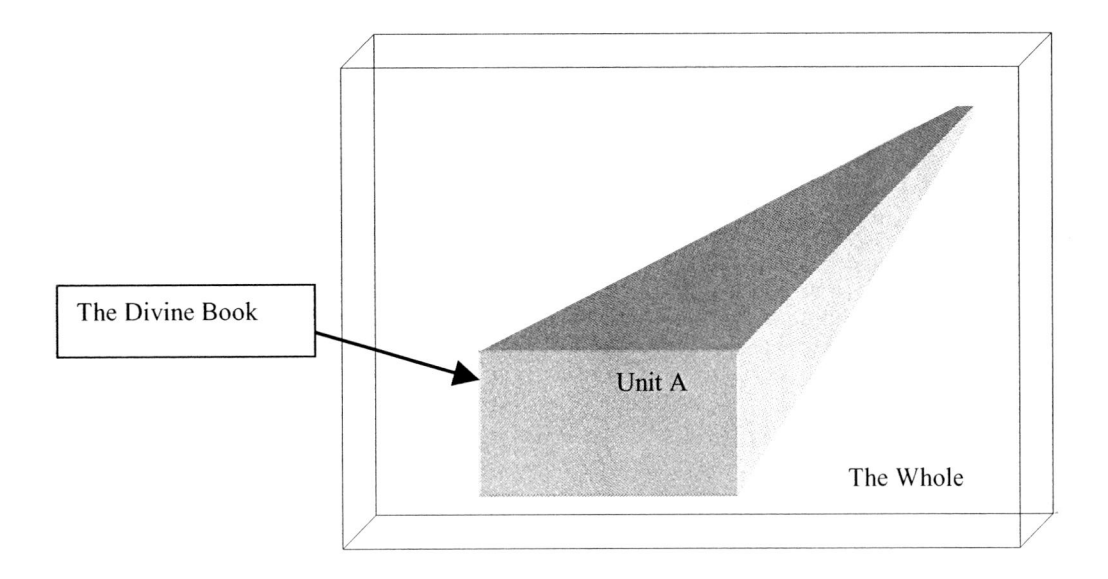

The Divine Book → Unit A

The Whole

And then, since 'the' Divine Book contains 'all knowing' we in essence have:

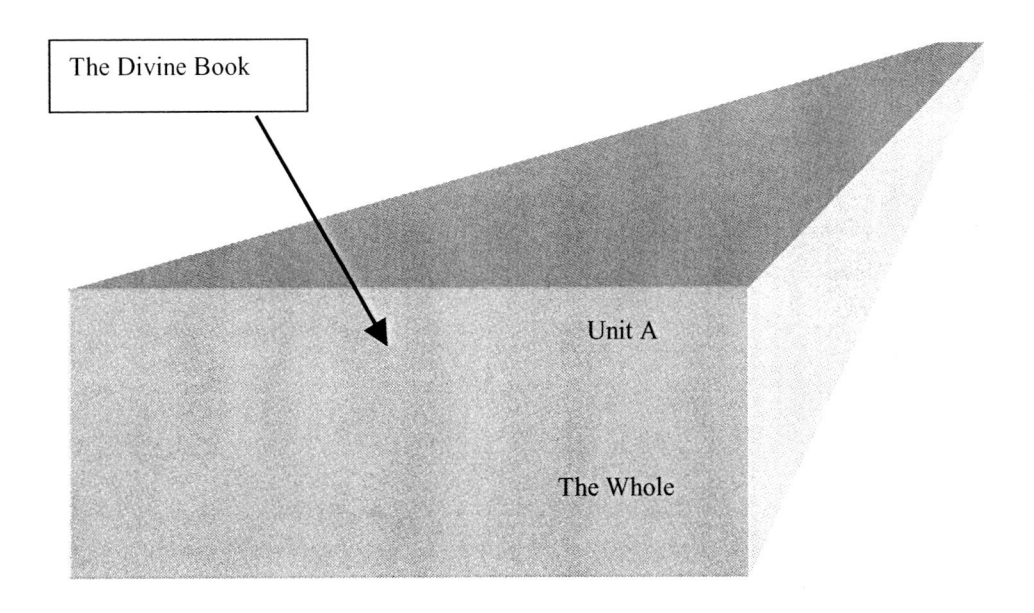

The Divine Book ↓

Unit A

The Whole

The War & Peace of a New Metaphysical Perception

The second diagram suggests a series of books:

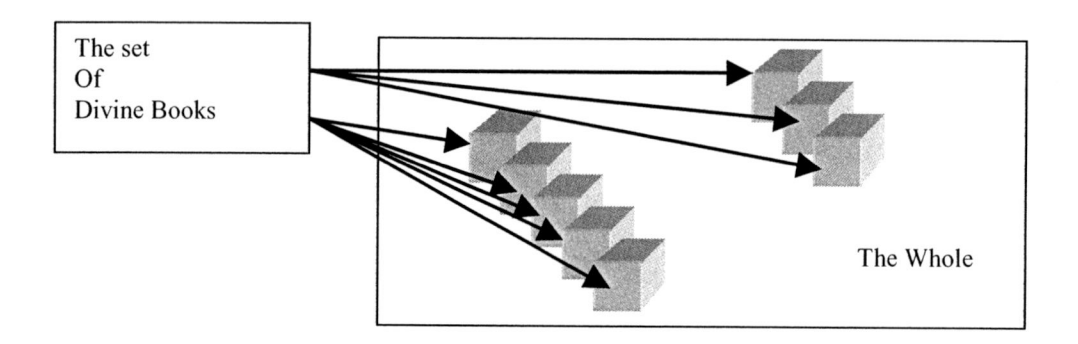

One could depict the concept of an 'emerging/evolving' 'knowing, depict the concept of 'emerging/evolving' books as"

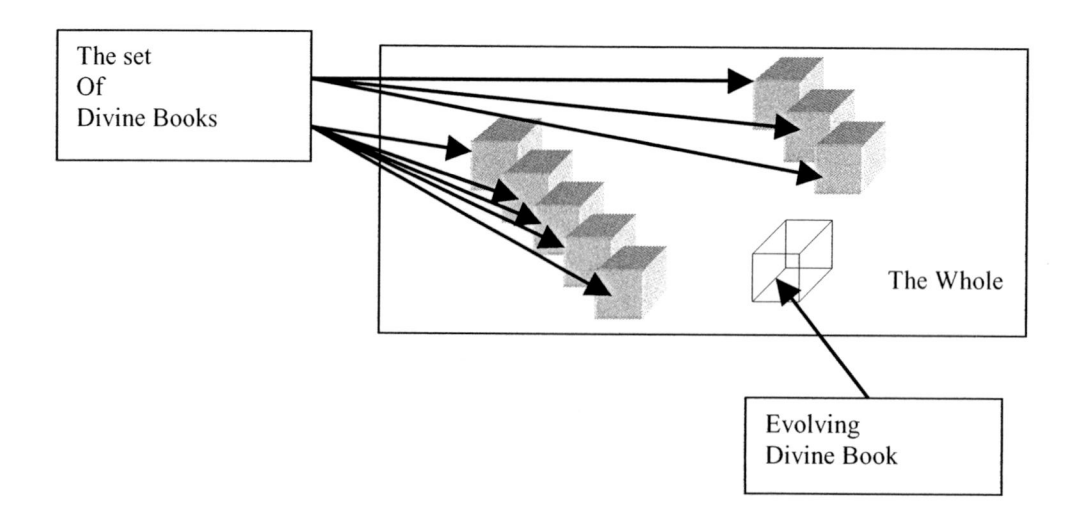

Now isolating the 'evolving' Divine Book in order to facilitate it's evolving uninfluenced by what is, we obtain:

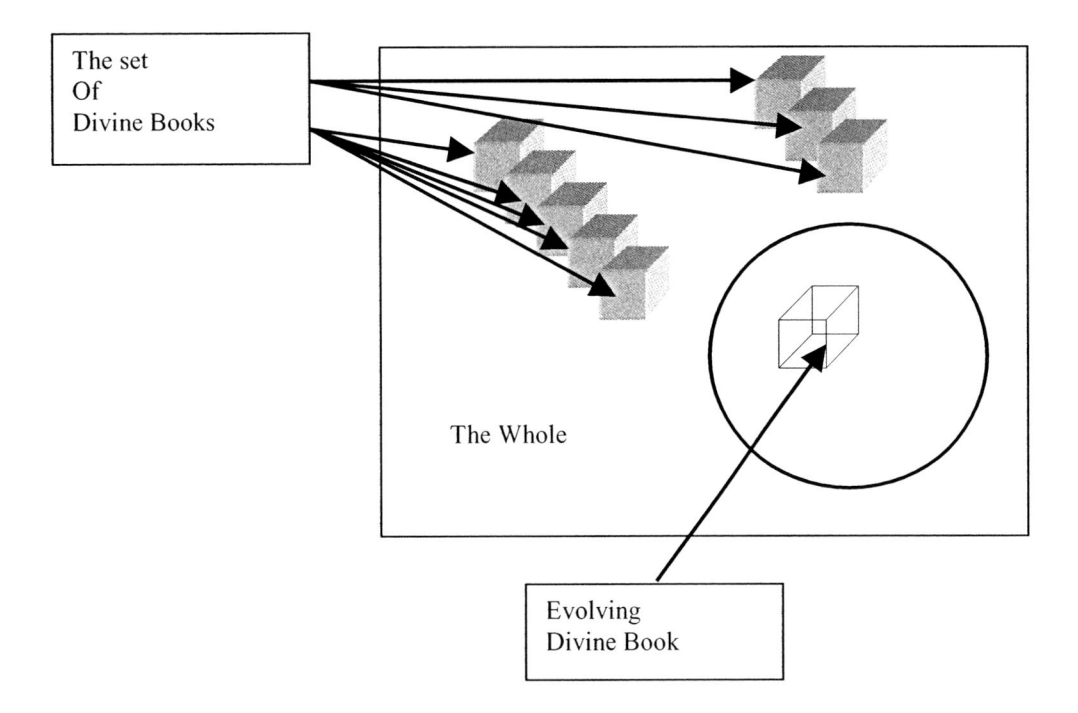

We are back to the concept of abstraction existing 'outside' the physical. Once again, we are back to the solution we examined in Tractate 1: Zeno and Seamlessness. Again, we find ourselves confronted with the concept of the 'real' and the 'real illusion' coexisting as was discussed in Tractate 1. The diagram clearly demonstrates the relevancy of the solution we examined within Tractate 2: Aristotle and Cartesian Systems, the concept of 'relative first truth' as opposed to Aristotle's implied existence of 'a' 'first truth'.

Determinism is determinism, predestination is predestination, the book is the book, and divine foreknowledge is foreknowledge be it divine or otherwise.

Philosophically, it has often been said that life is but a book already written within which living entities of reality can no more see what is to come than can the characters in a book.

If one should open the book at page 15 today or tomorrow, the results are the same. The characters on page 15 have no idea regarding what will happen on page 456 regardless of how many times the book has been read from cover to cover by the 'whole', by totality, by 'God'. Regardless of how many times 'God' rereads 'the book', the 'story' remains the same for Divine foreknowledge, as espoused by Boethius, remains Divine foreknowledge. Within 'Boethius' metaphysical system, regardless of the fact that the 'whole' may be found existing hunched over the book and rereading it for the hundred millionth time, the ending remains the same.

Some would say language is too limited to allow us the ability to understand what it is we cannot possible perceive. Again how ludicrous, if we can perceive the overall concept then the overall concept is not outside our ability to perceive the concept itself. 'A' concept may take some time to develop language capable of expressing the concept we perceive. It may take time to develop our understanding in order to express the concept we think we understand. It may take time to expand upon our perceptions in order to express what it is we sense our perceptions to be but which we have difficulty fully understanding. Regardless, if we do not 'presently' find it within ourselves to express what it is we 'perceive', eventually we will be able to express what it is we could not temporally express.

What does this have to do with Boethius? If we insist upon embracing the concept that there are things we conceptualize but will never be able to understand, then we shall remain ignorant of understanding not because we can 'never' understand but because we choose not to understand.

The only way to begin to understand the concept of 'determinism' and 'free will' existing simultaneously is through the process of remaining open and rejecting suggestions that we accept our lack of understanding as being simply a limitedness of our abilities. In short we cannot resolve the paradox of free will and determinism existing simultaneously until we dismiss Boethius' resolution to the issue as being simply something we have to accept, as being beyond our intellectual abilities.

Zeno, with the introduction of the paradoxes of time and space, reached the philosophical level of understanding what it is we sense but could not express in the time period of 500 BC. For two and a half millennium, we have been 'stuck' at this level. We have embraced Boethius' resolution to the problem, the concept of our limitedness, because we have been unable to express a solution to the problem. We are now at a point where we can begin to understand seamlessness existing simultaneously with multiplicity. We are now at a point where we can begin to understand how it is the physical world, multiplicity, can exist simultaneously with the abstract, seamlessness. Such understandings now begin to emerge through understanding the concept of seamlessness existing independent of multiplicity, through understanding that seamlessness, abstraction, exists independently of multiplicity, the physical, through understanding one existing 'inside' the other, through understanding a greater Reality existing 'outside' physical reality, through understanding the physical, multiplicity, existing immersed 'within' timeless existence itself.

What 'is being': Determinism - A location for *being* – action, process/reality – the universe

A location for Free Will to act: The process: individuality, 'being', becoming
A location of: What 'is being'

We have briefly examined the need as well as the rationality regarding 'a' location for both free will and divine foreknowledge

What then of determinism: Isn't determinism the same thing as divine foreknowledge? We often consider the two to be the same concept. Therein lies one of our problems regarding the paradoxical perception that free will and divine foreknowledge exist simultaneously as 'the' dominant form of action located 'within' the 'same' location.

The Error of Boethius

By classifying action into four classes, we find a separate location for determinism. Presently we have proposed:

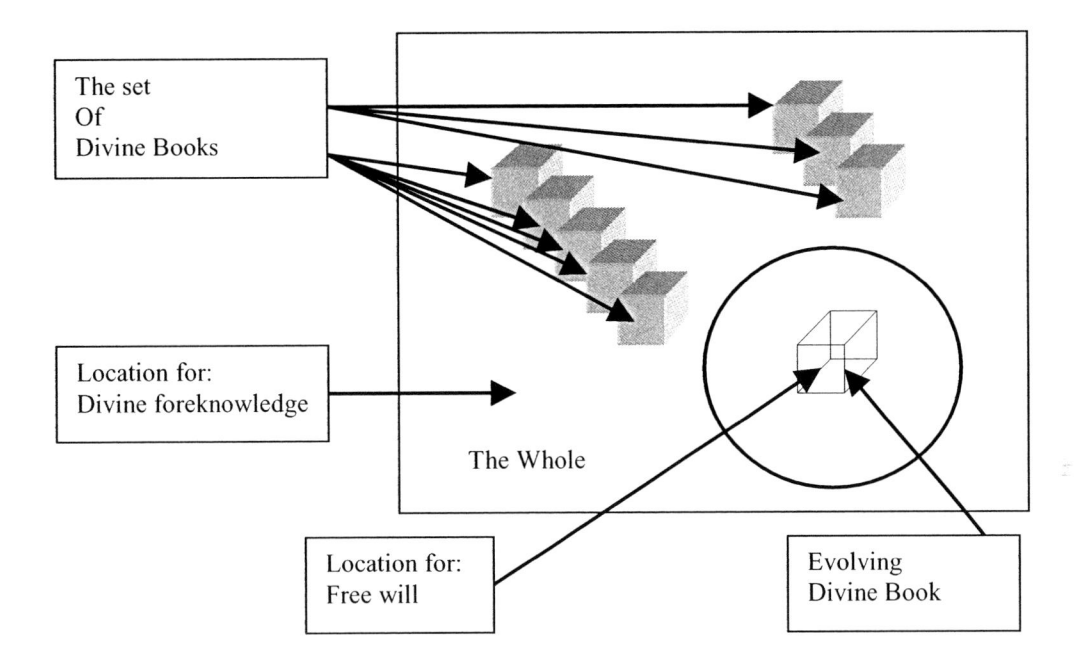

The War & Peace of a New Metaphysical Perception

So where does this leave us regarding 'a' location for determinism? We have 'a' location for which one of the four forms of action has not been attributed:

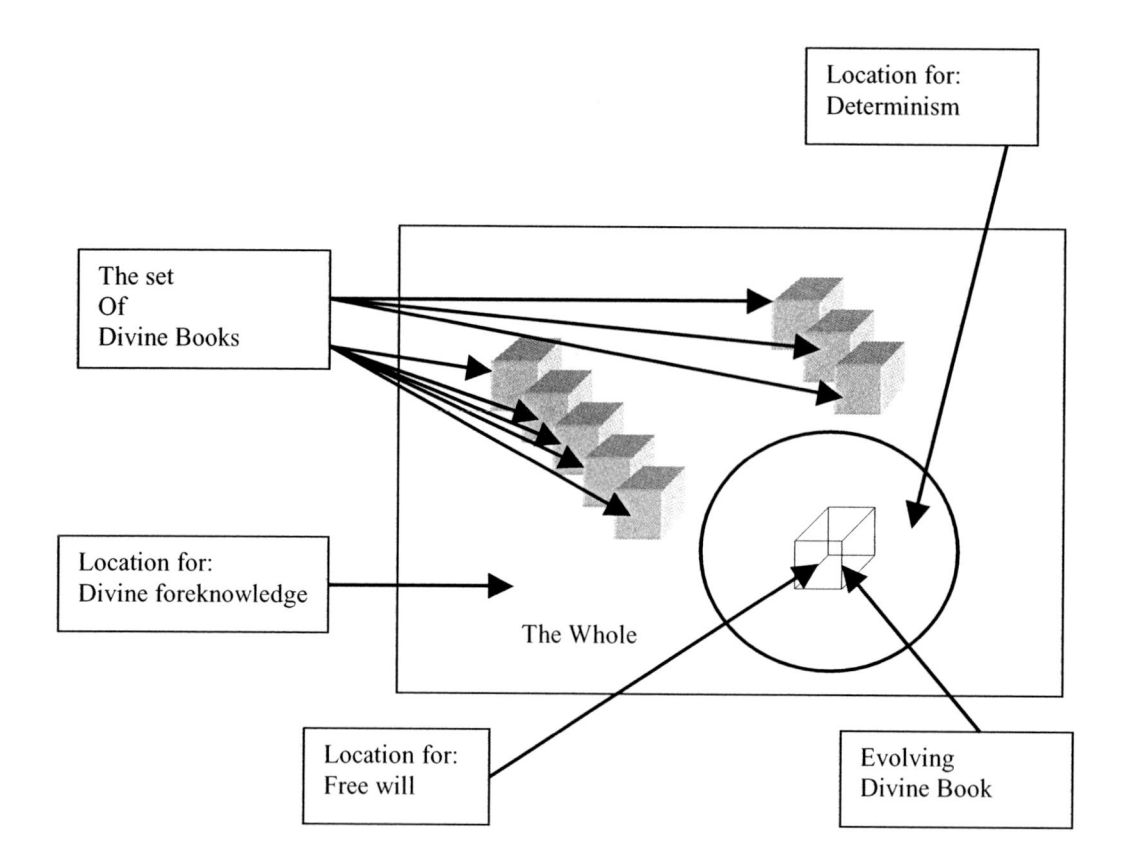

[Diagram: Shows "Location for: Determinism" pointing to a region; "The set Of Divine Books" with arrows pointing to several cube shapes; "Location for: Divine foreknowledge" pointing into "The Whole"; "Location for: Free will" and "Evolving Divine Book" pointing to a cube within a circle.]

Now we begin to understand what is meant by the concept: Determinism

Passive action:

    2. Actions bound by the laws of nature: What 'is being'

> Actions bound by the laws of nature are actions requiring no 'knowing'. Since these actions require no 'knowing' they are classified as forms of passive actions. These are actions taken by inanimate objects. Such actions also include the actions of animate entities that simulate the action of inanimate objects.
>
> Examples of actions bound by the laws of nature: When dropped from a cliff, a rock falls. When dropped from a cliff, you fall.

What 'is': Pre-destination/predestination - A location for being – existence of existence

A location for determinism to act, a location for free will to act, the process of the whole becoming, a location of What 'is'

What is 'intended': Determinism and free will simultaneously independent

What then are we to say regarding our fourth form of action: Actions bound by the laws of: The state of being: What 'is'?

This is perhaps the most interesting of the four forms of action for it is this very action, which makes the concept of separation of free will from divine foreknowledge possible.

Passive action:

1. The state of being: What 'is'

    The state of being is a form of action requiring no 'knowing'. The state of being is the most basic form of action. This form of passive action, the state of 'being' itself is the most elementary form of passive action. The primal state of existence is the most basic form of action. All other forms of action emerge from this most basic form of action.

    Examples of states of being: I exist. A rock exists.

Where are we to find such action? It would appear there is 'nowhere' to place such action other than 'outside' the system thus once again rendering the system an incomplete system.

To understand the fourth location it will help to first simplify the concept. We do so be examining a simple circle:

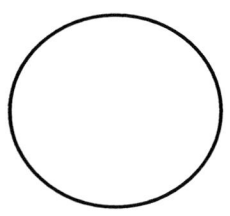

At first glance, it would appear the circle divides space into two regions:

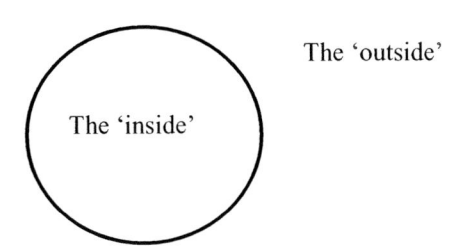

The 'outside'

The 'inside'

The War & Peace of a New Metaphysical Perception

Upon closer examination, we find this to be an incomplete perception. In actuality, the circle divides space into three regions:

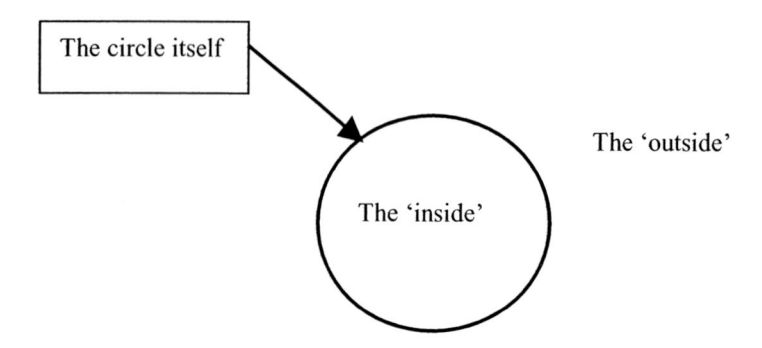

```
The circle itself ──────┐
                        ▼
                      ╱───╲        The 'outside'
                     │     │
                     │ The 'inside'
                      ╲___╱
```

With this in mind, we can reexamine our previous diagram and as we do so it becomes apparent that there is not only 'a' location for our fourth form of action but in fact there are three locations for our fourth form of action:

The Error of Boethius

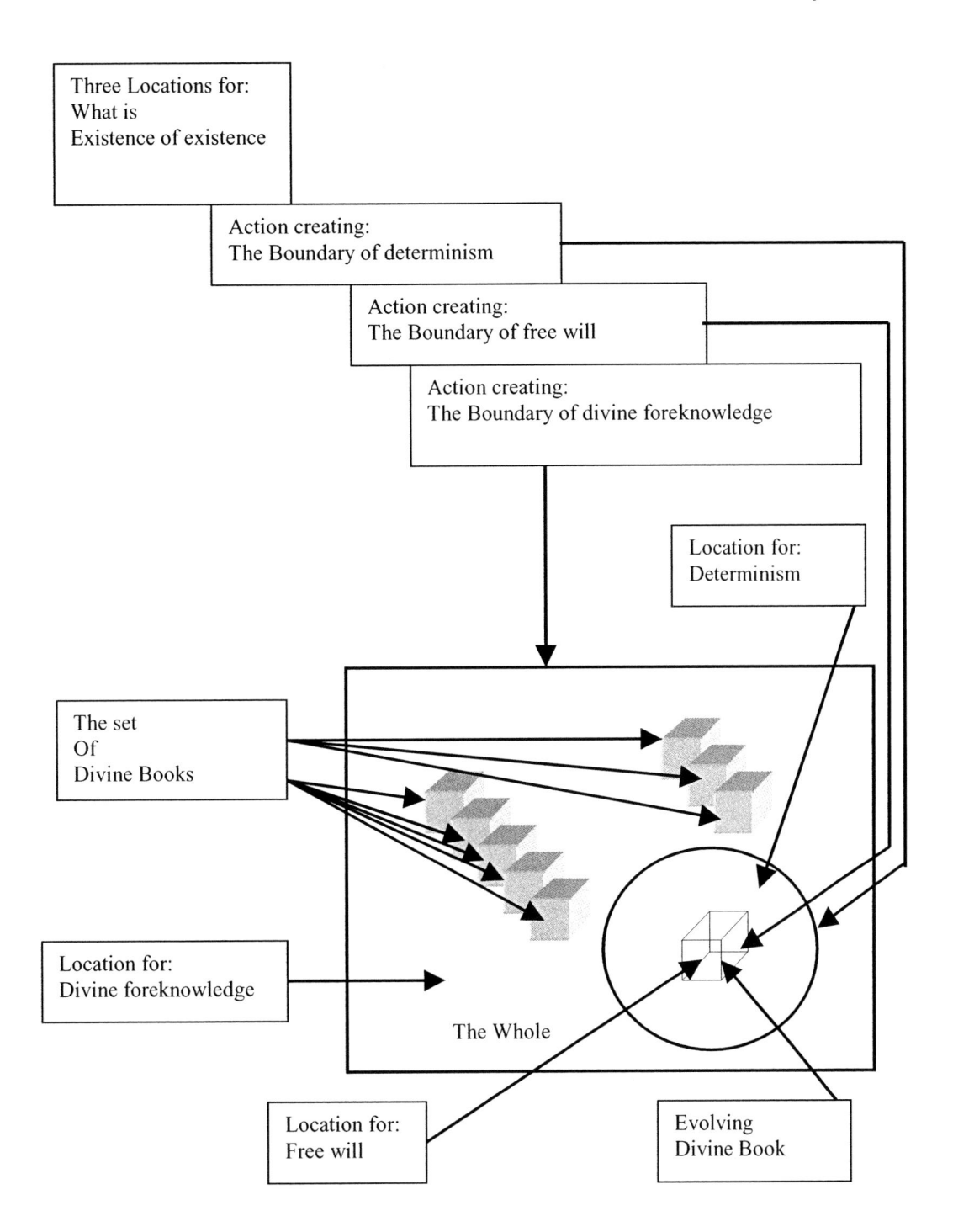

- Three Locations for:
  What is
  Existence of existence

- Action creating:
  The Boundary of determinism

- Action creating:
  The Boundary of free will

- Action creating:
  The Boundary of divine foreknowledge

- Location for:
  Determinism

- The set
  Of
  Divine Books

- Location for:
  Divine foreknowledge

- The Whole

- Location for:
  Free will

- Evolving
  Divine Book

The War & Peace of a New Metaphysical Perception

Functionality of action

Now we have a problem. We come back to our previous statement: 'Having classified action (classified action into distinct groups) in this manner, it is now possible to find a location for these four forms of action.

To refresh our memory regarding these groups we see we have two major groups each of which are further divided into two subgroups:

    I.   Passive action
            a.   States of *being*
            b.   Actions bound by the laws of nature
    II.   Active action
            a.   Actions bound by the laws of free will
            b.   Actions bound by the laws of determinism

At first glance it would appear there are three forms of active action and one state of pacifity. How is it 'action' bound by the laws of nature are passive when they involve motion. Metaphysically all forms of action, regardless of whether or not they are 'in' motion or simply existing, without 'knowing' are passive forms of action.

This then brings us back to our previous examination regarding the 'levels' at which actions are placed:

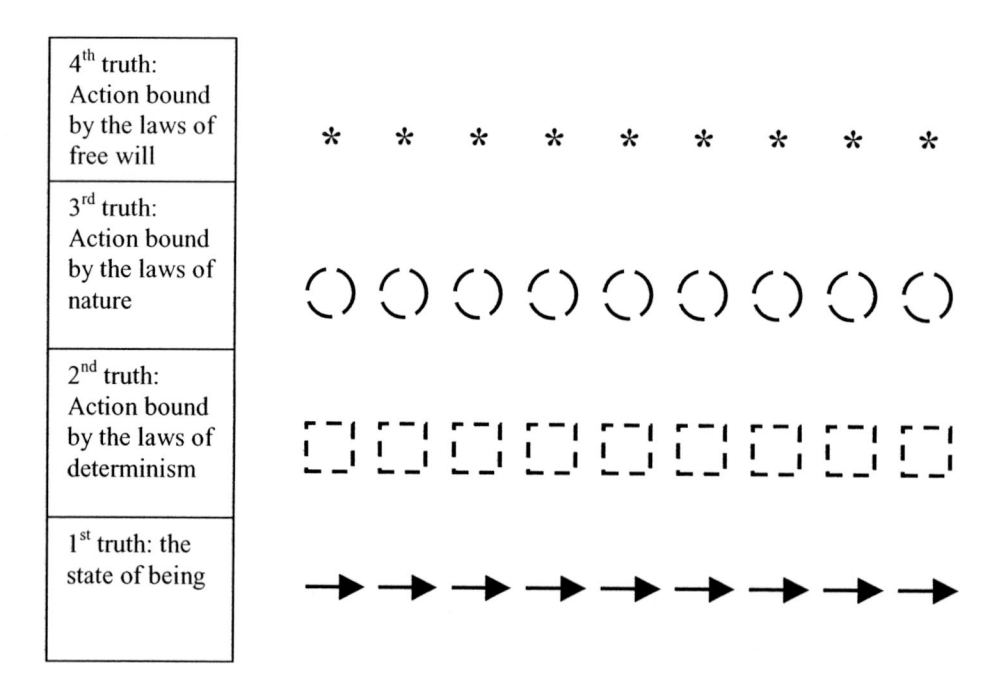

4th truth: Action bound by the laws of free will	* * * * * * * * *
3rd truth: Action bound by the laws of nature	( ) ( ) ( ) ( ) ( ) ( ) ( ) ( ) ( )
2nd truth: Action bound by the laws of determinism	⌐⌐ ⌐⌐ ⌐⌐ ⌐⌐ ⌐⌐ ⌐⌐ ⌐⌐ ⌐⌐ ⌐⌐
1st truth: the state of being	→ → → → → → → → →

Part II of this tractate found a new level of action being introduced into the model. As such the dynamics of the graphic has been expanded to include four action forms versus three action forms found in Part I of this tractate

The Error of Boethius

Two questions emerge from the information we have:

1. How is it possible one form of action is, can be, appears to be, more significant than another if all forms of action exist?
2. How can there be four simultaneous independent 'locations' for action when we 'know' of only two possible forms of action: the active and the passive forms of action.

Regarding question #1:

There is no rational answer to the question. The only way to answer the question is to simplify our diagram. Rather than 'level's of one dimension we will mold action into a two dimensional state:

We will begin the process through the application of Ockham's razor by removing the perceived relative values of significance we previously illustrated:

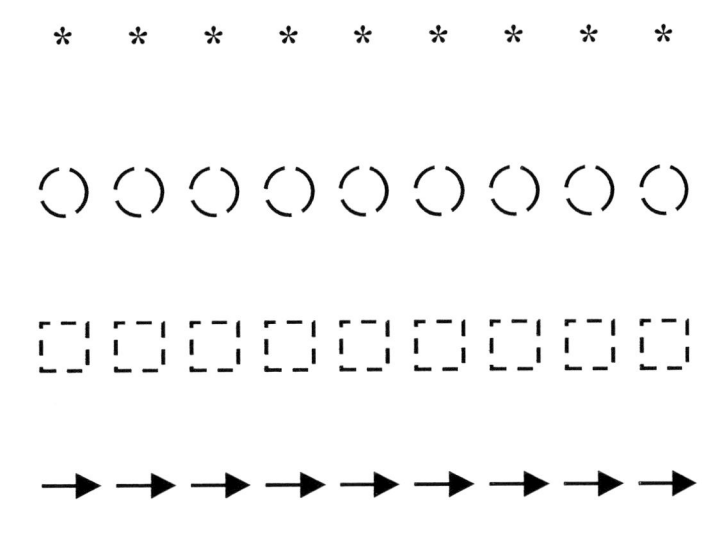

* * * * * * * * *

( ) ( ) ( ) ( ) ( ) ( ) ( ) ( ) ( )

[ ] [ ] [ ] [ ] [ ] [ ] [ ] [ ] [ ]

→ → → → → → → → →

Applying Ockham's razor once again, we obtain:

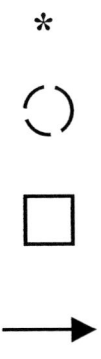

*

( )

□

→

If we then establish boundaries of existence for actions bound by the laws of nature, we obtain:

193

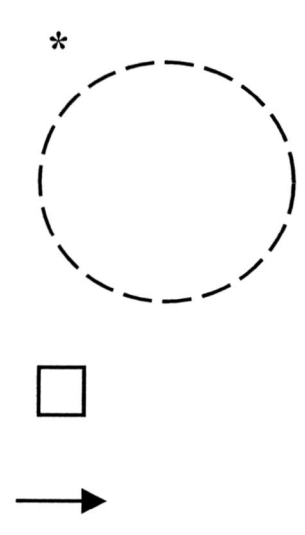

The War & Peace of a New Metaphysical Perception

If we continue to expand upon the boundaries enclosing actions bound by the laws of nature we obtain:

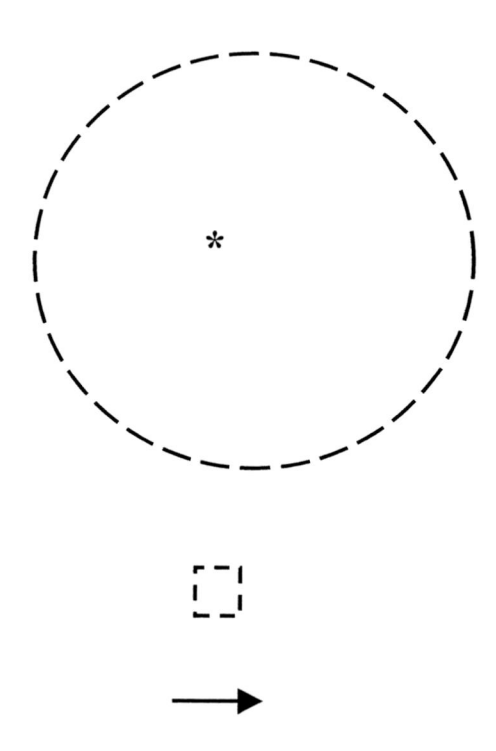

The Error of Boethius

If we then establish boundaries of existence for actions bound by the laws of determinism, we obtain:

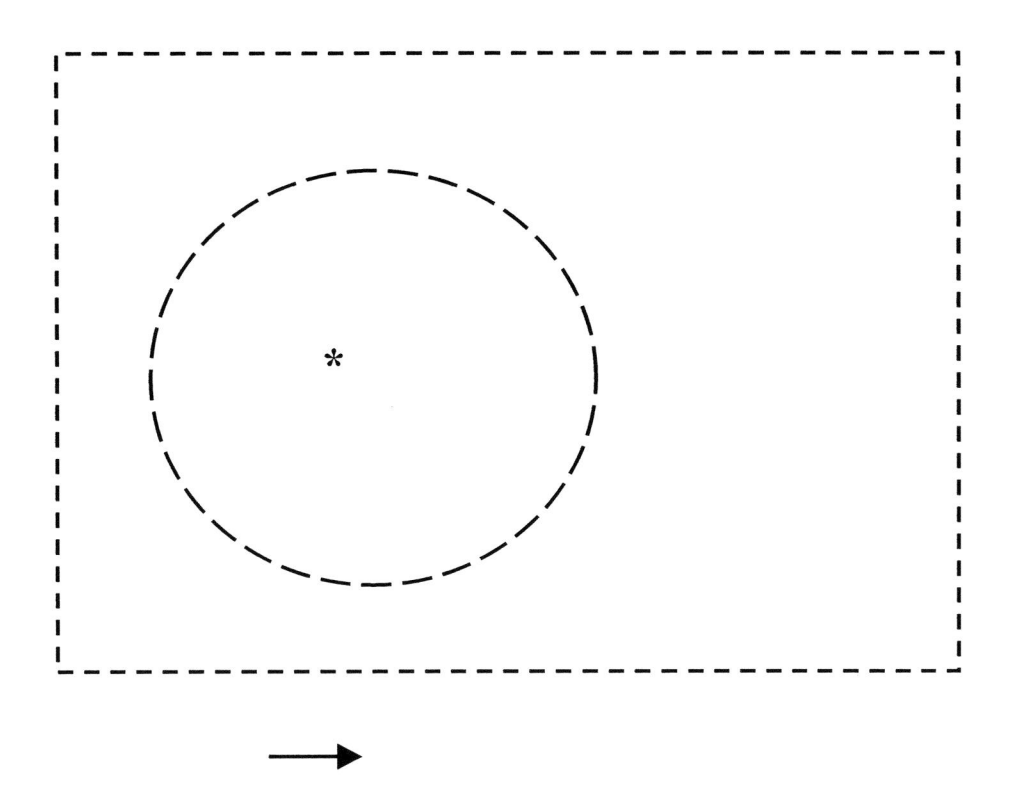

Now why expand the boundaries regarding actions bound by the laws of determinism beyond the boundaries of actions bound by the laws of nature? We do so first to respect Boethius' concept of divine foreknowledge being 'within'. The concept of actions being 'found' 'within' totality applies to all forms of action. We do so secondly because, as we shall see, it provides the means of resolving not only Boethius' paradox of free will versus determinism but it also resolves Zeno's paradox of seamlessness versus multiplicity. In addition, the action of expanding the boundary of actions bound by the laws of determinism in such a manner as to encompass actions bound by the laws of free will allows for the resolution of Aristotle's paradox. As we shall see in another tractate, this very perceptual process allows for the resolution regarding the paradox of a Kantian Cartesian system versus a Hegelian non-Cartesian system. In fact, such a perceptual model, provides a means by which we can resolve a myriad other metaphysical, ontological, and cosmological paradoxes as well.

The War & Peace of a New Metaphysical Perception

But back to the task we have been addressing, understanding 'location' of action.. The question then becomes: What then of:

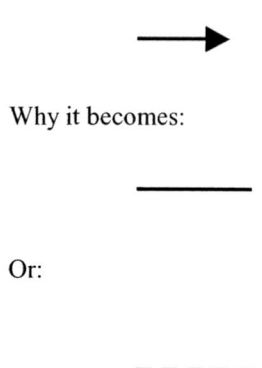

⟶

Why it becomes:

▬▬▬▬

Or:

▬ ▬ ▬ ▬

Whose 'location of existence becomes quite obvious when we remove the clutter and label the 'locations' of action:

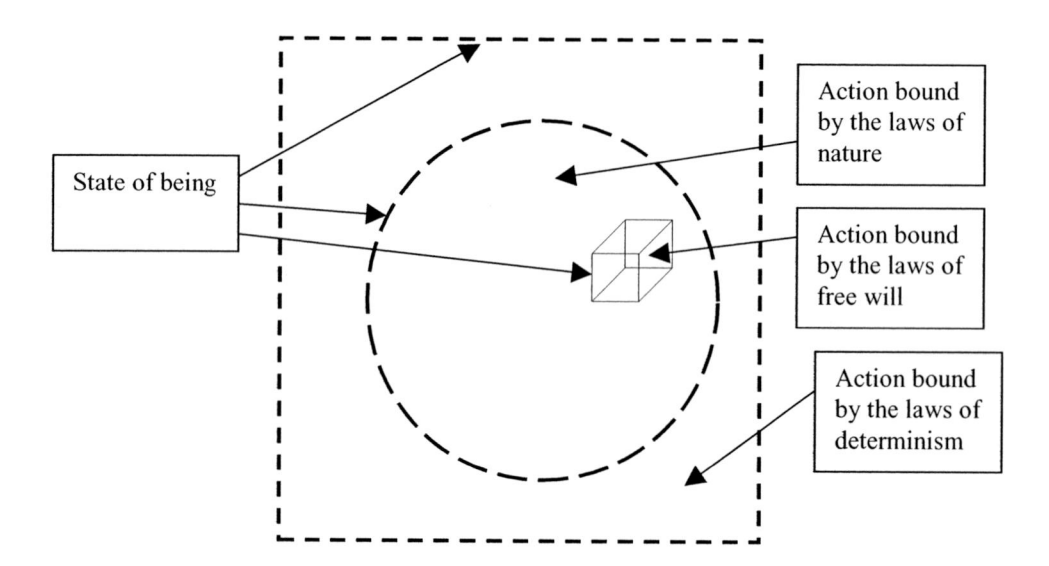

State of being

Action bound by the laws of nature

Action bound by the laws of free will

Action bound by the laws of determinism

This does not appear to answer question #2: How can there be four simultaneous independent 'locations' for action when we 'know' of only two possibilities? We understand the concept of the entity and the concept of the universe, our reality.

Perhaps this can more simply be explained through the examination of a circle:

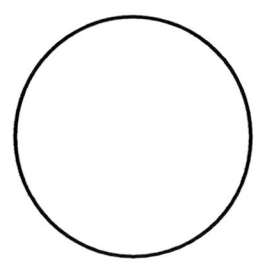

There appears to be two locations in this diagram:

1. The inside of the circle
2. The outside of the circle

In actuality, however, there are three locations to this diagram:

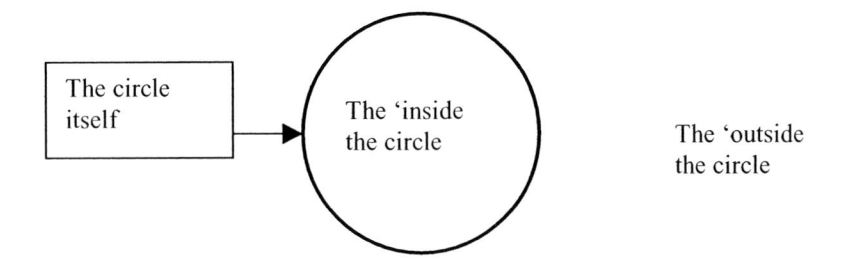

- The circle itself
- The 'inside' the circle
- The 'outside' the circle

With this in mind, we can then identify the four locations of our previous diagram:

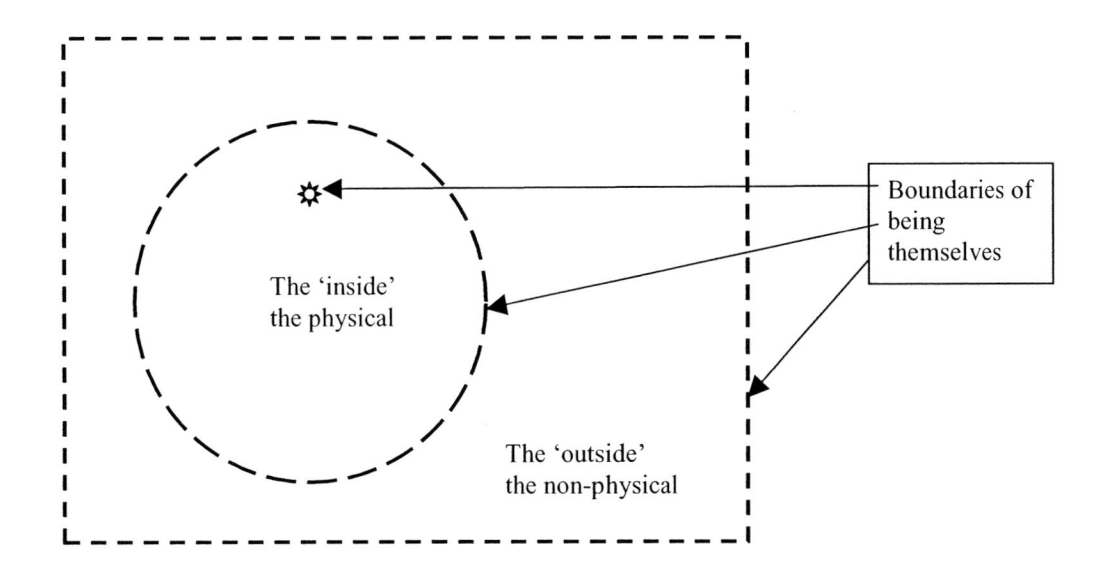

- The 'inside' the physical
- The 'outside' the non-physical
- Boundaries of being themselves

The War & Peace of a New Metaphysical Perception

But how can a 'location' implement 'action'? It cannot. What implements action are entities themselves. How then do we reconcile such a statement with the diagram above? We cannot if we retain Zeno's perception as discussed in Tractate 1: Zeno and Seamlessness:

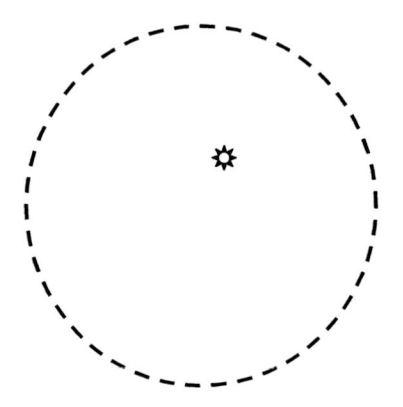

Nor can we reconcile such a statement if we retain Aristotle's perception as discussed in Tractate 2: Aristotle and Cartesian Systems:

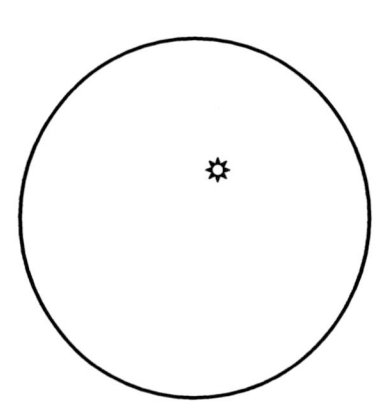

However, we can reconcile the questions:

1. 'But how can a 'location' implement 'action'?"
2. How can there be four simultaneous independent 'locations' for action when we 'know' of only two possibilities?

if we go back to the previous diagram:

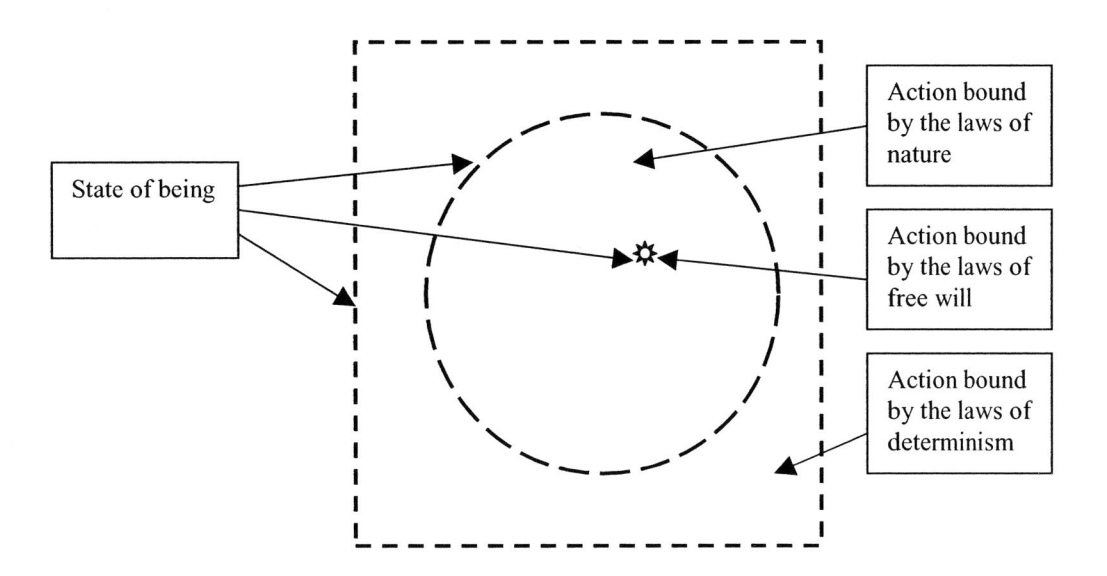

The entity 'within' the circle, within the physical obviously exists, obviously exists within a region of action bound by the laws of nature, intuitively exists within the region of action bound by the laws of free will – actions that do not defy the laws of nature.

Where, however, is the entity implementing action bound by the laws of determinism?

The solution becomes apparent when the entity whose actions are bound by the laws of free will as well as whose actions are bound by the laws of nature are terminated by the laws of nature themselves and thus moves into the non-physical, pure abstractual location of existence. As such, the diagram becomes:

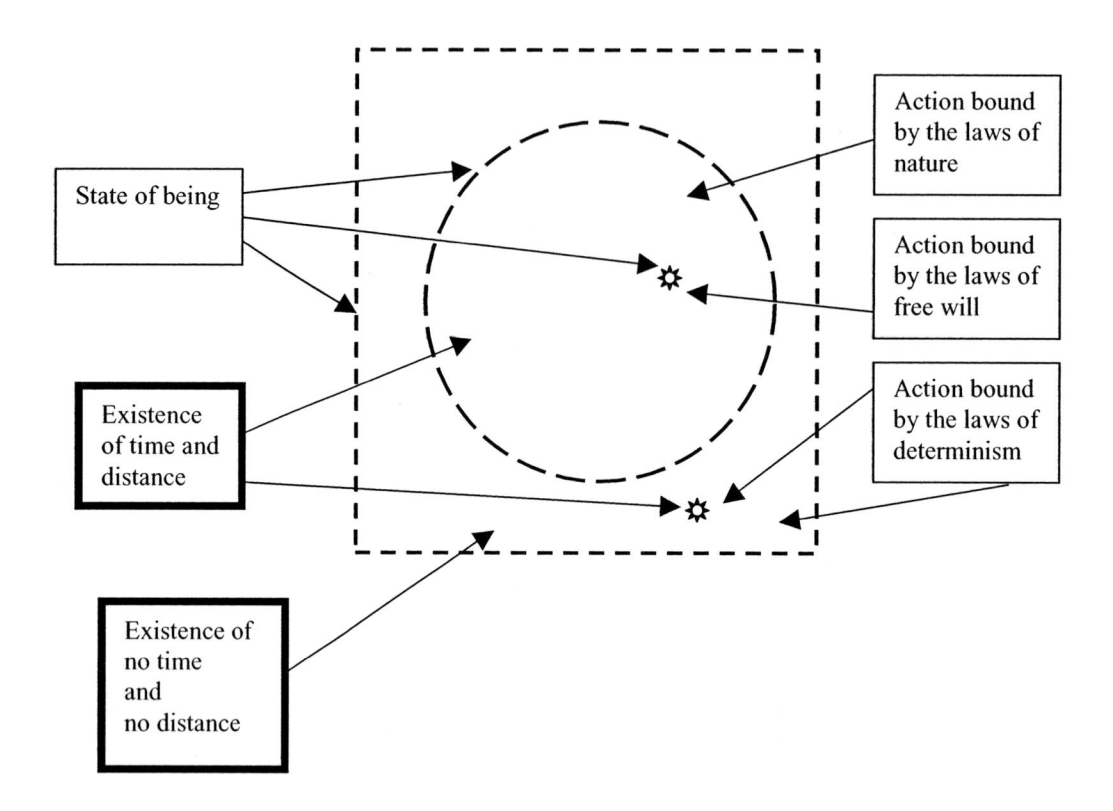

Why do the discussion of time and distance suddenly enter the discussion. Time and distance enter the discussion because we understand time and distance to be functions of the physical, functions of space, matter, and energy themselves. As such, the introduction of these concepts at this point in the discussion helps us to visualize, in a less theoretical manner, the metaphysical system suggested. This helps to initiate discussions immersed in pragmatism.

Locations for actions

Four questions arise with the establishment of forms of action:

There are four forms of action:

        a.   The state of being: a form of passive action
        b.   Actions bound by the laws of nature: a form of passive action
        c.   Actions bound by the laws of free will: a form of active action
        d.   Actions bound by the laws of determinism: a form of active action

The question: Why?

> Why the need for a location of action bound by the laws of being?
> Why the need for a location of action bound by the laws of nature?
> Why the need for a location of action bound by the laws of free will?
> Why the need for a location of action bound by the laws of determinism?

The short answers:

> What is
> What must be
> What could be
> What is is

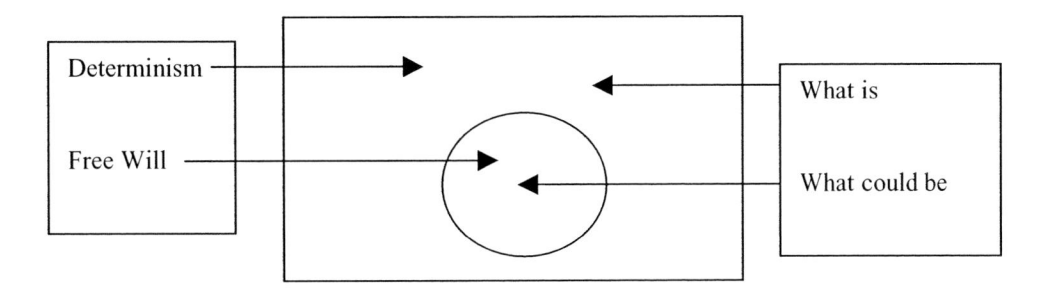

In order to expand our understanding regarding all this back and forth in terms of perceptual understanding, perhaps it would be beneficial to examine the concepts of divine foreknowledge, pre-destination, predestination, and determinism in a little more detail.

Divine foreknowledge, pre-destination, predestination, and determinism versus free will

Having touched upon the concepts free will, divine foreknowledge, pre-destination, and predestination it may help, before we move on with attempting to further resolve Boethius' paradox, to examine the four more closely as regards present day perceptions versus a new perception.

Divine foreknowledge:

The concept of divine foreknowledge suggests an awareness of all there was and all there is. The question arises does divine foreknowledge imply an awareness of all that will be. The very name 'foreknowledge' suggests that to be the case but is it necessarily the case?

The War & Peace of a New Metaphysical Perception

Present day perceptions:

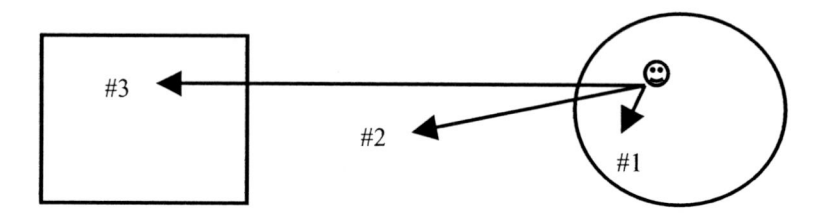

Within such a system, there is only one possible conclusion to the question: Does divine 'foreknowledge' imply not only an awareness of what was and what is but an awareness of what will be?

Since the location of all knowledge is 'contained' 'within #3, entrance of 'new' knowing unknown to an omniscient location would suggest the omniscient location is in fact a location without omniscience. The conclusion: Location #3, being omniscient, has no option but to have knowledge of what will be.

This perception is rational yet unexplainable when examined in the face of free will being free will. Thus Boethius' statement:

> ...'Therefore, all those things which happen without happening of necessity are, before they happen, future events about to happen, but not about to happen of necessity. For just as the knowledge of present things imposes no necessity on what is happening, so foreknowledge imposes no necessity on what is going to happen.
>
> 'The cause of this mistake is that people think that the totality of their knowledge depends on the nature and capacity to be known of the objects of knowledge. But this is all wrong.'...
>
> 'The point of greatest importance here is this: the superior manner of knowledge includes the inferior, but it is quite impossible for the inferior to rise to the superior.'...
>
> 'In the same way, human reason refuses to believe that divine intelligence can see the future in any other way except that in which human reason has knowledge.'...

becomes the rationale as to why this is so. Our lack of understanding is due to our limited perception relative to the Whole itself. We perceive the Whole as being what is found 'within' physical reality, within our universe.

Can such an argument be circumvented? A modification of our present perception through the simple process of shifting the location of the physical reality from being placed within a void into being placed within a region of abstraction will resolve the issue. The perceptual development of an abstractual region not only eliminates the questionable region of a void, region #2, existing 'outside' of regions #1 and #3 and thus simplifies the perception but the process of shifting the physical into existing 'within' the abstractual simplifies the repercussions regarding the concept of 'death' itself. Interestingly enough, the concept of 'death' does not just apply to unique entities of 'knowing' found 'within' the universe but applies to the unique entities of 'knowing' found 'within' the abstract should the universe itself 'die'.

The Error of Boethius

But why wouldn't the abstract shift into the physical as opposed to the physical shifting into the abstract? This discussion took place within Tractate 1: Zeno and Seamlessness.

Let's look in more detail at what we are suggesting.

The new perception:

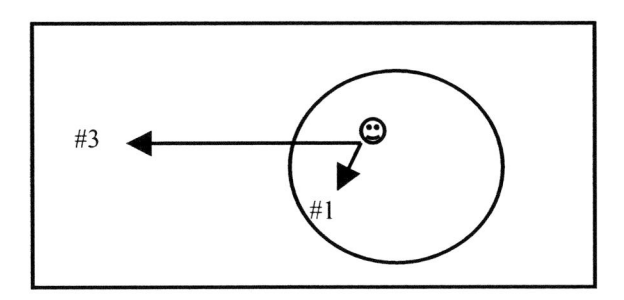

Within such a system, there is a new possibility regarding the question: Does divine 'foreknowledge' imply not only an awareness of what was and what is but an awareness of what will be?

Within such a system, since the location of all knowledge is 'contained' 'within' #3, entrance of 'new' unknown knowing into an omniscient location would not require entrance for it would already be 'within'. As such, the concept of what will be would be a part of what is and thus becomes a form of what is versus what will be.

However, wouldn't the entrance of unique entities of 'knowing' into #3 imply either a level of cardinality, an order of consecutiveness, or both? If we reexamine the diagram using a little more detail, we begin to find answers to just such questions regarding levels of cardinality and orders of consecutiveness.

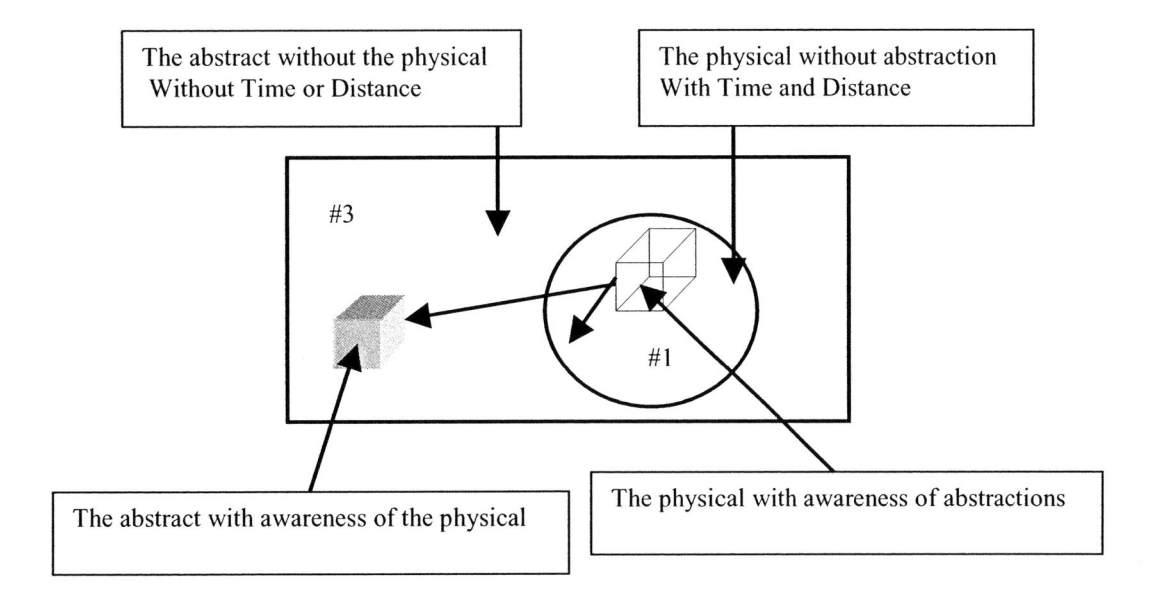

Such a perception does more than provide a symmetrical orientation to the perception we have of what we call our universe, what we call reality.

Such a perception explains how it is possible to gain an entrance of 'newness', an entrance of what 'will be' into what 'is' without our present understanding of 'newness' following 'oldness', without the need of our present understanding of consecutive order and our present understanding of 'levels' of cardinality in terms of individual significance.

When 'newness', what 'will be', enters region #3, 'newness' carries with it an understanding of time and distance but enters a region lacking time and distance. As such, independent packets of knowing have no relative primal order upon which they depend once within region #3.

The same concept applies to relative concepts of 'worth'. This concept will be examined in detail within Tractate 4: Copernicus. In the mean time, let us return to the concept of 'free will' becoming simply a state of what 'is' within such system and thus the concept of what 'will be' no longer becomes an issue for region #3. The result: The concept, divine foreknowledge, becomes a possibility for region #3 while simultaneously being a non-issue for region #1.

This process is best described as a process of separation through inclusion as opposed to separation through exclusion. This concept is described in detail in Tractate 8: Russell. Although the process of separation through inclusion best describes the system, Tractate 4: Copernicus lays the foundation to understanding such a concept through its dialectic regarding centricisn versus non-centricism.

The new perception initiates an understanding regarding how it is 'free will' could exist simultaneously with 'divine foreknowledge'. This in turn allows us to discard Boethius' premise that humanity is capable of perceiving paradoxes including some of which humanity is incapable of resolving.

Thus, Boethius' statement:

> …'Therefore, all those things which happen without happening of necessity are, before they happen, future events about to happen, but not about to happen of necessity. For just as the knowledge of present things imposes no necessity on what is happening, so foreknowledge imposes no necessity on what is going to happen.
>
> 'The cause of this mistake is that people think that the totality of their knowledge depends on the nature and capacity to be known of the objects of knowledge. But this is all wrong.'…
>
> 'The point of greatest importance here is this: the superior manner of knowledge includes the inferior, but it is quite impossible for the inferior to rise to the superior.'…
>
> 'In the same way, human reason refuses to believe that divine intelligence can see the future in any other way except that in which human reason has knowledge.'…

is on the brink of finally being able to be discarded, at least for the time being. Interestingly enough, while we may be able to discard Boethius' concept regarding the limitedness of entities of 'knowing' we are able to retain Boethius' concepts regarding the simultaneous existence of 'free will' and 'divine foreknowledge'.

So much for 'divine foreknowledge', but what of pre-destination?

Pre-destination:

Pre-destination is the concept of individual entities of 'knowing' having a variety of locations to which the individual entities of 'knowing' can 'go'. In the case of pre-destination it would better be said: Pre-destination is the concept of individual entities of 'knowing' having pre-assigned locations to which they are sent irrespective of the desire of the individual entity of 'knowing', irrespective of the desire of any parts of the whole, and irrespective of the desire of the whole itself. Pre-destination applies to the situation where the entities of 'knowing' becoming separated from the physical should such a separation be possible.

Present day perceptions:

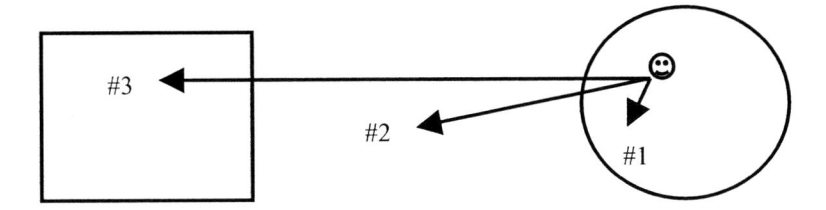

Within such a system, there are three possibilities: We are 'pre-destined' to enter one of three locations:

1. Upon death we may enter the universe. However since the universe is immersed 'within' time, since time is an apparent innate characteristic of a matter/energy system, then when time ends abstractual knowing has two possibilities
2. Upon death of the universe or before the death of the universe, abstractual knowing will enter either #2 or #3. If abstractual knowing enters #2 then abstractual knowing is alone, perhaps forever, fear enters the picture.
3. Upon death of the universe or before death of the universe, abstractual knowing will enter either #2 or #3. If abstractual knowing enters #3 then abstractual knowing no longer remains isolated, fear exits the picture

The criteria for entering #3: 'behavior' as pre-defined by 'men' or 'God'.

The new perception:

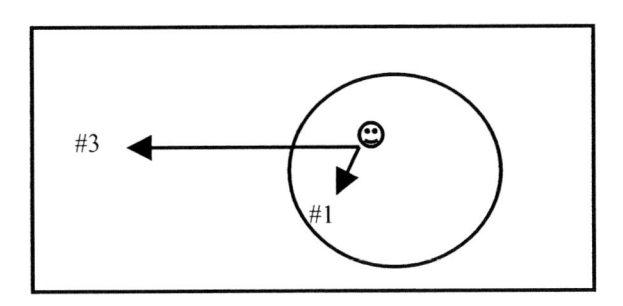

Two possibilities: We are 'pre-destined' to enter one of two 'locations'

1. Upon death, we may enter the universe. However since the universe is immersed 'within' time, since time is an apparent innate characteristic of a matter/energy system, then when time ends abstractual knowing has one possibility:
2. Upon death of the universe or before death of the universe, abstractual knowing will enter #3. If abstractual knowing enters #3 then abstractual knowing remains but no longer remains isolated, fear exists the picture

The criteria for entering #3: There is no criterion for entering #3, for there is no other possibility.

The implication is that pre-destination no longer becomes a pre-destined destination but rather the location is singular. Only one location exists although that location may be subdivided into various distinct perceptual subsets. The result of a perception of singularity: the elimination of the need to 'enter'. One is already 'in' the location of one's desired final destination.

If pre-destination no longer becomes pre-destined in the sense that a choice of one of several destinations is 'made' or is 'assigned for one's self by a second party other than one's self, what then of predestination?

The concept of pre-destination becoming obsolete is not the only resultant obsolescence the new perception, singularity of location, creates.

Predestination:

Present day perceptions:

> *Predestination: The doctrine that man's salvation or damnation was predetermined from eternity by God. When the doctrine holds that not only man's eventual disposition but every event of his life is predestined, the position is identical to a special kind of determinism.*[7]

Under an Aristotelian system, predestination suggests the 'divine book' has already been written. Predestination suggests, although one may not 'know' of one's future, the reader, the author, or both can certainly look ahead and discover what is to happen to the participants, the characters, 'within' the book. This concept, however, eludes the characters found within the 'divine book'.

The 'degree of action', possessed by the characters found within 'the divine book', separates predestination from various types and degrees of determinism.

Regardless of the degree of separation, however, all forms of predestination and determinism embrace the concept of 'a' 'divine book'. One form of 'divine book' may be more interactive than another but they all have 'an' ending.

The new perception:

Within a perceptual system of singularity subdivided into subsets, time and distance are not what complete individual entities of 'knowing', entities of individuality; find themselves immersed 'within'. Rather completed entities of 'knowing find time and distance immersed 'within' themselves. Time and distance find themselves immersed 'within' completed units of 'knowing'.

On the other hand, it is the 'forming', the 'evolving', 'incomplete' units of 'knowing' which find themselves immersed 'within' time and distance.

The perception of the whole system creates a new understanding as to the 'meaning' of predestination.

Before examining the new perception regarding predestination, let's reexamine the new perception regarding singularity of location. We will begin such an examination with a familiar diagram. The diagram is slightly different, however, from what we examined previously. In this diagram, the specific regions within which time and space can be found are identified. When examining such regions, do not overlook the significance regarding the difference between physically experiencing time and space versus abstractually perceiving time and space.

The War & Peace of a New Metaphysical Perception

Three Locations for:
What is
Existence of existence

Action creating:
The Boundary of determinism

Action creating:
The Boundary of free will

Action creating:
The Boundary of divine foreknowledge

Abstractually Perceiving Time and Space

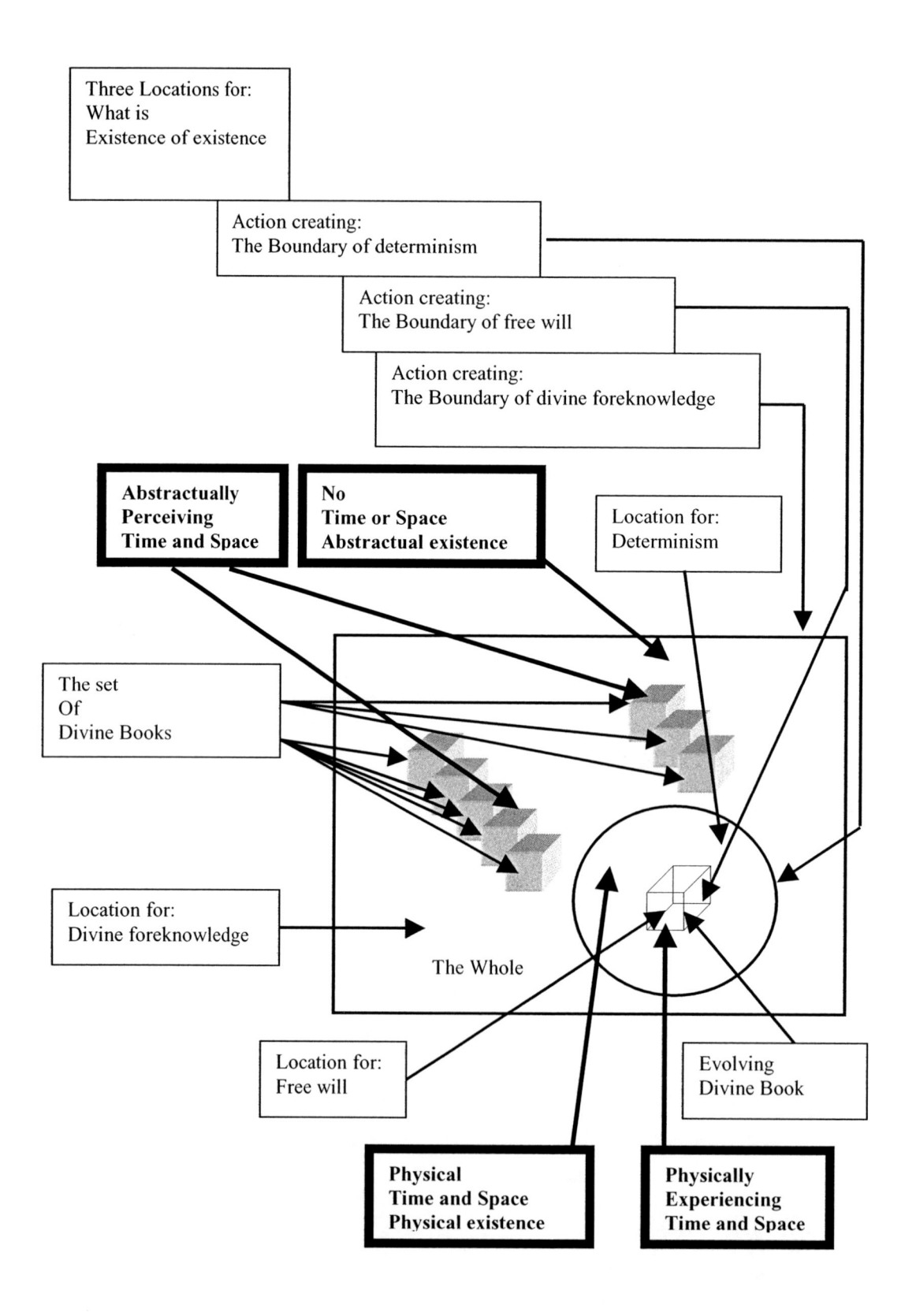

No Time or Space Abstractual existence

Location for: Determinism

The set Of Divine Books

Location for: Divine foreknowledge

The Whole

Location for: Free will

Evolving Divine Book

Physical Time and Space Physical existence

Physically Experiencing Time and Space

So what does this do to the concept of 'predestination'?
This perception moves predestination from being:

> *Predestination: The doctrine that man's salvation or damnation was predetermined from eternity by God. When the doctrine holds that not only man's eventual disposition but every event of his life is predestined, the position is identical to a special kind of determinism.*[8]

To being:

Predestination would now suggest the 'divine book' has not 'been' written but 'is being' written. Predestination suggests, although one may not 'know' of one's future, neither does the reader, neither does the author know of one's future for the future has not yet been written for the 'book' is written but on the other hand the 'book' is ever evolving within a 'location' of timelessness.

Predestination would now suggest absolutely NO entity can look ahead and discover what 'is to happen' to the participants, the characters 'within' the book. The concept of 'knowing' how the story ends eludes all entities of the system including the entity of the 'whole' system itself.

How can this be? The inability to understand the 'end' of the story becomes a characteristic of the system for the concept of time is not 'a' universal factor of the whole but rather time simply finds itself as 'an' aspect of subsets of the whole rather than being 'a' universal characteristic of the whole.

As such, the 'divine book' appropriately becomes the epitome of the lesser known children's novel: 'The Never Ending Story'. And just why would such a perception be 'appropriate'? It becomes appropriate for it moves us into understanding that we are not a subset of a 'static' 'whole' but rather we are a subset of a 'dynamic' whole and as such we do not have just a journey of exciting discover awaiting us but rather we have an 'endless' exciting journey of discover. Within such a perception, we will never run out of 'new' exciting experiences and fascinating previously unknown knowledge for 'newness' itself becomes an innate characteristic of the 'whole'. Such a perception represents the fountain of youth for our specie, for how can one ever grow old when presented with an endless emergence of new frontiers to placate our unquenchable thirst for new knowledge.

This new perception suggests the only form of 'predestination' lies in the concept of change itself. This new perception suggests we, as individuals and as a specie, are a part of this thing called 'eternal change' in a much greater degree than we have every previously conceived.

Within the new perception, although predestination and determinism embrace the concept of 'a' 'divine book', they embrace it as a 'Never Ending Story' for the 'divine book' no longer has 'an' ending.

How does this new perception affect the concept of determinism? Does determinism remain simply an extreme form of predestination, as we presently perceive it to be?

Determinism:

Present day perception:

> *When the doctrine holds that not only man's eventual disposition but every event of his life is predestined, the position is identical to a special kind of determinism*[9]

The War & Peace of a New Metaphysical Perception

Within an Aristotelian system, the statement is absolute not only in terms of what it implies but in terms of what it so succinctly states. As such, no more need be said regarding present day perceptions of determinism.

The new perception:

To best understand the concept of determinism as it applies to a perception of singular location composed of subsets, a diagram once again will be the best manner to initiate the discussion. This diagram may look familiar, as it well should by now, but the dialogue boxes are now filled with the four forms of action:

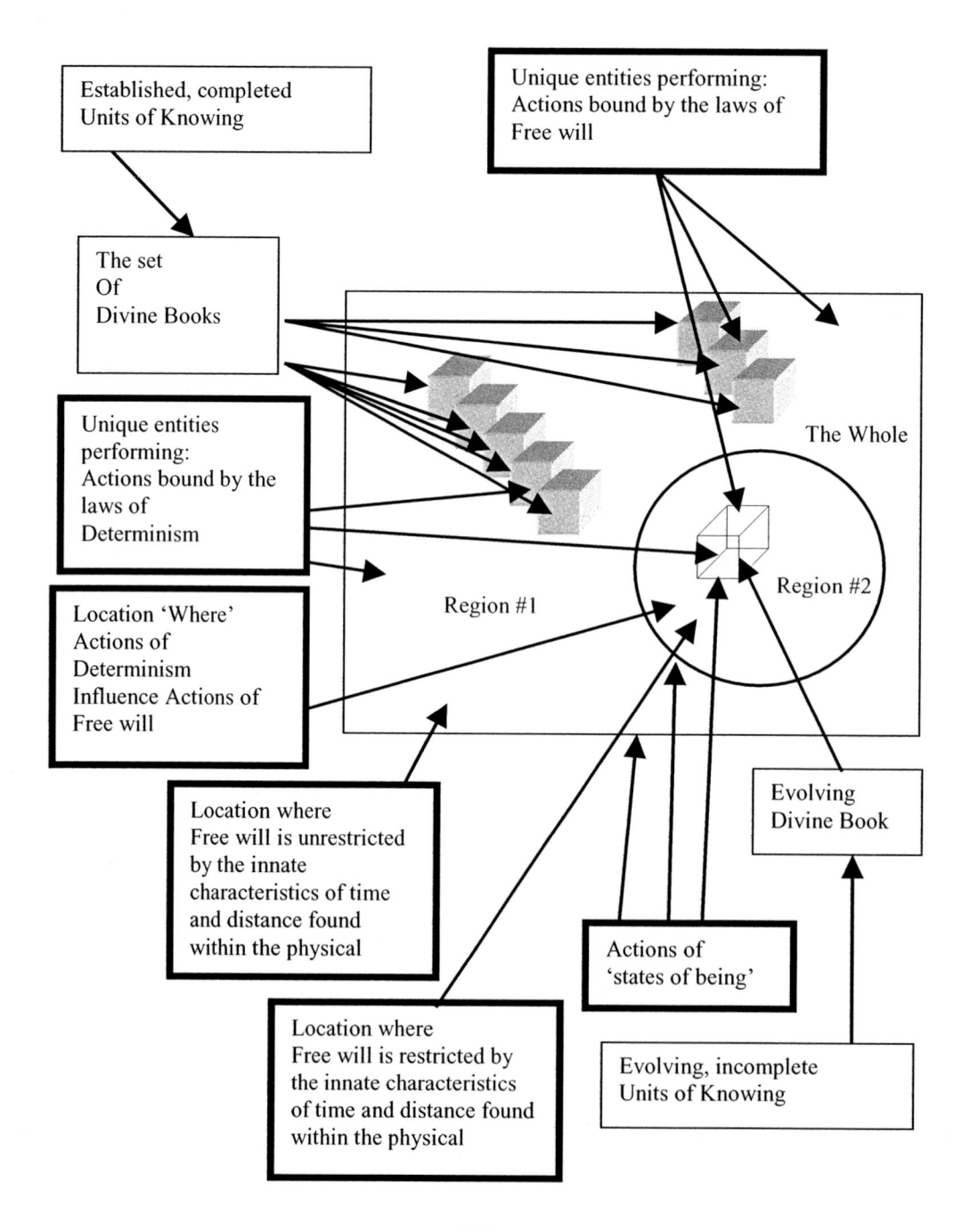

Now what is the difference between regions #1 and #2 in terms of determinism?

Region #2:

Within this region, within the region of the physical universe, actions bound by the laws of nature, actions which are subject to the laws of nature, actions observed and measured through the fields of science: physics, genetics, chemistry, etc.

Within this region, free will may operate but it does not operate unaffected by the laws of nature.

Region #1;
Within this region, within the region of pure abstraction, actions bound by the laws of nature are not found. As such, entities found 'within' this region have a much greater degree of potential acts they can 'perform' but the trade off is: They are unable to 'experience' 'originally'. Even though 'free will exists within this region, no unique, no original 'change' takes place because 'unique change' is a function of time and time is a function of the sub-entities rather than being a function of the whole.

In this section of the tractate, we have been giving a cursory examination to the concepts of divine foreknowledge, pre-destination, predestination, and determinism. One should note, that the concept of 'free will' has now been added to the equation. What of 'free will', does it change in terms of a 'new perception' as opposed to 'present day perception'? Absolutely, a perceptual change in our understanding of free will is where the heart and soul of this tractate lies. The understanding of a concept such as free will cannot be expressed in 'a' paragraph but rather takes a complete tractate to accomplish. The totality of this tractate is where a new understanding of free will lies.

With this in mind, we need to examine the concept of free will in detail. Before we do, however, let's examine the concept of determinism in a little more detail.

Internationality: the need 'for' a location of determinism

Actions bound by the laws of determinism: What 'has been'

Actions bound by the laws of determinism are active 'knowing' actions taken by a 'knowing' entity and are independent of the laws of nature. Actions of determinism are actions generated by a 'knowing' entity whose intended actions are to over-ride actions of free will generated by a second 'knowing' entity. Examples of actions bound by the laws of determinism are: I am, against my will, pushed off the cliff by an entity itself bound by the laws of free will.

Actions bound by the laws of determinism tend to establish 'gods' and 'God'. What is the difference between 'gods' and 'God'? 'gods' are 'beings', physical essences, 'higher order' 'beings' while God is an abstractual essence, 'higher order' 'Being'.

'beings' versus 'Being', what is the difference? In the sense of the four actions identified by metaphysics, nothing.

However, isn't there a difference of degree? Actually, there is no difference of degree. The action of overriding the free will of an entity is the action of overriding the free will of an entity. Isn't there a form of overriding the free will of an entity, which the entity in turn can overcome? If the entity whose freewill is being overridden manages to overcome the action of 'gods' or God and thus maintains its actions bound by the laws of free will, manages to maintain its desired course as originally intended, then its free will has not been overridden. As such, free will becomes the dominant action and determinism, although it remains an issue, becomes the recessive action.

Wouldn't an entity whose free will has been impacted by a 'god' or 'God' in an attempt to override the entity's free will, find its intended actions altered by those very attempts to override its initial actions in the first place? Certainly. Wouldn't such alterations be a form of 'overriding' the purity of action attempted by the entity attempting to initiate actions bound by the laws of free will? Absolutely. The degree of purity initiated by entities attempting to maintain their free will as well as the purity of actions initiated by entities of free will is not the issue here. Such concepts are discussions regarding what we call principles and issues regarding 'standing up for one's principles'.

With this having been said, we can now examine what actions bound by the laws of determinism really are. Such an examination brings us back to the four forms of action:

1. The state of being
2. Actions bound by the laws of nature
3. Actions bound by the laws of free will
4. Actions bound by the laws of determinism

Do not loose sight of the fact that within this tractate, the order given for the four forms of action in no way implies relative significance of one form of action over another. It may be too difficult to subconsciously overlook such a natural tendency without a little help. To assist us in recognizing the equality regarding all forms of action, lets restate the four forms of action and then proceed:

1. Actions bound by the laws of determinism
2. Actions bound by the laws of nature
3. The state of being
4. Actions bound by the laws of free will

The Error of Boethius

Through the aid of the concept of 'location', we can begin to examine the four forms of action:

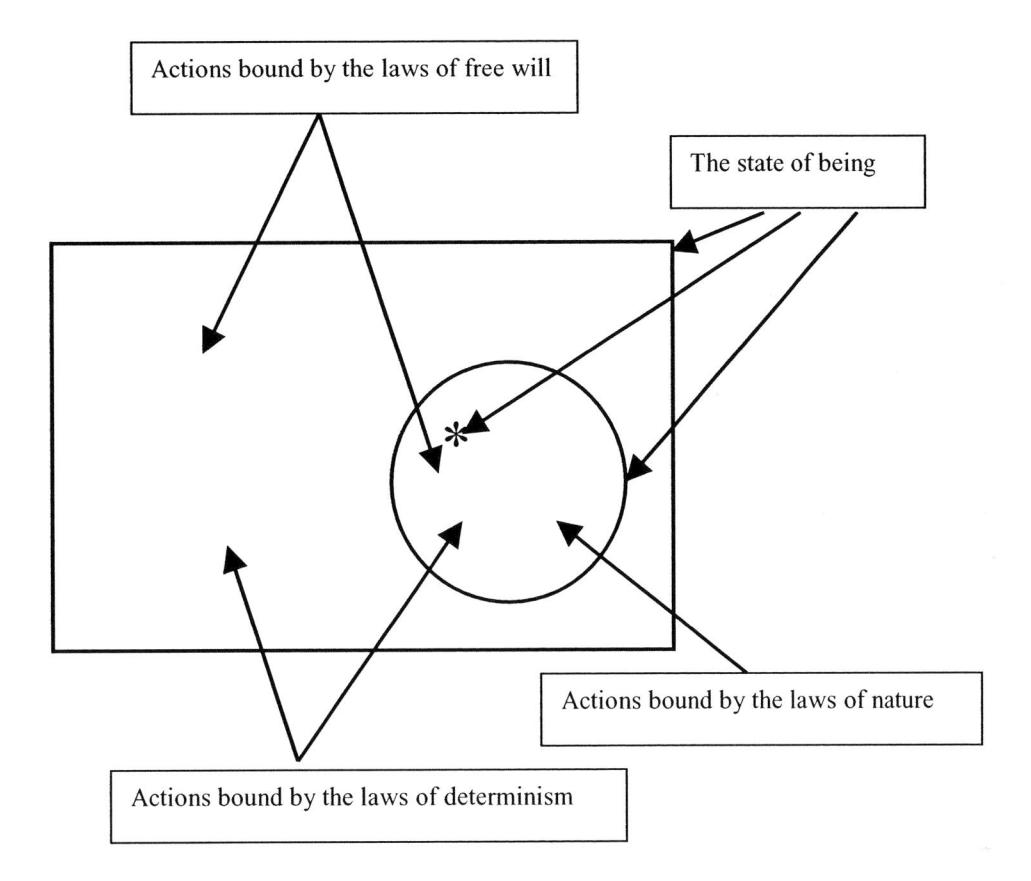

[Diagram: A rectangle containing a circle with an asterisk. Arrows point from four labeled boxes: "Actions bound by the laws of free will" (points outside the rectangle), "The state of being" (points to the circle), "Actions bound by the laws of nature" (points to the circle), and "Actions bound by the laws of determinism" (points outside the rectangle).]

With this diagram in mind, lets re-categorize our four forms of action:

Forms of determinism:

    1. Actions bound by the laws of nature
    2. Actions bound by the laws of determinism
    3. States of being

Forms of free will:

    4. Actions bound by the laws of free will

We have little difficulty acknowledging 'the state of being' exists.

We have little difficulty acknowledging, 'actions bound by the laws of nature' exist.

We have little difficulty acknowledging, 'actions bound by the laws of determinism' exist.

The War & Peace of a New Metaphysical Perception

We do, however, have a problem understanding forms of free will. For the time being, we are going to set free will aside and focus upon the other three forms of action.

As such our previous diagram now becomes:

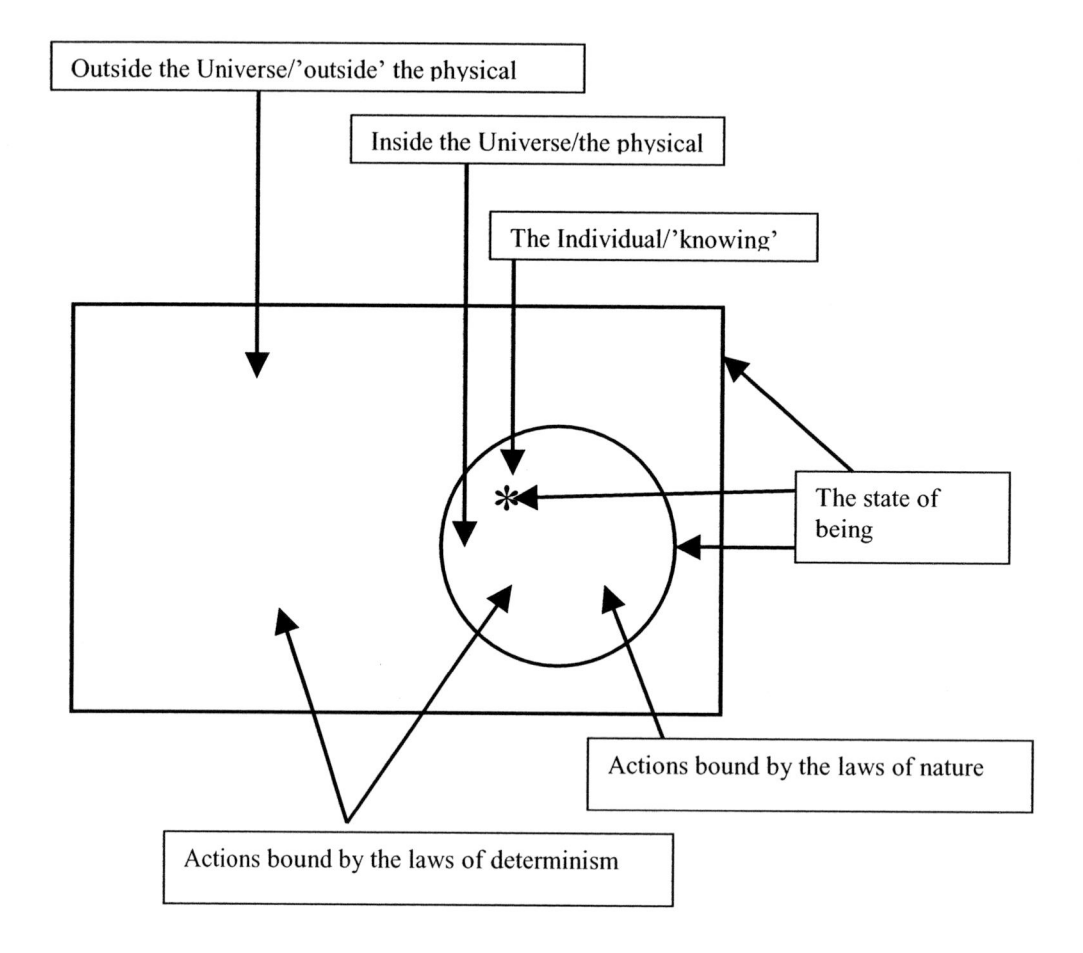

```
┌─────────────────────────────────────────┐
│  Outside the Universe/'outside' the physical │
└─────────────────────────────────────────┘
           │
           │    ┌──────────────────────────┐
           │    │ Inside the Universe/the physical │
           │    └──────────────────────────┘
           │              │
           │              │   ┌──────────────────────┐
           │              │   │ The Individual/'knowing' │
           │              │   └──────────────────────┘
           ▼              ▼              │
                                         ▼
                    ┌──────────────────────┐
                    │    The state of      │
                    │       being          │
                    └──────────────────────┘

              ┌──────────────────────────────┐
              │ Actions bound by the laws of nature │
              └──────────────────────────────┘

         ┌──────────────────────────────────┐
         │ Actions bound by the laws of determinism │
         └──────────────────────────────────┘
```

Earthquakes, volcanoes, waves, wind, starlight, gravitational pull, etc. are all forms actions bound by the laws of nature. These actions are, in present day society, perceived as neutral actions but actions nevertheless. They are perceived as actions, which affect entities of 'knowing'. For the most part, however, they are actions whose pre-existing laws we, entities of knowing, find affecting ourselves in a neutral manner. These forms of actions originate in response to the 'laws' of nature and are not 'initiated' in a conscious manner planned by the natural entity of the mountain, the star, the ocean, the atmosphere.

I am, you are, the mountain is, the lake is, the house is, the tree is, etc, are all forms of actions represented by the passive action: the state of being. These actions are in present day society, perceived as neutral actions but actions nevertheless. They are perceived as actions, which effect entities of 'knowing', but for the most part, are actions whose pre-existing laws we exist 'within' rather than being actions unit entities intentionally, 'knowingly', willingly, and consciously initiate in a physical sense.

214

The Error of Boethius

Murder, rape, verbal-abuse, genocide, physical assault, etc are, from the perspective of the victim, all forms of actions bound by the laws of determinism since the actions are not 'controlled' by the victim. These action, are in present day society, perceived as aggressive actions, forms of action. They are perceived as actions, which affect entities of 'knowing'. Such actions are actions the entity does not 'wish' to have forced upon it. In the pragmatic sense, there is little arguing such actions occur within the physical, but what of such actions existing outside the physical? Outside the physical 'actions bound by the laws of determinism' do not exist for to exist and be 'effective' in an 'affective' manner actions bound by the laws of determinism must have a medium of action. Such a median is the physical itself. Without the physical, abstraction as well as any entity of pure abstractual existence need not submit to unsolicited actions of other purely abstractual existence.

With this in mind, we can examine the concept of divine foreknowledge as 'the' ultimate form of action bound by the laws of determinism. Abstractual existence is what determinism lies 'within' and the abstract is the means and the location within which established consciousness, 'being' itself, exists timelessly and within which established consciousness, 'being', understands its very timelessness.

When observing human behavior and interactions, it becomes obvious where free will does not lie. While free will may lie not only within actions bound by the laws of nature, and within actions bound by the laws of determinism, and within actions bound as states of being, free will in the purest sense lies 'within' itself, within the entity itself.

With this in mind, we come to the concept of free will itself:

Potentiality: the need 'for' a location of free will

It is the 'entity', which 'performs' the action not the 'region'. Thus, the previous diagram needs to be expanded to include 'entities' within the abstract, to include units of knowing of what is uniquely perceived and uniquely experienced. As such, the diagram becomes:

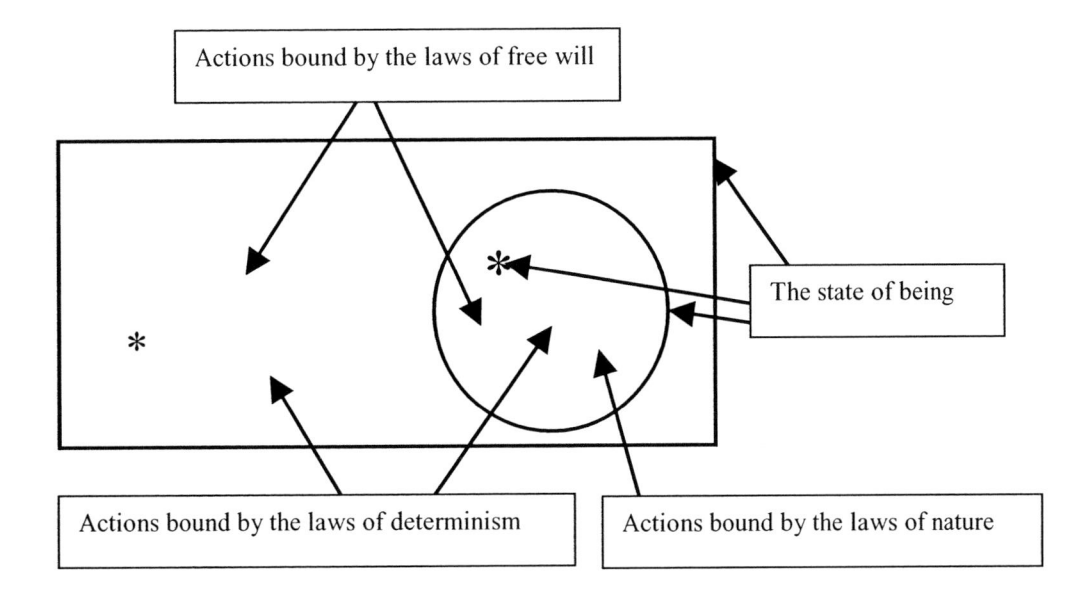

The War & Peace of a New Metaphysical Perception

Now we are ready to discuss the issue of free will and determinism existing simultaneously in two versus one location.

The potential 'to be', action bound by the laws of free will, tends to establish self preservation as 'the' ultimate form of action since the physical existence is what free will lies 'within' and since the physical is the means by which and the location within which virgin consciousness, 'being' itself, emerges and expands its very self.

Action bound by the laws of free will is not an 'absolute', rather action bound by the laws of free will are actions that we 'perceive to be occurring':

Perceive to be occurring:

    a. Perceive: active
    b. to be: passive
    c. occurring: active

This state, the passive sandwiched between states of the active, replicates a dynamic metaphysical systems as opposed to static metaphysical systems

Dynamic metaphysical system: 'being' *being* 'Being'

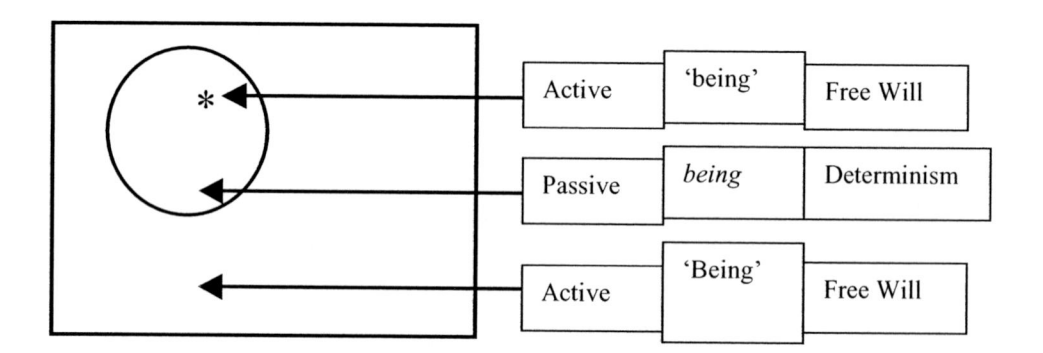

	Active	'being'	Free Will
	Passive	*being*	Determinism
	Active	'Being'	Free Will

So why is this a 'dynamic' metaphysical system? It is dynamic because it provides a means for 'growth'. All is 'known' except 'what is to be'.

Static metaphysical system:

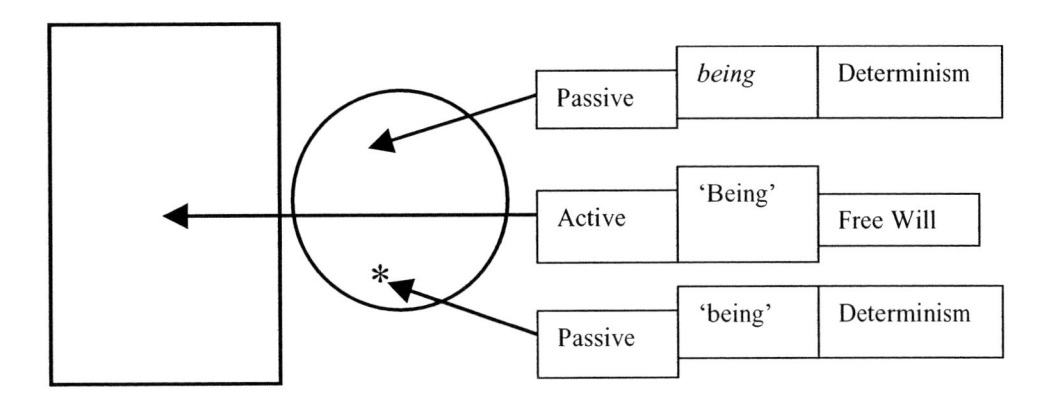

[Diagram: Static metaphysical system showing a rectangle on the left, a circle in the middle with arrows connecting to three labeled boxes on the right: "Passive — *being* — Determinism", "Active — 'Being' — Free Will", and "Passive — 'being' — Determinism". An asterisk (*) appears in the lower portion of the circle.]

So why is this a 'static' metaphysical system? It is static because it provides no means for 'growth'. All is 'known'.

With this in mind, once again we come back to:

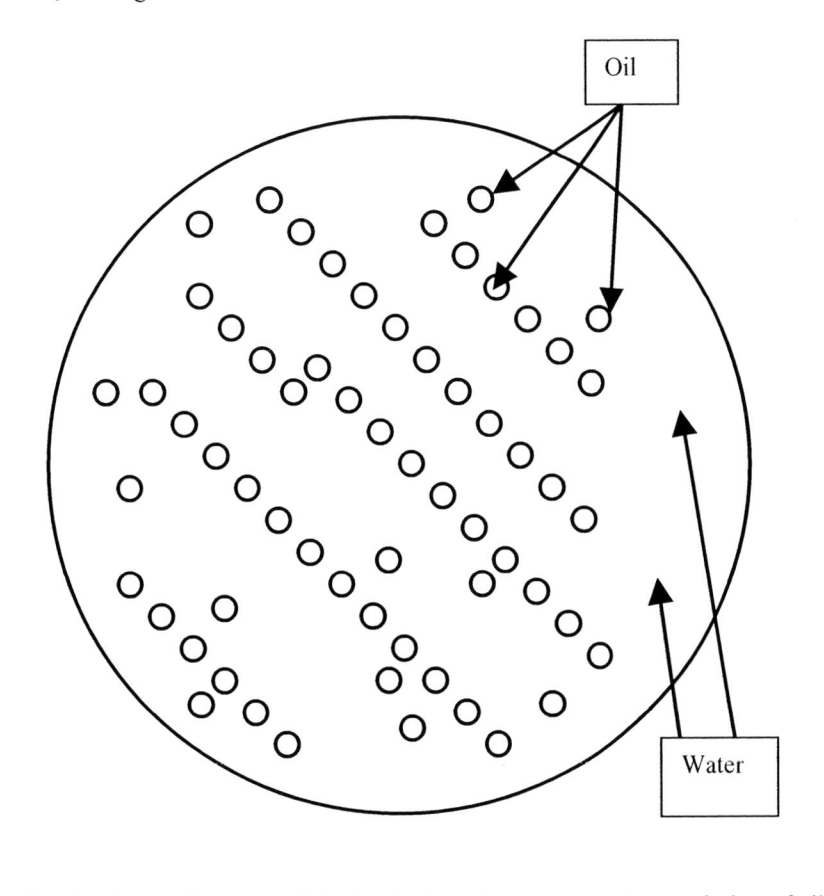

[Diagram: A large circle filled with small circles (o), with arrows pointing inward from a box labeled "Oil" and arrows pointing outward to a box labeled "Water".]

We will now dissolve the confinement of the border in order to remove the confusion of oil having an affinity to its container. As such, we obtain

The War & Peace of a New Metaphysical Perception

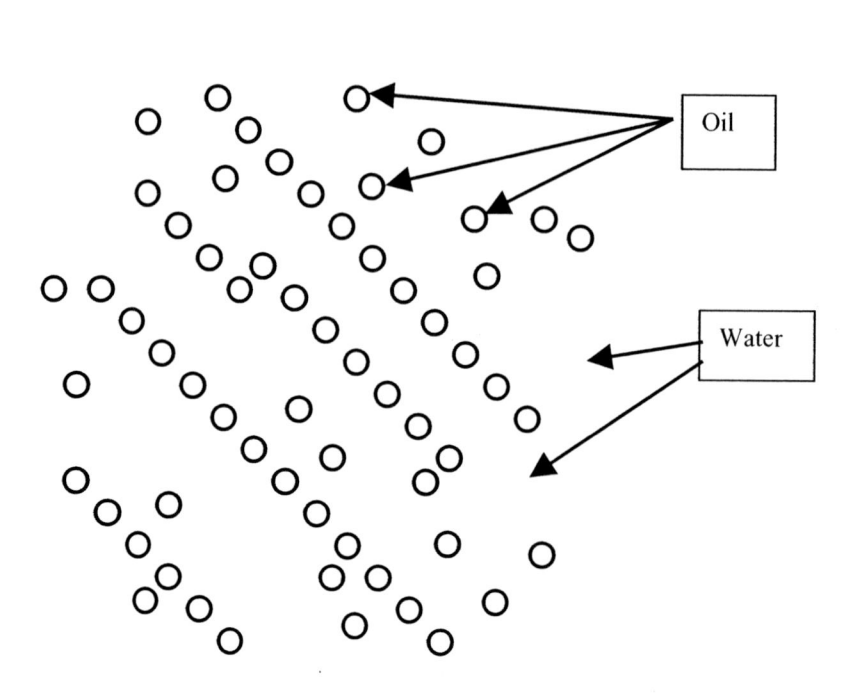

We then create 'a' system by adding a boundary, which has no affinity for either oil or water. We do so simply for convenience. We thus obtain:

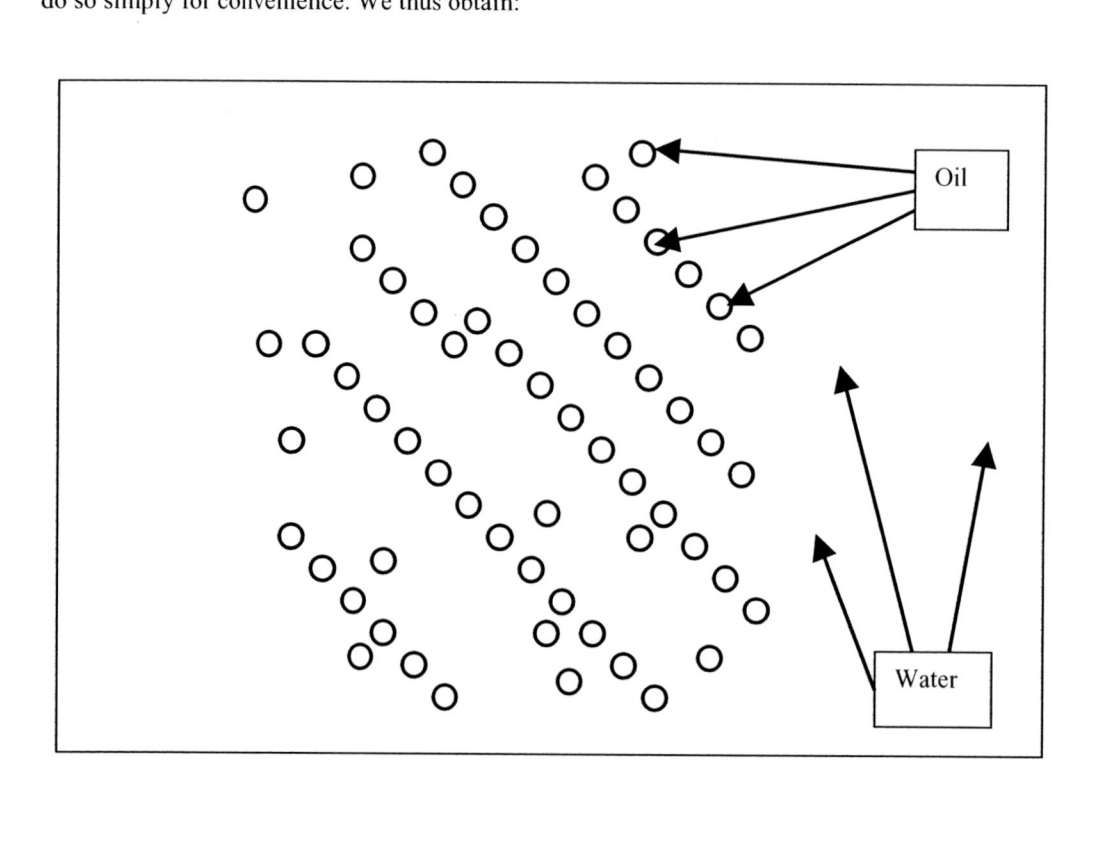

We then call oil by its correct symbolic name and do the same for water.

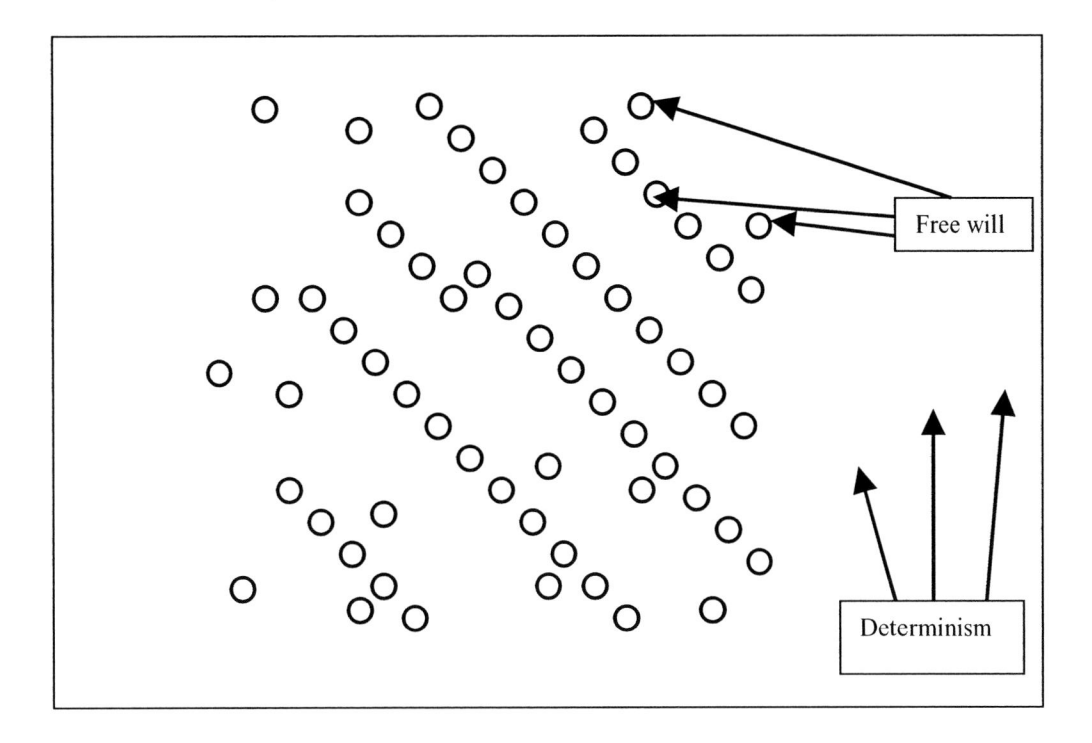

We then simplify using Ockham's razor:

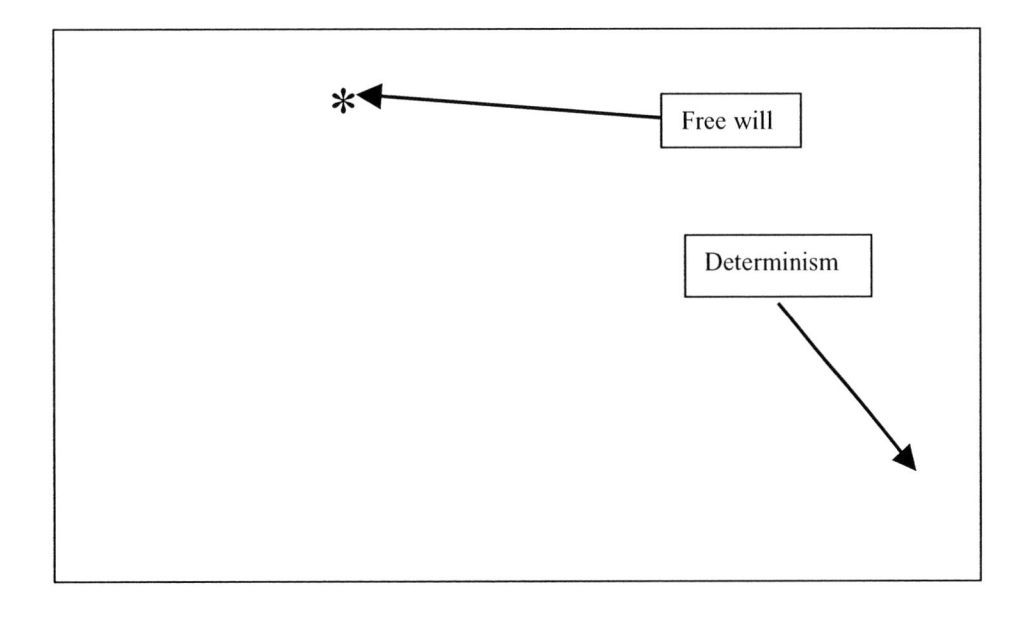

If we then create a 'location for free will to function within a realm of space and time, we then obtain

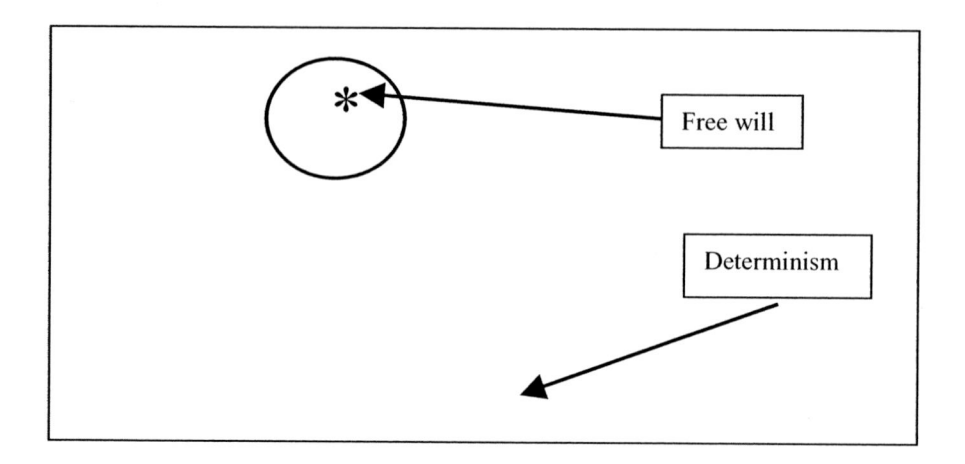

Once again we come back to the model of 'being' *being* 'Being'.

Nothing: the need 'for' a location of nothing

We have discussed the concepts regarding the existence of free will and the existence of 'divine foreknowledge'. We have discussed the concepts regarding a 'location' for free will and a 'location' for 'divine foreknowledge'. The natural extension of such dialectic would appear to move into the direction of examining the existence of 'nothingness' and the 'location' for 'nothingness'.

To move into the direction of such a discussion, however, would deprive us of completing the task at hand. The task at hand is finalizing our understanding as to how we can reasonably and rationally resolve the paradox regarding the simultaneous existence of 'free will' and 'divine foreknowledge'.

The issue regarding 'nothingness' is extremely important and is not to be ignored. As such, the examination of 'nothingness' will be examined in the Tractate 4: Copernicus. Why discuss the issue of 'nothingness' within the Tractate 4: Copernicus? We will examine the concept of 'nothingness' within the Copernicus Tractate because it is Copernicus who unwittingly led us away from understanding nothingness itself.

The Book of Divine Foreknowledge

Boethius' system introduces us to the Book of Divine Foreknowledge:

The Error of Boethius

Hidden deep within the 'Book' is free will

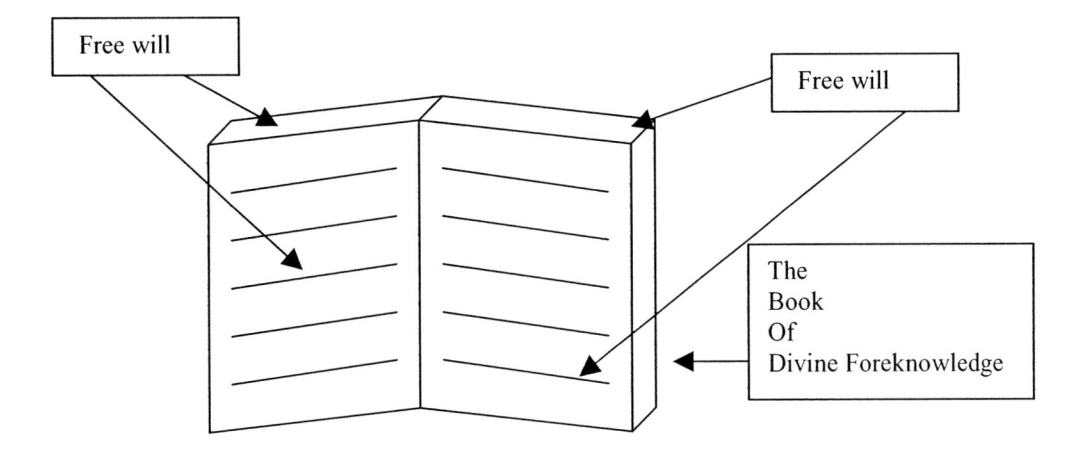

```
     Free will                              Free will


                                              The
                                              Book
                                              Of
                                              Divine Foreknowledge
```

Within the book, one is free to make choices of their own preference but the choices are already 'known' by the ultimate Knowing, 'known' by 'Omniscience'.

Religions would suggest the book is a form of encyclopedia of the whole; the book is a source of all knowledge.

If the book is a source of all knowledge, then Boethius is correct in his assumptions regarding the limits of men. If such is the case, then humanity can perceive of paradoxes whose solutions will never be know to humanity due to the limits 'placed' upon humanity not by itself but rather due to limits 'placed' upon humanity by a 'superior' Being.

If we find a means of resolving the contradicting paradox regarding the simultaneous existence of divine foreknowledge and free will, then we will, for the present, have removed the limits humanity places upon itself. If we can find an alternative solution to Boethius principle relegating humanity to a 'limited' status, then we will be ready to move on and free philosophy and metaphysics of its present constraints, thus opening the doors of not only truly new and exciting philosophical and metaphysical perceptual developments but we will have opened the doors of truly new and exciting cosmological and ontological perceptual developments as well.

This then leaves us with discussing the remaining two possibilities:

Which came first the chicken or the egg?

Which came first determinism or free will?

This question is very similar to the question, which surfaced in Tractate 1: Zeno and Seamlessness. In this Tractate, the question arose: Does the abstract exist 'within' the physical or does the physical 'exist' within the abstract?

The War & Peace of a New Metaphysical Perception

The Location of Free Will

Perceived 'free will' located 'within' the physical:

We understand free will to apply to active forms of actions. Previously we categorized actions into two forms:

> Forms of action:

> Passive:
> 1. State of being
> 2. Actions bound by the laws of nature

> Active:
> 3. Actions bound by the laws of free will
> 4. Actions bound by the laws of determinism

Since the two forms of actions: states of being and actions bound by the laws of nature are actions we do not perceive as being actions generated by forms of consciousness, we will set them aside and concentrate upon the other forms of action, free will and determinism.

Free will 'within' the physical:

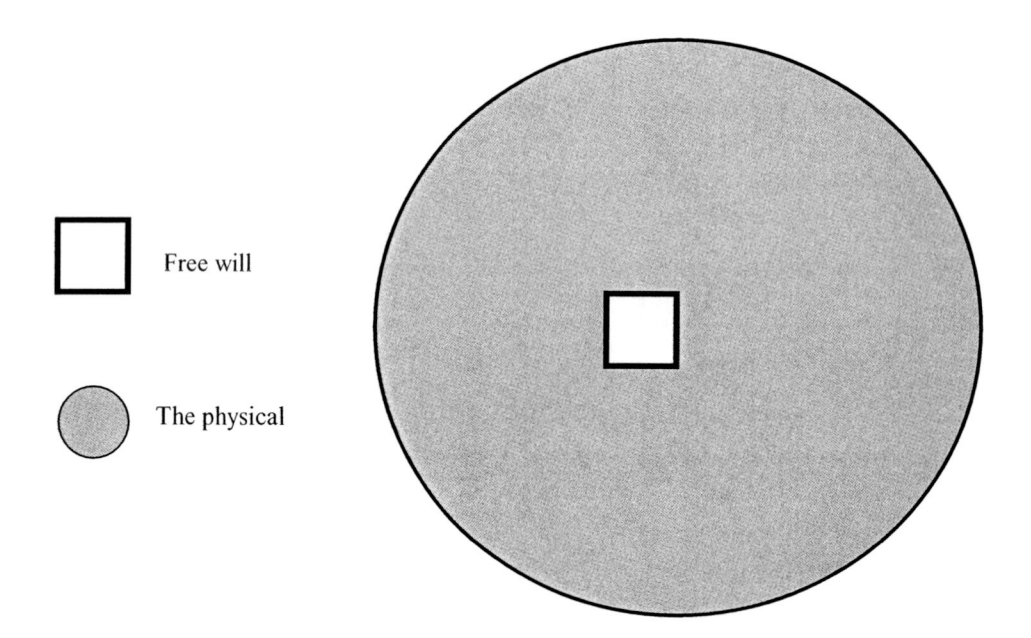

□ Free will

● The physical

And it is within the physical we perceive abstraction to exist. Love, hate, jealousy, joy, awe, inspiration, knowledge, consciousness of consciousness, ….

But what of:

Free will 'within the abstract

Since free will is an abstract concept we will use the same geometric configuration to represent abstraction:

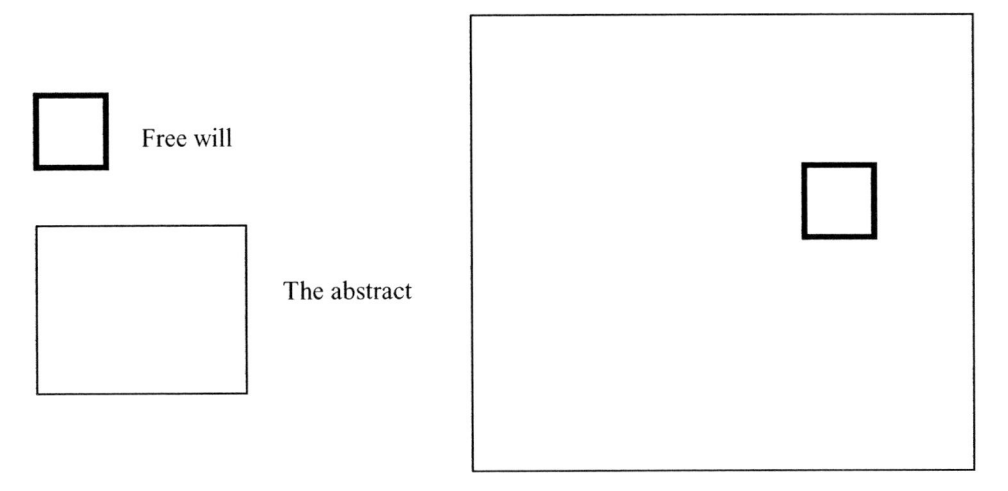

If free will is to be free will, the individual must be the individual and as such, multiplicity becomes:

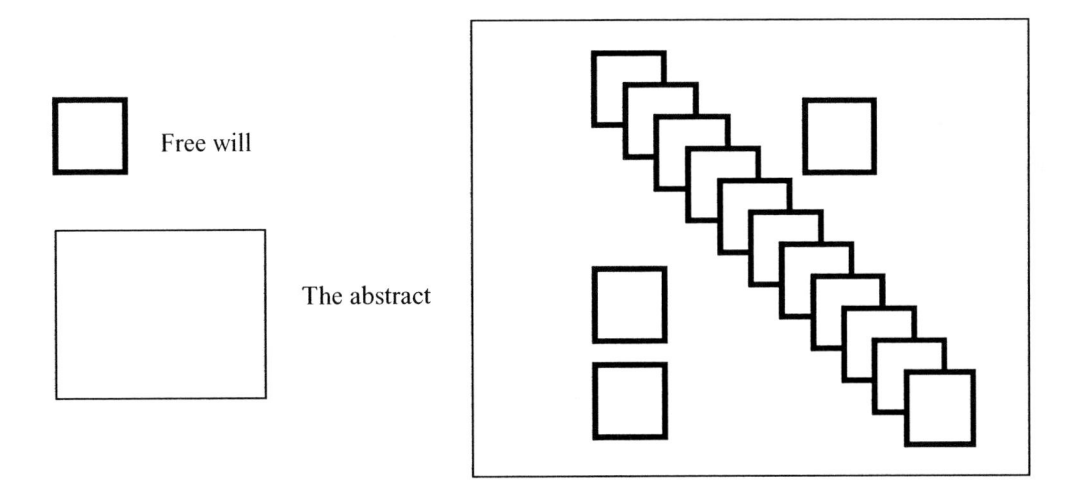

So it is, we come back again to the whole being the sum of its parts yet being the whole, having its own distinct identity. Thus giving rise, once again, to our understanding that in this type of metaphysical perception the whole is 'greater' than the sum of its parts.

The War & Peace of a New Metaphysical Perception

The parts are original entities of 'knowing' having experienced originally within the physical. As such, it is more accurate to portray the latter diagram as:

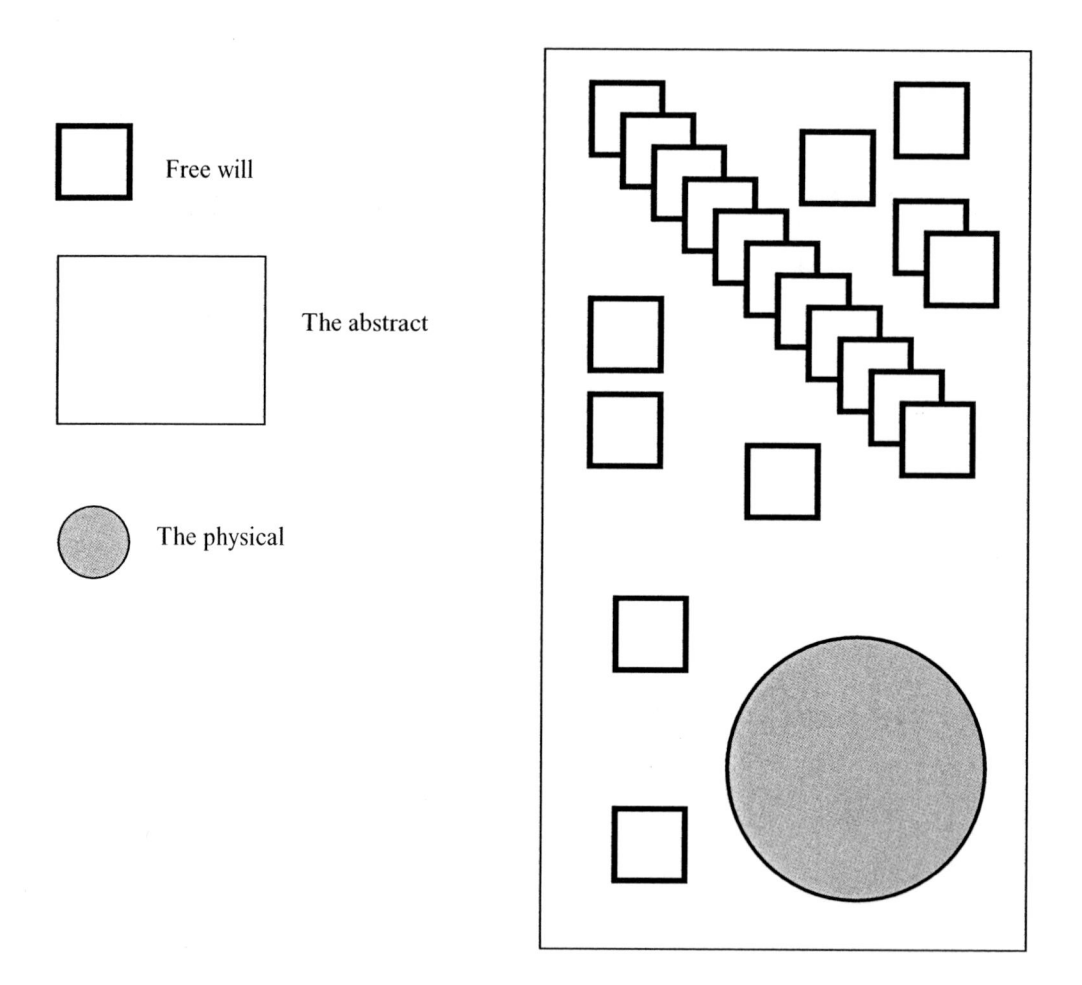

Free will

The abstract

The physical

The Error of Boethius

Where then is free will found in relation to the physical? It is found 'within' the physical just as it is found 'within' the abstract. As such, we obtain:

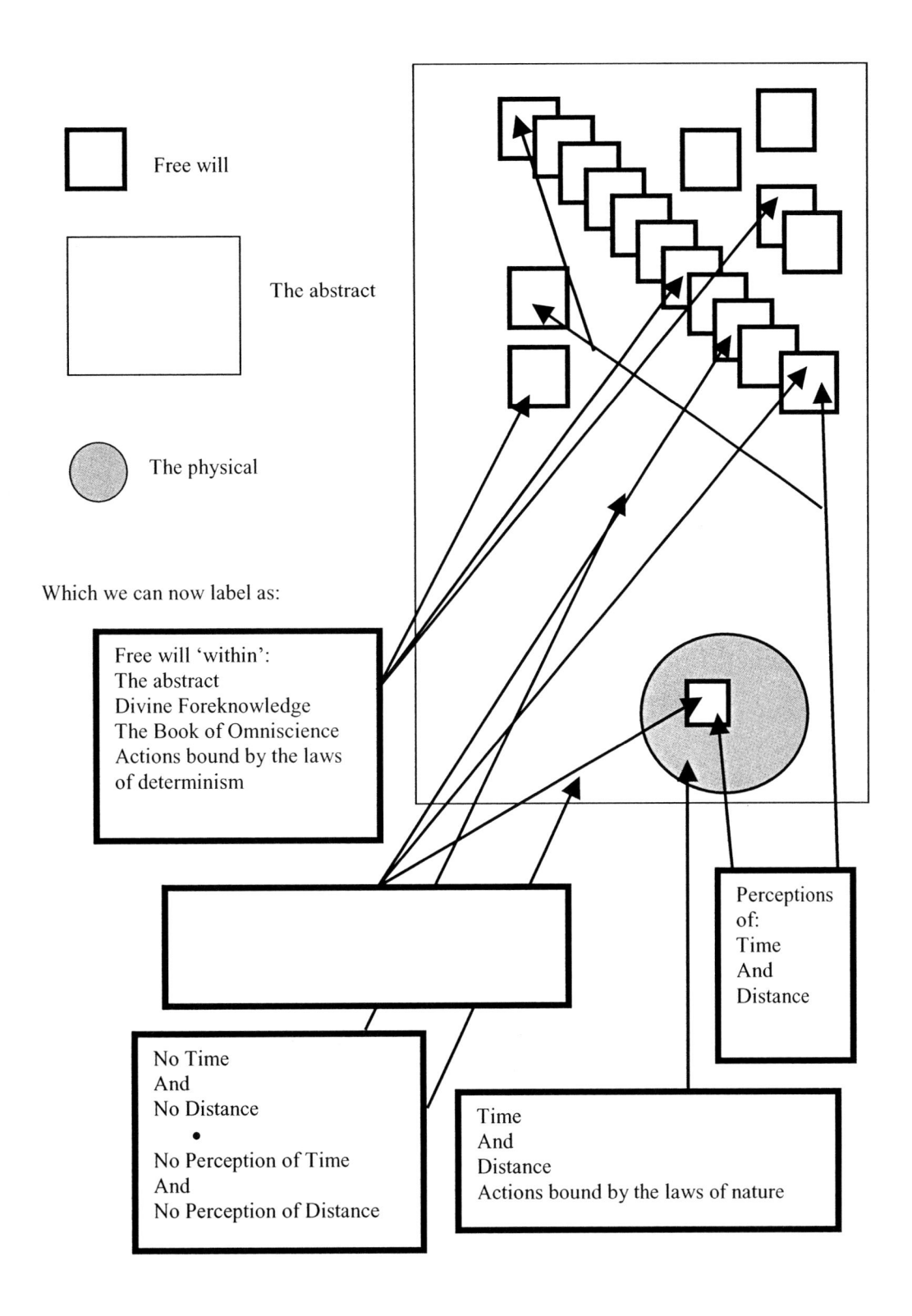

☐ Free will

☐ The abstract

● The physical

Which we can now label as:

Free will 'within':
The abstract
Divine Foreknowledge
The Book of Omniscience
Actions bound by the laws of determinism

No Time
And
No Distance
•
No Perception of Time
And
No Perception of Distance

Perceptions of:
Time
And
Distance

Time
And
Distance
Actions bound by the laws of nature

And what of the passive actions categorized as: states of being? These actions are represented by the black boundary lines of the three forms of action symbolized by the small square, the circle, and the large rectangle.

The location of Determinism

The large rectangle:

The latter diagram defines the location of determinism. Determinism is found in the whole, the large rectangle.

Entities of 'knowing' can travel 'within' the whole as they so choose and experience everything including all abstractions they so desire to experience for they are no longer confined by the restraints of time and distance. 'Knowing' of all entities is open to all to experience for the abstract cannot be hidden from the abstract.

The whole is the whole and is 'knowing' of its wholeness. So it is the whole is the sum of all its parts in addition to being an entity in and of itself.

The whole grows with the growth of virgin 'knowing' and this 'new' 'knowing' adds to the whole.

Sequentiality is not an issue of the whole, for sequentiality is a function of time and distance and since time and distance are not an innate characteristic of the whole of abstraction, ordinal sequentiality are not innate characteristics of the whole.

Both the whole and the individual entities of 'knowing' are incapable of awareness of what is not and what is not is what 'virgin knowing' is to become through free will.

The circle:

The latter diagram defines the location of determinism. Determinism is found in the physical, the circle, both through actions bound by the laws of nature and actions bound by the laws of determinism.

The square:

The latter diagram defines the location where determinism is not. Determinism is not found in the square. Determinism is not found 'within' free will.

The Error of Boethius

The misnomer of 'free will'

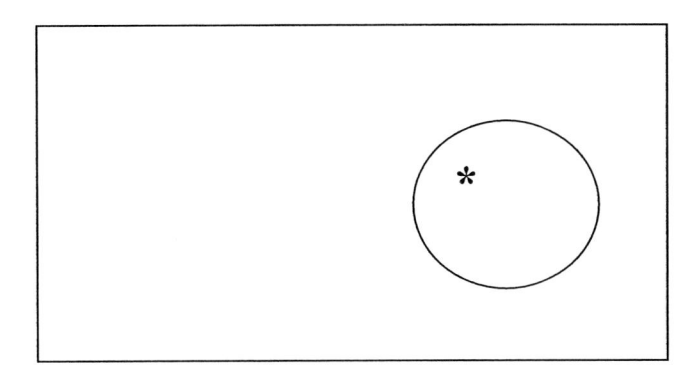

If 'free will' was established as action independent the action of determinism then is free will really 'free will' or just another form of determinism? If such were the case, then free will would have been established by determinism and thus free will would have been established through the act of determinism. If free will is found within determinism then was free will established 'after' the fact of determinism's existence?

On the other hand, perhaps 'free will' void determinism initiated determinism. Perhaps determinism was established as a 'storage' location for free will.

At this point in time, it cannot be determined which of the two, free will or determinism, came first. Nor would it seem, are we capable of determining if neither is the case. We are presently incapable of determining if one came before the other or if the two 'came' into existence simultaneously.

In actuality, the three options regarding which came first, free will, determinism, or both simultaneously, are not as impossible to discuss as one might think.

The third choice:

> Simultaneous emergence of free will and determinism would suggest an existence before either form of 'active action', determinism or free will, existed. But is it possible for there to be a from of action, other than either passive action or active action. Is it possible for there to be a form of action other than the four forms of action we discussed: States of being, actions bound by the laws of nature, actions bound by the laws of determinism, and actions bound by the laws of free will?

> If one wishes to proceed with such an argument one must be able to describe such action in order for this dialectic to proceed. . In the absence of such a description, we will let the possibility of such a possibility stand but we will ignore the dialectic of such a possibility until the description of some form of action, other than passive or active action, emerges. Having set such a possibility aside, we should then proceed with the dialectic

A point of information: This work regarding The War and Peace of a New Metaphysical Perception will not ignore the argument: what came 'before' free will and determinism. The immersion into this very concept initiates the totality of the last chapter: Chapter 18: The End of the Beginning – Theoretical Metaphysics.

This then leaves us with discussing the remaining two possibilities:

Which came first the chicken or the egg?

Which came first determinism or free will?

This question is, in essence, no different from the question, which surfaced in Tractate 1: Zeno and Seamlessness. In this Tractate, the question arose: Does the abstract exist 'within' the physical or does the physical 'exist' within the abstract? One may refer to Tractate 1 if one chooses but rather than reiterate what came before, it is time to begin to address a summary of the issue of free will versus determinism.

It appears an extraordinary number of concepts will be addressed in the manner of 'refer to what was previously…' or addressed as 'later we will…'. Unfortunately, this is a correct observation. Space and time are both limited by the concept known as a 'Tractate'. It is the concept of space and time, which confines us to the parameter of limited discussions. It is the concept of ''tractate', which limits us to staying on task rather than chaotically diverting our attention away from the discussion at hand, which is understanding how it is we became confined, caged, in the first place. It is only through understanding the concept of how it is we are 'caged' by limitations of creative understanding, that we can begin to explore the means of unlocking the door of our cage and stepping 'out' into the realm of free space once again.

Part of unlocking the door to this cage of philosophical confinement lies in exploding the perception of Boethius:

> 'It is not allowed to man to comprehend in thought all the ways of the divine work.' [10]

Perceptions generated by Boethius lead to slamming shut the doors of perceptual 'knowing' and locking it shut. Free will lies behind the door labled: 'It is not for us to know.'lead to multiple perceptions such as: 'If man were intended to fly, God would have given him wings.'

The misnomer regarding free will lies in the perception : Some people think free will is never interrupted or superceded. But as we have seen, there are two forms of action which often interfere with free will:

1. Action bound by the laws of nature
2. Actions bound by the laws of determinism

Actions bound by the laws of nature often supercede the desire to accomplish the actions bound by the laws of free will.

Actions bound by the laws of determinism often supercede the desire to accomplish actions bound by the laws of free will.

The ultimate extreme of both forms of action, actions bound by the laws of nature and actions bound by the laws of determinism, is exemplified as action which terminates actions bound by the laws of free will found within individual entities existing through action bound by the laws of the state of being.

Letting go

It is time for us to let go of Boethius' metaphysical system. Previously we could not let go of Boethius' perceptions because we had nothing to fill the vacuum 'letting go' would create. We could not let go of the concept:

> 'The point of greatest importance here is this: the superior manner of knowledge includes the inferior, but it is quite impossible for the inferior to rise to the superior.'...

It is now time to let go of such perceptions. We have an alternative set before us regarding a perception of free will and determinism. We have an alternative which provides the means of 'letting go' the concept that it is humanity who defines what it is we cannot 'know'. It is time to file Boethius' concept regarding the 'limits' of humanity, the limits of 'beings' found within the universe, away as a part of the annals of history:

We come to the first paragraph of this Tractate:

Free will confined within the boundaries of determinism is simply an illusion of free will.

> 'There can be little question that Boethius, more than any other philosophic author, helped the great Schoolmen to retain a general comprehensive view of the world as a whole, in spite of the distractions of their minute inquiries.'[11]

At this point in time, philosophers have not resolved the issue. On the other hand, at this point in time, philosophers have refused to embrace the rationality of a 'whole' enveloping the physical. As time has demonstrated, two and a half millennium of time, we cannot resolve some of our greatest philosophical paradoxes without the use of both the rationality and the reasonableness of such concept.

Until philosophy moves to the level of accepting its primary tool, reason, as being itself a legitimate tool, the paradoxes will remain paradoxes. Is the lack of being able to resolve the major paradoxes addressed within the Tractates of the work, The War and Peach of a New Metaphysical Perception, a negative? It is only a negative if one believes stagnation is a negative.
Why is it a 'negative' action to take the position: It is unimportant to resolve the issue of free will versus divine foreknowledge. Why is clinging to the concept that the relationship between free will and divine foreknowledge found within Boethius' paradox a negative? Why is refusing to face perhaps one of the most influential paradoxes to confront us for the last twenty-five hundred years a potential negative? The answer to all these questions lies in our abhorrence toward the concept that we are a stagnant specie.

We have addressed three forms of paradoxes: Tractate 1: seamlessness versus multiplicity, Tractate 2: one first truth versus multiple first truths, and now Tractate 3: free will versus divine foreknowledge. In each instance it has been argued that we can resolve the paradox through the means of expanding our perceptual understanding reason, metaphysics, philosophy, can provide.

In the past, we have been unable to resolve many philosophical paradoxes because the greatest paradoxes deal with abstractions and abstractions are not 'physical' in nature. As such, these paradoxes are not measurable for they are not items characterized by time and space.

Abstractions are capable of comprehending time and space but time and space are not capable of comprehending abstractions.

The War & Peace of a New Metaphysical Perception

To resolve abstractual paradoxes embracing characteristics of time and space, one presently has only the tool of reason at one's disposal.

Until we resolve the major paradoxes encompassing the interrelationships of the abstractual and the physical, the paradoxes will remain. The negative aspect of a state of stagnation is the state within which such a state leaves us, units of knowing. We remain mired at an established level of understanding.

Are there other levels of understanding awaiting us? Indubitably, and we, you and I, you and I together, will be left wanting in terms of rising to this new level of understanding until we find the means of resolving the primitive paradoxes presently facing us.

So what next? One thing is certain; we have not come to the end of our understanding regarding the issues of great paradoxes facing humanity. Our next step is to step 'out' beyond the issue of space itself.

It must be stated at this point that such a statement is a misconception for we cannot step 'out' beyond a region of infinite space. As we shall see in Tractate 4: Copernicus, we can only step 'into' a realm of infinite space and as we shall see, it is only by confining ourselves that we can free ourselves of confinement.

So it is free will may very well not be found 'within' 'the' System ' but rather free will may very well be found 'within' 'a' system 'itself 'contained' 'within' a 'greater' System.

Are we creating a paradox? It is only a paradox if one does not understand the solution to the paradox Copernicus espoused the paradox of Centricism versus non-Centricism.

We now understand that

Boethius is a vital link in moving our perceptual understanding forward regarding the 'system' being filled with determinism, into that of being 'the' system filled with both determinism and free will. As such, both free will and determinism, with the help of Boethius, now have a location within which each dominates. As such, the understanding regarding the role of free will and determinism as well as the understanding regarding the interrelationship between free will and determinism no longer remain in a state of confusion. Even more interestingly, the existence of such an interrelationship is not only recognized as a significant aspect of the 'larger' system but it is now understood how free will and determinism interact one with the other.

---

[1] Boethius, The Consolation of Philosophy, Penguin Books, 1969, England, Victor Watts, Merton College, Oxford.
[2] Oxford: Concise Science Dictionary, 1996.
[3] Boethius, The Consolation of Philosophy, Penguin Books, 1969, England, Victor Watts, Merton College, Oxford.
[4] **Question:** I understand what you mean by this. However, an ambiguity still remains. In quantum theory, many "theoretical" particles are "expected" to exist, even though they have yet to be measured. **Answer:** True, however, science has the perception that if it exists, it is measurable. It may not be measurable today, it will be measurable sometime in the future. Science attempts to validate 'theoretical' particles existing by finding a means of proving their existence through measurement.
[5] Boethius: The Consolation of Philosophy, IV, 6

[6] Boethius: The Consolation of Philosophy, Penguin Classics, 1969, p167 – 169.
[7] Dictionary of Philosophy and Religion, William L. Reese, 1980.
[8] Dictionary of Philosophy and Religion, William L. Reese, 1980.
[9] Dictionary of Philosophy and Religion, William L. Reese, 1980.
[10] Boethius: The Consolation of Philosophy, IV, 6
[11] Boethius, The Consolation of Philosophy, Penguin Books, 1969, England, Victor Watts, Merton College, Oxford.

Tractate 4

The Error

Of

Copernicus

❖

The Paradox of:

❖

Centrist Systems

•

The Need for:
A Point of Origination

1.   1543 AD Copernicus – The Error of:
   Centrist Systems – a new perception 2000 AD

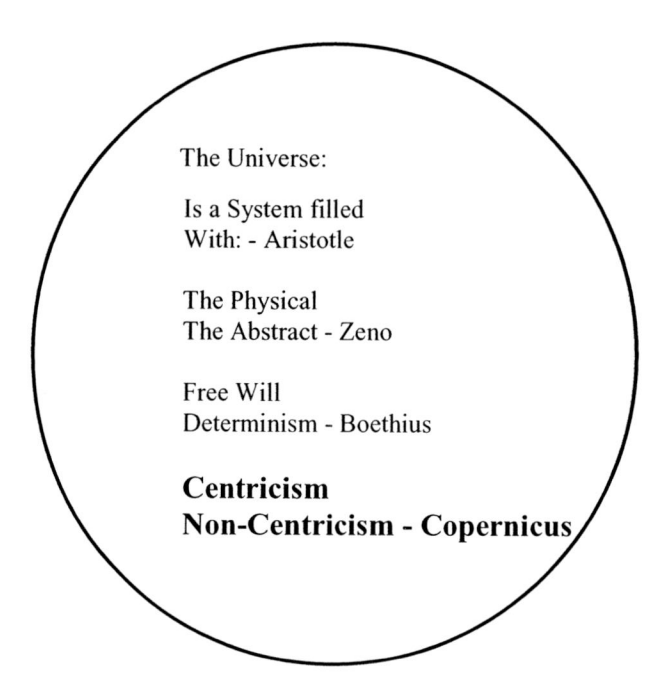

> The Universe:
>
> Is a System filled
> With: - Aristotle
>
> The Physical
> The Abstract - Zeno
>
> Free Will
> Determinism - Boethius
>
> **Centricism**
> **Non-Centricism - Copernicus**

The error: The paradox of Centricism

The perception: Copernicus moves our perceptual understanding regarding the system being filled with Centricism into that of being 'the' system filled with Centricism and non-Centricism. As such, Centricism and non-Centricism, with the help of Copernicus, now have a location within which they can be found. However, the understanding regarding the role of both centricism and non-centricism as well as the understanding regarding the interrelationship between Centricism and non-Centricism not only remain in a state of confusion but even more disconcerting, the existence of such an interrelationship is not recognized as a significant aspect of the 'larger' system.

It is this state of confusion which will be specifically addressed within this tractate.

Contents

Part I: Part I: The Paradox of Centricism and non-Centricism

Introduction I
Introduction II
Pre-Copernican
Post-Copernican
Copernicus' paradoxes

Part II: Resolving the paradox of Centricism with a new metaphysical perception

Centricism
A location of centricism
A location of non-centricism
The dynamics of centricism
    Stepping 'out': into Centricism: Independence
    Stepping 'in': 'beyond' Centricism: Independence
The dynamics of non-centricism
The law of inverse proportionality
The 'location' of 'nothingness'
Virgin physicality/'virgin physical life'
Virgin consciousness/'virgin abstract knowing'
Stepping 'in' beyond Centricism: Dependency
Stepping 'into' Centricism: Independence
The significance of insignificance: Random Sequencing
The explosive nature of the potentiality of knowing
Removing a piece of Randomness
Boethius' metaphysical system and why we can now file it away as a part of the annals of history
Archimedean Points
Philosophical infinities
A bag of marbles is not dependent upon sequential time
A unit of knowing is not a marble

Terms/concepts

'fundamental building block' of the abstract
'fundamental building block' of the physical
'inverse proportionality'
'Virgin physicality/'virgin physical life'
Aristotelian Points
Centricism
Hegel's 'open' dynamic non-Cartesian system
Kant's 'closed' dynamic Cartesian system
Non-centricism

The War & Peace of a New Metaphysical Perception

Tractate 4
Copernicus – The Error of
Centrist Systems

Part I: Creating the paradox of a Centrist System

Introduction I

With the scientific understanding of the sun being the Cartesian[1] point of origin, the point (0,0,0) as opposed to the individual being the Cartesian point of origin, the individual was literally put into motion.

By moving the concept of the center from being a man, to the center being the sun, Copernicus in essence created the perception of humanity having lost its sense of being the center. Such a perceptual development introduced two concepts into our understanding of the universe. First: we now perceived the universe to have a center, scientifically speaking. Second: Philosophically speaking, we now perceived the universe to be the whole within which 'a' center could be 'found'.

Before Copernicus' revelations, we had philosophically perceived 'the center' to be that of 'knowing'. Pre-Copernicus, we perceived the human id not only 'representing' the center of reality but 'being' the center of reality. With Copernicus' observations, humanity lost its concept of being the center and as such, philosophy/reason found itself being moved from the forefront to being place behind science/observation, and eventually being removed from second place in line to being placed third in line. This second transition of moving from second place to third place occurred with the cultural elevation of God/religion via Christianity, Islam, etc to second place.

How does Copernicus' development of Centricism and non-centricism differ from the Aristotelian development of Cartesian and non-Cartesian? The Aristotelian system of Cartesian and non-Cartesian emerged as a static physical system while the Copernican concepts of Centricism and non-Centricism moved the perceived Aristotelian 'static' system into a perceived 'dynamic' system of movement.

With the acceptance of the Copernican system, everything became objects in motion and all motion took place around a center, thus centricism. In fact, with the acceptance of Copernican system, everything became objects of motion centered around the Aristotelian point of origin.

The Aristotelian system led to the Copernican system, which was to lead to the Kantian system. This historical evolution was to open up the concept of system to Kant's dynamic 'closed' Cartesian system. Kant's system would in turn open up the concept of 'systems' and allow for the development of Hegel's suggestion of 'the' system being a dynamic 'open' non-Cartesian system.

The development of both Kant's and Hegel's systems in turn created the potential acceptance of a new metaphysical model which was to follow their innovations. The new system model which was to follow Kant's 'closed' dynamic Cartesian system and Hegel's 'open' dynamic non-Cartesian system was a model perceived as a 'dynamic open non-Cartesian system powered by a dynamic closed Cartesian systems' or better labeled as 'being' *being* 'Being' or more generically speaking, symbiotic panentheism.

However, we are moving too rapidly, therefore let's begin again:

Introduction II

Copernicus was not a philosopher but Copernican perceptions immensely influenced philosophical thought.

The perception initiated by Copernicus: The system is a location for Centricism as well as for non-Centricism. This perception moved Aristotle's Cartesian perception from that of being a static system to that of being a dynamic system and in essence introduced the concept of Centricism co-existing with non-Centricism within our universe, within our reality.

As we found with Aristotle, scientifically introducing two extremes of a concept may assist the workings of science but it can greatly befuddle our abstractual perceptions of philosophy and religion.

To unravel the philosophical and religious riddle introduced through the elevation of the significance of Centricism to that of non-centricism, we must first understand the pre and post scientific perceptions existing before Copernicus' Centricism was established as a scientific 'fact'.

Pre-Copernican

Before Copernicus, the center of existence resided with the individual. One might even suggest that pre-Copernicus, the center of existence resided 'within' the individual.

The individual was the center of 'knowing' since the individual was where 'knowing' resided. This is not implying that gods or God were not recognized entities. Rather it suggests that gods and God were perceived to be humanistic in form or at the very least capable of presenting themselves as such.

Pre-Copernicus, 'knowing' was the center of existence. Zeno acknowledged this with his suggestion that although abstraction might be a separate entity found 'within' the universe, it existed as a separate entity nonetheless.

Philosophy, religion and science all reinforced each other in terms of the center. Philosophy viewed the individual as the center of reason, the center of knowing. Religion viewed the individual as the center of attention, the arena around which the gods centered their attention. Science viewed the individual as the center of all that exists, the heavenly bodies all revolved around the individual, revolved around 'knowing', revolved around awareness.[2]

Now it was understood that men did move from place to place. However, it was also presumed by groups of men, that the heavenly bodies revolved around their particular group, revolved around their particular location of 'home'.

Post-Copernican

With Copernicus, the center of physical reality began to move outward from the individual. Science/ observation began to seek the center and as the process of seeking the center evolved, the center was found to move 'outward', move away from humankind.

The understanding regarding 'where' the center was 'located', moved from being 'within' the individual to being... well, we no longer knew where the center was to be found. It was the center we now sought to find.

The War & Peace of a New Metaphysical Perception

With Copernicus, the sun became the center of the concrete/physical. In spite of the fact that the sun now becomes the center, the concept of 'the center' remains and as such, the universe eventually evolves into being the concept with a center via the big bang. Confusion over the centrist perception not only remains in terms of the concrete but the concept of centricism remains in terms of perceptions regarding abstractual concepts. Humankind 'looks to' the center of all things: the center of the concrete and the center of all abstraction.

Scientifically the center was 'probably' 'out' there somewhere. The quest for the scientific holy grail became the quest to find the center, the quest to find the primary origin of both the universe and life. The more science looked, the further removed the center became from the individual. In the macroscopic sense the center moved from the center of 'knowing' found within the individual to the sun, to the center of the galaxy, to the center of the universe. In the microscopic sense the center moved from the center of 'knowing' found within the individual to the cell, to the nucleus of the cell, to the nucleus of the atom, to the quark, to…

As the search for the center moved away from abstractual 'knowing' and into the physical, science took off as 'the' source of knowledge. As the reputation of science being the legitimate tool for finding the 'center' increased, the legitimacy of philosophy and religion diminished.

The further the center became removed from the individual the more insignificant the individual became. Insignificance was not necessarily increasing in terms of human behavior but insignificance was increasing in terms of humanity's own perception regarding the rationality of human significance.

As time progressed, tolerance and respect due the individual was increasing but tolerance and respect were not increasing due to the increase in the rational understanding regarding why such respect should exist but rather tolerance and respect were increasing based upon the argument: We should tolerate and respect each other because.. 'Because why?', was the question and the answers centered around answers such as: Because we say we should. Because we believe we should. Because that is the way I want to be treated. Because God said we should. Because…[3]

Where were the answers involving the rationality of such behavior? The further we moved the center away from ourselves, the further removed the rationale regarding tolerance, respect, human compassion, abstract hedonism became removed from our understanding these very aspects of human knowing.

Our significance became simply a grain of sand in the beach of time as the center of origination moved further and further outward from ourselves.

As the center moved further and further away from ourselves, we lost the understanding regarding our significance for our significance became lost in time, space, and perceptual understandings regarding the limitlessness of reality versus Reality. Reality, with an upper case 'r' became lost and as such religion and philosophy became confused, humankind became lost and confused.

Energy – matter are dualities of the physical universe. Time – distance are dualities of the abstractual universe. Both dualities are dualities of our personal universe. Are they the only forms of physical existence or abstractual existence found within our personal universe? We are not naive enough to believe, with a fair amount of certainty, that this is not the case regarding abstractional concepts found within our personal universe. We are naïve enough to believe, with a fair amount of certainty, that is the case regarding physical concepts found within our personal universe.

Why are energy and matter something in which we 'believe' regarding the physical but time and distance are not something in which we 'believe' regarding the abstract? We believe the physical to be composed of only matter and energy because that is all we can observe/measure at this point in time. We believe the abstract is composed of more than time and distance because there are more than these two ideas of which we are consciously awareness regarding 'knowing' itself.

One may say, however: We can measure time and distance. That is true, and so it is we may find time and distance to be aspects of the physical, to be innate characteristics of the physical[4], to be aspects unique to the physical rather than aspects of abstractual existence itself. That too, however, is another topic. Are we going to postpone our discussion of such a topic as we have so many others? Yes and no, for we have already touched upon this very idea in both tractates one and two and we will delve into the concept of time and distance within practically every tractate found within Book II of this trilogy.

For the time being, however, we must stay on task and examine the concept of Centricism and non-Centricism, which Copernicus has so eloquently placed before us.

Copernicus' paradoxes

First a person's home, then city, country, continent, planet, sun, and galaxy 'had a center', was 'the' center. Now it is the origination of the Big Bang, which is the center. The origination of the Big Bang is now the point of origination, the center, we seek to 'find'. The 'primal atom', the point from which our universe began its expansion is what we desperately seek to find as we literally turn our earth into a massive radio telescope. It is the 'center' we seek to find as we send huge telescopes into orbit around our little inconspicuous planet.

The concept of a center, the concept of 'a' point of origination, haunts us because we perceive time to be the one and only true existence. We have no perception of the concept regarding a 'location' of timelessness.

The only way to eradicate or change the perception we have of ourselves is to change our perception. To be truly a change, such a perceptual shift must metamorphize our present understanding regarding our immense insignificance into becoming an understanding of our phenomenal significance.

Such a task is no easy matter. Such a task cannot emerge from science/observation; rather such a metamorphosis must emerge from philosophy/reason and in particular from metaphysics. It is observation of the physical/science whose function it is to aid us in understanding the degree of our insignificance. It is reason/philosophy, metaphysics in particular, whose function it is to aid us in the understanding the degree of our significance.

Why is this the case? This is the case because science deals with the physical and philosophy deals with the abstract. Again, we see the validity of Zeno's assertion that both the physical and the abstract exist as independent entities dependent upon one another.

Where then does our third means of developing perceptions enter the picture? Religion, our ability to believe, our third means of developing perceptions, finds its function lies in aiding us in believing what it is we observe and what it is we find reasonable. This is not to say that everything we observe or reason is 'fact'. Rather it simply says: If we cannot believe in anything we observe or believe in anything we reason, then there is nothing but religion itself left in which we can believe.

The War & Peace of a New Metaphysical Perception

We presently have a fairly secure scientific/observational understanding regarding who we are and how it is that we, humans, awareness, a packet of knowledge, an entity of abstractual consciousness, function as an entity of abstractual consciousness existing in a region where we are immersed in time rather than time being immersed within ourselves. Since we basically understand the concept that our physical essence lies within time and space, we will not be examining such a concept within the limits of this tractate.

We presently, however, do not understand who we are and how it could be that we, humans, awareness, a packet of knowledge, an entity of abstractual consciousness, could function as an entity of abstractual consciousness existing within a region where we are not immersed in time but rather time is immersed within us. The understanding of this concept will be the focus of our attention in Part II of this tractate.

What do the two previous paragraphs have to do with Copernicus, Centricism, and non-Centricism?

The first 'We presently…' paragraph deals with Copernicus' initiation of Centricism being the principle found within our universe, found within our reality. It is this concept, which fundamentally defines Zeno's concepts of 'multiplicity' discussed in Tractate 1.

The second 'We presently…' paragraph deals with Copernicus' inadvertent initiation of potential non-Centricism being the principle found 'outside' the universe, found 'outside' our reality, found 'within' the greater Reality. It is this concept, which fundamentally defines Zeno's concepts of 'seamlessness' discussed in Tractate 1.

How do we begin to understand such an alien concept as time existing 'within' us when we exist in a region of timelessness? How does such a concept even begin to relate to Copernicus himself? The whole concept of understanding such seemingly non-understandable concepts had its foundation laid within Tractates one, two, and three. Zeno, Aristotle, and Boethius all influenced our way of thinking and as such subconsciously directed us to a conclusion regarding Copernicus' revelations, conclusions Copernicus may have also deduced but by no means stipulated in his observations.

> Copernican astronomy: The system of astronomy that was proposed by the Polish astronomer, Nicolas Copernicus (1473 –1543) in his book, *De revolutionibus orbium coelestium*, which was published in the month of his death and first seen by him on his deathbed. It used some elements of 'Ptolemaic astronomy', but rejected the notion, then current, that the earth was a stationary body at the centre of the universe. Instead Copernicus proposed the apparently unlikely concept that the sun was at the centre of the universe and that the earth was hurtling through space in a circular orbit about it.[5]

What was it Copernicus suggested that had such a great influence upon our philosophical train of thought? Copernicus moved the concept of 'center' beyond our reach and it has remained beyond our reach ever since.

The concept of center moved off our planet, moved beyond our ability to 'go there'. As our abilities to 'go there' expanded, the 'center' of our 'known' reality moved further and further from our reach. One thing that did not change, however, was our perception that a center to 'it all' could be found and so it is we look for the origination of 'Om' the sound emanating from the center of origination itself, the sound originating from the center of the universe itself, the sound originating from the center of reality itself.

Since Copernicus, we have clung to the concept of centricism and rejected the very idea of a non-centrist existence. So it is, abstraction and the physical remain as Zeno's seamlessness and Zeno's multiplicity confined 'within' reality. So it is we ignore the concept of a greater 'Reality'. So it is the Aristotelian concept of the physical and the abstract being 'contained' within the lesser reality of the physical universe maintains its status of authenticity while the potential existence of a greater Reality, a reality with no center maintains its status as an occult form of metaphysical existence.

How sad it is that we have allowed the once proud intellectual arena of metaphysics to fall to such a lowly status. How sad that we have wrapped ourselves within the boundaries of the physical, only to feel its wrappings shrink in upon our psyche and sense our sanity slipping into a form of mimicry Gerard so aptly describes.

We must find the means of cutting the wrappings confining our psyche. We must emerge from the imprisonment of our own making or we shall surely collapse what small sense of abstractual hedonism still exists and we shall find ourselves completely seduced by the charms of physical hedonism.

The War & Peace of a New Metaphysical Perception

Part II: Resolving the paradox of Centricism with a new metaphysical perception

Centricism

Philosophically we have been immersed within the concept of centricism since time began.

1. We have seen ourselves as the center of concern.
2. We have seen our tribes as the center of sociological development
3. We have seen 'Om' as the center of the universe.
4. We have seen the Earth as the center of the universe.
5. We have seen the Sun as the center of the solar system.
6. We have seen the nucleus as the center of the atom.
7. We have seen God as the center of creation.
8. We have seen ourselves forever searching for the center, for the origination point of the universe.

Philosophically and religiously, Centricism has not disappeared just because Copernicus scientifically demonstrated that the earth is not the center of the solar system. We still seek the center.

We are not only scientifically, but philosophically and religiously enamored with the concept of 'a' 'center'.

We understand there is a location for multiplicity. We now understand there may well be 'a' separate location for the 'lack of multiplicity'/seamlessness. (Tractate 1: Zeno)

We have now seen there is a location for the physical. We have seen there may well be 'a' separate location for abstraction. (Tractate 2: Aristotle)

We have observed there is a location for free will. We have observed there may well be 'a' separate location for determinism. (Tractate 3: Boethius)

By the end of this tractate, we will be able to make a fourth statement. We will be able to state:

We recognize there is a location for centricism. We recognize there may well be 'a' separate location for non-centricism. (Tractate 4: Copernicus)

The rationality regarding our universe, our reality, being a part of a larger 'Reality', grows with each tractate.

The Error of Copernicus

A location of centricism

With Zeno, Aristotle, and Boethius, we understand the characteristics of the universe to be:

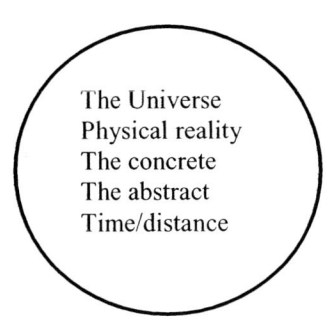

```
   The Universe
   Physical reality
   The concrete
   The abstract
   Time/distance
```

Time and distance exist 'within' the physical because time and distance are innate characteristics of matter and energy[6]. We can add the abstractual understanding regarding the concept of Centricism to this graphic since Copernicus elevated the concept of Centricism to the level of being a basic principle of science for many centuries following his observations.

The graphic may therefore be expanded as:

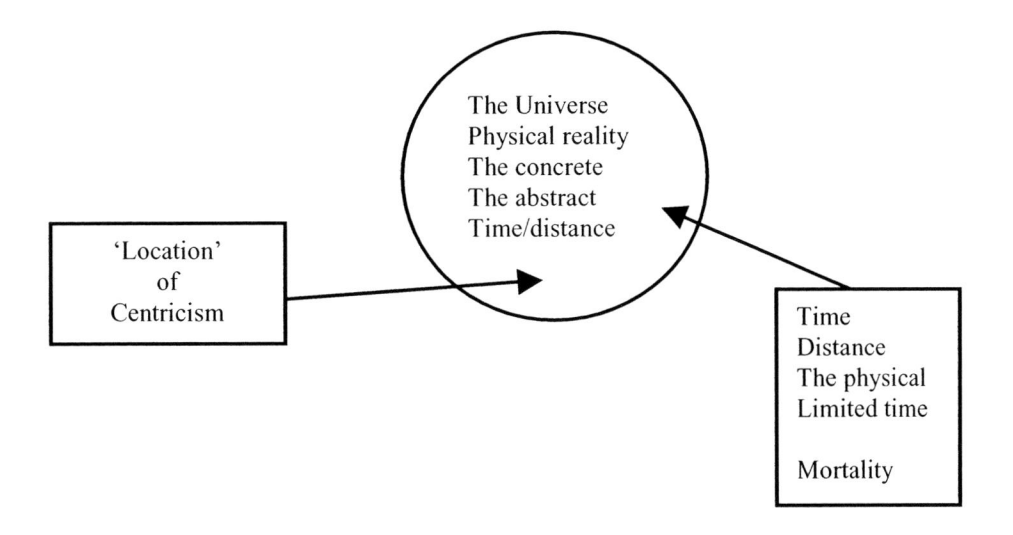

```
                      The Universe
 'Location'           Physical reality
    of       ──▶      The concrete
 Centricism           The abstract
                      Time/distance
                                      ◀──  Time
                                           Distance
                                           The physical
                                           Limited time

                                           Mortality
```

Rather than spend large quantities of time building a rational for the existence of an 'outside' to the universe, let's simply add an outside to the universe. To better understand the rationale for such a leap, one needs to retrace their steps and read Tractates 1, 2, and 3.

With this said we can move immediately into the next section and add the 'outside' to the graphic.

A location of non-centricism

The location of non-centricism:

The characteristics:

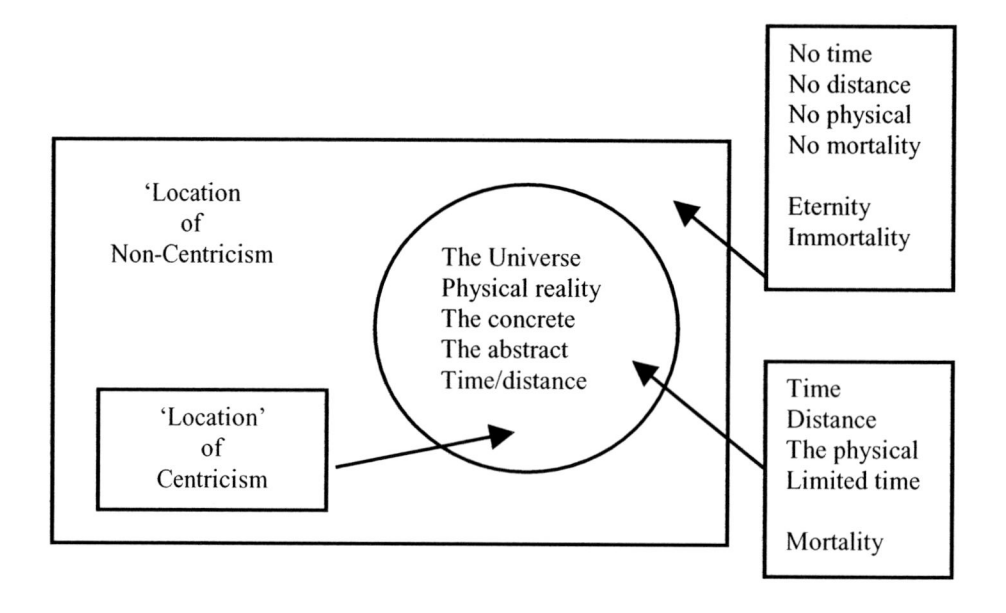

```
┌─────────────────────────────────────┐      ┌──────────────┐
│                                     │      │ No time      │
│   'Location                         │      │ No distance  │
│      of          ╭─────────╮        │      │ No physical  │
│  Non-Centricism  │         │◄───────┼──────┤ No mortality │
│                  │The Universe      │      │              │
│                  │Physical reality  │      │ Eternity     │
│                  │The concrete      │      │ Immortality  │
│                  │The abstract      │      └──────────────┘
│  ┌──────────┐    │Time/distance     │
│  │'Location'│    │         │        │      ┌──────────────┐
│  │    of    │────┼────────►│        │      │ Time         │
│  │Centricism│    ╰─────────╯        │      │ Distance     │
│  └──────────┘                       │◄─────┤ The physical │
│                                     │      │ Limited time │
│                                     │      │              │
│                                     │      │ Mortality    │
└─────────────────────────────────────┘      └──────────────┘
```

Time and distance exist 'within' the physical because time and distance are innate characteristics of matter and energy. Time and distance do not exist 'outside' the 'location' of the physical since time and distance are innate characteristics of the physical and the physical cannot be found 'outside' the physical itself

The dynamics of centricism

Centricism involves two primary concepts: time and distance. Without time and distance no center can be found.

Time and distance invoke the concept of motion, finding, seeking, looking for, reaching for, … the point of origination, the point (0,0,0), …

The Error of Copernicus

To understand the dynamics of Centricism, let's remove the location where Centricism is not the dominating concept:

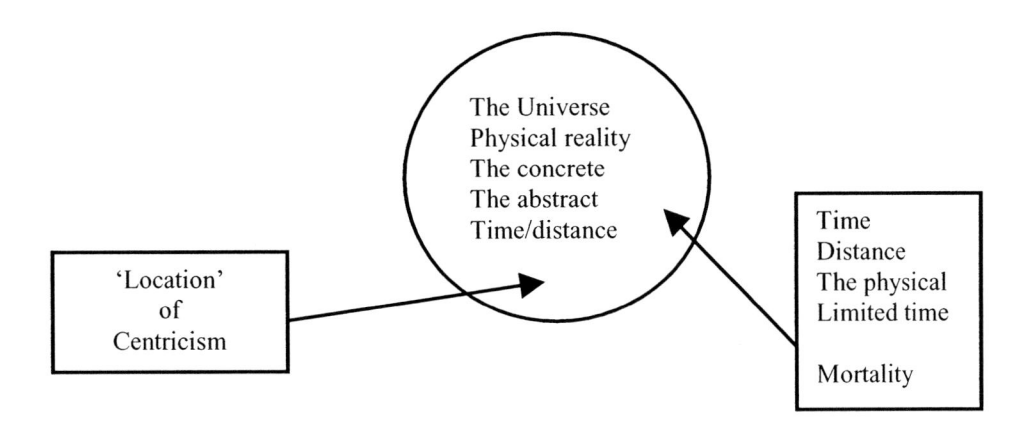

```
                          ┌─────────────┐
                         / The Universe  \
                        |  Physical reality|
   ┌──────────┐         |  The concrete   |         ┌──────────────┐
   │ 'Location'│────────▶|  The abstract   |◀────────│ Time          │
   │    of    │         |  Time/distance  |         │ Distance      │
   │ Centricism│         \               /          │ The physical  │
   └──────────┘           └─────────────┘           │ Limited time  │
                                                    │               │
                                                    │ Mortality     │
                                                    └──────────────┘
```

We understand the dynamics of the universe to be what the dynamics of the universe are as perceived by ourselves and what we, at this point in time, perceive the universe to be is a region permeated with the concept of beginnings leading to endings. We understand the initial step in the process is the concept of 'beginning' for without 'a' 'beginning' we cannot rationalize an 'ending' to what it was which we were focusing our thinking process or meditation upon.

Not only do we perceive the universe to be filled with concepts of beginning – end but science perceives the universe itself to be affected by such linear events as beginning – end. In fact, many scientists are looking for the very process of beginning – end, which they believe, may apply to the universe itself. Other scientists, unable to understand the answer to the question, 'What existed before the universe?' are attempting to understand the mechanism required which would explain the concept of the universe having 'no' beginning and 'no' ending.

The major hurdle confronting scientists today in terms of building a workable model of a 'timeless' universe is time itself. Time appears to permeate our universe from one end to the other. Time in fact appears to be an innate characteristic of matter and energy themselves.

It was Einstein who suggested: $E = mc^2$. 'c' being the velocity of light in a vacuum is simply d/t and thus not only are matter and energy implied to be directly dependent one upon the other but matter and energy are demonstrated to be absolutely related to both space/distance and time.

As such, as long as we perceive the model of the universe to be a model depicting the universe to be 'filled' with matter and energy, we will perceive the universe to be 'filled' with time.

Does this imply we must discard our perception of the universe existing in order to resolve the paradox of Centrist systems, resolve the paradox of all 'thing's having a point of origination? We cannot discard our perception of the universe existing and expect such an action to be 'acceptable' to beings 'existing' within such a location. We can however build a metaphysical model, which leaves the universe temporarily intact and functioning for trillions of years or more. We can build a metaphysical model, which demonstrates a function for such an existence and as such, a function for the entities found 'within' this subset of the whole, found 'within' the element we call 'our' 'reality', the universe.

The War & Peace of a New Metaphysical Perception

How does one accomplish such abstractual tasks? One takes the first step and accepts the characteristics of time, and thus the characteristics of matter, energy, and space, to be infinite within its own characteristics of time itself but finite 'because' it is just that: time.

At first glance, this may appear a strange action to take, but the precedent of accepting apparent dual contradictory characteristics is an idea that has already been set by science. It was science that first suggested we accept the characteristics of a photon to include characteristics of both matter and energy.

Since science established the concept of potentially accepting dual contradictory characteristics, there is no reason we cannot apply the concept of duality to time, space, matter, and energy. In the metaphysical model suggested of an 'outside' to the physical, we are applying the duality of infiniteness and finiteness to the concept of this new metaphysical perception. Time is infinite for it has no end until the end occurs and time is finite in nature for time is limited to the concept of time itself.

Many would object to such a contradictory statement regarding time. Many would argue: There is no way such a perception can be 'proved'. That is the same argument humanity used to explain why man cannot fly, why man cannot get to the moon, etc.

To continue our examination of a new metaphysical perception we are going to do what individuals such as the Wright brothers and Van Braun did. We are going to ignore critics and explore the uncharted. We are going to explore the concept that time is infinite by means of its linear characteristic but finite by means of its own existence.

Having made the decision to accept the duality of finiteness and infiniteness of time, we will accept the same of matter, energy and distance/space. But why accept the same of three new concepts, the concepts of matter, energy, and distance/space? We place the same parameters upon matter, energy, and distance/space as we do upon time because science directly ties the four together through the mathematical language of science via the equation $E = mc(2)$. When science distances itself from their own basic perception and replaces the perception of $E = mc(2)$ with a new perception expressed mathematically and accepted by the scientific community universally then we will metaphysically have to reexamine what it is that we are about to do in establishing a new metaphysical perception.

With this having been said we are now ready to explore the dynamics of a non-centrist location. We will do so by first establishing such a location.

So again, we come back to:

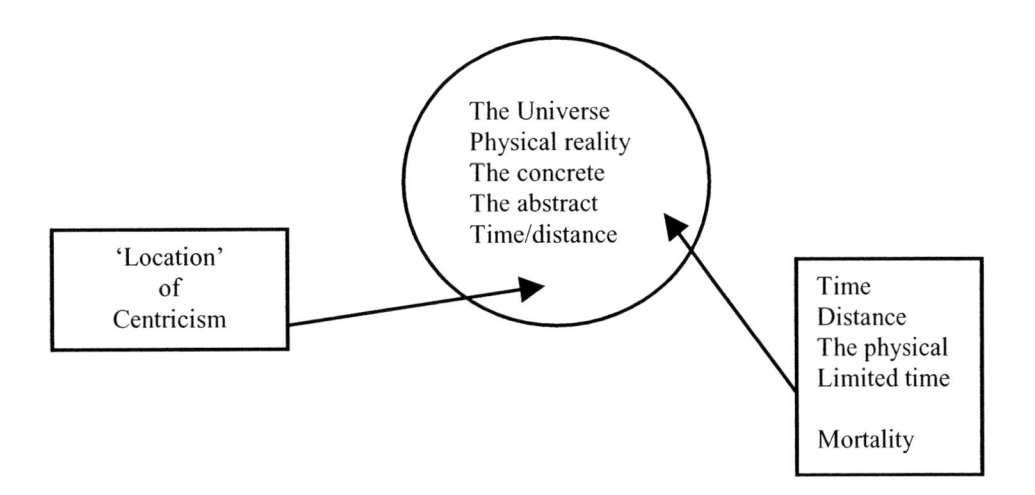

```
                    ┌─────────────────┐
                    │  The Universe   │
                    │ Physical reality│
                    │  The concrete   │
                    │  The abstract   │
                    │  Time/distance  │
                    └─────────────────┘
   ┌──────────┐           ↑    ↖        ┌──────────┐
   │'Location'│           │             │   Time   │
   │    of    │───────────┘             │ Distance │
   │Centricism│                         │The physical│
   └──────────┘                         │Limited time│
                                        │          │
                                        │ Mortality│
                                        └──────────┘
```

in order to build our location of non-Centrism.

We build the location of non-Centrism through the simple action of designating a location of non-Centrism:

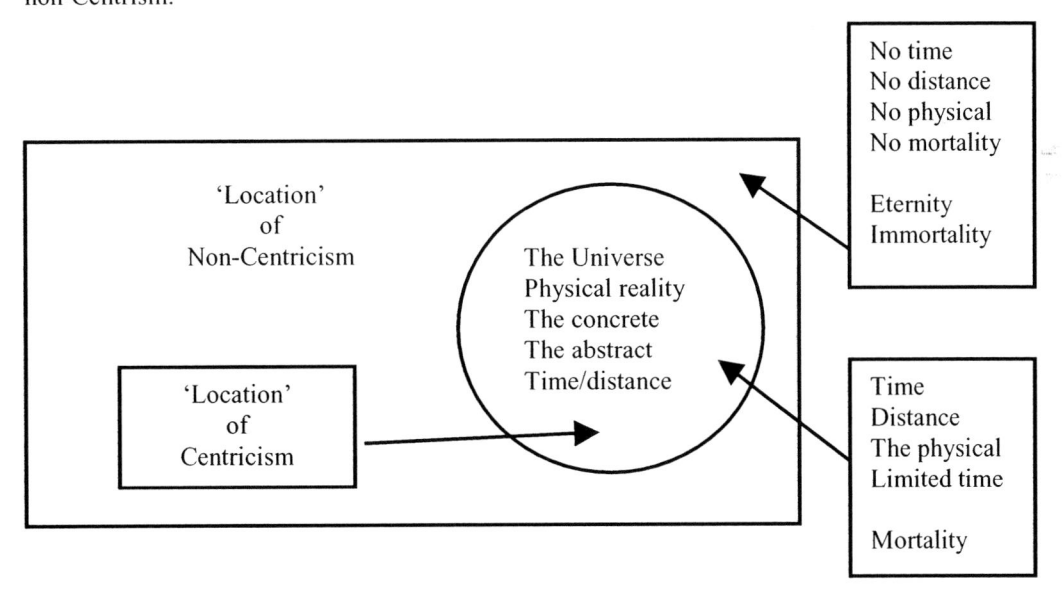

```
                                              ┌──────────┐
                                              │ No time  │
                                              │No distance│
                                              │No physical│
                                              │No mortality│
                                              │          │
                                              │ Eternity │
                                              │Immortality│
                                              └──────────┘
 ┌─────────────────────────────────────────┐       ↑
 │       'Location'                        │       │
 │           of                            │───────┘
 │      Non-Centricism                     │
 │                   ┌─────────────┐       │
 │                   │ The Universe│       │
 │                   │Physical reality│    │
 │    ┌──────────┐   │ The concrete│       │    ┌──────────┐
 │    │'Location'│   │ The abstract│       │    │   Time   │
 │    │    of    │──▶│Time/distance│───────┼───▶│ Distance │
 │    │Centricism│   └─────────────┘       │    │The physical│
 │    └──────────┘                         │    │Limited time│
 │                                         │    │          │
 │                                         │    │ Mortality│
 └─────────────────────────────────────────┘    └──────────┘
```

The first question, which arises, is: Why place the location of non-Centricism 'outside' the physical, outside the universe, outside 'reality'? We are not going to address that issue in detail in this tractate since it was examined in detail in Tractates 1 and 2.

It should be stated at this point, however, that the diagram is not intended to suggest that Centricism can only be found within the universe and therefore cannot be found 'outside' the universe. Nor does the diagram suggest that non-Centricism can only be found 'outside' the universe and therefore cannot be found 'within' the universe. What the diagram suggests is that it is Centricism which is the predominant characteristic found 'within' the universe and that it is non-Centricism which is the predominant predominant characteristic found 'within' the region 'outside' the universe.

Having said this and having established the location of non-Centricism, we can now begin an examination of the dynamics regarding the 'location' we call a location for non-Centricism.

The dynamics of non-centricism

A region of non-centricism lacks four primary elements found within a region where centricism dominates. Non-Centricism lacks the pervasive presence of time, space/distance, matter, and energy. Ignoring concepts of matter and energy for now, we can begin an examination of abstractual concepts of time and distance. Extracting the concepts of matter and energy from the region of centricism will allow us to examine the dynamics of time and distance/space.

The concept of a beginning, an origination, the origin, loses its meaning within a region we call non-Centricism. In a region where matter and energy do not exist as a part of the universal fabric, time and distance/space are elements, which in turn do not exist as part of the universal fabric. Without the perceived abstractual concepts of time and distance/space, the concept that a center can be found loses its validity as a fundamental principle of existence and thus the understanding of the concept of a non-centrist location begin to emerge.

How is it possible to find the lack of time and distance within the universe?[7] The only way to find such a 'location' within the physical is to look to the non-physical, look to abstraction.

Is this to say the 'location' of non-centricism is found within the physical? No, rather it is to say we have within our reality the indication that a 'location' of non-centricism does exist. We have, within our physical reality, non-centrist concepts which we can observe but which we cannot measure physically. We have, within our physical reality, non-centrist concepts we believe but which defy faith. We have, within our physical reality, non-centrist concepts we find logical but which reach beyond our rationality.

In spite of our primitive understandings regarding abstractions, we refuse to acknowledge the possibility of there existing 'a' location where abstractions can exist 'outside' the physical.

Our refusal to acknowledge the possible existence of 'a' location where abstractions exist outside the physical partially emerges from the implications such an existence implies. Time and distance are concepts that provide the means by which we understand what it is to move from 'here' to 'there'. Zeno described such movement as incremental elements of multiplicity. Zeno, however, did not ignore the abstractual. Zeno, through his introduction regarding the paradox of space and time, introduced the concept of seamlessness.

Seamlessness, the lack of time and the lack of distance, invokes the scientific concept regarding the lack of motion. Without 'a distance' through which to move, motion becomes a perceived contradiction and time becomes an unnecessary element. Without the existence of time and distance/space, the concept of motion becomes irrelevant. The concept of motion in and of itself creates the need for time within which to move from point B to point C. Thus without distance/space and time, motion becomes irrelevant.

The lack of time and distance does not, however, become a problem just for science. A lack of a point of origination for motion, a lack of a beginning, in essence, a lack of creation becomes what at first glance might be perceived as a fatal blow for religion. In fact, however, it does no such thing.

Philosophy, in particular metaphysical models, in a region void time and space/distance, experiences similar apparent setbacks, as do science and religion. Without time, philosophically and metaphysically, the problem of a beginning as initiated by a linear progression of time would appear to suggest there is no need to find the source of knowledge, no need to seek 1st truth, no need to look for 1st cause, no need to reach for the meaning of life itself.

Movement involving relocation through the process of incremental multiplicity, which the physical incorporates, need not be one of relocation from one physical location to another physical location.

There are two forms of movement. There is physical movement, which is characterized by the principle of multiplicity and there is abstractual movement, movement characterized by the principle of seamlessness. Abstractual movement can be found in the 'location of Centricism' and might better be characterized as simply a process of thought displacement.

Although abstractual movement, thought displacement, seamlessness of motion, can be found within a location of Centricism, such movement would best describe the primary form of motion found within the 'location' of non-Centricism.

To best understand such concepts let's examine the concept of physical motion existing within the location of Centricism.

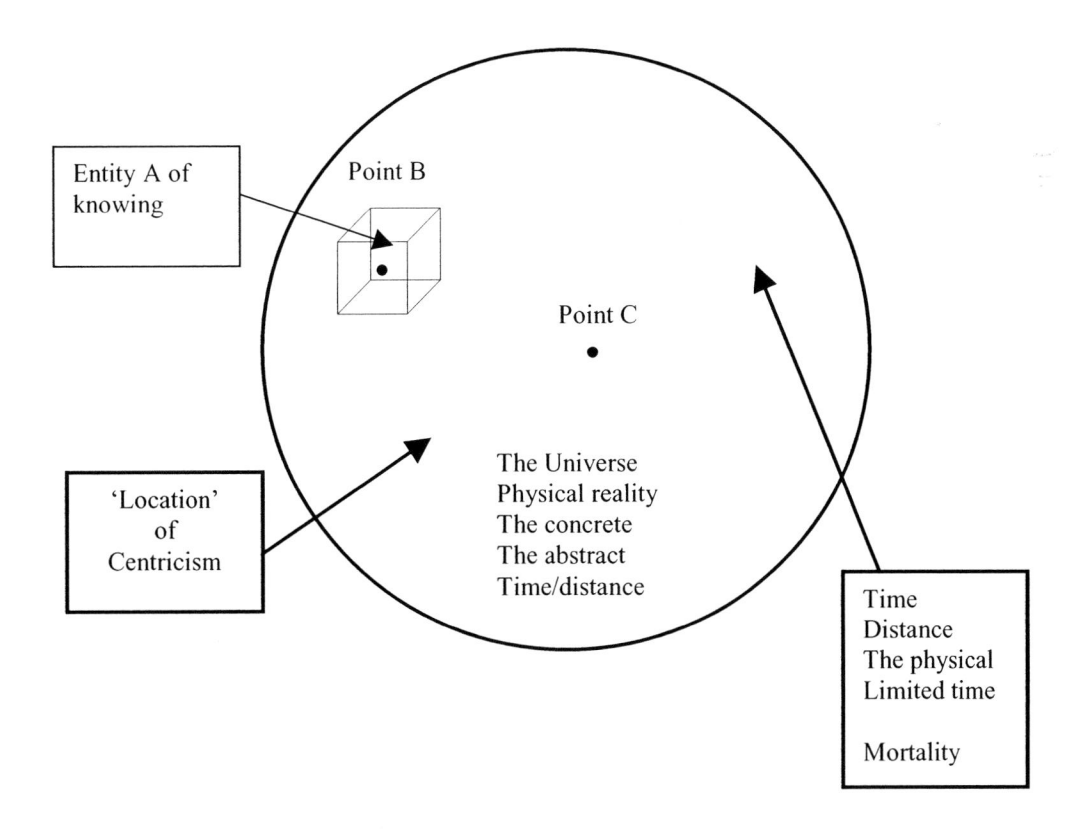

The War & Peace of a New Metaphysical Perception

For the entity of 'knowing - A' to move from point B to point C, 'A' must traverse distance/space, which takes the function of time to accomplish since distance/space is a characteristic of matter/energy, which produce the innate characteristic of time itself.

This process of 'physical movement' is what could be explained as an orderly process of sequential actions or simply sequential orderliness.

Little more need be said regarding such movement since we are quite familiar with this type of motion, which surrounds us on a daily basis.

This brings us to examining 'motion' within' the location of non-Centricism. In fact, such an examination leads us directly to understanding just why such a location is called non-Centricism.

To understand movement within non-Centricism, we must rebuild the location of non-Centricism. To do so we will take the latter graphic and expand it through the inclusion of the location of non-Centricism:

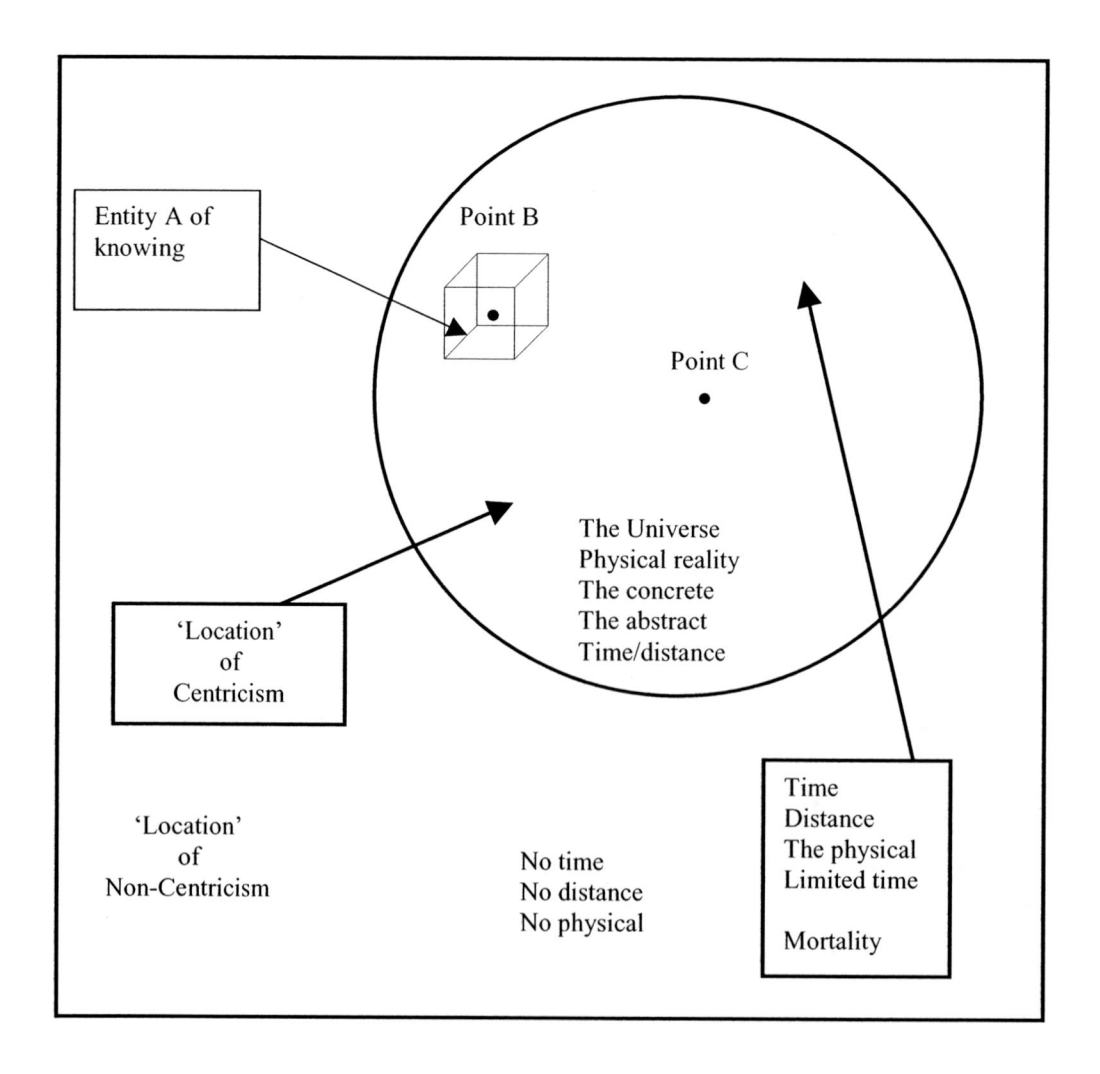

The Error of Copernicus

To simplify the discussion we will extract the region we have already explored. If we remove the physical, we obtain:

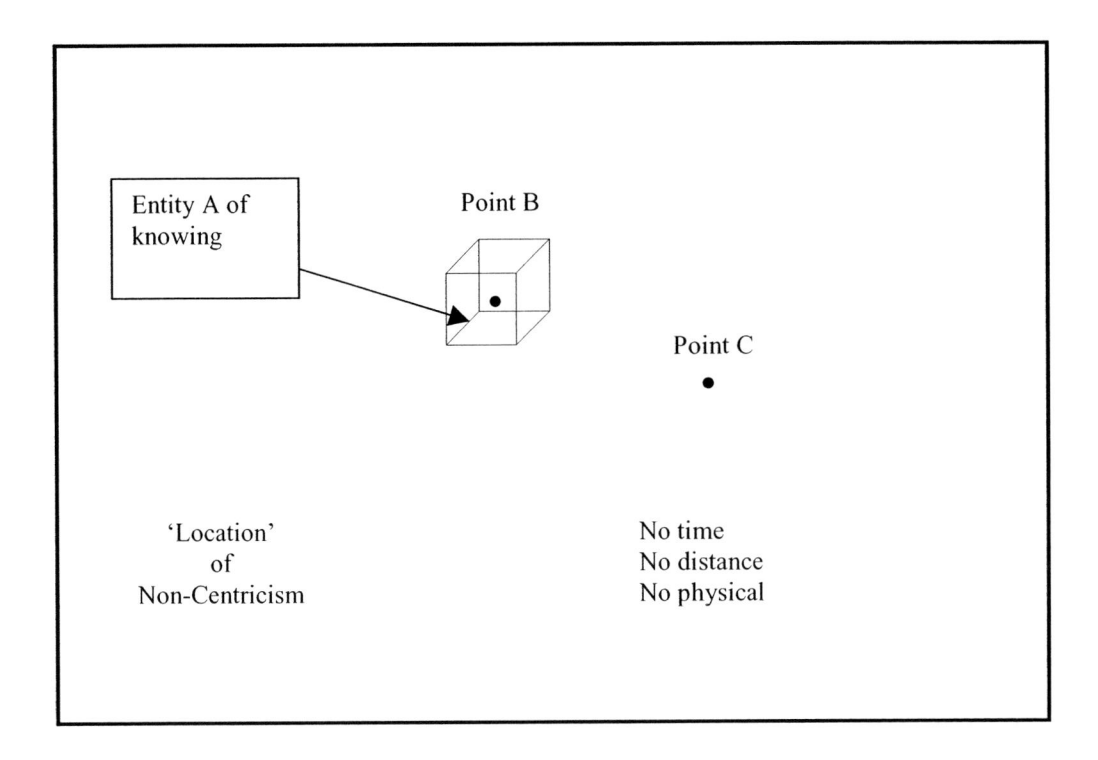

```
┌─────────────────────────────────────────────────────────────┐
│                                                             │
│   ┌──────────┐       Point B                                │
│   │ Entity A │        ╱▱╲                                   │
│   │    of    │───────▶│•│                                   │
│   │ knowing  │        ╲▱╱                                   │
│   └──────────┘                                              │
│                                                             │
│                                  Point C                    │
│                                    •                        │
│                                                             │
│      'Location'                 No time                     │
│          of                     No distance                 │
│    Non-Centricism               No physical                 │
│                                                             │
└─────────────────────────────────────────────────────────────┘
```

Having removed the physical, time, and distance/space, we obtain a location where points B and C still exist but to go from point B to Point C takes no time since there is no physical distance between them.

The ramifications of such a perception may better be understood in terms of the interaction, which occurs between several entities of knowing.

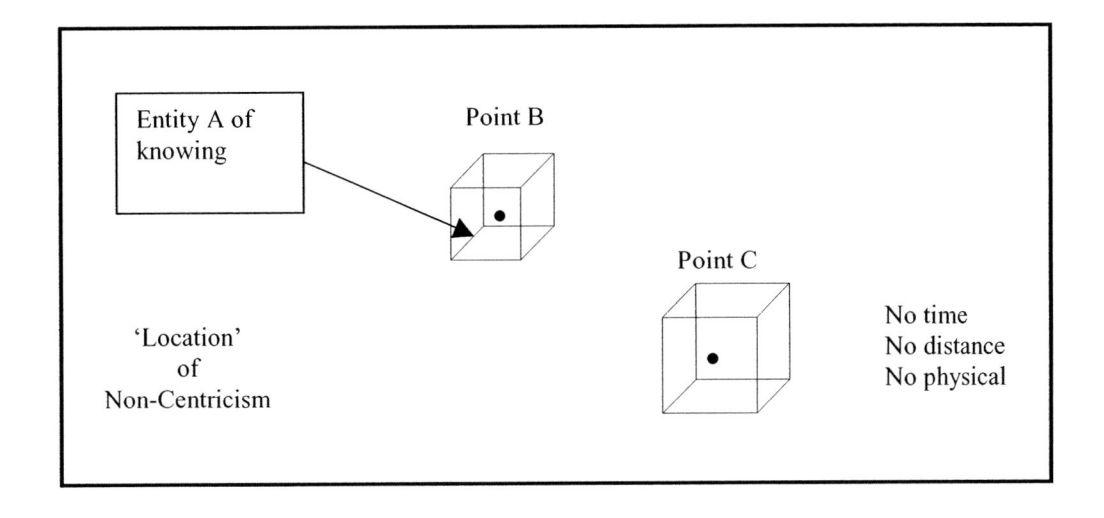

```
┌─────────────────────────────────────────────────────────────┐
│                                                             │
│   ┌──────────┐       Point B                                │
│   │ Entity A │        ╱▱╲                                   │
│   │    of    │───────▶│•│                                   │
│   │ knowing  │        ╲▱╱                                   │
│   └──────────┘                                              │
│                              Point C                        │
│                                                             │
│                               ╱▱╲        No time            │
│                              │•│         No distance        │
│      'Location'               ╲▱╱        No physical        │
│          of                                                 │
│    Non-Centricism                                           │
│                                                             │
└─────────────────────────────────────────────────────────────┘
```

The War & Peace of a New Metaphysical Perception

In essence, this depiction now becomes:

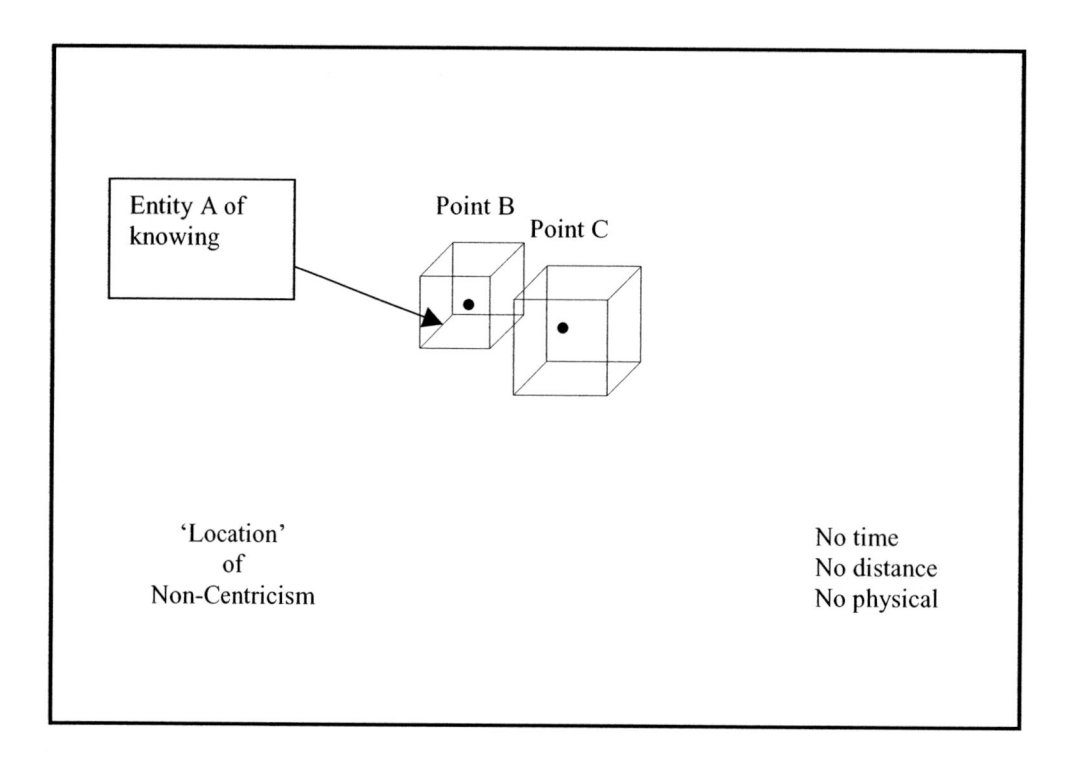

```
┌─────────────────────────────────────────────────────────────┐
│                                                             │
│   ┌──────────┐                                              │
│   │ Entity A │         Point B                              │
│   │    of    │              Point C                         │
│   │ knowing  │──────▶ ┌──┐                                  │
│   └──────────┘        │ •│┌──┐                              │
│                       └──┘│ •│                              │
│                           └──┘                              │
│                                                             │
│                                                             │
│           'Location'                           No time      │
│               of                               No distance  │
│          Non-Centricism                        No physical  │
│                                                             │
└─────────────────────────────────────────────────────────────┘
```

The 'distance' between point B and C no longer exists 'between' points B and C.

Distance/space and time do not disappear. Distance and time remain but remain as abstractual items of knowing found within the knowing of each entity itself. Each entity of knowing which experienced time and space through the process of 'traveling' through time and space, traveling through the physical, traveling through reality, traveling through the universe, has retained its awareness and understanding of just such experiencing.

The Error of Copernicus

Lets examine the graphic with many entities of knowing:

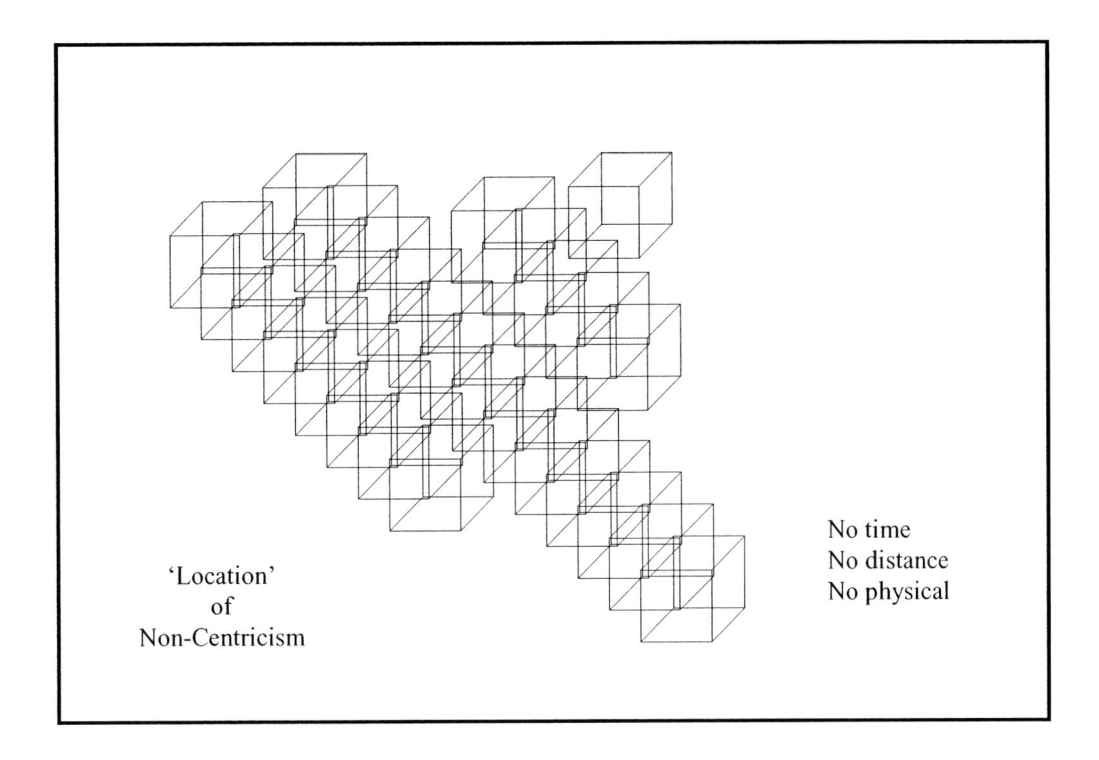

'Location' of Non-Centricism

No time
No distance
No physical

Such a perception initiates an understanding regarding what might be called a form of Brownian movement of thought, of abstraction. Brownian abstractual principles may in fact, apply equally to abstractual concepts found within a region of non-Centricism as it applies to physical concepts found within a region of Centricism.

Metaphysical perceptions now begin to emerge as the foundation of free will and the individual.

Within a location of Centricism:

1. Sequential orderliness of thought, sequential orderliness of cause and effect, emerges as a universal characteristic of Centricism
2. One can impact 'what is' and what 'will be' or what 'could be' since 'what is' is too short a time to exist and 'what will be' or 'what could be' do not yet exist.
3. One develops as a unit of unique knowing through the action of free will which eventually adds to the location of non-Centricism
4. One retains one's own unique self but can expand upon what it is one understands with the incorporation of the understanding of one's own self in relationship to what exists around one's self. This expansion is limited in scope by the limits of what exists as opposed to the non-existence of 'what will be'.

Within a location of non-Centricism:

1. Non-sequential randomness of thought, non-sequential randomness of cause and effect, emerges as an expansion of perceptual possibilities found as a universal characteristic of non-Centricism
2. One can impact 'what was' and 'what is'. Experiences such as the existence of Hitler's actions and Gandhi's actions exist and thus create the personality of the whole itself.[8]
3. One develops the potentiality of the non-Centricism location through the introduction of one's unique knowing acquired through 'present' actions invoked while in the realm of space/distance and time found within the realm of Centricism.
4. One retains one's own unique self but can expand upon what it is one understands with the incorporation of unique units of knowing which exists around one's self. This expansion, is unlimited in scope by the infinite potential of newness 'what will be' affords the region of non-centricism.

These statements incorporate the concept of orderliness and randomness. In the Western scientifically oriented society, the term 'orderliness' is viewed as a positive characteristic and the term randomness is viewed as a negative characteristic.

Within this tractate, the concept of positive and negative characteristics are not the issues being addressed. Rather we are examining the very basics of existence itself.

The law of inverse proportionality

Science speaks of the principle of symmetry: For every action there is an equal and opposite reaction, positives and negatives, up and down, matter and anti-matter, energy and ? (anti-energy?). Religion initiated this principle with its concept of 'good' and 'evil'. But what of philosophy, what is it philosophy has put into place regarding the principle of symmetry?

It might be stated that in terms of symmetry, philosophy has put forward the concept of life and death. Such a perception initiates the concept of death being a form of 'evil', death being a negative as opposed to the positive of life.

If we were to graph such perceptions, we would obtain:

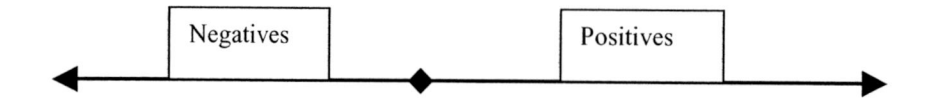

Scientifically:

◄─────── [Negatives] ◆ [Positives] ───────►

If one then combines the positive with the negatives one obtains:

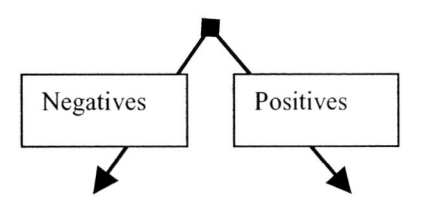

```
        ■
       ╱ ╲
      ╱   ╲
┌──────────┐  ┌──────────┐
│ Negatives│  │ Positives│
└──────────┘  └──────────┘
     ↓            ↓
```

And then

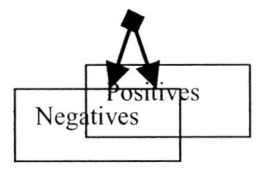

```
         ▼
        ╱╲
   ┌───┴──┴───┐
   │  Positives│
┌──┴───────┐  │
│ Negatives│  │
└──────────┴──┘
```

And finally:

▼

Or:

O

'Nothing'

The same process can be applied to other scientific perceptions: For every action there is an equal and opposite reaction, up and down, matter and anti-matter, energy and ? (anti-energy?).

The War & Peace of a New Metaphysical Perception

Applying the principle of symmetry to 'good' and 'evil' becomes the central aspect of many religious perceptions regarding the 'eternal' conflict of 'good' and 'evil'.

Philosophically if we apply the same concept of symmetry to 'life' and 'death' we obtain:

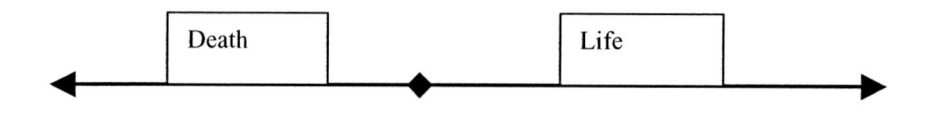

```
        ┌──────┐           ┌──────┐
        │ Death│           │ Life │
        └──────┘           └──────┘
◄───────────────────◆─────────────────────►
```

This makes no rational sense in terms of our present day perceptions regarding 'death'. Scientifically death means 'end'. What then has philosophy to offer our understanding regarding the perception of life and death in terms of the principle of symmetry?

Philosophy has nothing to offer our understanding regarding life and death but confusion and uncertainty. This confusion and uncertainty spills over to religion and science. The perception diagramed, having no rationality associated with it, causes the very principle of symmetry to take on the perception of being a faulty principle. The perception regarding the principle of symmetry being flawed, attaches a sense of doubt to the scientific and religious principles involving symmetrical perceptions.

If one philosophically accepts death for what it is, one obtains:

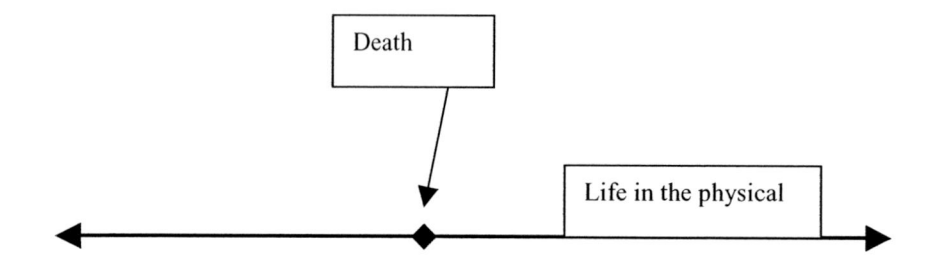

```
              ┌──────┐
              │ Death│
              └───┬──┘
                  │       ┌───────────────────┐
                  ▼       │ Life in the physical│
                          └───────────────────┘
◄─────────────────◆────────────────────────────►
```

And then:

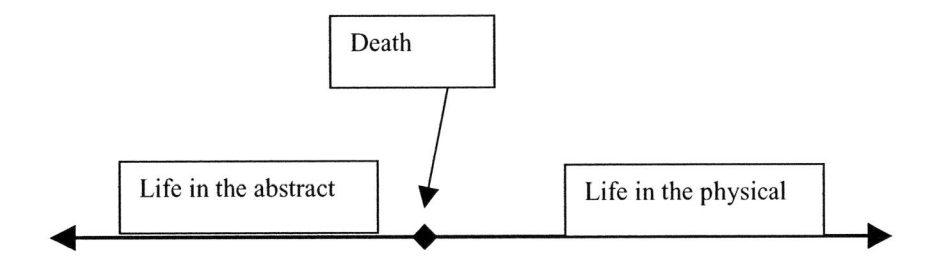

```
                    ┌─────────┐
                    │  Death  │
                    └────┬────┘
                         │
                         ▼
┌──────────────────┐           ┌──────────────────┐
│ Life in the      │           │ Life in the      │
│ abstract         │           │ physical         │
└──────────────────┘           └──────────────────┘
◄────────────────────────◆────────────────────────►
```

This perception moves 'death' from being the opposite of 'life' to being a 'cross-over' point as opposed to a form of existence. Why does such a graph suggest that death becomes a 'cross-over point' as opposed to a form of existence itself? Death has no past and no future. Death is an existence in the present.

If we apply the same graphic actions to this philosophical depiction as we did to scientific depictions we obtain:

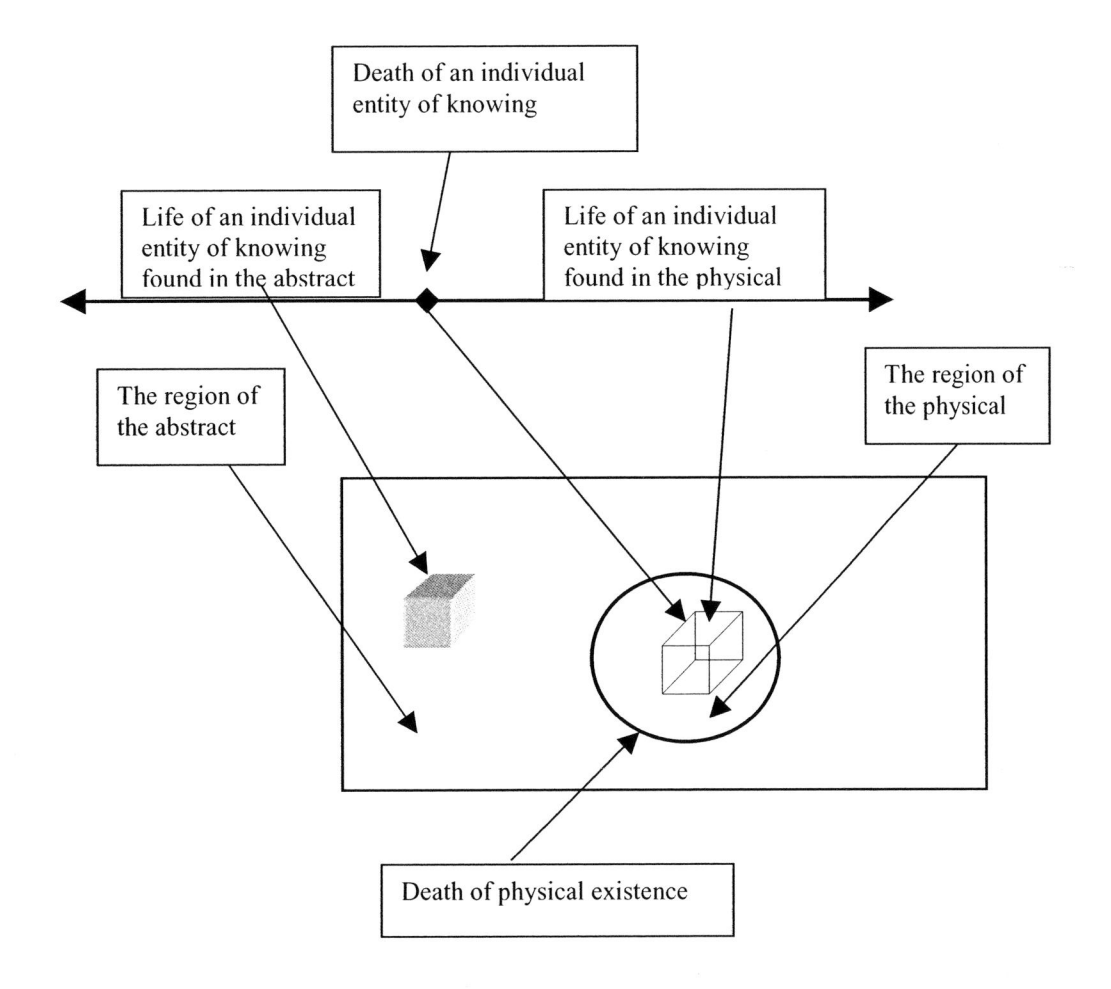

The War & Peace of a New Metaphysical Perception

Which, applying the graphics demonstrating the scientific summation of the concepts positive and negative, we obtain:

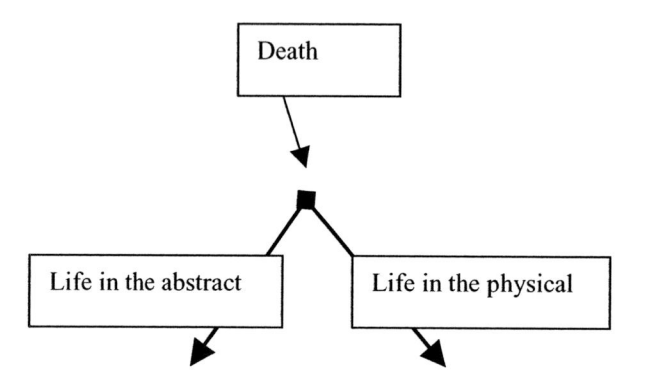

And then

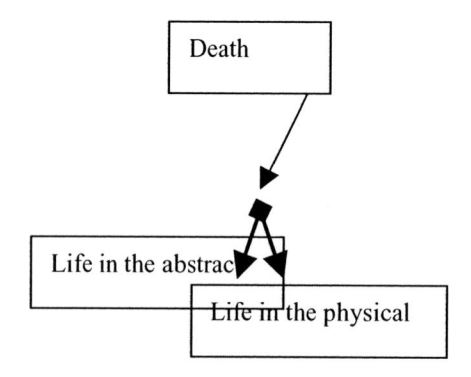

And finally:

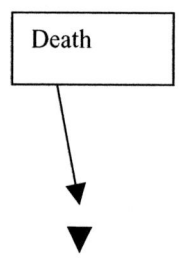

The Error of Copernicus

Or once again:

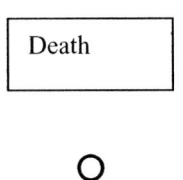

$$\boxed{\text{Death}}$$

$$\bigcirc$$

'nothing'

Such a philosophical perception may seem insignificant until one realizes it brings philosophy into line with science and religion. It is philosophy, which takes a lesson from religion/believing and science/observing means of developing perceptions. Is such a lesson important for philosophy? Absolutely. Philosophy has been 'stuck' long enough in terms of resolving its most prominent paradoxes. It is time for philosophy to resolve its most perplexing puzzles and move on. Philosophy has no reason to fear its becoming an outmoded form of perception. Resolving the most intriguing philosophical paradoxes will not bring an end to philosophy. Other paradoxes are awaiting discovery but these other paradoxes must wait for philosophy to accomplish its present task, the task of understanding the relationship between the abstract and the physical. Once accomplishing this task, philosophy will find that new, exciting, and even more challenging frontiers await. Such an event occurred with science and it will occur with philosophy.

How can philosophy accomplish its desire to resolve the philosophical paradoxes confronting it for the last twenty-five hundred years? Philosophy simply needs to expand its concept of 'reality' to that of 'Reality'. Philosophy simply needs to embrace the physical with the abstract:

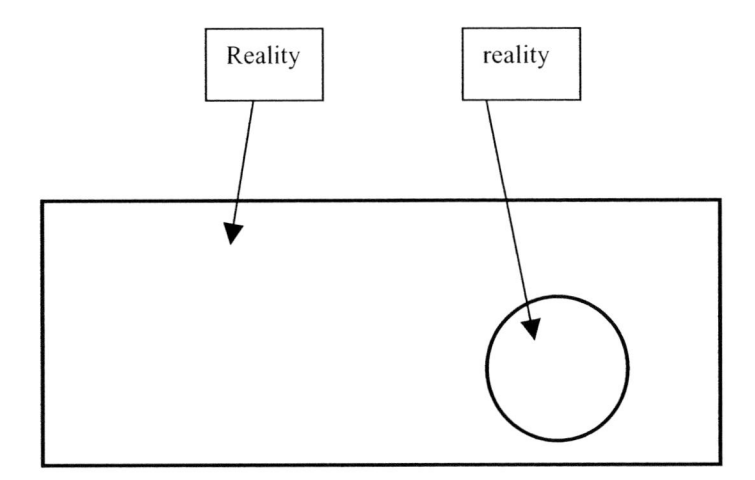

The War & Peace of a New Metaphysical Perception

And place the individual entity of 'knowing' where we know it to be, within the physical:

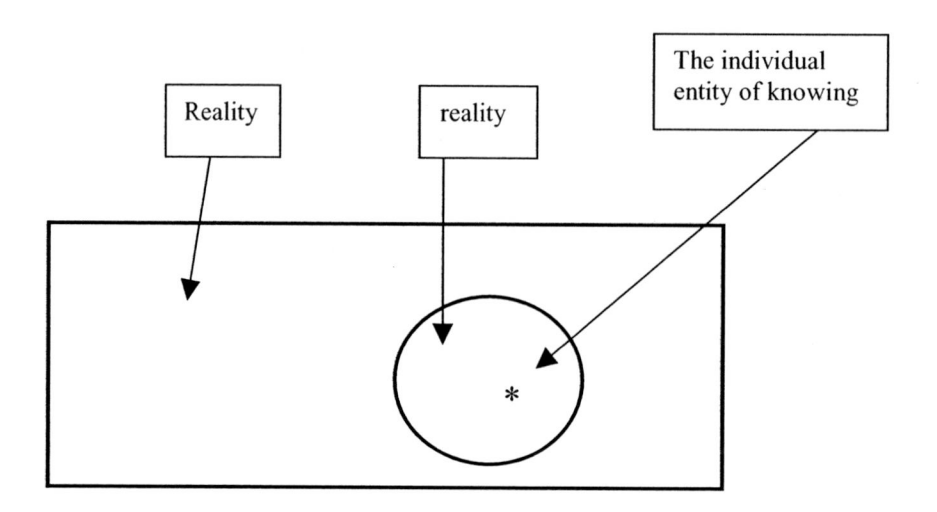

```
        [Reality]        [reality]         [The individual
                                            entity of knowing]
   ┌──────────│───────────────│────────────────│──────────┐
   │          ▼               ▼                │          │
   │                       ╭─────╮             │          │
   │                      (   *   )◄───────────┘          │
   │                       ╰─────╯                        │
   └──────────────────────────────────────────────────────┘
```

Which is the metaphysical system of 'being' *being* 'Being', symbiotic panentheism.

With the application of the principle of symmetry to philosophy, we find the paradoxes of philosophy become manageable and allow philosophy to move on with its task of providing science and religion new perceptions and paradoxes intended to challenge their creative thought and development.

This process does not appear to be a form of 'inverse proportionality'. This segment of the Tractate appears to deal with the law of symmetry. Therefore why title it: 'The law of inverse proportionality'?

Philosophy has an obligation to advance thought into active forms of imagery rather than cement thought into static forms of imagery. The law of symmetry, as we saw demonstrated, suggests all concepts, be they physical or abstract, can be reduced to 'nothingness' itself. This is not what is being implied by the progressive diagrams illustrated within this section.

What is being implied is something new. What is being implied is the existence of an active form of imagery. What is being suggested is that the abstract exists within the location of abstraction and the abstract also exists within the location of the physical. One location becomes the 'real' and the other becomes a 'real illusion' yet at the same time, the 'real illusion' becomes the 'real' and the 'real' becomes the 'real illusion'. Which is which depends upon one's point of reference. This concept was fully addressed within Tractates 1, 2, & 3. As such, we will not explore such a discussion other than to say:

> Philosophically speaking, 'all' does not reduce to 'nothingness', rather 'nothingness is the mirror separating one side from the other, separating the 'real' from the 'real illusion'. As such, the principle of symmetry rather than being the principle of symmetry is suggested by metaphysics to be the law of inverse proportionality.

This is no insignificant statement. This statement could revolutionize scientific and religious perceptions. And who said philosophy had nothing new to offer our perceptual development?

But why use the analogy of nothingness representing a mirror as opposed to nothingness being a location of reductionism where all reduces to the lack of everything including the lack of nothingness itself. A mirror is functional. It is not a glass separating one from the other. If one views oneself in a mirror and spends some time examining the opposing image, one realizes that the image is not the same as the object. With some detailed observation, the person viewing their image realizes that their right hand is the images left hand. Thus, a transformation takes place between the object and the emergence of the object's image as projected by the mirror.

In essence, a form of inversion of the object becomes the image and thus becomes the law of inverse proportionality. This proportion will become an important element in the two tractates, Tractate 7: Hegel and Tractate 9: Einstein.

The 'location' of 'nothingness

The left becomes the right and the right becomes the left at the boundary. Where is this boundary? The boundary is best described as a mirror. When looking into the mirror one will notice that as one lifts their right hand the mirror image lifts its left hand. As one scratches one's right ear the mirror image scratches its left ear.

It is often quoted that the eye is the mirror into the soul of a man. What then of the eye one views when looking into the mirror? Is it one's own soul or the soul of the whole, the soul of God Itself into which one peers?

And what mirror is it of which we speak when speaking of 'nothingness itself' It is nothingness which separates the 'Real' from the 'real'. It is nothingness, which acts as the boundary separating the 'real' from the 'real illusion' (Tractate 1: Zeno). It is nothingness, which acts as the boundary separating the Cartesian from the non-Cartesian (Tractate 2: Aristotle). It is nothingness, which acts as the boundary separating 'free will' from 'determinism' (Tractate 3: Boethius). And now we in essence are exploring the concept of nothingness separating Centricism from non-Centricism (Tractate 4: Copernicus).

What is perceived by us as 'nothingness' has its location as the mirror itself. Nothingness is and nothingness functions as the zero point on a number line. Nothingness allows one side to 'see' the other side, to see the image as we saw in the Tractates dealing with the concepts Boethius, Aristotle, and Zeno placed before us. Each philosopher had a dilemma with which to deal and each dealt with their particular philosophical dilemma in their own unique manner.

Zeno, Aristotle, Boethius, and now Copernicus could not see the mirror just as we cannot see the mirror as we gaze into the mirror itself. They each 'gazed into the mirror and saw what they wanted to see. They saw their right hand scratching their right ear and we, humanity, followed their lead. We, humanity, assumed what they had to say was true and we followed in their footsteps as if the truths they espoused were in fact 'truths' when in fact they were simply perceptions, their own personal perceptions, as best they were able to describe them. We assumed what they had to say was fact when in fact it was simply the best they could express the facts they had available to them personally.

> We know in part, and we prophesy in part.
> But when that which is perfect is come, then that which is in part shall be done away.
> When I was a child, I spake as a child, I understood as a child, I thought as a child: but when I became a man, I put away childish things.
> For now we see through a glass, darkly, but then face to face: now I know in part: but then shall I know even as also I am known[9].

The War & Peace of a New Metaphysical Perception

To look in a mirror is not to look in a mirror but to look at the inverse of the image, the left becomes the right and the right becomes the left.

Looking into nothingness does not cause us to see into what lies beyond the barrier of our reality but rather allows us to see a vision of what lies there.

To introduce a new concept into the picture, it will be helpful to revert to a simpler diagram than the ones that have been evolving. As such, to understand the concept regarding the 'location' of nothingness we will revert to the diagram:

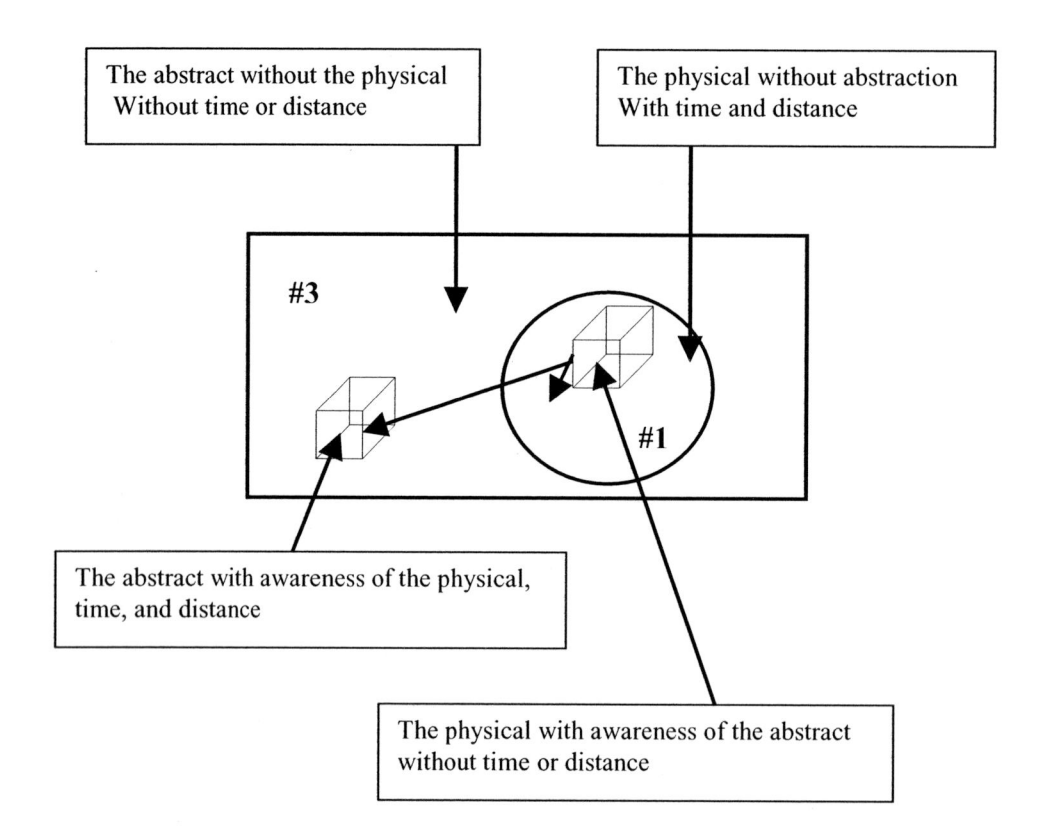

```
┌─────────────────────────────┐       ┌─────────────────────────────┐
│ The abstract without the    │       │ The physical without        │
│ physical Without time or    │       │ abstraction With time and   │
│ distance                    │       │ distance                    │
└─────────────────────────────┘       └─────────────────────────────┘
```

[Diagram: box labeled #3 containing a cube, with arrows to a circle labeled #1 containing another cube]

```
┌─────────────────────────────┐
│ The abstract with awareness │
│ of the physical, time, and  │
│ distance                    │
└─────────────────────────────┘

              ┌─────────────────────────────┐
              │ The physical with awareness │
              │ of the abstract without     │
              │ time or distance            │
              └─────────────────────────────┘
```

The question now becomes: If nothingness exists, then where 'could' it exist? To understand such a discussion it becomes necessary to answer three questions:

1. Does 'nothingness' exist?
2. What is 'nothingness'?
3. Where is 'nothingness' found?

Why this order to the questions? The concept regarding the very existence of nothingness evolves even before we define it because it was Boethius who suggested:

> 'The cause of this mistake is that people think that the totality of their knowledge depends on the nature and capacity to be known of the objects of knowledge. But this is all wrong.'…

'The point of greatest importance here is this: the superior manner of knowledge includes the inferior, but it is quite impossible for the inferior to rise to the superior.'...

'In the same way, human reason refuses to believe that divine intelligence can see the future in any other way except that in which human reason has knowledge.'...

'... it is quite impossible for the inferior to rise to the superior.', which in turn implies it is quite illogical for the 'inferior', 'ourselves', to perceive of either a concept or 'something' which is imperceptible to the 'superior'[10],

•

1. Does 'nothingness' exist?

We perceive of 'nothingness' as the lack of 'something'. Since we perceive of 'nothingness' as a lack of even abstraction itself, it would seem it exists. The very removal of 'nothingness' undermines all our present day fundamental cosmological, ontological, and metaphysical debates starting with Boethius himself.

Is the existence of 'nothingness' itself an absolute? Strangely enough, removing 'nothingness' from our present metaphysical model leads to the eventual termination of the system itself, leaving 'nothingness' in place of the metaphysical model we removed. In such a scenario, 'nothingness' becomes 'something'. In essence, a paradox arises equaling that which Boethius wrestled, equaling the paradox regarding free will versus divine foreknowledge.

Within the perspective of the new metaphysical system of 'being' *being* 'Being', removing 'nothingness' leaves the system intact. Thus, under such a scenario, 'nothing' becomes just that 'nothing'. Within this type of metaphysical system, NO paradox arises.

•

2. What is 'nothingness'?

Nothingness is nothing. Nothingness is a void of all.

1. Nothing is a lack of matter.

    Since matter is perceived to be 'something'. Nothingness, therefore, must 'contain' no matter.

2. Nothing is a lack of energy.

    With the development of Einstein's equation demonstrating a direct relationship between matter and energy, energy is perceived to be 'something'. Nothingness, therefore, must 'contain' no energy.

3. Abstraction is perceived 'to be'.

    Nothingness is the lack of all, a void of all. If abstractions are a 'part' of nothingness, then nothingness is no longer 'nothingness'. Any existence capable of being subdivided into sub-parts is equal to the sum of its parts. As such, any existence capable of being subdivided is by definition not 'nothingness' for by definition it is no longer a 'void' of all but rather a sum of all.

The War & Peace of a New Metaphysical Perception

What then is 'nothingness'? Nothingness is definitely not matter. Nothingness is not energy. Nothingness does not appear to be abstraction. It appears nothingness is closer to being energy than matter. Nothingness appears to be even closer to what we perceive to be abstraction than it is to being energy. In all likelihood however, nothingness may be our first glimpse into what acts as the fundamental unit of existence itself.

It is easy to come off task at this point. Moving into a dialectic regarding the topic of nothingness being the fundamental unit of existence itself, becomes an almost irresistible act. However, our task - within this tractate - is to explore the concept of Centricism versus non-Centricism. As such, we must return to work.

•

3. Where is 'nothingness' found?

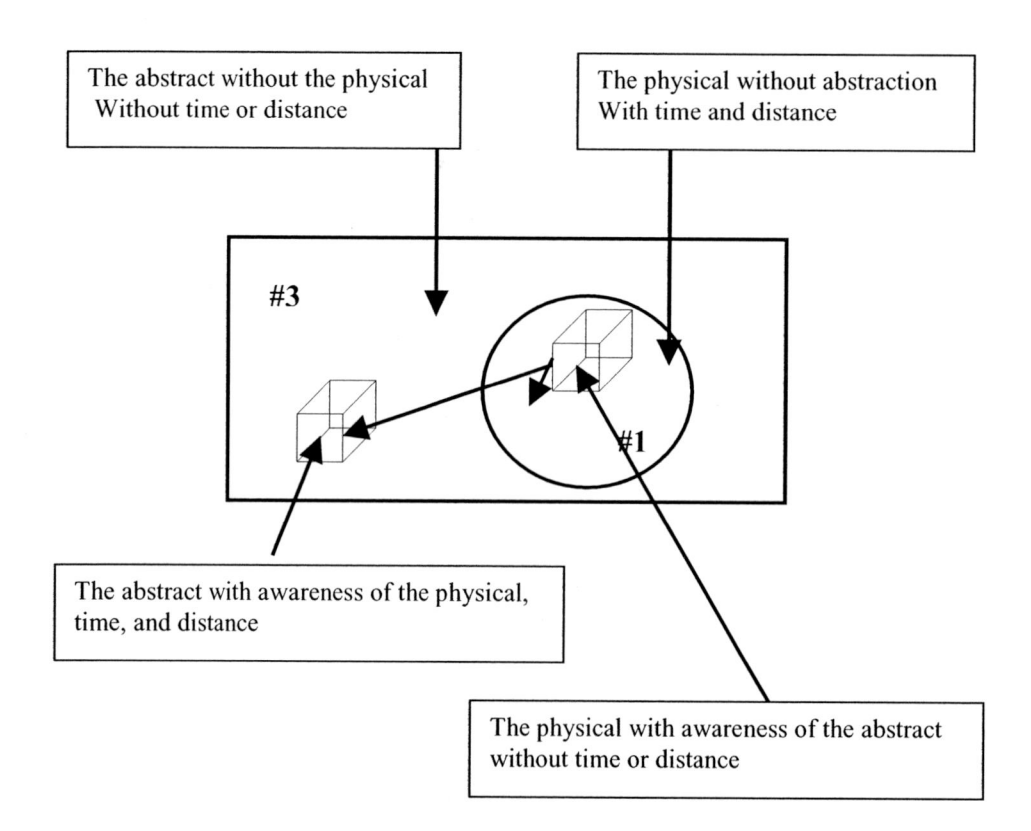

```
┌─────────────────────────────┐          ┌─────────────────────────────┐
│ The abstract without the    │          │ The physical without        │
│ physical                    │          │ abstraction                 │
│ Without time or distance    │          │ With time and distance      │
└─────────────────────────────┘          └─────────────────────────────┘
                │                                       │
                ▼                                       ▼
┌───────────────────────────────────────────────────────────────────┐
│  #3                                                               │
│                                                                   │
│                                         ╱─────────╲               │
│                                        ╱   ┌──┐    ╲              │
│        ┌──┐                           │    └──┘     │             │
│        └──┘ ◄──────────────────────── │        #1   │             │
│                                        ╲           ╱              │
│                                         ╲─────────╱               │
│                                                                   │
└───────────────────────────────────────────────────────────────────┘
        │                                        │
        │                                        │
┌───────────────────────────────┐     ┌───────────────────────────────┐
│ The abstract with awareness   │     │ The physical with awareness   │
│ of the physical,              │     │ of the abstract               │
│ time, and distance            │     │ without time or distance      │
└───────────────────────────────┘     └───────────────────────────────┘
```

    a. Can 'nothingness' be found 'outside' region #3?
    b. Can 'nothingness' be found 'outside' region #1?
    c. Can 'nothingness' be found 'within' region #3?
    d. Can 'nothingness' be found 'within' region #1?

a. Can 'nothingness' be found 'outside' the whole, 'outside' region #3?

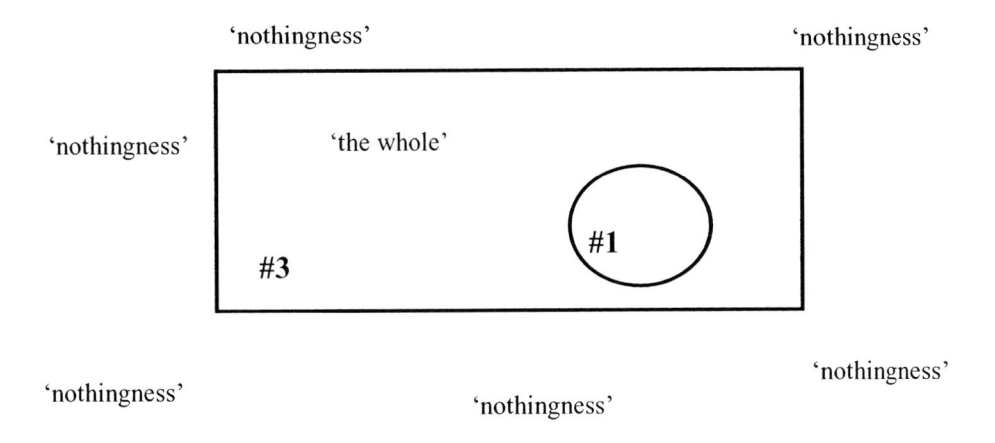

Since 'nothingness' in this graphic 'lies' 'outside' 'the whole' the whole to be the whole must expand to include what lies beyond it to remain 'the whole'. As such we obtain:

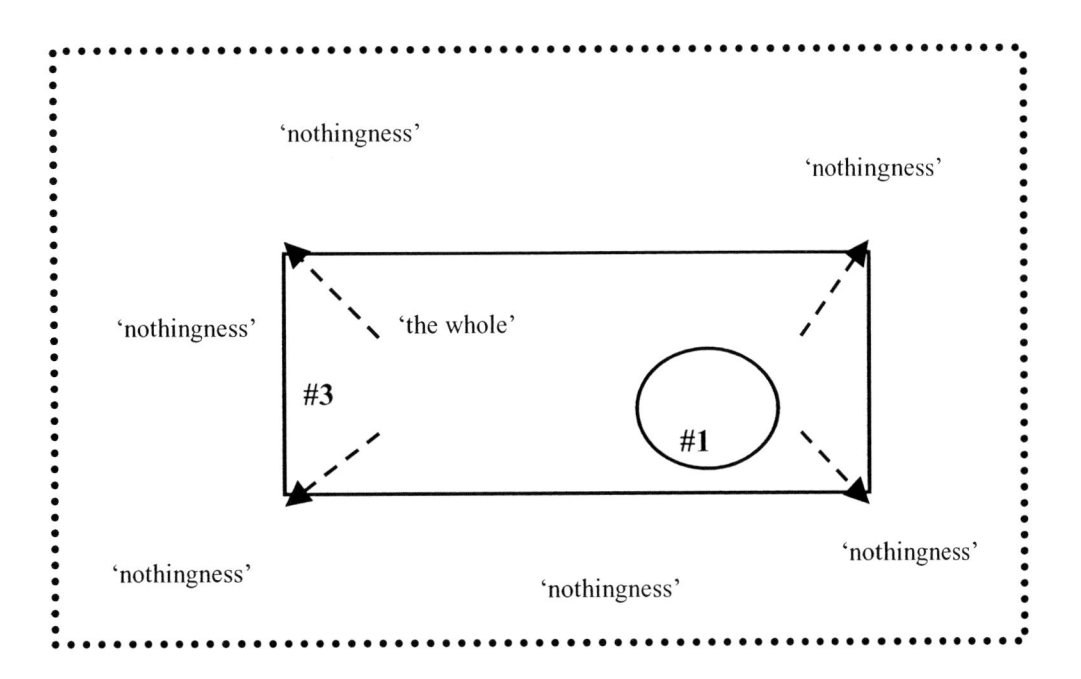

As such the 'whole' now becomes:

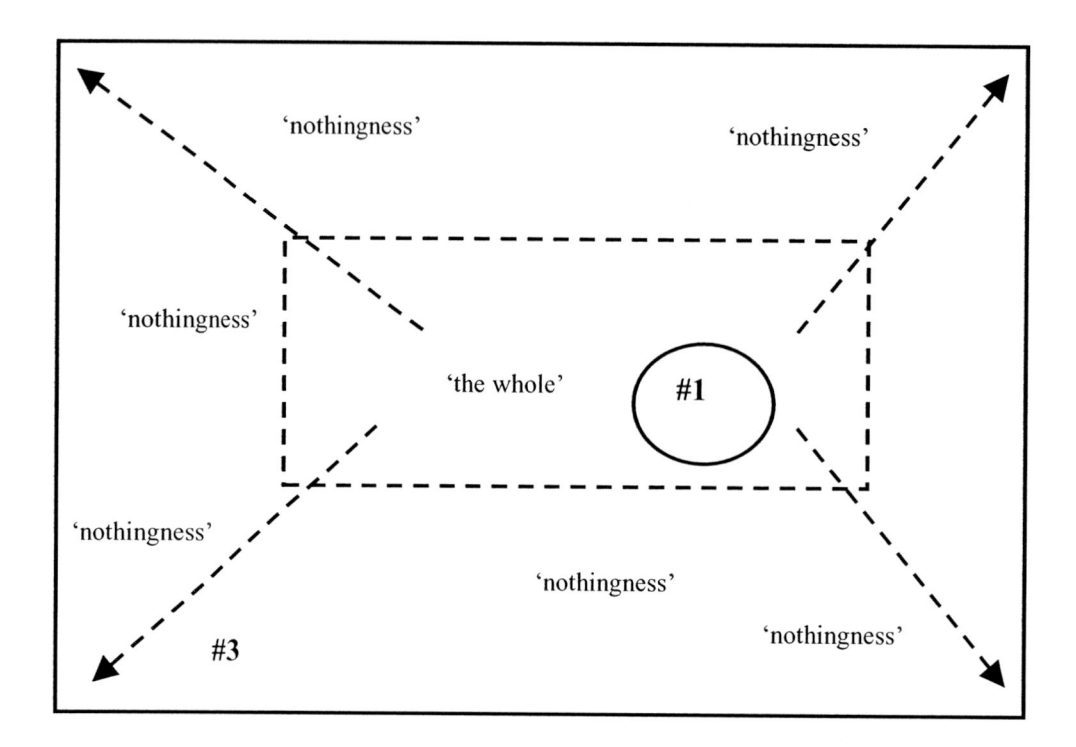

```
        ↖               'nothingness'        'nothingness'              ↗
         ＼                                                            ／
          ＼      ┌─ ─ ─ ─ ─ ─ ─ ─ ─ ─ ─ ─ ─ ─ ─ ─ ┐
           ＼    │                                  │
  'nothingness'  │                                  │
                 │                                  │
                 │    'the whole'      ⬭ #1         │
                 │                                  │
                 │                                  │
            ／   └─ ─ ─ ─ ─ ─ ─ ─ ─ ─ ─ ─ ─ ─ ─ ─ ┘    ＼
  'nothingness' ／                                            ＼
         ／              'nothingness'                          ＼
        ↙                                    'nothingness'       ↘
            #3
```

The significant result is that it appears 'a whole without 'nothingness'' is different from 'a whole with 'nothingness''.

If 'nothingness' exists, it appears to 'lie' 'within' 'the whole'. If one places 'nothingness' 'outside' the 'whole', the 'whole' must expand to include 'nothingness' or it is, by definition, no longer the 'whole'

Therefore in terms of the question: Can 'nothingness' be found 'outside' the whole, 'outside' region #3? The answer is 'nothingness' does not exist 'outside' the whole at least from all possible perspectives of the whole itself.

If such is the case, the question arises: Does 'nothingness' have a function? As we are about to explore, nothing lacks function within the whole, including 'nothingness' itself.

d. Can 'nothingness' be found 'inside' the physical, 'within' region #1?

'd'? Is this not out of order. Alphabetically, yes it is out of order. Order, however, is not the point here. In fact what we are about to do is examine the concept beginning with the 'furthest' 'outward' reaches of which we can possibly conceive, followed by the furthest 'inward' reaches we can possibly conceive. In short, we are examining the furthest extremes conceivable for 'nothingness'. Having done so we will then examine 'nothingness' in terms of the more moderate points of view.

The Error of Copernicus

We will begin exploring the inner most extremes of 'nothingness with our last graphic.

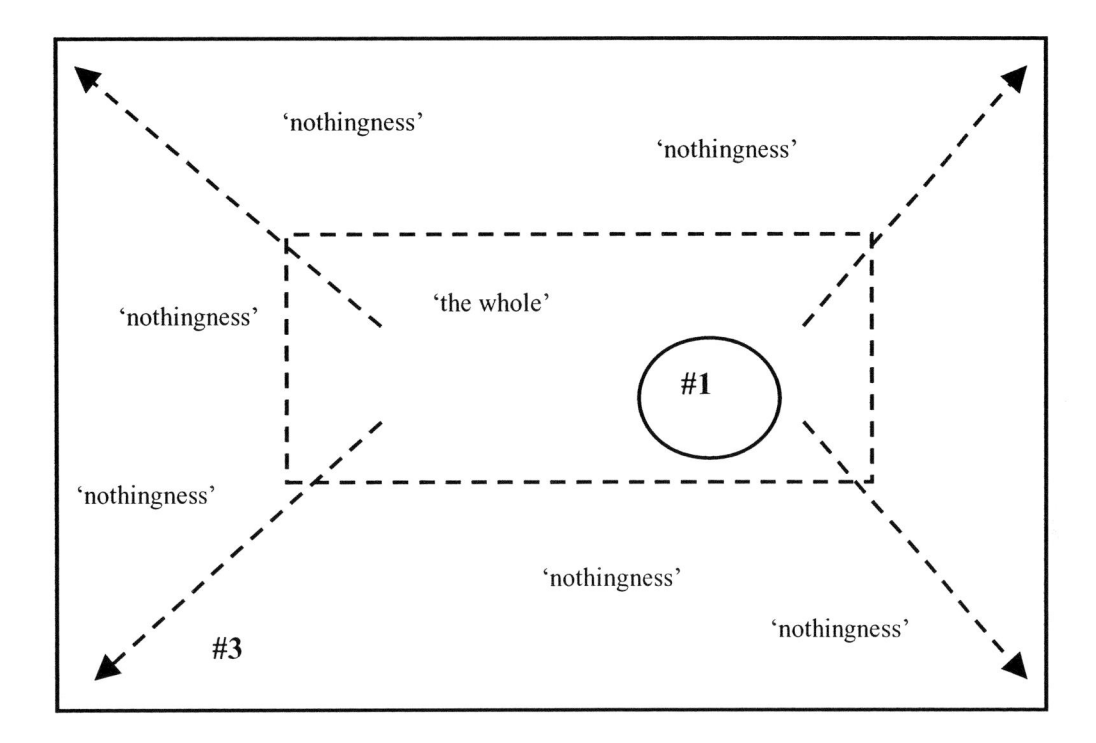

'nothingness'

'nothingness'

'nothingness'

'the whole'

#1

'nothingness'

'nothingness'

'nothingness'

#3

'nothingness'

To better depict the process of examining 'nothingness' in terms of the inner most extreme, we will remove the 'outer' aspect of our drawing and enlarge region #1:

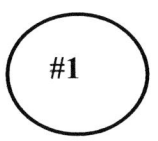

#1

We will not enlarge region #1:

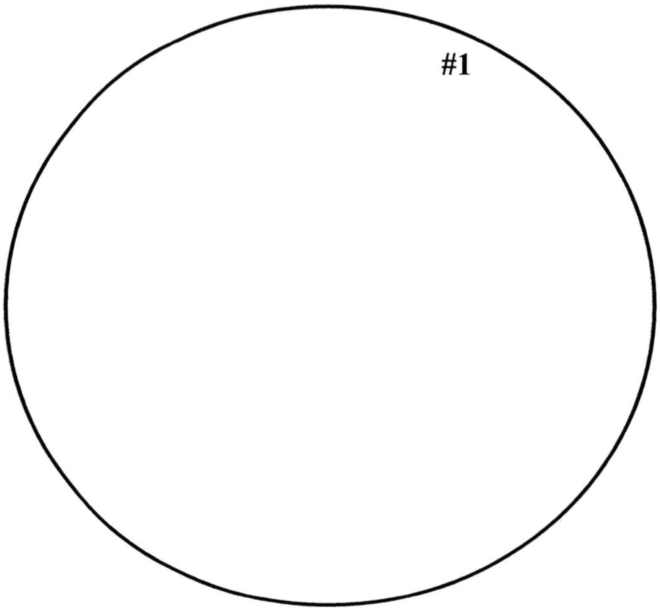
#1

We recognize this as the physical. We often label this region, the universe. Taking the region for what it is we will label it and place a representative of nothingness within this universe.

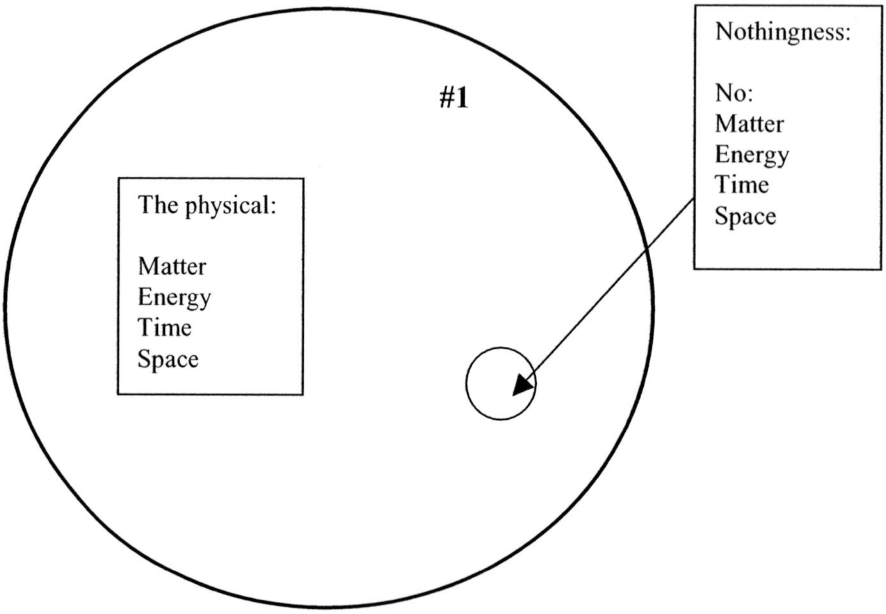
#1
The physical:
Matter
Energy
Time
Space
Nothingness:
No:
Matter
Energy
Time
Space

The Error of Copernicus

A vacuum is unnatural state of nature but we are not discussing a vacuum, we are discussing a region of nothingness. Not only is nothingness a lack of matter, but nothingness is a lack of energy. We can move to an even greater extreme, for nothingness is not only the lack of matter and energy but nothingness is a lack of matter, energy, and abstractions. Thus time and space would be absent within a region of nothingness.

Some would argue the lack of space and time cannot be found anywhere within the region of the universe and therefore such a concept is irrelevant. Time and space appear to be an innate characteristic of matter and energy. Some would disagree and say matter and energy are innate characteristics of time and energy. This is the old puzzle: which came first – the chicken or the egg? In this particular puzzle, the subject deals with innate characteristic and as such becomes: Are time and space innate characteristics of matter and energy, or matter and energy innate characteristics of time and space?

Since time and space are missing 'within' the region of 'nothingness', the region takes up no time and space and thus is in essence non-existent from the perspective of the region of the physical.

Therefore in terms of the question: Can 'nothingness' be found 'inside' the physical, 'within' region #1? The answer is 'nothingness' does not exist 'inside' the physical at least from all possible perspectives of the physical itself.

It might be feasibly possible to either find or create a region in the universe lacking matter and energy but it does not appear to be feasibly possible to find or create a region in the universe lacking time and space for time and space appear to be the very fabric of the universe itself.

    b.   Can 'nothingness' be found 'inside' the whole, 'within' region #3?

The War & Peace of a New Metaphysical Perception

To better understand the answer to this question we must refer back to a diagram found in section: The dynamics of non-Centricism:

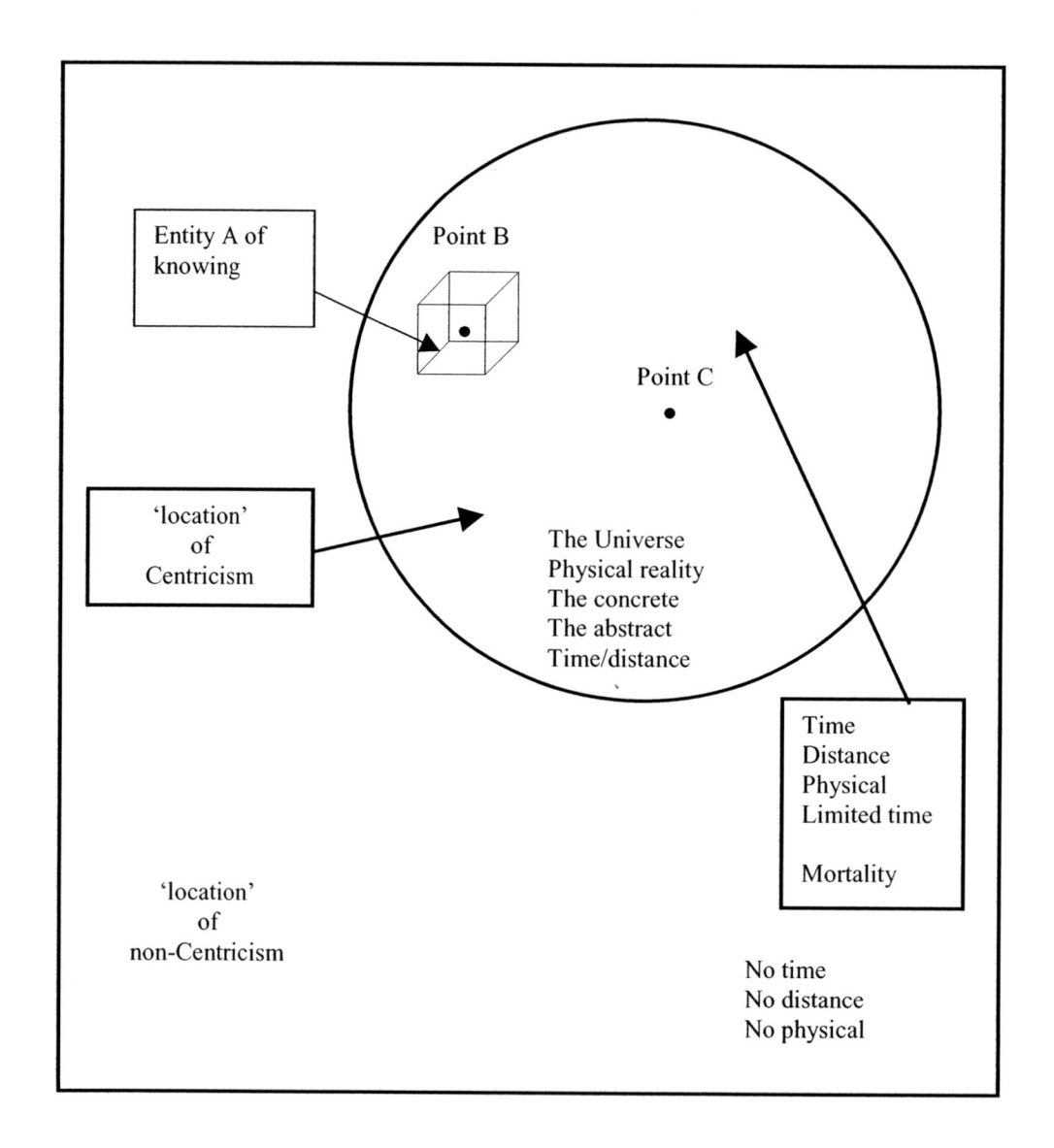

Entity A of knowing

Point B

Point C

'location' of Centricism

The Universe
Physical reality
The concrete
The abstract
Time/distance

Time
Distance
Physical
Limited time

Mortality

'location' of non-Centricism

No time
No distance
No physical

The Error of Copernicus

We will 'reduce' the graphic to a more manageable form and then add 'nothingness' within region 3:

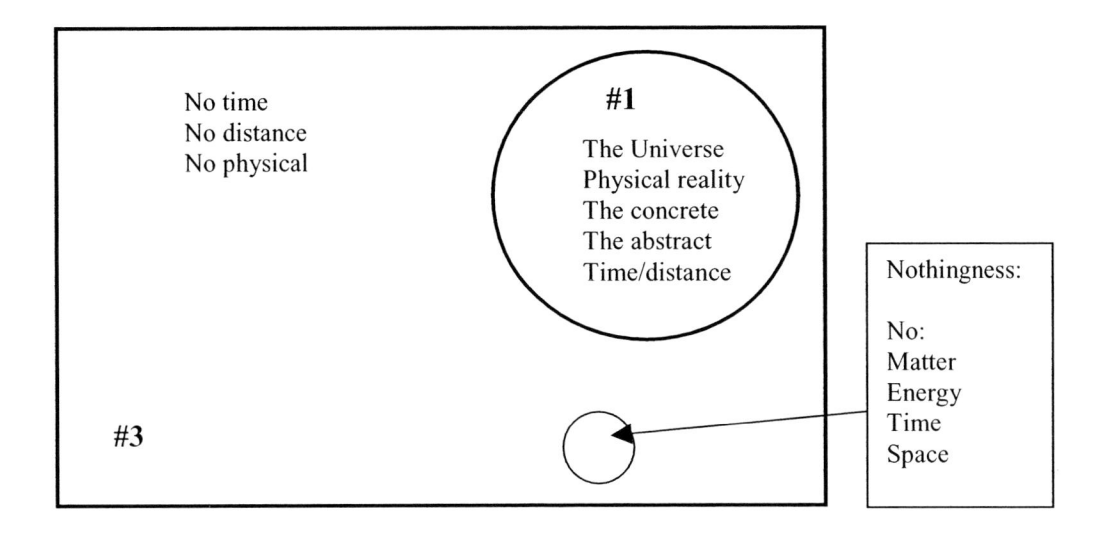

[Diagram: A large rectangle labeled #3 contains the text "No time / No distance / No physical" on the upper left and a circle labeled #1 containing "The Universe / Physical reality / The concrete / The abstract / Time/distance". A smaller circle in the lower right of region #3 is connected by an arrow to a box labeled "Nothingness: No: Matter Energy Time Space"]

This concept is understandable if one acknowledges an 'existence' of the physical lying within the non-physical, lying within the abstract. The question now becomes: Does abstraction lie within 'nothingness'? The answer would appear to be: If 'nothingness' is truly 'nothingness' then abstraction itself would be found to be absent 'within' 'nothingness'.

Could such a region exist 'outside' the physical but 'within' the abstract? The answer appears to be: Yes it is conceivable for the lack of matter, energy, time, space, and all abstraction to exist within a region of abstraction itself.

Therefore in terms of the question: Can 'nothingness' be found 'inside' the whole, 'within' region #3? The answer is 'nothingness' does not exist 'inside' the physical at least from all possible perspectives of the physical itself but 'nothingness' could lie within abstraction, could lie within region #3 if it lies outside region #1.

In short, it might be feasibly possible to either find or create a region within pure abstraction lacking matter, energy, time, and space since time and space are not what the fabric of which the abstract is composed

    c.   Can 'nothingness' be found 'outside' the physical, 'outside' region #1?

At first glance, this would appear to be the same question as 'b. Can 'nothingness' be found 'inside' the whole, 'within' region #3?' Questions 'c' and 'b' however, are significantly different questions.

Again, graphs will simplify our understanding of the question.

The War & Peace of a New Metaphysical Perception

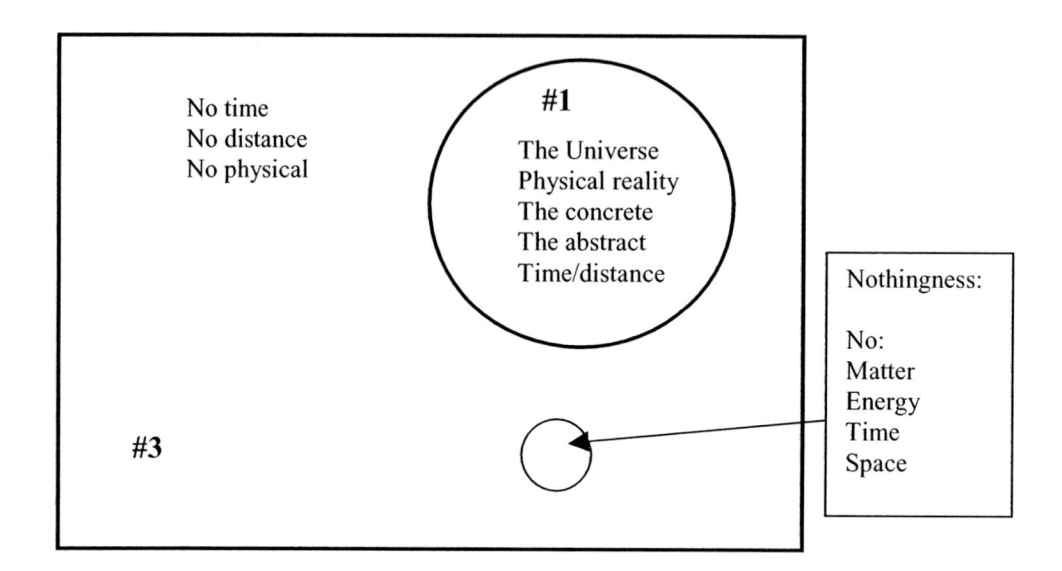

[Diagram: A large rectangle labeled #3 contains "No time / No distance / No physical" on the left, a circle labeled #1 with "The Universe / Physical reality / The concrete / The abstract / Time/distance", and a small circle pointing to a box labeled "Nothingness: / No: / Matter / Energy / Time / Space"]

Before we go any further, let's reiterate a concept presented in Tractate 1: Zeno. The concept: A circle divides existence into three regions: The inside of the circle, the outside of the circle, and the circle itself. We must also reiterate two basic principles of geometry: The first concept: A circle is composed of an infinite number of points in a plane located equidistant from 'a' point, the center. The second concept: 'a' point is a location in space having no dimensions, having no length, breadth, or depth

With this in mind, we will compress the contents of the circle, compress the universe, apply the contraction aspect of the Big Bang Theory to our diagram.

If we compress the border, separating the physical and the abstract we begin to see the expansion of a region lacking matter, energy, time, and space. In fact, if we follow the logic of 'b. Can 'nothingness' be found 'outside' the physical, 'outside' region #1?

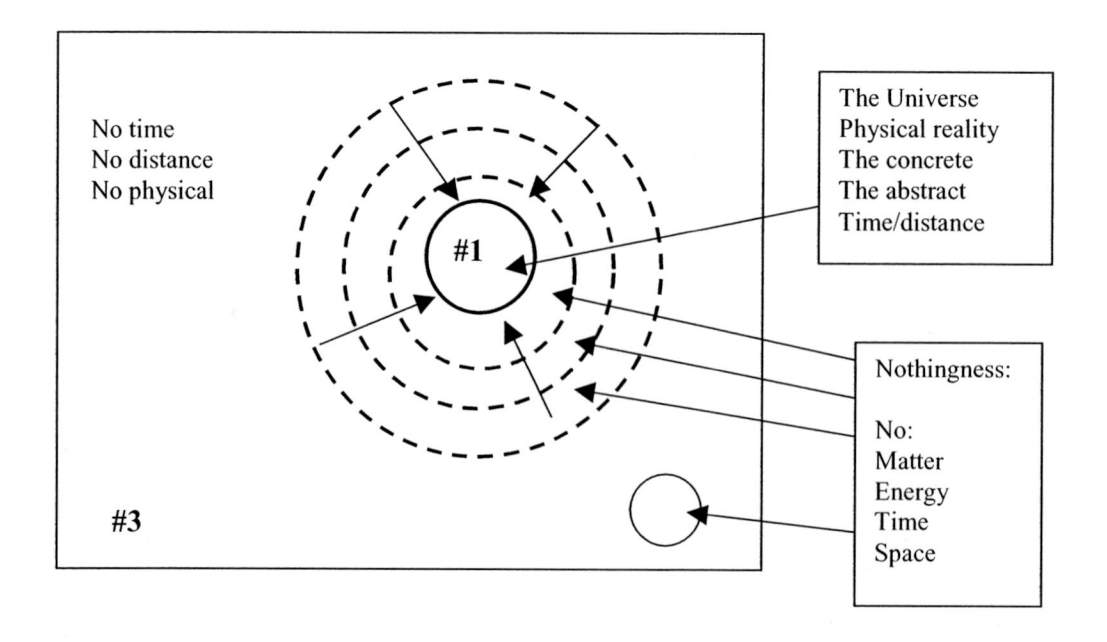

[Diagram: Similar rectangle labeled #3 with "No time / No distance / No physical" on the left, concentric dashed circles with arrows pointing inward to a small circle labeled #1, pointing to box "The Universe / Physical reality / The concrete / The abstract / Time/distance", and another small circle pointing to "Nothingness: / No: / Matter / Energy / Time / Space"]

The Error of Copernicus

Now we can understand that no matter how much the universe expands or contracts, it remains immersed within a bed of nothingness and therefore takes up 'no more space' if it becomes infinitely large than it does if it becomes infinitely small. The reason for this is that it lies 'within' 'nothingness' which 'contains' no time or space, which lacks time and lacks space.

But wouldn't the universe then lie directly in the abstract? No, for time and space are abstractual and as we have previously demonstrated in this Tractate, 'nothingness' is not only the lack of matter and energy but 'nothingness' is the lack of all abstractions.

The significance of such a concept now emerges:

The region 'separating' the physical from the abstract has no dimension. Matter, energy, time and space do not exist 'within' 'nothngness' and therefore the boundary separating the physical and the abstract is, from the perspective of the physical as well as from the perspective of the abstract, non-existent.

Now we see that not only can 'nothingness' be found within the whole but in terms of the universe, in terms of reality, in terms of the physical which contains time and space, 'nothingness' can be found in two places:

1. Adjacent to and therefore separating the universe, separating reality, separating the physical, separating multiplicity, separating Cartesianism, separating free will, separating Centricism, separating all aspects of the physical from the abstract
2. Non-Adjacent to the universe

Both 1 and 2 have their own implications.

Statement 1 implies 'nothingness' is the mirror separating the physical and the abstract. Statement 1 suggests a 'location' where the physical and the abstract face one another just as one faces oneself when gazing into a mirror.

Statement 2 implies the existence of multiple 'realities'. Statement 2 implies the potential of universes existing which do not have time and space as the fabrics of their universes but rather the fabrics of other universes may or may not be composed of other abstractual concepts than the abstractual concepts of space and time.

The War & Peace of a New Metaphysical Perception

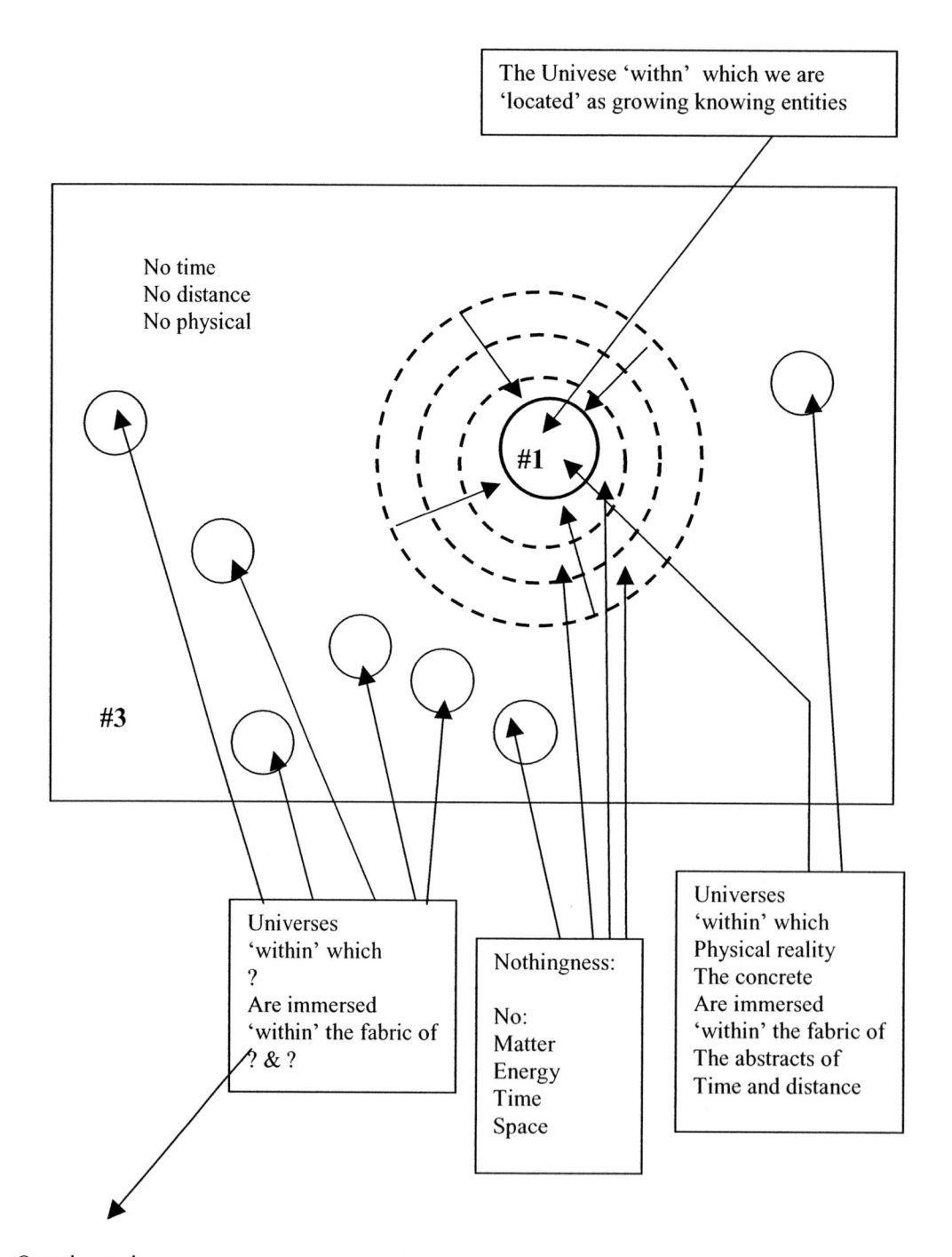

[Diagram with the following labels:

- "The Univese 'withn' which we are 'located' as growing knowing entities" (pointing to #1)
- "No time / No distance / No physical"
- "#1" (central circle)
- "#3"
- "Universes 'within' which ? Are immersed 'within' the fabric of ? & ?"
- "Nothingness: No: Matter Energy Time Space"
- "Universes 'within' which Physical reality The concrete Are immersed 'within' the fabric of The abstracts of Time and distance"]

Questions arise:

Is the first question mark replaced by the physical? It may be but it need not be. This capability allows the whole to be much more complex than if the answer were simply yes.

The second question which arises is: Are the remaining two question marks the abstractual concepts of time and distance/space? Again the answer is the same, they may be or they may not be.

Is there anything we can say about the three question marks? Yes, we can be fairly certain the last two question marks are forms of abstractions since the reality of universes is that they all lie 'within' abstractual existence.

The questions then become: Is either the basic concept of centricism or the basic concept of non-Centricism or both simultaneously for that matter, found to be an innate characteristic of 'nothingness' itself?

Centricism is a characteristic. As such Centricism must apply to 'some' concept be it physical or abstractual.

The concept of 'characteristics' do not apply to 'nothingness' rather the void of characteristics apply to 'nothingness'. Characteristics cannot 'characterize' 'nothingness', since 'nothingness' is neither physical nor abstractual. As such, it is only 'within' 'nothingness' where we find the lack of one or the other or both Centricism and non-Centricism.

Where do understandings regarding the characteristics of 'inverse proportionality', 'nothingness', 'entities of knowing', 'Centricism', and 'non-Centricism' lead us? Such understandings lead us toward comprehending the interaction as well as the interrelationship of the elements of the 'whole'. Since by definition we are a part of the whole, such understandings lead us toward comprehending the interaction as well as the interrelationship of ourselves to the whole..

Before we can explore such interrelationships and interactions, we have two other concepts, which need addressing.

Virgin physicality/'virgin physical life'

The concept: 'Nothingness' found 'within' the physical, found 'within' region #1 is 'Centricism' itself. In fact, 'nothingness' found 'within' the physical is the 'fundamental building block' of the physical, is a concept for the field of science/cosmology to explore.

We find ourselves in the middle of a dialectic regarding the differences of existing within a region of Centricism (region #1) and a region of non-Centricism (region #3). The similarities of the two regions, as well as the significance one region imposes upon the other, are the concepts we are attempting to understand. We can begin our understanding by making a simple statement:

> 'Nothingness' found 'within' the physical, found 'within' region #1, is centricism itself.

The War & Peace of a New Metaphysical Perception

To understand the concept: 'Nothingness' found 'within' the physical, found 'within' region #1, is centricism itself, we will once again rely upon graphics:

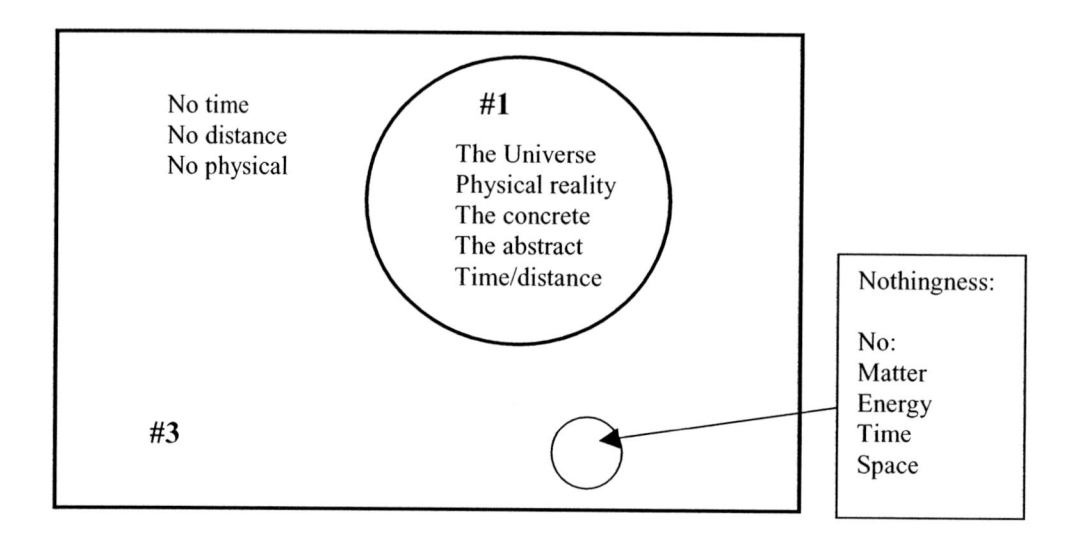

```
┌─────────────────────────────────────────────────┐
│                                                 │
│  No time         ╱‾‾‾‾‾╲                        │
│  No distance    │  #1   │                       │
│  No physical    │       │                       │
│                 │ The Universe                  │
│                 │ Physical reality              │
│                 │ The concrete   ┌────────────┐ │
│                 │ The abstract   │Nothingness:│ │
│                 │ Time/distance  │            │ │
│                  ╲_____╱         │ No:        │ │
│                                  │ Matter     │ │
│                                  │ Energy     │ │
│                              ○───│ Time       │ │
│  #3                              │ Space      │ │
│                                  └────────────┘ │
└─────────────────────────────────────────────────┘
```

We will now expand the universe to include 'nothingness':

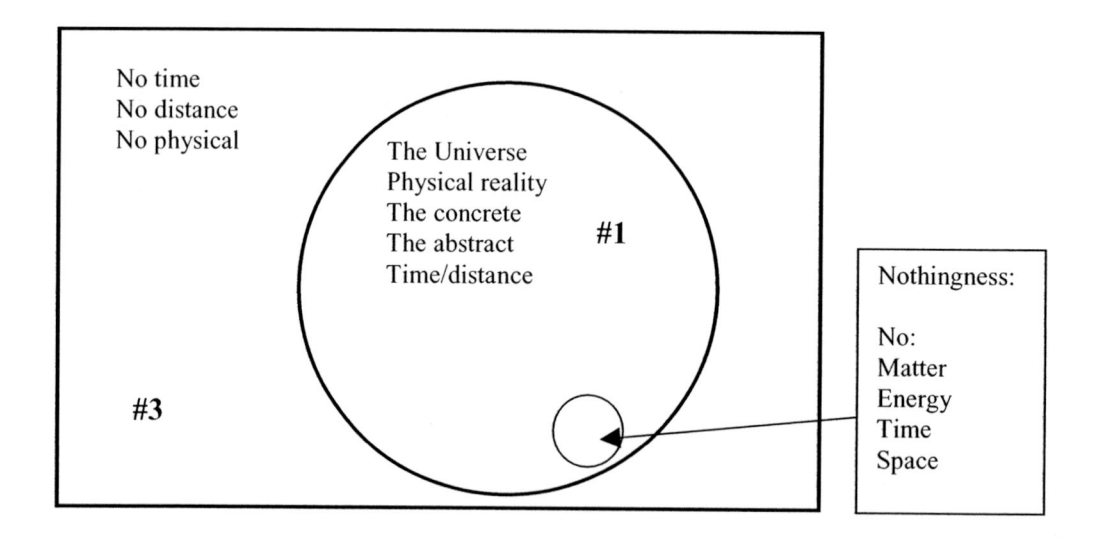

```
┌─────────────────────────────────────────────────┐
│                                                 │
│  No time       ╱‾‾‾‾‾‾‾‾‾‾‾╲                    │
│  No distance  ╱              ╲                  │
│  No physical │  The Universe  │                 │
│              │ Physical reality                 │
│              │  The concrete      #1            │
│              │  The abstract                    │
│              │  Time/distance  ┌────────────┐   │
│               ╲               ╱│Nothingness:│   │
│                ╲             ╱ │            │   │
│                 ╲_____╱  │ No:        │   │
│                          ○─────│ Matter     │   │
│                                │ Energy     │   │
│  #3                            │ Time       │   │
│                                │ Space      │   │
│                                └────────────┘   │
└─────────────────────────────────────────────────┘
```

As we have discussed previously, nature abhors a vacuum and as such rushes to fill the vacuum. But nature acts symmetrically and as such nature rushes to fill the vacuum equally from all 'directions' until the vacuum is no longer a vacuum. The point is the vacuum collapses from the 'outer' edge toward the 'center'. Within the physical, 'nothingness' is the location towards which all 'things' move to find the center.

'Nothingness' becomes the epitome of the center itself. 'Nothingness' becomes the center for as 'nothingness' becomes 'occupied' and its radius diminishes to non-existence itself, 'nothing' has occurred no 'space' was lost and no 'distance' traversed. Since no distance was traversed, no time was taken to fill the region of 'nothingness'. This statement can be made when referring to time for time is not an element, is not a part of the fabric of which 'nothingness' is composed since by definition 'nothingness' is the void of all including not only matter and energy but also distance and time.

What then is: 'Virgin physicality/'virgin physical life'? 'Virgin physical life' is physical life at the point of centricism's formation. 'Virgin physicality' begins just before formation but just after it pre-existed as separation. 'Virgin physical life' is the point of origination, is physical life 'before' it has gained the ability to physically function as singularity of existence versus multiple independent existence of components. 'Virgin physicality' is physical existence as 'a' unit versus existence as separate components 'capable' of combining to form 'a' unit. 'Virgin physical existence' is in essence nonexistence, is in essence nothing, is in essence 'nothingness' itself. 'Virgin physicality/'virgin physical life' is the moment 'before' space, time, matter, energy forms of experience become a part of knowing and thus knows nothing of its own self for its own self has yet to begin its process of knowing. The lack of knowing existing immediately before the process of knowing begins is where 'virgin-ness' lies. Virgin-ness lies at the center of 'nothingness' itself. Cosmologically and ontologically, centricism thus finds its ultimate source of centricity.

What then of the universe? Science and religion with their principles of symmetry and creation would suggest the same concept can be applied to this thing we call 'virgin physicality'. Again, however, this is a discourse for science/cosmology and religion/ontology to explore. Our task is metaphysical in nature and although our discussion may have direct implication for science and religion, it is not the scientific nor the religious aspects we are to pursue.

What then are we attempting to explore? We are attempting to explore the concept of knowledge becoming 'knowing' knowledge, consciousness of 'knowledge'.

We will, therefore, modify our graphic by replacing the symmetrical circle within which we find three dimensions, four dimensions, and may in the future find five, six, and more dimensions. with a unit entity of 'knowing': In short, we are about to explore the concept of: Virgin consciousness/'virgin abstract knowing'.

Virgin consciousness/'virgin abstract knowing'

We can now make a second statement regarding the concept of 'nothingness'

      'Nothingness' found 'within' the abstract, found 'within' region #3 is 'non-Centricism' itself.

It could be said that the statement: 'Nothingness' found 'within' the abstract is the 'fundamental building block' of the abstract. is a concept for the field of religion/ontology to explore.

We find ourselves in the middle of a dialect regarding the differences of existing within a region of Centricism (region #1) as explained by cosmology and existing in a region of non-Centricism (region #3) as explained by ontology. This is the very point of metaphysics. Metaphysics listens to both cosmology and ontology and attempts to resolve the issues keeping the two apart.

Before we can make the leap of resolving the basic differences between ontology and cosmology, we must allow the metaphysical understanding regarding the ontological perception of

The War & Peace of a New Metaphysical Perception

'nothingness' to emerge just as we allowed the metaphysical understanding regarding the cosmological perception of 'nothingness' to emerge.

To understand the concept: 'Nothingness' found 'within' the abstract, found 'within' region #3, is non-Centricism itself. we will once again rely upon graphics:

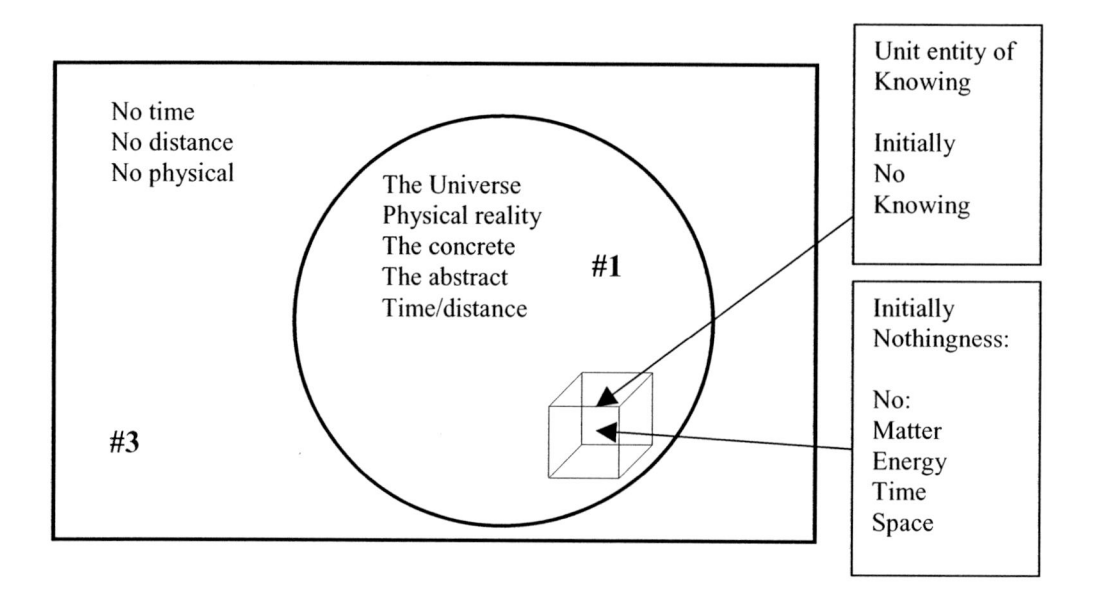

```
┌─────────────────────────────────────────┐   ┌──────────────┐
│                                         │   │ Unit entity of│
│   No time                               │   │ Knowing      │
│   No distance                           │   │              │
│   No physical     The Universe          │   │ Initially    │
│                   Physical reality      │   │ No           │
│                   The concrete          │   │ Knowing      │
│                   The abstract   #1     │   └──────────────┘
│                   Time/distance         │   ┌──────────────┐
│                                         │   │ Initially    │
│                            ┌──┐         │   │ Nothingness: │
│                            │  │◄────────┼───│              │
│   #3                       └──┘         │   │ No:          │
│                                         │   │ Matter       │
│                                         │   │ Energy       │
│                                         │   │ Time         │
│                                         │   │ Space        │
└─────────────────────────────────────────┘   └──────────────┘
```

As the entity moves through time and space, it gains an 'awareness' of experiencing. The entity begins to 'fill' up with both knowing and awareness of its knowing. Eventually, the entity becomes 'full'. The 'fullness' of the entity does not terminate the entity's existence in the physical. Rather the termination of the entity's existence in the physical completes the filling of the entity.

This does not imply the entity has 'room' for more knowing, for the entity is always 'full'. Rather the physical termination is the termination of the 'process' of acquiring knowledge by the knowing of the entity.

The Error of Copernicus

Unit entity of Knowing

Upon Termination Filled with:
Knowing of Knowledge

Unit entity of Nothingness:

Upon Termination Filled with Knowing of:
Matter
Energy
Time
Space

No time
No distance
No physical

The Universe
Physical reality
The concrete
The abstract
Time/distance

#1

#3

Unit entity of Knowing

Initially
No
Knowing

Initially Nothingness:

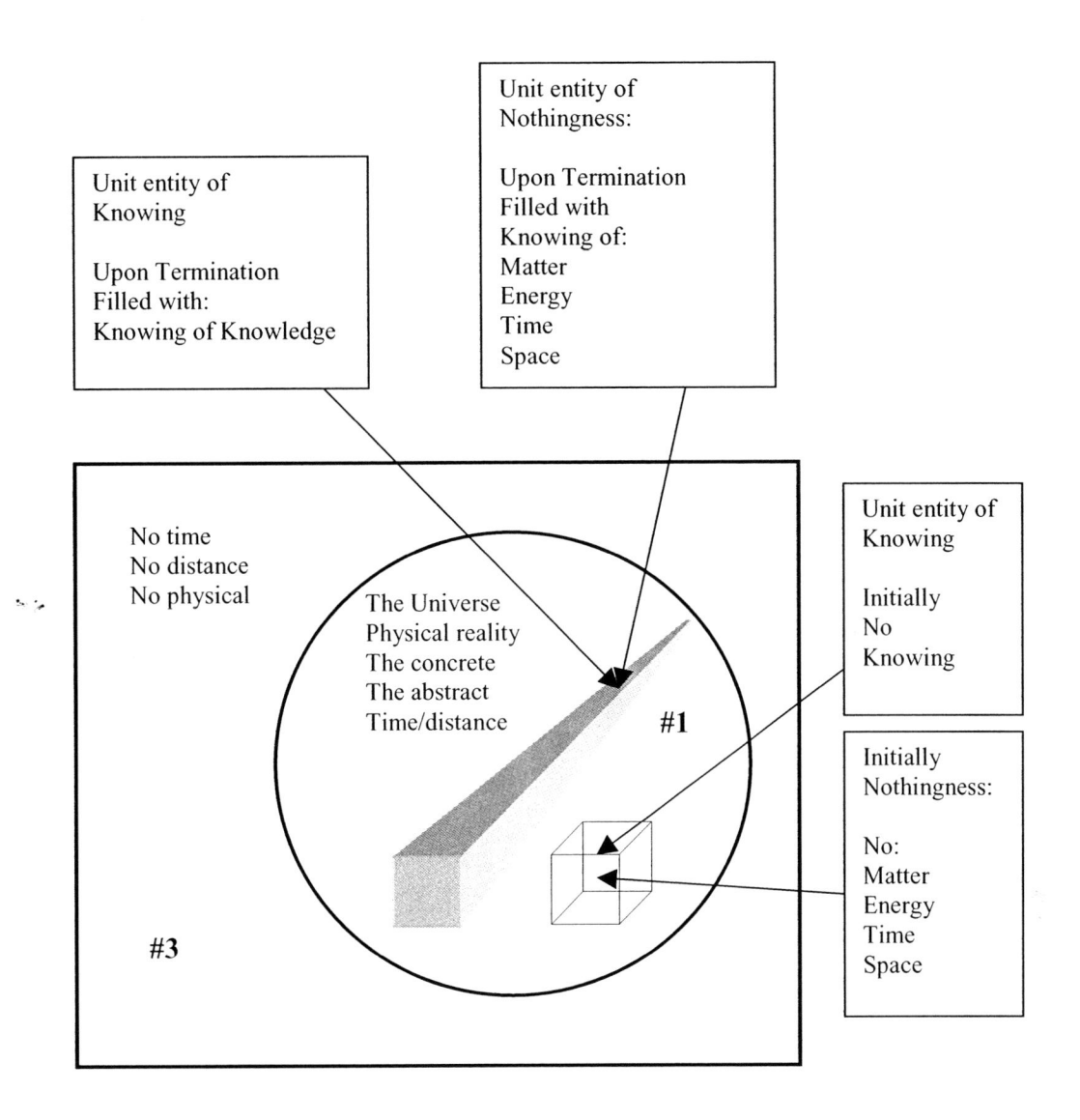

No:
Matter
Energy
Time
Space

We can depict the completion of the process as a 'filled' versus an 'empty' unit. Regardless of the 'amount' of knowledge 'contained' within the entity of knowing, the concept of the entity being completely filled is complete with the termination of gaining knowing unique to the entity of knowing.

Likewise, regardless of the 'amount' of knowledge 'contained' within the entity of knowing the concept of the entity being completely empty while in the process of gaining knowing unique to the entity of knowing is in essence 'empty' relative to the potential to gain knowledge by the entity of knowing. The only limit imposed to the continued increase in knowledge forced upon the unit of knowing is the termination of the process itself.

Some would call this termination of the growth process of 'knowledge' by the unit of knowing, death. There is nothing inappropriate regarding this label. However, to say we 'know' what death is, is inappropriate for we can only speculate regarding such a meaning. In this Tractate, we are exploring the very meaning of the term death, from a different direction than that which society

The War & Peace of a New Metaphysical Perception

presently comes. We are exploring the perception of death - exploring the perception of the mirror separating the physical and the abstract from the point of view of a new metaphysical perception.

What then is: Virgin consciousness/'virgin abstract knowing', 'virgin abstract knowing' is knowing at its point of origination, is knowing 'before' it has gained any knowledge and thus its knowing knows nothing. Virgin consciousness/'virgin abstract knowing' is the moment 'before' space, time, matter, and energy forms of experience become a part of knowing. Virgin consciousness knows nothing of its own self for its own self has yet to begin its process of knowing. The lack of knowing existing immediately before the process of knowing begins is where 'virgin-ness' lies. Virgin-ness lies at the center of the 'nothingness' of knowing itself. Metaphysically, centricism thus finds its ultimate source of centricity.

Stepping 'in' beyond Centricism: Dependency

Now as much as it may appear logical to begin examining the entities of knowing within region #1, we are going to begin examining the entities of knowing from region #3. To do this we will simply move the entities of knowing out of region #1 and into region #3.

In essence, we are going to step 'out' into non-Centricism. We are going to allow the two forms of unique knowing of knowledge to step 'out' into non-Centricism.

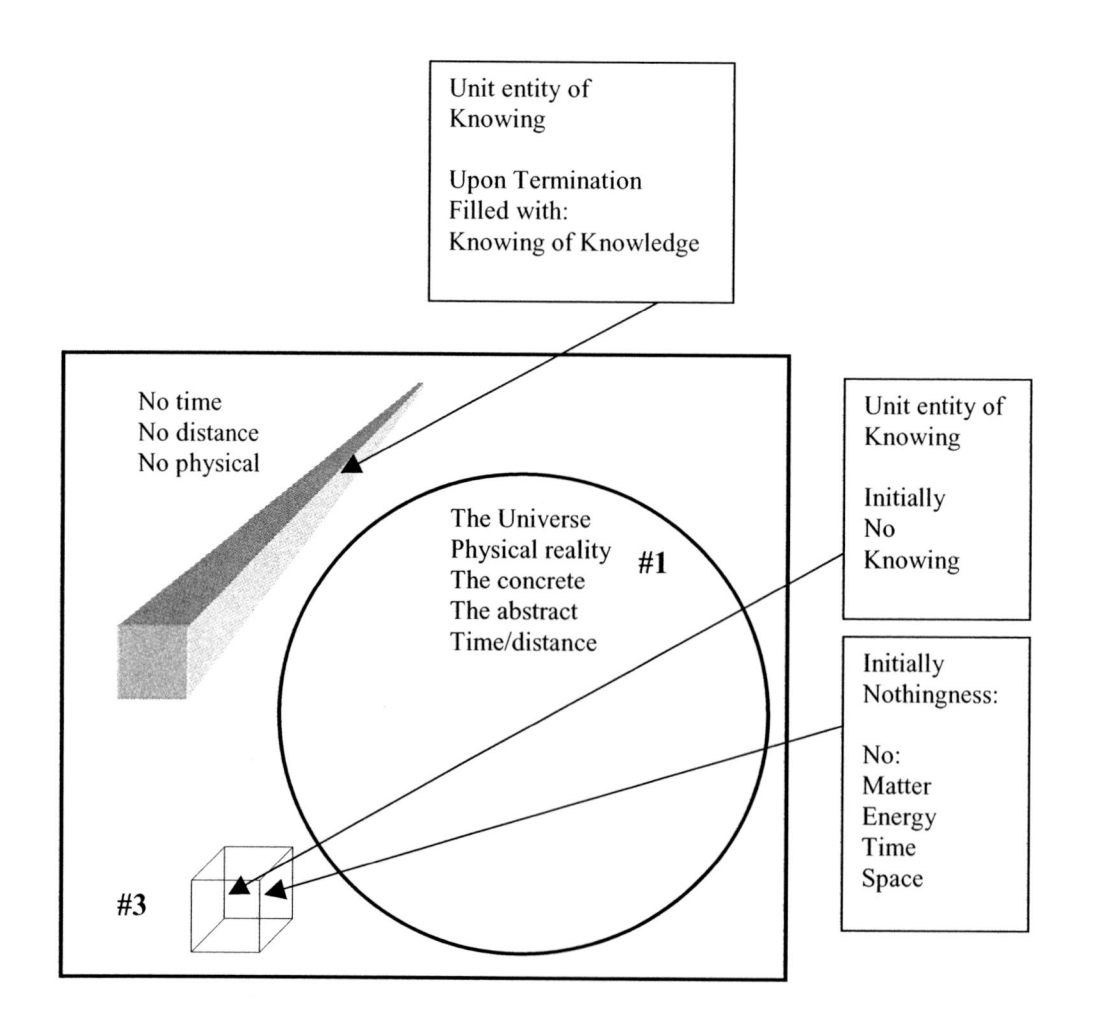

Since the 'empty' unit, the 'virgin entity of knowing', has absolutely nothing abstractual or otherwise within it, it takes up no space or time and thus we can now simplify the graphic:

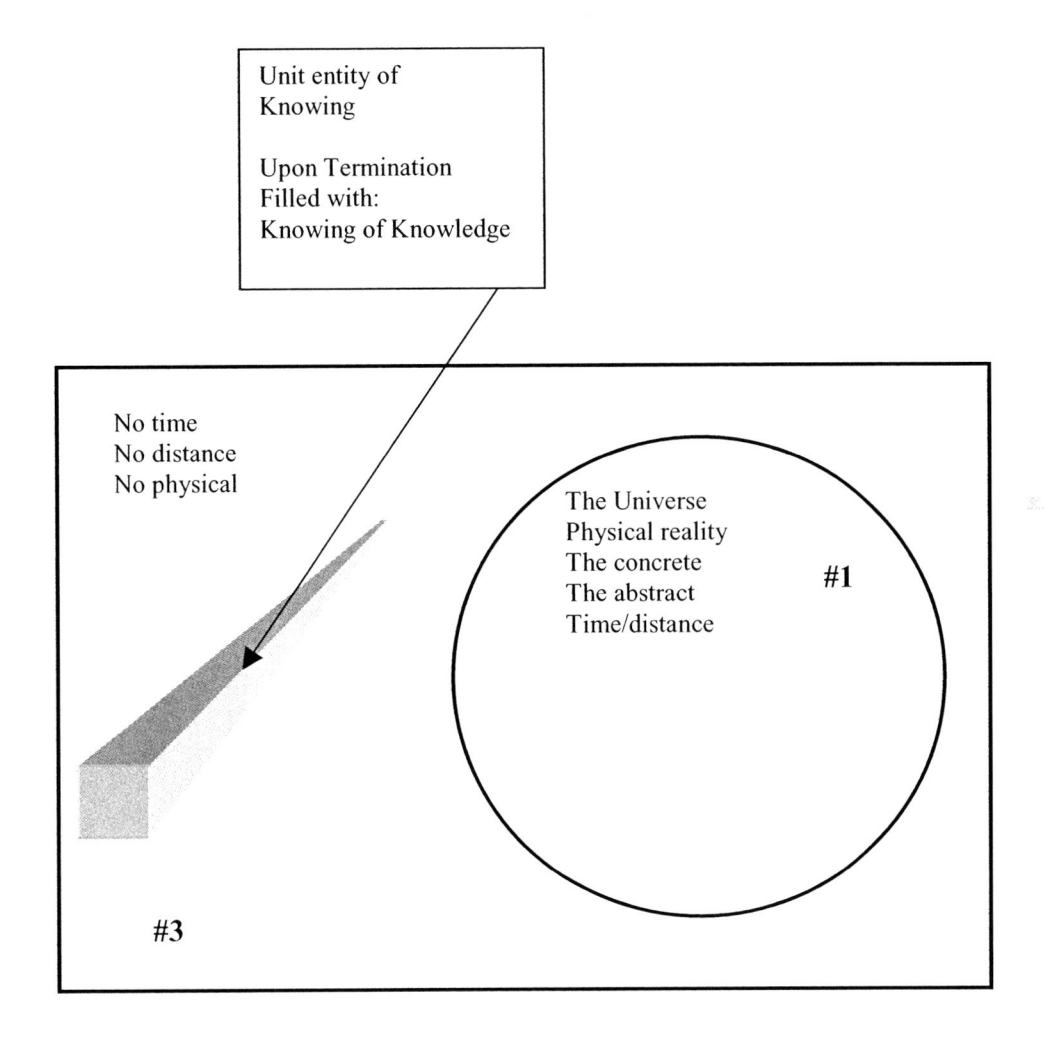

Unit entity of Knowing

Upon Termination Filled with: Knowing of Knowledge

No time
No distance
No physical

The Universe
Physical reality
The concrete
The abstract
Time/distance

#1

#3

With the aid of this graphic, we can now begin to understand the interrelationship between existing entities found within region #3. We can now begin to understand the very concept of not only the very existence of non-Centricism itself but we can begin to understand the process as well as the potentiality of non-Centricism.

Existence within non-Centricism:

We will take the latter diagram and reduce region #1, the location of Centricism since we are concerned with region #3. In addition we will expand upon the number of entities of knowing which have evolved through the process of 'traveling', experiencing region #1 – the location of space, time, matter, energy…:

The War & Peace of a New Metaphysical Perception

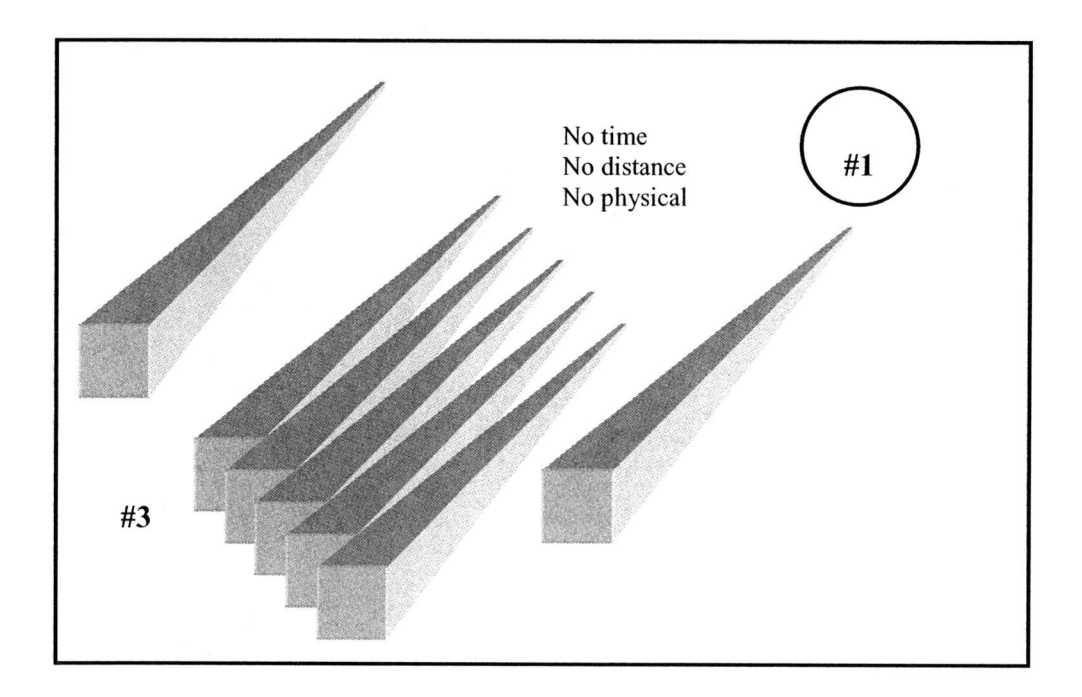

No time
No distance
No physical

#1

#3

The entities of knowing:

1. Are each unique in and of themselves due to their unique experiencing and assembly through time and space or whichever abstractual fabric should exist within the 'universe' from which they emerge
2. Do not vary in size since relative to the whole, each is relatively the same in size
3. May appear to vary regarding their 'distance' apart but since they are immersed in a location void distance, in essence the 'distance' separating them does not exist. They are, therefore, all equidistant – no distance apart
4. Are independent of beginning – end parameters since they are immersed in a void of time and space, immersed within a form of non-Centricism

Process

5. Take no 'time' to get from one to another since there is no 'distance' to traverse
6. Are capable of 'knowing' one another completely since they are not knowledge but passive unique experiencing of knowledge assembled by the active process of knowing and whose process remains an integral part of themselves since the passivity of knowledge is nothing without active process of knowing

Potentiality

7. Are capable of incorporating 'new' entities of unique knowledge, knowing, and experiencing
8. Partial summations of knowing as well as complete summations of knowing are as varied as the potential combinations of existing entities and the parts of existing entities allow. This is known as 'Omniscience'.

9. Potentiality within region #3 is, due to #1 – 8 is limited to what is and therefore is 'dependent' one entity upon another entity, which exists as opposed to what 'might' exist.

Dependence thus becomes the principle of region #3.

It must be acknowledged that the concept of existence 'within' non-Centricism is a difficult concept to comprehend. But why shouldn't it be. We are after all immersed 'within' Centricism' and as such find time and space to be concepts expanding 'outward' from 'a' point of reference which varies from conscious knowing to conscious knowing.

What must not be lost within the exploration of the unfamiliar, however, is that within a location void the fabric of space and time, 'correct' sequencing is not a fundamental principle since 'correct' sequencing is an aspect of time and space found within our personal universe.

Region #3 therefore is a location where our unique experiencing depends upon what others have to offer us to experience versus our forming our own experiencing for our own unique experiences are what they are and our own uniqueness cannot change without the infusion, embracing, union of another's unique knowing.

Divine intervention? Perhaps. Who is to say what the whole is capable of doing with its creation: the universe, our reality.

Nevertheless, how can an 'all knowing' entity be all knowing if it doesn't know 'all things'?

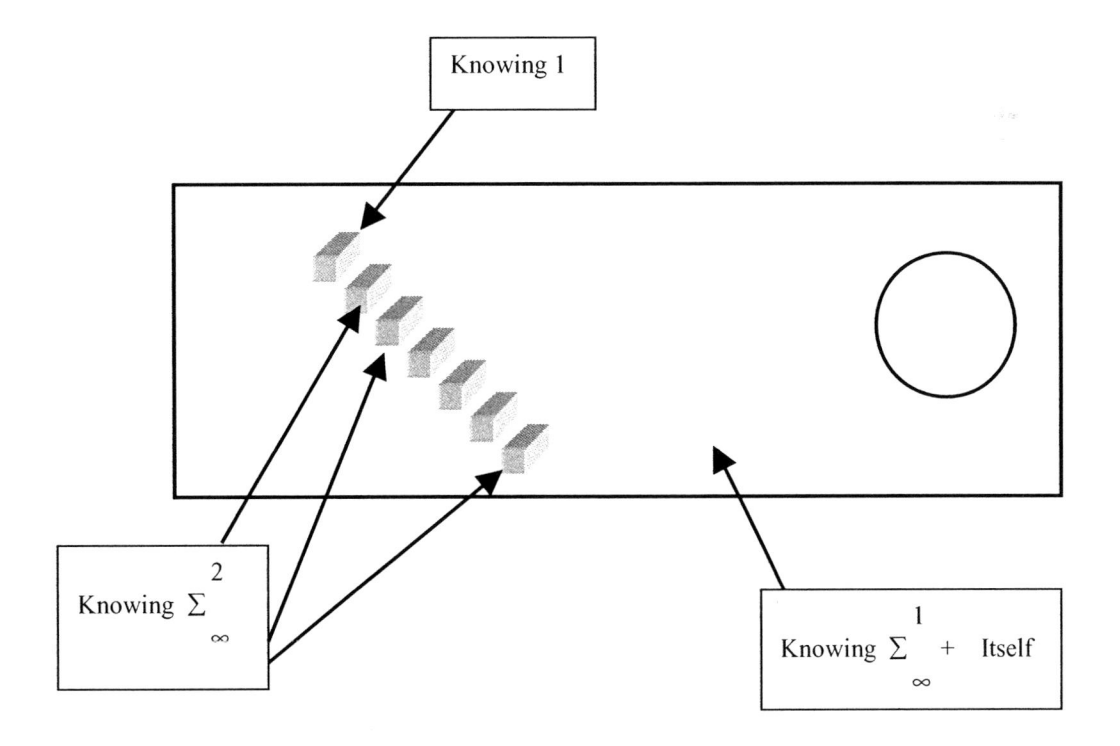

$$\text{Knowing 1}$$

$$\text{Knowing } \sum_{\infty}^{2}$$

$$\text{Knowing } \sum_{\infty}^{1} + \text{ Itself}$$

The War & Peace of a New Metaphysical Perception

Doesn't this diagram imply 'all Knowing' doesn't know what 'will be' and doesn't this in turn imply time exists in 'all Knowing'?

The concept of what 'will be' only exists 'within' time and if we review what we had previously learned of time, we find time to be 'located' within two locations:

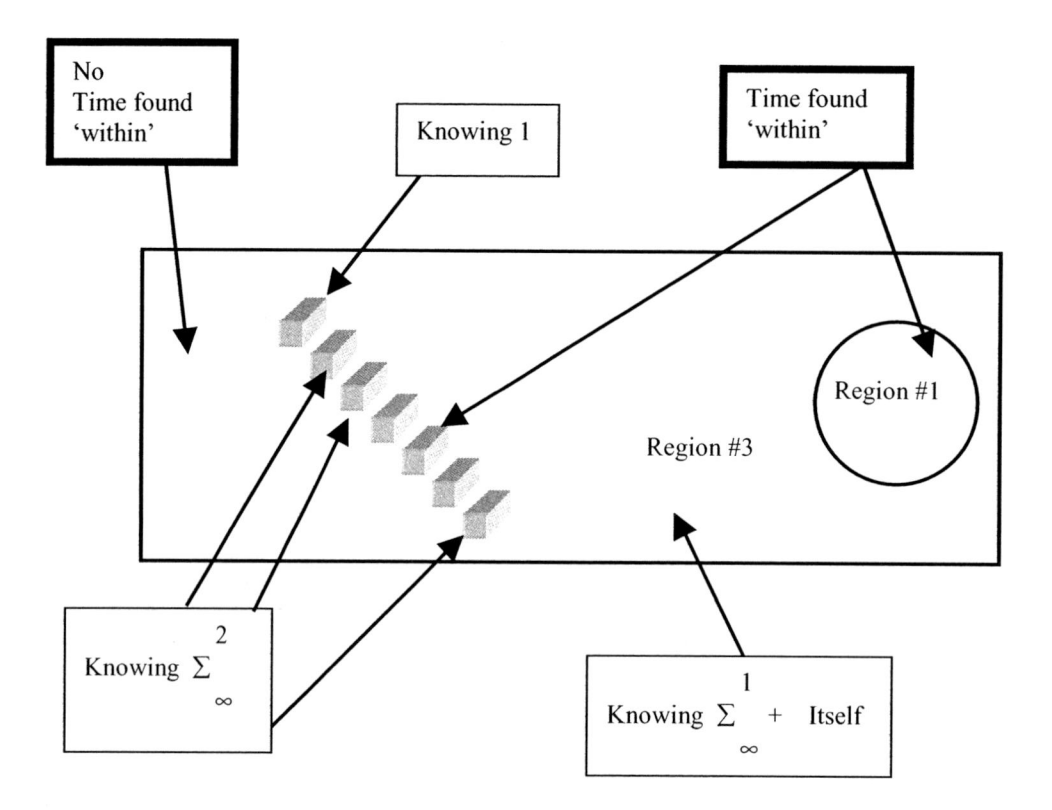

[Diagram with labeled boxes: "No Time found 'within'", "Knowing 1", "Time found 'within'", "Region #1", "Region #3", "Knowing $\sum_{\infty}^{2}$", "Knowing $\sum_{\infty}^{1}$ + Itself"]

Since time is not found either as an innate characteristic of region #3 nor as a medium of region #3 'within' which subsets of region #3 find themselves immersed, there is no concept of 'what will be' to be found in region #3.

This is not to say time is not found 'within' region #3, rather it demonstrated time is not an all-pervasive characteristic, a universal medium of region #3. Time is found in region #3 in two distinct location of which we are presently capable of perceiving. Time is found 'within' entities of 'knowing', which have evolved out of the 'universe', and time is found as a medium of the universe within which entities of 'knowing' move from being 'virgin' entities of 'knowing' to being complete entities of 'knowing'.

Where then does the 'Book of Divine Knowledge' find itself to be in terms of the metaphysical system of singular location, 'being' *being* 'Being'?

284

The Error of Copernicus

Stepping 'into' Centricism: Independence

Having stepped 'in' beyond Centricism and into the region characterized by non-Centricism, let's now step 'out' of non-Centricism and into Centricism – Independence. To do so we will begin where we initiated the understanding of region #3:

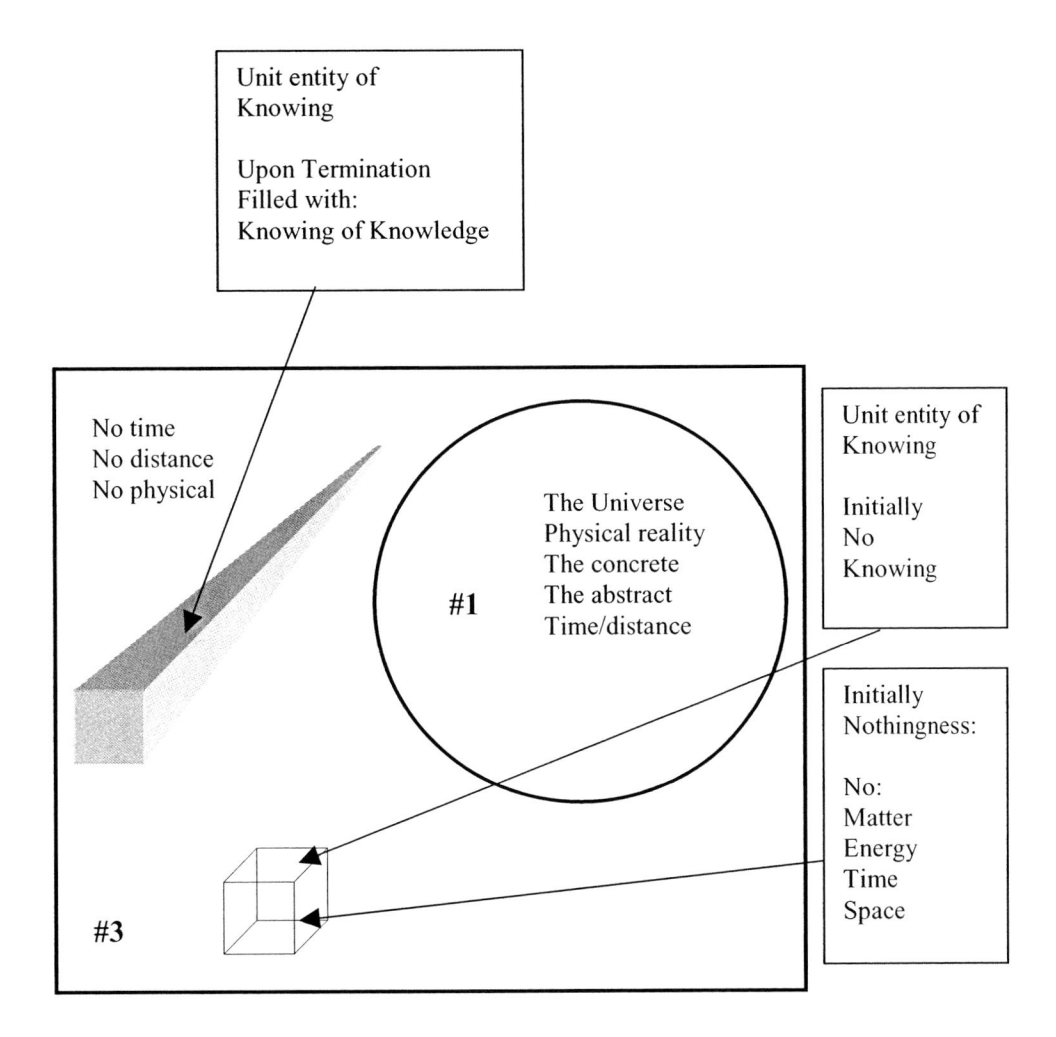

Unit entity of Knowing

Upon Termination Filled with: Knowing of Knowledge

No time
No distance
No physical

#1
The Universe
Physical reality
The concrete
The abstract
Time/distance

Unit entity of Knowing

Initially
No
Knowing

Initially Nothingness:

No:
Matter
Energy
Time
Space

#3

The War & Peace of a New Metaphysical Perception

By moving 'into' Centricism we are in essence moving 'beyond' non-Centricism/dependency and into Independency. As such our graphic now becomes:

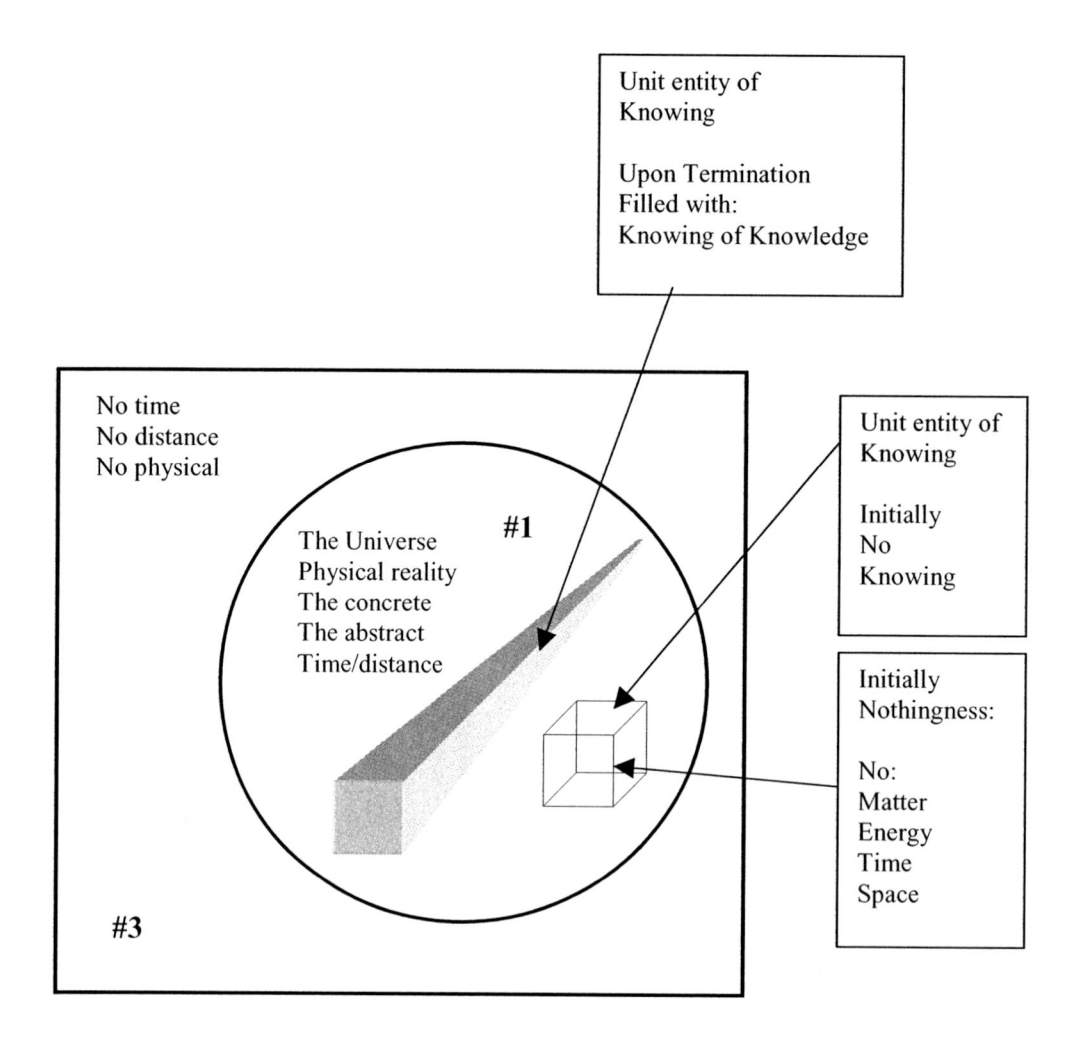

Diagram labels:

- Unit entity of Knowing / Upon Termination Filled with: Knowing of Knowledge
- No time / No distance / No physical
- The Universe / Physical reality / The concrete / The abstract / Time/distance — #1
- Unit entity of Knowing / Initially No Knowing
- Initially Nothingness: / No: Matter / Energy / Time / Space
- #3

Region #1 is a location where our unique experiencing begins at the point of nothingness and forms in a unique manner to ourselves based upon our own unique experiences.

As we previously discussed, upon termination of the journey of knowing within time and space, the entity is no longer 'empty' or partially 'empty' of knowledge. This leads us to our next step. We are going to remove the 'filled' entity of knowing since we are focusing upon the 'process' of knowing and how it interacts with the concept of Centricism, which Copernicus so aptly entrenched in the field of science.

The Error of Copernicus

As such, our graphic becomes:

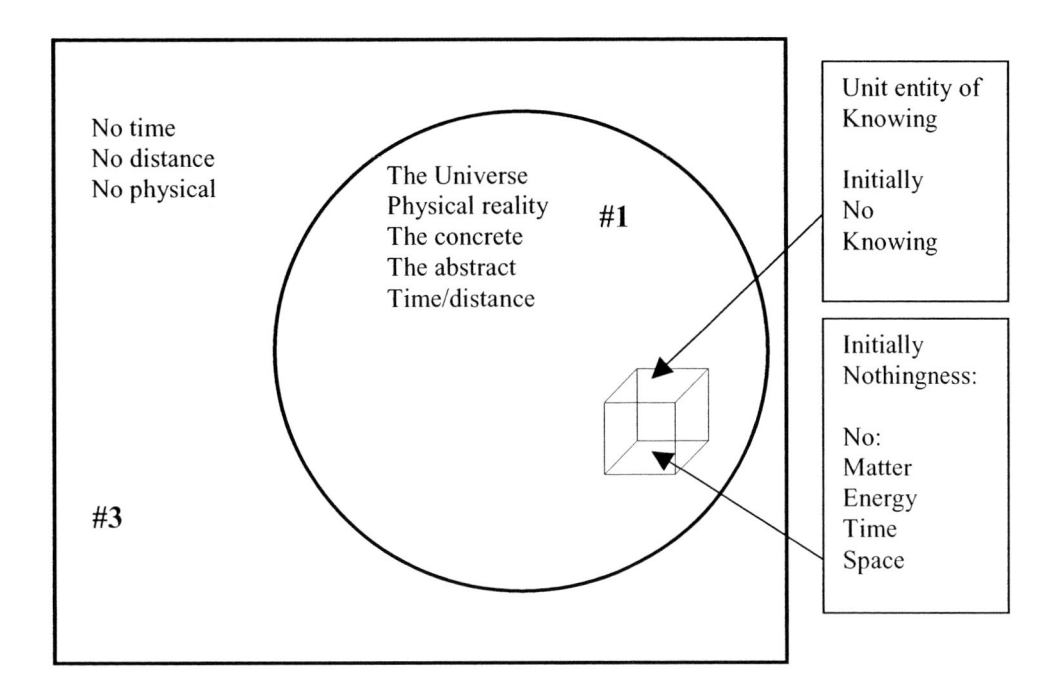

```
No time
No distance
No physical

    The Universe
    Physical reality    #1
    The concrete
    The abstract
    Time/distance

#3
```

Unit entity of Knowing

Initially No Knowing

Initially Nothingness:

No:
Matter
Energy
Time
Space

The 'empty' unit, the 'virgin entity of knowing' has absolutely nothing abstractual or otherwise within it at only one point in time. The 'virgin entity of knowing' is empty when it is simply 'process'. Until the process of knowing begins, the entity is in a state of passivity and only enters the active state of *being* when it makes the step beyond being in a passive state to being in an active state. A detailed discussion of such states was explored within Tractate 2: Aristotle.

Since we discussed the concept of a passive state of knowing in Tractate 2, we will proceed to examine the active state of knowing, the process of filling an abstractual unit of active knowing with the substance it needs to exist as an entity, the substance of knowledge and experience.

The entity exists enmeshed in the fabric of time and space/distance since time and space are the very fabrics of region #1.

With the aid of this graphic, we can now begin to understand the interrelationship between existing entities found within region #1. We can now begin to understand the very concept of not only the very existence of Centricism itself but we can begin to understand the process as well as the potentiality of Centricism.

Existence within Centricism:

We will take the latter diagram and reduce region #3, the location of non-Centricism since we are concerned with region #1. Since region #1 is located 'within' region #3, the only way to do this while expanding region #1 is to apply the concept of relativistic size of region #1 compared to region #3. In addition to modifying the relative size of each region, we will expand upon the

The War & Peace of a New Metaphysical Perception

number of entities of knowing which evolve through the process of 'traveling', experiencing region #1 – the location of space, time, matter, energy…:

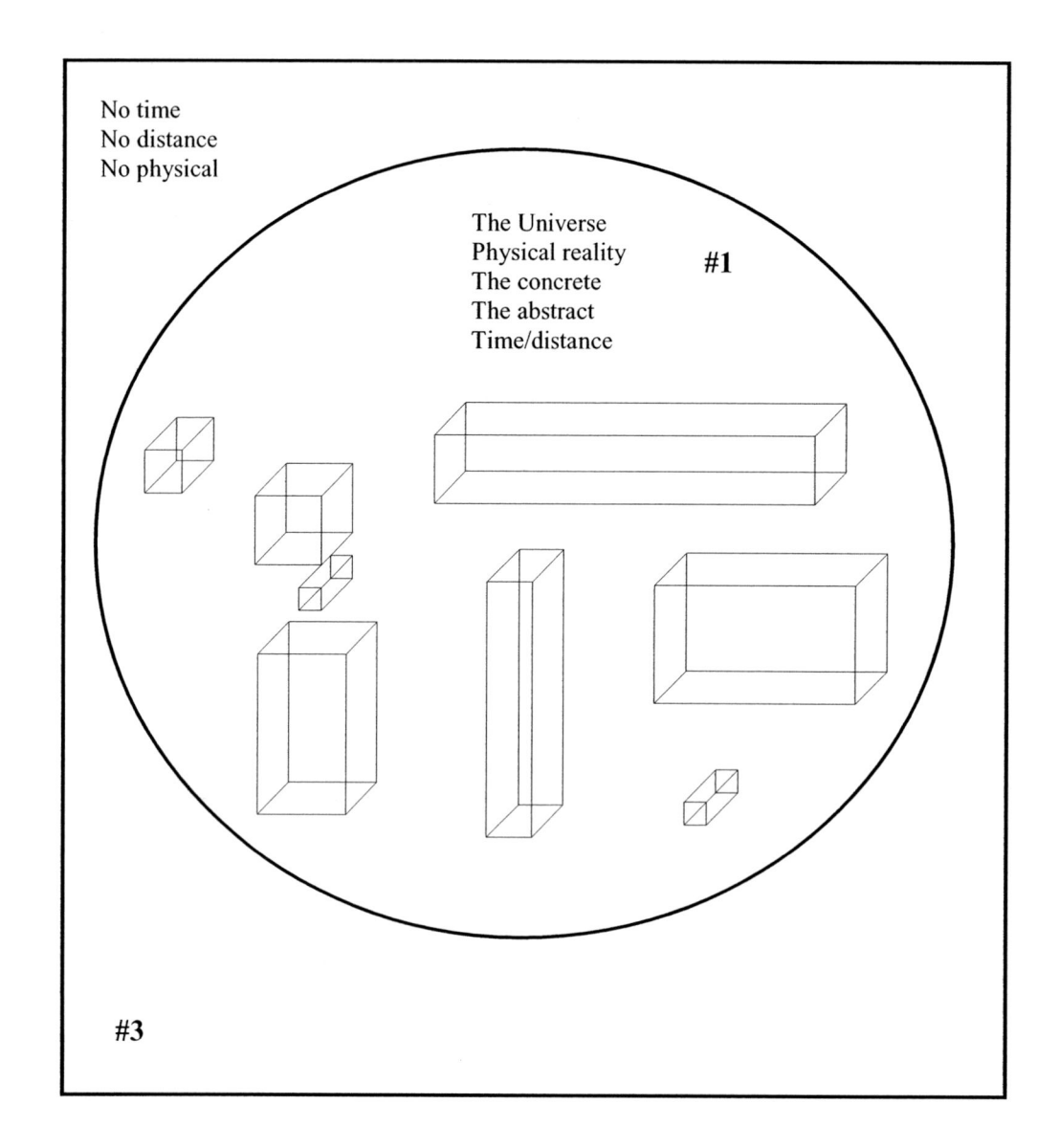

No time
No distance
No physical

The Universe
Physical reality
The concrete
The abstract
Time/distance

#1

#3

The entities of actively growing knowing:

1. Are each unique in and of themselves due to their being in the process of acquiring unique experiencing as they move through time and space. Each entity of knowing has its own unique perceptions and experiencing assembled uniquely by the linear progression of the multiple facets of both time and space or whatever abstractual fabric should exist within the 'universe' from which the entity of knowing emerges
2. Vary in size since relative to each other they contain vastly different 'quantities' of knowledge and contain vastly different experiences.

3. Not only may appear but do vary regarding their 'distance' apart since they are immersed in a location whose very fabric is composed of distance. In essence, the 'distance' separating them does exist. They are therefore all separated by varying degrees of distance no two distances of which are equal
4. Are dependent upon beginning – end parameters since they are immersed in time and space, are immersed within a form of Centricism

Process

5. Take 'time' to get from one to another, to get from one place to another, since there is 'distance' to traverse
6. Are incapable of 'knowing' one another completely since they are not complete forms of knowledge but rather are actively and uniquely experiencing knowledge and being assembled through the active process of knowing and experiencing uniquely. The process itself becomes uniquely an integral part of themselves since the active process of gaining knowledge is the creation of the perception of knowledge and experiencing through the process of knowing itself.

Potentiality

7. Are incapable of incorporating other 'newly' developing entities of unique knowledge, knowing, and experiencing for their process of 'forming' has not yet ended and therefore any new knowledge and experiencing 'affects' the very formation of the entity itself is in the process of 'becoming'.
8. Partial summations of a unique entity of knowing as well as the complete summation of the unique entity of knowing is as varied as the potential combinations the parts of 'a' particular unique entity of developing knowing can allow confined to itself. This is known as 'limited' knowing.
9. Potentiality within region #1 is, due to #1 – 8, limited to the abstractual and ? and ? fabric of a particular universe. In 'our' case, potentiality regarding formation of unique entities of knowing is limited to what time, space, matter, and energy will allow. Since uniqueness is a quality acquired by the active process of knowing itself, each entity of knowing is unique and becomes so independent of one another

Independence thus becomes the principle of region #1.

This is not to say that individuals are not dependent upon one another in society. What it says is that the very concept of uniqueness is a quality of existence itself and is not a characteristic 'given' by one individual to another.

Centricism is not a difficult concept to comprehend because we are, after all, immersed 'within' Centricism', and as such we not only observe but experience time and space to be concepts expanding 'outward' from 'a' point of reference which varies from conscious knowing to conscious knowing.

What must not be lost within the exploration of the familiar, however, is that within a location whose very fabric is that of space and time, 'correct' sequencing is a fundamental principle. One cannot die unless one is first born, one cannot wake up unless one first goes to sleep, one cannot swim unless one first goes into the water. Granted the term 'cannot' may be too strong a term to use in these particular examples but the concept of 'correct' sequencing is an aspect of time and space and as such is something all of us within our personal universe understand.

The War & Peace of a New Metaphysical Perception

Region #1 therefore is a location where our unique experiencing does not depend upon what others have to offer us to experience. Rather our own experiencing is in the process of 'becoming' as uniquely experienced by ourselves. Our own unique experiencing and knowledge as viewed uniquely through our own knowing is becoming what it is - our own uniqueness. We are in the process of becoming rather than being what we finally are to be. We can change with the infusion, embracing, union of experiencing space and time while immersed within matter and energy.

Divine intervention? Perhaps. Who is to say what the whole is capable of doing within its creation: the universe, our reality.

How can an 'all knowing' entity be all knowing if it doesn't know 'all things'?
\

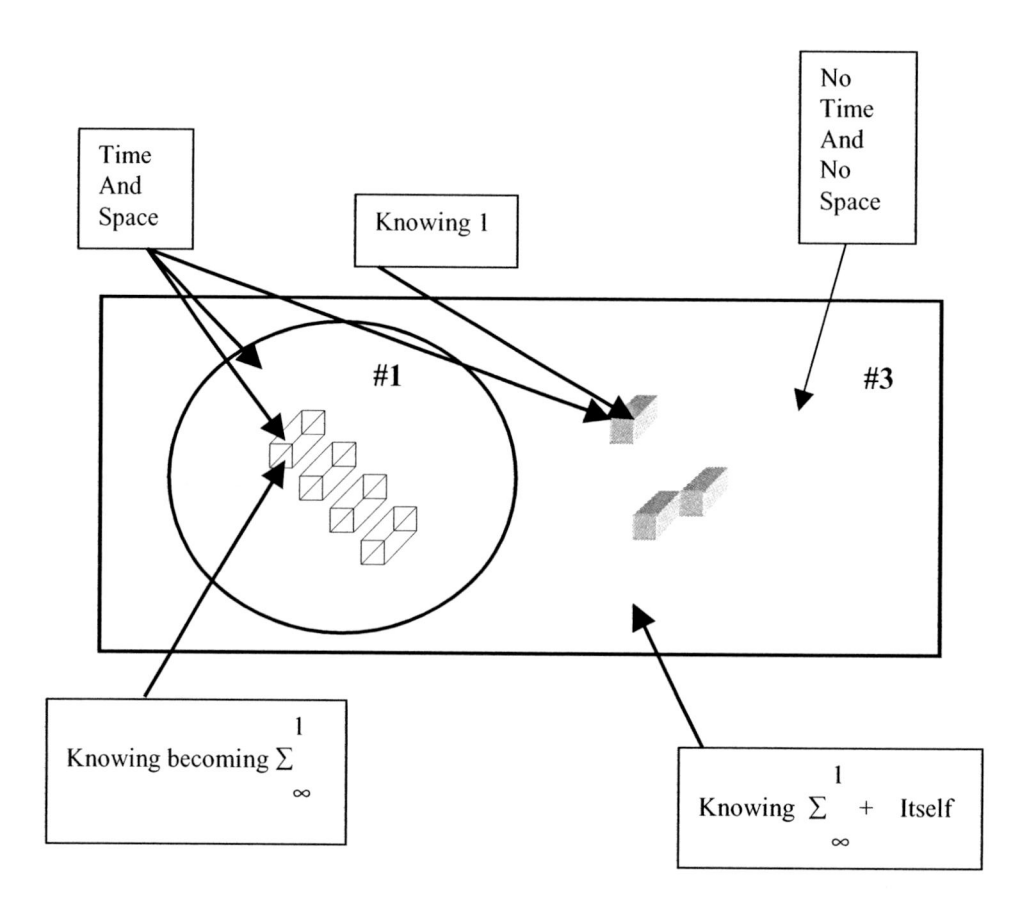

Again we must ask: Doesn't this diagram imply 'all Knowing' doesn't know what 'will be' and doesn't this in turn imply time exists in 'all Knowing'?

Again, we must reply: The concept of what 'will be' only exist 'within' time. If we review what we had previously learned of time we find time to be 'located' within two locations:

The Error of Copernicus

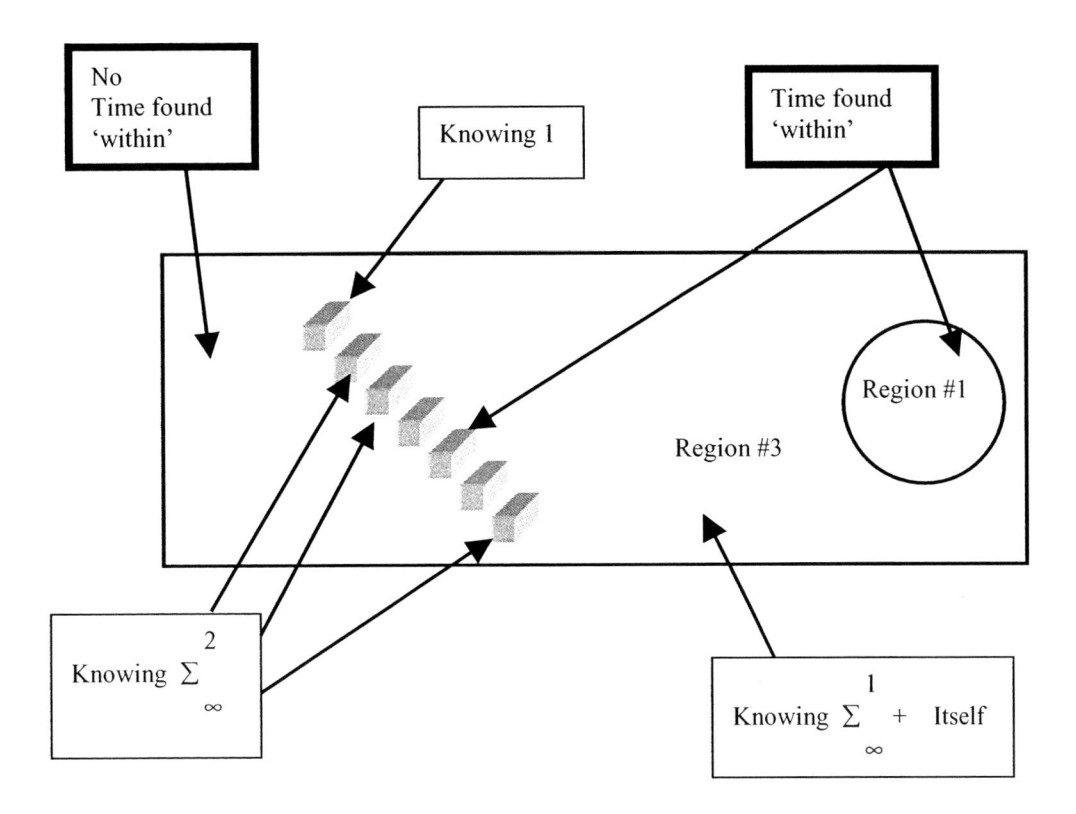

[Diagram: A rectangular region labeled "Region #3" contains a circle labeled "Region #1" and a series of shaded cube/house shapes. Labels point to various parts:
- "No Time found 'within'" points into Region #3
- "Knowing 1" points to the cubes
- "Time found 'within'" points to Region #1 and to the cubes
- "Knowing $\sum_{\infty}^{2}$" points to the cubes
- "Knowing $\sum_{\infty}^{1}$ + Itself" points to Region #3]

Since time is not found either as an innate characteristic of region #3 nor as a medium of region #3 'within' which subsets of region #3 find themselves immersed, there is no concept of 'what will be' to be found in region #3.

This is not to say time is not found 'within' region #3, rather it demonstrated time is not an all-pervasive characteristic, a universal medium of region #3. Time is found in region #3 in two distinct location of which we are presently capable of perceiving. Time is found 'within' entities of 'knowing', which have evolved out of the 'universe', and time is found as a medium of the universe within which entities of 'knowing' move from being 'virgin' entities of 'knowing' to being complete entities of 'knowing'.

Where then does the 'Book of Divine Knowledge' find itself to be in terms of the metaphysical system of singular location, 'being' *being* 'Being'?

The significance of insignificance: Random Sequencing

There is really no place to begin with such a topic. Perhaps that is a fitting observation considering the topic itself: randomness.

We have, however, little choice but to begin if we are to understand the significance of insignificance.

So lets begin:

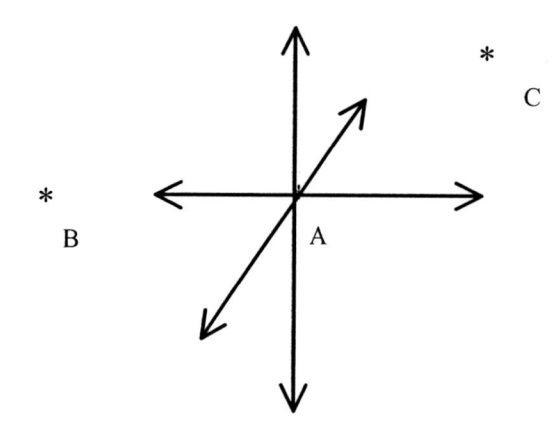

* B ⟷ A
(with vertical and diagonal axes at A)
* C

Or:

(axes at B) ⟶ * A
* C

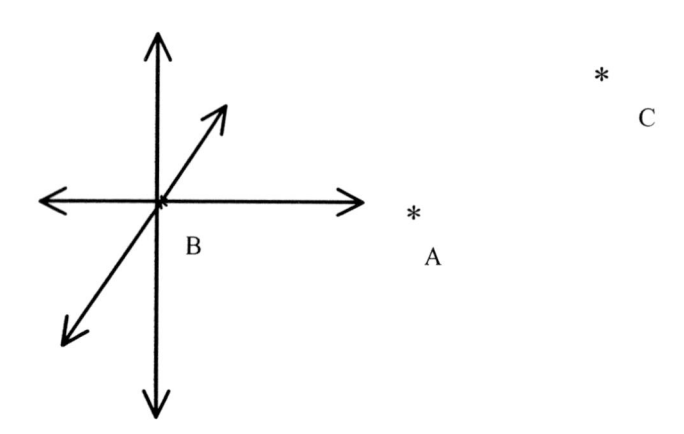

Or:

```
        ↑  ↗
        │ ╱
   ←────┼*────→
        │╱      C
        ╱│
       ↙ │
         ↓
```

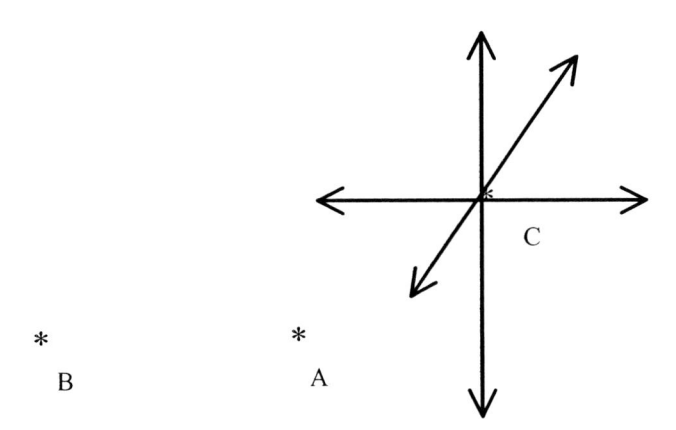

       *   *
      B   A

The potential names of points A, B, and C using the Cartesian coordinates (X, Y, Z) grows as the number of locations for the origin increases. The number of locations of the origin grows exponentially as the number of dimensions grows linearly.

One could begin with one point and zero dimensions. By doing so one observes

*
A

Since a point has no length, depth, or height, point A has zero dimensions.

By adding one dimension we obtain: zero dimensions + one dimension = one dimension but the potential names for 'a' point becomes infinite in nature:

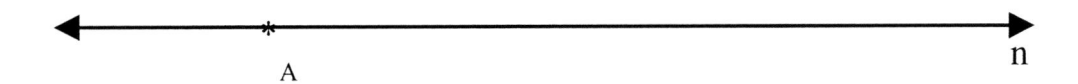

←─────────*─────────────────────────────→
       A   n

The point A has the potential to be located anywhere upon line n. The concept of one dimension being the only existence creates a line, line n, which is infinite in length. Point A has the potential of being located anywhere upon line n since, by definition, point A has no length. Point A could move along line n, however, point A need not move to change position relative to line n, line n could move relative to dimensions 2, 3, 4 ... which exist to us but not to the situation we are discussing. Such a statement is neither a paradox nor an untruth. As we, you and I can readily attest to, just because 'a' dimension and its components are not aware of other dimensions does not mean other dimensions do not exist.

If we now add a second dimension, we can observe the nonlinear growth of potential points of location for point A.

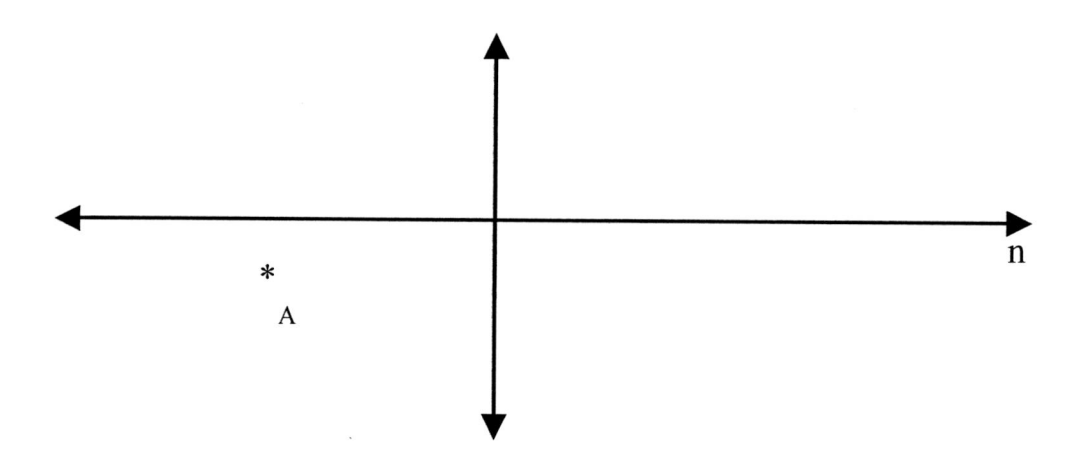

```
                    ↑
                    |
    ←───────────────┼───────────────→ n
         *          |
         A          |
                    ↓
```

So it is two and then three dimensions can be understood to exponentially grow the perceptual potential coordinates for point A. If we presume point A can move or if point A is presumed to be static in its location the same results of exponential growth for the names of point A can be understood to increase if we presume the X and Y axis move.

If we then factor in the name of point A changing with time, again the perception regarding point A's contribution to the space/time relationship causes another exponential increase in the coordinate names point A could acquire.

But what does this have to do with abstractual concepts of free will, determinism, significance and insignificance?

This progression of thought regarding the exponential expansion of perceptual spatial location generated through increasing numbers of dimensions leads us to the rudimentary mindset which will help us understand the exponential expansion of the totality of perceptual 'knowing' generated through increasing numbers of unique entities of 'knowing' evolving out of free will.

The Error of Copernicus

To understand the connection let us look at a unit entity of awareness, a unit entity of 'knowing' as it develops within the physical:

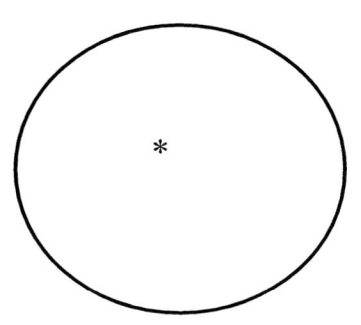

Virgin awareness, virgin 'knowing', begins with no 'knowing' and expands through experiencing within the universe. As such, it could be drawn as:

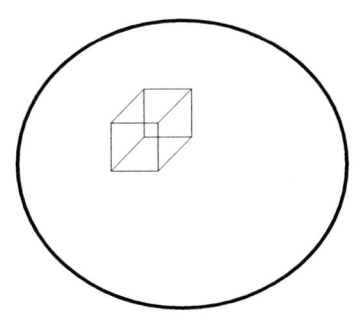

The transparency of the rectangular prism represents the ability of the physical to continue to affect and form the entity of 'knowing'. The entity of knowing continues to grow, experience, and formulate its completeness of unique 'knowing 'until it' dies. At the point of its no longer being capable of continuing to grow its summation of awareness, we obtain what could be diagramed as:

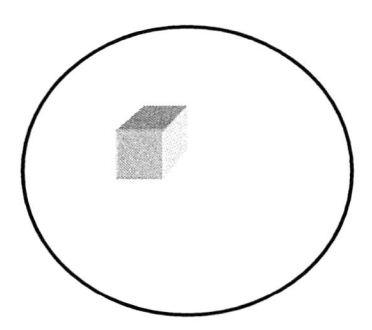

The War & Peace of a New Metaphysical Perception

The ability to initiate actions of free will combined with the ability to experience actions bound by the laws of nature generate the unit of unique abstractual perception which has developed.

Now lets remove the influence of the physical since, as symbolized by the 'filled' rectangular prism, the sensory mechanism has been removed from the individual unit of perceptual development. This removal of the physical does not imply the abstractual uniqueness of the unit of 'knowing' just 'goes away'. In fact, the implication of 'being' *being* 'Being' implies quite the contrary. As such, we obtain the following:

Unit A

We have removed physical reality in order to study the entity of awareness. We will label this entity: unit A. Keep in mind. Unit A is no longer a Virgin point of 'knowing' but rather a point of 'knowing' having its own unique perceptual 'outlook' which has been developed through the influence of an almost infinite number of abstractual interactions. Such interactions have been generated through the actions of both free will initiated by itself and initiated by actions of free will generated by other units of 'knowing', as well as generated by actions bound by the laws of nature.

In essence, the unit of abstraction indicated above is 'filled' with various perceptions, desires, wants, loves jealousy, greed, compassion, etc. One must also recognize the unit to be just that: 'a unit'. It is. It is unique. It has 'wholeness' of perception that is unique in and of itself.

Before we move any further, one will find it interesting to note that if Unit A is the whole of existence, then:

1. The potential perceptual development of the whole is simply that of unit A
2. The number of abstractual existences are infinite in number but limited to what is found in unit A
3. Perceptions of time and distance can be found 'within' unit A but not 'outside' unit A for there is nothing 'outside' unit A
4. The 'whole' is identical to unit A and as such has the same perceptions as unit A
5. The 'whole' has the power of unit A and no more
6. The 'whole' has the same 'knowing' as unit A and no more
7. The 'whole' has the same 'presence' as unit A and no more

Sound familiar? The discussion evolves out of Tractates 1, 2, and 3: Zeno, Aristotle, and Boethius.

The Error of Copernicus

In order to address our understanding of what we mean by the whole we will enclose unit A within the whole:

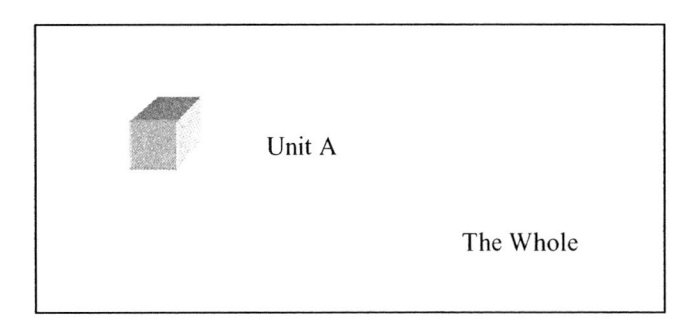

```
┌─────────────────────────────────────┐
│                                     │
│     ▮  Unit A                       │
│                                     │
│                      The Whole      │
│                                     │
└─────────────────────────────────────┘
```

It is obvious the whole is Unit A. It is also obvious time and distance are abstractions found 'within' unit A for the elements necessary to generate the concepts of time and distance are no longer present. Time and distance are elements of space and matter both of which had been removed when we erased the circle which represented the physical reality of the universe.

What then happens if a second unit of 'knowing' is added to the system above?

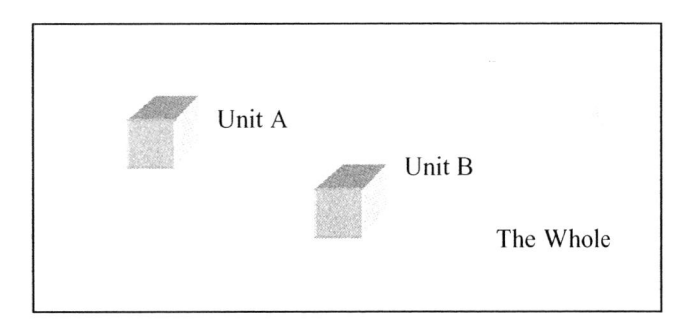

```
┌─────────────────────────────────────┐
│                                     │
│          ▮  Unit A                  │
│                  ▮  Unit B          │
│                                     │
│                      The Whole      │
└─────────────────────────────────────┘
```

Now we no longer can say:

1. The potential perceptual development of the whole is simply that of unit A
2. The number of abstractual existences are infinite in number but limited to what is found in unit A
3. Perceptions of time and distance can be found 'within' unit A but not 'outside' unit A for there is nothing 'outside' unit A
4. The 'whole' is identical to unit A and as such has the same perceptions as unit A
5. The 'whole' has the power of unit A and no more
6. The 'whole' has the same 'knowing' as unit A and no more
7. The 'whole' has the same 'presence' as unit A and no more

The War & Peace of a New Metaphysical Perception

We must now say:

1. The potential perceptual development of the whole is that of unit A, unit B, or unit A + unit B
2. The number of abstractual existences are infinite in number but is no longer limited to what is found in unit A, rather it is limited to what is found in unit A, unit B, or unit A + unit B
3. Perceptions of time and distance can be found 'within' unit A or found 'within' unit B but not 'outside' unit A and/or unit 'B' for there is nothing 'outside' unit A and unit B
4. There is now something found 'outside' unit A and that is not only 'unit' B but the summation of unit A + unit B
5. The 'whole' is identical to unit A, or unit B, or unit A + unit B and as such has the same perceptions as unit A or unit B or unit A + unit B
6. The 'whole' has the power of unit A or unit B or unit (A + B) and no more
7. The 'whole' has the same 'knowing' as unit A or unit B or unit (A + B) and no more
8. The 'whole' has the same 'presence' as unit A or unit B or unit (A + B) and no more

It becomes apparent that the increase in the varieties of combinations of the whole increase not on a linear basis but rather on some form of geometrical or exponential basis. If we expand our units of unique 'knowing' developed under the laws of free will, we obtain three units of unique knowing and as such obtain:

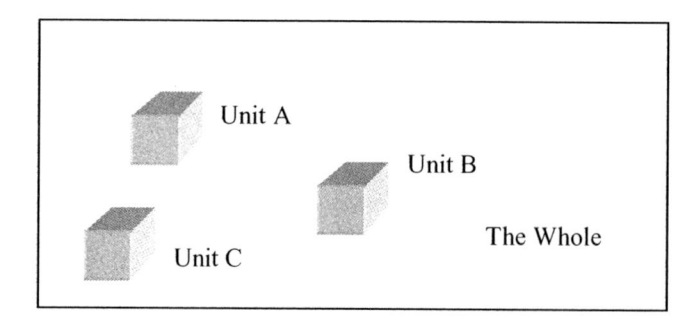

At this point, we could reevaluate the results of the above using the same format we previously used. This process however becomes beset with even more verbiage than previously. To minimize this problem of verbiage we will examine the results of the above using more diagrams.

The Error of Copernicus

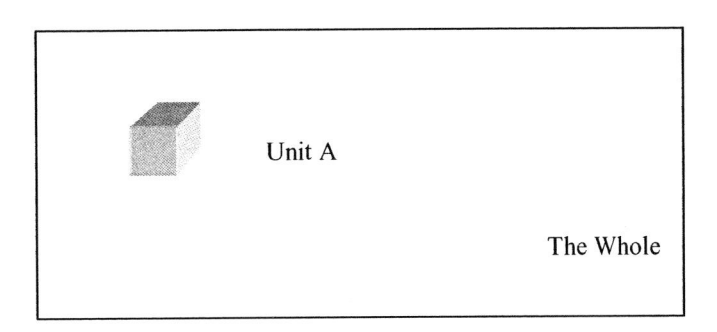

We will now open unit A and pour its 'substance' into the Whole.

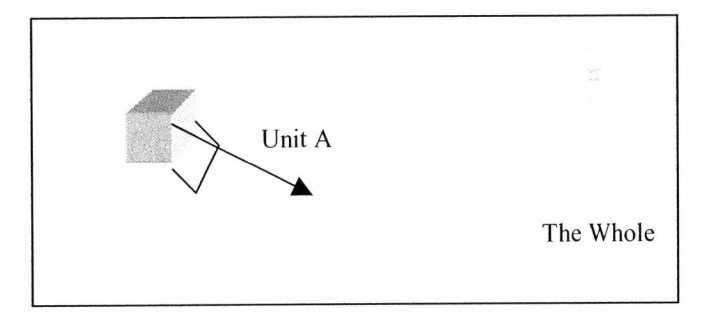

Example 1: If Unit A only

Possibilities for the Whole:

    1. A

Example 2: If Unit A and Unit B only

Possibilities for the Whole:

    1. A
    2. B
    3. AB
    4. BA

Before we go to example three, we should address the question of why the potential for BA? AB and BA are not the same even though time and/or distance are not 'active' elements of the whole. Time and distance are elements of Unit A and Unit B. As such, should the contents of A and B be released 'into' the Whole, then time and distance become options with which the Whole can develop its own unique perceptions.

The War & Peace of a New Metaphysical Perception

At first glance, it would appear the characteristic of cardinality would only be relevant if one speaks in terms of sequencing physical perceptions generated through the element of cardinality innately found in spatial cardinal concepts of distance or if one speaks in terms of sequencing abstractual perceptions generated through the element of cardinality innately found in the abstractual cardinal concept of time.

The perceptions generated through the potential combinations of A and B are not A, B, and AB but also BA. A fifth state of the whole itself exists. This fifth state of being is the summation of some sequential form of A and B independent of the perception developed through an order of sequencing.

Having said this we then obtain a new perspective for the possibilities for the whole, which in turn will allow us to move to example three.

Example 2 corrected:

Possibilities for the whole:

1. A
2. B
3. AB
4. BA
5. the whole

Example 3:

Possibilities for the whole:

1. A
2. B
3. C
4. AB
5. BA
6. BC
7. the whole of A and B
8. ABC
9. ACB
10. BAC
11. BCA
12. CAB
13. CBA
14. the whole of A and B and C

There is a pattern developing here. The mathematics of it are much to difficult to explore in this tractate. However, a simplistic example can be demonstrated by following a similar yet much more simplistic sequence:

Example 1:

A

Example 2:

A, B, AB

Example 3:

A, B, C, AB, AC, BC, ABC

Example 4:

A, B, C, D, AB, AC, AD, BC, BD, CD, ABC, ABD, ACD, BCD, ABCD

As one examines the increase in potential possibilities generated by the sequence one begins to appreciate the significance of each unit.

If there is only one unit, the unit is the whole, there is nothing greater.

If 'a' second unit is added the number of potential possibilities expands by two not one, expands to three.

If 'a' third unit is added the number of potential possibilities expands by four not one, expands to seven.

If 'a' fourth unit is added the number of potential possibilities expands by eight not one, expands to fifteen.

Any one unit of growth may or may not be greater than another. The size of the unit is not what is important here but rather what is important is the very fact that an additional unit has been added. Mathematically we see the pattern as being:

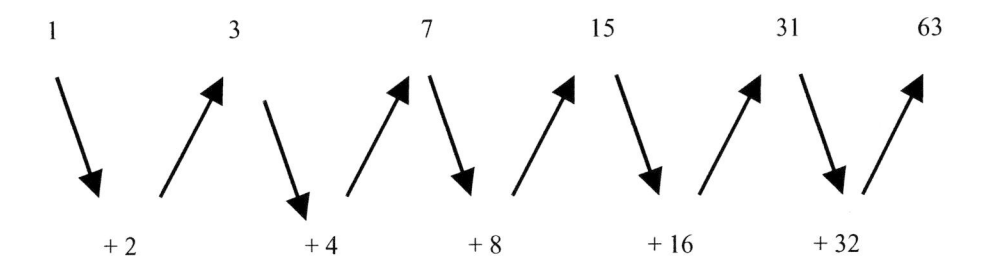

```
   1        3        7        15        31        63
    \      /\      /\       /\        /\       /
     \    /  \    /  \     /  \      /  \     /
      \  /    \  /    \   /    \    /    \   /
       \/      \/      \ /      \  /      \ /
      + 2     + 4     + 8      + 16     + 32
```

As one can see, the potential increases non-linearly. Each unit added has tremendous repercussion upon the potential of the whole. Each unit added has tremendous significance to the whole. Each unit added impacts the whole more than once, more than itself.

The War & Peace of a New Metaphysical Perception

But where is the individual unit here? It appears to be lost. It appears to be lost not because it is lost but because we have not fully expanded upon the pattern.

If we more fully expand the pattern to be what it is, we obtain:

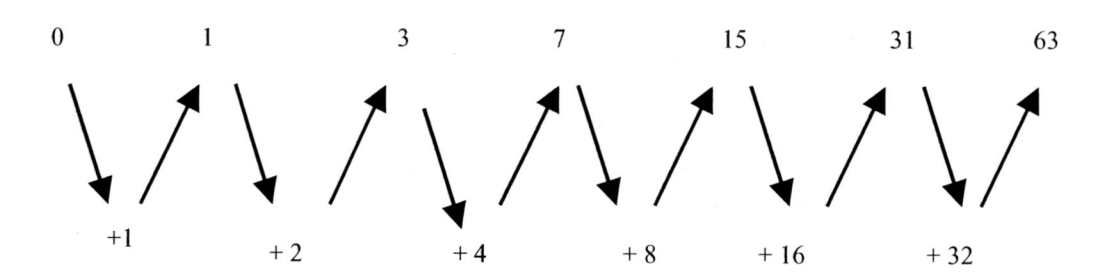

```
0        1        3        7       15       31       63
   +1       +2       +4       +8      +16      +32
```

This does not appear to fit the pattern unless we adjust the pattern accordingly:

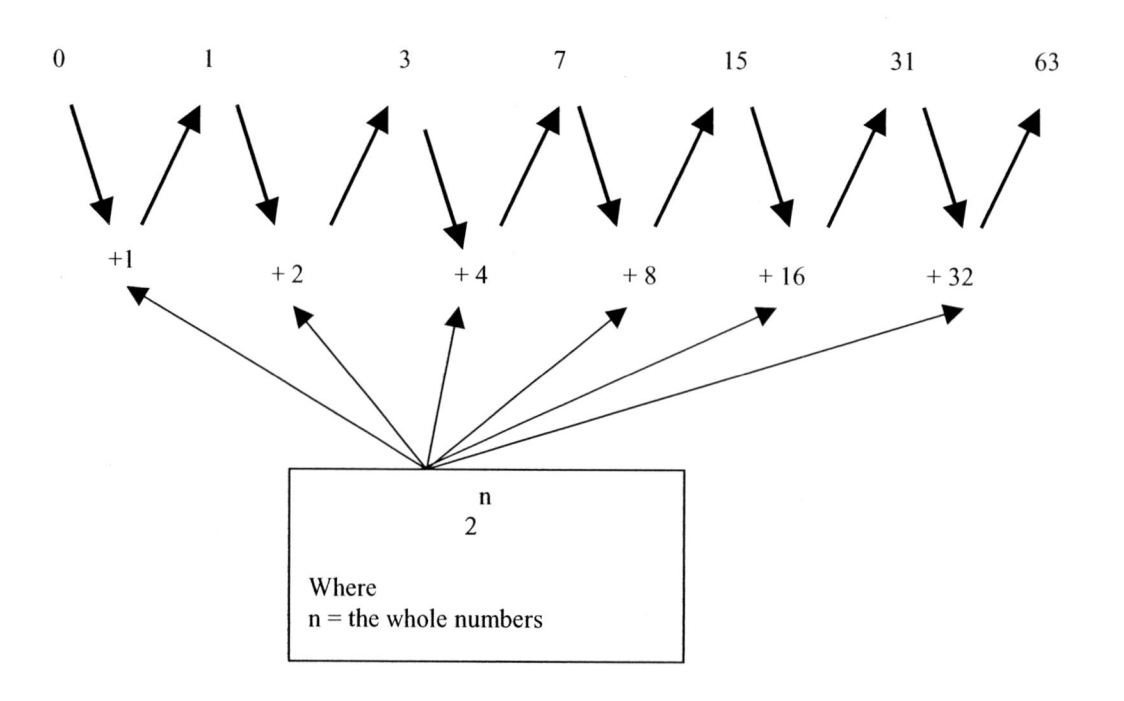

```
0        1        3        7       15       31       63
   +1       +2       +4       +8      +16      +32
```

$$\frac{n}{2}$$

Where
n = the whole numbers

All of a sudden, we see the base for what it is. The base, the foundation, is built upon the individual unit since 'n' is the epitome of individuality itself. 'n' is the set of unit numbers in their very completeness of form. 'n' is the set of natural numbers beginning with one and extending into infinity as a set comprised of increasingly large numbers of whole, complete units based upon 'a' whole unit itself.

As we can see, the growth is not geometric but exponential.

Is this an anomaly or is this the very concept upon which the growth of the whole itself is built when one speaks of 'all knowing'? Within the system of 'being' *being* 'Being', this is not an anomaly but rather the foundation of total knowing, the whole itself.

Under the metaphysical system of symbiotic panentheism, 'being' *being* 'Being', the very perceptual abilities of the whole grow exponentially with each unit of knowing added to it. Furthermore, the growth is not based simply upon the pattern diagrammed above but rather the pattern leaps beyond this potential by a factor of:

The whole of A + the whole of A and B + the whole of A and B and C + ...

So it is each individual unit added may be added to such a large number of others that it appears insignificant compared to the whole but it is in fact 'the' element which increases the whole exponentially over the huge 'potentiality of 'knowing'' it had been previous to the individuals addition to the whole.

Doesn't the concept of 'previously' imply an element of time and sequencing? No and that is the very reason the concept such as alphabetical sequencing, a concept of sequencing 'controlled' by time becomes a limit not imposed upon the whole of abstraction itself. The result of course is an even greater form of exponential growth applying to the whole than the form of exponential growth we demonstrated.

Suddenly, through an understanding of a new metaphysical system – through an understanding of a non-Cartesian system powered by a Cartesian system – through an understanding of 'being' *being* 'Being', through an understanding of a system of determinism powered by free will, we begin a new understanding regarding the very significance of the seemingly insignificant.

Humanity, the individual, begins its upward climb out of the depths of insignificance and into the glory of significance itself.

The explosive nature of the potentiality of knowing

Adding 'a' piece of knowing creates an explosion of potential combinations over and above what existed previously. As each new piece of knowing is added, the addition creates an exponential expansion of potentiality to which the next piece of knowing can add its potentiality of growth to the whole.

Potentiality now becomes a situation of 'expanding', increasing, potential growth itself on an exponential basis as opposed to an 'expanding', increasing potential growth on a geometrical basis.

As such, the whole of knowing, the whole itself, moves from simply 'being' to 'Being'. The whole itself now gains not just the potential to grow but gains the potential to grow in a potentially explosive manner. The difference may best be understood as that of the difference in existence of a substance, the explosive nature of the substance gun powder and the explosive nature of fission, and the explosive nature of fusion and now: the explosive nature of knowing.

What does this have to do with Centricism and non-Centricism? It is the very concept of Centricism, which limits the potentiality of the Whole itself. It is Centricism which limits our potential significance. And the further away we appear to be from the center of the whole, the less significant we perceive our significance itself to be.

The War & Peace of a New Metaphysical Perception

This was not the intent of Copernicus as he reevaluated the concept regarding the 'location' of the center. As little as Copernicus had expected to influence our very understanding regarding the significance of the individual, his work involving the search for the center of the physical was to impact humanity's most fundamental perception regarding the value of the individual and its own specie.

Removing a piece of Randomness

To understand the significance regarding the impact removing a piece of knowing from the whole has upon the whole itself, one must not begin by removing what one find at the left but at the right of the graphic:

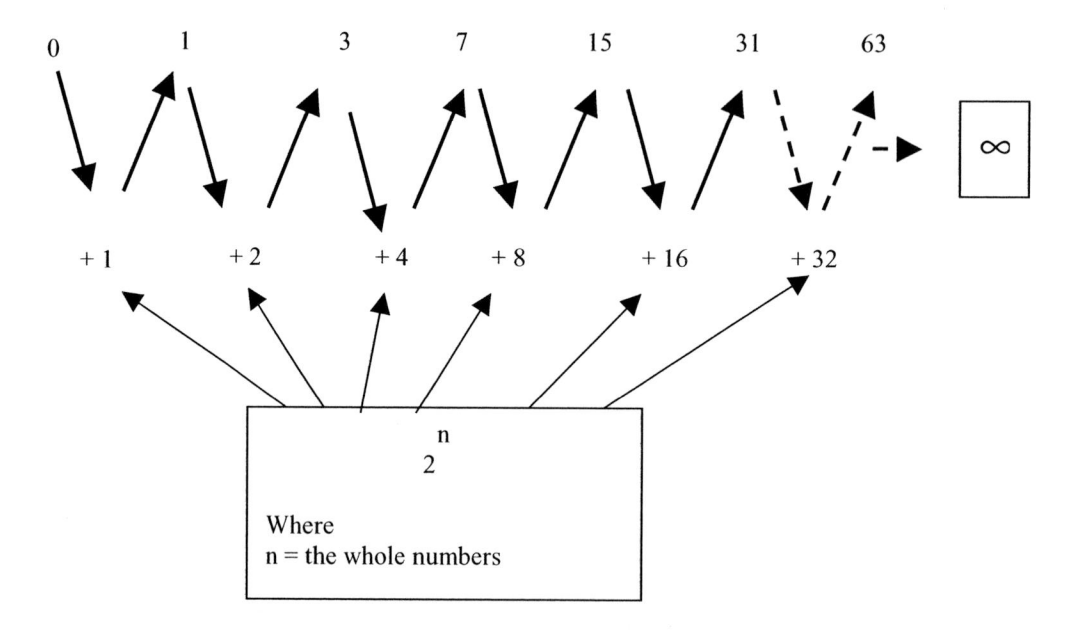

And with that the significance of removing, losing, terminating, interfering with, 'cutting short', a piece of knowing's potential once it has 'become', speaks for itself. Interfering with the development of a unit of knowing affects the outcome of what the Whole is.

Boethius' metaphysical system and why we can now file it away as a part of the annals of history

We must now come back to the diagram representing the 'location' of free will and the 'location' of determinism in order to understand why it is we can finally relegate Boethius' metaphysical system to the annals of history, relegate Boethius' metaphysical system to that of being a history book as opposed to being a current philosophical theme.

This aspect of Tractate 3: Boethius, was put on hold until we were able to expand our understanding regarding Centricism and its affect upon units of knowing addressed within this tractate. We can now return to the concept of free will and determinism for a short summation as

The Error of Copernicus

to why Boethius' metaphysical system can now be filed away in the archives of interesting historical paradoxes.

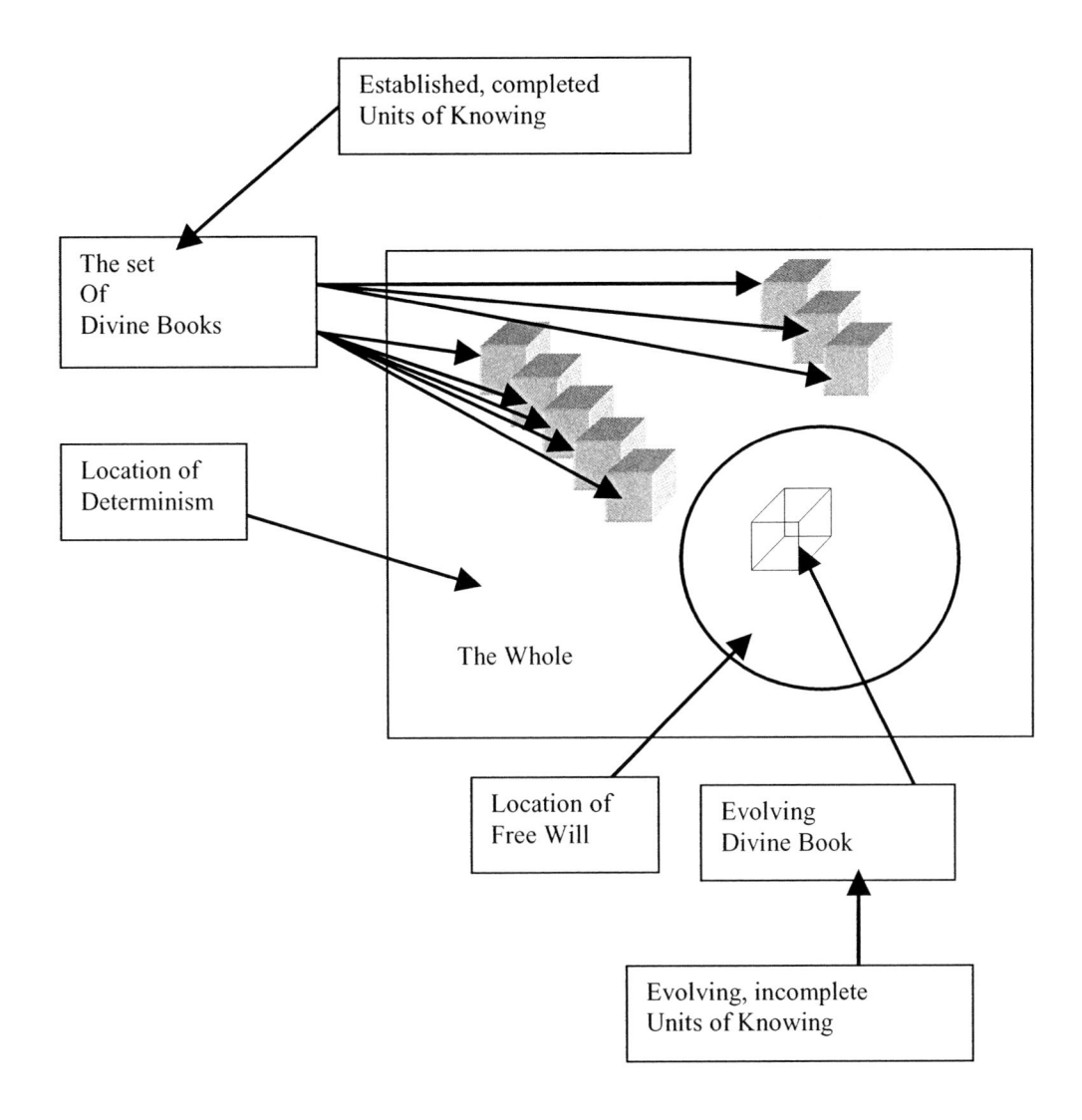

Established, completed Units of Knowing

The set Of Divine Books

Location of Determinism

The Whole

Location of Free Will

Evolving Divine Book

Evolving, incomplete Units of Knowing

The War & Peace of a New Metaphysical Perception

As we have done so often before, we find ourselves in need of simplifying the diagram. Simplifying we obtain:

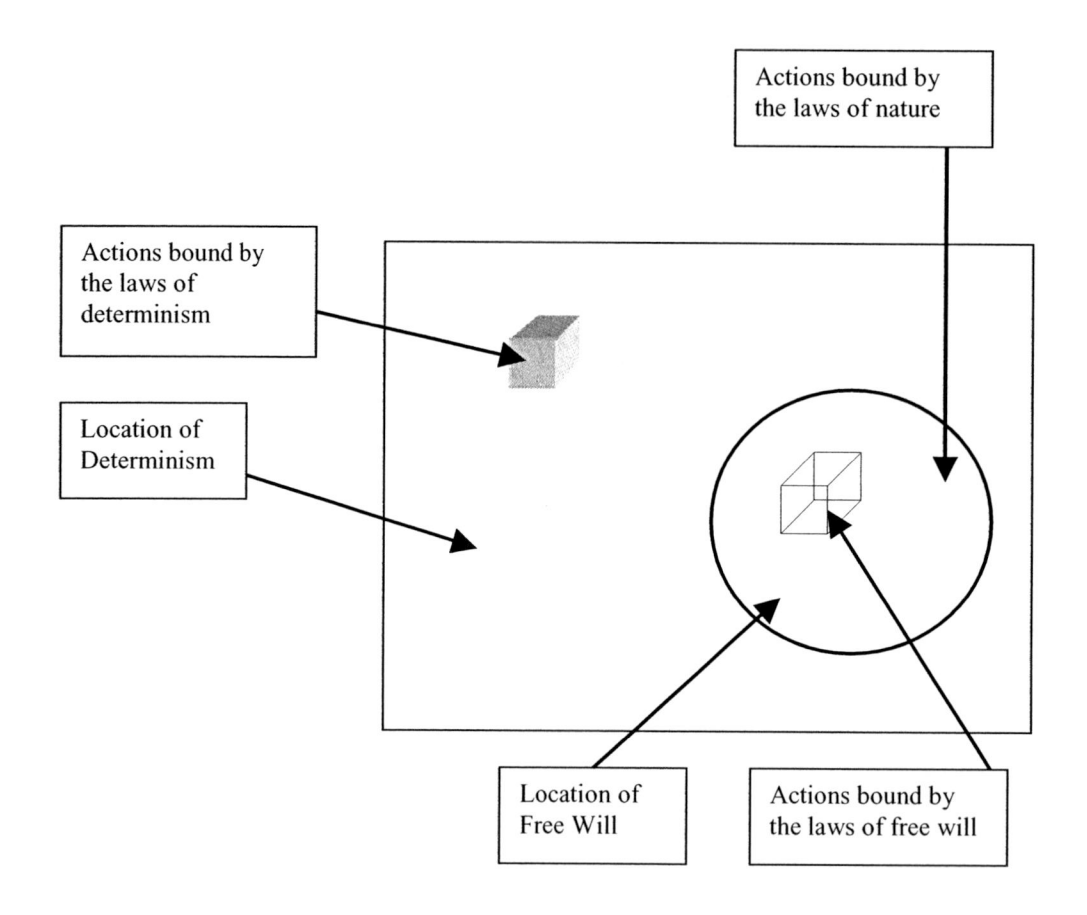

Actions bound by the laws of nature

Actions bound by the laws of determinism

Location of Determinism

Location of Free Will

Actions bound by the laws of free will

New questions now begin to emerge. Questions emerge which had no opportunity to emerge under the confines of Boethius' system where determinism was bound 'within' the same confines as free will.

The Error of Copernicus

Is the whole confined by actions bound by the laws of free will? Graphically we now understand such a question to be represented as:

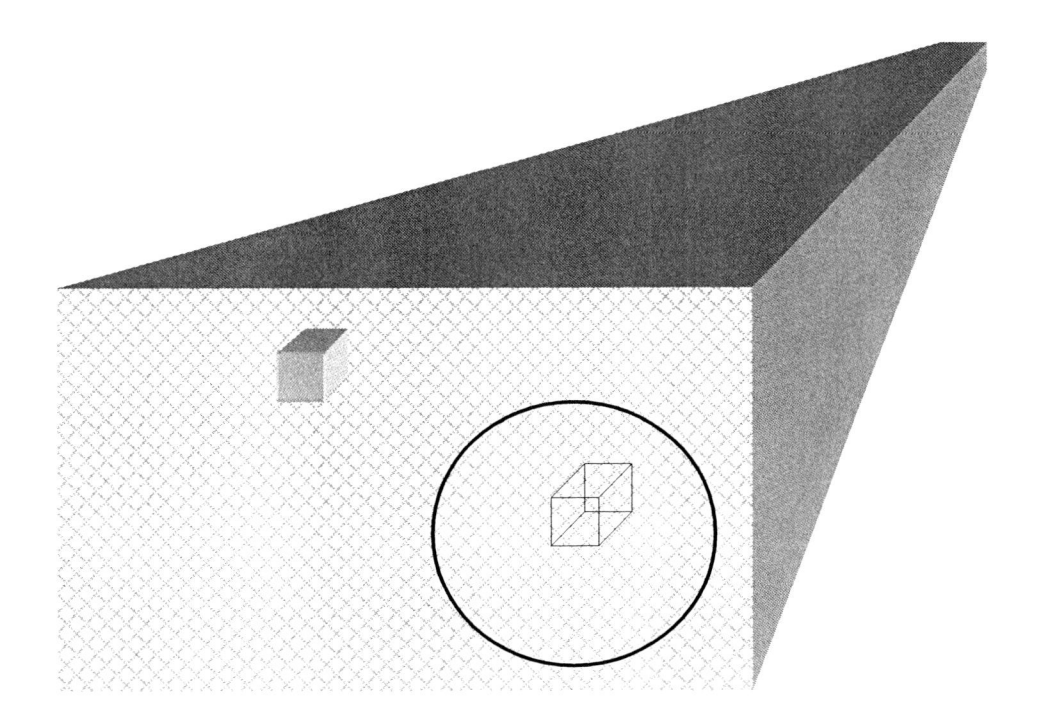

The War & Peace of a New Metaphysical Perception

Is the whole confined by action bound by the laws of determinism? Graphically we now understand such a question to be represented as:

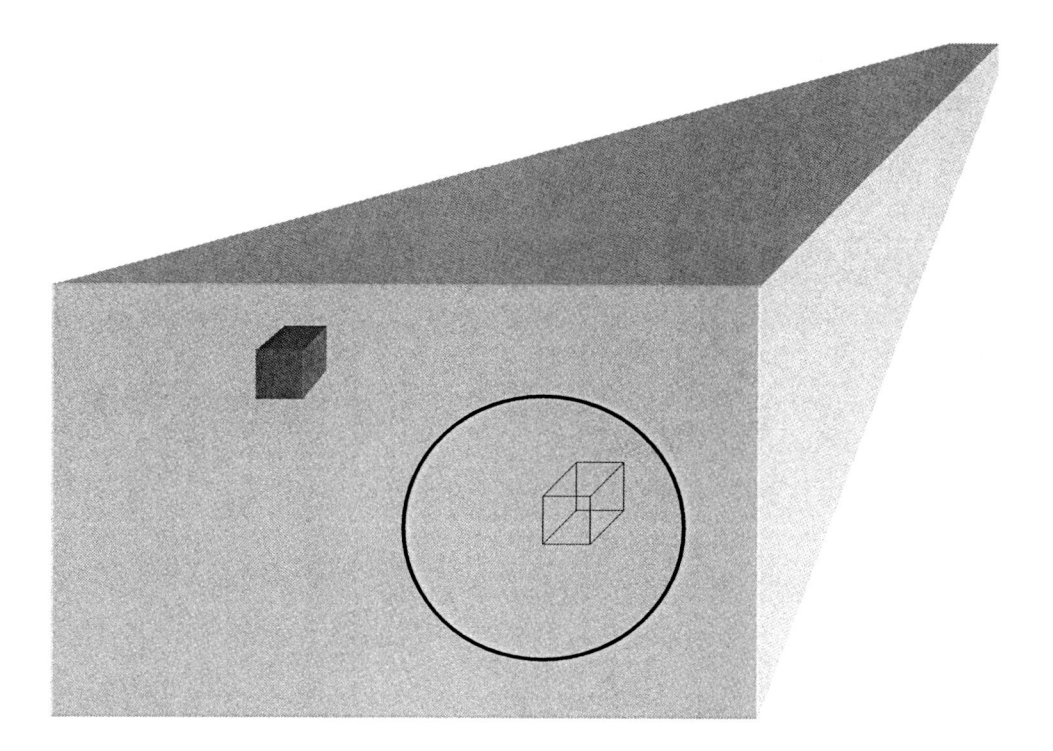

Is determinism found 'within' the location of free will? Graphically we now understand such a question to be represented as:

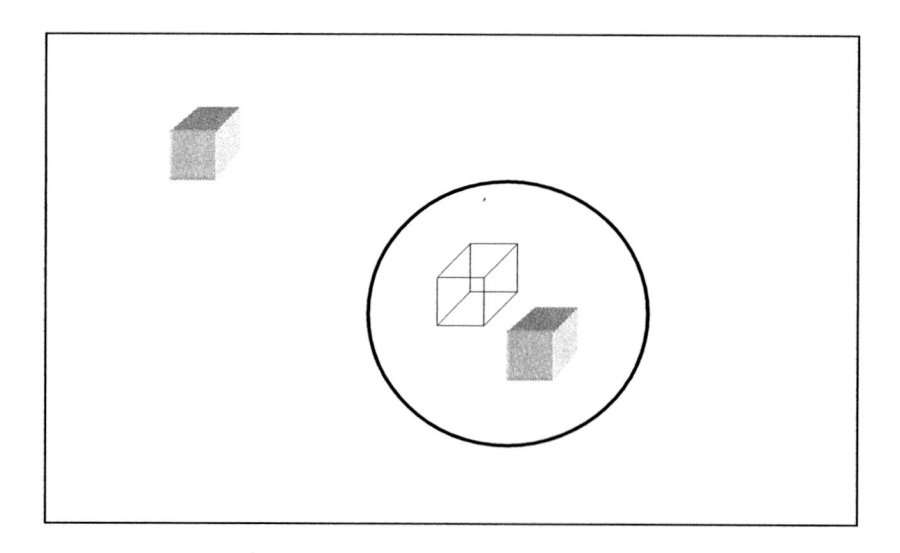

Is free will found 'within' the location of determinism? Graphically we now understand such a question to be represented as:

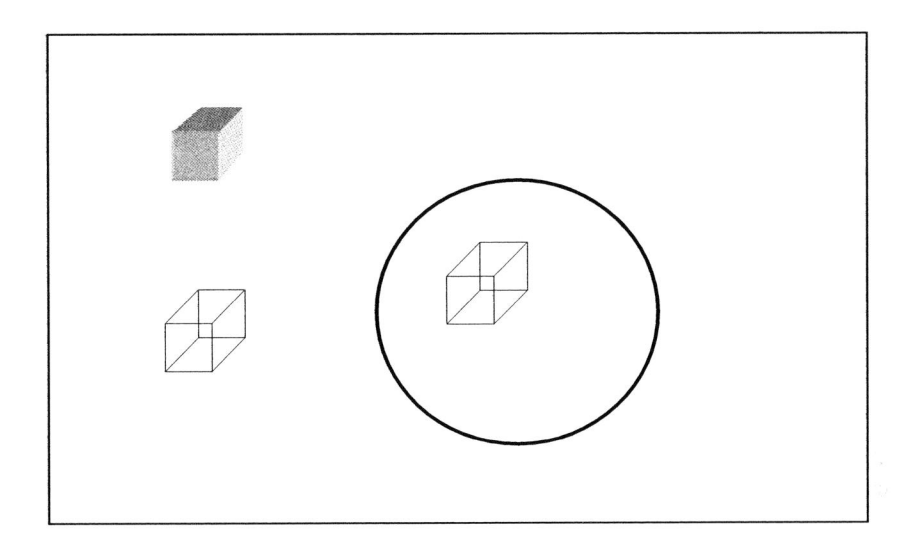

Etc., etc., etc.

The questions, not the answers, have only been presented. The questions are limitless, the answers now become intuitively understandable through the application of the new metaphysical perception: 'being' *being* 'Being' or generically speaking 'symbiotic panentheism.'

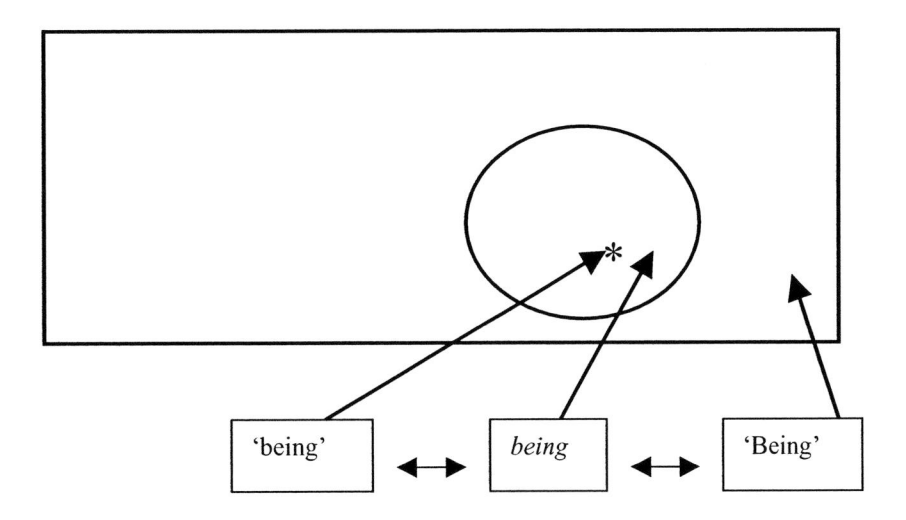

Some of these questions are not metaphysical in nature but rather are ontological in nature. It is for this very reason that this new metaphysical perception of a non-Cartesian system being powered by a Cartesian system appears to relegate Boethius' system to the annals of history.

Boethius' system appeared to leave metaphysics in a state of stagnation while this new perception opens up an almost infinite array of new metaphysical thoughts as well as philosophical thoughts in general.

But what of the answers to the given questions? How can one possible bring up such topics of discussion and then leave the reader in a state of suspended anticipation? For the time being, we have little choice but to proceed with this work regarding The War and Peace of a New Metaphysical Perception. However, if it is of any solace, these questions will come up again in Tractate 18: The End of the Beginning – Theoretical Metaphysics Emerges.

For the time being, however, we must get back on track or we will never get done with the examination of many of philosophy's greatest paradoxes and how it is we can now resolve them and as such relegate not just Boethius' paradox but a large number of paradoxes to the annals of history.

Archimedean Points

Archimedean Points are referred to by Husserl as 'the' Archimedean Point. The Archimedean Point is the unshakable foundation of human knowledge.[11]

It is 'within' the individual, be it the subset of the whole as 'the individual' or 'the whole' as the individual, 'within' which, the 'unit' of knowledge is found. In addition, it is 'within' the individual, be it the subset of the whole as 'the individual' or 'the whole' as the individual, 'within' which, the process of knowing knowledge is found. The concept of 'being' *being* 'Being' now becomes two 'substantives', or two universals as Russell would say, interacting upon each other via the verb.

The universals, substantives: 'being' and 'Being'
The verb: *being*

All three are elements of the system. To rephrase it, we have a system of: three in one.

The Error of Copernicus

So it is:

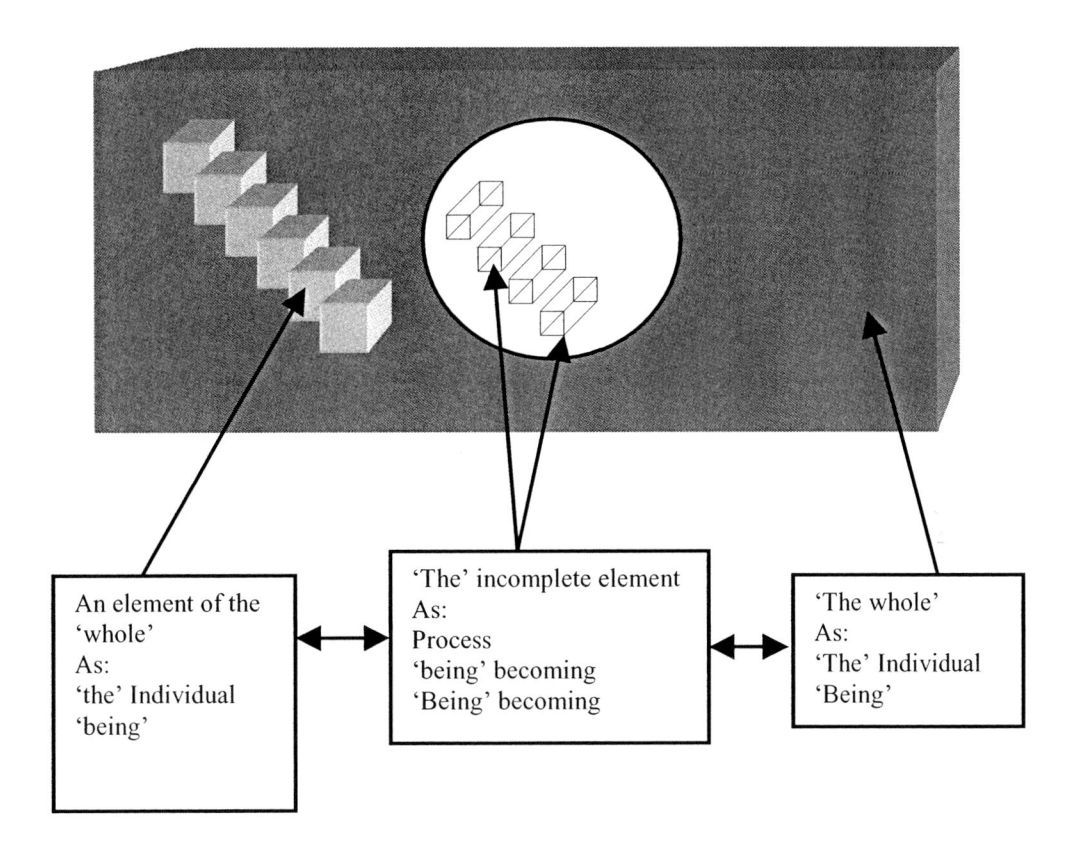

| An element of the 'whole' As: 'the' Individual 'being' | ↔ | 'The' incomplete element As: Process 'being' becoming 'Being' becoming | ↔ | 'The whole' As: 'The' Individual 'Being' |

So it is each entity of knowing becomes 'a' first truth in relationship to itself, in relationship to the whole, and in relationship to the universe/reality

So it is 'infinite relative 1st truths' emerge within 'finite relative 1st truths' within 'a' 1st truth.

The War & Peace of a New Metaphysical Perception

Philosophical infinities

Juxtaposition of infinities thus emerges as an essential element of the new metaphysical system 'being' *being* 'Being'. The concurrence of ontological infinities, cosmological infinities, and metaphysical infinities arises out of the understanding of this new metaphysical perception.

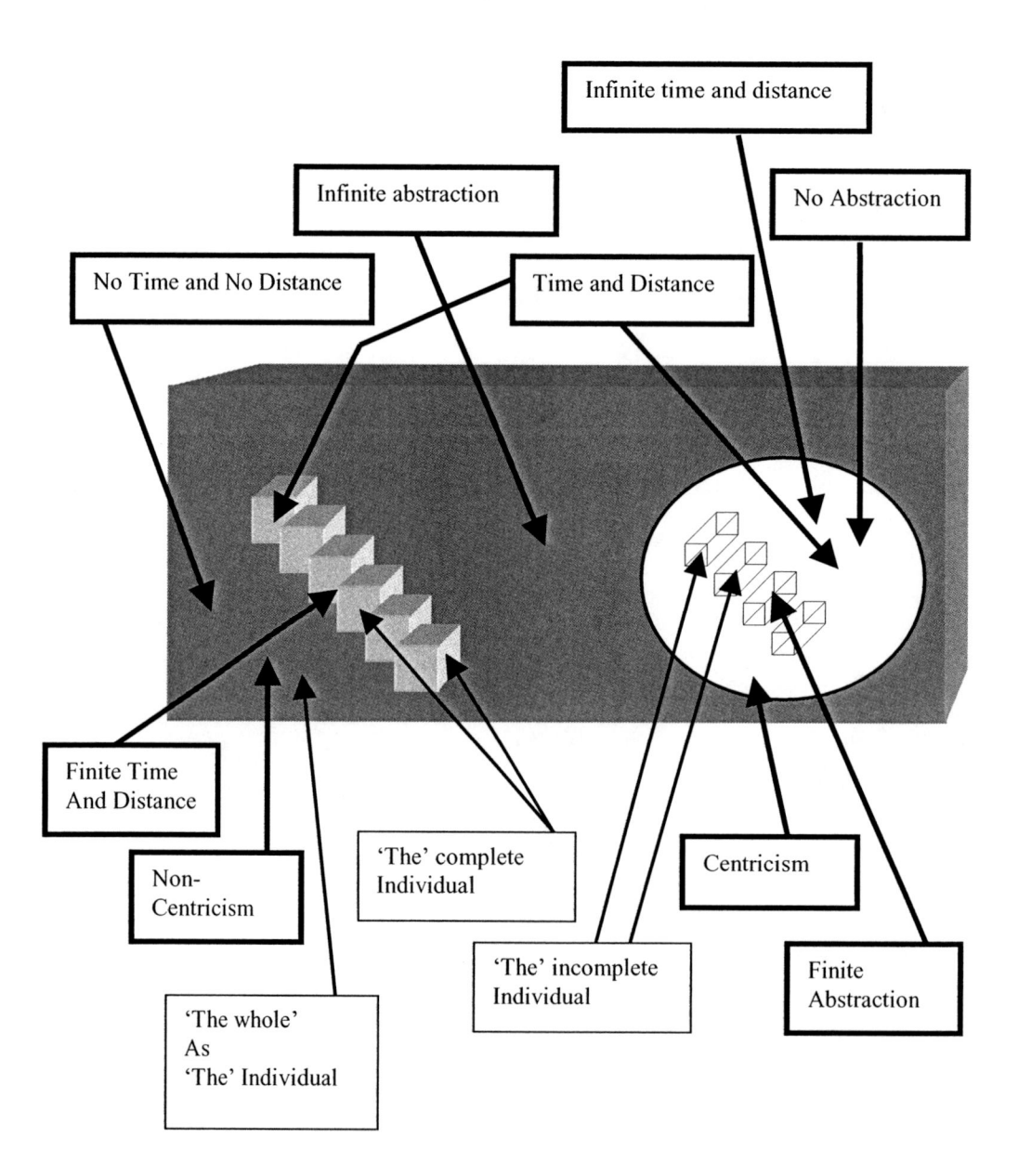

We can simplify the above diagram as:

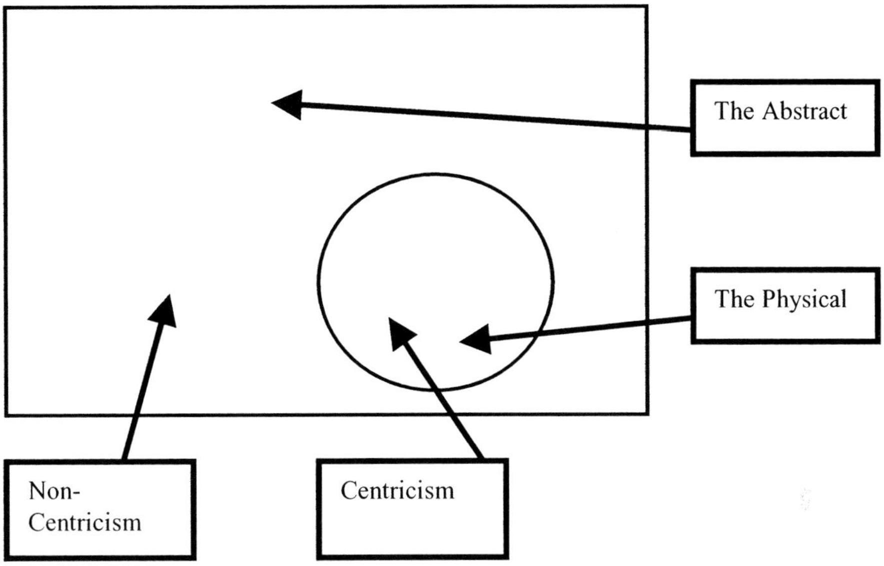

The Abstract
The Physical
Non-
Centricism
Centricism

Such an understanding will lead us into a discussion of Kant's Centricism and Hegel's non-Centricism in Tractates Six and Seven respectively.

The latter diagram evolves through the process of reality/the physical itself being 'experienced' through a process, which can be depicted as:

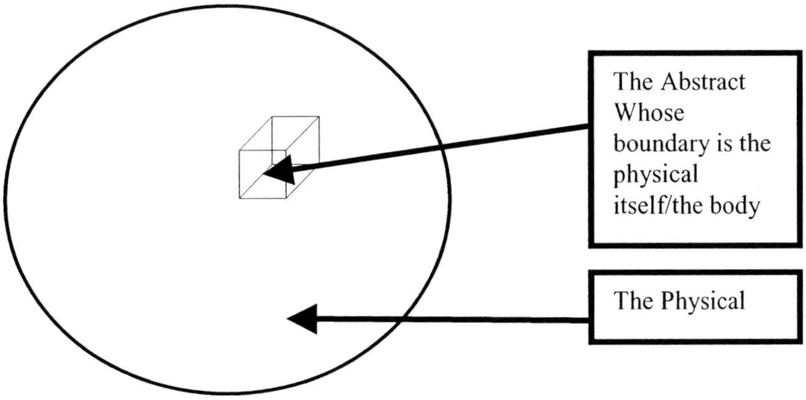

The Abstract
Whose
boundary is the
physical
itself/the body
The Physical

The War & Peace of a New Metaphysical Perception

Which, when placed back into its former diagram, becomes:

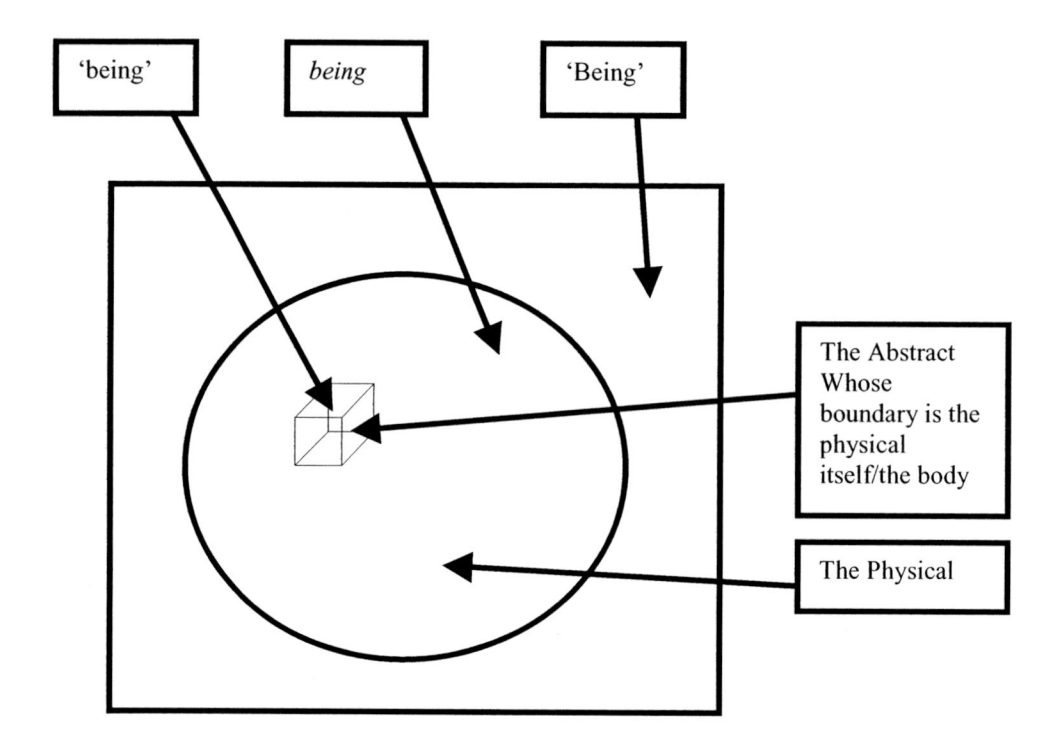

[Diagram: Three labeled boxes at top — 'being', *being*, 'Being' — with arrows pointing into a square containing a circle containing a small cube. Labels on the right: "The Abstract Whose boundary is the physical itself/the body" (pointing to the cube) and "The Physical" (pointing to the circle).]

Or 'being' *being* 'Being', centricism within non-centricism, Cartesian within non-Cartesian, non-Cartesian powered by Cartesian, non-centricism powered by centricism, 'Being' powered by 'being' through *being*.

The Error of Copernicus

This in turn becomes:

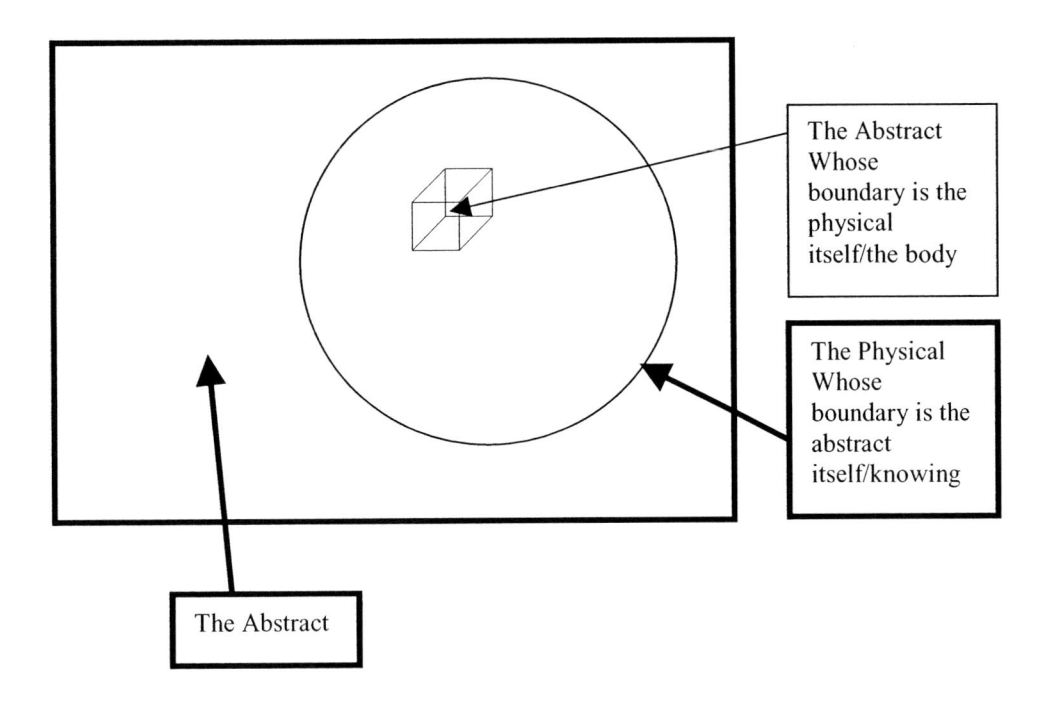

- The Abstract Whose boundary is the physical itself/the body
- The Physical Whose boundary is the abstract itself/knowing
- The Abstract

Or to put it more generically:

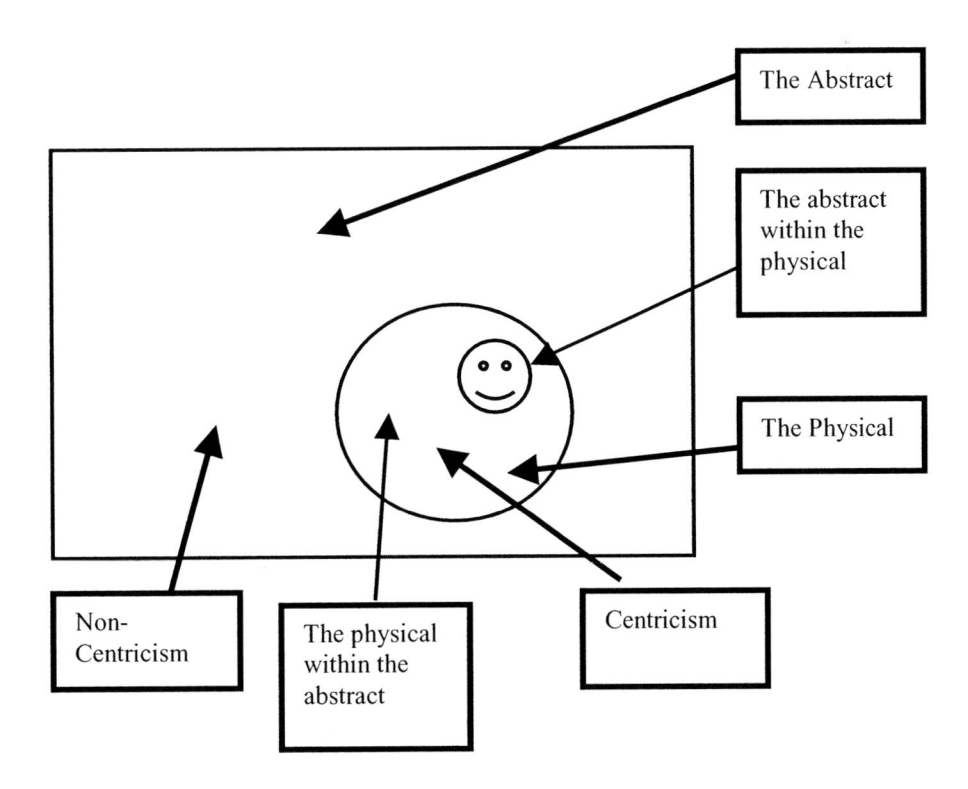

- The Abstract
- The abstract within the physical
- The Physical
- Non-Centricism
- The physical within the abstract
- Centricism

315

The War & Peace of a New Metaphysical Perception

A bag of marbles is not dependent upon sequential time

Remove the universe, remove the physical and we have:

Round out the unit of knowing:

Duplicate the units of knowing:

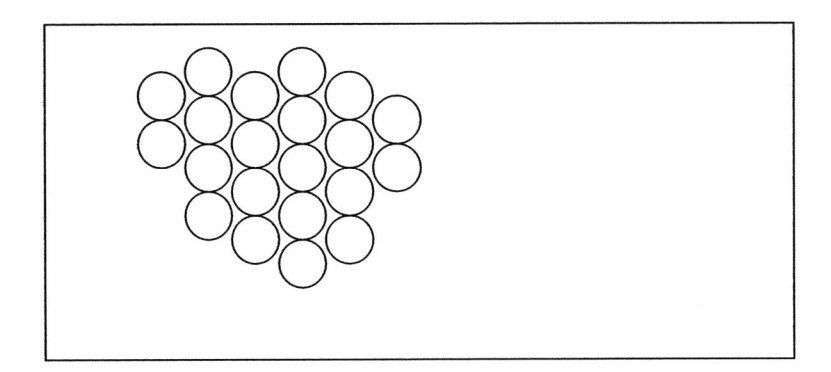

Resize your container

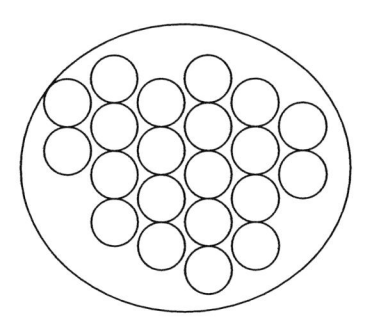

And you have a bag of twenty-one marbles

So what? So, the twenty-one marbles are not dependent upon time for their existence. If you put your hand in the bag and mix the marbles, you may have rearranged the marbles but you still have twenty-one marbles. Not only do you have twenty-one marbles but each marble is as it was as opposed to is where it was.

Now lets place time into the picture.

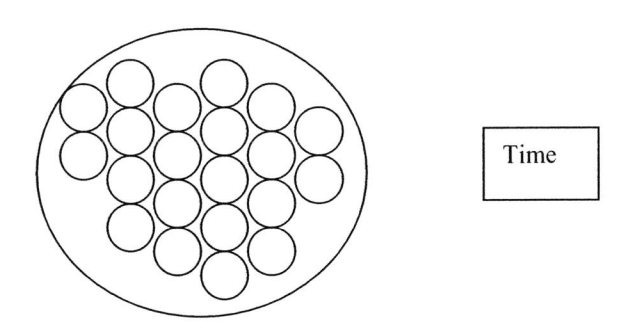

The War & Peace of a New Metaphysical Perception

The question becomes: Where does time fit into the graphic? The marbles went through a process of emerging as individual entities, unique individual entities. Each marble emerged out of non-existence. Each marble uniquely crystallized. Each has its own distinctive appearance. Granted each marble may look like the others at first glance but each marble is unique and can be identified as its own self upon close examination. So once again, where is time found to exist in the graphic?

Time is found as an element of the process of development of each marble. Thus:

The surroundings 'within' which the marble is immersed is void time in terms of the marbles very existence. Does time affect the existence of the marble? Physically time affects the physical existence of the marble but time does not affect the fact that the marble was what it was. Time only affected what the marble became on its way to being what it is.

Thus time remains a factor found 'within' the marble but time does not affect the abstractual existence of the marble.

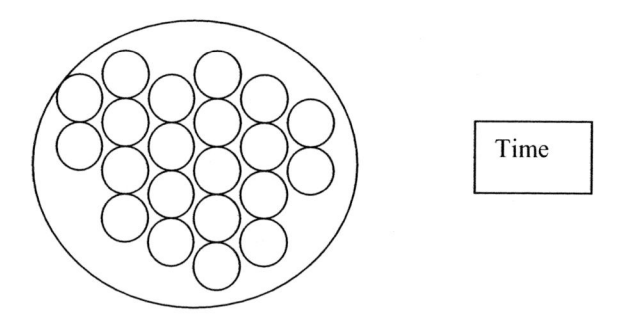

Now lets apply the concept to a unit of knowing.

A unit of knowing is not a marble

Units of knowing are not marbles but units of knowing do have some similarities to marbles. Each unit of knowing was formed in its own unique manner through becoming, as was the marble. Each unit of knowing is unique because it existed through time and had its own unique summation of input as an entity of knowing. Each unit of knowing may have a similar appearance at first glance but upon closer examination, each unit of knowing is found to be unique.

As such, the bag of marbles might better be represented as stones in a Kaleidoscope, which adds uniquely to the potential of the whole and what it is the whole becomes. Now using the word 'becomes' may lead one to believe that time is a factor found to surround the marbles but that is not the case. The bag of marbles is simply a bag of marbles and has the potential to have an overall appearance of but one summation if the bag contains but one marble. As the number of marbles increases beyond the total of one and becomes two, then three, then four, etc. so to grows the potential summation alternatives of the whole.

This growth is not geometric but rather exponential. The point being made here, however, is not that the summation of potentiality grows but that time is not a factor of the potential but rather time is the essential element of the growth of the sub-unit emergence itself rather than an element of the whole as the whole.

So, what of units of knowing not being marbles?

Let's reexamine the bag of marbles and apply uniqueness to the marbles in terms of apparent knowing. As such, the bag, for convenience purposed, becomes a rectangular window and the marbles become irregularly shaped objects representing 'uniqueness'.

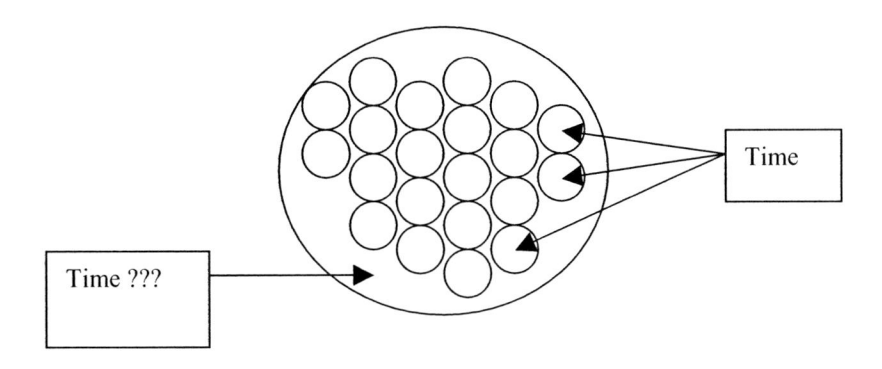

Becomes:

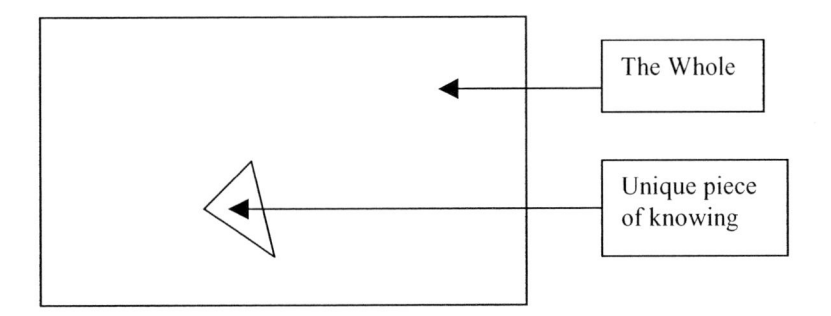

The triangle can of course rotate in any direction and as such the appearance of the whole changes. To simplify the process we will work only in terms of two-dimensional space.

The War & Peace of a New Metaphysical Perception

Adding another unique piece of knowing:

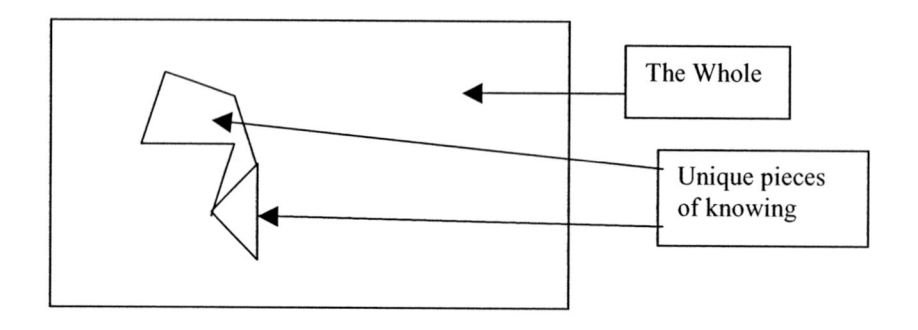

Add another unique piece of knowing:

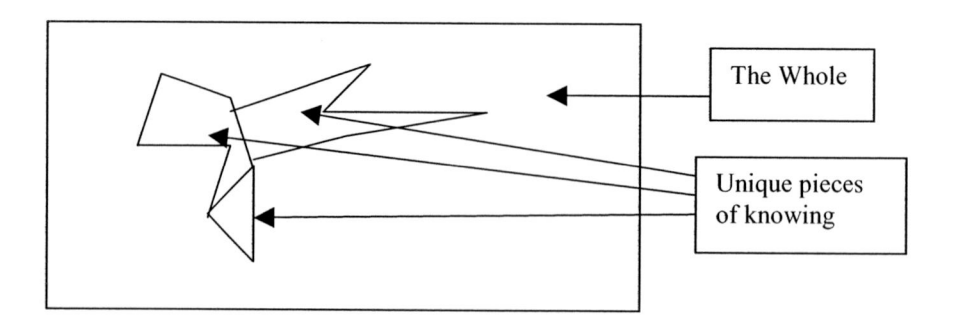

The Error of Copernicus

And so it is the picture grows. Keep in mind, however, that the picture has the potential to shift just as it does in a Kaleidoscope. However, where do the units form? They form through time. As such, time must have a location within which to exist.

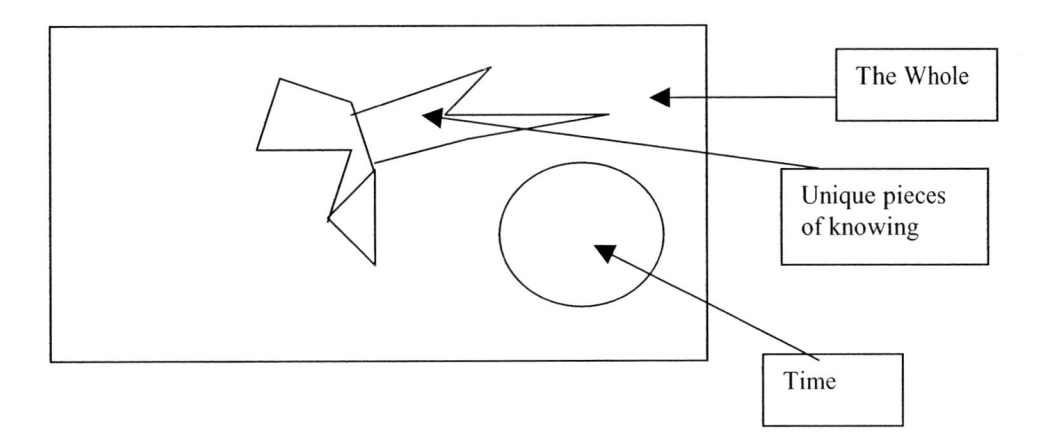

Within time unique pieces of knowing emerge from being virgin knowing to being a unit of knowing:

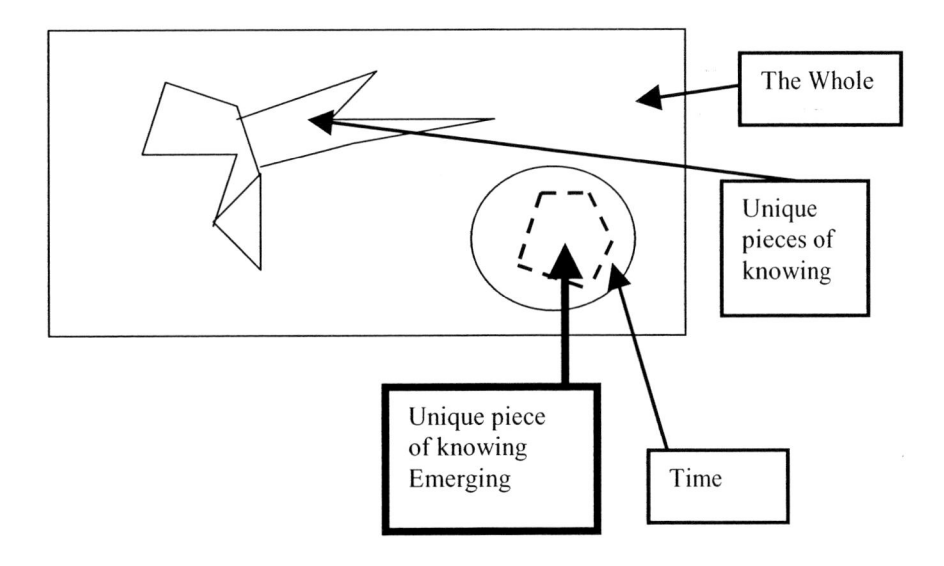

It is reaching the point where we must leave Copernicus and move on with other paradoxes. As such, the final question becomes: What does this have to do with Centrist systems and Copernicus?

Centrist systems have a center, a central point from which unique pieces of knowing expand upon themselves, central points from which unique pieces of knowing emerge. It is the 'unique unit of knowing', with its own unique experiencing, with its own unique knowledge which emerges from

The War & Peace of a New Metaphysical Perception

a Centrist system, emerges from 'the', 'a' physical universe and 'enters' the existence 'beyond' the physical, 'beyond the universal fabric of space and time. The universes of which we have familiarity, which forms our particular type of unit, is one whose very fabric of apparent universality is time and space/distance which itself may be an innate characteristic of matter and energy.[12] Whether or not it is time and space/distance that are the innate characteristic of matter and energy or matter and energy that are the innate characteristic of time and space/distance is not the point of this tractate. The point is:

> Centrist systems have a center, a central point from which unique units of knowing expand beyond and upon themselves, central points from which unique units of knowing emerge. It is the 'unique units of knowing', which through their own unique experiencing, emerge from a Centrist system, 'the', 'a' physical universe and become a part of the non-centrist system.

This statement can be rephrased as:

> Centrist systems have a center, a central point from which unique units of knowledge expand beyond and upon themselves, central points from which unique units of knowledge emerge. It is the 'unique unit of knowledge', which through its own unique formation, knowledge itself emerges from a Centrist system of knowledge formation, from 'the', 'a' physical universe and becomes a part of the non-centrist system of total knowledge.

If we return to our marble analogy, we can begin to grasp a clearer image of what is being said:

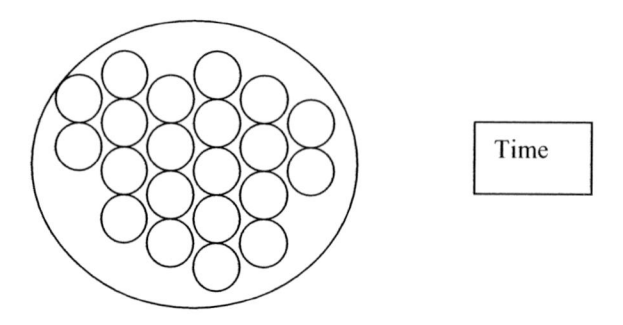

This becomes:

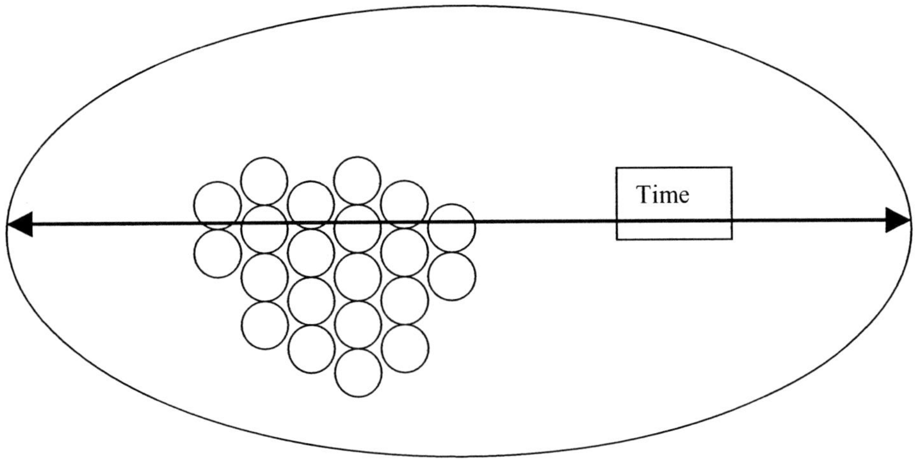

Which becomes:

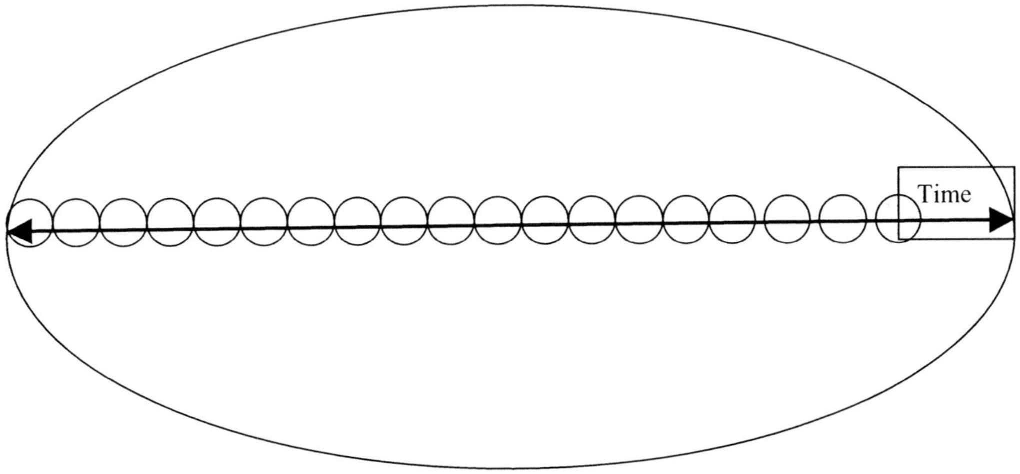

We can now see how it is that time becomes a part of each unit entity of knowing which travels through our universe of centrist systems.

The War & Peace of a New Metaphysical Perception

This however is not the end of the analogy for we have twenty-one marbles. The center is what is called the origin, is called the present, is defined as: What is:

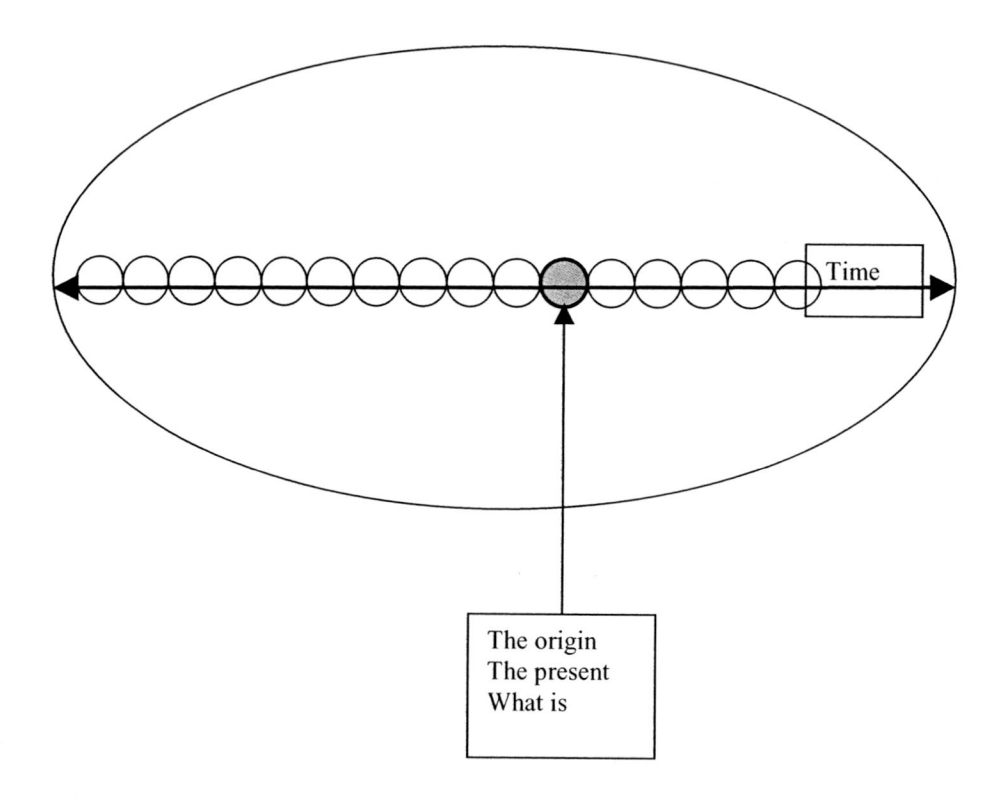

[Diagram: an ellipse containing a horizontal arrow labeled "Time" with a row of twenty-one circles along it; the center circle is shaded gray and points down to a box labeled "The origin / The present / What is"]

The left of the center units, the left of the present are units, which have already "become". We refer to such a concept as the past or 'what was'.

The right of the center unit, the right of the present are units, which have yet to "become". We refer to such a concept as the future or 'what could be'.

The concept of the right being 'what could be' versus 'what will be' is a very important aspect of the future events. 'What could be' implies free will of the individual. 'What will be' implies determinism.

It would be interesting running this train of thought under the premise of 'what will be'. That scenario, however, belongs with Boethius and we are not going back there. We must stay on track of following history and where it has led us, is leading us, and 'could' lead us. Let it be noted, however, that in the case of the 'what will be' scenario, the marbles to the right of center are all pre-filled with a predetermined pattern. As such the potentiality of kaleidoscope of patterns is limited to 'what is' rather than being unlimited by 'what could be'. Within such a scenario, infinite finites supercedes finite infinites (see Tractate 2: Aristotle).

The Error of Copernicus

Returning to the task at hand, we then obtain:

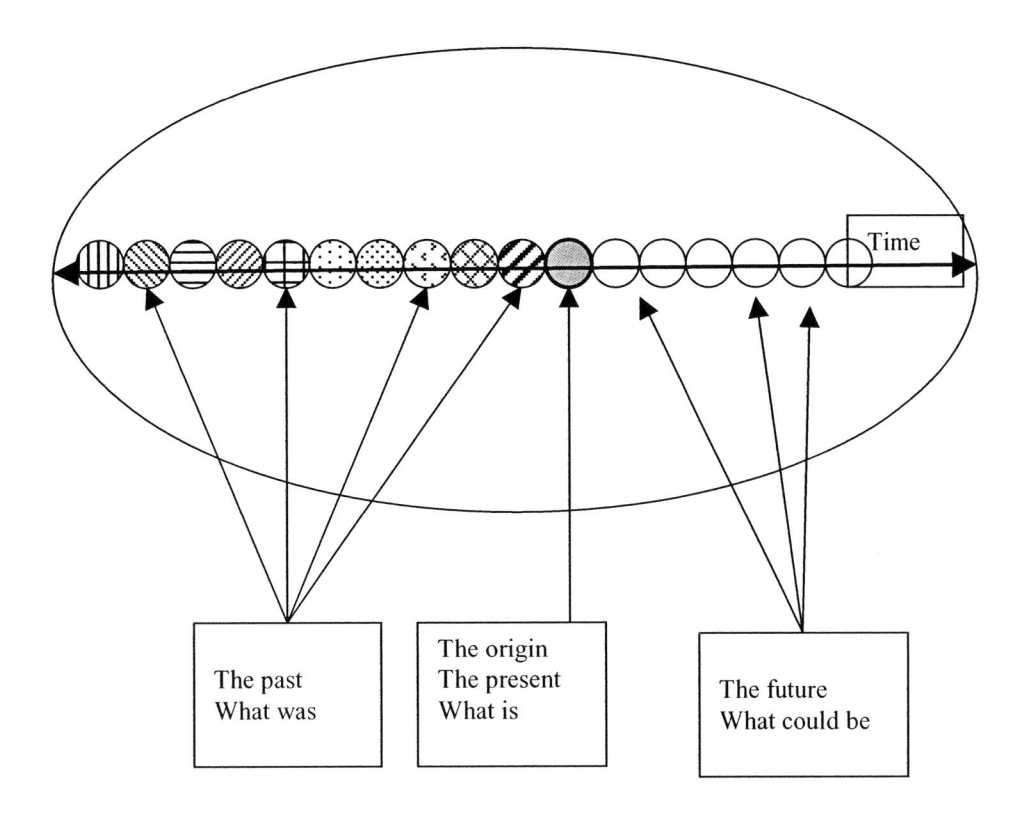

The past
What was

The origin
The present
What is

The future
What could be

Now of course we recognize the left side as not only being the stones of the Kaleidoscope existing within the void of time and space/distance yet 'containing' perceptions of time and space/distance. We can, therefore redo our graphic and in doing so we find we have:

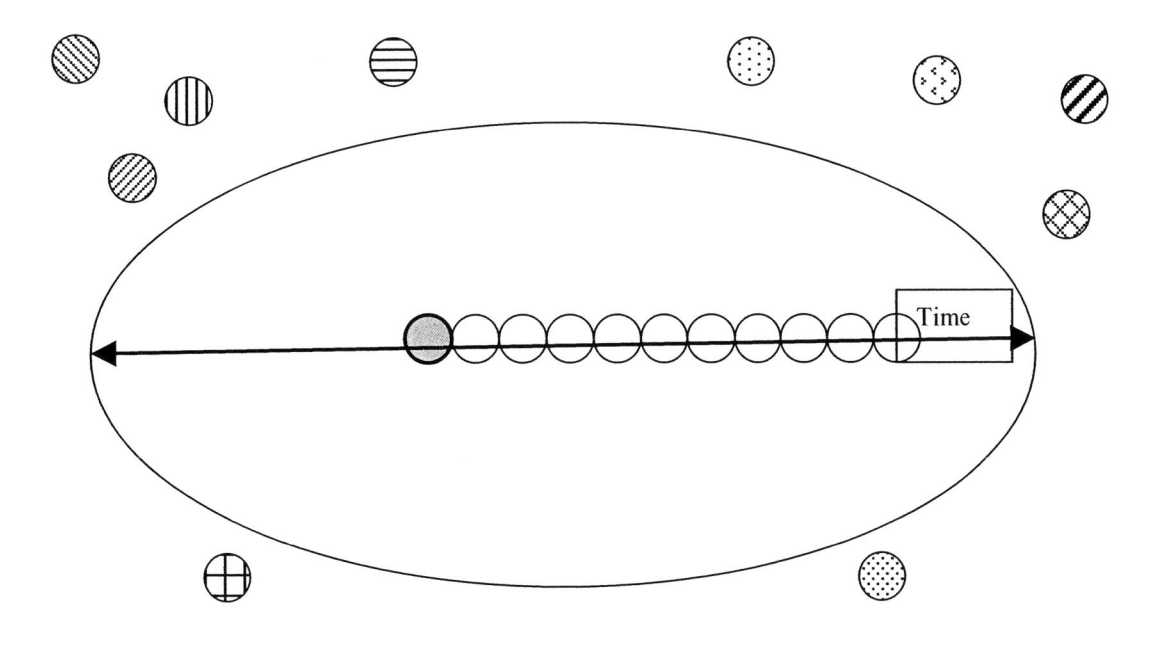

The War & Peace of a New Metaphysical Perception

As the marbles roll through space and time, they become unique one from another. This is a two dimensional depiction. One must not lose track of the concept that even in a two-dimensional depiction time has many degrees of latitude regarding 'where' it is headed:

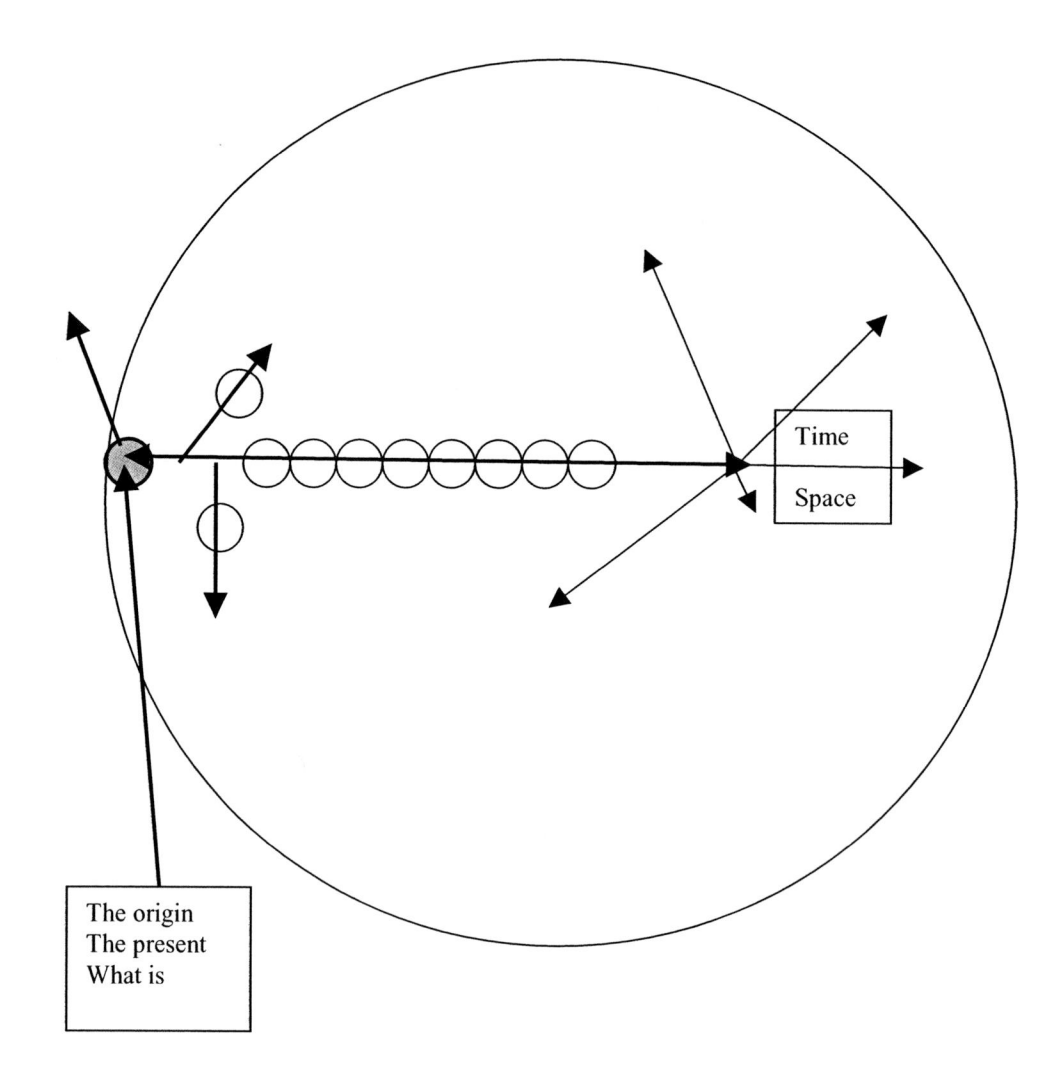

Time
Space

The origin
The present
What is

The Error of Copernicus

In essence, we have:

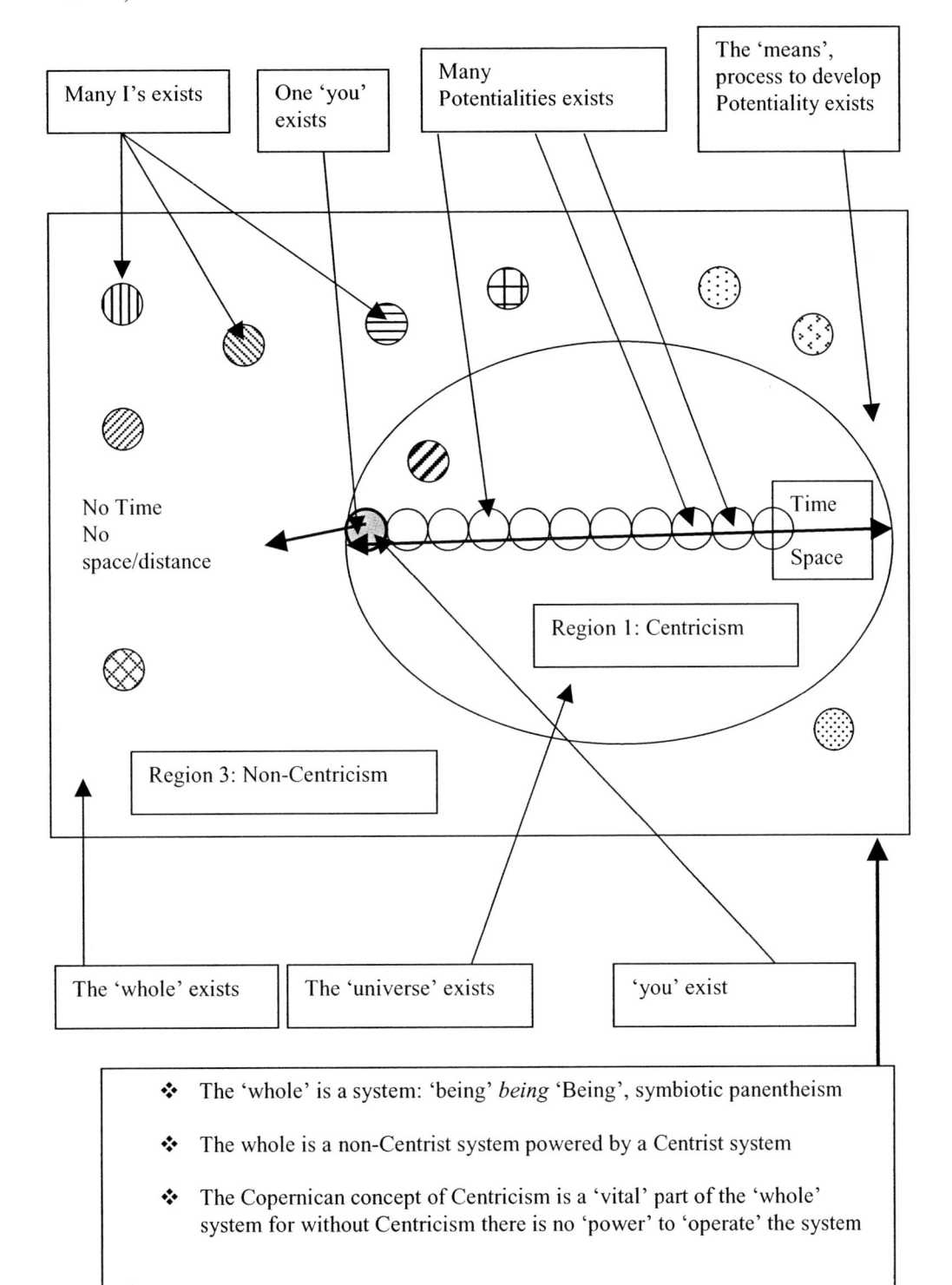

- Many I's exists
- One 'you' exists
- Many Potentialities exists
- The 'means', process to develop Potentiality exists

No Time
No space/distance

Time
Space

Region 1: Centricism

Region 3: Non-Centricism

- The 'whole' exists
- The 'universe' exists
- 'you' exist

- ❖ The 'whole' is a system: 'being' *being* 'Being', symbiotic panentheism
- ❖ The whole is a non-Centrist system powered by a Centrist system
- ❖ The Copernican concept of Centricism is a 'vital' part of the 'whole' system for without Centricism there is no 'power' to 'operate' the system

The War & Peace of a New Metaphysical Perception

We now understand that

> Copernicus is a vital link in moving our perceptual understanding forward regarding the 'system' being filled with Centricism into that of being 'the' system filled with Centricism and non-Centricism. As such, Centricism and non-Centricism, with the help of Copernicus, now have a location within which they can be found. And now, the understanding regarding the role of both Centricism and non-Centricism as well as the understanding regarding the interrelationship between Centricism and non-Centricism no longer remain in a state of confusion. Even more interestingly, the existence of such a interrelationship is not only recognized as a significant aspect of the 'larger' system but is now understood as to how such an interrelationship interacts one with the other.

---

[1] Aristotle initiated the elementary form of Cartesianism, which might better be termed 'static Cartesianism'. Although some discussion of 'static' Cartesianism will occur in this tractate, a detailed explanation of what the concept means to metaphysics can be found in Tractate 2: The Error of Aristotle.

[2] **Question**: This paragraph suggests philosophy, science, and religion were equals. Before Copernicus, philosophy did enjoy an independent status apart from religion. However, by the medieval period, philosophy was used to support – and not compete with – religious views. It wasn't until the emergence of science, as an independent area of study, that philosophy once again regained its independence. At that point – philosophy, religion, and science – all became independent of each other. With this in mind could you explain what you are attempting to imply? **Answer**: We have at our disposal three means of developing perceptions. We have science/observation, religion/belief, and philosophy/reason. Each of the three, throughout the unfolding of time, wanes and ebbs in terms of its 'apparent' significance one to the other. But in truth each is, uniformly through time, equal to the other in significance and any universally stable perception we develop has no choice but to be confirmed by the three equally. We will never, as individuals or as specie, accept the validity of a metaphysical model if it is a model: We find unsupportable by either direct or indirect observation, interpolation or extrapolation, and induction or deduction. We find to be unbelievable. We find to be unreasonable.

[3] **Question**: Because the foundations of political philosophy were being established during this period, I don't perceive the process of the "Why" as being a random and unimportant event. I agree that, during this period, we "settled" for different models of cooperation and agreement, rather than a larger metaphysical understanding. However, these earlier "models" did help establish an atmosphere whereby later philosophers could propose more advanced "models'. As such, can you clarify what you mean by 'random' and 'unimportant' events? **Answer**: Metaphysically speaking, no 'foundation of reason' was being laid down to rationalize the concept regarding 'tolerance and respect due the individual'. The understanding of 'a' metaphysical model from which a natural emergence of such a perspective would occur had not been laid out for students of philosophy to examine. Granted the emergence of political philosophy was just emerging but that is not the point. Political philosophy is no more a foundation of reason than is religion or science. The foundation for the concept regarding 'tolerance and respect due the individual' can be found in science/observation, religion/faith, and philosophy/reason. Philosophy/reason, itself has 'a' foundation and that foundation is the most basic, the most primitive, the most primal of foundations. This most primal, most basic of

foundation is the understanding of 'a' metaphysical system which explains the very fundamental dynamics existing between ourselves as abstractually knowing individuals and what lies beyond the physical itself.

[4] **Question**: Can you clarify? **Answer**: Up to and through Copernicus, the West, for the most part, 'believed' time and space/distance were aspects of the physical. Such perceptions dominated not only scientific thought, but also religious and philosophically thought. With the advent of Kant, however, such philosophical perceptions underwent the same type of traumatic inversion as occurred to science and its concept of Centricism with the advent of Copernicus.

[5] Oxford Concise Science Dictionary, 1996

[6] **Question**: Can you clarify? **Answer**: Up to and through Copernicus, the West, for the most part, 'believed' time and space/distance were aspects of the physical. Such perceptions dominated not only scientific thought, but also religious and philosophically thought. With the advent of Kant, however, such philosophical perceptions underwent the same type of traumatic inversion as occurred to science and its concept of Centricism with the advent of Copernicus.

[7] **Question**: "…lack of time and distance"? Can you explain? **Answer**: All forms of physical existence are tied to time and space. Physical existences find their very existence defined by four coordinates: the three dimension of space and the dimension of time. Without space and time physical objects could not exist, as we know them to be, physical. Abstract concepts on the other hand are not dependent upon the physical quality of space nor the physical quality of time. Granted some abstractual concepts are dependent upon an abstractual understanding of space and time but they are, however, not dependent upon the very existence of the physical qualities of space and time themselves.

[8] **Question**: Can you clarify? **Answer**: No, other than to say that omniscience by definition leads to the summation of knowing, summation of motivation of action. As such, Gandhi and Hitler, both of whom impacted human awareness through two opposing points of view, became a part of total knowing. The result, the summation of knowing, omniscience, incorporated the aspects of both men as well as the horrendous number of ripples both men initiated which in turn became, are still becoming, will continue to become part of the summation of knowing and thus mold the very personality of the summation of knowing itself.

[9] Genesis 32:30, 8:2

[10] Boethius: The Consolation of Philosophy, Book V, section IV.

[11] **Question**: Can you expand on this statement? **Answer**: Husserl would suggest all things can be stripped away from reality until only one primary concept remains. Such a process would leave the most fundamental of foundations. Such a foundation would be termed 'the Archimedean Point' from which all else emerges.

[12] **Question**: Can you clarify? **Answer**: Up to and through Copernicus, the West, for the most part, 'believed' time and space/distance were aspects of the physical. Such perceptions dominated not only scientific thought, but also religious and philosophically thought. With the advent of Kant, however, such philosophical perceptions underwent the same type of traumatic inversion as occurred to science and its concept of Centricism with the advent of Copernicus.

Tractate 5

The Error

Of

Leibniz

❖

The Paradox of:

❖

Perfection

•

The Need for:
Theodicy

The War & Peace of a New Metaphysical Perception

1.   1716 AD Leibniz - The Error of:
         Perfection

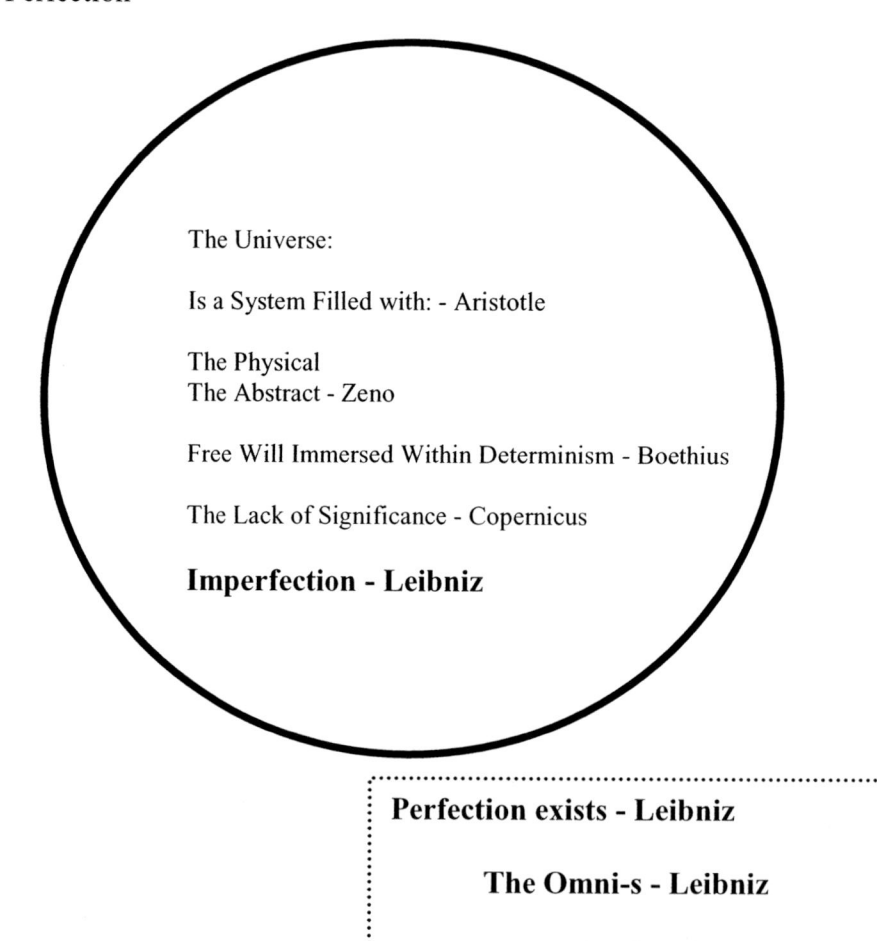

> The Universe:
>
> Is a System Filled with: - Aristotle
>
> The Physical
> The Abstract - Zeno
>
> Free Will Immersed Within Determinism - Boethius
>
> The Lack of Significance - Copernicus
>
> **Imperfection - Leibniz**

Perfection exists - Leibniz

The Omni-s - Leibniz

1. **Omnipresence**
2. **Omnipotence**
3. **Omniscience**
4. **Omnibenevolence**

The error: The paradox of Theodicy – Omnibenevolence

The perception: Leibniz moves our perceptual understanding regarding the system being filled with both 'imperfection' and 'perfection' into that of being 'the' system filled with 'imperfection' and 'perfection' being found elsewhere. As such, imperfection and perfection, with the help of Leibniz, now have a location within which they can be found. However, the understanding regarding the role of imperfection and perfection as well as the understanding regarding the interrelationship between imperfection and perfection not only remain in a state of confusion but even more disconcerting, the existence of such an interrelationship is not recognized as a significant aspect of the 'larger' system.

It is this state of confusion which will be specifically addressed within this tractate.

Contents

Part I: Creating the paradox of a Perfect System

Introduction
Errors created through the passive process of definition
'Defining' theodicy
    First
    Second
    Third
Error through the active process of extrapolation as opposed to the passive process of definition

Part II: Resolving the issue with a new metaphysical perception

The Core: Omniscience
The first shell: Omnipotence and Omnipresence
Leibniz and the error of addition
The Second Shell: Answers to three questions
The location of 'imperfection'
The Location of 'perfection'
Conclusion

Terms/concepts

Minimal extreme of knowing
Omnibenevolence
Omnipotence
Omnipresence
Omniscience
Perceptual knowing
Puristic non-relativistic values of abstraction
Sub unit of knowing
Theodicy

Tractate 5
Leibniz – The Error of
Perfection

Part I: Creating the paradox of a Perfect System

Introduction

This tractate, Tractate 5: Leibniz and Theodicy, appears relatively unimportant when compared to the voluminous material found within the previous tractates. One must not forget, however, that we are dealing with abstractual concepts within the complete work of The War and Peace of a New Metaphysical Perception of which this tractate is an element.

Abstractual concepts are not measured in terms of physical dimensions and thus cannot be compared one to another in our customary fashion. Abstractual concepts just are and as such abstractual concepts have not only no relative value of physical size one to the other but have no relative value of importance one to the other.

Why then examine the concept of Theodicy which was introduced so eloquently by Leibniz rather than other 'more important' aspects of Leibniz' work? There it is again, the almost inescapable desire to place relative value upon one idea as opposed to another.

So again we will ask the question but remove the concept of 'relative value' from the question:

> Why then examine the concept of Theodicy?

The concept of theodicy, as introduced by Leibniz, created a beacon which metaphysicians felt obliged to follow as they worked throughout the following centuries. Metaphysicians, by embracing the concept that 'perfection' as defined by ontologists, in truth lost their way and simply perceived themselves to be metaphysicians when in actuality they became ontologists masquerading as metaphysicians.

Such 'metaphysicians' examined the personality of 'God' versus the fundamental characteristics of 'the whole' system 'within' which we, elements of perceptual knowing, find ourselves to exist. Metaphysics does not deal with the personality of the whole but rather metaphysics deals with the basics, with what is. Ontology deals with the abstractual personality of the whole which emerges from the existence of the whole itself.

So for a third time:

> Why then examine the concept of Theodicy?

It is theodicy we must examine in order to understand how we are to redirect the 'masquerading metaphysician' back to becoming a purist, a legitimate metaphysician as opposed to being a ontologist masquerading as a metaphysician.

It is Leibniz who introduced the concept of 'perfection' and 'imperfection' and labeled such a concept with a unique term of its own, theodicy.

The Error of Leibniz

At first glance, one will notice that this tractate is 'shorter' than the previous tractates. Upon closer scrutiny one will also notice this tractate does not take on the same unemotional dialectic approach as the first four tractates.

In terms of the shortness of the tractate, there is no doubt the tractate is 'shorter.' The concepts with which the work, The War and Peace of a New Metaphysical Perception, deals are abstractual in nature and as such 'perfection' and 'imperfection' are found to be, metaphysically speaking, non-relativistic in nature.

Should one feel uncomfortable with the concept of puristic non-relativistic values of abstraction, one may find comfort in reexamining the diagram introducing this tractate. Upon doing so, admirers of Leibniz may find comfort in observing that although the tractate regarding Leibniz may be 'shorter' than the other tractates of this work, The War and Peace of a New Metaphysical Perception, Leibniz and the concept with which he dealt take up more space within the diagram and require the listing of his name more frequently than any other philosopher. In addition, the diagram credits Leibniz with having established the first thought of there being a distinctly separate and independent 'location'[1] existing 'isolated from' the physical.

So much for the 'shortness' of the Leibniz' tractate, but what of the emotional approach versus the less objective approach found within the tractate itself as 'compared' to the first four tractates? Leibniz introduced a very emotional concept, the concept of humanity, the concept of all forms of abstractual knowing being 'imperfect' versus simply 'being' in the puristic sense of the word. Such personal
re-characterization of our very essence deserves its own unique emotional response. Leibniz, through his work, re-characterizes our, humanity's, actions as being 'imperfect'.

Leibniz creates the concept of imperfection becoming a location of the lack of 'perfect quality' through the emergence of a new location. As the new location emerges, its characteristic becomes defined: Perfection exists. As such the concept of 'omni…' spreads to action as well as knowledge, power, and presence. Through Leibniz, 'Separation through exclusion'[2] becomes a necessity.

And where will examining Leibniz and theodicy take us? It will take us to the metaphysician who perhaps was the first philosopher since Leibniz to discard the façade of being 'an ontologist working in the guise of a metaphysician'. It will take us to the work of Immanuel Kant himself.

Leibniz attempted to create a term to resolve what he considered to be a paradox underscoring religious and philosophical thought.

> *Theodicy, a term introduced by Leibniz to characterize the topic of God's government of the world in relation to the nature of man. The problem is the justification of God's goodness and justice in view of the evil in the world.*[3]

He attempted to compartmentalize the contradictory discussion regarding the concept of a 'perfect' 'Being' being 'perfectly good' while allowing 'evil' to exist, while allowing evil to take place, while allowing evil to be created 'within' It's personal creation which 'lesser' 'beings' call 'the universe'.

But Leibniz failed to recognize that as soon as he accepted the first three forms of 'omni-', omniscience, omnipotence, and omnipresence, than the fourth form, omnibenevolence, became an invalid concern to both religion and philosophy.

Error created through the passive process of definition

The concept of omnibenevolence is irrational if one accepts the first three forms of 'omni-', omniscience, omnipotence, and omnipresence. 'But,' one may say, 'what if I do not accept these three characteristics of God?' Then the question becomes, 'Just which one of the 'omni-' does one not accept?'

If we begin with the whole, God, not only does 'a' definition emerge but the concept of 'definition' itself emerges.

By definition, God exists and is simply (yes, it is simple) the whole: all knowledge – omniscience, all power[4] – omnipotence, and all presence[5] – omnipresent. So the question restated, now becomes, 'If you are rejecting any one of the three, which 'omni-' concept would you reject? Would you reject: omniscience - the summation of knowledge, or omnipotence - the summation of power, or omnipresence - the summation of presence.

Should one dismiss any one of the three forms of 'omni-', one by definition no longer has the concept of God in mind, rather one has some 'other' concept in mind.

Leibniz made an error when he assumed the existence of omnibenevolence was one of the 'omni-' traits of the whole, of God. He did not examine the rationality of such an existence. He did not examine its impact upon the other three forms of 'omni-existence'. Had he done so, he would have immediately concluded that the concept he was about to label was incompatible with the other forms of omni-existence. As such, he would have led the discussion of theodicy in the direction of demonstrating the irrationality regarding the concept of God allowing 'evil' to occur. Had Leibniz been more conscientious, he would have lead the direction away from blaming God for 'allowing' 'evil' to occur, to placing the blame where it belonged, with you and I, not God.

Leibniz was wrong on two accounts. He was wrong both in terms of 'defining' theodicy and in terms of the 'process' he used in establishing the legitimacy of theodicy. This mistake was one that led to many misperceptions over the next three centuries and it was often these perceptions, which lead to misguided actions, abusive actions, inhumane action, we inflicted upon each other. Many abusive actions have taken place because of our misperceptions that it is God who 'allows evil' to exist and descend upon humanity.

Such a perception allows us to shirk our sense of responsibility for our own actions.

It was our misperception that we were not responsible for 'evil', which allowed many abuses to be generated by society, governments, religions, sciences, philosophies, and individuals while the rest of us shrugged our shoulders and went on about what we considered to be more important business.

Because of this, it is important to reexamine Leibniz's development of the term theodicy. It is time we reexamine our presumptions regarding the legitimacy of the idea that God allows 'bad' things to happen to 'good' people. With this reexamination will come the understanding that it is you and I, not God, who allow 'evil' to happen to 'good' people. With this reexamination will come an understanding that some 'evils' are not 'evils' but rather simply experiences and natural processes. These natural 'evil' events we are forced to experience we label as 'evil' when in fact they are simply random natural events.. This is not going to be a pleasant process to follow for it will end in our understanding what it is we do not want to accept. It will lead to the understanding that we, you and I, are responsible for 'evil', not God. It will do something, which the work of Leibniz did not do, it will force us to grow up and take responsibility for ourselves.

Let's examine the irrelevance of theodicy from both the perspective of definition and then from the perspective of process.

'Defining' theodicy

In order to examine the flaw regarding the concept of theodicy one must first understand where the heart of the matter lies. The heart of this concept lies in the Greek prefix, 'omni-' meaning all.

By definition, theodicy defines God as having a fourth characteristic. Defining theodicy is an attempt to expand our knowledge of what God is. Religions say God is omnipresent (all-present), omnipotent (all-powerful), and omniscient (all-knowing). Now along comes Leibniz who introduces a fourth 'omni' into the equation. Because of the prominence of Leibniz, everyone says, 'Oh, yeah that is a problem." And no one stands up and says, 'Wait a minute, Leibniz, this fourth 'Omni-' term is irrelevant and therefore your development of the term theodicy is irrelevant.

The problem with Leibniz's definition is threefold:

First:

If God is omnipresent as all major religions of the world today say, then God is everywhere. If God is everywhere then we are in God. As such we are a part of God. Objections immediately arise, 'No, we are a part of the universe.' But if God is omnipresent – all present, then the universe is inside God, a part of God and you, being within the universe, must be considered a part of God.

The War & Peace of a New Metaphysical Perception

Metaphysically as opposed to Ontologically such a concept graphically becomes:

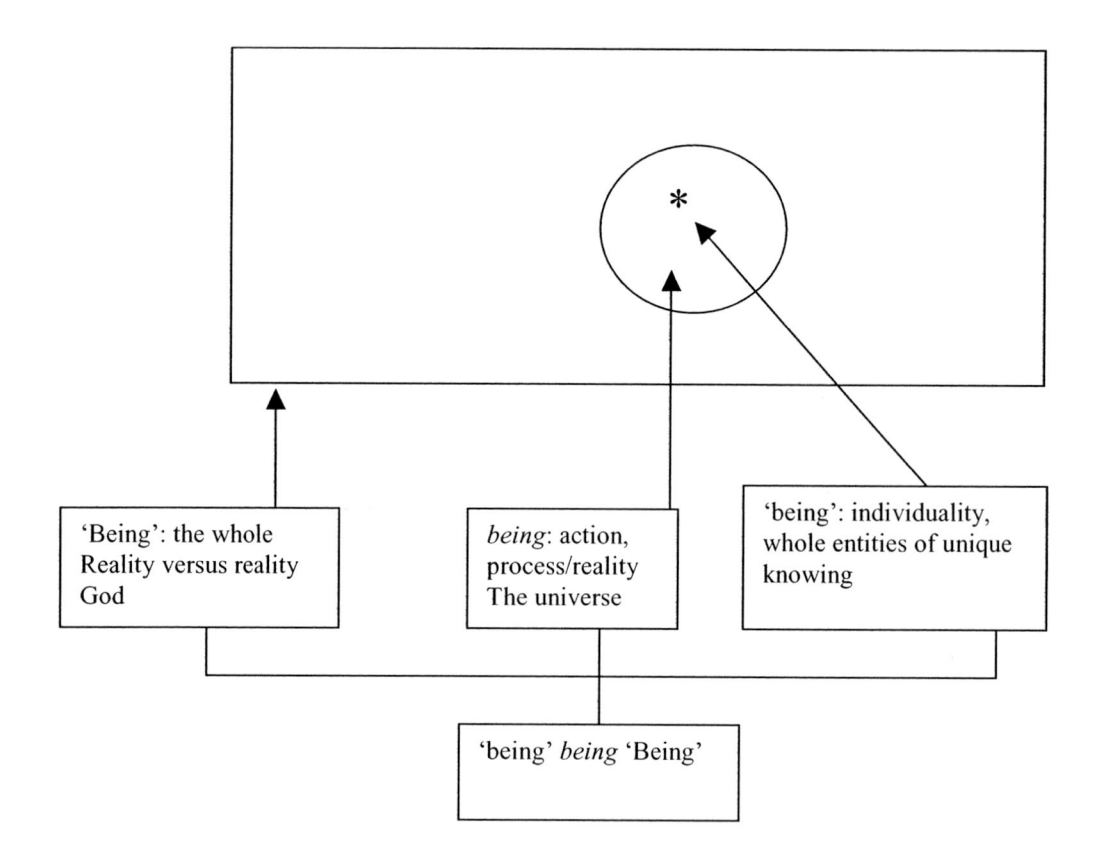

```
┌─────────────────────────────────────────┐
│                                         │
│                    ╭─────╮              │
│                    │  *  │              │
│                    ╰─────╯              │
│                     ↑  ↑                │
│                        ╲                │
│        ↑                ╲               │
└────────┼─────────────────╲──────────────┘
         │                  ╲
┌────────────────┐  ┌──────────────┐  ┌─────────────────────┐
│ 'Being': the whole│  │ being: action,│  │ 'being': individuality,│
│ Reality versus reality│ process/reality│ │ whole entities of unique│
│ God            │  │ The universe │  │ knowing             │
└────────┬───────┘  └──────┬───────┘  └──────────┬──────────┘
         │                 │                     │
         └─────────────────┼─────────────────────┘
                           │
                  ┌────────┴────────┐
                  │ 'being' being 'Being'│
                  └─────────────────┘
```

Once again the objections drown out the discussion, 'There is evil in the universe and God is a perfect being therefore the universe.must lie outside God. God must transcend the universe. It is the only way to resolve this paradox.' But is it? Could it not be resolved by perceptualizing the universe being within God but God not being within the universe? In this particular reference to God, we are not speaking of God's 'presence'; rather we are speaking of the 'whole' of God. In other words, we are simply acknowledging the validity of 'omnipresence' being one of the characteristics of God. At the same time, we are stating there is more to God than what is found, sensed, and experiences within the limitation of our universe. If one is to accept this concept of the omnipresence of God, then one can accept the concept that the universe must be within God. Thus one may remain committed to the concept that part of the definition of God incorporates the concept of omnipresence and thus understand how it is that God, as a whole, is not in the universe.

Second

Leibniz accepted the concept that 'evil' could not exist in a perfect being and proceeded from there.. But if we are to accept the main premises of religions, including the concept of omnipresence, than there is nowhere else for 'evil' to exist. 'Evil' as well as 'goodness' must exist 'within' God. As such, humanly judgmental forms of 'omni's' are not forms we can assign as basic characteristics of God.

The major religions of the world believe the universe was made from 'nothing'. Interestingly enough, science itself, through quantum mechanics, is leaning in this direction. As such the physical, having been created from 'nothing', is nothing. Therefore, what we perceive to be, what we perceive as being the physical, is in actually a form of 'nothing' just as Eastern religions have always stipulated. Such a concept was addressed in detail in Tractate 1: Zeno and Multiplicity and Seamlessness.

Does such a concept imply you are nothing? Absolutely not, unless one perceives one's essence to be the physical, as opposed to the spiritual, the soul, an abstract form of existence. It is abstraction, which now takes on the form of true reality, rather than what we call the concreteness of our perceived universe being the totality of 'Reality'.

If one accepts the concept of the soul being abstract and thus one's true essence being abstract, as all major religions profess, than it can readily be seen that the very dissolving of the universe, the dissolving of matter, energy, space, and time, back into it's original form of nothingness leaves one's essence, the abstract, as an entity existing within the omnipresent whole, within God. Again we come back to the concept of your being an abstraction and God being an abstraction. Again we come back to the concept of your being a part of the whole, of total abstraction. Again we come back to the concept of your being a part of God, for how can total abstraction be total without including your abstraction? How can the whole be whole without you? How can God be all knowing, omniscient, without your knowledge and your experiences? Knowledge is power, so how can God be all powerful, omnipotent, without your knowledge? In other words God cannot be God without you. You are definitely important to God for you, by definition, are what make God, God.

But what does this have to do with good and evil and the paradox of a 'perfect being' containing evil or allowing evil to take place within It?

If the universe originated from nothing and can regress back to nothing than it is, in essence, nothing. You are in the universe. As such, the physical form you take, takes on the form of the universe, the characteristics of the universe, is in essence 'nothing'. On the other hand, the abstractual form you take, takes on the characteristics of God, your abstraction, your awareness of your every experience gleaned from the universe, your awareness of the universe itself, is a part of God. As such, you and I, others, may be pieces of God, made in the image of God. Granted you are temporarily isolated from the 'whole', but you remain a part of the 'whole' nevertheless. When it is understood that you and others are cut off from and then separated from the 'whole', from God, through 'a process of inclusion'[6] by the void of space and time[7], by emptiness, is it any wonder so many of us feel isolated from God.

Definition leads to understanding of evil and our creating it. We affect God for we carry awareness of action generated from within a physical existence obtained 'within' an existence of space, time, matter, and energy, into the real world of God. We, as individual units of knowing, as individual units of action directed by free will (See Tractate 3: Boethius and Free Will)[8], are responsible for all the 'evil', which exists in God.

The War & Peace of a New Metaphysical Perception

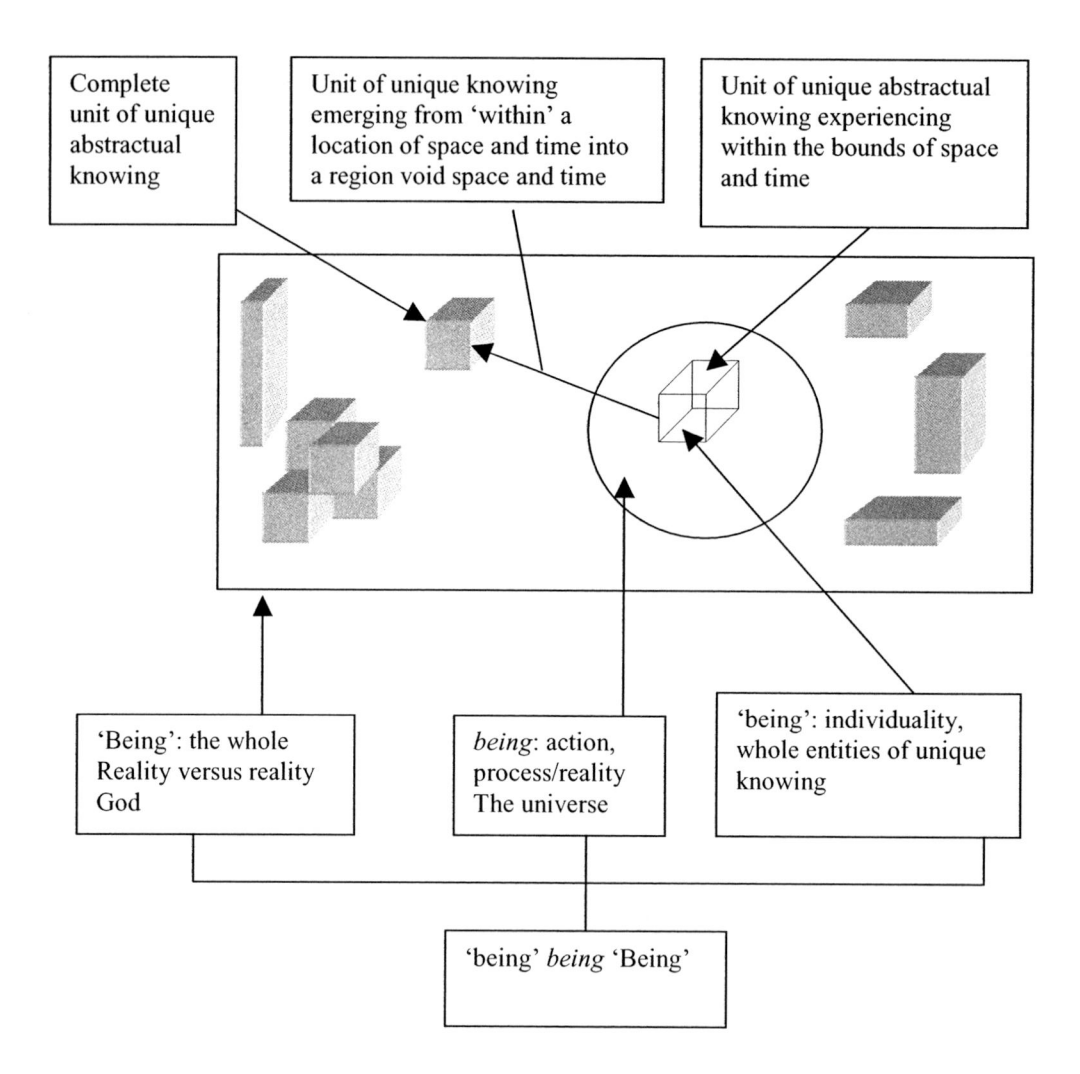

| Complete unit of unique abstractual knowing | Unit of unique knowing emerging from 'within' a location of space and time into a region void space and time | Unit of unique abstractual knowing experiencing within the bounds of space and time |

| 'Being': the whole Reality versus reality God | *being*: action, process/reality The universe | 'being': individuality, whole entities of unique knowing |

'being' *being* 'Being'

The same argument applies to the 'good'. But it is not the 'good' with which the concept of theodicy is concerned. It is the debate regarding the relationship between 'evil' and God and how such a relationship affects humankind with which theodicy is concerned. And it is here that Leibniz erred. It is at this point that Leibniz, having defined theodicy, should have turned the debate away from the concept of the relationship between 'evil' and God and how this relationship affects humanity and into the direction of the relationship between 'evil' and humanity and how the relationship affects God rather than how it affects ourselves.

Third

To create a term, which accelerates a paradoxical dilemma, embracing the very soul of the individual, is one thing, but to develop such a term based upon the foundation of another obscure term, omnibenevolence is quite another. Such obscurity does nothing but distance the concept of the original term, theodicy, from the ensuing chaos. As soon as one begins to formulate a discussion regarding theodicy that in any way proves threatening, the term of omnibenevolence is thrown into the fray and focuses the attention away from theodicy. And as soon as one switches to the concept of omnibenevolence the term theodicy is thrown into the fray and focuses the attention away from omnibenevolence..

So as not to fall into this trap, let's instead steadfastly focus in on omnibenevolence, the foundation of theodicy itself. Let's examine just why it is that omnibenevolence is not one of the 'omni-' characteristics of God.

By definition God is the 'whole'. Unless religions are willing to let go of the three characteristics they have associated as characteristics of God, omniscience – all knowing - knowing all, omnipotence – all powerful - having the power to do anything, and omnipresence – all presence - present everywhere, then we will have to assume they are part of the definition of God. Science and philosophy use this definition as their starting point when debating religion regarding the legitimacy of the concept of God. Since religions have not unilaterally agreed to change their primary definition of God, we have no choice but to proceed from there. To proceed with this dialectic on any other basis would undermine not only religions but the very purpose of discussing this issue.

With this established let's examine the implications of the concepts of 'omni-' and then examine why it is relevant to apply the prefix 'omni' to knowledge, power, and presence but irrelevant to apply the prefix 'omni' to benevolence.

Error through the active process of extrapolation as opposed to the passive process of definition

Definition is one means by which concepts of perception can be established and legitimized. Process is another. There is no doubt that establishment of the legitimacy of a perceptual concept through definition is a process, but it is a passive process. The other form of establishing the legitimacy of a perceptual concept is through an active process. In this case the process would be what we would call the process of extrapolation.

'Omni-' means all. 'All' implies the other extreme of nothing. As we understand it, knowledge, knowing, exists. If knowledge, knowing, exists, even if it is infinite, it is possible for there to be a total summation of knowledge – knowing. It is possible for there to be the universal set of knowledge or what we might call the 'whole'. On the other hand, the least amount of knowledge, knowing, is no knowledge, no knowing, no existence of knowing, no existence. Whether this state of existence exists or not is debatable. But we are not here to examine that particular issue. We are here to examine the issue regarding the validity of theodicy. As such we must look at the very minimal extreme of knowledge's existence, the very minimal extreme of knowing.

On one end of the extreme of knowing appears to be the whole. On the other end of the extreme of knowing appears to be none, no, zero knowledge. There is, however, no apparent knowing existence we are presently capable of perceiving which is the opposite of a knowing existence.. As such there is no apparent existence of negative knowledge, negative knowing. There is knowledge about negative things but no apparent knowledge about the opposite of knowledge.

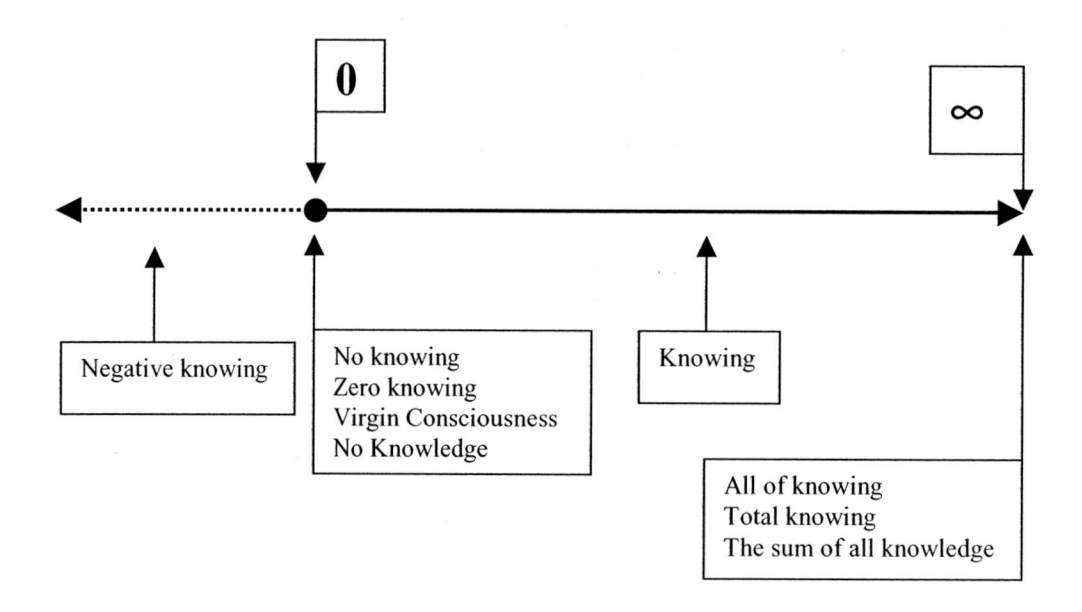

The War & Peace of a New Metaphysical Perception

```
         0                                              ∞
         ↓                                              ↓
◄·······················•────────────────────────────────►
    ↑              ↑                  ↑                 ↑
┌─────────┐  ┌──────────────┐    ┌─────────┐
│ Negative│  │ No knowing   │    │ Knowing │
│ knowing │  │ Zero knowing │    └─────────┘
└─────────┘  │ Virgin Consciousness│
             │ No Knowledge │
             └──────────────┘
                              ┌──────────────────────┐
                              │ All of knowing       │
                              │ Total knowing        │
                              │ The sum of all knowledge │
                              └──────────────────────┘
```

Knowledge therefore reaches from the one extreme to another. The terms, infinity and zero represent the extremes. The extremes reach from the concept of an infinite quantity of the item, to the possibility of there being none at all, no knowing, no existence, the rejection of Descartes', 'Cogito, ergo sum, I think, therefore I am.'. It does not get any less than none at all.

As such the 'whole', the summation, total knowledge is a concept that exists for knowledge. This in turn makes the 'whole' the greatest possible accumulation of knowledge of which we are capable of understanding, perceiving. It is, therefore, logical to assign the concept of omniscience to the most all-encompassing entity of which we can conceive.

This perception of 'omni-' applies similarly to the concepts of power and presence. We cannot conceive of anything less than zero power, no power, and we cannot conceive of anything less than zero presence, no presence. As such the concepts of omnipotence and omnipresence take on a legitimate form of being a possible characteristic for God, for the 'whole'.

What about benevolence? One may say benevolence also has a maximum of infinity and a minimum of zero. But does it? When we think of 'good' we think of its opposite evil. Benevolence is unlike knowledge, power, and presence for benevolence does not stop at zero on the line of continuance. Benevolence, 'good', on a line of continuum moves past zero and accelerates into the region of its opposite, 'bad'. The continuum upon which benevolence is located is a line not a ray and it extends in both directions infinitely far. In addition benevolence does not have a starting point which is a constant. Its starting point fluctuates with the fickleness of what the social perceptions of 'right' and 'wrong' define it to be depending upon the culture, times, and convenience of humankind. For example, taking a life may be murder (wrong) in one case, but socially correct in another (war, capital punishment)

One may say, 'The extremes of knowledge, power, and presence also extend infinitely far in two directions.' But does it? How can one have something less than no knowing, no power, no presence. There is nothing of which we, as a specie, presently conceive that applies to the concept of the opposite of power and presence.

As such 'omnibenevolence' does not apply to the concept of God unless one rejects what our specie has developed as characteristics of God over the last ten millennia. It is not our place, within this discourse, to say this cannot be done, but on the other hand neither is it our place, within this discourse, to say this can or should be done. As such we are limited, in this discourse by the constraints of time and space, to discuss one small error of philosophy.

The War & Peace of a New Metaphysical Perception

Part II: Resolving the issue with a new metaphysical perception

There is a fundamental flaw in both the process of definition and the process of extrapolation Leibniz used when he created the term theodicy.

Theodicy adds a fourth characteristic to God, omnibenevolence

There are two means of developing perceptions of God. One can develop a perception of God through the passive process of definition as was addressed in Part I of this tractate or one can develop a perception of God through the active process of extrapolation. Extrapolation is most commonly used in terms of two-dimensional lines n a planar graph or two-dimensional lines in three-dimensional space. However, extrapolation can also be used in terms of three-dimensional forms in three-dimensional space immersed in the fabric of time and space creating what we call 'real' perceptions.

Developing a perception of God, through the active process of extrapolation, is much like putting together a solid three-dimensional puzzle. Three-dimensional puzzles need to start with the inner piece, the core, the origin, and is considered the foundation of the puzzle.

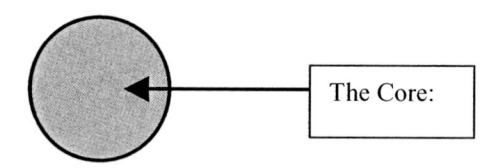

If one does not place the core first, then one is forced into building the first shell around an empty inner core.

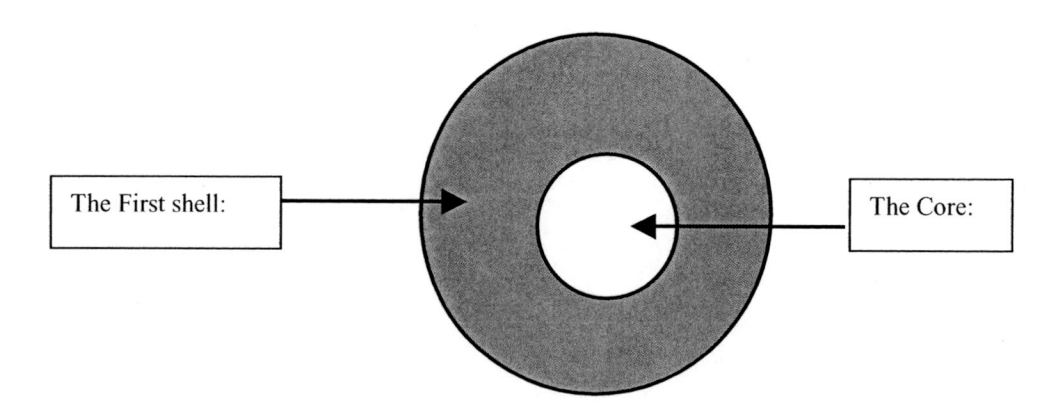

Once a shell is built around an empty core one cannot go back and fill in the core without dismantling the puzzle and starting over. Such a process is unstable and eventually will collapse upon the originators, be they religions, philosophies, or scientific theories.

So where does one begin in terms of putting together an abstractual understanding of a three dimensional puzzle of God? One does not begin with 'faith' nor does one begin with 'observation'. One begins with 'reason'.

Faith cannot act as the core for faith is diversified. Faith varies with culture, race, time, etc. This is not to say one ignores faith for one cannot begin with a statement of what the core is unless one has 'faith' in what it is one reasonable 'believes' makes up the core concept of God.

Observation cannot act as the core for very act of observing may in fact 'change' what it is one 'observes'. Such a concept is not only reinforced by the present day perception of 'critical philosophy' but by the scientific concept known as: The uncertainty principle. In addition, if we cannot demonstrate in an observable fashion what it is we establish as a 'reasonable' core, the concept we profess to be the core loses its very characteristic of being reasonable and thus losses its potential to be a believable core concept. In short such a core is unsubstantiated by science – what we observe, religion – what we believe, and philosophy – what we reason.

The core and the first shell therefore emerge out of the most primitive concepts found within our perceptual knowledge.

One would be truly arrogant to think they, personally, can build, create, the primary pieces: the core and the first shell of the puzzle.

This is where Leibniz erred. Leibniz was arrogant enough to believe he was both capable and intelligent enough to dismantle what humanity had spent thousands of years putting into place. Leibniz believed he alone could reestablish humanity's core concept of God.

When building his model of God, Leibniz presumptuously removed the core piece of the puzzle humanity had put into place. Having done so, Leibniz then proceeded to dismantle the first shell humanity had placed around the core.

Leibniz then, arbitrarily, replaced the core and first shell with his own version of a core, which he believed, should then act as 'the' metaphysical model of God humanity should accept as their starting point for understanding 'what' God was.

The term God is being used not as a religious/ontological term but as a philosophical/metaphysical term. Before one can understand God ontologically one must understand God metaphysically. Leibniz did not make this distinction and this was where he made his mistake in terms of understanding God through the active process of extrapolation.

Thus Leibniz moved the study of God from the traditional model of metaphysics into being the study of God from the new model of ontology. Thus it is metaphysicians became ontologists masquerading as metaphysician. Granted such masquerading had been, with the blessing of the church, occurring prior to Leibniz but it was not until Leibniz that the core of omniscience, a metaphysical term, was replaced with a core of omnibenevolence/theodicy, an ontological term

The War & Peace of a New Metaphysical Perception

Graphically such a transformation would appear as:

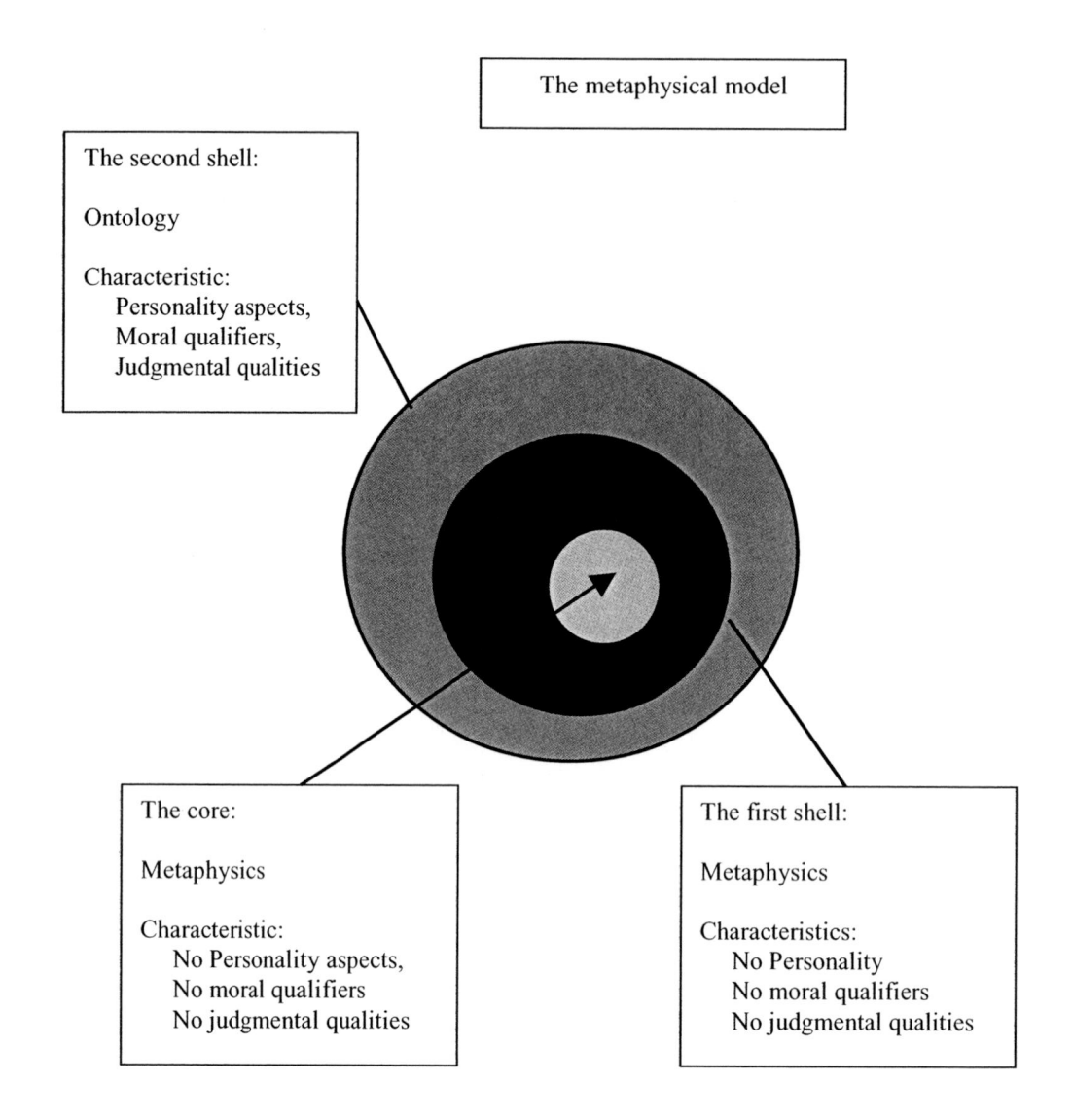

The metaphysical model

The second shell:

Ontology

Characteristic:
    Personality aspects,
    Moral qualifiers,
    Judgmental qualities

The core:

Metaphysics

Characteristic:
    No Personality aspects,
    No moral qualifiers
    No judgmental qualities

The first shell:

Metaphysics

Characteristics:
    No Personality
    No moral qualifiers
    No judgmental qualities

With the aid of Leibniz, transforming into the ontological model:

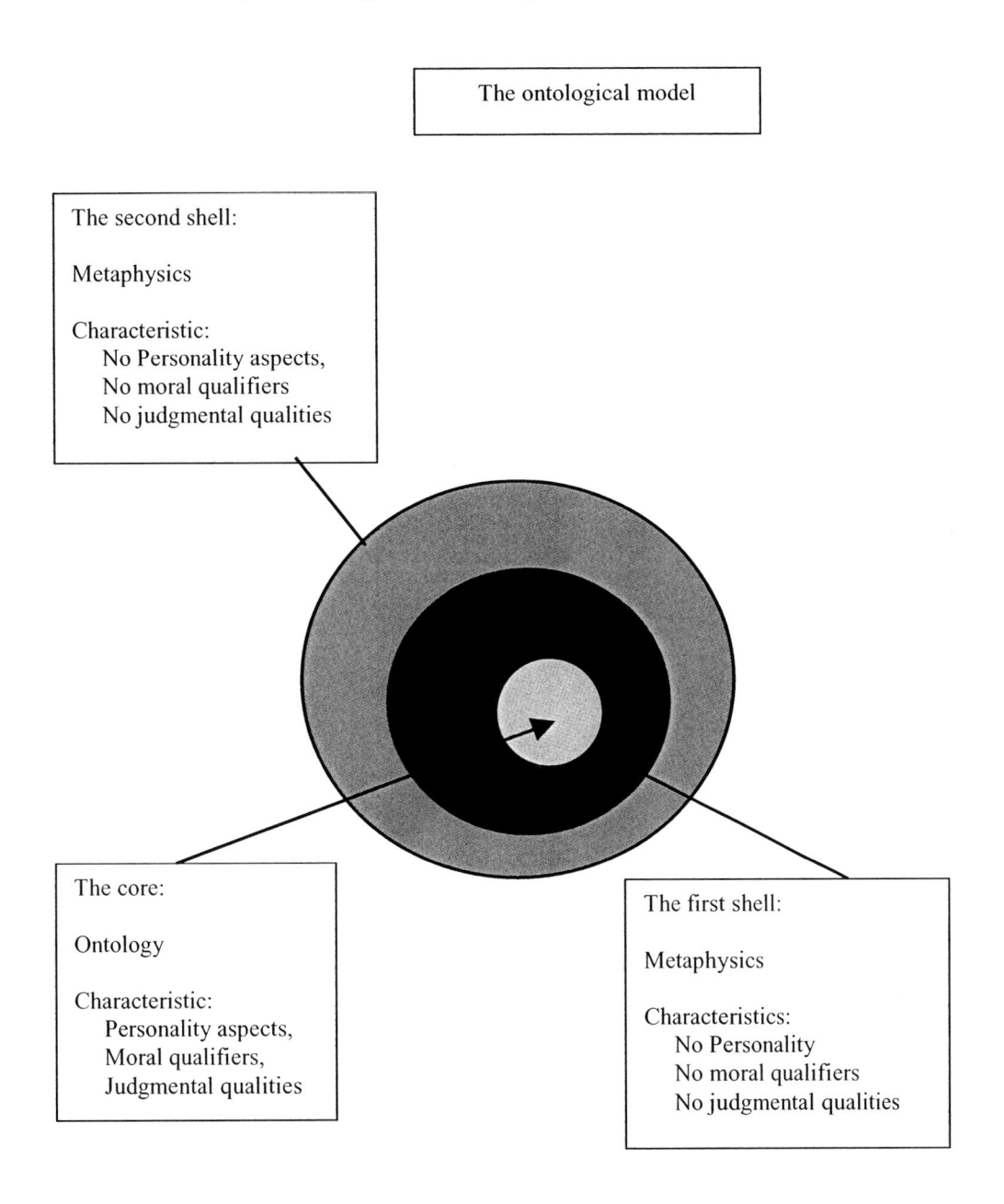

The ontological model

The second shell:

Metaphysics

Characteristic:
　No Personality aspects,
　No moral qualifiers
　No judgmental qualities

The core:

Ontology

Characteristic:
　Personality aspects,
　Moral qualifiers,
　Judgmental qualities

The first shell:

Metaphysics

Characteristics:
　No Personality
　No moral qualifiers
　No judgmental qualities

It had taken our specie tens of thousands of years to put the core and first shell into place.

So let's look at the active process of building an understanding of God through extrapolation in order to understand how Leibniz went 'wrong'.

Placing the first piece the core of the puzzle:

The Core: Omniscience

What was it our specie had been working to establish as their understanding of the essence of God? The primary piece, the core, comes from one of the 'omni-' concepts. The piece was omniscience, not just knowing, not just knowledge, but rather 'all' knowing, 'all' knowledge.

Such an aspect involves no 'personality trait', is 'non-judgmental in nature', involves no 'moral' qualifiers. Such an aspect is simply a state of existence or is not a state of existence. Something either is 'all' knowing or it is not 'all' knowing.

Thus the core emerges out of metaphysics as:

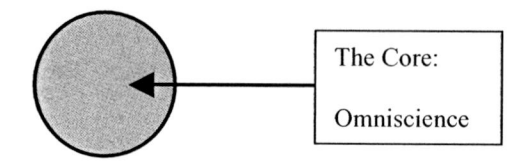

The Core: Omniscience

Without 'knowing', without awareness of itself, without knowing itself, God would have no significance, rather God would just 'be'. Without awareness of itself, God would simply be a 'passive' form of existence as opposed to an 'active' form of existence. The concept regarding 'active' versus 'passive' action will be more fully addressed in Tractate 6: Kant.

We as a specie, then expanded our idea of God as we evolved and grew. We expanded our idea of God to be a 'very' knowing entity and finally into being what we conceive God to be today which is the summation of all knowing, all knowledge and the self-awareness of Its being so . In short we have expanded God to be the 'whole' of all we believe we are capable or incapable of discovering. This is the core foundation of religions today. This not to say religions have not added various characteristics of personality, moral qualifiers, and judgmental quantifiers to God for they have taken the foundations of metaphysics and expanded upon the basics metaphysics has established as the foundation of a metaphysical definition of God. These additions, however, fall into the field of ontology rather than metaphysics.

All characteristics added to a perception of God are not ontological in nature for many such characteristics form shells beyond the layers ontology applies to the core and first shell formed by metaphysics.

It is reason/philosophy which must sort through what it is we observe/science and what it is we believe/religion and choose what it is which most reasonably acts as the core characteristic of God. As such it is 'all' knowing, knowing of all, the summation of knowledge which most reasonable acts as the core created through the process of 'active' extrapolation.

And why is this the case? Without 'knowing', without awareness, no process of extrapolation could occur let alone any form of 'active' extrapolation.

So the first piece, the core, is the concept of omniscience. Without any knowledge and awareness of it, the knowing of knowledge, there would be no 'God' as we conceive of the idea today.

After placing the core, the next task becomes building the first shell regarding our understanding of 'what' God is.

The First Shell: Omnipotence and Omnipresence

After placing the core piece, where does one go to find the pieces, which will form the first shell encompassing the core piece of omniscience? One again goes to the depository of knowledge built by humanity. But why go to the depository of knowledge built by humanity? Could there not be another source other than human knowledge? Perhaps but such a source is not available to us at this time.

A shell around a core is naturally more expansive than the core. The first shell appears to expand upon the core. But the first shell, in actuality does not expand upon the core but rather only appears to do so. In truth the first shell encompassing the core, protects the purity of the concept of the core itself. The first shell helps us as a specie to understand the core. This shell is composed of humanly crafted concepts placed around the core in as close a proximity to the core, as we are humanly capable of doing.

As such, this shell must contain concepts as closely allied to the core as possible in order to not contaminate or compromise the core concept we have metaphysically/philosophically/reasonably, cosmologically/scientifically/observationally, and ontologically/religiously/believably built of regarding the whole itself.

To discard the product we obtained through the use of the only perceptual tools we appear to possess as a specie, reason – observation – belief, is an action which leaves us with no foundation of action from which we launch our effort to understand not only our physical reality but to understand our abstractual Reality.

As a specie, we have attempted to attain this proximity in order to expand the puzzle. As a specie, we have subconsciously attempted to construct the core and first shell in such a way that no 'air' pockets of irrationality would be trapped between the core and the first shell we put into place. We did not want air pockets which would warp our picture of God.. We were truly sincere in our desires to know 'what' God, what the whole was in order to understand 'what' we were and 'why' we existed.

The shell we finally established as a specie was composed of two humanly understandable concepts, power and size. Neither of these 'had' to be put into place for the core, omniscience, implied both. We however, as a visual creature, wanted desperately to understand, to visualize God, for we recognized that to do so was the key to our most haunting questions: Where are we? What are we? Why do we exist?. We recognized size to be a pictorial concept and being a visual creature we felt the need to be able to picture the size of God, in order to better understand God.

The War & Peace of a New Metaphysical Perception

As such, the first shell is composed of the concept of size. God must be big enough to 'contain' all knowledge, knowing, and awareness of its knowing.

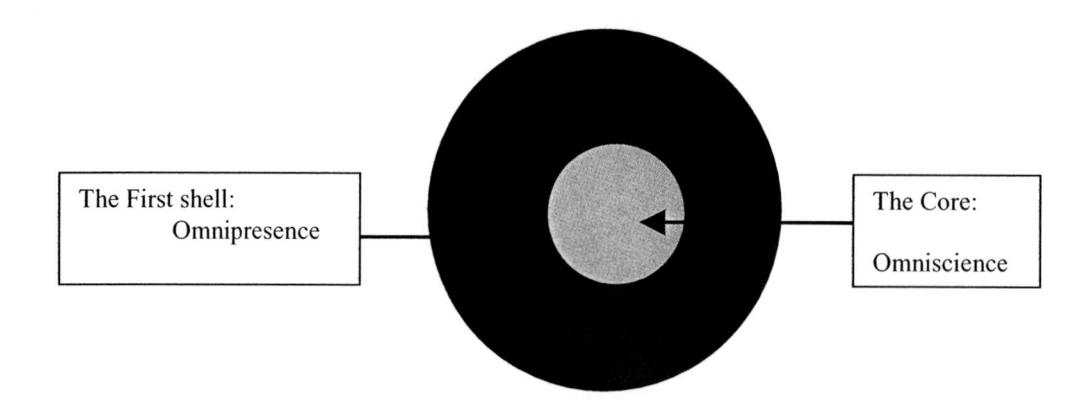

| The First shell: Omnipresence | | The Core: Omniscience |

Size was a puzzle piece characterized by the same three principles as omniscience:
1. Concepts of omni's help us as a specie to visualize a perception of what we hoped was a 'true', accurate picture of God.
2. Concepts of omni's are nonjudgmental in nature.
3. Concepts of omni have had a beginning point. In other words omni's were composed of a continuum stretching from zero to infinity.

The question then became, were there any other pieces of the puzzle that should or could be used to build the first shell, which was to wrap around the core concept of God, omniscience. Were there any other pieces, which could be used as a protective layer for omniscience?

After thousands of years of looking, our specie found what it considered to be just such a piece. We found a piece that helped us visualize God, was nonjudgmental, and had a beginning point of zero, an end point of infinity, and was implied by the core concept of omniscience. This piece was the summation of power, all power, omnipotence.

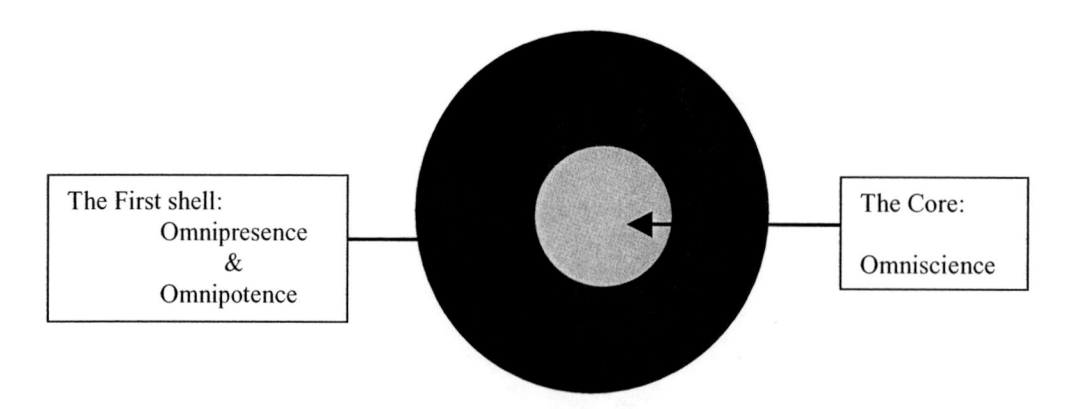

| The First shell: Omnipresence & Omnipotence | | The Core: Omniscience |

As a specie, we recognize the concept of power but we do not recognize the concept regarding the opposite of power. The question arises: Is power used for 'evil' purposes the opposite of power used for 'good'? That is not the issue we are addressing. What we are addressing is the concept of power itself and who would deny that having the ability to perform, having the ability to initiate 'evil', 'bad', 'inappropriate', and 'abusive' actions is any less a form of simple, pure, raw power than the having the ability to perform, having the ability to initiate 'good', 'nice', 'appropriate', and 'warm' actions.

As such there is power and there is a summation of power. Power can be understood to exist and be diminished all the way down to a point of having no power at all, zero power, but after that we cannot conceive of power being reduced any further. We can reduce power to the point of no power, pure power, without debating, without being judgmental, in terms of reducing it any further.

Leibniz and the error of addition

Leibniz added omnibenevolence to the first shell.

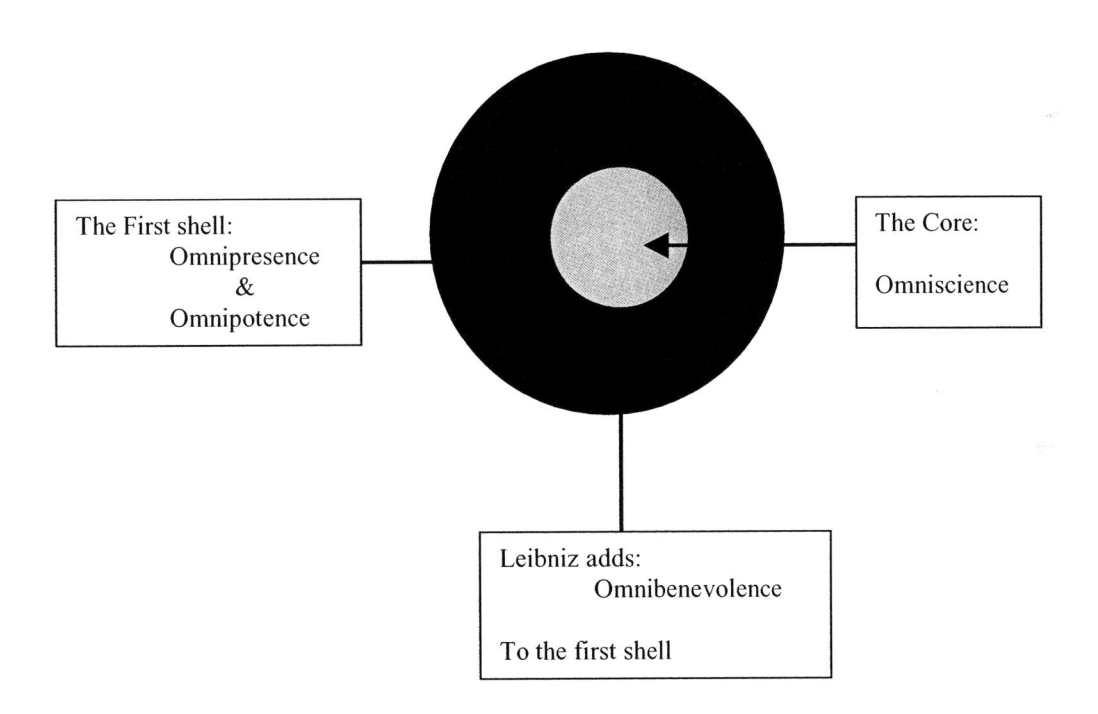

```
The First shell:            The Core:
  Omnipresence              Omniscience
       &
  Omnipotence

        Leibniz adds:
        Omnibenevolence
        To the first shell
```

Leibniz did not add omnibenevolence to the first shell based upon reason but rather Leibniz added omnibenevolence to the first shell based upon his personal perception that such a characteristic logically belonged with other impersonal, nonjudgmental, nonmoralistic characteristics of God.

Such an action is based upon faith rather than reason and faith is the perceptual tool of ontologists.

Thus it is, Leibniz began his examination regarding his concept of theodicy. It is from the very definition of the term theodicy that Leibniz, as a philosopher, should have begun to ask the question, 'Does the concept of 'omnibenevolence' belong as a part of this first shell?'

The War & Peace of a New Metaphysical Perception

If Leibniz had began his examination of the concept of theodicy with such a question, he would have recognized that 'omnibenevolence' does not meet the same standards we expected of omnipotence and omnipresence.

The three standards we required of the puzzle pieces forming the core and first shell ware:

> Standards required of the puzzle piece forming the core and first shell:
>
> 1. Concepts of omni's help us as a specie to visualize a perception of what we hoped was a 'true', accurate picture of God.
> 2. Concepts of omni's are nonjudgmental in nature.
> 3. Concepts of omni have had a beginning point. In other words omni's were composed of a continuum stretching from zero to infinity.

Omnibenevolence meets the first criteria of the first shell. Omnibenevolence helps us visualize, form a picture of God, but omnibenevolence is a judgmental concept. Benevolence depends upon one's point of view. What is benevolent and what is not benevolent depends upon ones culture, religion, personal perception, time in history and therefore does not meet the second criteria required of the pieces to be placed in the first shell.

But what of the third point required of various forms of 'omni's'?

> 3. Concepts of omni's have a beginning point. In other words omni's are composed of a continuum stretching from zero to infinity.

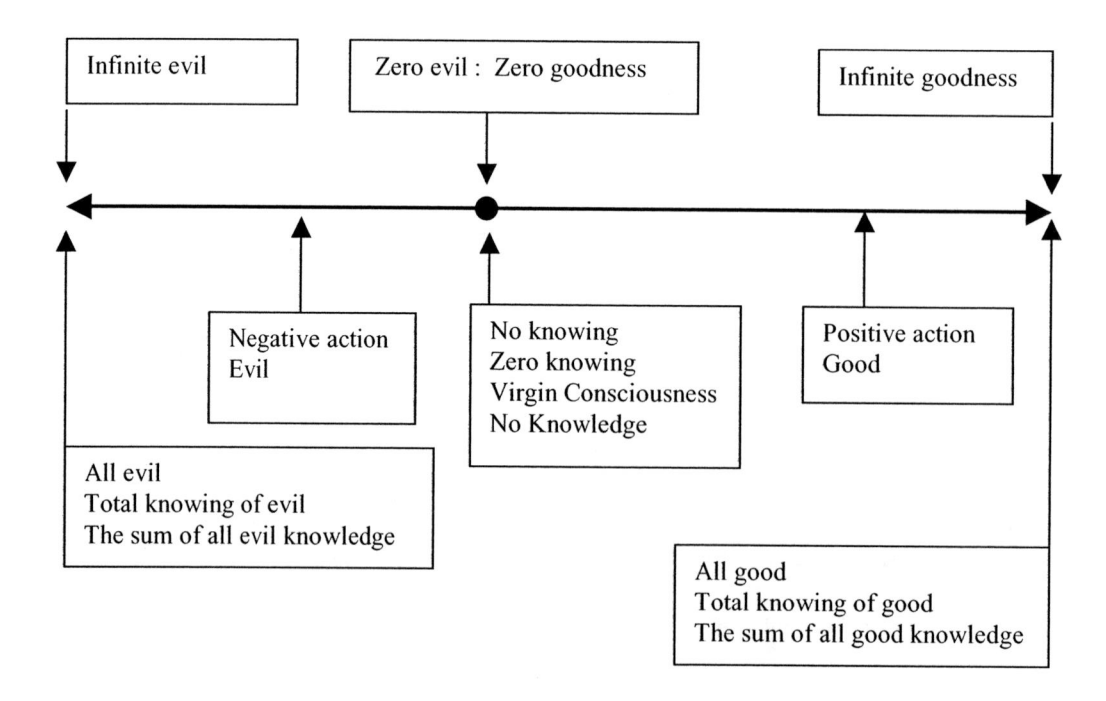

```
    Infinite evil          Zero evil : Zero goodness         Infinite goodness
         │                            │                              │
         ▼                            ▼                              ▼
    ◄────────────────────────────────●──────────────────────────────────►
                    ▲            ▲       ▲             ▲
                    │            │       │             │
              Negative action    No knowing       Positive action
              Evil               Zero knowing     Good
                                 Virgin Consciousness
                                 No Knowledge

    All evil
    Total knowing of evil                      All good
    The sum of all evil knowledge              Total knowing of good
                                               The sum of all good knowledge
```

It is clear from the graphic that omnibenevolence does not fit the parameter set out by the third characteristic required of the various forms of omni's. Omnibenevolence is not only subject to the concept of judgment but omnibenevolence, rather than finding itself beginning at the point zero and moving to infinity, finds itself having no beginning point and two rather than one point of infinity.

Omnibenevolence did not fall within the standards required by the passive action of definition required of a term encompassing the prefix, omni. In addition, omnibenevolence did not rise to all three standards required of a term encompassing the prefix, omni by the active action of extrapolation.

Leibniz ignored the requirements, which both active action and passive action placed upon our most fundamental metaphysical understandings of God. Leibniz striped away the first shell of God. He then took these two pieces, omnipotence and omnipresence, and mixed them with the concept of omnibenevolence. By doing so, Leibniz developed a less cohesive mixture of omni's to apply to the core of omniscience.

Leibniz then proceeded to mold and form this new but less cohesive mixture around our core concept of God. Due to the substandard qualities of this new omni mix, Leibniz created a bubble of air between the first shell and the core surrounding our understanding of God, and the result has been the rotting away, drying out, cracking of the first shell. This in turn has initiated a form of dry rot within the core itself.

The result has been the acceleration of hostility, anger, and rage individuals feel towards God which are perpetuated by the perception that God 'allows' 'evil', 'bad' things to happen to 'good' people. The natural extension of such perceptions leads to the belief that God does not 'care' about us.

It is time to remove omnibenevolence from the mix composing the first shell regarding our understanding of God. It is time to reestablish the fundamental metaphysical characteristics of the first shell as it had previously been. It is time to move on in our efforts to understand God, understand ourselves, and understand our responsibilities to the whole within which we find ourselves to exist, so we can fulfill these very responsibilities.

It is only natural to ask several questions at this point. Are we willing to let go of theodicy being a metaphysical characteristic as Leibniz established? Are we willing to accept the concept of omniscience, omnipresence, and omnipotence as the first key pieces leading to the understanding of God: If the answer is yes, then the question becomes, 'What next?'

If omniscience is the core and omnipotence and omnipresence compose the first shell surrounding omniscience, than what is the composition of the next layer, the composition of the second shell regarding our understanding of God?

The Second Shell: Answers to three questions

Do we have any ideas regarding what the second shell should be?' Subgroups of humanity thought it might be composed of their particular religious dogmas. These dogmas ranged from Hinduism, Christianity, Islam, Buddhism, Judaism, Wickam, New Thought, Zorasticism, etc. But religion proved to be not only 'inter' and 'intra' adversarial but adversarial towards our natural desire to observe/science and our natural desire to reason/philosophy.

The War & Peace of a New Metaphysical Perception

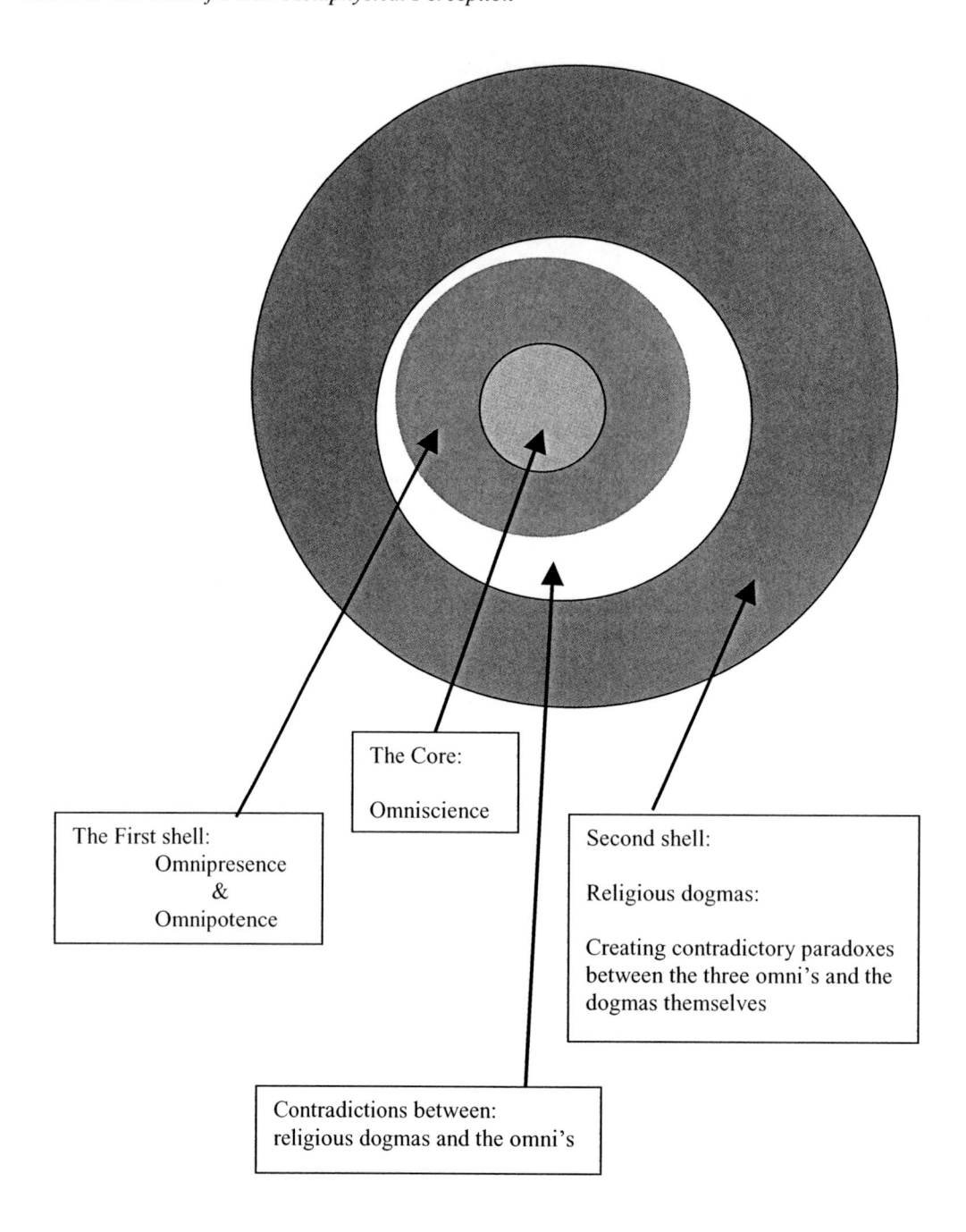

The Core:

Omniscience

The First shell:
Omnipresence
&
Omnipotence

Second shell:

Religious dogmas:

Creating contradictory paradoxes between the three omni's and the dogmas themselves

Contradictions between: religious dogmas and the omni's

In spite of the adversarial positions religious dogmas took, these subgroups of humanity insisted upon placing such dogmas around the first shell, omnipresence, omnipotence, and the core of omniscience. This second shell is in place even today.

The very fact the second shell of religious dogmas and the first shell of the omni's are not a tight fit is indicated by the insurmountable contradictory dilemmas constantly emerging out of the philosophical, scientific, and religious obfuscating dilemmas generated when attempting to reconcile the religious dogmas, scientific models, and philosophical theories with the metaphysics of the omni's.

The Error of Leibniz

The same process of attempting to build a second shell occurred with science and it's concept of Aristotelian passive observation and with philosophy and its concept of Kantian active observation. Neither religion nor science nor philosophy appears able to adequately build a second shell alone. It appears we will need to build a second shell incorporating all three forms of perception.

It appears the core and first shell must by definition as well as by the active action of extrapolation remain the domain of metaphysics. But, one may ask: Are not concepts of omniscience, omnipotence, and omnipresence aspects of religion versus being aspects of metaphysics? No, for the concept of the summation of knowing, summation of knowledge, summation of the whole, summation of power – the ability to act, is nothing short of the summation of what it is we observe/science and the summation of what it is we believe/religion emerging out of the most basic foundation of our ability to reason. In short the foundation is metaphysical in nature.

It is from metaphysics itself that we find religion, science, and yes even philosophy itself emerges.

The War & Peace of a New Metaphysical Perception

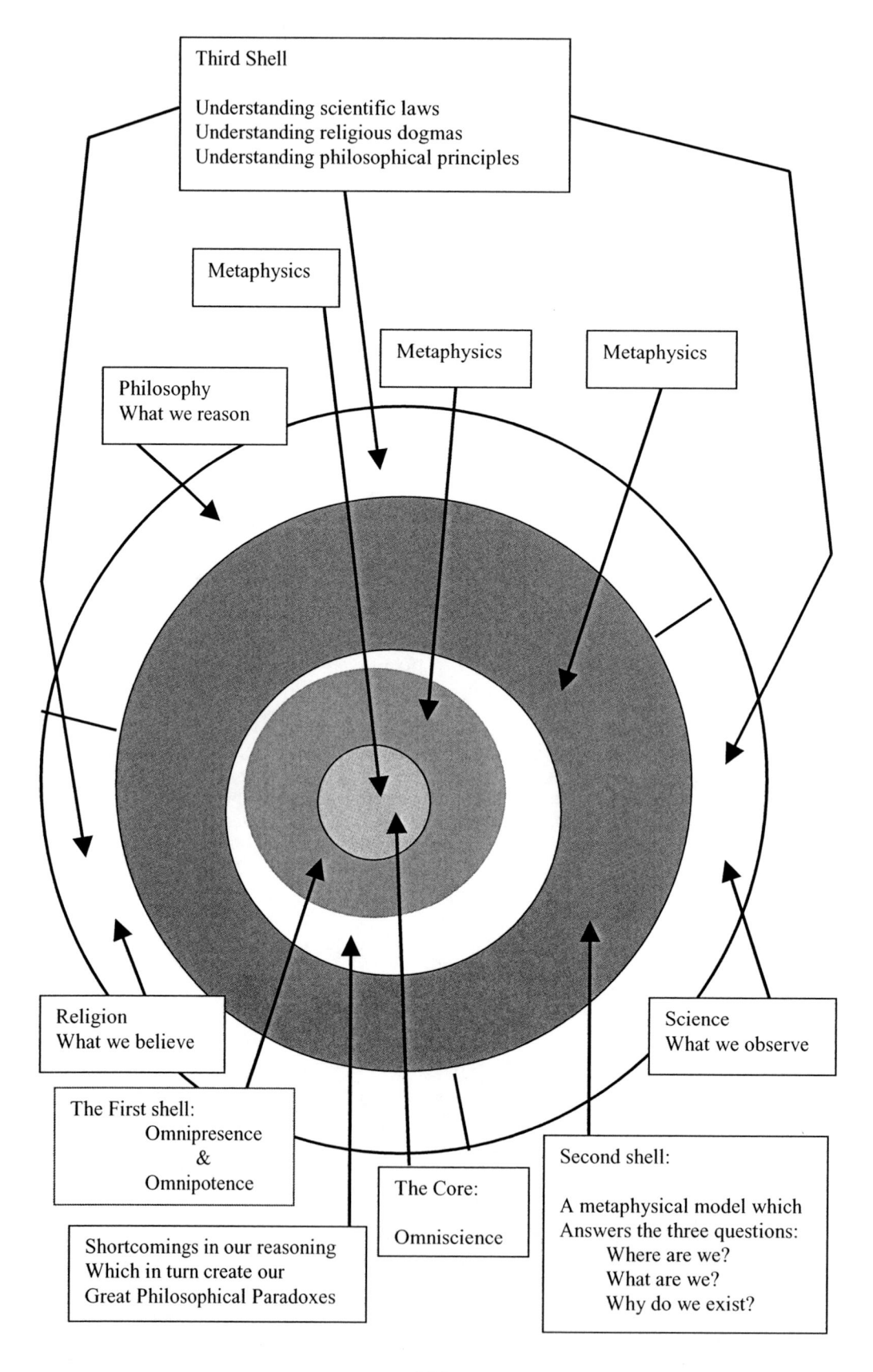

Third Shell

Understanding scientific laws
Understanding religious dogmas
Understanding philosophical principles

Metaphysics

Metaphysics

Metaphysics

Philosophy
What we reason

Religion
What we believe

Science
What we observe

The First shell:
   Omnipresence
   &
   Omnipotence

The Core:
Omniscience

Second shell:

A metaphysical model which
Answers the three questions:
   Where are we?
   What are we?
   Why do we exist?

Shortcomings in our reasoning
Which in turn create our
Great Philosophical Paradoxes

There appears to a complete form of shell missing between the first shell and the third shell we have constructed. This incomplete second shell should be composed of a metaphysical system, which answers the three questions: Where are we? What are we? and Why do we exist? Our present metaphysical systems do not seem to fit well with the first shell and core which metaphysics has established. Despite all our attempts to establish a metaphysical system which answers the three basic questions which have haunted our specie for what seems to be time eternal, there appears to be a lack of a consensus between ourselves as individual members of our specie in terms of 'Where it is we think we are.' 'What it is we think we are.' and 'Why it is we think we exist.'

As a specie we appear to be historically leaning towards the concept that the second shell may be composed of fragmented pieces of science, religion, and philosophy. These fragmented pieces all appear to be simultaneously providing us with an understanding of the three questions.

Where are we?

> Science, religion, and philosophy all appear to suggest: We are located within the whole.

What are we?

> Religion, philosophy, and science all appear to suggest: If we are located within the whole, then we are a piece, we are a part of the whole.

Why do we exist?

> Philosophy, science, and religion all appear to suggest: If we are in within the whole and if we are a part of the whole, then we exist to interact with the whole, we exist to aid the whole in being what it is the whole itself is.

The War & Peace of a New Metaphysical Perception

Graphically we can demonstrate such a perception as:

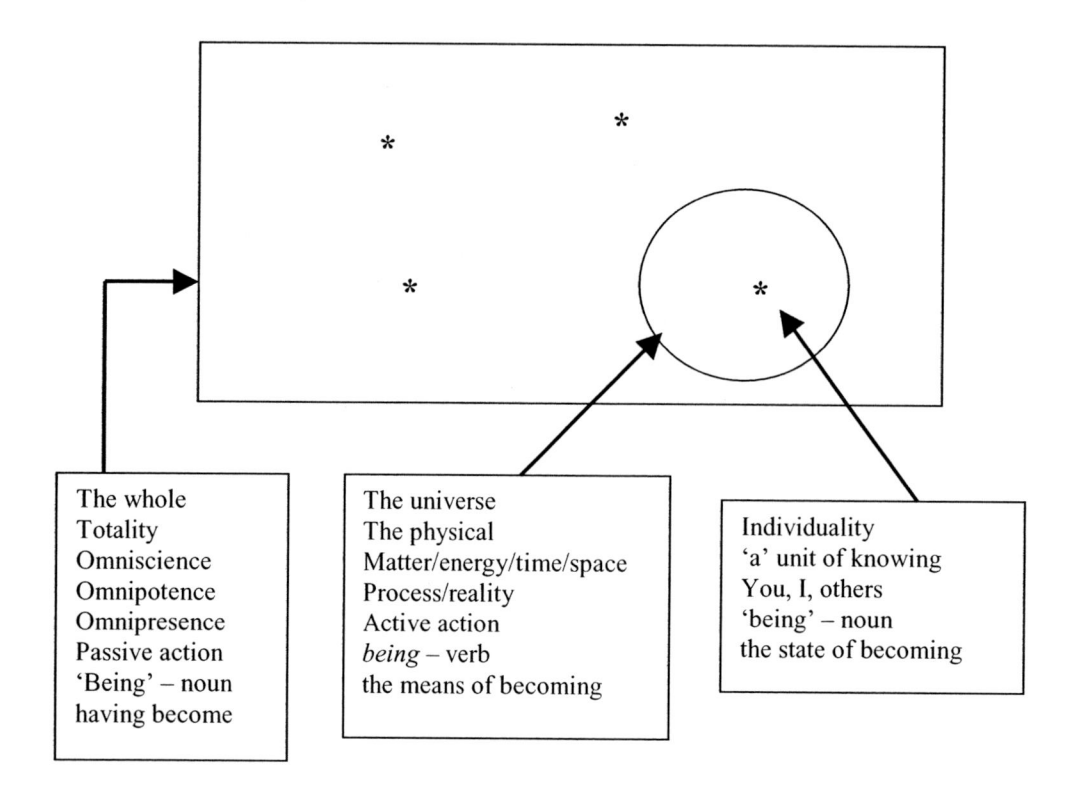

The whole	The universe	Individuality
Totality	The physical	'a' unit of knowing
Omniscience	Matter/energy/time/space	You, I, others
Omnipotence	Process/reality	'being' – noun
Omnipresence	Active action	the state of becoming
Passive action	*being* – verb	
'Being' – noun	the means of becoming	
having become		

Such a perception is best described metaphysically as 'being' *being* 'Being'.

The location of 'imperfection'

The question regarding Leibniz then becomes: If imperfection exists, where does imperfection lie within such a system, within a system of 'being' *being* 'Being'?

The Error of Leibniz

Imperfection lies in two locations:

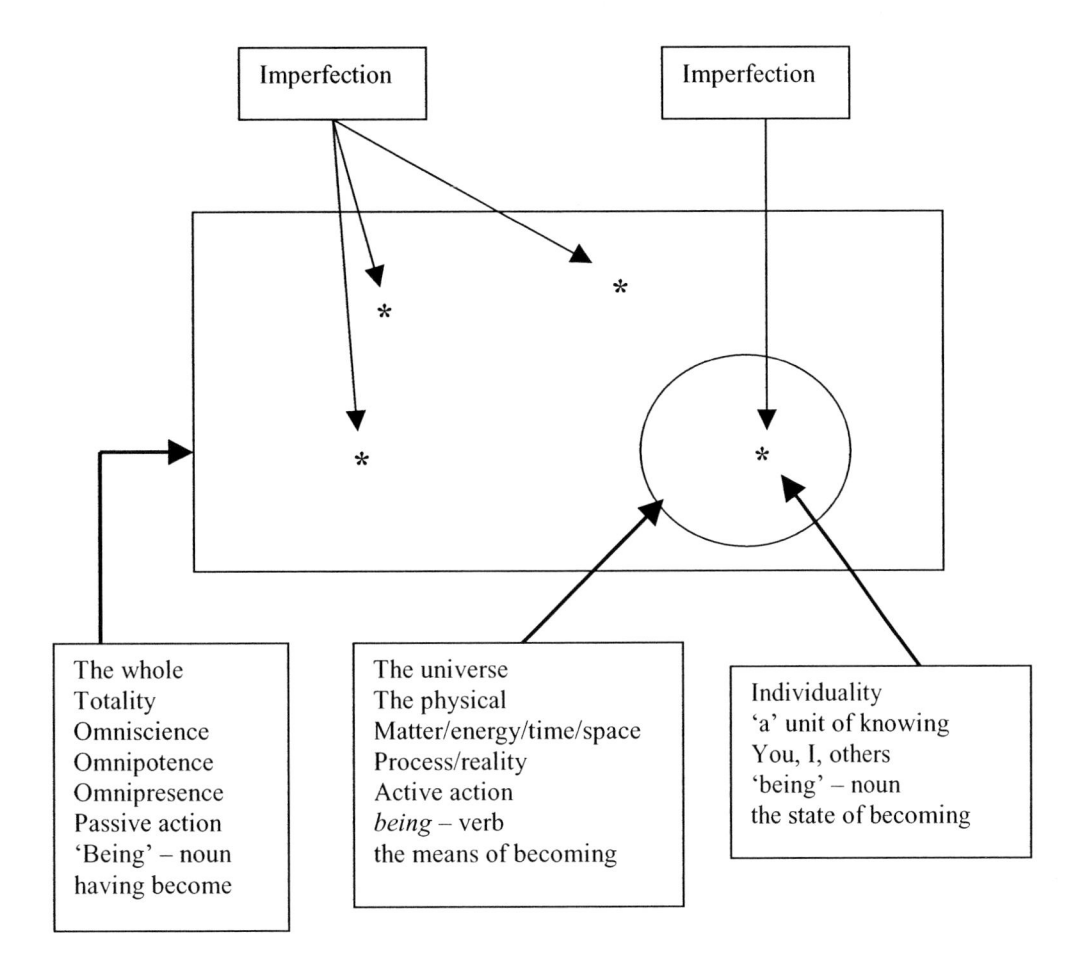

```
        ┌──────────────┐         ┌──────────────┐
        │ Imperfection │         │ Imperfection │
        └──────┬───────┘         └──────┬───────┘
               │                        │
               ▼                        ▼
        ┌─────────────────────────────────────────┐
        │         *              *                │
        │                                         │
        │                         ┌─────┐         │
        │    *                    │  *  │         │
        │                         └─────┘         │
        └─────────────────────────────────────────┘
```

The whole	The universe	Individuality
Totality	The physical	'a' unit of knowing
Omniscience	Matter/energy/time/space	You, I, others
Omnipotence	Process/reality	'being' – noun
Omnipresence	Active action	the state of becoming
Passive action	*being* – verb	
'Being' – noun	the means of becoming	
having become		

Imperfection lies 'within' the sub unit of knowing found inside the whole but outside the location of its development and imperfection lies 'within' the sub unit of knowing found inside the whole but inside the location of its development.

Imperfection is found within the sub units because the sub unit is less than the whole and therefore does not rise to the level of the whole because of the very fact that it is not the whole and by the very definition of 'sub unit', can never be 'the' whole.

The Location of 'perfection'

The second question regarding Leibniz then becomes: If perfection exists, where does perfection lie within such a system, within a system of 'being' *being* 'Being'?

The War & Peace of a New Metaphysical Perception

Perfection lies in one location:

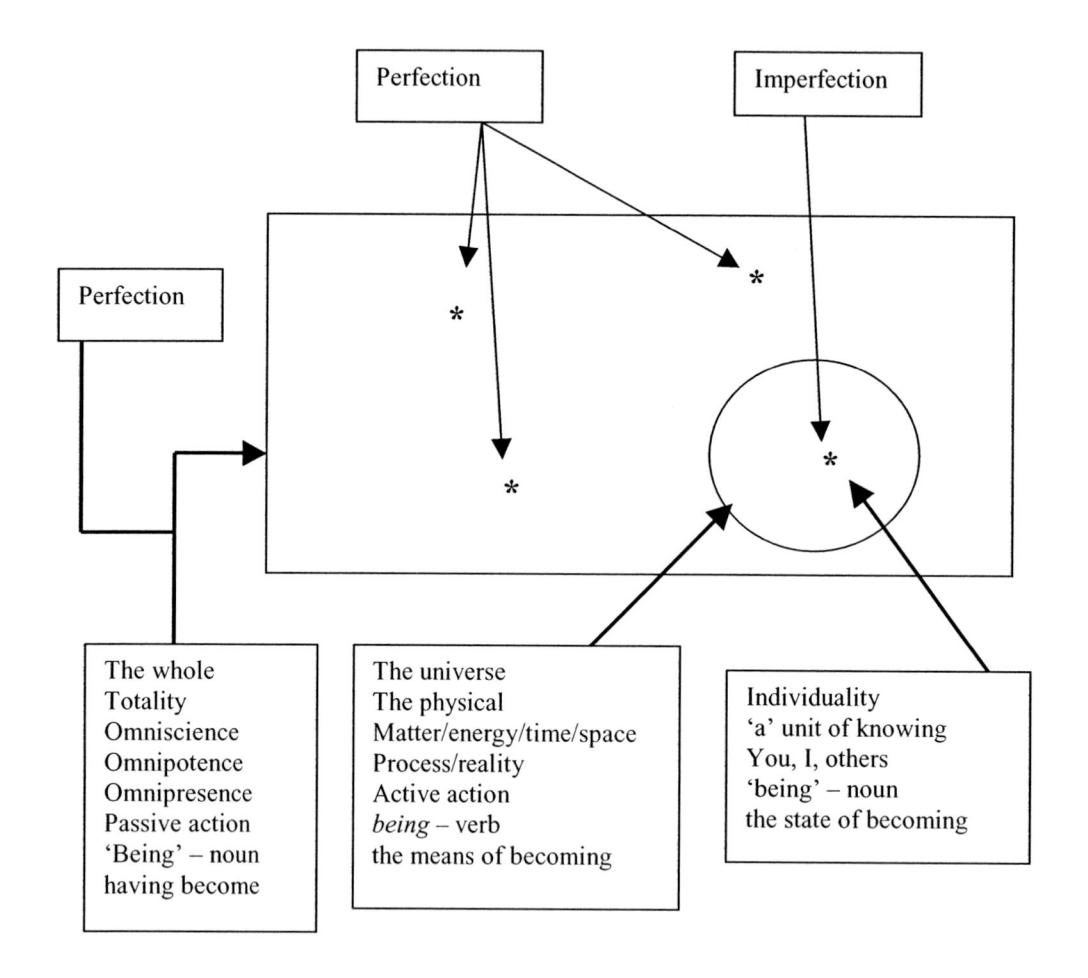

```
                    ┌──────────────┐      ┌──────────────┐
                    │  Perfection  │      │ Imperfection │
                    └──────┬───────┘      └──────┬───────┘
                           │    ╲                │
    ┌──────────────┐       │     ╲               │
    │  Perfection  │       ▼      ╲              │
    └──────┬───────┘       *       ╲             │
           │                        ▼            ▼
           │                        *      ⎛     *  ⎞
           │                               ⎝        ⎠
           ▼                                  ▲
                                              │
                                              │
┌─────────────────┐  ┌────────────────────┐  ┌──────────────────────┐
│ The whole       │  │ The universe       │  │ Individuality        │
│ Totality        │  │ The physical       │  │ 'a' unit of knowing  │
│ Omniscience     │  │ Matter/energy/     │  │ You, I, others       │
│ Omnipotence     │  │   time/space       │  │ 'being' – noun       │
│ Omnipresence    │  │ Process/reality    │  │ the state of         │
│ Passive action  │  │ Active action      │  │   becoming           │
│ 'Being' – noun  │  │ being – verb       │  │                      │
│ having become   │  │ the means of       │  │                      │
│                 │  │   becoming         │  │                      │
└─────────────────┘  └────────────────────┘  └──────────────────────┘
```

Perfection lies 'within' the whole as the whole. Perfection is the whole for all that is is the whole. The whole is perfectly what it is. The whole is a perfect impression of itself, a perfect resemblance of what is, a perfect appearance of 'all'. The whole is the only 'location' 'within' which a perfect semblance of what perfection is

But cannot the same be said of each and every sub unit? Isn't each sub unit a perfect semblance of itself? Absolutely, but we are discussing the concepts of 'perfection' and 'imperfection' and by definition:

> Perfection: From the Latin *perfectio* meaning 'completeness' or 'completion'[9]

As such the caption having read 'imperfection' in terms of the sub unit of knowing found 'within' the whole but 'outside' the location of development of the sub unit of knowing has been relabeled 'perfection' for such a sub unit is both perfect and imperfect simultaneously.

It is only the whole, which strictly retains the label perfection, and it is only the sub unit found located 'within' the whole and 'within' the location of development which strictly retains the label 'imperfection' for it has not yet attained 'completion'. It has not yet attained 'completeness'.

But one may argue that the 'whole' appears to 'change' within the metaphysical system of 'being' *being* 'Being' and thus it would appear the whole should strictly retain the label of 'imperfection' for it appears to be an active dynamic system and thus is never reaching 'completeness'. The issue regarding the whole changing while simultaneously not changing is an exhaustive issue which will be addressed in the more appropriate tractate, Tractate 6: Kant and its subsection: 'How something which is unchangeable can change and remain unchangeable'. But why wait for the tractate regarding Kant? We will wait for Kant because it was Kant who moved the metaphysical perception of a passive static Aristotelian system into being an active dynamic Kantian system.

Conclusion

Religiously, scientifically, and philosophically the metaphysical perception of 'being' *being* 'Being' is best described as symbiotic panentheism. Such a term incorporates three aspects:

Panentheism:

1. Religiously: all in God
2. Scientifically: all in the whole
3. Philosophically: all in Being

Symbiosis:

1. Scientifically: The elements of the whole interact with the whole to make the whole what it is in terms of the whole being an active whole
2. Religiously: God and humanity interact one with the other
3. Philosophically: 'being' interacts with 'Being'

The War & Peace of a New Metaphysical Perception

The fusion power of the two terms lies in the power of reason as directed by metaphysics itself. Such an understanding becomes clearer when demonstrated graphically:

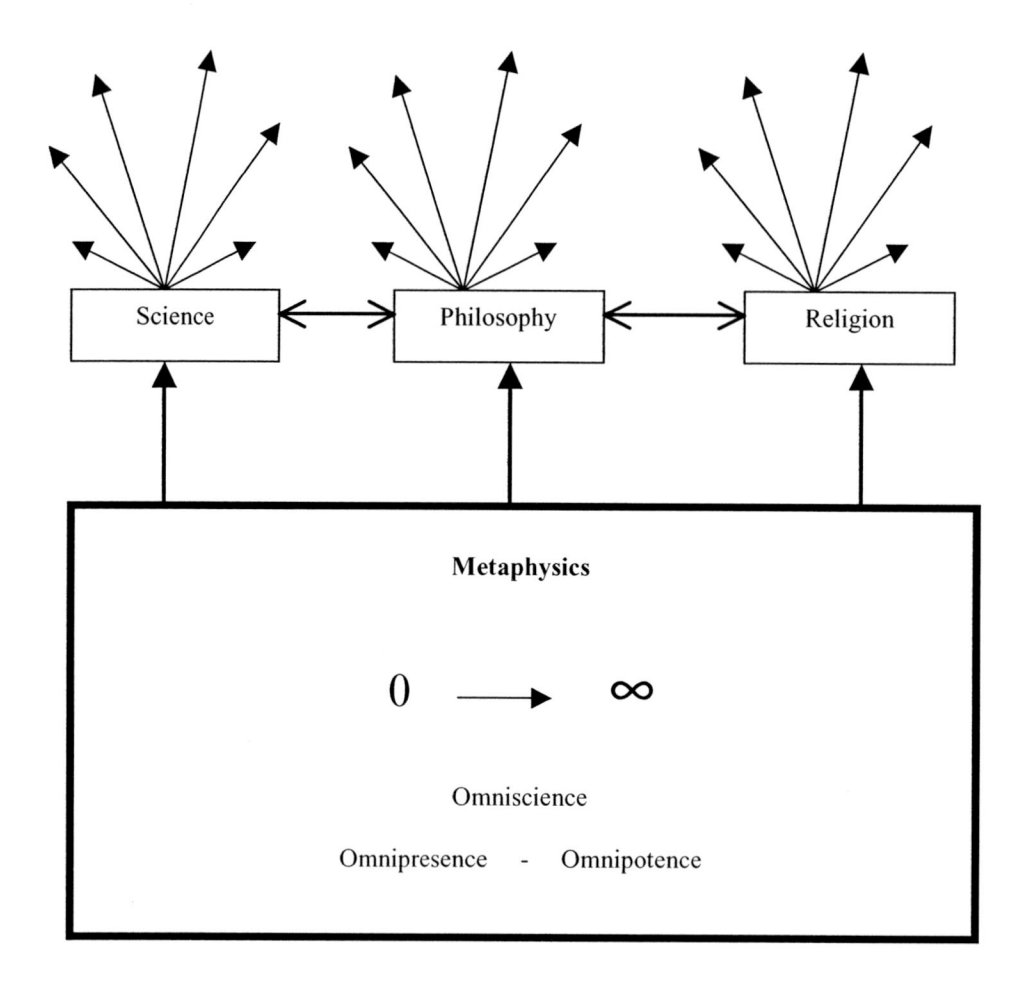

```
        Science  <--->  Philosophy  <--->  Religion
           ↑                ↑                  ↑
  ┌─────────────────────────────────────────────────┐
  │                   Metaphysics                    │
  │                                                  │
  │                  0  ───▶  ∞                      │
  │                                                  │
  │                    Omniscience                   │
  │                                                  │
  │           Omnipresence  -  Omnipotence           │
  └─────────────────────────────────────────────────┘
```

The second shell is best described as a metaphysical system, which explains what it is we have observed, believed, and reasoned throughout the ages. Such a shell is based upon the metaphysical concepts describing the 'overall' picture of the whole. Be that as it may, we have not yet come to a consensus as to just what it is all of our perceptual tools, reason, observation, and faith have in common. Such a state of confusion does not exist because we 'cannot' come to a consensus regarding the existence of a metaphysical system capable of answering the three fundamental questions but rather the lack of a consensus exists because we have not made a concerted coordinated effort to do so.

We have not made a concerted effort to find acceptable answers to each of the three questions that have been haunting us ever since we began asking the questions. We have not composed the answers to these questions because we have not made a concerted effort to find a metaphysical understanding which bridges the gap between the concept of the three omni's and our three most haunting of questions.

The Error of Leibniz

This is not to say there have not been great philosophical, religious, and scientific thinkers who have made a concerted effort of their own to resolve the issues. Tractates 1, 2, 3, 4, and now 5 have examined such great thinkers and offer a resolution to the issues which they have attempted to address but been unsuccessful at resolving.

Tractates 6 – 12 will address the issues other great individual thinkers such as Kant, Russell, Hegel, Einstein, etc. have to offer.

The lack therefore of a concerted effort has not been due to some individuals but rather the lack of a concerted effort has been due to our collective desire to do so.

The means of finding this second shell, which bridges the interrelationship between the three omni's and the three fundamental questions haunting our specie, is to find 'a' metaphysical model which answers the three fundamental questions which face religion, science, and philosophy simultaneously. Pitting the model against our greatest of philosophical paradoxes can test the model of such an understanding. If the model cannot resolve these paradoxes then we are not yet ready to move onto other paradoxes awaiting more advanced metaphysical dilemmas that surely await us.

It appears it may serve us well to begin the process of building this second shell in order to fill in the air pocket between our visualization of the most basic fundamentals of God and the shell composed of the three basic questions religion, science, and philosophy are all attempting to resolve. It appears this second shell, this metaphysical model, may be the means of understanding omniscience, omnipotence, and omnipresence as it applies to ourselves. It appears that the second shell, a comprehensive universal (literally universal) metaphysical system, may in fact be the means through which we are to understanding the answers to the questions: 'Where are we? What are we? And, Why do we exist?'

What does finding the model of a universal metaphysical system have to do with Leibniz and theodicy? We have looked at a universal metaphysical model which might very well act as a primitive understanding, which might well resolve the paradoxes placed before us by Zeno, Aristotle, Boethius, and Copernicus. We are now about to enter the debate of paradoxes placed before us by Kant, Hegel, Russell, Einstein, Heidegger, Philosophy, and Society. But historically we have come to Leibniz and his concept of theodicy and it is the concept of God 'allowing' 'evil' things to happen to 'good' people, which brings our metaphysical discussion to a complete halt unless we acknowledge that the personality of God is not the issue of metaphysics. The issue of metaphysics is the issue regarding only the neutral characteristics of the whole itself and how it is these neutral characteristics of the whole interact with the neutral characteristics of the sub elements of the whole, interacts with ourselves, that is of concern to the field of metaphysics.

This process appears to be neutral in nature and so it is, but this does not imply ethics cannot emerge from such a discussion for in fact the most fundamental foundation of ethics itself is what it is that emerges out of such a discussion.

Before we can mold the second shell involving the perceptual tools of faith, observation, and reason, the mutual concepts regarding the religious, scientific, and philosophical characteristics of God must all come together simultaneously and fit our model of God. Leibniz concept of theodicy, omnibenevolence, does not fit the requirement and thus must be discarded in order to get back to our discussion oriented towards building a universally acceptable model, a metaphysical system of the whole of Reality.

Perfection, does it exist? The whole is perfect from the point of view of the whole for the whole is purely and simply the whole. The whole is what the whole is. Does the whole have a sense of 'moral' obligation? At first glance such a statement would appear to be a metaphysically ludicrous statement but is it? If the whole is composed of knowing subunits and is a 'living' thriving entity, then wouldn't the whole feel a sense of obligation to the subunits to which it owes its very ability to 'grow', 'change', find variety itself? If such is the case then not only does such a question become ontologically significant but such a question becomes metaphysically significant for no longer are we dealing with simply a 'static' whole but we are dealing with an active dynamic whole whose very active dynamic state depends upon subunits of knowing which develop within the whole itself.

Imperfection, does it exist? Imperfection exists from the point of view of the sub elements, which judge the status of the whole from the point of their personal perceptions. Can the subunit ever 'judge' the whole as the whole when the subunit is simply a 'part' of the whole and cannot see the whole as the whole? Yes but only from the point of view of the limited perception from which the subunit is capable of viewing the whole. As such the subunit develops 'judgmental' perceptions of the whole such as 'good' and 'evil'. Ontologically such 'judgmental' developments are not actions overreaching the bounds of the subunit, however, metaphysically such 'judgmental' developments do overreach the bounds of the subunit and as such must be put aside when discussion the base foundation upon which religion, science, and philosophy themselves must be built.

It appears the next step must be a concerted attempt to find Kant's categorical imperatives and that is exactly what will take place in Tractate 6: Kant.

And what about the concept of theodicy, which Leibniz had coined? Theodicy/omnibenevolence appears to belong to the ontologists as opposed to the metaphysician. It appears to belong in a shell which lies somewhere beyond the second shell.

Had Leibniz not been so infatuated with his own creation, he may have seen that his piece of the puzzle did not belonged in the first shell with omnipresence and omnipotence. Had Leibniz not been so arrogant he himself may have concluded that his creation of theodicy did not belong in either the first or the second shell protecting the core concept of omniscience, did not belong as a characteristic to be found in any metaphysical understanding of God.

It may appear there is much negativism involved with the misstep of Leibniz. Be that as it may, all is not negative when we look to Leibniz and his concept of theodicy for:

We now understand that

>Leibniz is a vital link in moving our perceptual understanding forward regarding the 'system' being filled with 'imperfection' into that of being 'the' system filled with, metaphysically speaking, neither 'perfection' or 'imperfection'. As such, 'perfection' and 'imperfection', with the help of Leibniz, now no longer exist as elements of a metaphysical system but rather exist as elements of an ontological dialectic which itself lies beyond the boundaries of all three fields of metaphysics: theoretical metaphysics, practical metaphysics, and metaphysical engineering.

---

[1] Location here is different than what most of us are accustomed to for location here refers to an abstractness such as love, joy hate, evil, etc. which do not take up any space or time. This is unlike concrete items such as chairs, electrons, light, magnetic forces etc., which occupy both space or time or both. simply where knowledge, knowing exists.

[2] 'Separation through exclusion' versus 'separation through inclusion' will be fully addressed in Tractate 8: Russell
[3] William L. Reese, Dictionary of Philosophy and religion, Humanities Press, 1996.
[4] Knowledge is power
[5] Where there is any knowledge by definition it becomes part of the presence of God.
[6] 'Separation through exclusion' versus 'separation through inclusion' will be fully addressed in Tractate 8: Russell
[7] The concept regarding the void of space and time will be fully addressed in Tractate 6: Kant
[8] See Tractate 3: Boethius and Free Will
[9] William L. Reese, Dictionary of Philosophy and religion, Humanities Press, 1996.

Tractate 6

The Error

Of

Kant

❖

The Paradox of:

❖

A System Based upon a Foundation

•

The Need for:

The Void of Time and Space

The War & Peace of a New Metaphysical Perception

1.   1804 AD Kant - The Error of:
   Systems built upon a foundation

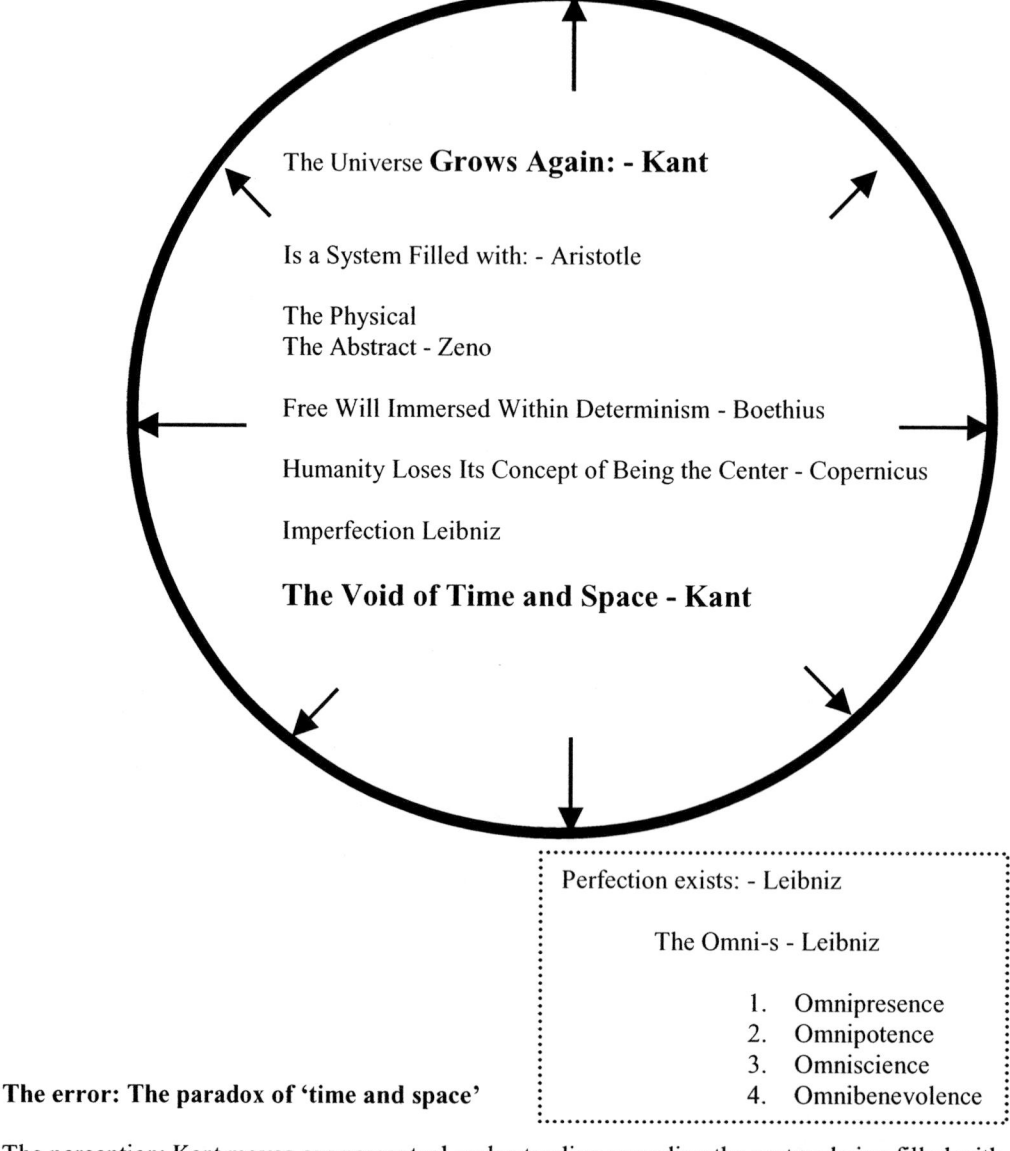

The Universe **Grows Again: - Kant**

Is a System Filled with: - Aristotle

The Physical
The Abstract - Zeno

Free Will Immersed Within Determinism - Boethius

Humanity Loses Its Concept of Being the Center - Copernicus

Imperfection Leibniz

The Void of Time and Space - Kant

The error: The paradox of 'time and space'

Perfection exists: - Leibniz

The Omni-s - Leibniz

1. Omnipresence
2. Omnipotence
3. Omniscience
4. Omnibenevolence

The perception: Kant moves our perceptual understanding regarding the system being filled with 'time and space' into that of being 'the' system filled with 'the void of time and space' and 'time and space'. As such, 'time and space', 'the void of time and space', passive observation, and active observation, with the help of Kant, now have a location within which they can be found. However, the understanding regarding the role of 'time and space', 'the void of time and space', passive observation, and active observation, as well as the understanding regarding the interrelationship between 'time and space', the void of time and space, passive observation, and active observation not only remain in a state of confusion but even more disconcerting, the existence of such an interrelationship is not recognized as a significant aspect of the 'larger' system.

It is this state of confusion which will be specifically addressed within this tractate.

Contents

Part I: The Paradox of the 'unknowable'

Introduction
Cartesian
So, do we need a 'system'?
'The' Missing Foundation
Boredom and knowledge
'Everything'
Passive observing
Active observing
Raising metaphysics up from the dead

Part II: Resolving the issue with a new metaphysical perception

Metaphysics and Cartesianism revisited
'a' Foundation
The need for 'a' whole
The whole does not change
A new meaning of the term 'everything'
How something, which is unchangeable, can change and remain unchangeable
The death of God
Analytic versus Synthetic 'a priori'.
The causal
The non-causal
The boundary separating the causal and the non-causal
The 'Absolute Zero' point of abstraction
The fusion of: $0 / \infty$ and $\infty / 0$
God does not change
The future does not exist
The past does not exist
What is exists
Resolving Kant's four antinomies
The prioritized natural emergence of the first two categorical imperatives
Morality versus categorical imperatives

Terms/concepts

Absolute Zero Point of Abstraction
Antinomies Active Observation
Cartesian
Cartesian system
Change
Causal
Endless Repetition
Foundation
Foundationless
Multi-dimensional Combinations of Tessellations
Non-Cartesian
Non-Cartesian system
Non-Causal
Passive Observation

Tractate 6
Kant – The Error of
A System Built Upon a Foundation

Part I: The Paradox of the 'unknowable'

Introduction

> *Werner Heisenberg: The brash German patriot was just 32 when he won the Nobel Prize for the uncertainty principle, which states that it is possible to know a subatomic particle's position or momentum, but not both. In simplified form, the principle means that the very act of observing something changes its behavior.*[1]

And so it is science makes a move to claim that it, science, originated such a concept when in actuality it was philosophy, which did so. So it is we obtain the false impression that science takes the lead in developing and innovating new perceptions regarding our reality when in fact it is philosophy which innovates new perceptions and it is science which follows and attempts to validate such new perceptions.

To find proof of the lead role philosophy plays regarding our perceptual development, one need but look back to 1770 and the work of Immanuel Kant who initiated a philosophical perception which was to be as far reaching in its impact upon philosophy and metaphysics as Copernicus' ideas were to science and cosmology.

> *After Hume had destroyed philosophy and any possibility of constructing a metaphysical system, Kant created the greatest metaphysical system of them all*[2].

Kant introduced a concept into philosophy known as 'critical philosophy'. Before Kant, Aristotelian views dominant philosophical perceptions. One could say: Until Kant, no other metaphysical perception existed other than 'passive observation' as described by Aristotle. Aristotle's metaphysical system, regarding the observer's passive effect upon matter and energy found immersed within space and time, remained in place for more than two thousand years, remained in place until Kant introduced the concept of active observation

Kant introduced the concept of a limited system located within infinite possibilities.[3] At first glance, such a statement appears paradoxical.

Regarding paradoxes, Wittgenstein stated:

> *'It is the business of philosophy not to resolve a contradiction by means of a mathematics or logic discovery but to get a clear view of the state of ... affairs before the contradiction is resolved. (And this does not mean that one is side stepping a difficulty.)*[4]

Wittgenstein believed philosophy has the responsibility to resolve paradoxes through an interpretation of what seems most reasonable. It is then mathematics and logic, which follow and validate or invalidate such a view.

It is the function of the philosophical field known as metaphysics to examine the concept of the whole. Is the physical the whole? If the physical is not the whole then what lies beyond the physical, meta – beyond, physics – the physical? Kant proposed a metaphysical system of limited existence 'containing' infinite possibilities. Such a perception is metaphysical in nature for it places a limit upon the whole leading to the question regarding what lies beyond the limit itself. Such a topic lies well beyond the parameters regarding a dialectic of space and time. In fact, such a topic lies beyond the parameters regarding a dialectic of the void of space and time. We will not ignore such a topic, rather we will address the topic of what lies beyond the limits of the whole in Tractate 18: The Emergence of Theoretical Metaphysics.

What then are we to examine within this tractate: Tractate 6: Kant and the Void of Space and Time? We are to examine space and time, the void of space and time, passive observation, active observation.

In spite of the pronouncements of philosophers to follow Kant, meta-physics, is not dead. Meta-physics has just been set aside while we await a new metaphysical system. Kant said we have no choice but to establish a more comprehensive metaphysical system before we relegate his system to the archives of ancient history. Such then becomes the task of this dialectic for it is the very purpose of this work, The War and Peace of a New Metaphysical Perception, to establish the rationality regarding a new metaphysical model.

As we shall see, however, the task of 'replacing' Kant's system is not to be attempted through the process of destroying Kant metaphysical model but rather the new model is established through the process of fusing Aristotle's, Kant's, and Hegel's model all into one metaphysical model.

Kant's metaphysical system presented many contradictions. Before we can replace Kant's system we must first examine Kant's system to, as Wittgenstein said:

> *'... get a clear view of the state of ... affairs before the contradiction is resolved*

It is both aspects, examination and replacement, which is the focus of this tractate.

Kant embraced the concept of an Aristotelian Cartesian system. A Cartesian system is one built upon 'a' 'foundation'. Kant, therefore, believed a metaphysical system must have 'a' first principle.

Kant's system:

> *Kant's critical philosophy is a syncretic theory bringing together in a single framework doctrines of realism and idealism. The philosophical movement following from his position, known as German idealism, includes....*[5]

> *...In all experience, there is someone who experiences the experiential subject, and the object, or what is experienced. We can distinguish between two approaches to experience: the claim that the mind is passive with respect to what it experiences, and merely registers what impacts upon it: and the converse claim that the mind is active with respect to its experience, so that in some sense the mind shapes what it experiences.*[6]

> *...The distinctive feature of German idealism is the claim, common to all great German idealists, that the subject is never passive but always active with respect to what it experiences.*[7]

The brief description of Kant's system, leads us to Kant's dilemma.

Before we delve into the substance of this tractate however, a few additional words would be appropriate regarding the direction this tractate is to take. This tractate is not to be a critique of

Kant's work; rather this tractate is an examination followed by an expansion of two of Kant's positions.

First: The universe evolves as our thoughts evolve.

Second: The concept of system is critical to metaphysics.

Regarding the first concept: The perception, the universe evolves as our thoughts evolve, provides the rationale as to why our understanding of the 'Greater' picture is so important. The concept that the universe evolves as our thoughts evolve implies we actively 'form' what 'will be' as opposed to the past Aristotelian perception that we are merely observers of 'what is'.

Regarding the second concept: Kant was the first to propose such an upside down concept as the universe itself evolving as our thoughts evolved. Kant turned metaphysics and thus philosophy on its head just as Copernicus turned cosmology and thus science on its head. Kant was the first metaphysician to step beyond the perceptual metaphysical perception of the day. Kant was able to step beyond the perception of the day regarding the observer passively observing. Kant, however, was unable to step beyond the perception of the day regarding the existence of an Aristotelian closed system. Such conflicting positions generated unwieldy metaphysical contradictions.

Kant innovated a perception incapable of being 'confined' within an Aristotelian closed system and thus found himself incapable of finding both first truth and his dearly sought categorical imperative.

It is these two concepts, first truth and categorical imperatives, that this tractate will examine and with the help of Hegelian concepts attempt to resolve.

In this tractate, as in previous tractates, we will focus upon a relatively few basic references. This is not intended to demean Kant's contribution to philosophy. Kant's work is extremely complex but the complexity of Kant's work is not the concern of this tractate. Rather the intent of this tractate is the same as previous tractates. The intent of this tractate is to examine the paradox this philosopher presented to us and then resolve the paradox created by the philosopher in order that metaphysics may move on from its seemingly endless state of stagnation.

To accomplish such a monumental goal, we have no choice but to simplify Kant.

Since we are not seeking an in-depth understanding of Kant, we are going to apply an extreme form of Husserl's reductionism in conjunction with the surgical application of Ockham's razor to Kant's metaphysical perceptions.

Through the application of techniques developed by both Husserl and Ockham, we should be able to apply Kant's metaphysical concepts to two aspects of Epistemology:

The subject	and	The predicate
Noun		Verb
Object		Process
Passive Action		Active Action
Knowledge		Knowing

Cartesian

Active/passive – Passive/active

A graphic will help us better visualize where it is Kant's system came to an abrupt halt. We will begin constructing the graphic from the point of view within which Kant found himself personally immersed:

Perception of Kant's day: Time exists.

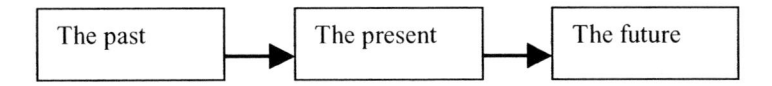

```
[The past] → [The present] → [The future]
```

If we add to this graphic, the existing Aristotelian perception of Kant's day we obtain:

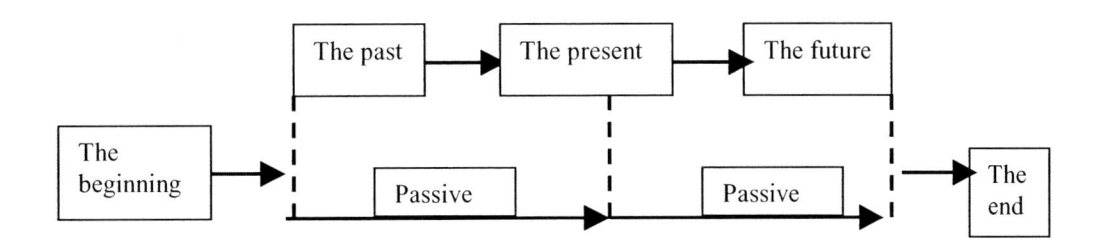

```
                [The past] → [The present] → [The future]
[The
 beginning] →      [Passive]           [Passive]         → [The end]
```

The graphic demonstrates the concept of time passing from 'what was' to what is' to 'what will be'. The 'beginning' demonstrates the 'creation' concepts of the day, demonstrates the cause and effect concepts of the day. The Aristotelian additions refer to the universe. The Aristotelian perception is comprised of two factors:

1. The universe exists and we can measure it through observing what it is.
2. The universe is what it was, is what it is, and is what it will be.

In other words: The universe is permeated with fundamental universal laws, which are both universal and predictable. Objects fell 'downward' yesterday. Objects fall 'downward' today. Moreover, Objects will fall 'downward' tomorrow. This might better be called the certainty principle as opposed to Heisenberg's present day 'uncertainty principle'

The universe in other words existed and we as observers observed in a passive fashion. Granted we could act within the universe and alter it through action but we could not alter the universe through simply observing the universe, nor could we in any way alter the laws of the universe through active action, rather our actions were limited by the laws of the universe themselves.

There is room in the graphic to indicate the passive past and the passive future for both occupy a 'span' of time. There is no room to indicate the passive present for the present is fleeting and in actuality 'occupies' no time. It is for this reason there are only two forms of passivity indicated. In fact, many Aristotelian believers would argue whether or not we altered the universe in any manner, ala the determinists.

The War & Peace of a New Metaphysical Perception

Kant then proposed a unique concept:

> *Kant drew an analogy between the critical philosophy and the work of Nicolas Copernicus.... Copernicus inverted the traditional claim for the relation between the earth and the universe. The critical philosophy depends on a revolutionary new concept, called the Copernican Revolution, which similarly inverts the relation between the subject and object, between the perceiver and the perceived. This general claim, namely that the mind of the subject, or perceiver, is active with respect to, and influences, what the subject perceives, is central to Kantian position and recurs, in different ways, throughout all later German idealism.*

This new perception regarding the universe, directly impacts the most basic philosophical concept regarding knowledge itself. In fact, it was philosophy, not science, which was to first find its most basic premises, turned upside down.

The concept of the observer changing 'what is' through simply observing 'what is' creates a scenario of the observer being 'active' in regards to the Aristotelian perception:

    a. 'What is' was.
    b. 'What is' is.
    c. 'What is' will be.

Kant's metaphysical system changes this to being:

    a. 'What is' was.
    b. 'What is' is.
    c. 'What is' may not be, 'what it presently is', in the future.

Thus Kant initiated the idea known as German idealism: The very fact that our observing changes what it is we observe. A scientific form of this was later to be called the 'the uncertainty principle'.

This leads us to modifying the graphic. As such the graphic becomes

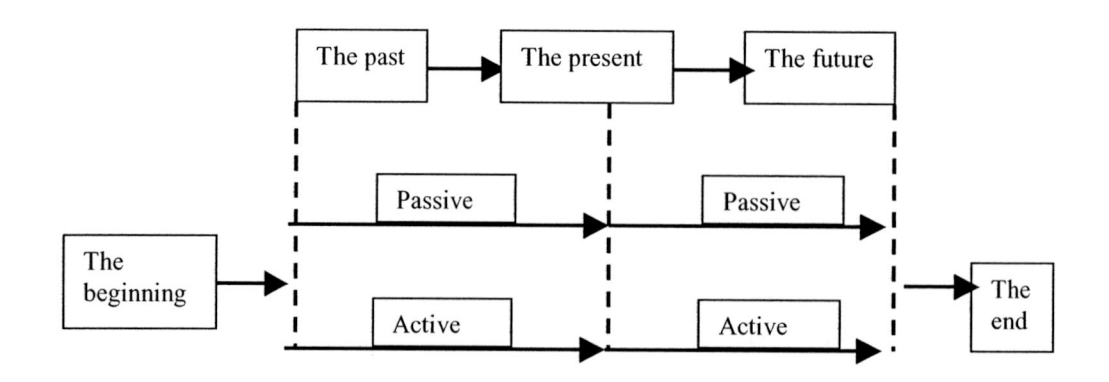

The 'passive' remains on the graphic because the passive remains as a perception found within present day society. Kant's suggestion of the 'active' in no way displaced the concept of the 'passive'. Even today Kant's perception of a 'new system' has not replaced the old Aristotelian system.

The new system proposed by Kant was both 'a system' and 'new'. Kant did not discard the concept that 'a' system existed. Kant was a firm believer that reality could be demonstrated through the process of modeling.

Copernicus inverted our view of centricism. With Copernicus, we began to understand that not all things revolved around ourselves. Kant inverted our view of knowledge. With Kant, we began to understand that
knowledge was not necessarily an absolute.

This presented a problem for Kant. Kant believed in what is known as a Cartesian System, believed in a foundation-based system, believed in a system based upon 'a' 1st truth. But what is this thing we call a 'Cartesian system'? A detailed examination of a Cartesian system is found in Tractate 2: Aristotle and Cartesianism. For the present, however:

> *.... With respect to the Cartesian concept of system. Descartes, in effect, insists on a foundation known to be true as the condition of knowledge*

Which brings us to the question: When analyzing metaphysics, do we 'need' a system?

So do we need a 'system'

> *...Philosophy has always been concerned with what is called the theory of knowledge, or epistemology. The theory of knowledge, more precisely, the problem of how to formulate a systematic theory of philosophy, is central to the critical philosophy. It is also the central thread linking the views of Kant, the post-Kantians, and Hegel.*[8]

It could be argued that knowledge can be understood in terms of the lack of 'a system' but the 'lack of a system' is simply another form of a system. The lack of any system is the least/greatest possible form of a system. The lack of 'a system' is a system so minimal the system is reduced to a system zero in size; the lack of 'a system' is so maximal in size the system extends beyond size. The lack of a system is simply a system so minimal it is 'no' system at all, nothing at all. It is a system so maximal it extends beyond the concept of size itself and thus size finds itself a part of the system rather than the system finding itself defined by size/space.

The War & Peace of a New Metaphysical Perception

There are an almost infinite variety of systems:

System A:

- The individual

I am: I exist and all else is but a figment of my imagination

System B:

◯ The universe

The universe is: The universe exists and all else is but a subset of the universe

System C:

▭ The whole

The whole is: The whole exists and all else is but a subset of the whole

And then there are variations of the sets:

- The individual

I am: I exist and all else is but a figment of my imagination

System: the individual

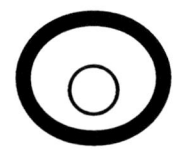

I am: I exist and all else is but a figment of my imagination.

The universe is but a part of me.

The universe

The universe is: The universe exists and all else is but a subset of the universe

The War & Peace of a New Metaphysical Perception

System: the universe

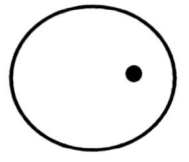

○ •

The universe is: The universe exists and all else is but a subset of the universe.

I am but a part of the universe.

▭ The whole

The whole is: The whole exists and all else is but a subset of the whole

System: the whole

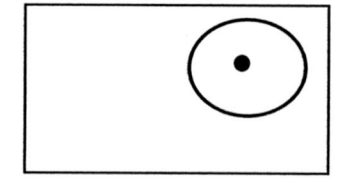

▭(○•)

The whole is: The whole exists and all else is but a subset of the whole.

The universe and I are but a part of the whole.

On the other hand, one may say: All three exist independently of the others and thus perhaps there is no system:

- The individual

I am: I exist and all else is but a figment of my imagination

○ The universe

The universe is: The universe exists and all else is but a subset of the universe

▭ The whole

The whole is: The whole exists and all else is but a subset of the whole

And thus the non-system becomes the ultimate extreme of each element existing independently from the other, multiple independent systems:

- The individual

○ The universe

There are many variations of the above graphic depicting a 'non-system' but one characteristic remains universal between them all: In a non-system metaphysical system, the elements remain independent one from the other. But as much as one would like to call the independence of existence of elements one from the other, a non-system, the fact remains that the very existence of the elements being independent of each other makes them a system. The system a non-system represents is the lack of dependency and orientation of one to the other within the system

The question once again is: Do we need a metaphysical system? The answer: There is no way around the concept of a metaphysical system other than to explain the metaphysical system as having a net sum of zero and even then we have a system which we reduce to zero, but it is 'a' system nevertheless.

In short:

Within the field of metaphysics, do we need a system? The answer: Yes we do. Kant understood this and that is why Kant so adamantly held to the concept that all metaphysical concepts, once fully understood, reduce to a system be it the least form of system, a system-less system, or .be it a more substantive form of system, a system.

Should the system be the least form of system, be a system-less system, then the system is foundationless, the system is what Hegel would call an 'open system, the system is what Aristotle might call a non-Cartesian system.

Should the system be of 'greater' form than the least form of system, be a system, then the system is based upon a foundation, the system is what Kant would call a 'closed system, the system is what Aristotle might call a Cartesian system.

Kant initiated the concept of the 'critical philosophy', but Kant could not explain such a concept in terms of 'a' system, or any system for that matter which met the criteria of 'system' historically existing up to and through his own time period. As such Kant, like Zeno (see Tractate 1: Zeno and Seamlessness), was left perplexed, was left holding his new and unique metaphysical perception void a system capable of rationally incorporating his concepts within itself, within 'a' system.

It is this most basic puzzle left unresolved by Kant that this tractate will resolve through the introduction of a new metaphysical perception, the metaphysical perception of a non-Cartesian system, as introduced by Kant, powered by a Cartesian system, as introduced by Aristotle.

The result: The emergence of a 'dynamic', active metaphysical system as opposed to a static, passive metaphysical system.

The result: A metaphysical system emitting the potentiality of fusion power versus a metaphysical system emitting the potentiality of fossil fuel combustion.

The 'Missing Foundation'

Kant could not find 'the' 1st principle

Kant was working within the realm of the Aristotelian system. Kant dramatically altered what metaphysics perceived to be the state of observation. Although Kant altered our perception of observation within the system from being a passive form of observation to being an active form of observation. Kant did not alter the system from being perceived as it had always been perceived, being perceived as a closed system.

The Error of Kant

It was Hegel who eventually modified Kant's system from being a 'closed' Cartesian system into being an 'open' Cartesian system.

A closed Cartesian system requires not only a 1st principle but requires a first principle found within the system. Since Kant perceived his system to be 'closed', Kant looked within to find the foundation for his system, the fundamental upon which his system was to be built.

1st principle found 'within' the system proved to be an elusive concept. The whole of the phenomena, the universe, appeared to exist; the element of the phenomenal, the individual, appeared to exist; the element of the noumenal, the individual, appeared to exist; and the whole of the noumenal, summation of knowing, causation, appeared to exist. Which was the 1st of the principles?

If the physical, the phenomenal, existed as Aristotle suggested, it existed, always existed, always will exist for without it there is nothing and nothing was not a concept the Greeks acknowledged as a logical state of existence:

The whole Greek universe rested upon this pillar. There is no void.[9].

If Kant was correct, the physical was not passive but active and our very existence within the universe, our noumenal existence existing within phenomenal existence changed the very essence and the very outcome of the phenomenal. Where then did 'the' initial change begin for the phenomenal world, the universe itself?
Did the physical, the phenomenal, the universe, initiate the abstract, the noumenal, or did the abstract initiate the physical? And if the physical initiated the physical what then becomes of the abstract should the physical no longer exist. And should the abstracted, God, have initiated the physical, what then becomes of the physical should the abstract no longer exist?

These were the very question facing Kant. These were the questions Kant was unable to answer through the implementation of his metaphysical system.

1st principle became as illusive to Kant as it did to Aristotle. The issue of 1st principle was no closer to being resolved by Kant than by Aristotle.

As we discussed in Tractate 2: Aristotle and Cartesianism, it became obvious that neither Kant nor Aristotle had the answer but rather each had a portion of the answer. The puzzle pieces were being created rather than the puzzle pieces being assembled.
But two pieces of the puzzle remained to be created: The function of 'nothingness' within a metaphysical system and the function of infinity within a metaphysical system.

Aristotle had elucidated region #1: The universe as a region is infinite in terms of time and space

Kant had elucidated region #2: The region within the individual incorporates a perception of the functionality of the concepts of time and space.

And now with this tractate, region #3: The region beyond the universe incorporates no universal fabric of space and time but rather incorporates the perceptions of the functionality of time and space as perceived by elements of multiplicity, individuality, found within itself.

But how is it the three regions exist and how is it the three regions depend one upon the other?

Like Zeno, Kant had a sense that there were two existences, the physical and the abstract, but Kant was unable to resolve how two regions, let alone three, could exist simultaneously and yet

The War & Peace of a New Metaphysical Perception

independently one from the other. This led to the issue of just what is 'the' foundation of the system. It would take Hegel to re-open the system before a new metaphysical system could evolve which would lead to a potential resolution to Kant's dilemma.

Just as quickly as Hegel's metaphysical model led to a logical resolution regarding the dilemmas Kant's metaphysical model produced, Hegel's metaphysical system led to its own unique dilemmas. As we shall see in Tractate 7: Hegel, Hegel would set the stage for the entrance of 'nothingness' and 'infinity' to emerge as critical elements of a metaphysical system while at the same time introducing the notion that the metaphysical concept of systems themselves were dead.

With the on vent of Hegel, we have the potential to 'compare' nothingness to the infinite, to 'compare' nothingness to $0 / \infty$, to 'compare' nothingness to $\infty / 0$. These strange concepts emerge as the last pieces of the puzzle necessary for a new metaphysical system which addresses the historical paradoxical issues which so long avoided resolution by philosophy.

But we are not yet to the point of examining Hegel's metaphysical model for it is Kant's dilemma we must address before approaching Hegel's paradoxical dilemma.

Kant suggested the very action of observing the universe affected the universe itself. This perception suggested we mold, influence, what the universe becomes. As such the universe evolves not only in a passive sense but in an active sense.

We examined the four states of action in Tractate 4: Boethius and Free Will. Within this tractate we found action to be divided as follows:

Four forms of action:

    Passive action:

1. Action as a state of being:

    The passive action of being is action in the form of the primal state of existence as opposed to other forms of action emerging from the primal state of existence

2. Actions bound by the laws of nature

    Actions bound by the laws of nature are passive actions taken by inanimate objects as well as actions that simulate the action of inanimate objects – a rock falls, you fall, a rock exists, you exist

    Active action:

3. Free will

    Active actions of free will are actions taken by a 'knowing' object, action which could go various ways and whose action was directed by the 'knowing' object of its own accord.

4. Determinism

    Active actions of free will taken by a 'knowing' object whose intended actions have been overridden by actions of free will generated by a dominating second 'knowing' object

These four forms of action now gain deeper meaning through Kant's development of active observation. The concept of throwing our Aristotle's passive observation, however, was not the intent of Kant. Although Kant believed in the existence of the noumenal, Kant also believed in the concept of the existence of the phenomenal, the universe:

Kant believed that what happens within this world is governed entirely by scientific law.[10]

Kant came up against the wall of Aristotelian thought, which had 'closed' the metaphysical system, see Tractate 2: Aristotle and Cartesianism. As such, Kant literally found himself bounded by the limits closed system imposes upon any metaphysical thinker. Being confined by limits a closed metaphysical system placed upon his own metaphysical system left Kant with apparently irresolvable contradictions of the before mentioned Active and Passive actions.

To begin to resolve Kant's dilemma through an alternate means as suggested by Hegel, one must begin by examining Kant's dilemma.

If two forms of action, active and passive, existed simultaneously 'within' the confinement of infinite time and space then four possibilities of active – passive existences emerged which needed addressing by Kant:

1. Passive – passive
2. Passive – active
3. Active - passive
4. Active – active

Kant began by accepting the Aristotelian limits to a metaphysical system,

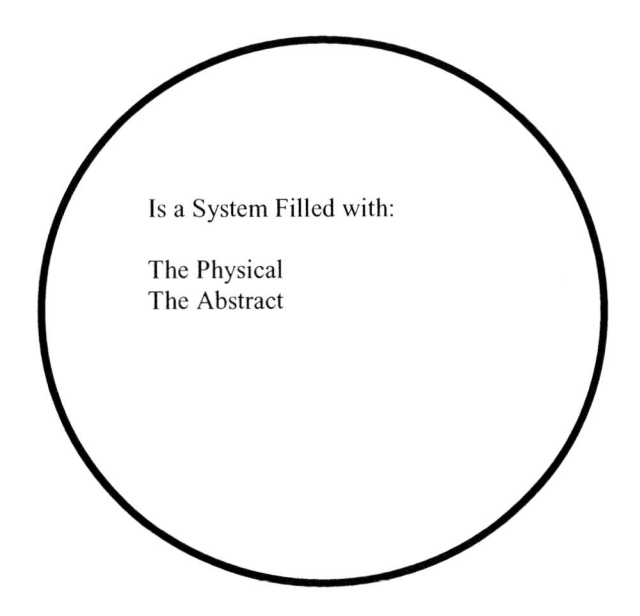

Is a System Filled with:

The Physical
The Abstract

The War & Peace of a New Metaphysical Perception

and then proceeded to modify the system:

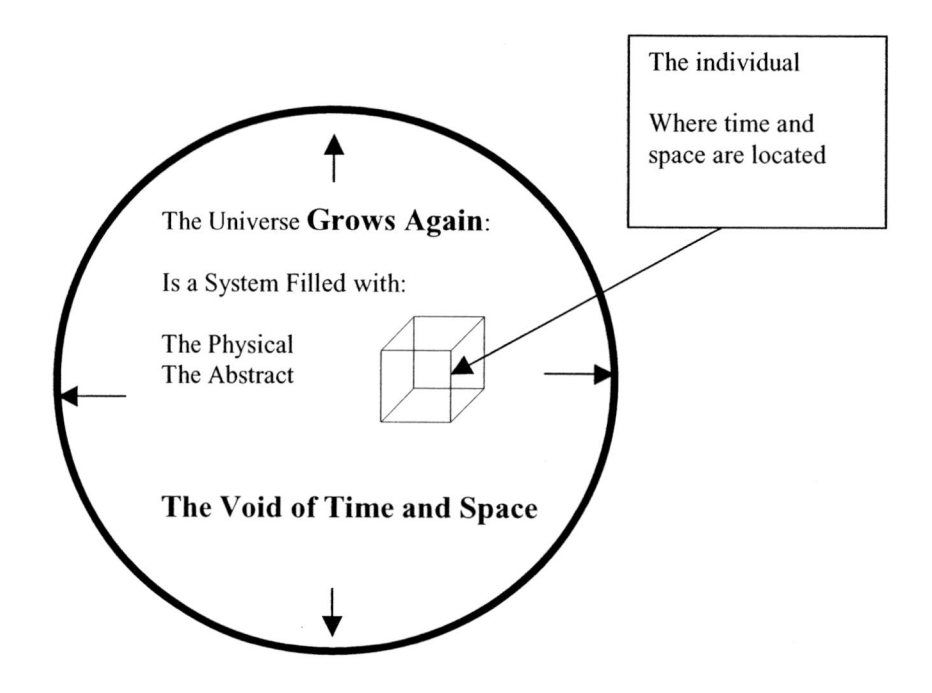

The Universe **Grows Again**:

Is a System Filled with:

The Physical
The Abstract

The Void of Time and Space

The individual

Where time and space are located

Having modified Aristotle's metaphysical system, Kant began looking for 'a', 'the', 1st principle, 'the' foundation for his closed Cartesian system.

With the conversion of the Aristotelian closed passive system into a Kantian closed active system came the dilemma regarding which of the four forms of active – passive interrelationships was the most probable?

The most minimal act found within the active – passive interrelationship is the simple act of existing without observing.

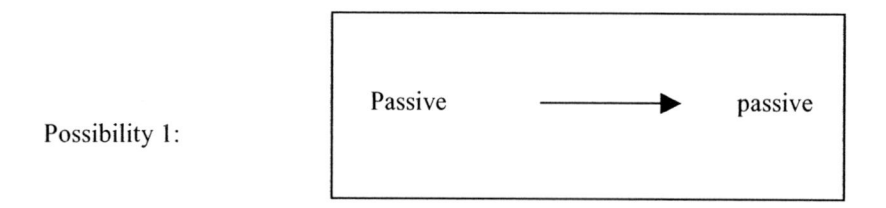

Possibility 1:

Passive ⟶ passive

As one views the graphics one must keep in mind that the act of observing a process is the most minimalist action one can impose upon the action – reaction process, upon the cause and effect process.

Possibility 2:

```
┌─────────────────────────────────┐
│  Observing                      │
│     the                         │
│      ↓                          │
│                                 │
│  Passive    ─────────▶  passive │
│                                 │
└─────────────────────────────────┘
```

Possibility 2 was the Aristotelian system.

The universe existed. The universe abided by physical laws.

Our presence as well as our observing the universe did not change the dynamics of the physical laws, did not change the net result of the universe of which we were an element.

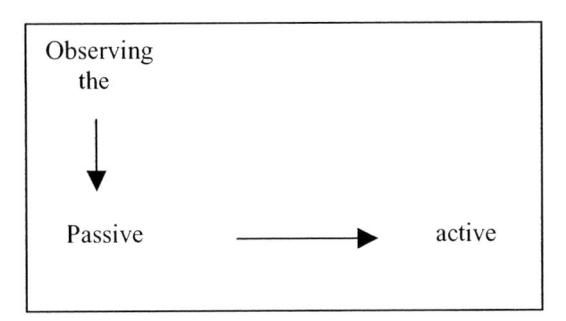

Possibility 3:

```
┌─────────────────────────────────┐
│  Observing                      │
│     the                         │
│      ↓                          │
│                                 │
│  Passive    ─────────▶  active  │
│                                 │
└─────────────────────────────────┘
```

This was the Aristotelian system becoming the Kantian system due to Kant simply making the assumption through observation.

The universe existed. The universe abided by physical laws.

Our observing, our presence within the universe changed the dynamics of the physical laws. Our observing, our presence within the universe somehow changed, in both the phenomenal sense and in the nominal sense, the net result of the universe of which we were an element.

Kant had difficulties finding 'a' foundation to his metaphysical system. Although Kant perceived the noumenal and the phenomenal to be at different 'levels' one to the other and thus separate one from the other, Kant did not perceive the two to be separate entities one from the other.

In other words, Kant retained the Aristotelian concept of the physical and the abstract being separate but bounded within the same confines as each other. Kant retained the same 'bounds' to his metaphysical system:

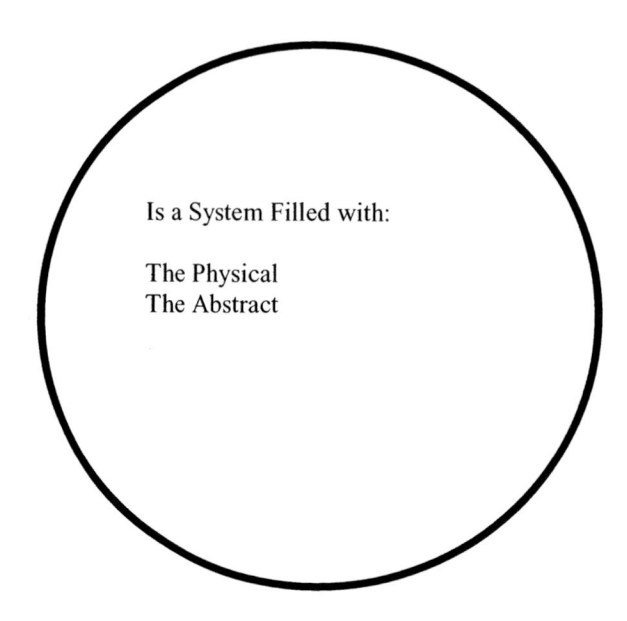

```
      ┌─────────────────────┐
      │  Is a System Filled with: │
      │                     │
      │  The Physical       │
      │  The Abstract       │
      └─────────────────────┘
```

A metaphysical system utilizing a common boundary of singularity creates the fourth possibility.

Possibility 4:

```
┌──────────────────────────────────┐
│        Observing                 │
│           the                    │
│            ↓                     │
│                                  │
│        Active   ───────▶  passive│
└──────────────────────────────────┘
```

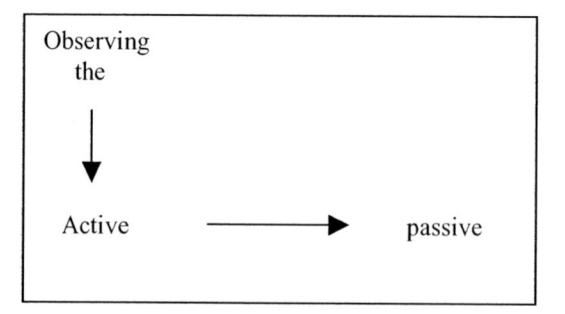

In essence this demonstrates Boethius' metaphysical system, which we addressed in detail within Tractate 3: Boethius and Free Will. Such a system represents the end product of free will being known to a 'higher' order Being through the process of divine foreknowledge.

Possibility 4 reinforces Boethius concept regarding the simultaneous existence of free will and divine foreknowledge. Possibility 4 reinforces the concept that all potential end results either 'do' exist or at the very least, are 'known' products.

An abstraction 'knowing' not only all that is but all that could be is a form of knowing incapable of creating 'unknown' results, incapable of creating 'unknown' knowledge. Acknowledging the omission of such a scenario leads us to Possibility 5:

Possibility 5:

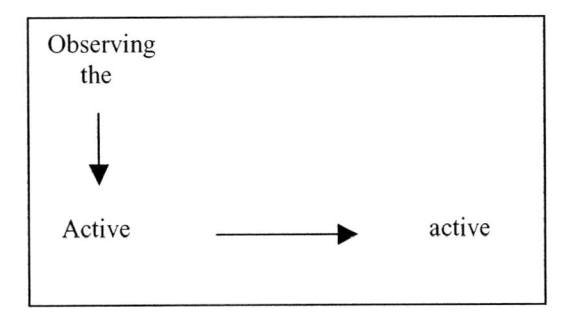

```
        Observing
           the
            ↓

   Active  ──────────▶  active
```

Possibility 5 suggests: The universe was always this way; we just didn't understand it to be such. As we shall see, such a scenario is what emerges from the new metaphysical system of 'being' *being* 'Being'. Such a scenario evolves through the process of merging the Aristotelian closed Cartesian system and the Kantian closed non-Cartesian system which Hegel converted into an open non-Cartesian system. In essence Possibility 5 fuses the Cartesian with the non-Cartesian into a single system of multiplicity which provides for the unique individuality of the two rather than choosing one over the other or fusing the two in a manner which compromises the uniqueness of each system.

The scenario from which five possible forms of existence arise exemplify the metaphysical dilemma facing Kant. Kant yearned to find 'the' foundation to his system but the foundation Kant so longed to find proved to be illusive. Other scenarios create similarly perplexing dilemmas. The concept of Cartesianism versus non-Cartesianism is another example.

Although we examined the concept of Cartesianism in detail in Tractate 2: Aristotle and Cartesianism, it may well behoove us to refresh our memory by briefly re-examining the concept of Cartesianism.

> We have already noted that Descartes links the concepts of system and foundation. For Descartes and for those who follow him on this path, there is no science without system, and no system without a foundation. To put the same point differently, in the Cartesian perspective the concept of system is the cornerstone of the entire affair, the condition *sine Qua non* of philosophy a science and , hence, of knowledge of any kind. The entire Cartesian edifice is sustained by the foundation that subtends it.[11]

The question then becomes: What is 'the' foundation of the system? Is it the universe? Is it myself? Is it you? Or is it the creator of the beginning? Each creates contradictions and thus Kant could not resolve which was 1st truth.

The point needs further emphasis for it is a critical issue regarding Kant's system:

> Kant insists that in his theory he intends to navigate between dogmatic affirmation and skeptical doubt[12]. If systematic form is essential to knowledge, then the critical theory does not escape skepticism, and the Kantian claim to dissipate Hume's doubts is simply dogmatic.[13]

There is no doubt there are many variations regarding a specific definition of Cartesianism. A few might fall into the following forms:

Cartesian: 1. a closed system 2. a system with a beginning 3. a system in a state of permanent equilibrium

1. a closed system: Aristotle's system followed the logic of 'what is is'. As such the only conceivable perception of reality was what is as opposed to what could be for what could be. The universe was in essence static. If the universe, the physical, dissolved into nothingness, nothingness would be all that remained. This led to the concept that the 'creator' of the universe was 'within' the universe, 'was' the universe. This is a pantheistic approach vs. a panentheistic approach. Panentheism as opposed to pantheism takes the approach: if the universe, the physical, dissolved into nothingness, nothingness may remain but this nothingness would be 'located' 'within' the creator, which would remain as the creator.

2. a system with a beginning: Aristotle's system conceived of a beginning to all that existed within the universe and ignored the concept of: What if the physical dissolved? What would remain? This was a senseless question to Aristotle for the concept of nothing did not exist, had been suppressed by the Greeks.

   The whole Greek universe rested upon this pillar. There is no void.[14].

   In essence Aristotle's system had no end and no beginning. It always existed and always would.

3. a system in a state of permanent equilibrium

   From an ontological point of view, this is not an arguable scenario for it makes no sense ontologically. Such a statement suggests all action becomes passive. And why is it such a scenario is illogical. Such a scenario establishes the scientific concept of entropy, which applies to the phenomenal/the physical, as 'the' direct analogy for the noumenal/abstraction. If such were to be the case, the abstract would, like the physical, find time and space to be innate characteristics of itself and thus find itself to be nothing other than simply another form of the physical. In short within such a scenario, the abstract would be simply another 'level' of the physical and thus the noumenal and the phenomenal would be in essence one in the same rather than separate entities one from the other.

   Within such a scenario, even the action of God becomes passive at some point.

We seem to be swimming in a sea with no land in sight. The waters of the ocean are but the endless problems, paradoxes, and contradictions within which philosophers find themselves immersed. The land, when it does appear to emerge before us, soon finds itself to be nothing but a mirage.

We can further understand Kant's dilemma by viewing a metaphysicians dialogue with a theist:

Part I: Metaphysical perceptions

Ok we agree upon one thing:

   1. *You exist*

Now you understand I did not initiate this Metaphysical discussion with the Descartes' principle of 'I exist' but you also understand that when you look at me and say the two words, 'You exist.', my existence becomes a recognized fact by you. By the way I hope you understand the significance of this approach. If the first principle is, 'I exist.', it is reinforced by only one entity, myself. When the first principle is, 'You exist.' then the concept of 'I exist.' becomes reinforced not by one entity, myself, rather the concept of my existence becomes reinforced by six billion you's out there looking at me and all saying to me personally, 'You exist..

I must emphasize here that I am not disagreeing with Descartes. I too agree the first principle is 'I exist.' I just do not agree with Descartes as to 'where' that first principle becomes the 'first' principle. That question in essence is the crux of the argument I am putting forward in my next work: The War and Peace of a New Metaphysical Perception. The article I sent you: Metaphysical Systems – On 'being' being 'Being' is Tractate 14: Metaphysical Systems of that work.

But back to the business at hand. What next? Since we agree 'You exist.' we now need a place to put you. Remember we have previously Husseraled, reduced, everything away, the earth, the moon, the sun, the galaxy, the universe itself, God Itself, even what remains, nothingness has been reduced away and all that is is 'you exist'

Now we could bring God into the equation but since I am directing this part of the discussion, I would prefer to leave God out of the equation a little longer. So then what? Well how about the universe? Can we agree to bring the universe back into the equation? Can we agree:

    2. The universe exists.

Now I am not saying the universe is real nor am I arguing the universe is simply an illusion, I am just suggesting it exist in whatever form you wish to think of it yourself. Your perceptions of what it is personally are not the issue here – that is a cosmological debate not a metaphysical debate. The issue is simply: Does the universe exist in some form or other or not?

To speed things along here (We are not face to face and thus the need for advancing the conversation – remember I am limited to only five more letters after this one) If you agree the universe exists in some form or another – real or illusionary or a real illusion as I would say, can we agree you are inside the universe?

    3. You are inside the universe.

Now I know we can get cute here and begin all types of debate regarding the universe but lets try to rise above the cute philosophical stuff and stay two reasonable rational men discussing a metaphysical point. If you would like to debate the concepts such as 'everything is simply a figment of my imagination, or your imagination, or whatever', lets do that later. The process we are taking leads us nicely into the heart of these cute and interesting discussions. In fact, this process we are taking not only leads us into these discussions but does so in a new, fascinating, and serious manner as opposed to our old, perplexing, and glib manner.

To summarize:

We agree:

    1. You exist

Can we agree:

> *2. The Universe exists (either in some 'form' or 'non-form')*
> *3. You exist 'in' the Universe.*

Part II: Personal perceptions

I have put additional thought into your solution regarding WWII. In addition to the more obvious problems regarding the 'lack' of understanding that not all humans are altruistic, another thought comes to mind. You say we could have sent a boatload of 3000 people to take the place of 3000 Jews in order to shame Hitler and his cronies (all shameless people by the way) into discontinuing their atrocious acts. If that did not work, we would repeat the action as often as it took to accomplish our ends – the termination of the act of the holocaust.

If, as this solution would imply, violence is so taboo under ALL circumstances that one should seek to actively, give up one's own life to oppose violence, then that brings up a question: Forgetting the self-inflected violence Jesus allowed Himself to be put through, what about the Jews?

(Interestingly enough you view the act of 'allowing' oneself to be violated as an act of pacifism as opposed to such an act being an act of active violence. This would seem to imply one should view oneself as 'lesser' in value than one views someone other than one's self. Why is it we cannot regard ourselves on a level of 'equal' value, 'equal' significance, having 'equal' purpose for existing. In regards to your question: was Jesus' act of allowing himself to be crucified an act of violence? Yes, emphatically yes. I would view Jesus' act of giving up his life as a conscious self imposed act of violence of the greatest degree, which, by the way, in my eyes only elevates the significance of his commitment to his teachings of 'love one another' I would regard this act to be the ultimate expression of commitment to his teachings: Love thy neighbor as thyself. He loved us so much He was willing to give up His own life in an excruciating manner of violence (and who can deny it was done very painfully) (Also note Jesus did not say: Love thy neighbor 'more' than thyself.') to show the degree of love for us and commitment towards his teachings.)

Scenario:

At the time before Christ, God had parted the Red Sea to allow an escape route to open up for the Jews. The Jews moved across the dry riverbed followed by the Egyptians.

There were three players involved here: the Jews, the Egyptians, and God. The Egyptians were threatening to kill the innocent, the Jews. The Egyptians could have stayed upon their banks of the River but choose not to. They were out to kill and maim the Jews. God had a choice, to kill the Egyptians or allow the Jews to be killed. God choose. God closed the waters of the Red Sea behind the Jews and drowned the army of the Egyptians.

Under you perception of pacifism, God should not have done this. Under your proposed plan, the Jews should have run back to the Egyptians, dispersed throughout their ranks, held their hands upward and cried out, 'We will not be a part of your actions, God.' They would have attempted to 'shame' God into acting differently.

Now this would have implied God did not know what he was doing, had no 'reason' for protecting the Jews, had no 'grand plan' but rather is a very emotional fellow who, like many of us, says: Do as I say not as I do.' (I am not implying by a 'Grand Plan' that determinism is the way of reality. In fact, as you will see later, I am stating quite the opposite.)

The question becomes why would God act in such a violent manner yet say violence is 'wrong'. Perceptually we have had no understanding regarding the solution to this paradox. We just say: Well God is God and as such God can, by definition, do what God wants to do and Who are we to question His actions? But this is exactly where the heart of metaphysics goes. No it does not go into the realm of questioning Him for his acts but rather questioning 'why' He acts as He does in order that we can understand, in order that we can emulate his behavior.

Metaphysics, for the religious metaphysician, accepts His acts and then attempts to build a simple model of what is, in order to understand how we can merge ourselves into becoming harmonious with God's creation. (Keep in mind there are non-religious metaphysicians also. These non-religious metaphysicians my not 'accept' the 'acts of God' but in essence they examine 'Being'. The two are in essence no different on a metaphysical level. They become 'different' on an ontological level. I am not ignoring your question regarding the differenced between metaphysics and ontology. But the question need not be addressed at this point. It will resolve itself as we proceed with the discussion. In fact, the question is the very orientation of the progress of this discussion.)

And why attempt to move into a harmonious existence with nature? Because such a state would logically lead us into the highest degree of efficiency in terms of accomplishing our very purpose for existence: more efficiently accomplishing the very reason we were 'created', the very reason we exist in the first place. There is little doubt in my mind that the closer we come to fulfilling our purpose the closer we will come to finding personal satisfaction, joy, happiness, love, tolerance... not only as individuals but as a specie.

(Keep in mind a 'lack' of purpose is, metaphysically speaking, as much a purpose as 'a' purpose itself.)

You do not need to reply to this aspect of the discussion, there is more than enough for you to do in Part I and II on your part. If you feel a need to reply, however, do not confuse it with your Parts I & II. A reply would fall under Part III for you.

Also take note the above statement is simply given to you to place in your head where it will begin brewing. It will become obvious later how such paradoxes are not paradoxes at all if one views them from a different perspective than we have presently. And after all, isn't this the very purpose of metaphysics: to resolve paradoxes we identify which expose the shortcomings of our present perceptions of reality?

And so the dialogue goes. The dialogue goes on endlessly and the mirage of 'a' foundation upon which we can build a metaphysical system remains, seemingly forever, but an illusion.

We glimpsed only three potential foundations to a metaphysical system: I exist, you exist, the universe exists. We did not even venture into the realm of the existence of causation itself, the existence of a 'creator' itself, the existence of God, the existence of 'Being' versus the existence of 'being'. Nor did we examine the potential of 'action' itself on the part of 'Being', 'being' and/or both 'Being' and 'being'

The War & Peace of a New Metaphysical Perception

The sea remains and we find ourselves still swimming within the same endless morass of questions, problems, contradictions, and paradoxes, which faced philosophers twenty five hundred years ago.

Zeno, Aristotle, Boethius, and Copernicus each provided us with the temporary sense of being washed upon the beach of solid perceptions. Such perceptions were only temporary and soon gave rise to the next wave of self-doubt regarding our significance in reality.

Now we see Kant before us and once again we sense land appearing before us. The question is: Is the land but another mirage? We have studied Kant for almost three hundred years and the answer appears to be: The land is but another mirage, however, upon closer examination, it appears another shore lies beyond the mirage of Kant. The new shoreline appears, as a shoreline comprised of the works of six philosophers rather than the isolated ghostly image emerging from the works of any one philosopher.

The ghostly image of the more promising shoreline appears to lie beyond Kant. This new shoreline is the new metaphysical perception of 'being' *being* 'Being'. Is this new ghostly image simply another mirage or is it a shoreline from which we can establish a beachhead for our assault upon new and exciting ontological, cosmological, and metaphysical adventures we are sure to find awaiting us once we have emerged from our ocean of self doubt, once we emerge from the sea of questions which have been washing over us since what seems to be time eternal?

Before examining this new shoreline, examining this new metaphysical perception in depth, we will have no choice but to conquer the crest of Kant. To do so we have no choice but to examine a few other aspects of Kant's metaphysical system. We might find it interesting to start the process by examining the concept regarding the 'boredom' of knowledge.

Boredom and knowledge

If there is a set known number of elements of knowledge, regardless of the immensity of the number of elements of knowledge involved, the number of combinations regarding the set number of elements of knowledge eventually leads to beginning the set number of combinations over once again.

Now regardless of whether time is endless or a void of time exists, the number of reruns becomes a factor of infinity, be infinity an exponent of the number of combinations or an exponent of the number of pieces of knowledge is not the issue.

What is the issue is that of boredom. 'Eventually' a knowing 'Being', with either infinite time or the void of time at its disposal, will find 'reruns' to be an issue with which it must deal. The issue with which it must deal is the same issue all 'knowing' entities must address when it comes to repetition. The issue is that of boredom - endless, repetitious boredom.

The Error of Kant

Aristotle's metaphysical system:

Kant's metaphysical system:

The Universe

Time

Individuality

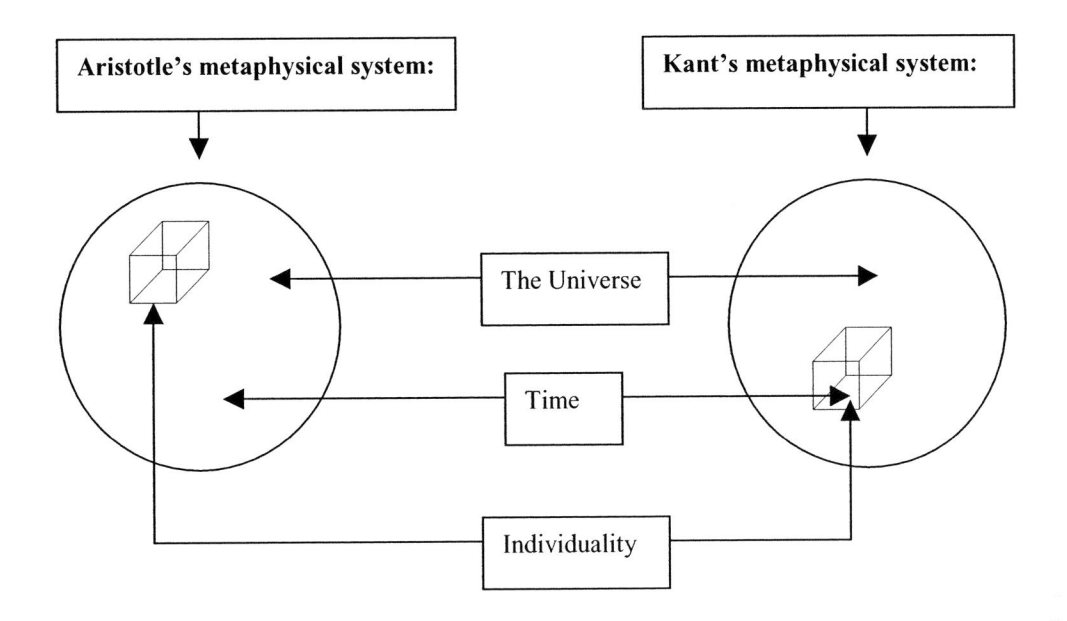

One difference between the two systems:

Aristotle: time is found 'within' the universe
Kant: time is found 'within' the unit of the individual

In both systems, the universe is 'the' system, 'the only' system. In such systems, there are two choices:

1. Time is limited

Or

2. Time is endless

Time being limited is not an option for Aristotle's system. In a system where time is the very fabric of the system, the end of time becomes the end of the system itself, leaving what? If the answer is leaving nothing then 'all' ends with the end of time, thus an irrational ending emerges from the given system where the system is 'all' and time is limited.

Time being endless is not an option for Kant's system. In a system where time is the fabric of the individual, the fabric of the system becomes 'knowing'. Whether 'All knowing' becomes the summation of 'all' knowing or the summation of 'all' knowing plus 'All knowing' is not the issue. The issue we are discussing is that of limited time and we understand time to be limited in terms of the individual for the individual, as an element of the physical, 'begins' and 'ends'. The result, the eventual sum of all knowledge emerges as a concept of 'divine' foreknowledge' which leads us to our previous dilemma of 'boredom' for in such a system 'reruns', boredom, becomes an issue.

The War & Peace of a New Metaphysical Perception

If we reexamine the two systems we can now interject the only rational argument, which gives both systems rationality:

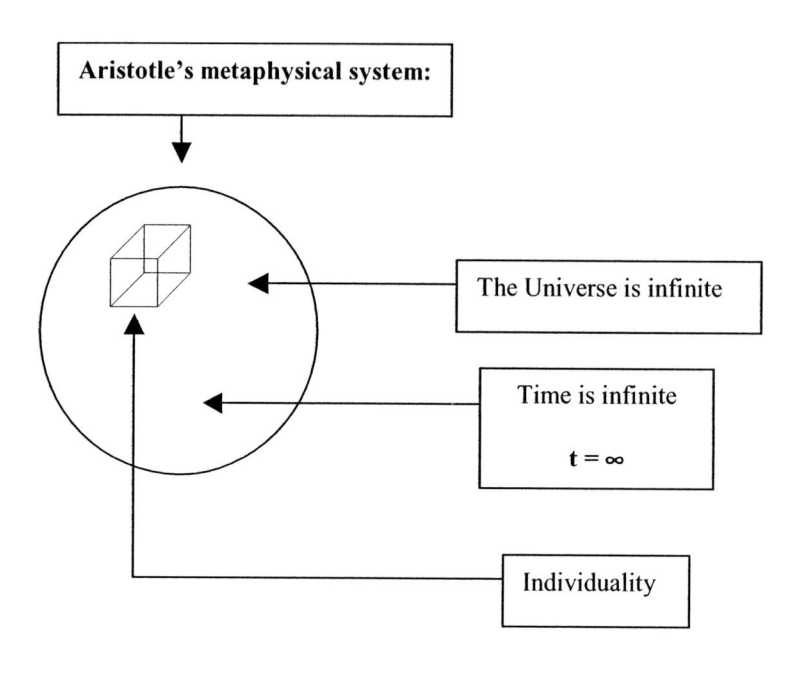

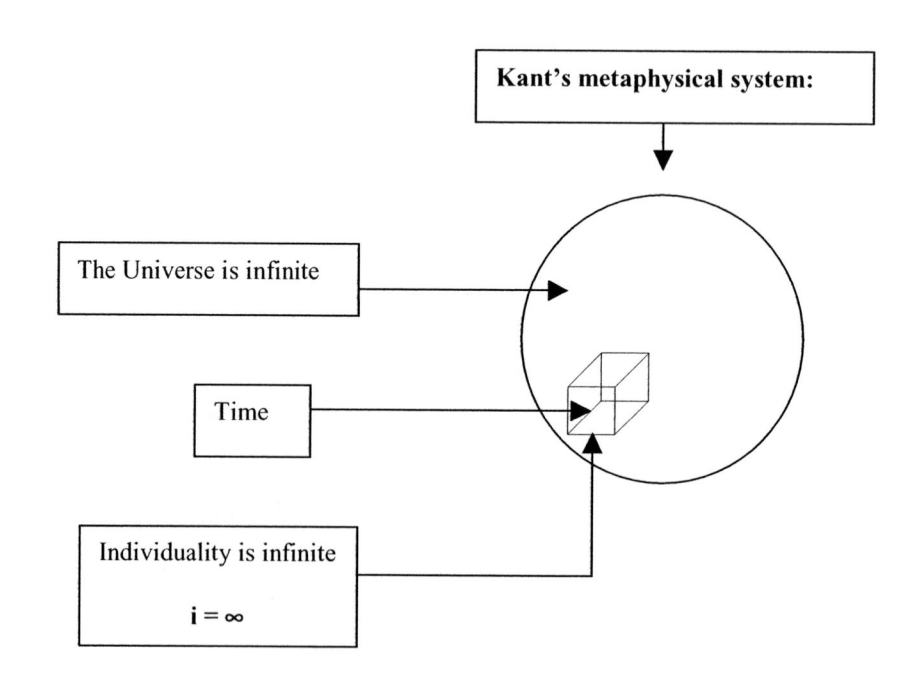

Aristotle's metaphysical system:

- The Universe is infinite
- Time is infinite
  $t = \infty$
- Individuality

Kant's metaphysical system:

- The Universe is infinite
- Time
- Individuality is infinite
  $i = \infty$

Without the interjection of infinity, both systems face the issue of termination. Such an issue is not an acceptable scenario for either system. Neither metaphysician acknowledges nor accepts the issue of their system eventually 'ending'.

This is the paradox of both systems: How does one rationalize the elimination of boredom? How does one rationalize the elimination of repetition? How does one rationalize the elimination of the infinite repetition of knowledge leading to the eternal state of boredom?

Time being endless is Aristotle's system:

Time being limited is Kant's system

But why is it assumed that there are only two choices: either there is endless time or there is limited time? In this tractate we will examine a third option: Endless time and limited time both existing simultaneously and independently one from the other while existing simultaneously and dependently one upon the other.

Before making a direct assault upon such a task, there are a few issues we need to address.

'Everything' equals passivity

The concept of 'what is' lies at the heart of the concept known as omniscience/passivity, which in turn lies at the heart of divine foreknowledge/passivity, which lies at the heart of determinism/passivity, which lies at the heart of… /passivity.

Passivity: living eternally in the past, living eternally in the present, the existence of no future. The past and present void the future equals passivity. It matters not if such an existence applies to sub-units of the whole, individual entities of knowing, or if such an existence applies to the whole of knowing.

Passive observing

In Tractate 3: Boethius and Free will, we discussed four forms of action:

Four forms of action:

Passive action:

1. Action as a state of being:

    Passive actions of being is the action of the primal state of existence as opposed to other forms of action emerging from the primal state of existence

2. Actions bound by the laws of nature

    Passive actions are actions taken by inanimate objects as well as actions that simulate the action of inanimate objects - a rock falls, you fall, a rock exists, you exist

Active action:

3. Free will

   Active actions of free will are actions taken by a 'knowing' object, action which could go various ways and whose action was directed by the 'knowing' object

4. Determinism

   Active actions of free will taken by a 'knowing' object whose intended actions have been overridden by actions of free will generated by a dominating second 'knowing' object

Kant brought us to the point where we are now ready to reevaluate this categorization of action.

Kant moved Aristotle's metaphysical system from being a passive form of system to being an active form of system.

A passive system is:

> *... the claim that the mind is passive with respect to what it experiences, and merely registers what impacts upon it ...*

Such a perception reinforces the validity of the categorization of action demonstrated.

Aristotle presumed that merely registering, observing an event, does not affect the event and therefore actions created by or subject to the laws of nature are actions predestined through the natural act of cause and effect itself.

Active observing

> *... and the converse claim that the mind is active with respect to its experience, so that in some sense the mind shapes what it experiences.'*

Kant 'turned the philosophical world upside down' by suggesting that merely registering, observing an event, actually affects the event.

Kant and therefore German idealism believes that the very act of 'observing' an object shapes what it is that is being observed. But is such an action a form of 'active' action? In reality it is no more active than an observation having no affect upon the event being observed.

If Kant's presumption is correct, and the uncertainty principle tends to indicate it may be, then in effect the event being 'changed' by observation is simply another form of natural event and subject to natural laws of which we at present are unaware exist.

Does the universe, do planets, does nature have awareness and as such decide to create natural catastrophes to intentionally offset the actions of humankind? Some individuals 'believe' this to be true. Is it a rational perception based upon science, reason, and religion? Such a debate is not the intent of this tractate.

The intent of this tractate is to understand how we can incorporate both Kant's critical philosophy, Kant's active abstract metaphysics and Aristotle's passive physical metaphysics into 'a'

The Error of Kant

metaphysical system which would simultaneously resolve the paradox Kant's system and the paradox Aristotle's system create.

Since we have addressed Aristotle's paradox in Tractate 2: Aristotle and Cartesianism, the intent is to now concentrate upon Kant's metaphysical system while at the same time acknowledging the basic validity of Aristotle metaphysical system.

Such a perception leads to a new categorization of action:

Four forms of action:

Passive action:

1. Action as a state of being:

    Passive actions of being is the action of the primal state of existence as opposed to other forms of action emerging from the primal state of existence

2. Actions bound by the laws of nature

    Passive actions are actions taken by inanimate objects as well as actions that simulate the action of inanimate objects - a rock falls, you fall, a rock exists, you exist

3. Determinism

    Active actions of free will taken by a 'knowing' object whose intended actions have been overridden by actions of free will generated by a dominating second 'knowing' object

Active action:

4. Free will

    Active actions of free will are actions taken by a 'knowing' object, action which could go various ways and whose action was directed by the 'knowing' object

Why is it that determinism becomes a form of 'passive' action? Action, which is controlled by 'intent' of the initiator of the action itself, is active action from the perspective of both the one producing the action and the event/object experiencing the action. Action uncontrolled is action found within the realm of the cause and effect cycle. The only forms of 'active' actions are actions controlled by the one being acted upon. In essence, actions which are 'active' are ones 'intended' by the 'creator of the action itself.

This is where free will lies. Free will lies in the ability to 'control' one's act, control one's intentional acts. What of the will of the whole as the whole? If the whole has consciousness, then the only form of active action generated by the totality of awareness are actions intentionally initiated by the whole itself.

For example: The fact an object falls 'downward' is most likely not an intentional act initiated by total awareness. It rather is a passive act simply following the laws of physics. It is doubtful that every act of an object 'falling' is intentional contemplated by the whole. It is not reasonable to expect the whole examines every single isolated event where a unit of mass is subjected to the gravitational potential of free fall and then decides whether or not to 'intentionally' allow the object to fall.

It is more probable, more reasonable to deduce that total awareness may have intended to initiate the dynamics required for a system of physical laws within which the physical operates in a form of passive dynamic action. An analogy to the process would be the situation of a person stepping into a car and turning the key with the intent of starting the complex interaction of pistons, valves, fuel injectors, energy transfer to the transmission, etc to begin in order to reach an objective. The objective: to go from here to there, wherever 'there' may be.

What then of totality? What is totality's objective in 'turning the key' to start the universe going. That is the issue we are to examine as we attempt to resolve the paradox Kant's system creates.

One may object at establishing such a seemingly impossible task. But one must not forget it is Kant we are examining and,

> *Kant insisted that although we cannot prove the world has a purpose, we must look upon it 'as if' it has a purpose.*[15]

Kant also held the view that humanity played a role in such a purpose.

> *Reading Leibniz, led Kant to see humanity as not only participating in nature, but over and above this participating in the ultimate purpose of the universe.*[16]

In this tractate, however, we are not going to refer to humanity in particular as 'the' participant in nature and participating in the ultimate purpose of the universe but rather we are going to refer to the concept of humanity as units of unique knowing filled with the concepts of space and time. The reason for this form of generalization is that our time in history differs from Kant's time in history.

During Kant's time in history, the concept of humans finding themselves confronted with entities of unique knowing from outside their own planet or for that matter from outside their own galaxy, was incomprehensible. Today such an encounter, such an existence, is no longer incomprehensible. In fact, we as a society are actually preparing scientifically for such an encounter. We are, however, avoiding such preparations both metaphysically and ontologically. This is perhaps the greatest sociological failure of our time.

The essence of this work, The War and Peace of a New Metaphysical Perception, is intended to lay the initial groundwork for just such preparations and it is the study of past metaphysical concepts, which acts as the means of allowing us to establish just such a foundation.

To accomplish such a task, we must return to the concept of Kant and metaphysical systems. Finding Kant's elusive foundation will lead us to resolving the metaphysical shortcomings of philosophers such as Zeno, Aristotle, Boethius, Leibniz, Kant, Hegel, Russell, Einstein, and Heidegger in order to establish the 'intra' as well as 'inter'-universal categorical imperatives, which will naturally emerge from a complete metaphysical system.

Kant could not find his categorical imperatives because Kant could not find 1st truth.. Kant could not verbalize the complete workings of his metaphysical system. The problem Kant had with all these issues emerged out of the fact that Kant's system lacked specific elements needed to complete his system.

The Error of Kant

It is the elements alluding Kant that we will establish. It is the missing elements, which we will add to both Kant's system and Aristotle's system in order to establish 'a' complete system.

In truth, it is not an addition of elements we will use as the means of finding a complete system but rather the more potent process of fusion, which we shall use.

Kant and Aristotle had no idea regarding the power of fusion. It is only in today's time period that we have been made aware of such phenomenal potential.

Before we can begin using the tool of fusion, however, we must resurrect an element of philosophy from the dead.

The place to begin such a process is with the understanding of the ramification of Kant's system. The ramification: the premature announcement regarding the death of metaphysics.

Raising metaphysics up from the dead

The perception exists that Kant believed Metaphysics died with the emergence of his 'system'. Such a perception emerges from the 'belief' that Kant's system is 'the' ultimate of systems. But was this the case or was Kant's perception simply that his 'system' was 'the' system and as such described the whole of all?

Kant perceived his system to be:

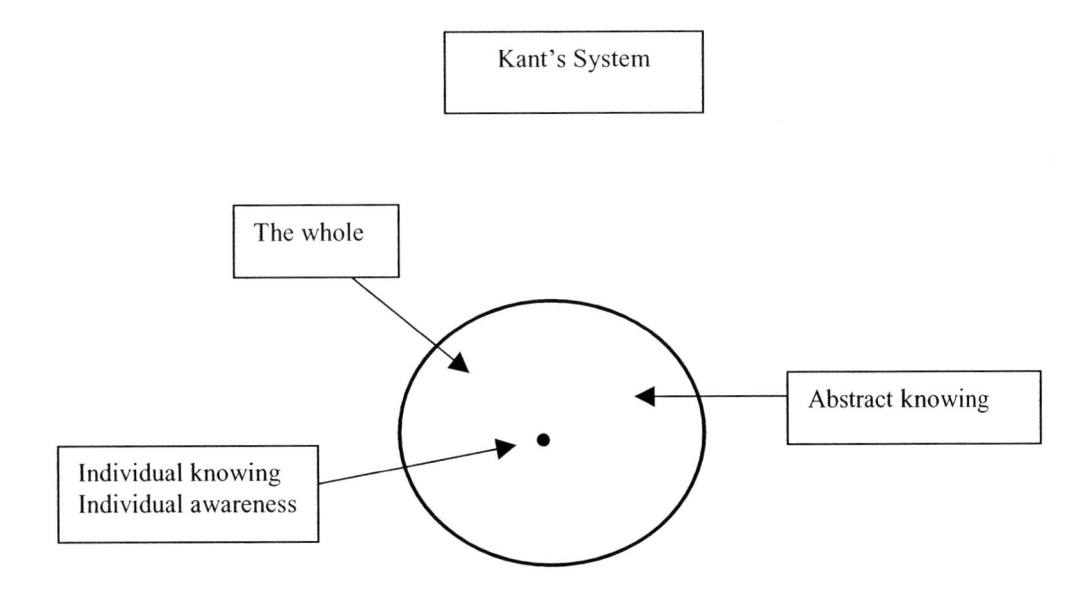

Kant's System

- The whole
- Abstract knowing
- Individual knowing / Individual awareness

As such, Kant visualized no 'outside' to his system since his system was the whole, accounted for the whole.

'Metaphysics' is a term coined by Aristotle. The term is comprised of two syllables: 'meta' – outside, 'physics' – the physical.

Kant visualized his abstract system as replacing the old Aristotelian physical system:

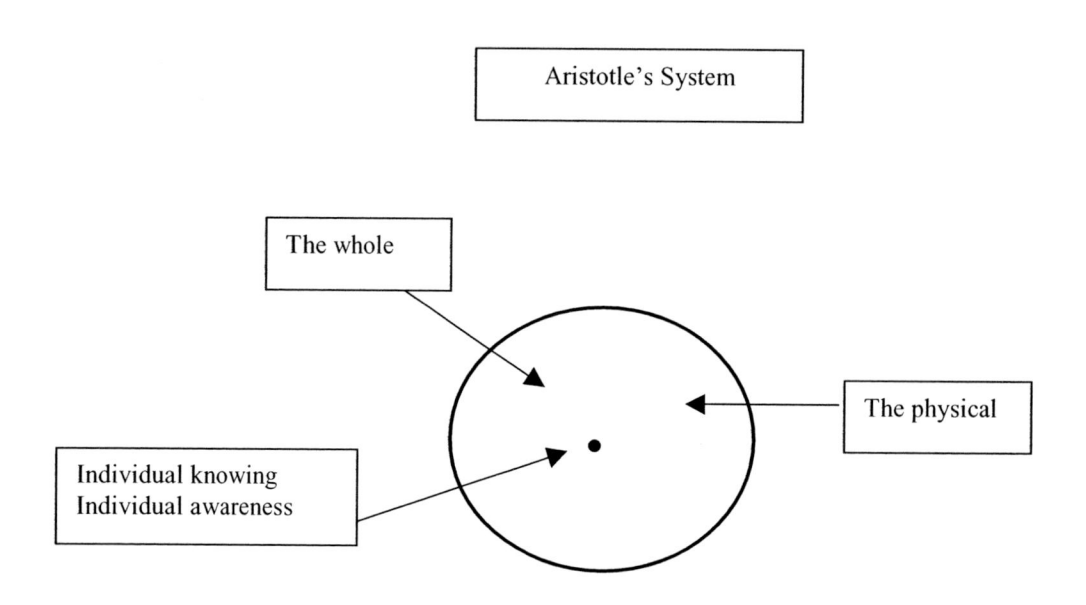

Aristotle's System

The whole

The physical

Individual knowing
Individual awareness

Kant's system was perceived to be the ultimate of metaphysical systems

In essence Kant and Aristotle had the same model. The variation, which occurred between the two, lay in the fabric comprising the medium of the two. The universal fabric found within Aristotle's system was the physical and the universal fabric found within Kant's system was the abstract. Again we see the paradox of Zeno, multiplicity versus seamlessness, comes once again to the surface.

This presented a problem, however, for Kant sought to find 'the' foundation of his system, sought to find first cause to his system, sought to find first principle.

It was in the basic quest to find first cause where Kant found his system to be lacking.

With the perception that Kant's system was not only the ultimate of systems but 'the' system itself, metaphysics died for having 'discovered' the ultimate of metaphysical systems there was now no need for the further study of metaphysics. Now metaphysics in actuality did not die for metaphysics is abstractual and as such cannot 'die' for abstractions are not affected by space or time.

Metaphysics can, like other minor points with phenomenal potential, be suppressed.

> The Aristotelian system was Greek, but the Judeo-Christian story of creation was Semitic – and Semites didn't have such a fear of the void. The very act of creation was out of a

chaotic void, and theologians like Saint Augustine who lived in the fourth century, tried to explain it {nothingness} away by referring to the state before creation as 'a nothing something' that is empty of form but yet 'falls short of utter nothingness.' The fear of the void was so great that Christian scholars tried to fix the Bible to match Aristotle rather than vice versa.[17]

But metaphysics, like nothingness, is simply a concept. Metaphysics is the study of what lies outside the physical and the interaction of the two: the physical and what lies outside the physical. It must be acknowledged here, at this point, that philosophy, science, and religion, have all three attempted to complicate the study of metaphysics. All three have attempted to cling to either a Kantian or an Aristotelian perception.

The problem generated by insisting upon one or the other perception can be eliminated in one simple move: Fuse the two. Fuse the Kantian and Aristotelian systems into one system: A non-Cartesian system powered by a Cartesian system.

Such a process gives us:

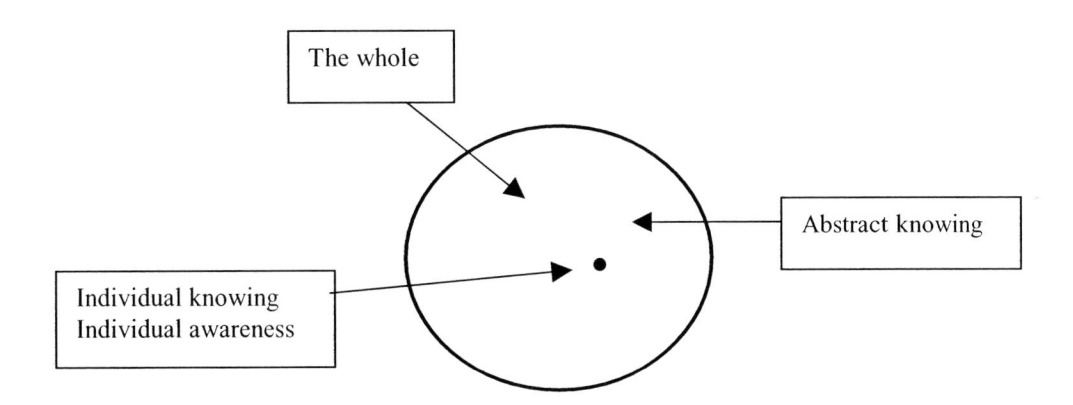

Kant

The whole

Abstract knowing

Individual knowing
Individual awareness

The War & Peace of a New Metaphysical Perception

Aristotle

- The whole → ●
- The physical → ●
- Individual knowing / Individual awareness → ●

Aristotle fused with Kant

- The whole 'Being'
- The physical *being* – action, process/reality
- Individual knowing, individual awareness 'being'
- The abstract

The result: Kant 'saw' beyond Aristotle. Kant's system remains intact. Aristotle's system remains intact.

The result: 'being' *being* 'Being'

With the understanding that the whole is the sum of its parts merged with the understanding of 'a' 'system' being active versus passive, in other words, not just existing but existing in a dynamic fashion, we obtain a system where the whole interacts with its parts and the parts simultaneously interact with the whole. Such a dynamic system becomes symbiotic in nature. As such we obtain a system where the whole is no longer equal to the sum of its parts but rather becomes 'greater' than the sum of its parts. Such a system, the Kantian merged with the Aristotelian, 'being' *being* 'Being, might, in a fusion of cosmological and ontological concepts, be termed: symbiotic panentheism.

In tractates 0 – 5, we have examined such a system in terms of its capability to resolve paradoxes evolving out of perceptions 'nothingness', abstraction/Zeno, physicality/Aristotle, divine foreknowledge/Boethius, Centricism/Copernicus, and omni-benevolence/Leibniz brought to the dialectics of philosophy, science, and religion. Now we are going to examine how such a 'metaphysical' system can resolve categorical imperatives'/Kant's dilemma while simultaneously acknowledging the genius of Kant.

The power of fusion thus initiates of a third metaphysical system (the first being the Aristotelian metaphysical system and the second being the Kantian metaphysical system): a non-Cartesian system powered by a Cartesian system.

At one point we 'believed' Aristotle's system was 'the' system. Later we 'believed' Kant's system was 'the' system. If it is true that history repeats itself, with the fusion of the two, we will once again fall into the error of 'believing' that the fusion of the two systems is 'the' system. Let's not delude ourselves a third time, however. We have not come to the end of metaphysics. Metaphysics is simply at the end of the beginning and about to enter the beginning of the 'body' of its work. Metaphysics is about to enter its most interesting of times, is about to write the transitional statement leading from Chapter one of metaphysics to chapter two of metaphysics found within the history book of metaphysics itself.

Part II: Resolving the issue with a new metaphysical perception

Metaphysics and Cartesianism revisited

We come back again to the concept of systems. Do we really need a system, as Kant believed to be the case? We will not belabor the point other than to make a few pertinent comments.

First:

> If we accept Kant's perception that we should be able to explain the concepts of metaphysics through the process of modeling a system, then it is a model, a system, we must seek.

Second:

> If we claim a system is not necessary, then it is a 'system less' system we must seek but that in itself is a form of system. A 'system less' system is the most minimalist form of system.

Third:

> Kant suggested: If we do not accept his system then we must proceed to establish another system.

All three issues are what are being addressed within this tractate. An alternative system to Kant's system as well as an alternative system to Aristotle's system is being proposed. As one examines the new system, one may object to the suggestion that a new system is being proposed. Such objections are invalid. As much as it may seem that the newly proposed system is but a fusion of two system, the Aristotelian system and the Kantian system, one must not lose track of the fact that Kant's system was simply a modification of Aristotle's system.

Kant moved Aristotle's closed system of passive action into being a closed system of active action. Kant moved the concept of time from the Aristotelian concept of being located within reality into time being located within the individual.

Metaphysics is no different than science or religion in terms of progressive growth. Metaphysical growth is simply the advancement of what it was we understood, into being something we now understand to exist. Thus for Kant to advance Aristotle's metaphysical system from being a closed passive system of action into being a closed active system of action, is no more valid or invalid in terms of advancing metaphysical understanding than to advance Kant's system of a closed active system into being an open passive system powered by an closed active system which exists as a subset of the open passive system.

The significance of this new system:

1. Not only does the concept of system remain intact but now the system itself becomes a 'growing' dynamic system in and of itself while retaining both concepts of passivity and action.
2. There is now an independent location for limited time
3. There is now an independent location for endless time
4. There is now an independent location within which 'nothingness' can logically be placed
5. There is now an independent location within which the infinite can be placed

6. Aristotle's system remains intact
7. Kant's system remains intact

In addition, and not any less significantly, this new system now finds itself accommodating free will. Free will now finds two regions from which it emanates:

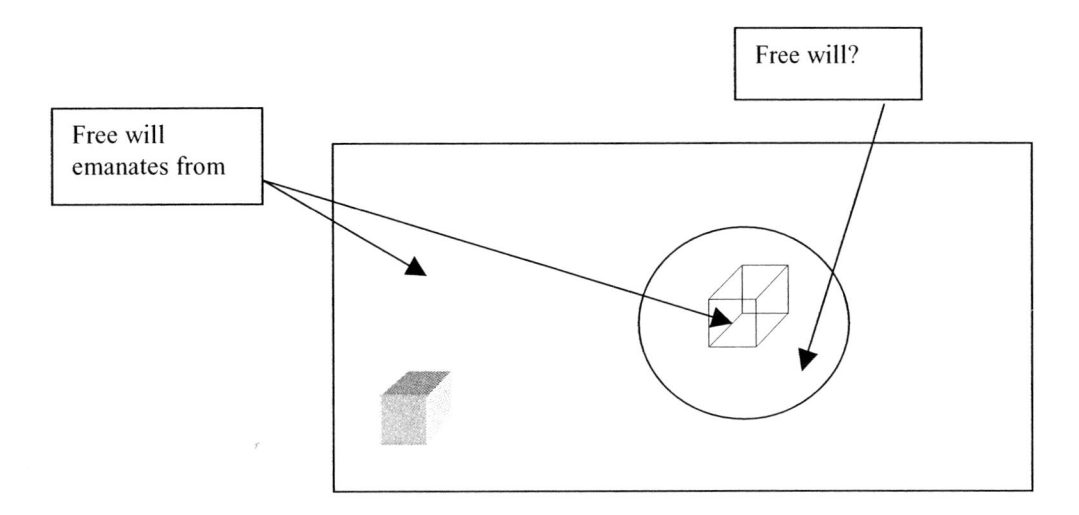

Whether or not the physical universe has free will of its own is not the question of metaphysics. Such a question is a question of cosmology and ontology.

In addition, this new system now finds itself accommodating determinism. Determinism now finds two regions from which it emanates:

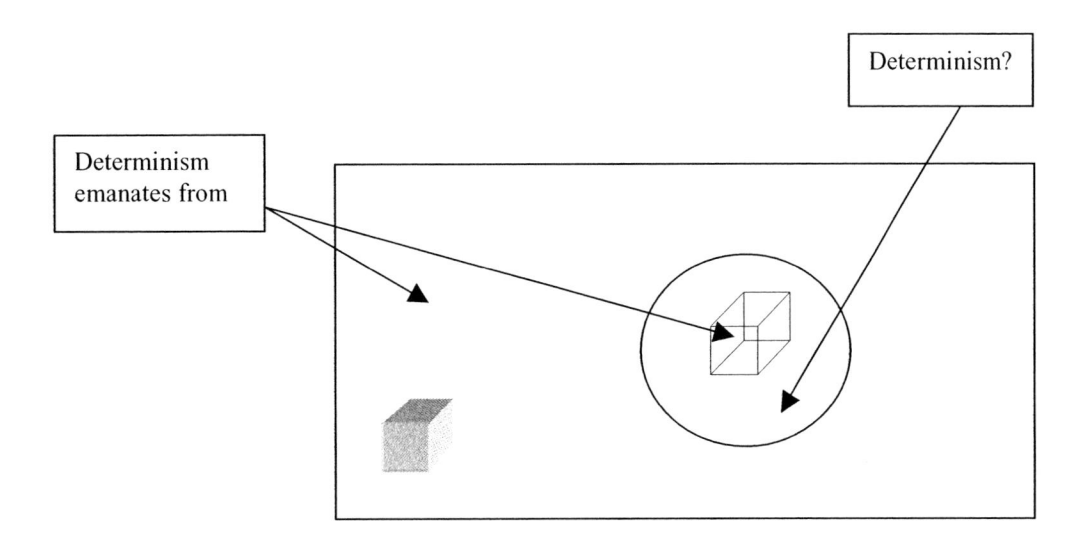

Whether or not the whole exerts its free will in a deterministic fashion 'within' the physical universe is also not the question of metaphysics. Such a question is a question of ontology and cosmology versus it being the question of the reverse nature, of cosmology and ontology, as the previous diagram regarding free will suggested vis-à-vis free will of the universe as an entity.

To make such limited claims as to the responsibility of metaphysics is by no means shirking the duty of metaphysics but rather further defining the very responsibility to which metaphysics must look. Metaphysics is the study of what lies 'beyond'/'outside' – 'the physical' and the interrelationship of such a region to ourselves and ourselves to it.

Metaphysics is not a study of what lies beyond the physical and how such a region interacts with the physical itself, nor is metaphysics the study of what occurs 'after' the physical no longer exists should such an occurrence be possible.

But what of Metaphysics and Cartesianism? What exactly does this have to do with Metaphysics and Cartesianism themselves?

Metaphysics

Over and over we come back to the concept of metaphysics: Meta - beyond, physics – the physical. Again and again one responds: We can never understand such a region for it lies beyond what we have 'seen' and therefore must 'contain' what it is which lies beyond our ability to 'ever' 'see'.

Be that as it may, we did not let this perception stop us from hypothesizing what lay 'inside' the atom. We did not let such a perception stop us from hypothesizing what lay 'inside' a neutron. We did not let such a perception stop us from hypothesizing what lay inside a 'quark'.

Metaphysics: the study of what lies beyond the physical.

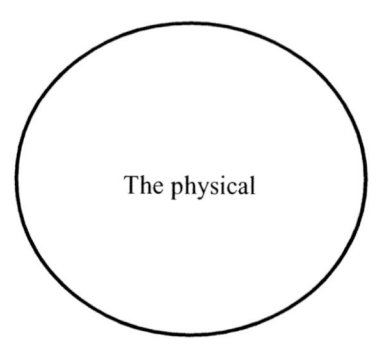

○ The physical

We know to be:

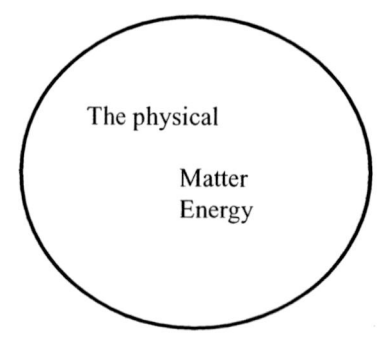

○ The physical
Matter
Energy

We postulate to be:

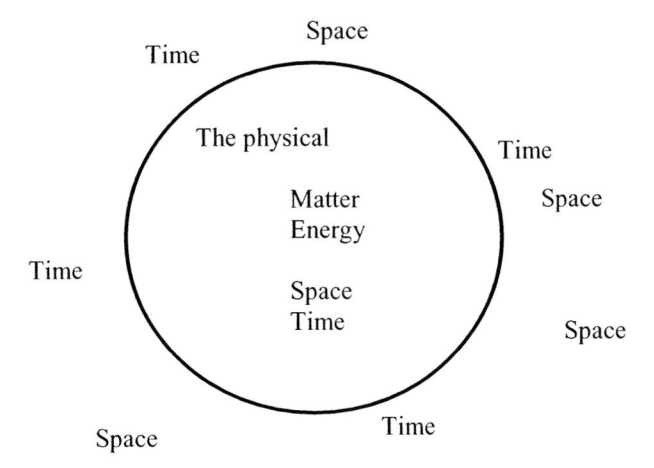

```
                    Space
         Time
                  ┌─────────┐
                  │The physical│    Time
                  │            │
      Time        │  Matter    │    Space
                  │  Energy    │
                  │            │
                  │  Space     │
                  │  Time      │    Space
                  └─────────┘
         Space         Time
```

Upon close scrutiny we know this to be an inaccurate depiction for space and time have been identified as fabrics of the universe. Therefore if space and time were where we said they were in the former diagram, we would have to expand the boundaries of the universe to include them, giving us:

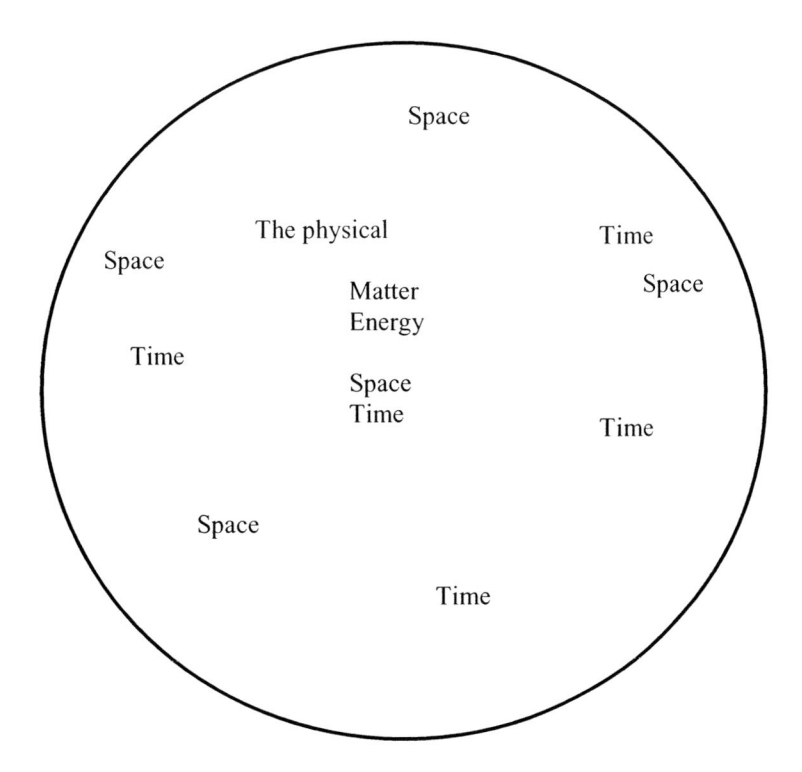

```
                     Space

              The physical
      Space                      Time
                                    Space
                Matter
                Energy
      Time
                Space
                Time             Time

         Space
                     Time
```

The War & Peace of a New Metaphysical Perception

Does this mean space and time, matter and energy, cannot be found 'outside the physical/the universe? Yes and no. Matter and energy, space and time cannot be found 'outside' the physical/the universe in the form of being the 'fabric', which exists as 'the fabric', which lies outside the physical/the universe just as 'the fabric' of what lies 'outside' the physical/the universe cannot be 'the fabric' of what lies 'inside' the physical/the universe. If 'the fabric' of the physical lay 'outside' the physical/the universe:

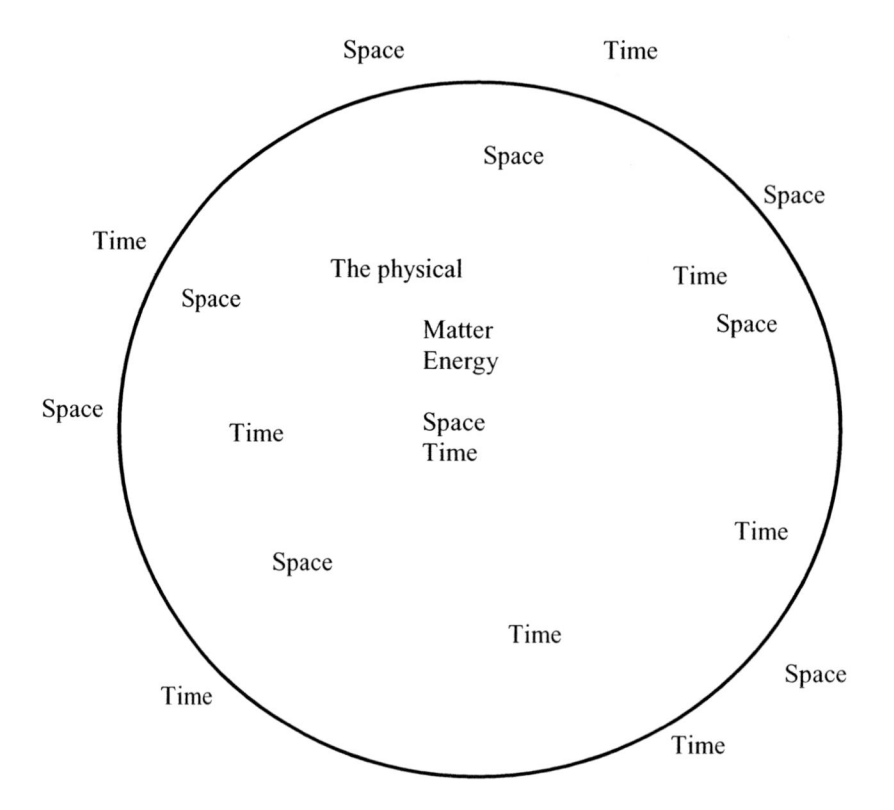

we would simply have to expand the physical/the universe once again:

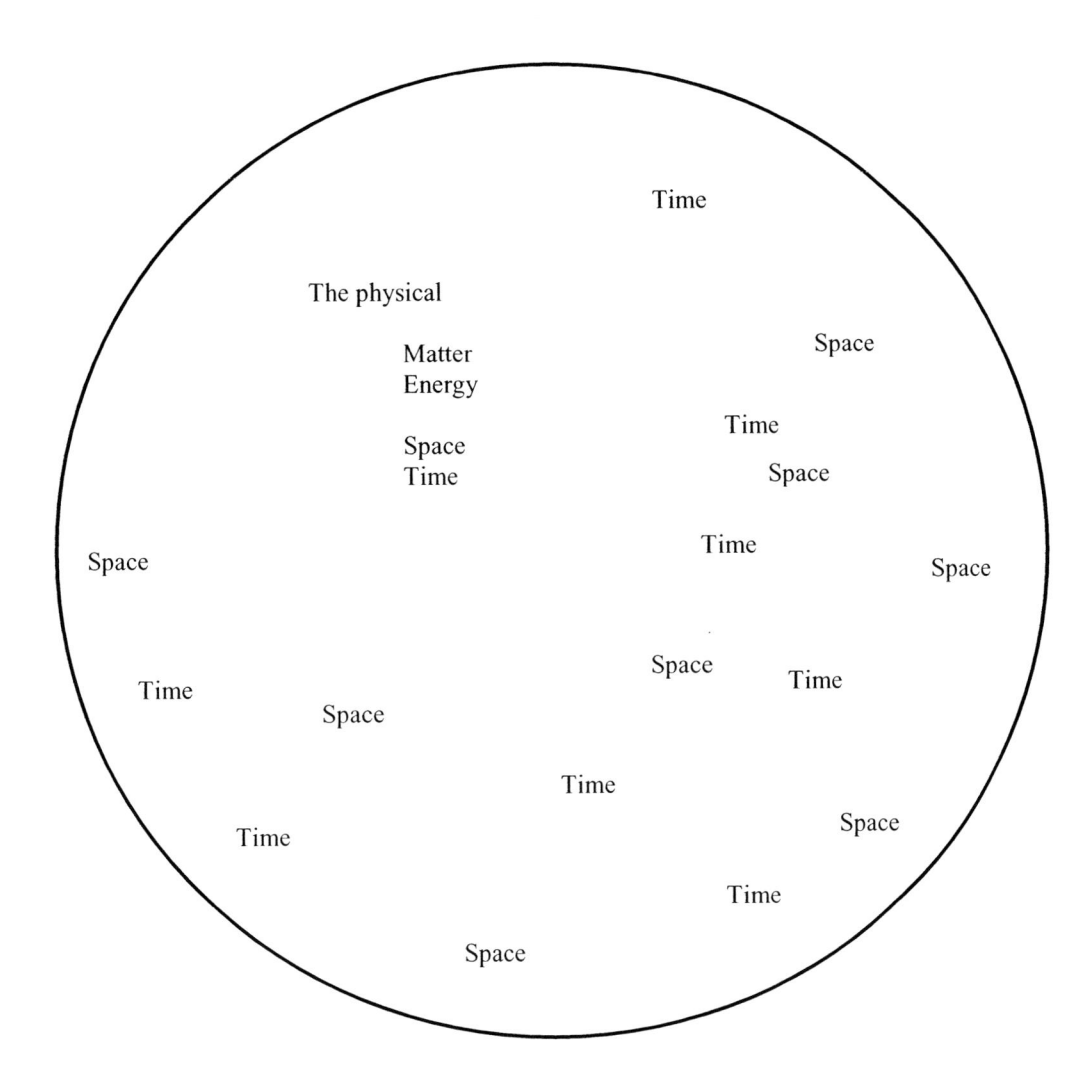

```
                         Time

         The physical
                                    Space
           Matter
           Energy
                                Time
            Space                    Space
            Time
                            Time
                                              Space
   Space

                                Space
                                         Time
   Time
              Space
                         Time
                                            Space
        Time
                                        Time
                   Space
```

So is there any way to 'know' what lies 'outside', what lies 'beyond' the boundary of the physical/the universe

From the given argument we can make a fairly good guess, hypothesize, as to what lies beyond the physical/the universe. We can be fairly certain that what acts as the fabric of what lies 'beyond' the physical/the universe is not a fabric of space and time, matter and energy.

But what type of fabric could exist other than space and time, matter and energy? Zeno gives us a good insight into an alternative fabric to space and time, matter and energy.

Space and time, matter and energy, spawn a product of cause and effect. Therefore lets now diagram what we perceive to be the physical composed of a space/time, matter/energy fabric and examine the results. To do so we will need to reduce the 'apparent' size of the physical/the

The War & Peace of a New Metaphysical Perception

universe in order to place what lies 'beyond' the universe in its appropriate location relative to the diagram:

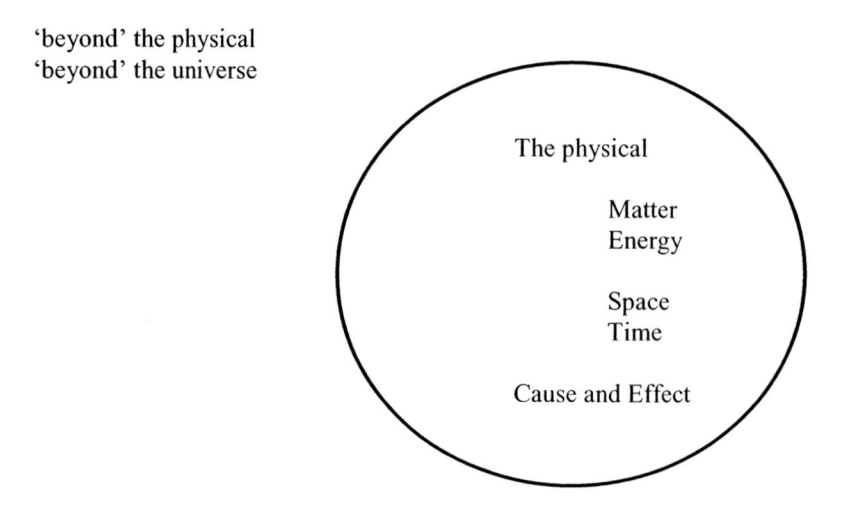

'beyond' the physical
'beyond' the universe

The physical

Matter
Energy

Space
Time

Cause and Effect

To assist our need to focus upon the task of examining what lies 'beyond' the physical/the universe, we will enclose what lies 'beyond' the physical and as such we obtain:

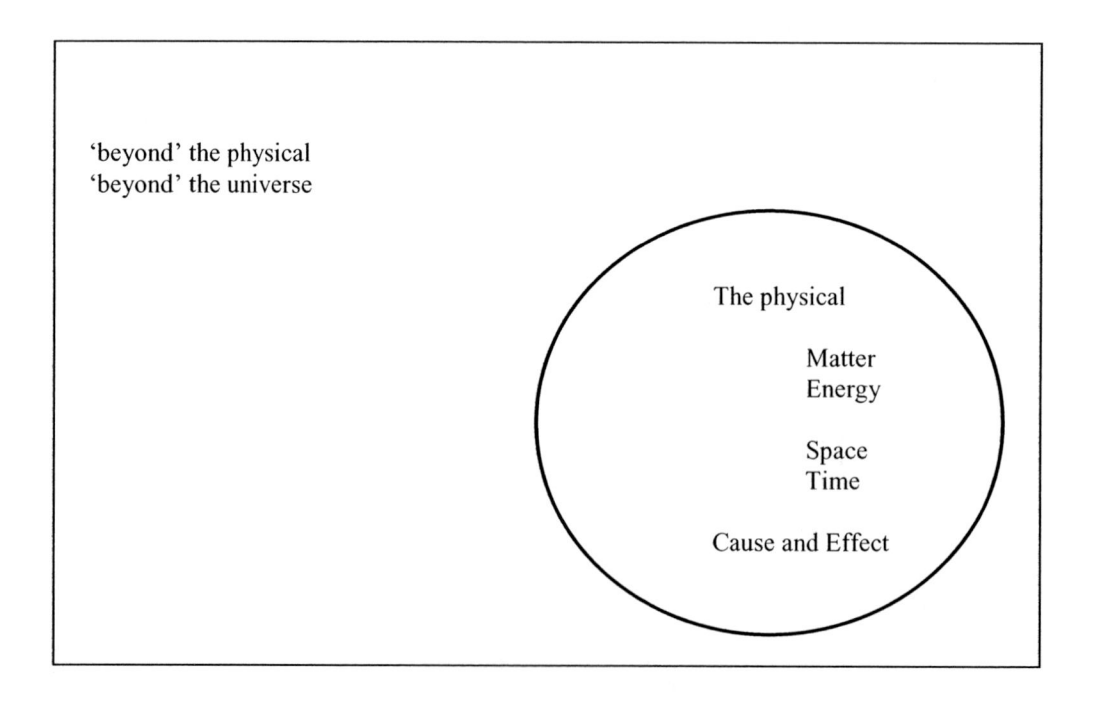

'beyond' the physical
'beyond' the universe

The physical

Matter
Energy

Space
Time

Cause and Effect

The Error of Kant

Now we know space and time are not the fabric of what lies beyond the physical, therefore we obtain:

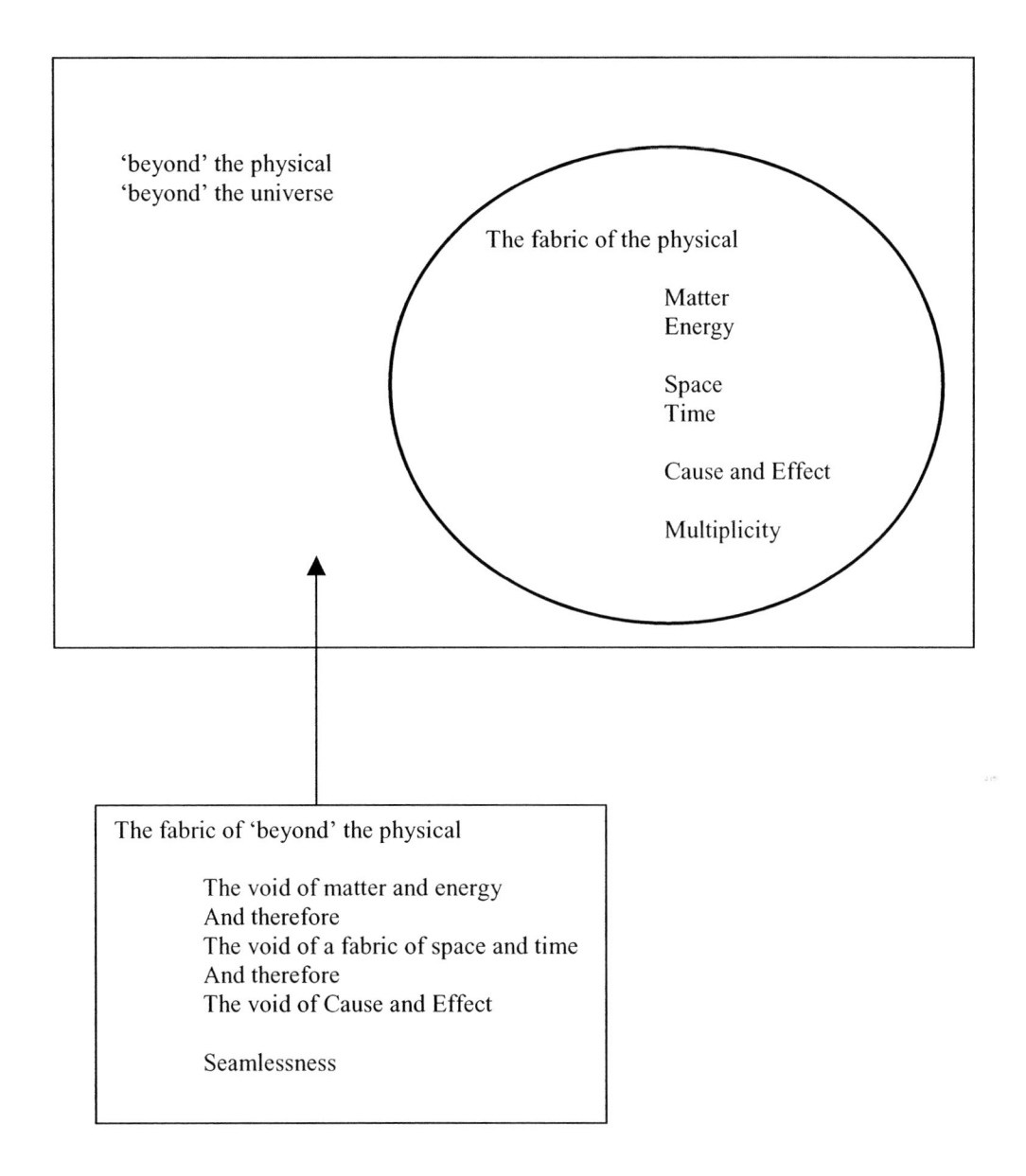

```
┌─────────────────────────────────────────────────────────┐
│                                                         │
│   'beyond' the physical        ╭───────────────╮        │
│   'beyond' the universe       ╱                 ╲       │
│                              │  The fabric of    │      │
│                              │  the physical     │      │
│                              │                   │      │
│                              │     Matter        │      │
│                              │     Energy        │      │
│                              │                   │      │
│                              │     Space         │      │
│                              │     Time          │      │
│                              │                   │      │
│                              │   Cause and Effect│      │
│                              │                   │      │
│                              │     Multiplicity  │      │
│                               ╲                 ╱       │
│              ▲                 ╰───────────────╯        │
│              │                                          │
└──────────────┼──────────────────────────────────────────┘
               │
   ┌───────────┴─────────────────────────────┐
   │  The fabric of 'beyond' the physical    │
   │                                         │
   │      The void of matter and energy      │
   │      And therefore                      │
   │      The void of a fabric of space and time │
   │      And therefore                      │
   │      The void of Cause and Effect       │
   │                                         │
   │      Seamlessness                       │
   └─────────────────────────────────────────┘
```

We now once again come back to Zeno and his concepts of seamlessness and multiplicity. But rather than obtain Zeno's concept of there being only 'one' location we find we have 'two' locations. The physical/the universe finds itself containing the fabric of cause and effect generated by matter and energy explaining Zeno's multiplicity and the second location, 'beyond' the physical/the universe, containing a fabric void cause and effect generated by matter and energy because matter and energy are aspects of the physical/multiplicity and thus we obtain a fabric of seamlessness generated by the lack of matter and energy, space and time, and cause and effect.

Once again the question: What lies 'beyond' the physical? Put more specifically: What lies 'beyond' the Cartesianism. The answer: What lies 'beyond' the Cartesian is the non-Cartesian.

> Cartesianism: Cause and effect, beginning and end, a foundation based sub-system.

> Non-Cartesianism: No cause and effect, no beginning and no end, a foundationless set.

Cause and effect, cause and effect, cause and effect: is the primary concept of Cartesianism – beginning/end, concepts

'a' foundation

Aristotle states that we are immersed within space and time from which emerges the concept of passive observation. Kant states that we are not immersed in space and time but rather that time and space are immersed in us from which emerges the concept of active observation.

In order to establish which is correct and thus take the subsequent step of 'building' a model of one's metaphysical system, one appears to then have little choice but to choose which is correct: Are we immersed in space and time or is space and time immersed within ourselves.

The obvious, however, is not always the most appropriate choice. There is a second, less obvious, choice. One can accept the accuracy of both and then establish one's metaphysical model. That is precisely what the system of 'being' *being* 'Being' does.

The Error of Kant

```
┌─────────────────────┐   ┌─────────────────────┐
│ Time and space - Kant│   │Time and space - Aristotle│
└─────────────────────┘   └─────────────────────┘
```

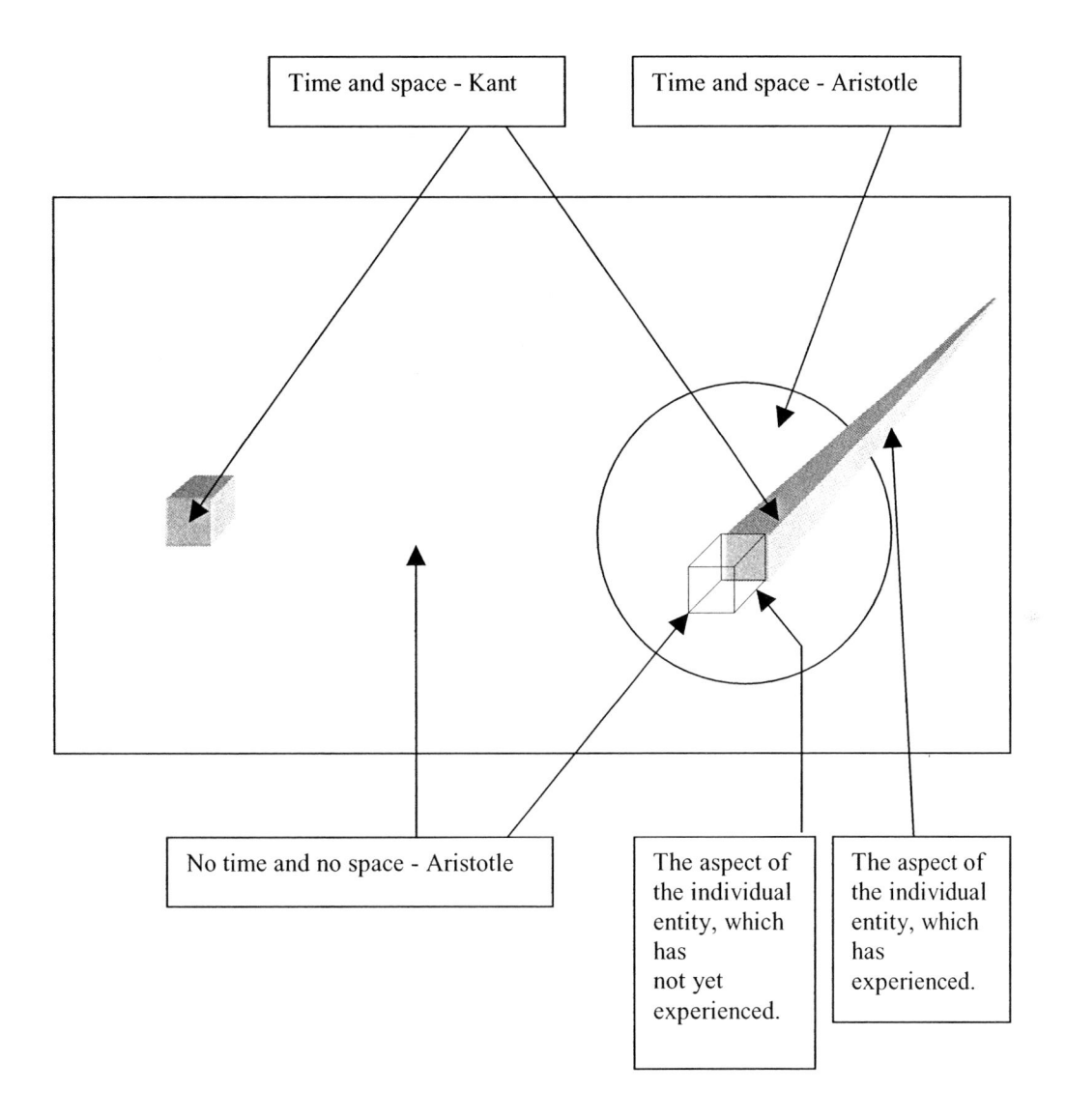

```
┌──────────────────────────┐   ┌──────────────┐   ┌──────────────┐
│ No time and no space -   │   │ The aspect of│   │ The aspect of│
│ Aristotle                │   │ the individual│  │ the individual│
└──────────────────────────┘   │ entity, which│   │ entity, which│
                               │ has          │   │ has          │
                               │ not yet      │   │ experienced. │
                               │ experienced. │   │              │
                               └──────────────┘   └──────────────┘
```

So it is, time and space are found within us and likewise we are found within time and space

We understand how we travel through space and time, but how does space and time become a part of our abstractual existence? Time and space become a part of our abstractual existence through our experiencing events within the parameters of space and time themselves. This begins with 'virgin consciousness' and ends wherever the ending of the travel through space and time may find itself to be.

Kant was at a loss to establish his system as a system for he perceived his system to be a modification of the Aristotelian system. In other words Kant perceived the universe to be the system. In addition Kant perceived his system to simply invert the Aristotelian system from being one of passivity to being one of action. The system, however, remained bound within the Aristotelian concept of being 'the' universe.

The War & Peace of a New Metaphysical Perception

Because Kant's system remained bound in Kant's perception of 'contemporary bounds', Kant could not find 'a' foundation, 'a' first truth, 'a' first cause, 'a' ….

With the new metaphysical system fusing Aristotle's system with Kant's system, 'a' foundation, 'a' first truth, etc now become multiple 'first' truths, multiple 'first' foundations based upon the concept of relativistic first principles established in detail within Tractate 2: Aristotle and Cartesianism.

Kant's quandary of being unable to establish which of the concepts, Causation exists, the universe exists, or I exist, is 'the' foundation upon which the other truths emerge disappears as a dilemma with the establishment of a metaphysical system where the three exists in separate locations as 'the' base foundation of their own existence:

'being' *being* 'Being'

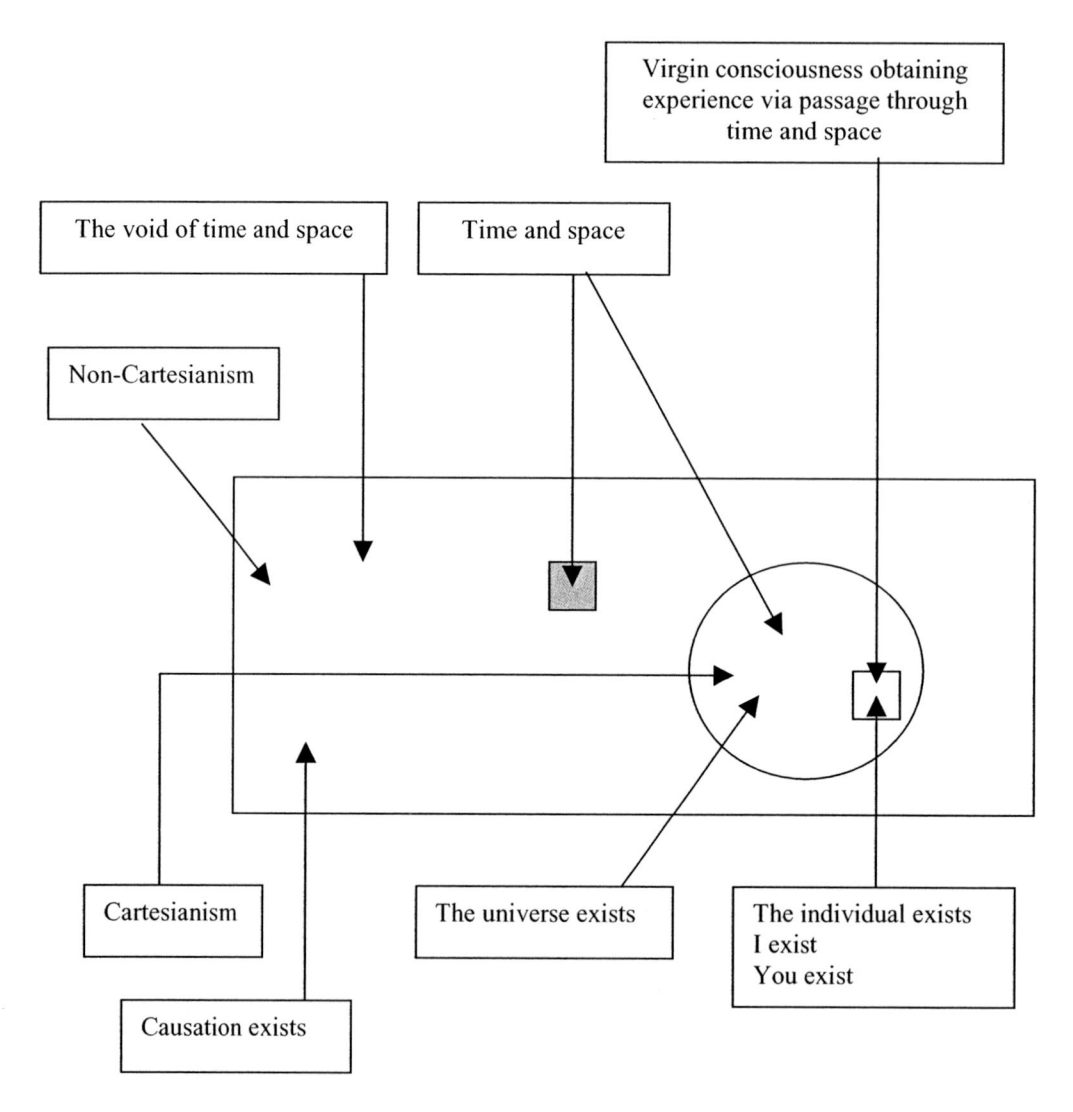

With such a system Kant no longer need find 'a' 1st principle for three 1st principles exist equally relative one to the other. Once again, for a more detailed explanation of the concept of relativistic 1st principle one should refer to Tractate 2: Aristotle and Cartesianism.

This then brings us to the concept of why we need 'a whole'.

The need for 'a' whole

We perceive there to be three aspects to time: the past, the present, and the future.

Such a perception leads us to the false perception that metaphysical perceptions are limited to three forms of possibilities: what was, what is, and what will be.

Such a perception, added to our perception of the universe being the only 'location', leads to chaos and thus confusion:

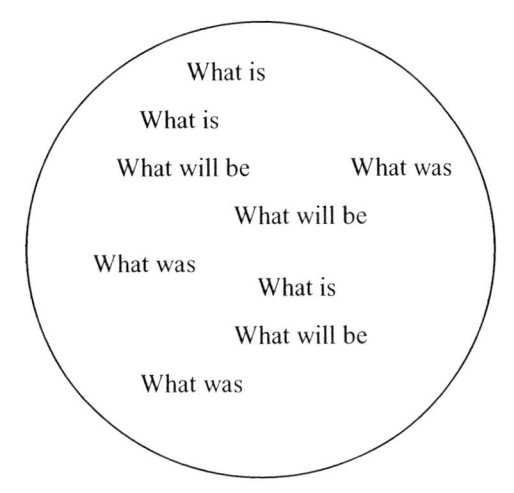

```
            What is
         What is
      What will be        What was
                   What will be
      What was
                What is
              What will be
         What was
```

The confusion is one of our own making. As such the chaos generated by confusion can be methodically organized by ourselves to bring order out of chaos. The order, however, can only be accomplished through the introduction of an additional metaphysical perception regarding time.

If we reexamine our perception of time we will see that in truth there are only two aspects of time: The present and the future. At first glance, such a statement would imply a process of subtraction rather than addition to our perceptions of time.

In truth, such a reordering of time creates a perception of time, which leads us to the more accurate perception of time. With such a reordering of time we begin to see time as having two aspects: 'what is' and 'what could' be

The War & Peace of a New Metaphysical Perception

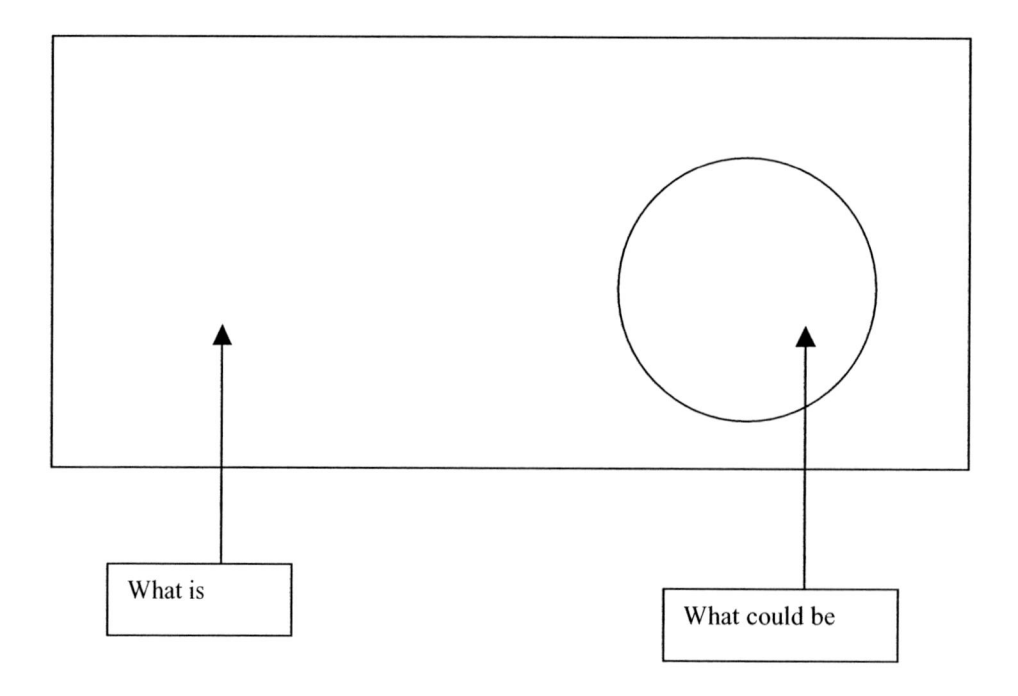

[Diagram: A large rectangle containing a circle in the upper right portion. Two arrows point upward from labeled boxes below—"What is" points into the rectangle (outside the circle), and "What could be" points into the circle.]

Now why use the phrase 'what could be' versus the phrase 'what will be'?

'What will be' indicates that it 'will be'. Such a statement cannot be denied, and therefore it must already be while it may not yet be. The result: What will be 'is' and as such simply is a part of 'what is'. 'What will be' is not 'potentiality' but rather predetermined and thus lies in the fabric of timelessness and spacelessness. 'What will be' is a part of what lies 'beyond' the physical/the universe.

What lies 'within' the fabric of space/time, cause and effect is "what 'could' be", potentiality. The cause will lead to an effect. In terms of the physical/multiplicity the effect is predictable. In terms of the non-physical/seamlessness/abstraction the effect is unpredictable, has potentiality of becoming what is not predictable.

We therefore now obtain:

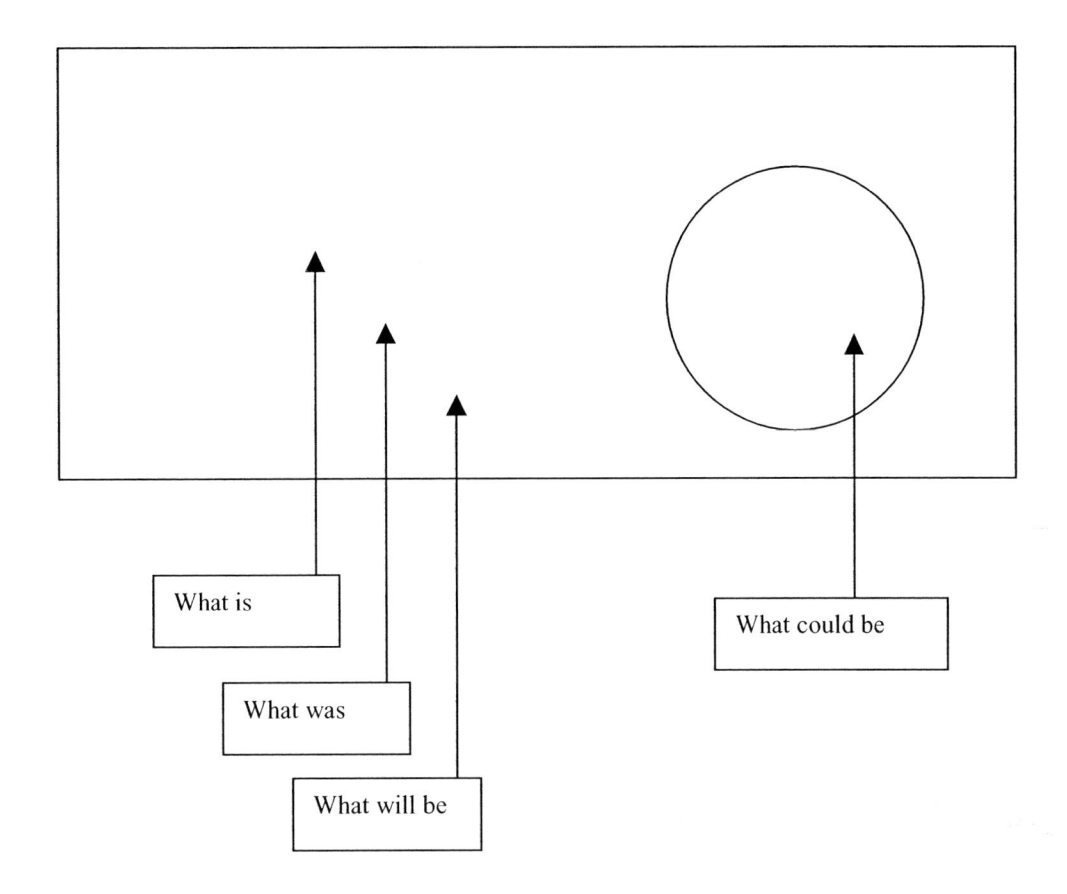

[Diagram: A rectangle with three arrows pointing up from boxes labeled "What is", "What was", and "What will be" into the rectangle, and a circle inside the rectangle with an arrow pointing up into it from a box labeled "What could be".]

And as such we begin to formulate an understanding regarding a 'need' for a whole, which rephrased becomes: We begin to formulate an understanding regarding a 'need' for a system.

Such a perception leads us to arguments reinforcing the new metaphysical perception of 'being' *being* 'Being'.

The whole does not change

Change is a concept of cause and effect not addition for addition is a concept tied to the premise of order emerging out of time, before and after linear progressions of events.

From the American Heritage Dictionary of the English Language, Third Edition, 1992:

>   Change vb. To cause to be different, to transform
>   Change int. To become different or alterations
>   Change n. The act, process, or result of altering or modifying

The War & Peace of a New Metaphysical Perception

There is a location of cause and effect, a location of first this then that, before and after, causing to be different. Such a location, by definition, requires time. For cause and effect to occur the effect must follow the cause.

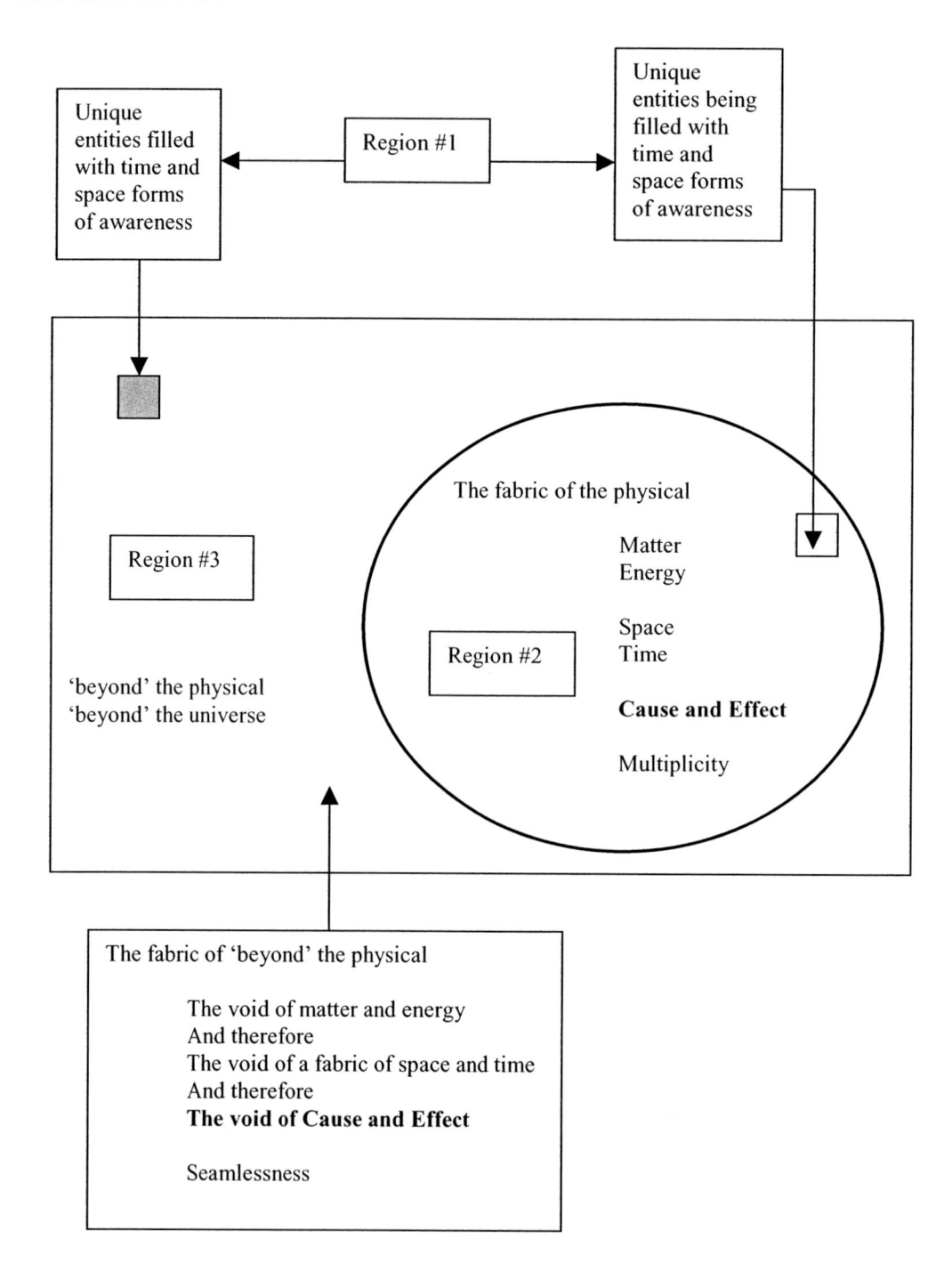

```
┌─────────────┐                              ┌─────────────┐
│ Unique      │                              │ Unique      │
│ entities    │                              │ entities    │
│ filled      │    ┌──────────┐              │ being       │
│ with time   │◄───│Region #1 │─────────────►│ filled with │
│ and space   │    └──────────┘              │ time and    │
│ forms of    │                              │ space forms │
│ awareness   │                              │ of awareness│
└─────────────┘                              └─────────────┘
       │                                             │
       ▼                                             │
┌──────────────────────────────────────────────────┐ │
│   ■                                              │ │
│                                                  │ │
│                      ╭─────────────────────╮     │ │
│                     ╱  The fabric of the   ╲    │ │
│  ┌─────────┐       │    physical           │    │ │
│  │Region #3│      │                         │◄──┘
│  └─────────┘      │         Matter          │
│                   │         Energy          │
│                   │                         │
│                   │   ┌─────────┐ Space     │
│                   │   │Region #2│ Time      │
│                   │   └─────────┘           │
│  'beyond' the      │                         │
│  physical          │      Cause and Effect  │
│  'beyond' the       │                         │
│  universe          │      Multiplicity      │
│                     ╲                       ╱
│                      ╰─────────────────────╯
│                              ▲
└──────────────────────────────┼───────────────────┘
                               │
         ┌─────────────────────────────────────┐
         │ The fabric of 'beyond' the physical │
         │                                     │
         │   The void of matter and energy     │
         │   And therefore                     │
         │   The void of a fabric of space     │
         │   and time                          │
         │   And therefore                     │
         │   **The void of Cause and Effect**  │
         │                                     │
         │   Seamlessness                      │
         └─────────────────────────────────────┘
```

Within region #1:

> Cause and effect do not exist but cause and effect experiences/perceptions develop

Within region #2:

> Cause and effect exist and emerge out of the presence of 'universal' time and space.

Within region #3:

> Cause and effect do not exist since the region is void the 'universal' fabric of time and space.

Region #3, lacking time and space as the universal fabric, does find time and space, and cause and effect, concepts imbedded within itself. It may likewise find infinite other forms of conceptual awareness imbedded within itself as developed by other forms of 'universes' whose universal fabric may be comprised of other abstractions than space and time.

Getting back on task, the question becomes: What happens to 'newness' 'added' to the whole? Doesn't such newness take on the aspect of change? 'Change from what?' one may ask. Change from what existed before? 'Before what?' becomes the question for there is no 'before' since there is no time 'within' which new knowing is added to the summation of knowing. There is no 'cause and effect', no 'first this then that', no 'before and after', no limit placed upon the entities of knowing other than what they find 'within' their own unique packets of experiencing and knowing they acquired through 'a' passage through the time and space continuum found 'within' our particular physical universe which itself is composed of a unique space/time universal fabric.

What then of change within region #3? There is no change with the 'addition' of 'a', or for that matter many, new unique entities of knowing. Rather what occurs is an exponential form of growth created by the increase in combination potentials of multiple dimensions tessellations of awareness. For further details one may refer back to Tractate 4: Copernicus and Centricism.

Change therefore does not occur in region #3, rather what occurs is increased potentiality of awareness. Increased potentiality of awareness is a form of growth but it is not a case of

> Change vb. To cause to be different, to transform
> Change int. to become different or alterations
> Change n. The act, process, or result of altering or modifying

The 'change' once occurring is no longer change but rather simply 'what is' and not 'what is' now as compared to 'before' for there is no 'before' for there is not universal fabric of time which is required for the concept of 'before' to exist.

What then of:

> Changeable adj. Liable to change
>
> Changeless adj. Constant

If entities of unique knowing are infused into the realm of the whole via the physical/the universe, then how is it such an event does not transform the whole, cause the whole to be different?

The understanding of such a question lies in taking a different approach to the question. As such we will rephrase the question to be:

> Does a system, void time and space as a universal fabric, change, 'become' different, 'evolve' from one to another state or does a system, void the universal fabric of time and space, simple exist from the point of view originating from 'within' the region void the universal fabric of space and time yet change from the point of view of the observer found immersed 'within' a universal fabric of time and space.

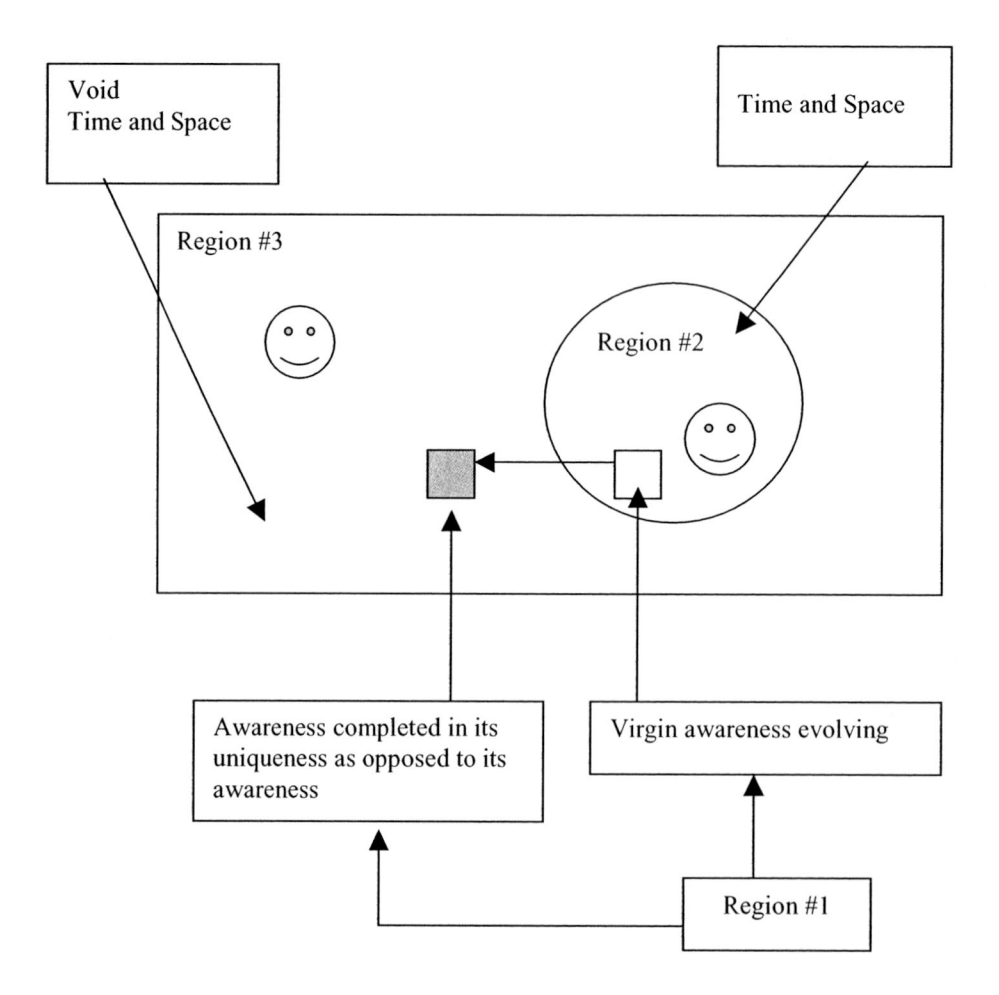

A new meaning of the term 'everything

'EVERYthing' now becomes just that, 'everything' in the generic sense. Everything becomes not only all things but all non-things. Everything now becomes: 'What was', 'what is', 'what will be', as well as 'what could be' should the 'could be' become. In other words, everything includes potentiality of what does not yet exist and is not yet conceived.

Thus everything now includes potentiality and thus has potential to be what it is not. We could say: Everything includes 'what will be' but that excludes 'what could be'. Without the 'what could

The Error of Kant

be', the system would find itself complete but complete without potentiality to be what it is not, complete without the ability of the potential to grow and thus incomplete as opposed to being complete.

The inclusion of the potential to grow takes place 'within' a region whose universal fabric is constructed of space and time but a space and time whose universal fabric incorporates space and time as separate entities of itself, separate elements found 'within' itself as opposed to a universal fabric of itself. These separate entities of 'growth' thus find themselves 'within' the void of a universal concept of cause and effect, beginning and end, first this than that, forms of the universal fabric.

The potentiality for growth thus begins with virgin consciousness, begins with the potentiality to expand into a form of unique knowing entity, expand into a potentiality of multiplicity. Thus 'I think therefore I am.' in essence emerges out of:

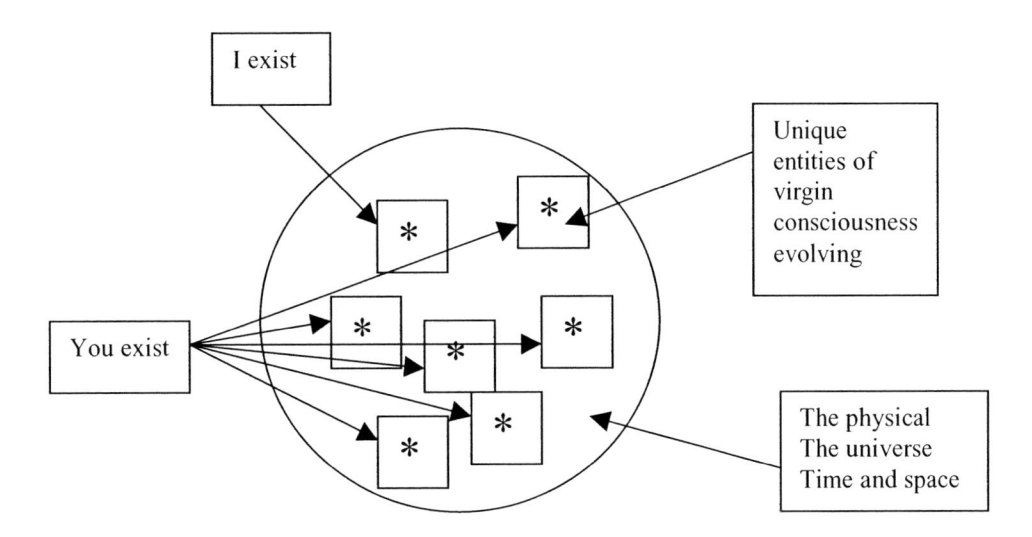

You think, therefore I am. Without 'you' there would be no 'I'.

Where then does 'I am.' take on its significance of primary importance?

The War & Peace of a New Metaphysical Perception

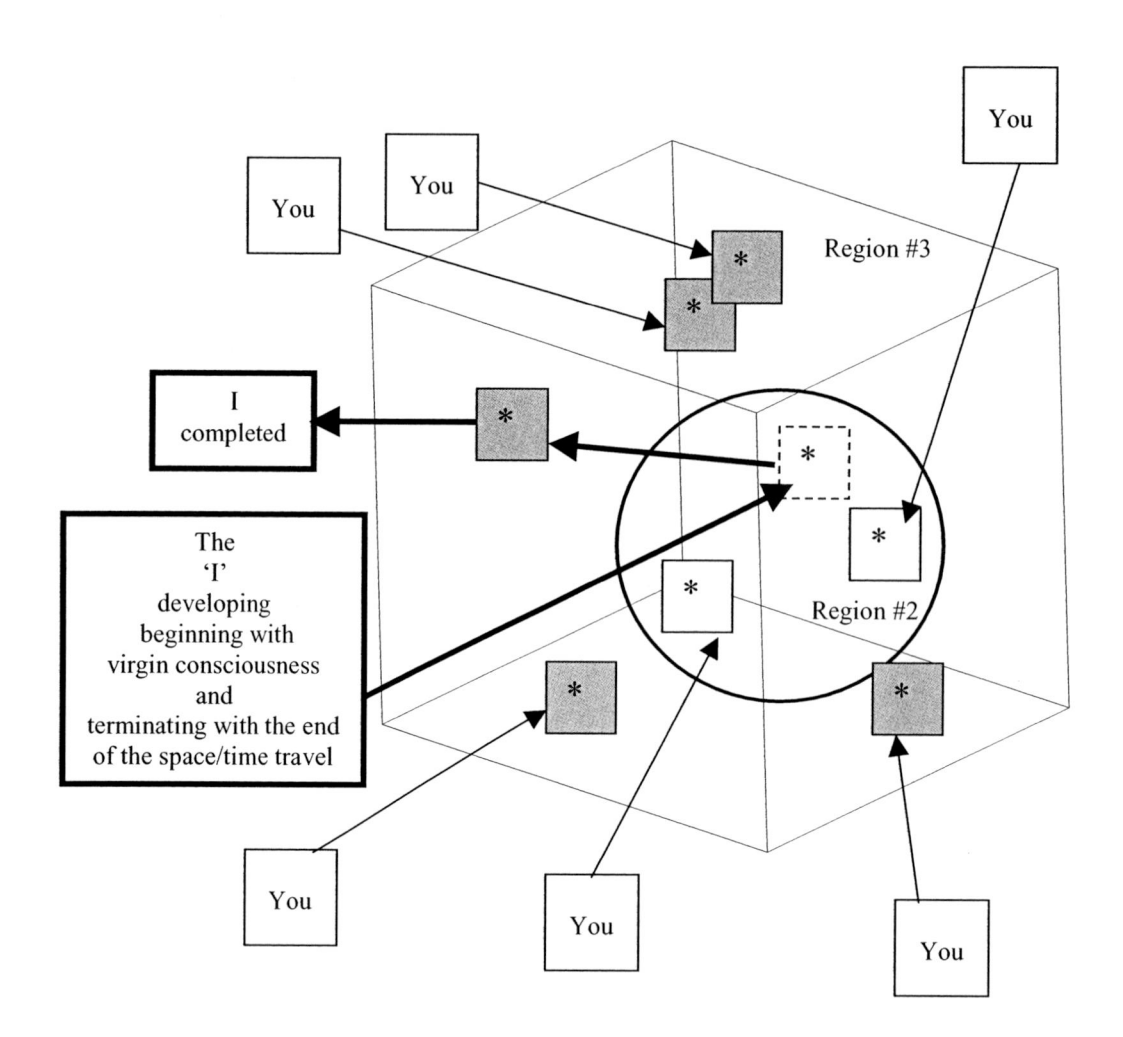

[Figure: Diagram showing a cube with Region #2 (circle) and Region #3, containing multiple "You" boxes connected by arrows to asterisk-marked squares, with boxes labeled "I completed" and "The 'I' developing beginning with virgin consciousness and terminating with the end of the space/time travel"]

Region #2:

Within region #2 of the metaphysical system of 'being' *being* 'Being', 'You think therefore I am.', evolves via Kant's conversion of Aristotle's passive system into an active system. It is Kant's perception that the physical, upon being observed, changes. Thus through your observations the physical/the universe becomes what the universe is and it is into this universe, which I step as a virgin consciousness and thus the many 'you' assists the means by which the 'I' is able to develop as it chooses to develop. Without the many 'you's' I would be an entirely different me for my choices would be entirely different.

Now this is not to say that I have no choice as to what I become, rather it simply says is that my springboard of choices emanates 'from' depends upon what 'you' made of it. The rest is up to the 'I', the 'me'.

Region #3:

Now the reverse takes place when we examine region #3.

Within region #3 of the metaphysical system of 'being' *being* 'Being', 'I think therefore you are.' evolves via a new metaphysical perception of an open non-Cartesian metaphysical system powered by a closed Cartesian System found 'within' the open non-Cartesian system. It is within this new metaphysical perception that the abstract, through my unique knowing, develops/changes. Thus through my observations of the physical, the universe became what the universe is and as such other 'I's' prepare space/time for other 'I's to follow. And it is through the unique development of the 'me' that the whole of abstraction, region #3 becomes what it is in terms of potentiality of combinations of perceptual summations including the whole of summation of knowing itself. It is out of the universe from which I step as a virgin consciousness developing and thus the many 'you' through the 'I' are provided the means by which the 'you' is able to develop into an exponentially greater number of multidimensional combinations of knowing tessellations. Without the 'I', not only the whole but 'you' would be entirely different for your choices of knowing 'what is' would be entirely different.

Such a development within region #3 is not a function of the multiplicity of time but rather is a function of the seamlessness, of time. Time capsules of 'being' travel in any direction adding to the potential variations and permutations of experience within the abstract, region #3.

Thus the statements emerge:

1. I think therefore you exist.
2. You think therefore I exist.

What then becomes of the statement:

I think therefore I am.

Such a statement remains intact for could I not think, I would in essence not exist in terms of my personal perception; I would not exist to me although I may exist to you.

In short the statement:

'I think therefore I am.'

is a statement of hope as opposed to a statement of fact, as opposed to a statement of actuality, as opposed to a statement of existence. The statement however is in error if taken as a statement of existence as opposed to being taken as a statement of perceptual existence.

The reason the statement remains as a cornerstone of logic is that without others 'knowing', my 'knowing' could gain no knowing.

From where then did God – 'the initial knowing' originate? That discussion must wait for Tractate 18: The End of the Beginning.

How something, which is unchangeable, can change and remain unchangeable

If we take a cross-section of the metaphysical system of 'being' *being* 'Being', we obtain a cross-section of timelessness:

The War & Peace of a New Metaphysical Perception

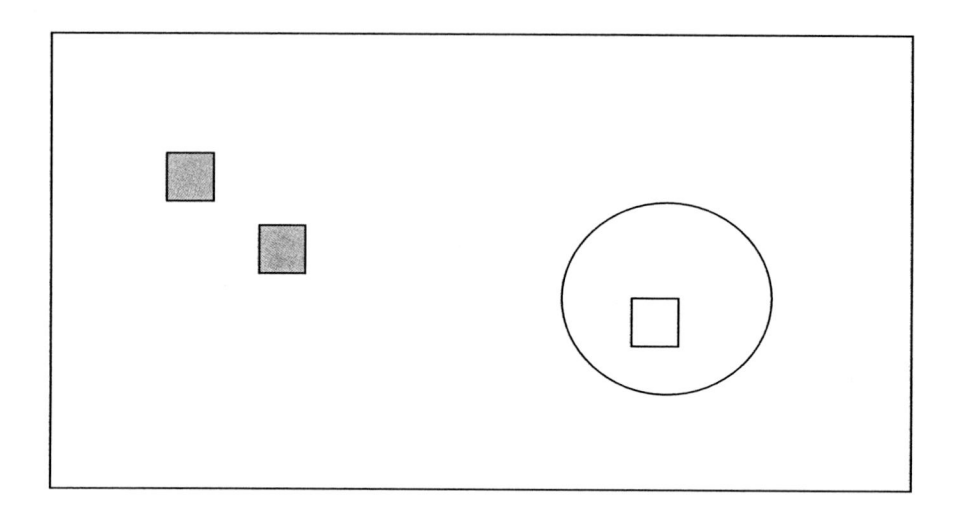

The system is what it is

We can now add an additional unit of knowing to the region outside the physical, outside the universe. Such a unit has evolved by means of its awareness having passed through the space/time continuum found within the physical/the universe. We thus obtain:

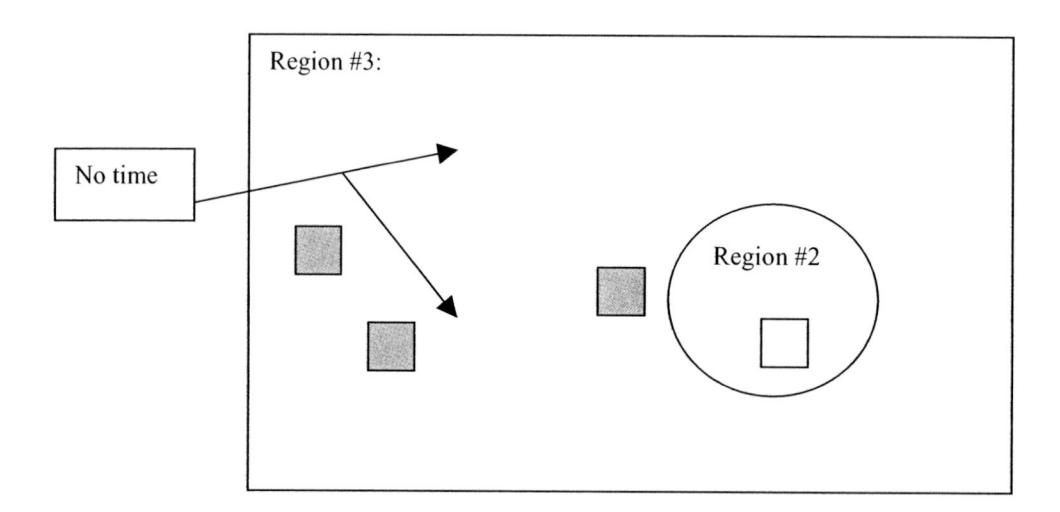

As we can see: The system is what it is and has not changed because no time exists between units and no time exists as a universal medium of the fabric within which the completed units of awareness, knowing, knowledge, find themselves to be.

In this state, one cannot be identified as 'having' existed 'before' another, for there is no 'before/after' concept to be found as a universal medium of region #3. The only location within which a medium of before/after concepts can be found to exists as the medium is within region #2 and within the individual units of knowing found within region #2 and region #3.

How then does the whole change? The whole, region #3 changes from our point of view since we are immersed within time. The whole from its point of view does not change but rather sees the state of 'change', growth, from simply the point of the constant 'what is'. There is no past and no future within region #3 for there is not time or space found within region #3 as a part of the universal medium of region #3.

Growth occurs within region #3 but not as a linear progression but simply as an explosion of randomness of combinations of knowledge which have the potential to be pieced together in a multitude of multidimensional possibilities of knowledge tessellations whose potential possible combinations explode exponentially in a continuous manner.

Permanent stagnation, static existence, passivity, it is not. 'Growth' it may be. 'Decay' it may be. One or the other it is under such a metaphysical perception of the whole system. The mechanisms for the explosion or implosion of multiply dimensional combinations of tessellations, the individual units of knowing themselves, developing through the process of passing through a medium of space and time.

Are there other means of exponential explosion or implosion? Perhaps, perhaps not. What might account for other means of exponential explosions or implosion? Other distinct universes having a different form of medium than the space/time medium found within our universe.

The death of God

The death of metaphysics - the death of God, is there any difference? Actually, no there is no difference. The death of metaphysics is the understanding that there is no such thing as metaphysics. Kant with his perception of the death of Aristotelian concepts of 'what is' initiates an understanding that our very observation changes what it is we observe. Such a perception implies the creation of God's, this thing we call the universe, is not His creation but our creation for we make the observations and God has nothing to do with observations for our observations are our creations not his.

1st principle then becomes ourselves not God. But without the universe we would have nothing to observe in a manner unique to ourselves and therefore the universe had to be here before we were here for without the universe there would have been nothing for us to observe in our own unique manner. We would therefore have had nothing from which to begin to develop our own unique individual observations and therefore the universe is 1st cause. On the other hand, we know we did not exist before some other we's existed for we are the product of the union of a sperm and an egg and therefore without this union 'we' would not exist as we are. Thus other 'we's', the you's, had to come before the present we's, before the 'I'.

So which came first: I, the universe, or God? Kant was unable to reconcile this argument. The old, which came first the chicken or the egg, became, metaphysically, which came first: the I, the universe, or the creator. Kant being unable to resolve this argument suggested he had a whole new system of metaphysics, which in essence was not a metaphysical system at all, yet was irrefutable.

The only logical conclusion he could draw was that metaphysics, as we knew it, was dead. However, since we knew of no other form of metaphysics than the form of metaphysics we had had previously, in essence metaphysics was dead.

Kant was unsure of what this meant. It was Hegel who was to come along and move us one step closer to understanding just what this meant.

But we are speaking of Kant, and thus it is Kant we must address.

As such, lets look at what the concepts of Kant's system suggest.

At this point we will acknowledge that is arguable whether or not Kant's system was actually a system since Kant was unable to satisfy his own personal expectations of a system. Kant believed 'a' system, to be a system, must produce 'a' first principle, 'a' foundation. Since Kant could not extract this most fundamental of requirements, the debate emerges as to whether or not Kant's system was truly a system at all.

Having acknowledged the issue regarding the validity of whether or not Kant's system actually was a system, let's began an analysis of Kant's proposed 'system'.

Analytic versus Synthetic 'a priori':

Were space and time innate characteristics of objects or were objects innate characteristics of space and time?

Kant suggested: Since we cannot perceive of objects without concepts of space and time but we can perceive of space and time without objects than it is objects which are the innate characteristic of space and time rather than the reverse.

In essence objects found themselves immersed within the medium of space and time.

Space and time therefore became the synthetic a priori of the physical. But did this establish space and time as the ultimate medium of metaphysics? If it did, it could be said metaphysics was dead for metaphysics dealt with three basic concepts: God, free will, and immortality. Some would suggest metaphysics dealt with knowing and knowledge but knowing and knowledge are aspects of God for by definition God is omniscient, omnipotent, and omnipresent. God is, metaphysically speaking 'all knowing' of knowledge and the awareness of all such knowledge, knowing. Immortality deals with infinite time and between all knowledge and time, space is filled up. Individual units of knowing, individuality, become an issue regarding elements of the whole, thus humankind in the form of individuals becomes an issue of metaphysics.

What of space? Space becomes the location of such knowing and such knowledge, be it space in the physical sense or space in the abstract form. Kant suggested space was not physical for physical objects were the innate characteristic of space and time not the reverse.

And what of actions of free will? Actions of free will became an issue dealing with the active form of action versus passive form of action regarding subsets of knowledge and thus God, free will, and immortality became issues of metaphysics.

If the physical emanates from space and time and if space and time was all there was, God was space and time. As such, God perceptually emerged as being dead for space and time were not 'knowing' entities but rather brain dead abstractions.

It then followed that metaphysics was dead for immortality, being an element of time, became a part of the unknowing and free will became a part of an unknowing space and time. What then of God? Why God was an unknowing fabric, medium of space and time, within which 'all' was found.

Kant could not resolve his own paradox. The logical conclusion, which was to be drawn: God was dead.

The Error of Kant

Philosophers following Kant thus assumed metaphysics to have expired.

> On the other hand, the people whose business it is to ask why, the philosophers, have not been able to keep up with the advance of scientific theories. In the eighteenth century, philosophers considered the whole of human knowledge, including science to be their field and discussed questions such as: Did the universe have a beginning? However, in the nineteenth and twentieth centuries, science became too technical
> l and mathematical for the philosophers, or anyone else except a few specialists. Philosophers reduced the scope of their inquiries so much that Wittgenstein, the most famous philosopher of this century, said, 'The sole remaining task for philosophy is the analysis of language.' What a comedown from the great tradition of philosophy from Aristotle to Kant![18]

As such, philosophers of the nineteenth and twentieth centuries believed: If Kant could not resolve his own paradox, then the only feasible explanation as to why Kant could not do so was because:

Metaphysics was dead.

God was dead.

> *This idea, that God is in fact nothing but an idea of our own making for use within our moral practice, is a thought Kant repeatedly expressed in his very last years.*[19]

Kant did not seek to resolve the issue he should have been seeking:

> If objects lie within the medium of space and time, are innate characteristics of space and time than is there a synthetic a priori of space and time? Is there a medium such that space and time cannot be conceived of being without the existence of this new medium itself? In other words is there a medium from which space and time emerge, is immerged within?

The answer to such a question could conceivable resolve the paradox Kant established, resolve the concept of the lack of a foundation for Kant's system yet leave Kant's system intact. This sounds like a lot of hypothetical impossibilities and the reason it sounds as such is due to the fact that Kant was examining his system rather than a new perception, which had not yet been proposed.

The next logical step of this tractate then becomes: to examine this new system and to examine whether or not such a system resolves Kant's dilemma.

The War & Peace of a New Metaphysical Perception

We begin with:

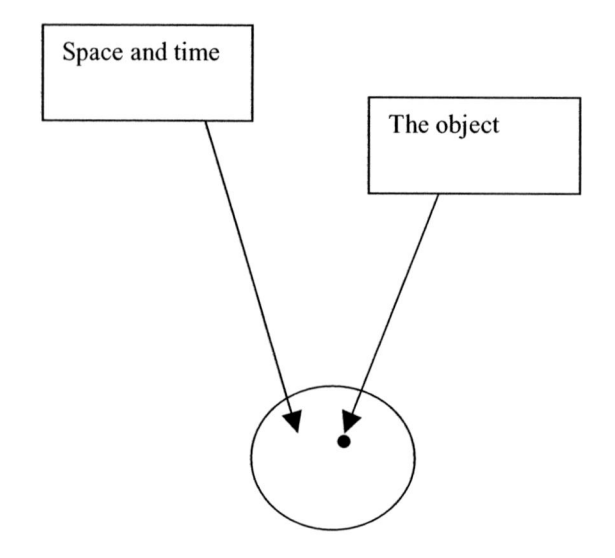

This is Kant's perception. Now lets add an outside to the system:

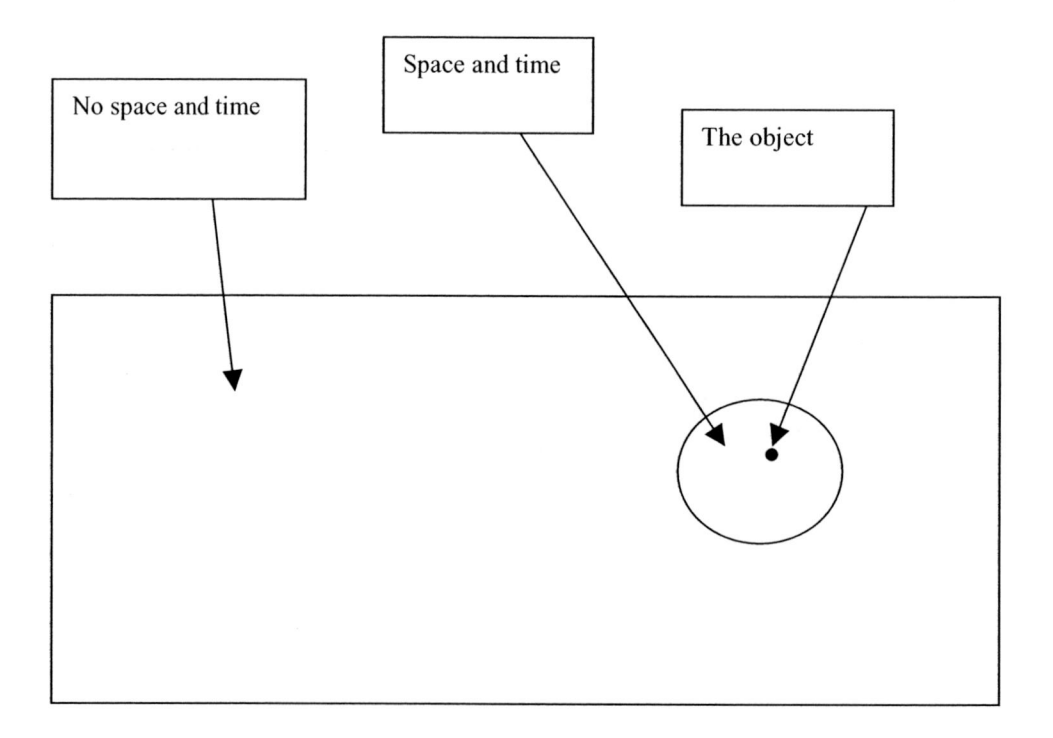

The Error of Kant

Since space and time exist within the median of no space and time what then is the medium within which space and time find themselves existing? It could be that space and time exist in what we think of as abstractual knowing, a form of active abstraction existing in a medium of passivity itself. But aren't space and time abstractual? Perhaps, but are they a form of knowing? As far as we know space and time are not a form of knowing but rather 'unknowing' abstractions. As such it would be possible that the knowing, awareness, of space and time concepts would graphically appear as:

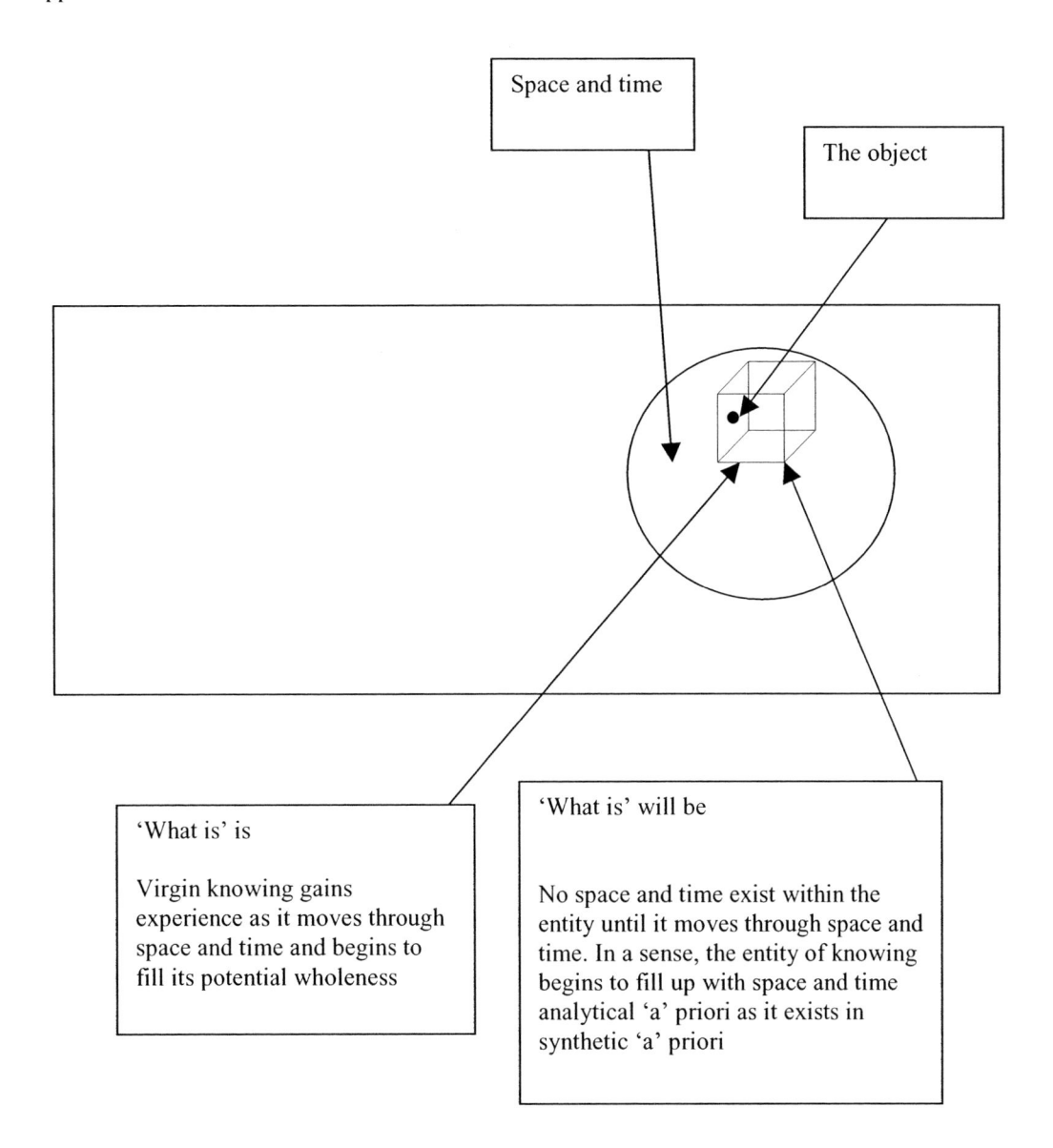

Space and time

The object

'What is' is

Virgin knowing gains experience as it moves through space and time and begins to fill its potential wholeness

'What is' will be

No space and time exist within the entity until it moves through space and time. In a sense, the entity of knowing begins to fill up with space and time analytical 'a' priori as it exists in synthetic 'a' priori

The War & Peace of a New Metaphysical Perception

Now does this necessarily mean the knowledge, which exists no longer, exists? No for with the concept of 'being' *being* 'Being', symbiotic panentheism, we find synthetic 'a' priori now becomes apparent to Kant's questionable system. The new addition of an outside to space and time, a synthetic 'a' priori to space and time takes on its own functionality and becomes:

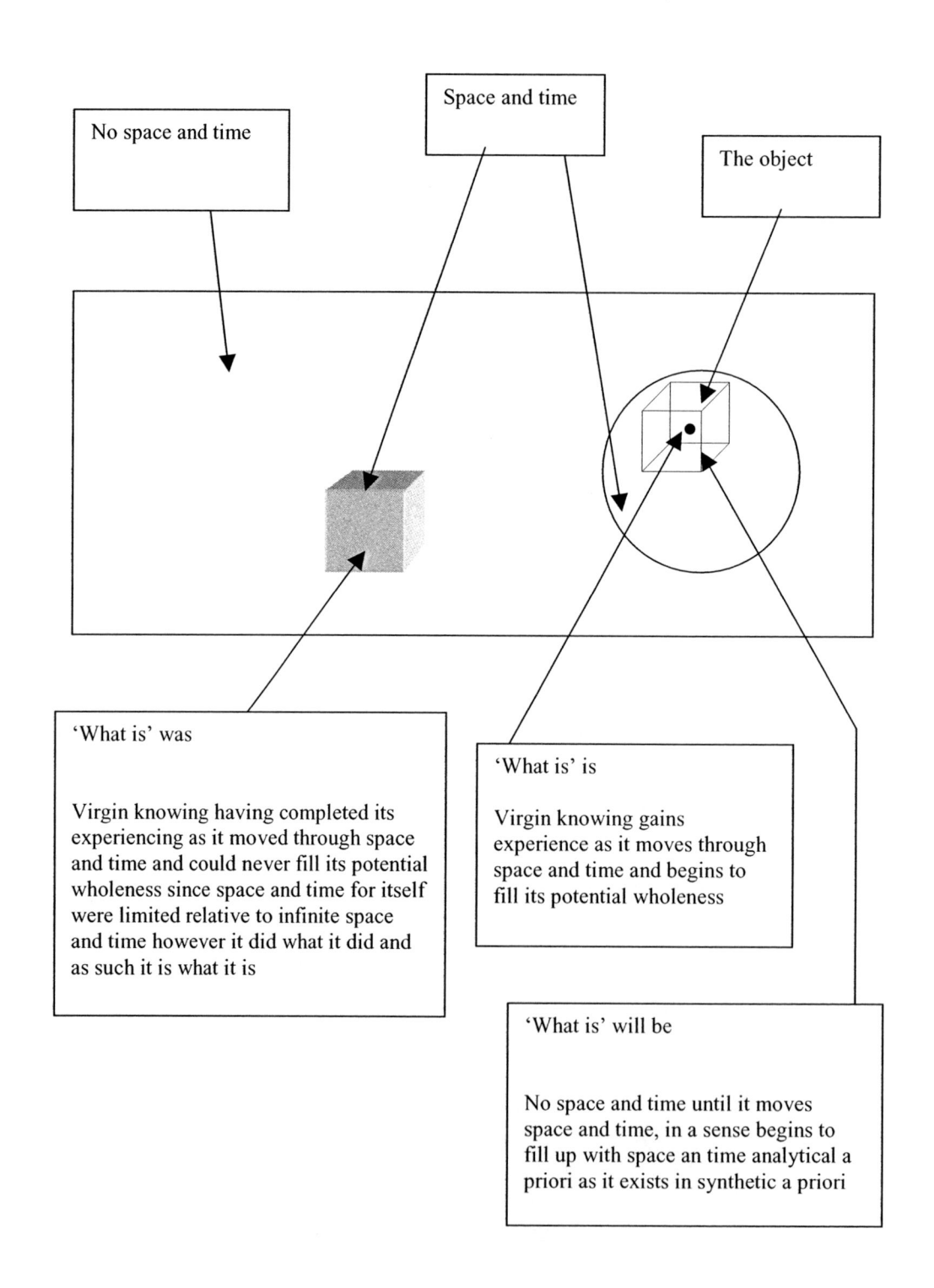

No space and time

Space and time

The object

'What is' was

Virgin knowing having completed its experiencing as it moved through space and time and could never fill its potential wholeness since space and time for itself were limited relative to infinite space and time however it did what it did and as such it is what it is

'What is' is

Virgin knowing gains experience as it moves through space and time and begins to fill its potential wholeness

'What is' will be

No space and time until it moves space and time, in a sense begins to fill up with space an time analytical a priori as it exists in synthetic a priori

The Error of Kant

Time now becomes an analytical 'a' priori to 'Knowing', the whole, and the concept of individual 'knowing' becomes an analytic 'a' priori to space and time through the analytic emanations of objects emerging from space and time itself. In essence we obtain 'knowing' *knowing* 'Knowing'. We obtain 'knowledge' of 'Knowledge'. We obtain the 'active passive active' sandwich. We obtain 'being' *being* 'Being'. We obtain circular understanding of not just the significance of 'Bering' to 'being' but of 'being' to 'Being'. We obtain an understanding of a symbiotic relationship, a symbiotic functionality between 'being' and 'Being' through the very action of being.

To better understand how it is a physical being interacts within an unobservable abstractual existence we must examine three concepts: The Causal, The non-Causal, and The Boundary between the Causal and the non-Causal.

The Causal

Almost everyone exists within the causal

The Causal is the realm of cause and effect. I like the effect; I examine what created the effect. I react by repeating the casual actions, which cause the effect I enjoyed. I go fishing. I catch a fish. I enjoyed catching the fish so I go fishing again. I enjoyed it again so I buy a boat of my own so I can go fishing. I go fishing. I catch a fish. I enjoyed catching a fish...

The process can be diagramed as:

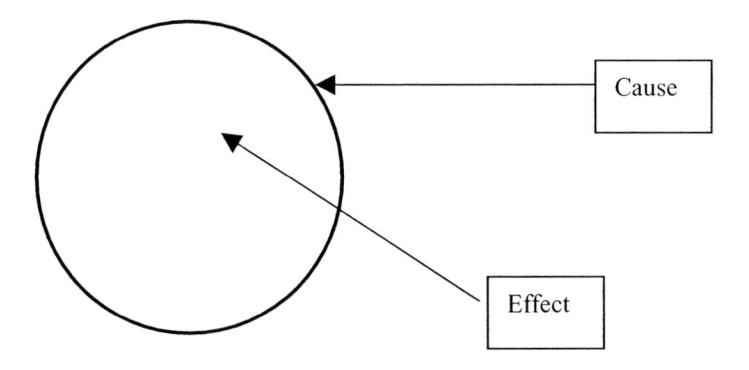

This in no way implies the action of fishing requires no intelligence. Rather this explanation suggests the act of catching a fish is enjoyable and thus it creates the desire to do it again. It is a Cause and Effect sequence of actions driven by a desire to repeat the action as opposed to being driven by the need to understand 'why' one 'should' repeat the sequence of actions.

To better understand the Causal we will expand upon the region representing the Causal. The black region represents Cause and the gray region represents Effect. Effect is placed 'inside' cause since effect is action of the past, action which has occurred due to the cause.

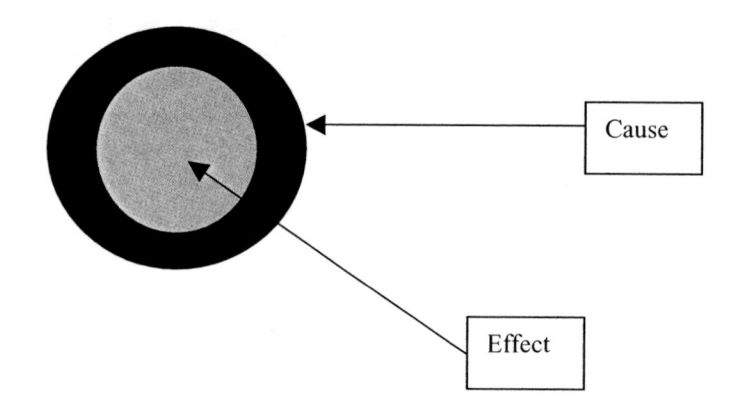

[Diagram: black ring with grey inner circle; arrow labeled "Cause" points to the black ring; arrow labeled "Effect" points to the grey inner area.]

But why not reverse the diagram?

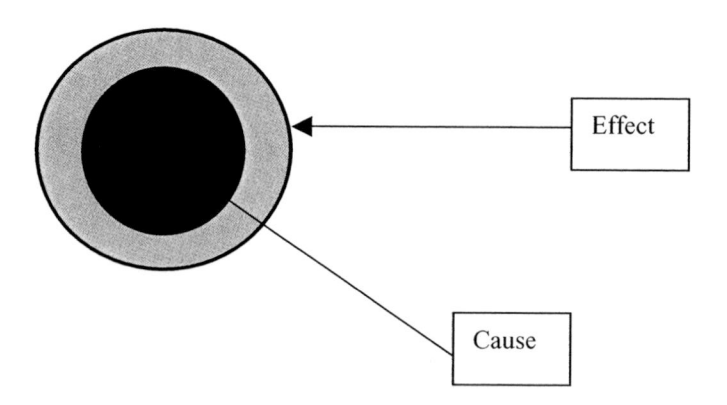

[Diagram: grey outer ring with black inner circle; arrow labeled "Effect" points to the black inner area; arrow labeled "Cause" points to the grey outer ring.]

We are inside the universe, or so it appears to modern day cosmology, ontology, and metaphysics. Therefore we will portray actions to lead to reactions beginning with the creation giving us the effects of which take place 'within' giving us the former diagram rather than 'without' us portrayed by the latter diagram.

We therefore begin with:

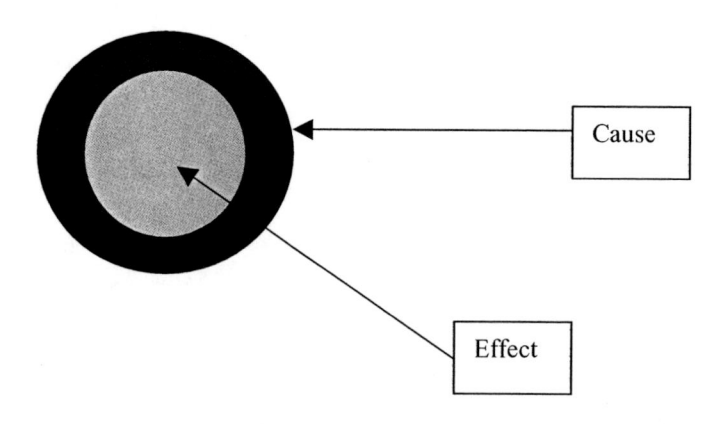

[Diagram: black ring with grey inner circle; arrow labeled "Cause" points to the black ring; arrow labeled "Effect" points to the grey inner area.]

Now let's introduce the concept of understanding. The understanding that we will introduce is understanding that one reacts to the Cause with free will. The insertion of such a concept is the acknowledgement that we have a certain amount of 'control' over our desires; we have some semblance of free will. The degree of free will is not the issue here. What is of issue is the acknowledgement due the concept of awareness, due the concept of understanding, due the concept of conscious 'knowing'. The diagram now becomes:

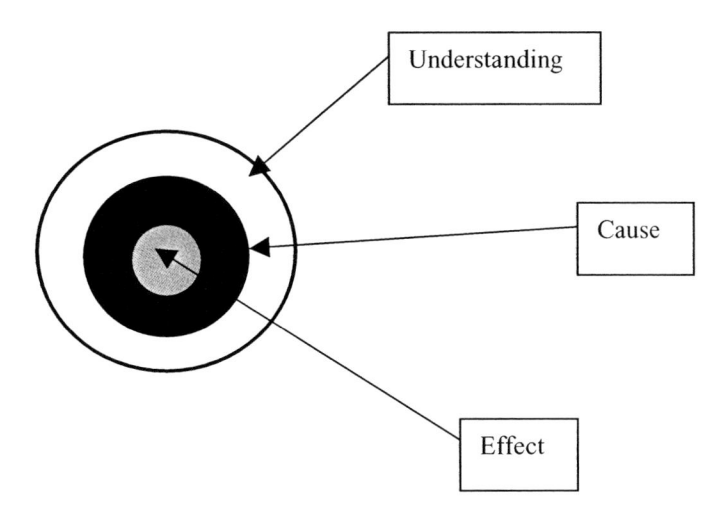

The basic diagram is a simplistic representation of Cause and Effect actions. The physical is filled with such actions of Cause and Effect. They not only act intra-entity but inter-entity.

The War & Peace of a New Metaphysical Perception

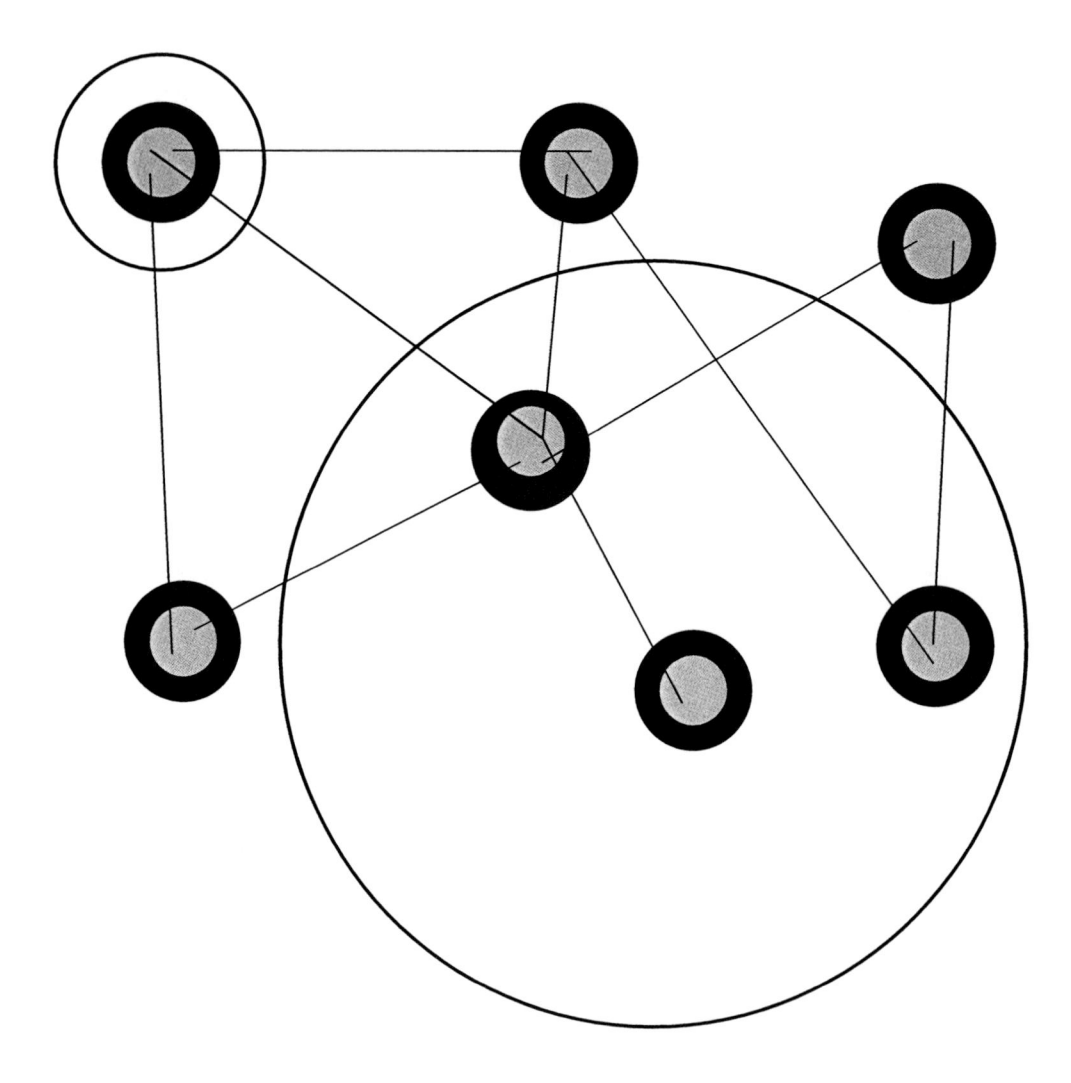

Of the three regions, it is the region of 'knowing', the region of understanding which interests us for it is 'knowing' which Kant was attempting, yet failed, to understand with his metaphysical system of 'critical philosophy'.

Since we are interested in the Causal at this point we will expand the Causal experiencing of the entity while ignoring the non-Causal, ignore the region represented by the colorless region.

The Causal entity, be it human or otherwise, developing Causally takes on, in a simplistic sense, the following appearance when factoring in outside as well as internal interactions:

The Error of Kant

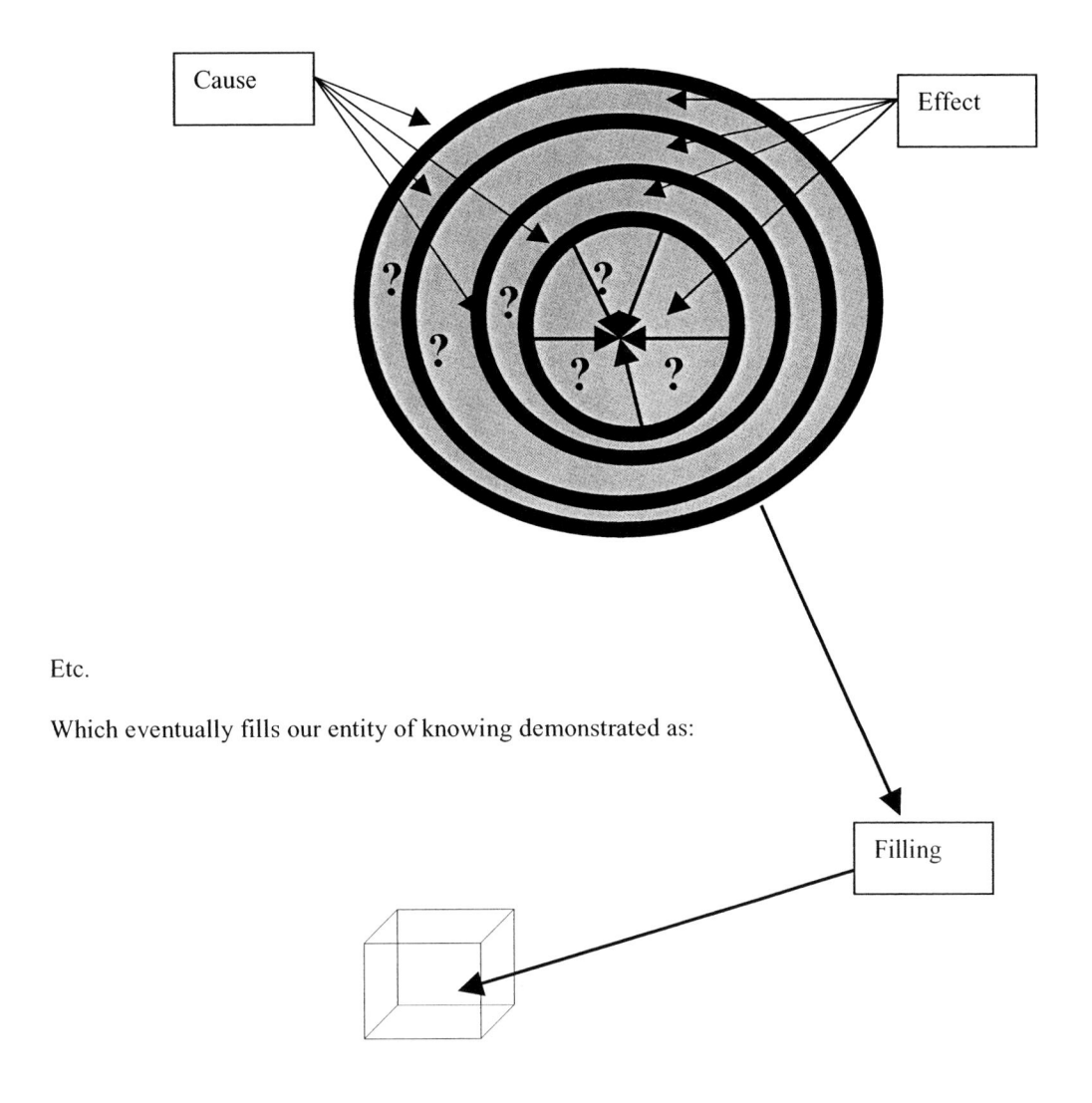

Etc.

Which eventually fills our entity of knowing demonstrated as:

This entity of knowing runs throughout not only this tractate but all Tractates to date: Tractates 0 – 6.

Understanding the graphic of the entity acting in the Causal, we are now ready to move to the concept of the non-Causal.

The War & Peace of a New Metaphysical Perception

The non-Causal

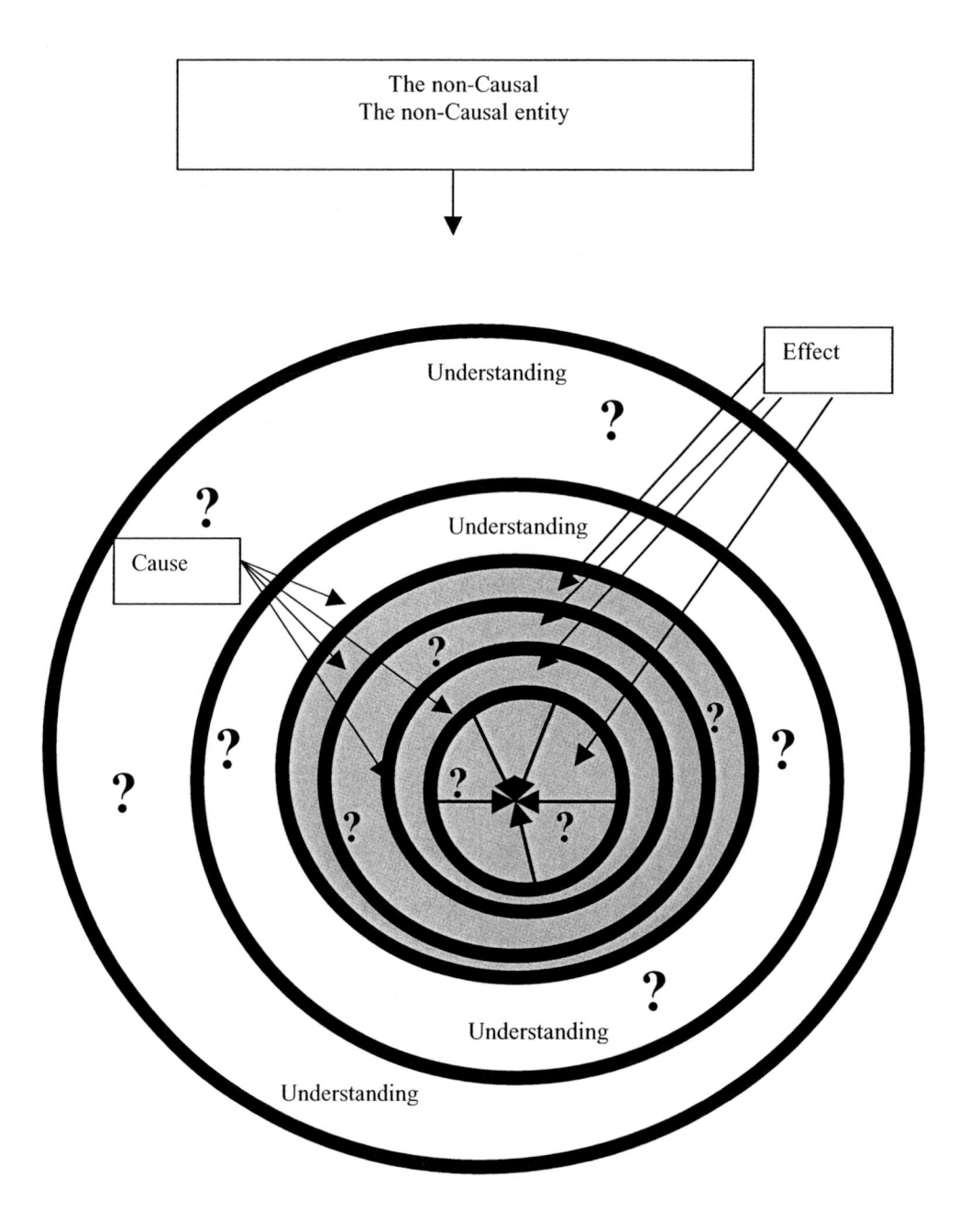

The Error of Kant

> The non-Causal
> The non-Causal entity
> The metaphysician: in particular, the metaphysician exploring the general realm of
> **Practical Metaphysical**

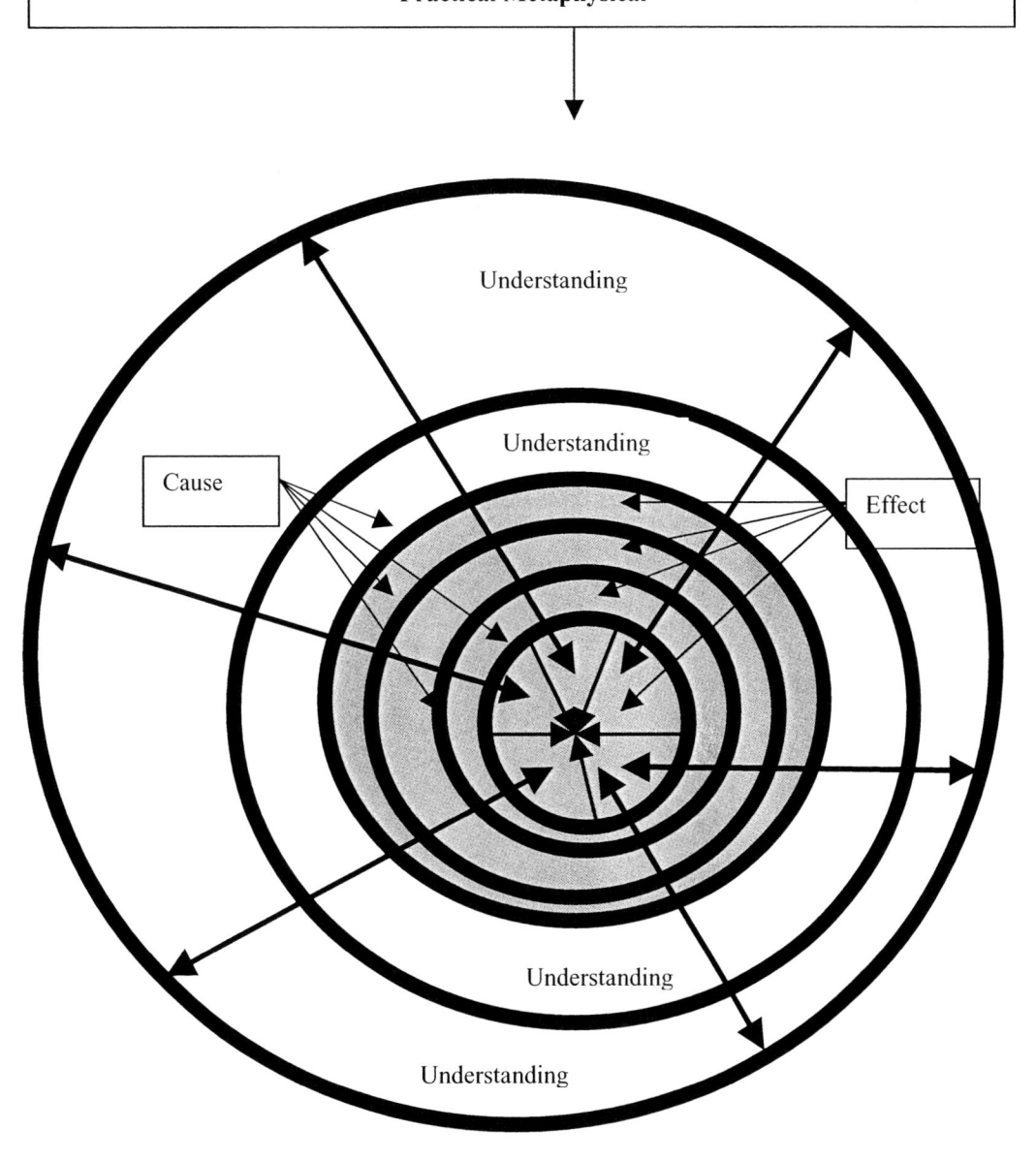

The War & Peace of a New Metaphysical Perception

The non-Causal
The non-Causal entity
The metaphysician: in particular a metaphysician exploring the realm of
Metaphysical Engineering

Understanding

Understanding

Cause

Effect

Understanding

Understanding

The Error of Kant

The non-Causal
The non-Causal entity attempting to understand what lies in the outer reaches of the
The Metaphysician: in particular a Metaphysician exploring the realm of
Theoretical Metaphysics

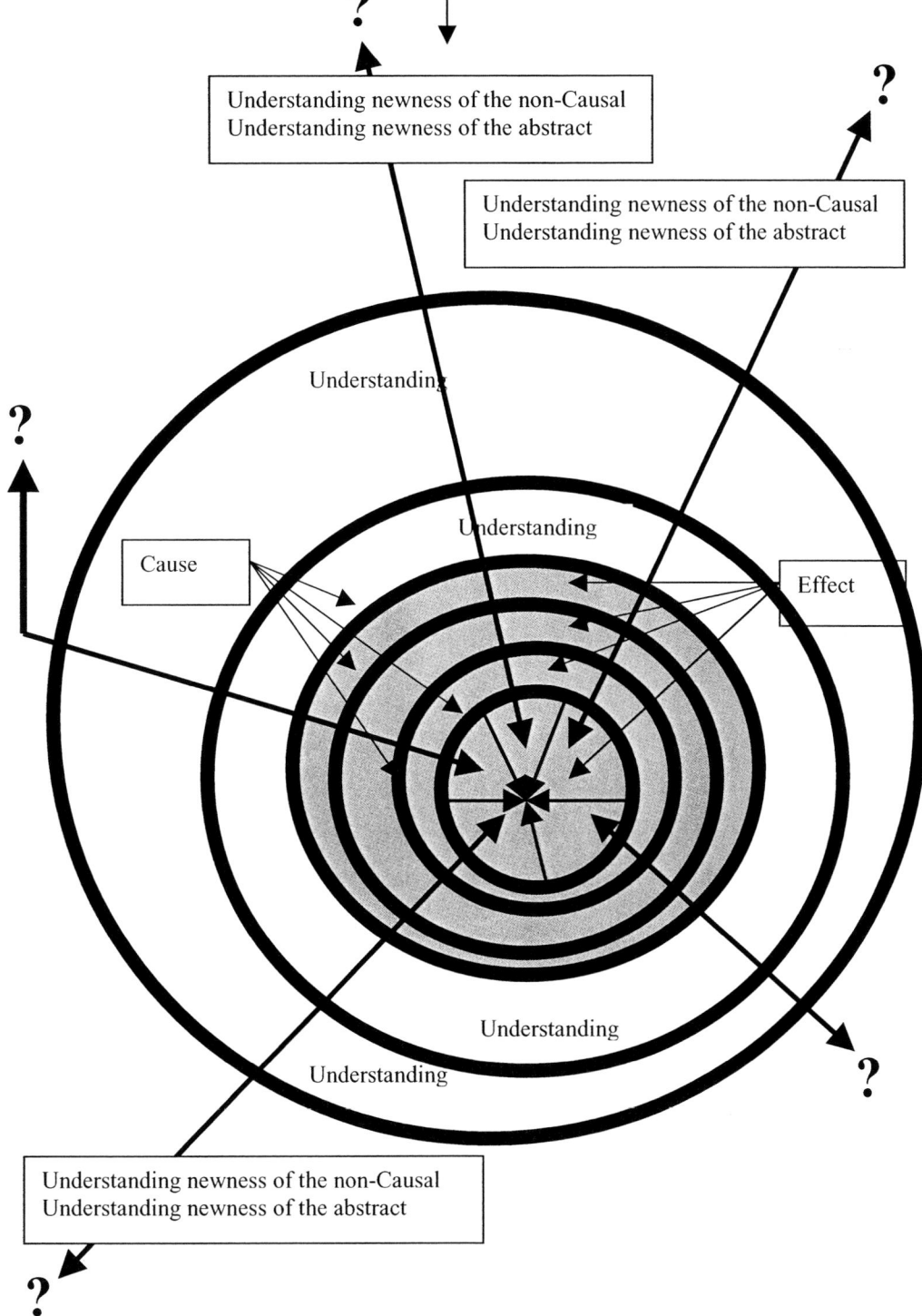

Understanding newness of the non-Causal
Understanding newness of the abstract

Understanding newness of the non-Causal
Understanding newness of the abstract

Understanding

Understanding

Cause

Effect

Understanding

Understanding

Understanding newness of the non-Causal
Understanding newness of the abstract

The metaphysician is not just a non-Causal individual but rather the metaphysician is a non-Causal individual who explores how the two, the abstract and the physical, the Causal and the non-Causal, interact.

With this understanding regarding the task of the metaphysician, we can now begin to understand the task uniquely confronting experts specializing in the three fields of Metaphysics. Such an understanding is not an exercise in futility nor is it an exercise in the realm of fantasy.

The lack of understanding regarding the process of subdividing the tasks of various metaphysicians is in fact the very reason Kant had difficulty formalizing his metaphysical system.

Metaphysics now becomes subdivided into three realms:

The Practical Metaphysician:	One who understanding and defines how the Causal and the non-Causal work as a whole as described by the Theoretical Metaphysician.
The Metaphysical Engineer:	One who lays out, constructs, or manages social systems founded upon the work of the Practical Metaphysician, founded upon an understanding of how the Causal and the non-Causal interact which in turn is based upon a metaphysical understanding of the whole.
Theoretical Metaphysician:	One who expands the understanding of the Causal and non-Causal interrelationship and thus provides expanded metaphysical perceptions with which the Practical Metaphysician can work.

Kant understood what his task was in terms of being a Theoretical Metaphysician but Kant could not understand how Theoretical Metaphysics related to Practical Metaphysics nor could he understand just how his system of Critical Philosophy could be applied to reality itself through the process of Metaphysical Engineering.

Had Practical Metaphysics and Metaphysical Engineering been defined, Kant may have followed his theoretical perceptions to their obvious conclusions. We will examine such a trail within Tractate 10: Heidegger. Having observed the results his theoretical metaphysical system produced, Kant would have had no choice but to backtrack to his initial assumptions and then modified his theoretical system.

Eventually Kant, through the use of such a process, would have produced a viable system or Kant would have done as Zeno did: Kant would have proclaimed, he did not have the answer regarding 'the' viable system and would leave the task to future metaphysicians.

This would have resulted in:

1. Philosophy continuing to recognize the significance of metaphysical research rather than proclaiming the demise of metaphysics.
2. Establishing the understanding of future theoretical metaphysicians that perhaps 'the' metaphysical system incorporated both Kant's active and Aristotle's passive forms of action.

In addition to Kant's lack of understanding regarding the three fields of metaphysics, Kant was caught up in the perceptions of the day. Kant believed his system was a system of singularity as opposed to multiplicity. Kant believed his system outlined the whole system, however, Kant was unable to model his system because he, as all metaphysicians up through his time, believed 'a' system, any system in order to be considered to be a system was required to fulfill the Aristotelian principle: all systems can be reduced to 1st principle.

Kant could not find 1st principle within his system. To Kant, a system, which continually changes, changes with the very observation of passive observation itself, is a fluid, dynamic, system within which it is impossible to identify 1st principle.

Within Kant's metaphysical system, the individual cannot exist without the universe, the universe cannot exist without the creator, and the creator depends upon the observations of the individual for its change. In essence we have a vicious circle with no beginning and no end:

Such contradictions defy the parameters of a 'Cartesian' system, defy the parameters of a 'closed' system, defy the parameters of an Aristotelian system.

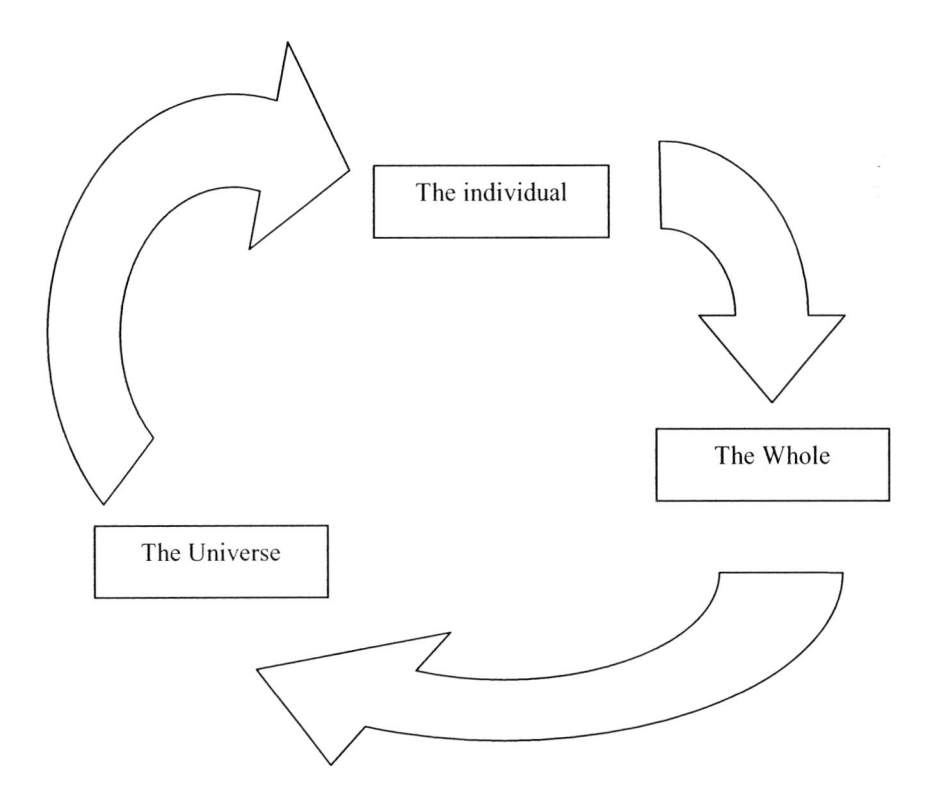

```
        The individual
              ↓
  ↑      The Whole
  ↑           ↓
  The Universe ←
```

Within Kant's metaphysical system there appears to be no 1st cause, no 1st principle, no 1st truth. Kant was stymied and that is, for the most part where Kant left his metaphysical development. The abrupt termination of the theoretical aspect regarding the further development of Kant's metaphysical system was no different than what had occurred to Zeno when he simply said: Seamless ness and multiplicity exist but I have no idea of how it is they do so independent of each other. All I know is that it is obvious they do so. The function of theoretical metaphysicians is to expand our understanding regarding the abstract and the physical. Zeno did this. Aristotle did this, Boethius did this, Copernicus did this Leibniz did this, and now we see Kant did this also.

Our examination of philosophical history is not yet done. As we shall see, 'being' *being* 'Being; symbiotic panentheism, is not a quantum leap in the development of theoretical metaphysics but rather simply one small step beyond those remaining for us to examine: Hegel, Russell, Einstein, Heidegger, Husserl, Hawking, and Ockham.

To better understand Kant's dilemma and the solution to the dilemma we must examine one more region. We must examine the boundary between the Causal and the non-Causal.

The boundary between the Causal and the non-Causal

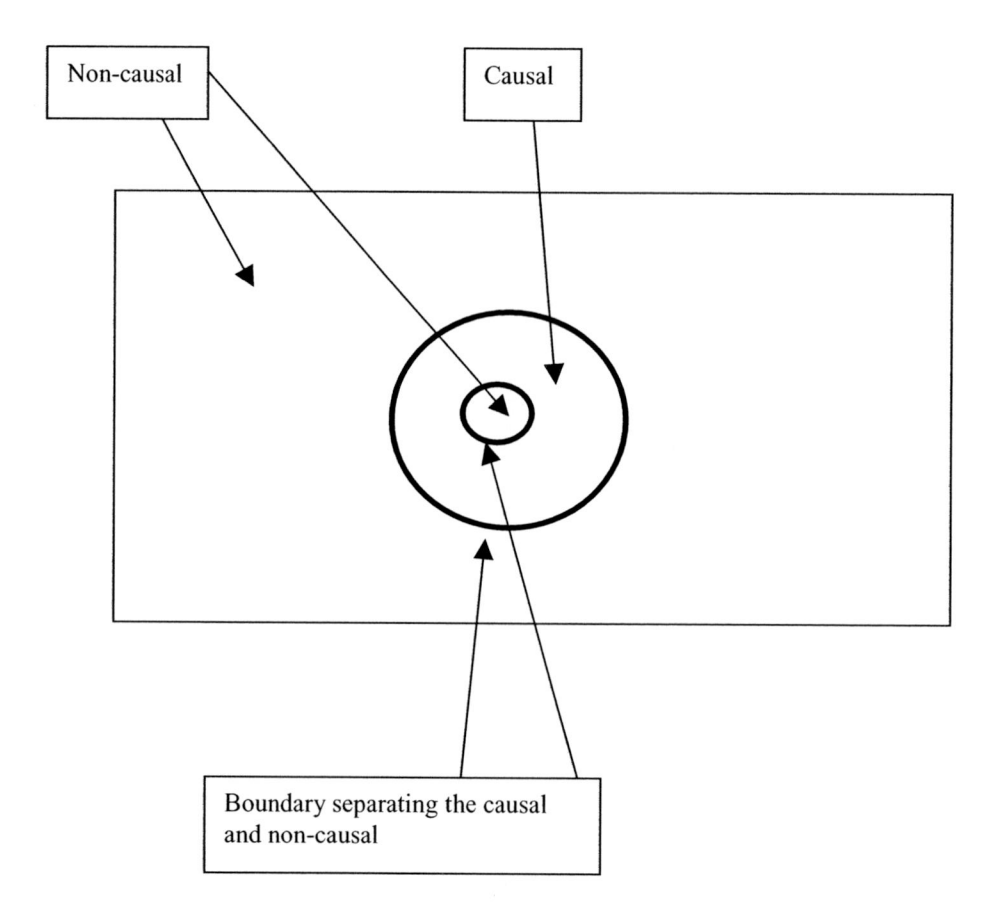

What we have is the causal sandwiched between the non-causal. There is another way of saying this however. It could be said the non-causal is separated from itself through a process of separation through inclusion.

Why would totality separate a portion of itself from itself? Interesting question and one that has been addressed generically in 'Trilogy I' and will be addressed in detail in future tractates. However, the intent of this tractate is to discuss Kant and the paradox his critical philosophy places before us rather than discuss the purpose of the separation.

So what of the boundaries?????

In the physical we examine multiplicity/individuality and theorize/wonder about seamlessness/singularity. In the abstract we must do the reverse. In the abstract we must examine seamlessness and theorize/wonder about multiplicity.

What does such a statement mean?

Lets begin by examining the more familiar of the two. We will examine the location where multiplicity is the more obvious, perhaps the more dominant characteristic. That location is of course, our reality, the universe.

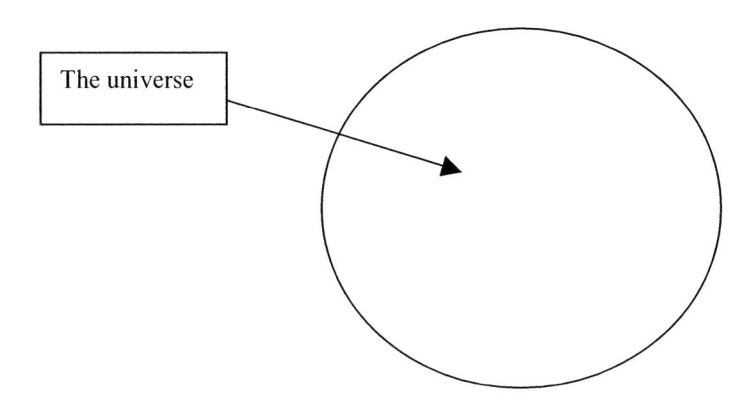

[Figure: A box labeled "The universe" with an arrow pointing to a circle]

Within the universe we observe through a process of examining cross sections of time. In short we take multiple cross sections and by examining them we can project as to what might happen within future cross sections. If we find our projections are correct we attempt to establish laws allowing us to make even more futuristic projections.

It is the cross sections, which dominate our thoughts. It is the cross sections, which we categorize, photograph, examine, and file away for future references. All the while we wonder about the 'seamless'. We wonder what it means to be void multiplicity., wonder what seamlessness means in terms of a totally seamless abstractual flow of reality.

Kant led us to the apogee of such wonders. Kant theorized what it means to reformulate our perceptions of the abstract into an active system where everything found within the system impacts the system. Kant went so far as to say that even the simply act of observing the system impacts the system. This was contrary to the metaphysical system existing at the time. The Aristotelian system of the time maintained that the system was passive and thus the observer did not impact the system through observation.

In essence Kant suggested it is significant to understand the seamlessness of totality when examining the 'whole system'. Since Kant had no other location within which to place such an observation, Kant found he had no other choice but to place such an observation within the universe. Such a choice however suggests that a selection had to be made regarding Kant's metaphysical system being 'the' system or Aristotle's metaphysical system being 'the' system.

The War & Peace of a New Metaphysical Perception

This brings us back again to Zeno's paradox: Which is it, seamlessness or multiplicity?

This brings us back to our graphic and allows us to add an additional parameter:

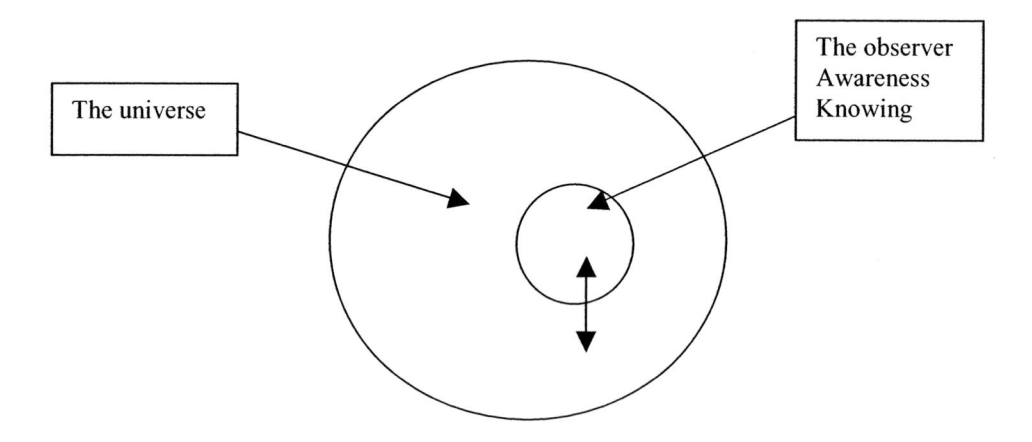

Now we see the physical affects the observer and the observer affects the physical. In essence, the physical affects the abstract and the abstract affects the physical. As such we begin to understand the meaning of our previous statement:

> *In the physical we examine multiplicity and theorize/wonder about seamlessness/abstraction.*

If there is no observer then there is no impact of the observer upon the physical and as such the physical functions simply within the parameters of physical laws. As such we can and logically do take cross sections of the universe and examine them for what they are, cross section of a physical immersed in space and time. The very fact that the physical is immersed in the fabric of space and time allows us to take the cross section of time itself. In fact it is logical to do so within the universe itself, within the physical itself.

But what of the abstract, the non-causal? Is it found only 'within' the causal and how is it to be examined? Can we take cross sections of the non-causal and examine them as we take cross sections of the physical and examine them? This brings us back to the statement:

> *In the abstract we must do the reverse. In the abstract we must examine seamlessness and theorize/wonder about multiplicity.*

This statement suggests the examination of the abstract becomes a form of reverse process to the process we find functional in the physical.

If we take a previous statement:

> *...the physical affects the observer and the observer affects the physical.*

The Error of Kant

And shift some of the words we get a glimpse of the solution to our previous statement regarding the abstract. Shifting the words we obtain:

…the observer affects the physical and the physical affects the observer.

For this to happen we need to add the following to our graphic:

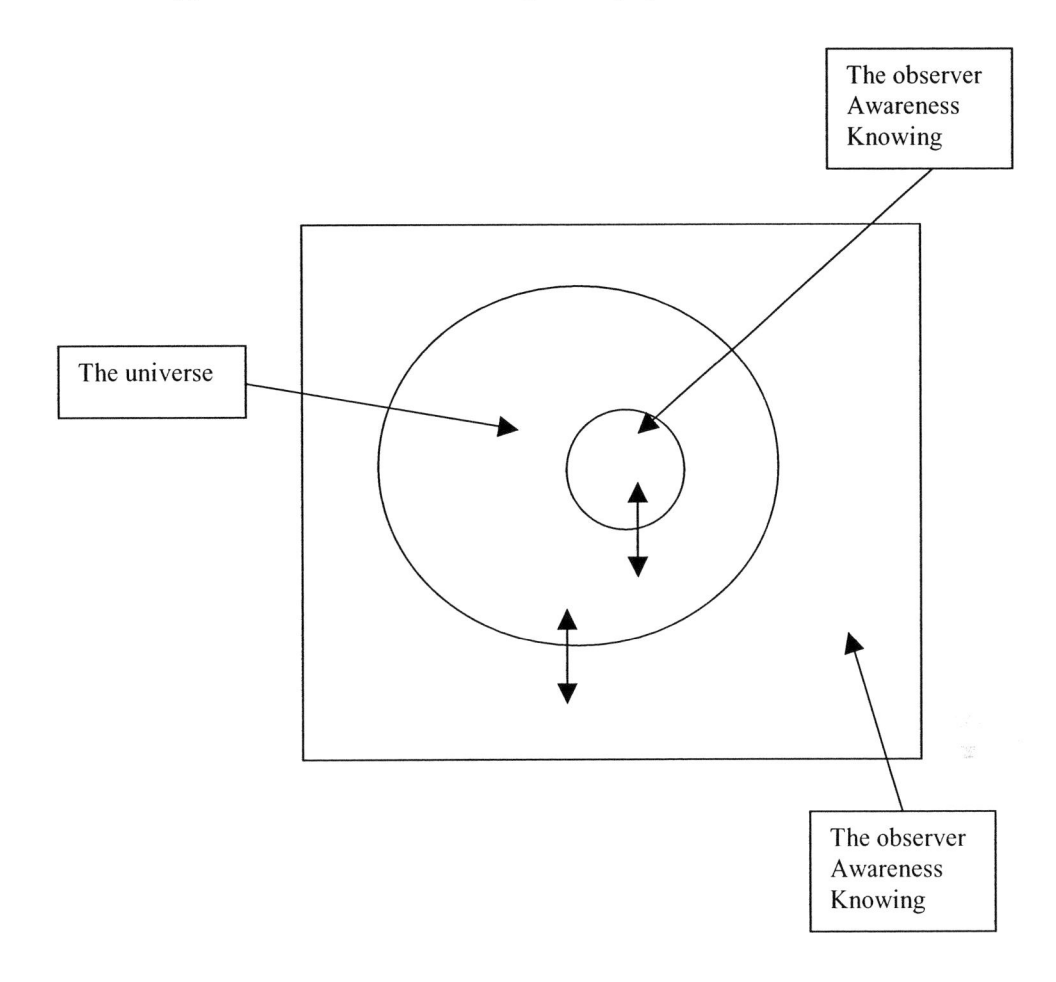

[Diagram: A square labeled with arrows pointing to "The universe" (outer circle) and "The observer Awareness Knowing" (inner circle and outer square), with bidirectional arrows between them.]

So it is the physical once again becomes sandwiched between the abstract. The result is that Kant's system leads us towards a duel system not a single system. Kant's system leads us towards 'being' *being* 'Being'

So what do we observe if we take a cross section of the abstract? We see:

1. What is
2. The future does not exist within the abstract.
3. The future has no potentiality within the abstract void a universe whose fabric is time.
4. The past exists
5. The present exists
6. The future does not exist
7. What 'is' is

445

The War & Peace of a New Metaphysical Perception

8. What 'was' is
9. What 'will be' is
10. What 'could be' is not
11. Potentiality is not

The 'Absolute Zero' point of abstraction

Just as the physical has its point of 'absolute zero', so too does abstraction.

The point of absolute zero for the physical is speculated by science to be '0' degrees Kelvin. This is more definitively defined as the point when all energy is equally distributed universally both macroscopically and microscopically.

What then is the absolute zero point of the abstract? The absolute zero point of abstraction is when all knowledge is equally distributed within the abstract. If no new knowledge is introduced into the system the system soon reaches a point of equilibrium similar to the equilibrium reached at absolute zero Kelvin in the physical. In short, rather than a lack of fresh energy transfer from one physical entity to another, we find a lack of fresh knowledge transfer from one to another. Put in a different manner: We find stagnation is achieved.

Is there 'an' energy source to keep the physical system dynamic? That is the realm of science and science has no answer to this question at this point in time.

Is there 'a' knowledge source to keep the abstract dynamic? This is the realm of metaphysics and metaphysics had no theory up to and through the combined efforts of Kant and Hegel. But what about now at this point in time? Beginning with the turn of the millennium, metaphysics has a theory regarding the source of such knowledge. The theory is 'being' *being* 'Being', symbiotic panentheism, a fusion of the Kantian/Hegelian and Aristotelian systems as presented in this work: The War and Peace of a New Metaphysical Perceptions.

The absolute zero point of multiplicity is attained when the stagnation point of energy transfer is achieved.

At this point all motion stops and time and distance cease since no relative motion is occurring. Time after all is:

$$v = \frac{d}{t}$$

or

$$vt = d$$

And if d, distance, is something no longer travelable and thus no longer measurable, it no longer exists and as such 't' no longer exists. What then of 'v'? 'v' is simply a coefficient and as seen in the first formula becomes:

$$v = \frac{d}{t}$$

where d = 0, t = 0

$$v = \frac{0}{0}$$

Which is significantly different than either $0/\infty$ or $\infty/0$

Due to the constraints of time we will leave the phenomenal metaphysical potential of $0/0$ to Tractate 8: Hegel.

The fusion of: $0/\infty$ and $\infty/0$

First: Kant

$0/\infty$

Finite time / Infinite knowledge

Infinite knowledge within Finite time

The War & Peace of a New Metaphysical Perception

We now come back to Kant's metaphysical system:

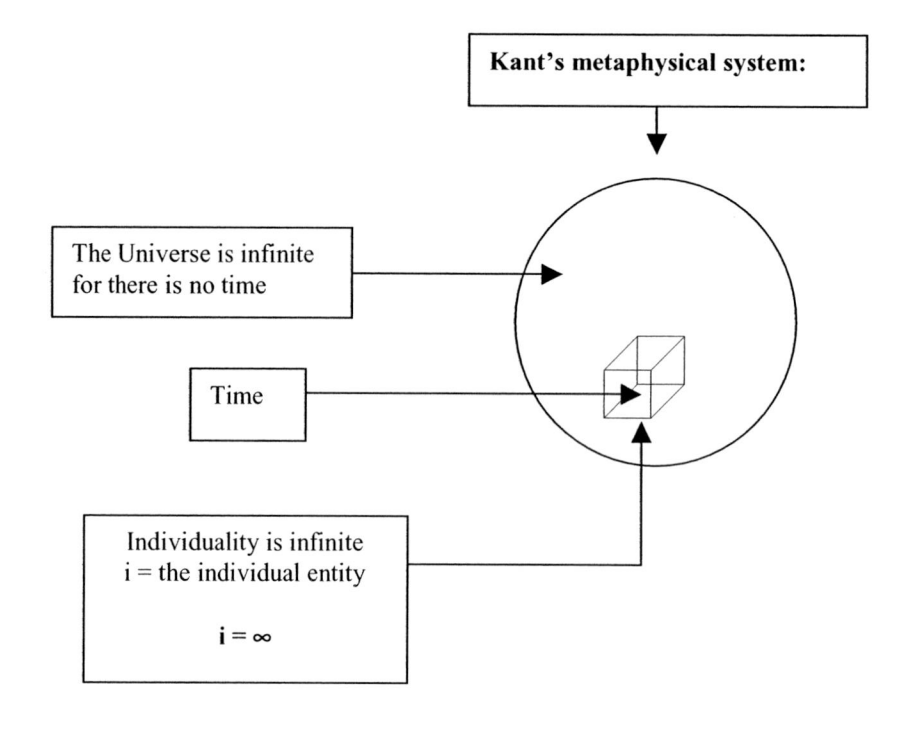

Kant's metaphysical system:

The Universe is infinite for there is no time

Time

Individuality is infinite
i = the individual entity

i = ∞

Universe / endless knowledge

The universe is '0' for the universe, without the observer, is simply passivity of observation

0 = ∞

0 / ∞ = 0

Which brings us back to boredom, endless repetition.

Second: Aristotle

∞ / 0

Infinite time / Finite knowledge

Finite knowledge within infinite time

We now come back to Aristotle's metaphysical system:

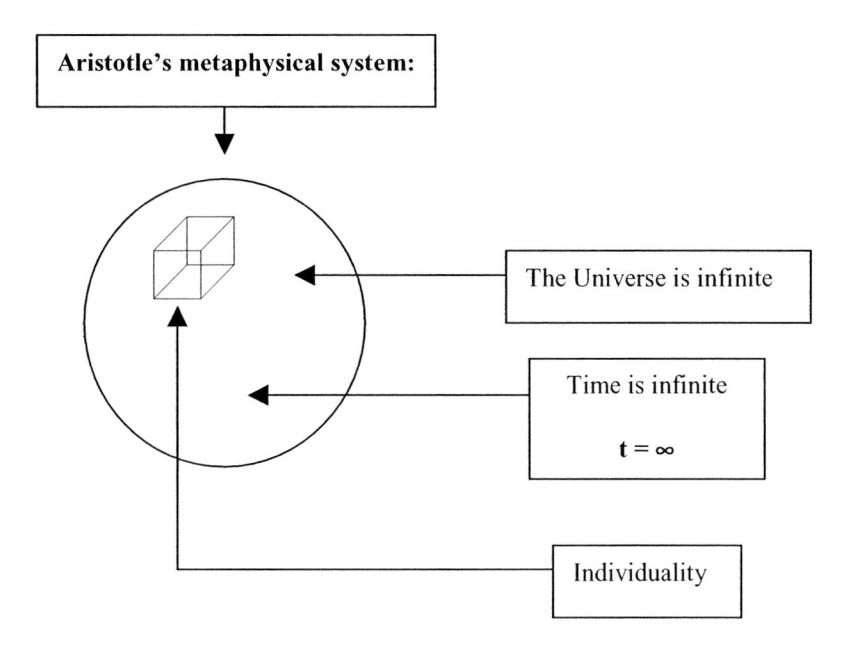

Aristotle's metaphysical system:

→ The Universe is infinite

→ Time is infinite

$t = \infty$

→ Individuality

Universe / limited knowledge

The universe is '∞' for the universe, without the observer, remains throughout infinite time as it is, passive.

$$\infty = 0$$

$$0 = \infty / 0$$

Which brings us back to boredom, endless repetition.

The question becomes: How do we eliminate the boredom????

The War & Peace of a New Metaphysical Perception

Third: the fusion of the two

The elimination of endless repetition, the elimination of boredom

| Time is infinite

$t = \infty$ | | Time is limited to what is 'found' 'within' the individual

$t = 0$ |

$\infty / 0$ $0 / \infty$

Infinite time / Finite knowledge   Finite time / infinite knowledge

Finite knowledge within infinite time   Infinite knowledge within finite time

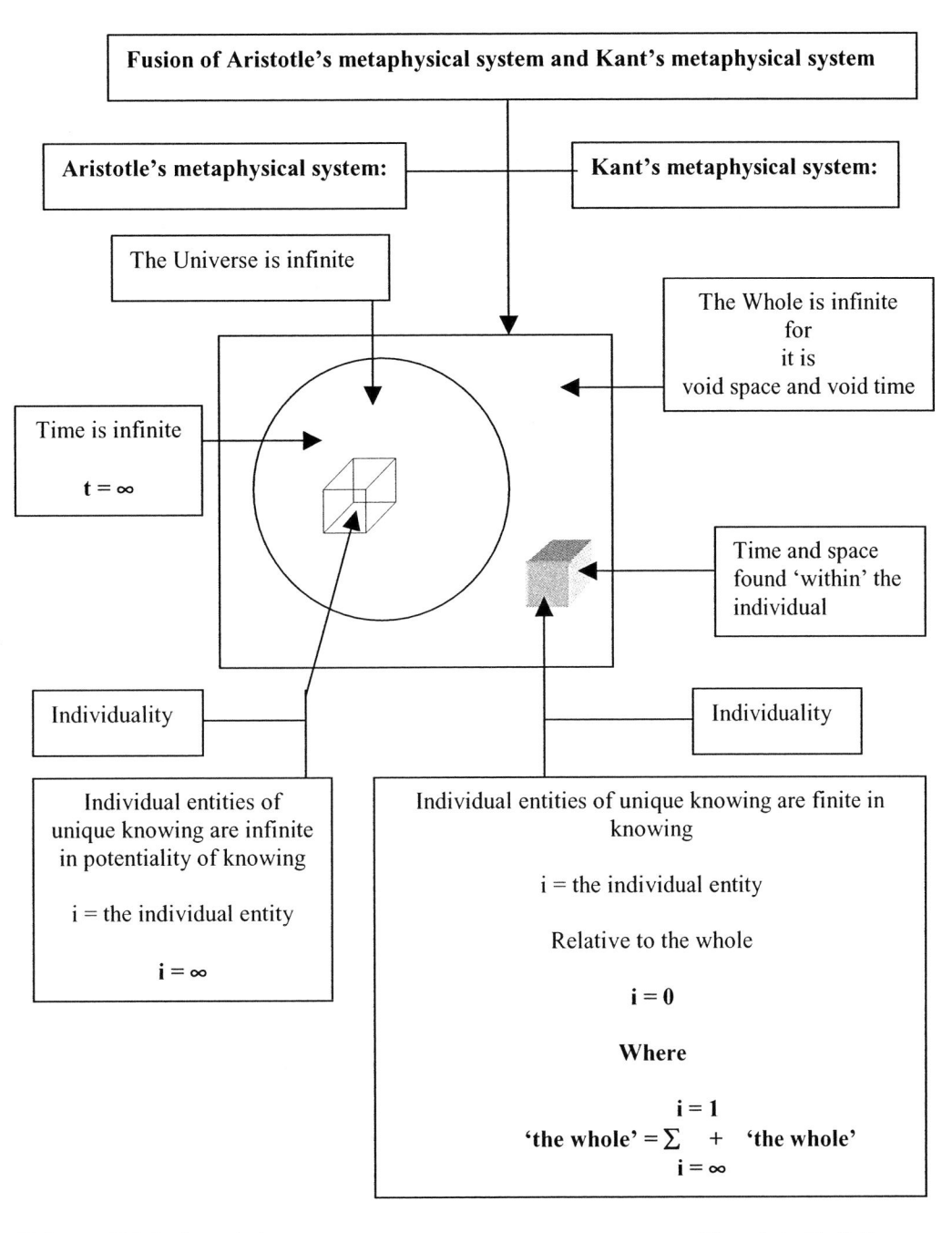

The Error of Kant

Fusion of Aristotle's metaphysical system and Kant's metaphysical system

Aristotle's metaphysical system:

Kant's metaphysical system:

The Universe is infinite

The Whole is infinite for it is void space and void time

Time is infinite

$t = \infty$

Time and space found 'within' the individual

Individuality

Individuality

Individual entities of unique knowing are infinite in potentiality of knowing

i = the individual entity

$i = \infty$

Individual entities of unique knowing are finite in knowing

i = the individual entity

Relative to the whole

$i = 0$

Where

$$\text{'the whole'} = \sum_{i=\infty}^{i=1} + \text{'the whole'}$$

Universe / Finite knowledge
knowledge

The universe is '0' for the universe, whole,
without the observer, experiences

only passive action

The whole / infinite

The whole is '∞' for the

with active action of the observer,
has infinite potential of knowledge

(continued on next page)

451

The War & Peace of a New Metaphysical Perception

The whole is '0' for the whole, universe without active action of the observer the remains as it is. potentiality of

The universe is '∞' for the with the active action of observer has infinite 'newness'

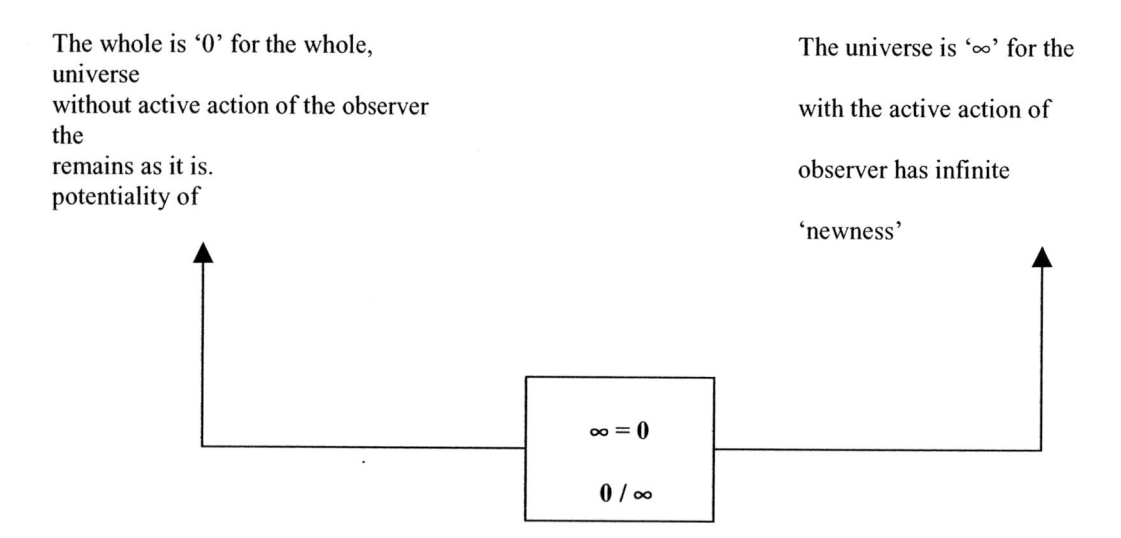

$$\infty = 0$$
$$0 / \infty$$

The result of fusing the two systems into a complete system:

> The elimination of endless repetition, boredom, stagnation, ...

The result of fusing the two systems into a complete system:

> The emergence of birth, change, renewal, ...

At last we achieve the elimination of the most insidious form regarding the four states of existence. We eliminate the existence of the simple state of being as the dominant form of existence. We eliminate the perception of permanent equilibrium, multiplicity, the passive, physical objectives being the point towards which all action tends and in its place we find change, seamlessness, the active, abstractual objectives being the point towards which all action tends.

The two states of existence remaining are both similar in nature for each embraces the state of our new constant called change:

1. Growth
2. Decay

What does the new metaphysical system of 'being' *being* 'Being' suggest regarding the two remaining states of existence? The fusion of the Kantian system and the Aristotelian system suggest we best think long and hard about our responsibilities for the choice of the two remaining forms of existence is dependent upon us, is up to us to decide as to which will prevail through the application of free will itself.

God does not change

Collective Thought, 'Being', 'God' reaches it's point of 'absolute zero' when it reaches it's point of no longer changing.

Keep in mind however that there is no time, distance, space, matter, or energy found in the fabric of abstraction within which the universe is imbedded verses there being time and distance existing as the fabric of the universe, existing as the fabric 'within' which matter and energy are immersed.

The Error of Kant

We are not debating the concept, of which is which. We are not debating whether time and distance are innate characteristics of matter and energy or whether matter and energy are innate characteristics of time and distance.

What we are examining is the apparent paradox of change occurring in a region incapable of changing. Such a statement emerges from this new metaphysical system where there is a 'location' for the void of time and the void of space since what is 'is' and 'what could be' has potentiality but as yet 'is not' rather 'what could be' is simply capable of potentially being.

Any newness of knowledge must be just that 'new' and thus incapable of being 'known' by an 'all knowing', omniscient, entity in terms of 'divine foreknowledge'.

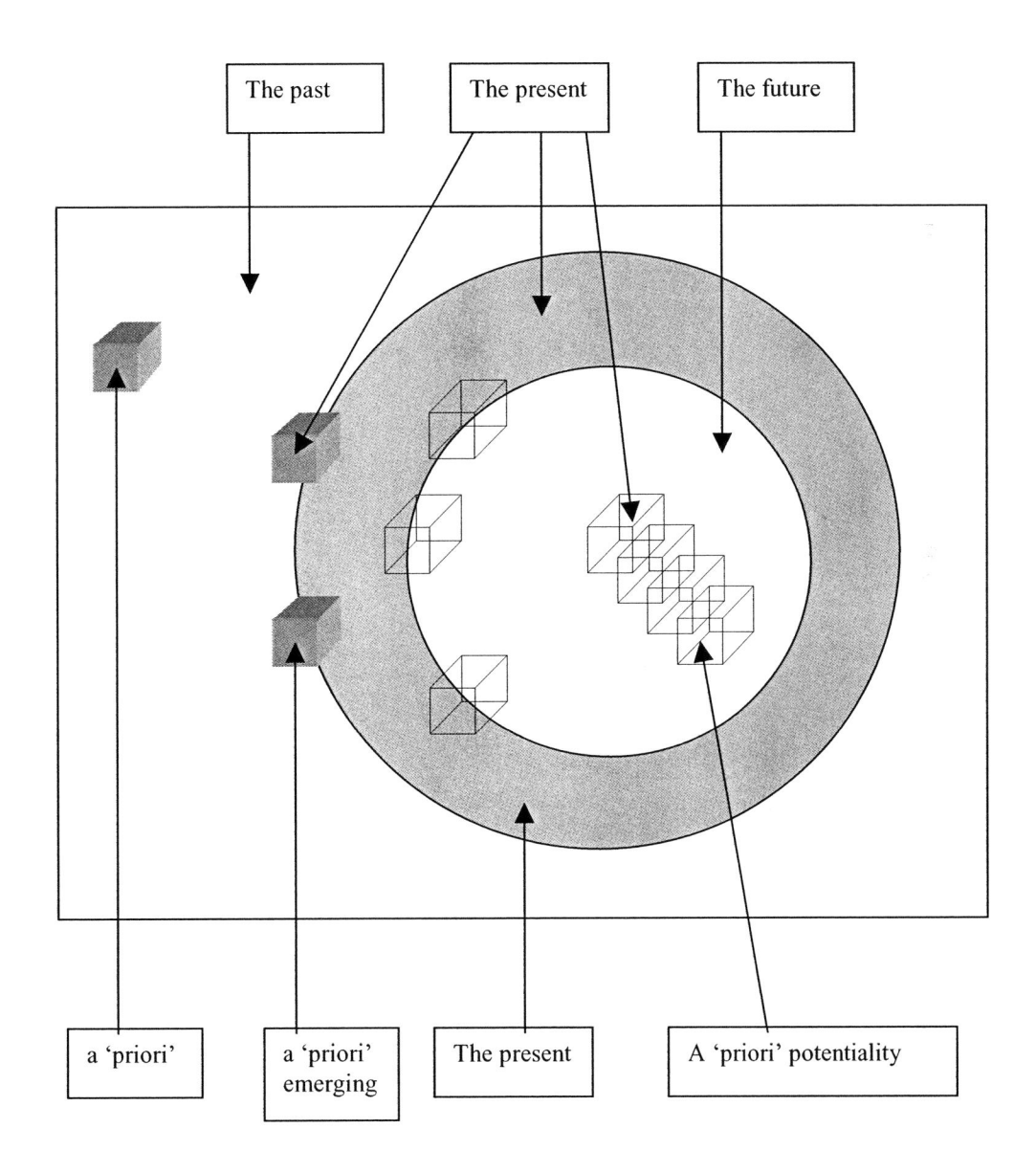

The War & Peace of a New Metaphysical Perception

The future does not exist

Only the present exists. Potentiality in the present exists only as potentiality. We call such emergence of potentiality: the future. Storage of the present exists, we call it the past. But the past is gone and we cannot change it. The future is yet to come and until it comes we cannot impact it. We can only impact the present. Only the present exists as location of cause and effect.

Lets re-examine the drawing with knowledge as our focus:

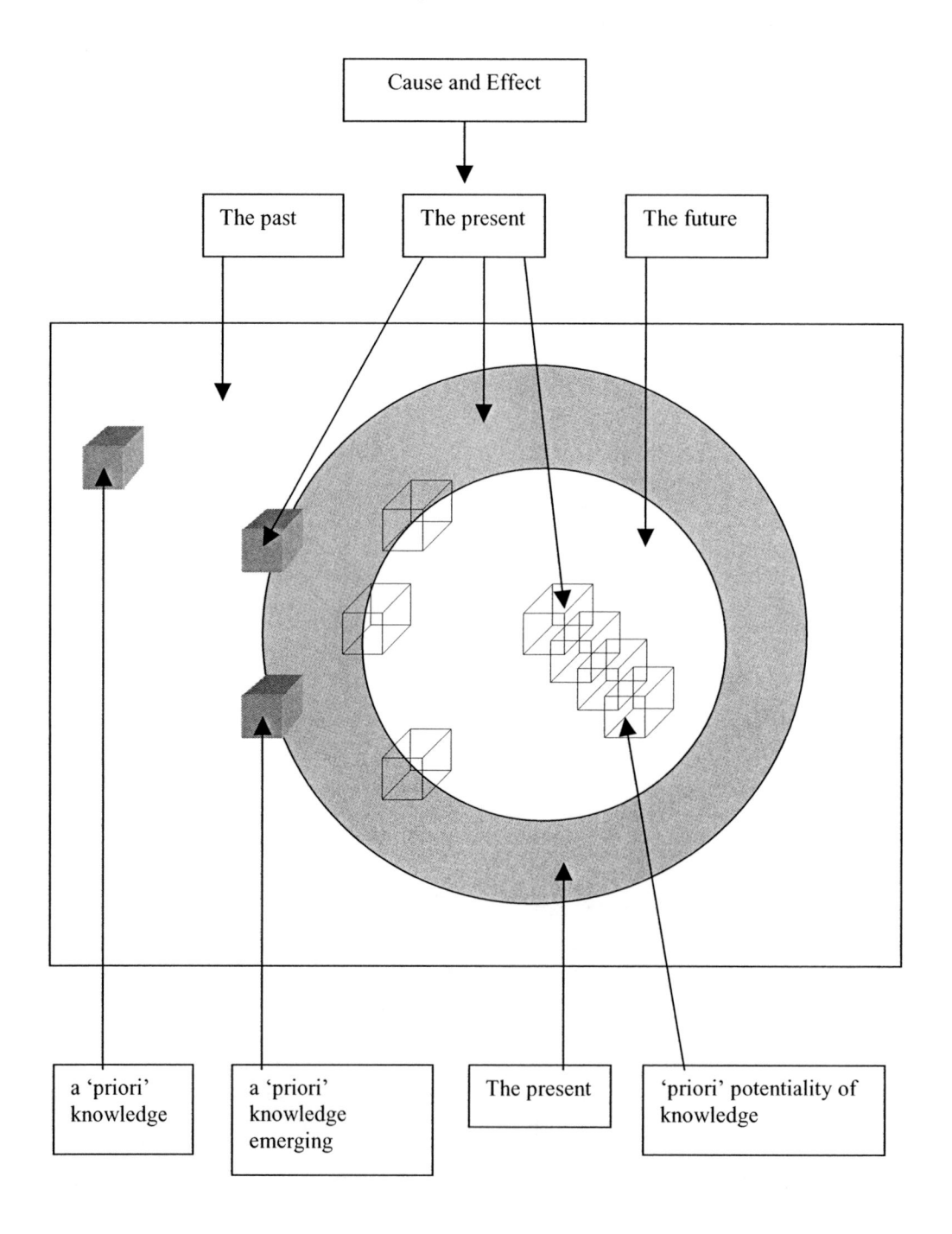

The Error of Kant

If we expand upon the apparent existence of the present, we obtain:

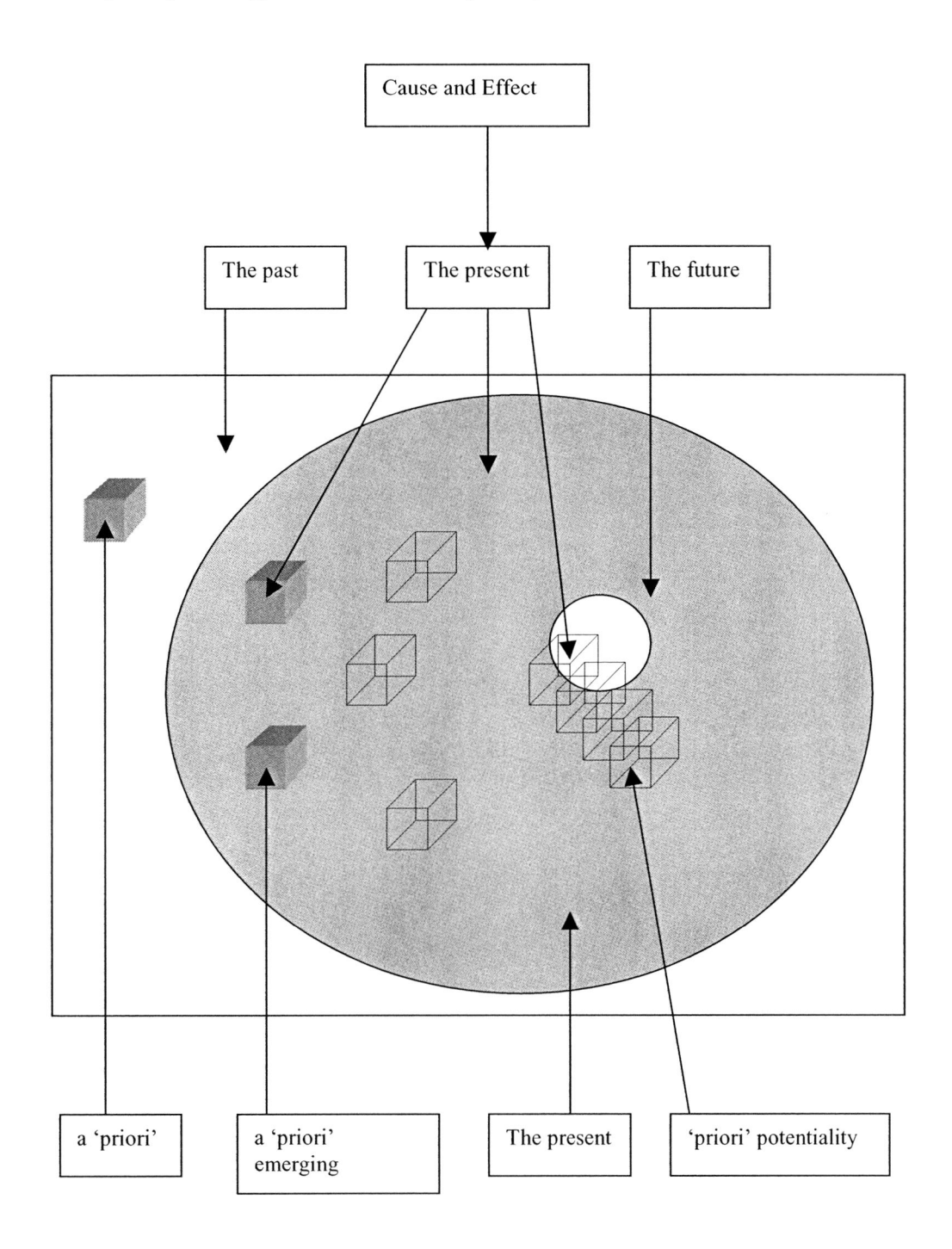

As small as potentiality becomes it has in fact not become any smaller for it never was.

As large as the present appears to become within the whole it takes up no space for the present is but a fleeting moment in time so small it is no more distinguishable from the whole of knowledge than a point is distinguishable from the whole of space.

If the future does not yet exist, we can examine the metaphysical system of a non-Cartesian system powered by a Cartesian system, 'being' *being* 'Being', symbiotic panentheism, through the process of examining 'still' shots of the system. In essence we can view the active system by examining cross sections of this active system through a picture of the system in a passive form. Keep in mind, however, that the system is not passive/stagnant but rather active/dynamic.

As such let's look at one such passive graphic of the dynamic system. We will examine the system in terms of what happens to the future when we take a passive slice of the system.

The Error of Kant

We recognize the graphic as being what we had previously diagramed:

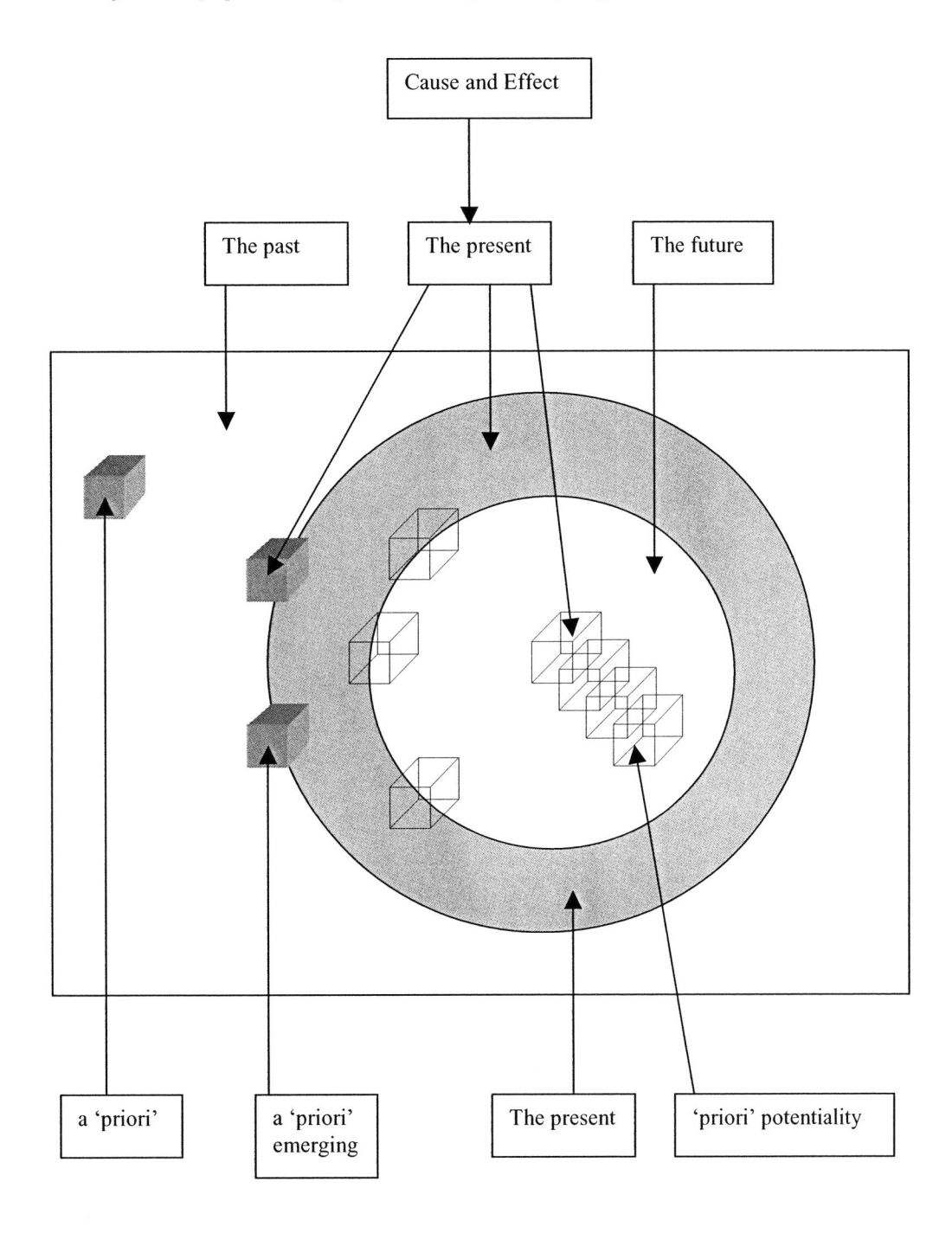

| Cause and Effect |
| The past | The present | The future |
| a 'priori' | a 'priori' emerging | The present | 'priori' potentiality |

Because this is a slice of what exists, we can remove the elements, which do not pertain to the picture since they do not exist in terms of existence itself but rather exist only in terms of potentiality.

The War & Peace of a New Metaphysical Perception

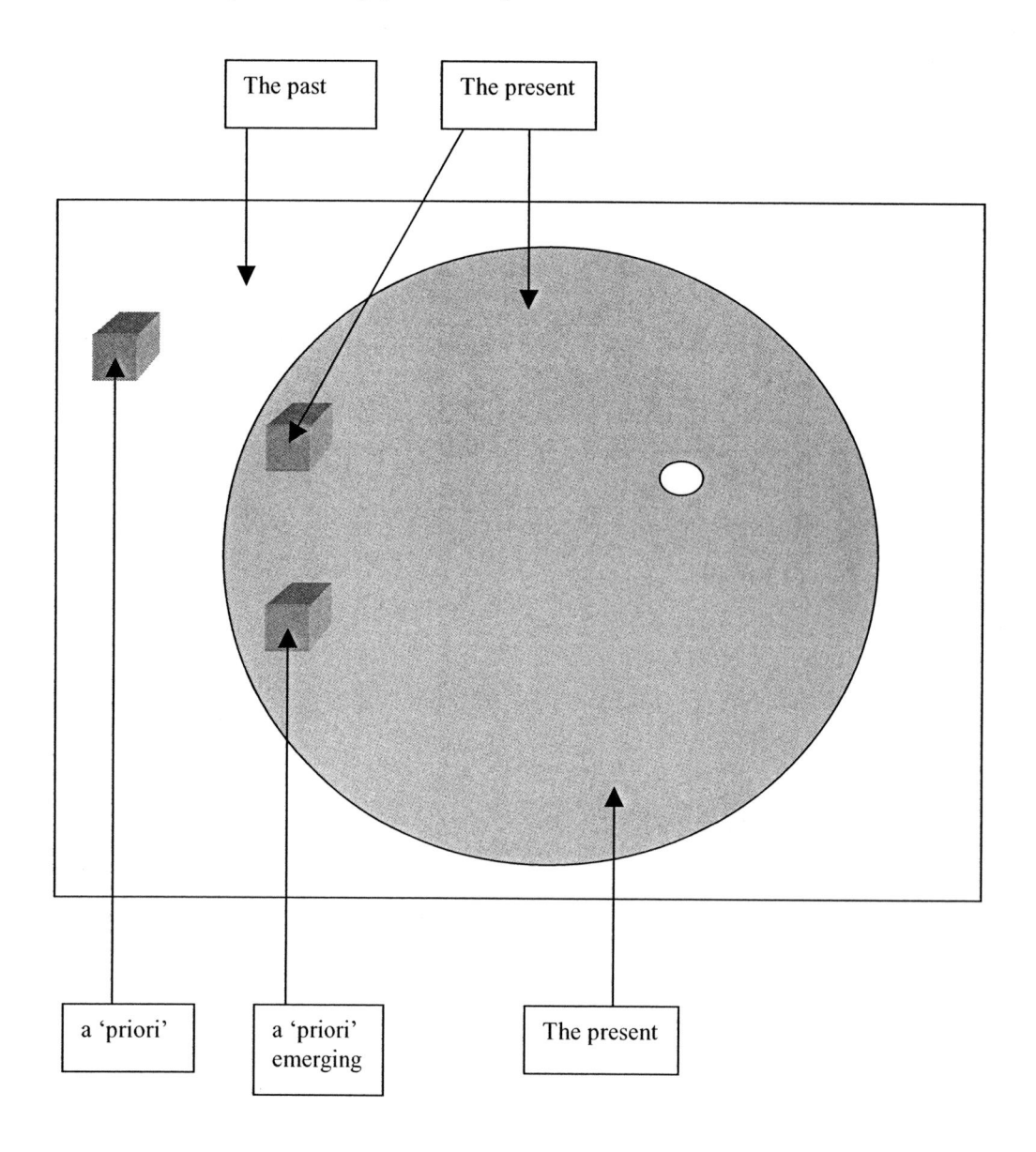

The past	The present	
a 'priori'	a 'priori' emerging	The present

The Error of Kant

In fact the bubble of potentiality disappears and the past merges into the present for the past becomes what presently is. We thus obtain:

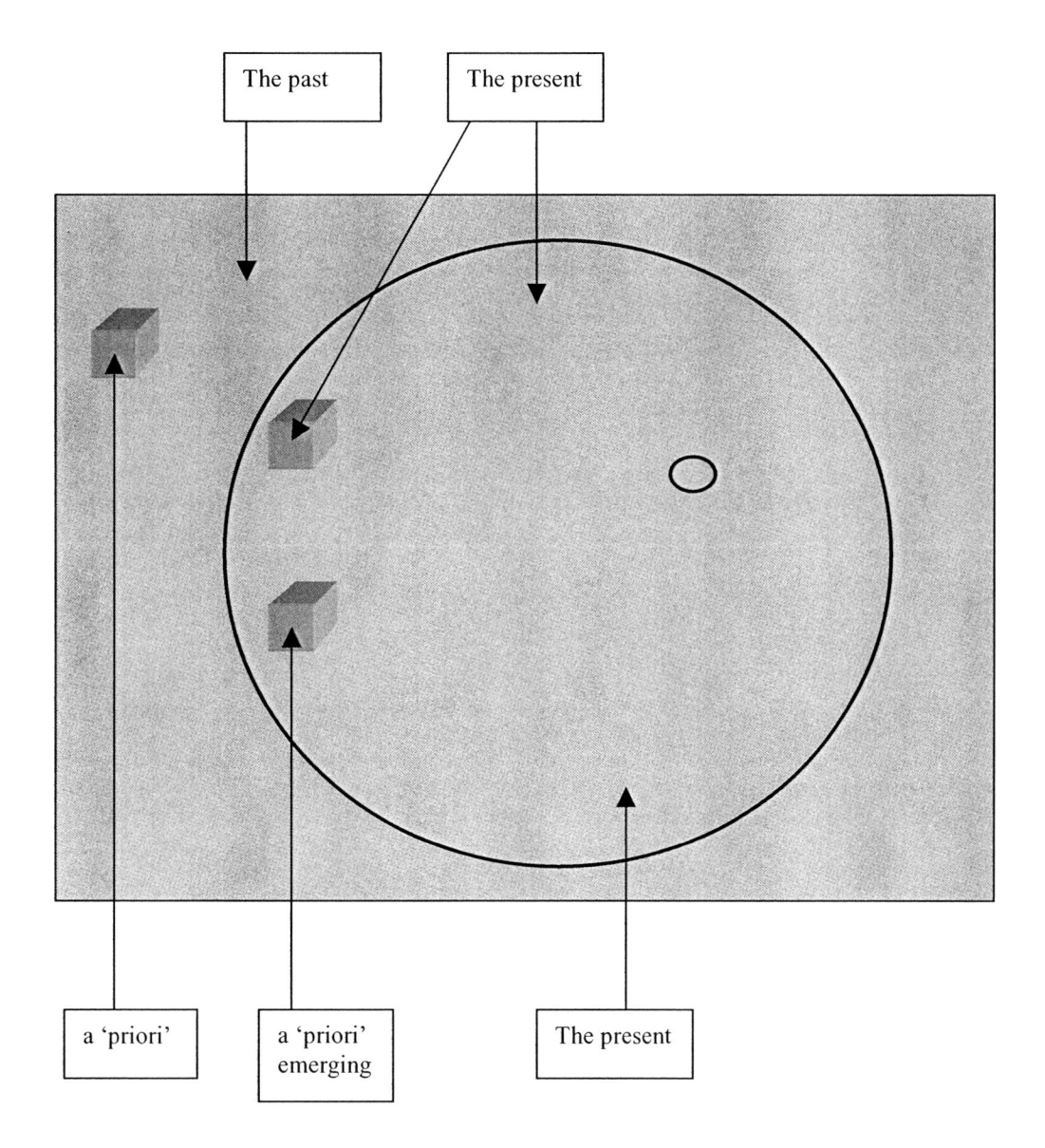

The past | The present

a 'priori' | a 'priori' emerging | The present

The War & Peace of a New Metaphysical Perception

Such a graphic arises out of the metaphysical system of 'being' *being* 'Being', symbiotic panentheism

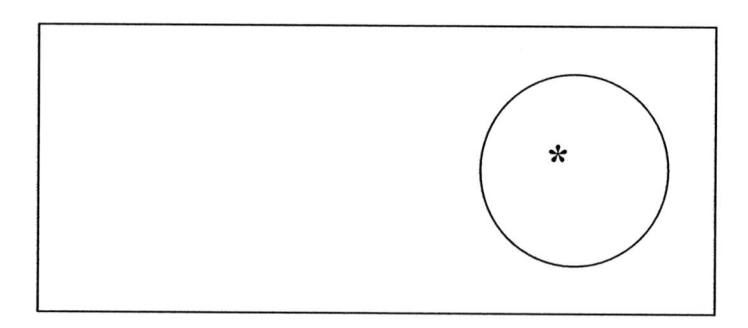

'being' *being* 'Being'

One may recognize the graphic of 'being' *being* 'Being' as a more simplistic negative/inverse image of the previous diagram.

What does such a system imply about the current theoretical concept of parallel universes infinitely branching off from each 'choice' we make. Does another universe begin at the juncture of each of our decisions?

Such a concept is not being dismissed as 'an impossibility', however, within the metaphysical system of 'being' *being* 'Being', such an occurrence would now have 'a' location 'outside the physical/the universe 'within' which it could function in an active manner. Such an occurrence might take the appearance of:

The Error of Kant

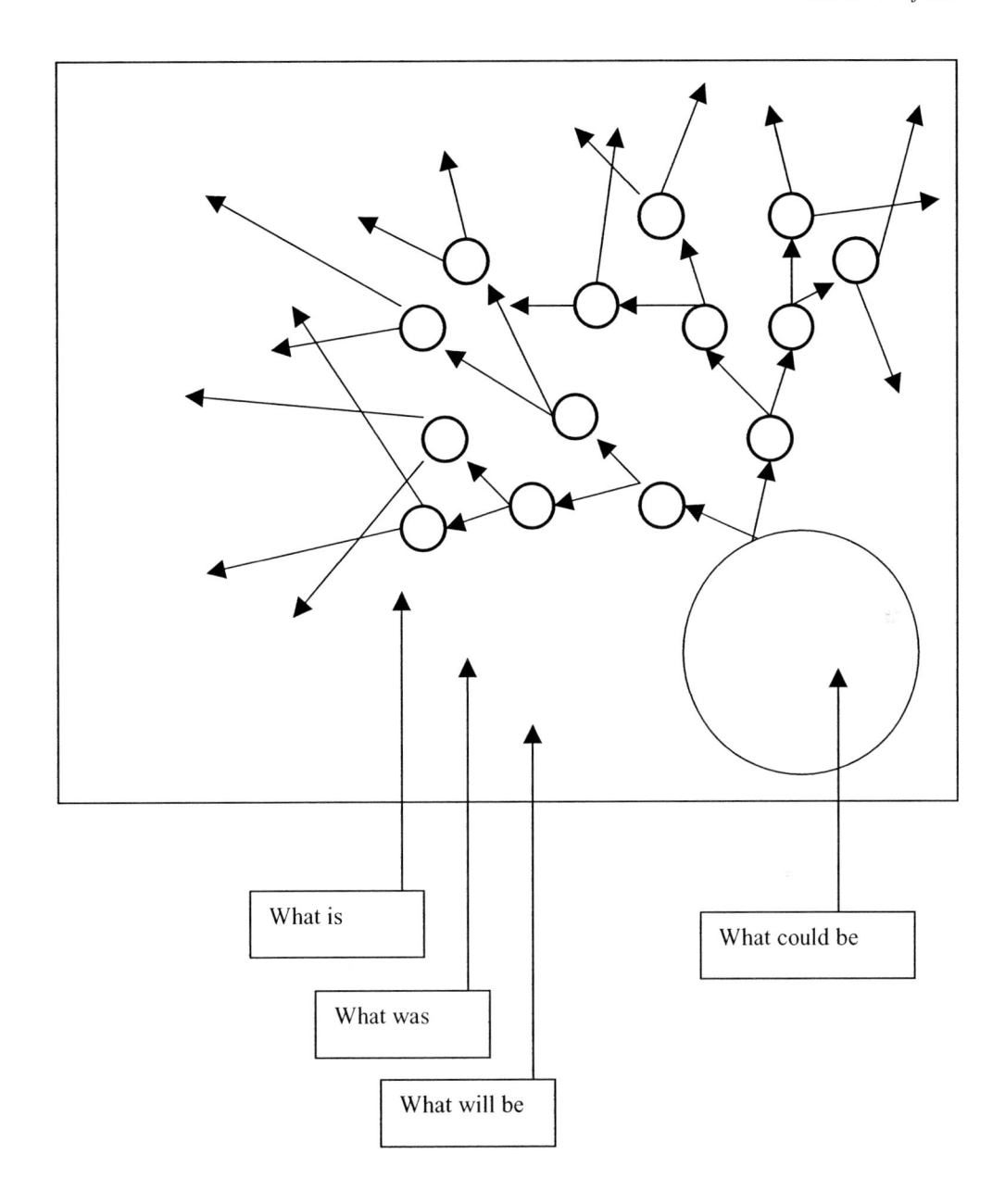

[Diagram with boxes labeled "What is", "What was", "What will be", and "What could be" pointing to regions of a branching arrow diagram]

Such existences, should they in fact occur, would belong to the region of 'what will be' versus "what 'could be'"

As we can see, within a metaphysical system of 'being' *being* 'Being', the future only takes on a function when the system is dynamic through the process of action itself. The obligatory branching 'off' of other universes from the original 'choice' simply makes the obligatory branch itself pre-determined. Since we discussed 'pre-determinism' within the Tractate 3: Boethius and Free Will, we will not go there other than to say such existences are not examples of potentiality but rather examples of absolutism. More of absolutism and its component of minimalism as represented by the absolute zero of the absolute can be found within the section, ' The 'Absolute Zero' point of abstraction', found previously within this tractate.

The past does not exist

What of the past? How can we say the past does not exist? When we take a cross section of the given dynamic system of 'being' *being* 'Being', we obtain an understanding that the present expands to include the past. We observed a similar occurrence when we observed the result as the present moved inward to occupy the position of the future. The process demonstrated that the future, in a passive system, does not exist.

Such an understanding explains why the small bubble of the future can now be completely removed. Simultaneously we now understand how it is the present expands to incorporate 'what was' within the region of 'what is' for the past was and the past now is. The graphic then becomes:

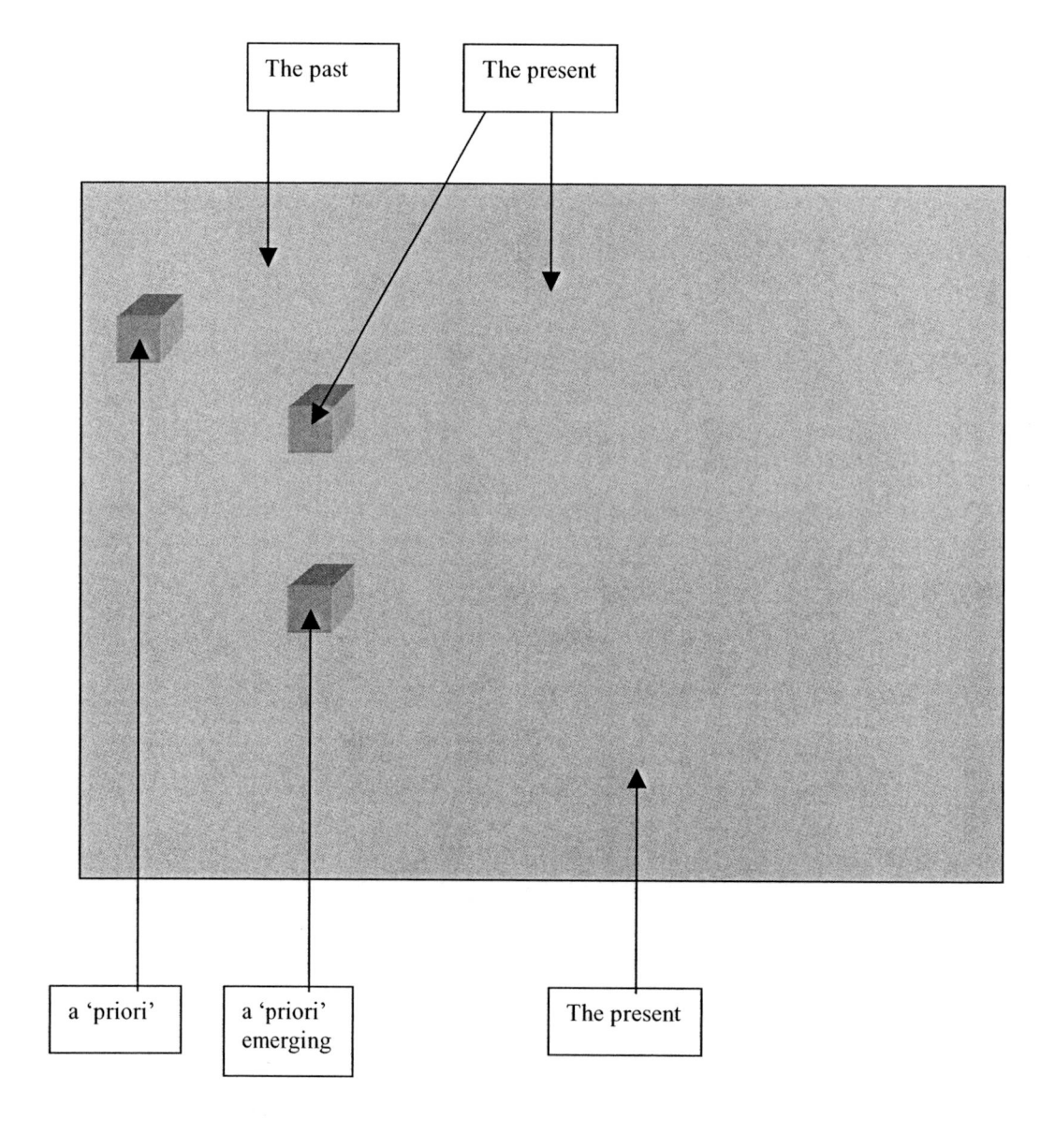

The Error of Kant

Such a depiction is what it is, a graphic cross section of a dynamic system, a passive view of the system.

What is exists

If we move the system back into the mode of being a dynamic system, we come back to:

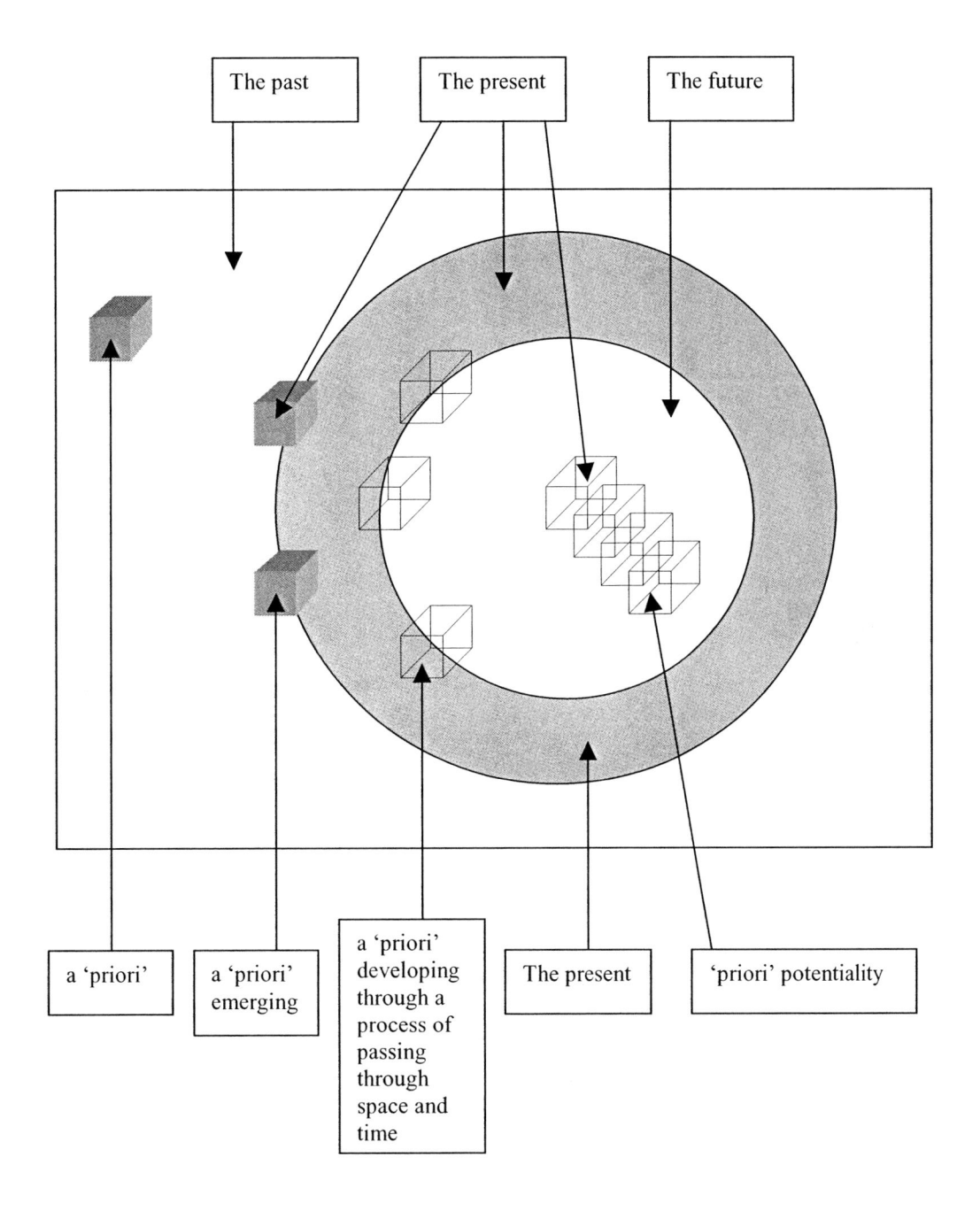

| The past | The present | The future |

| a 'priori' | a 'priori' emerging | a 'priori' developing through a process of passing through space and time | The present | 'priori' potentiality |

463

The War & Peace of a New Metaphysical Perception

If we then reduce the present, a period of time so short it is but an illusion – albeit a 'real illusion' - of time, to what it truly is within a dynamic system, we obtain:

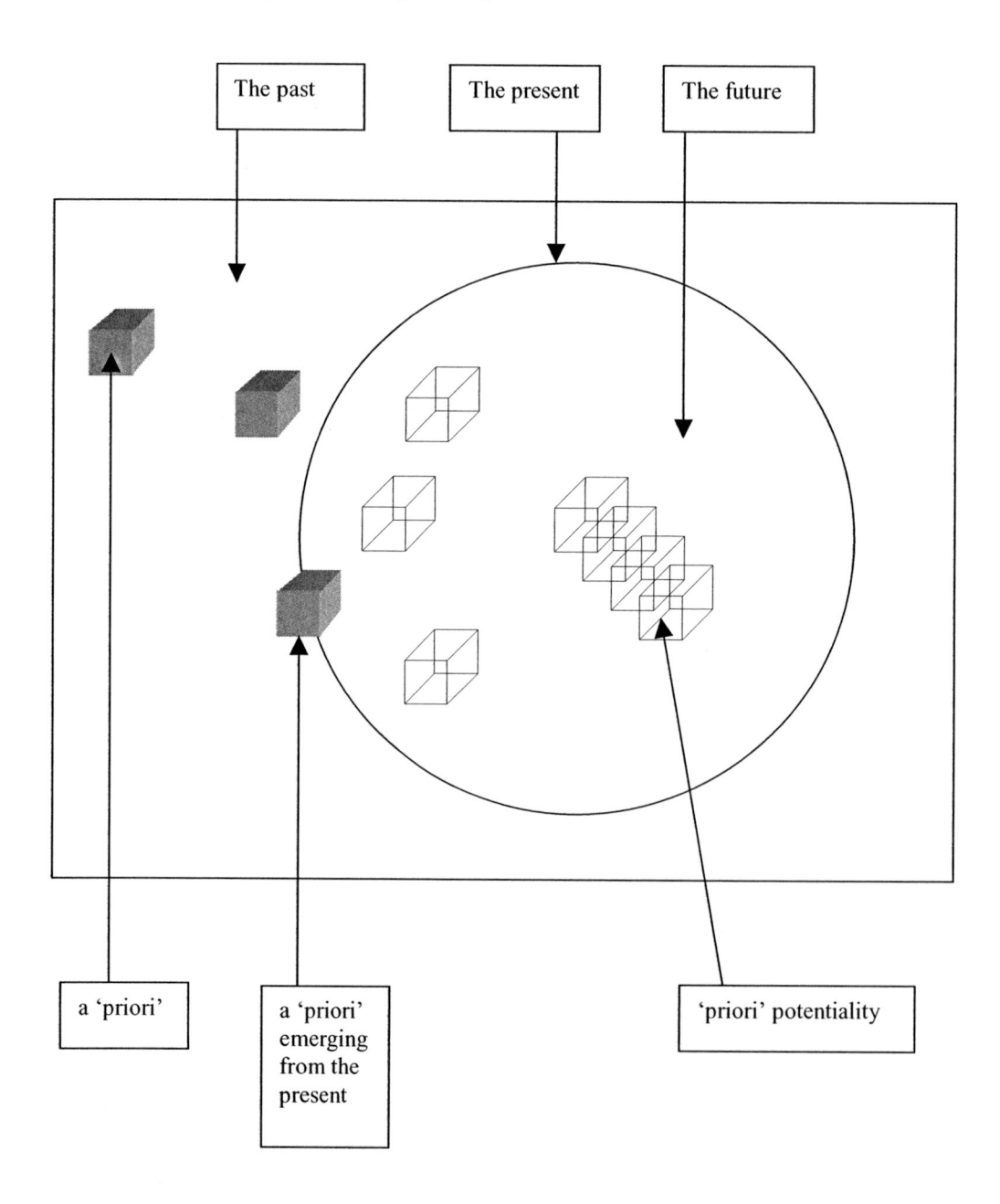

[Diagram: boxes labeled "The past", "The present", "The future" pointing into a rectangular area containing a circle. Inside the circle are outlined cubes (future/potentiality); outside the circle are shaded cubes (past). Labels below point to: "a 'priori'", "a 'priori' emerging from the present", and "'priori' potentiality".]

This diagram demonstrates the present to be just what the present is, such a small element of existence that it in essence does not exist 'in' anything rather it is an 'active' boundary separating potentiality from existence.

Such a representation is appropriately expressed by the graphic depiction of a circle, where the inside of the circle is the future/potentiality and the outside of the circle is the past, what exists. The circle itself is composed of points equidistant from a single point of potentiality. Since all

The Error of Kant

points have no length, depth, or width, the circle itself is in essence non-existent or simply a separation of 'what is' and 'what could be'.

Simplified in terms of regions this becomes:

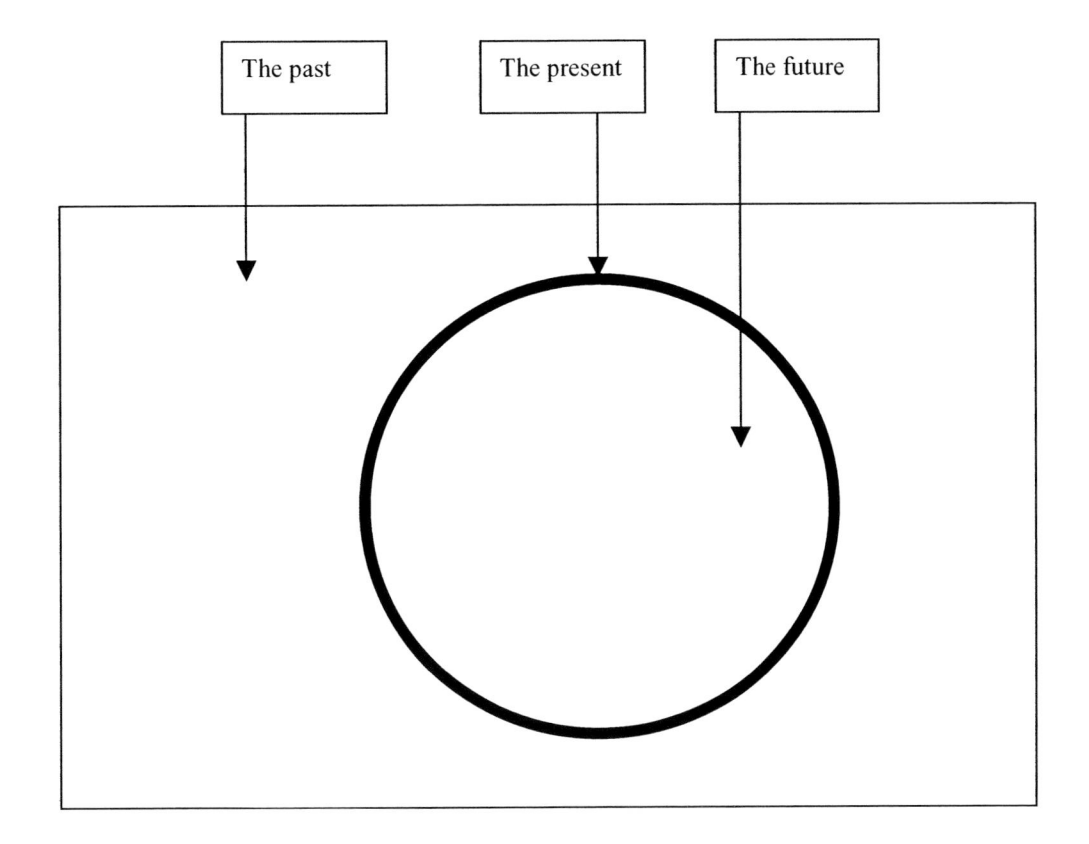

The War & Peace of a New Metaphysical Perception

In terms of knowledge, as a passive system, this becomes:

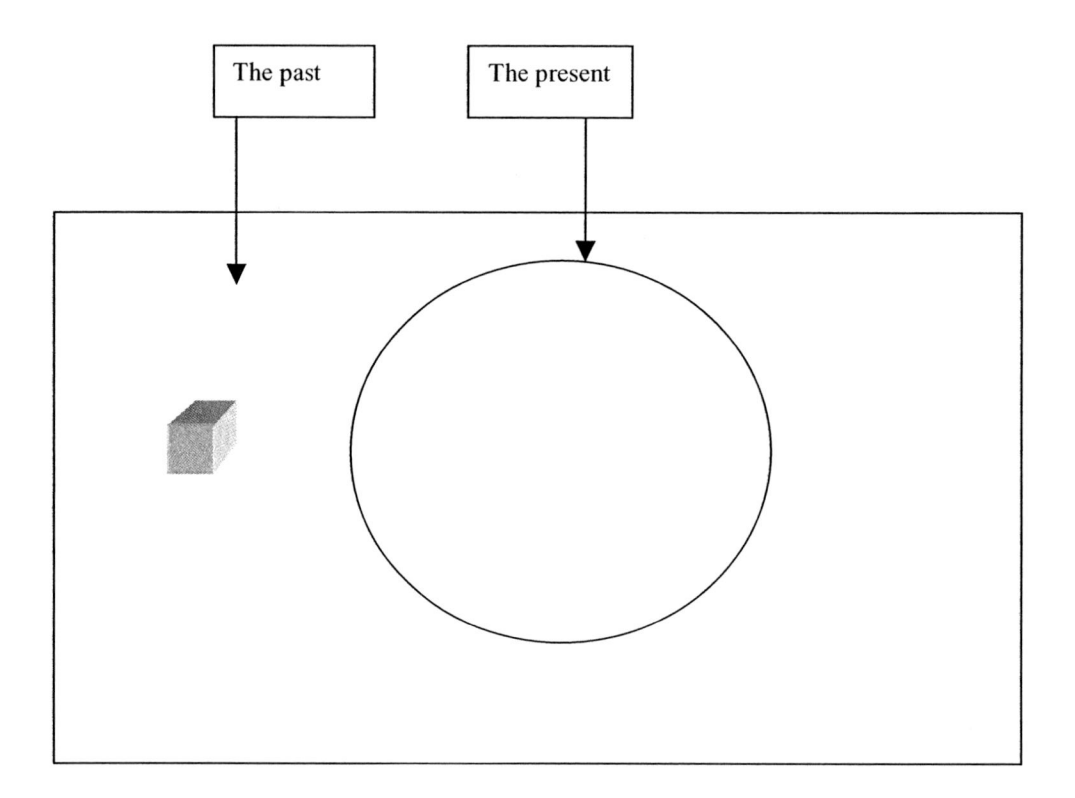

Or simply "being' being' and since this is a passive system, action becomes simply the state of being and thus non-italicized form of being representing action.

The Error of Kant

If we move the passive representation of the system to that of being a dynamic system of active action, we obtain:

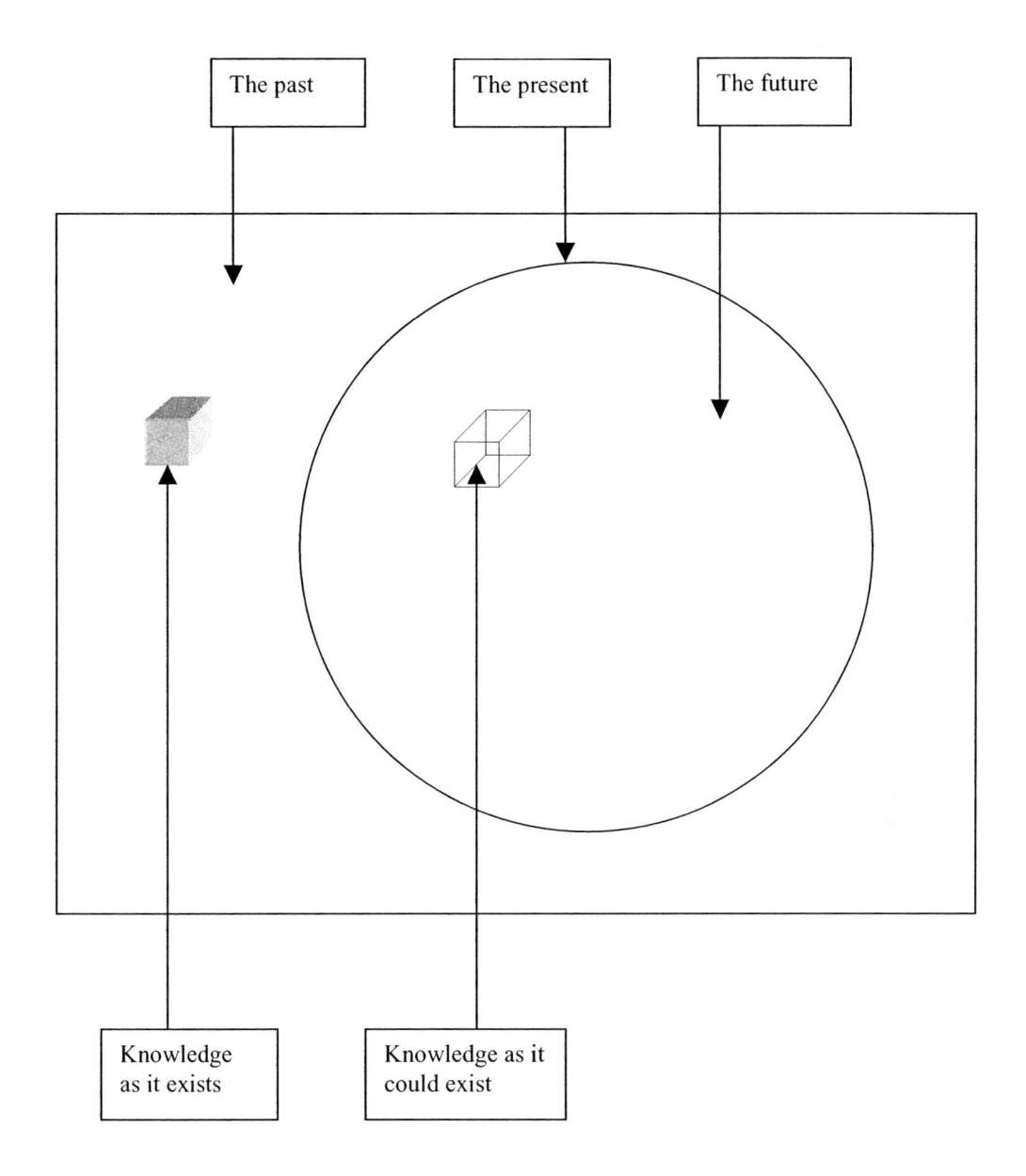

```
     The past          The present         The future
         │                  │                  │
         ▼                  ▼                  ▼
┌────────────────────────────────────────────────────┐
│                                                    │
│                  ╱─────────────╲                   │
│                 ╱               ╲                  │
│                │                 │                 │
│      ▓▓▓       │      ▢          │                 │
│       ▲        │      ▲          │                 │
│       │        │      │          │                 │
│       │         ╲    │          ╱                  │
│       │          ╲───│─────────╱                   │
└───────┼──────────────┼─────────────────────────────┘
        │              │
   ┌─────────┐   ┌─────────────┐
   │Knowledge│   │Knowledge as it│
   │as it exists│ │could exist   │
   └─────────┘   └─────────────┘
```

Or 'being' *being*, where being is italicized to represent action in a dynamic sense, an active sense. With the addition of potentiality/the future, we retain knowledge as it exists and obtain knowledge, as it could exist.

The War & Peace of a New Metaphysical Perception

If we then add an interrelationship of the whole to its parts and the parts to the whole, we obtain:

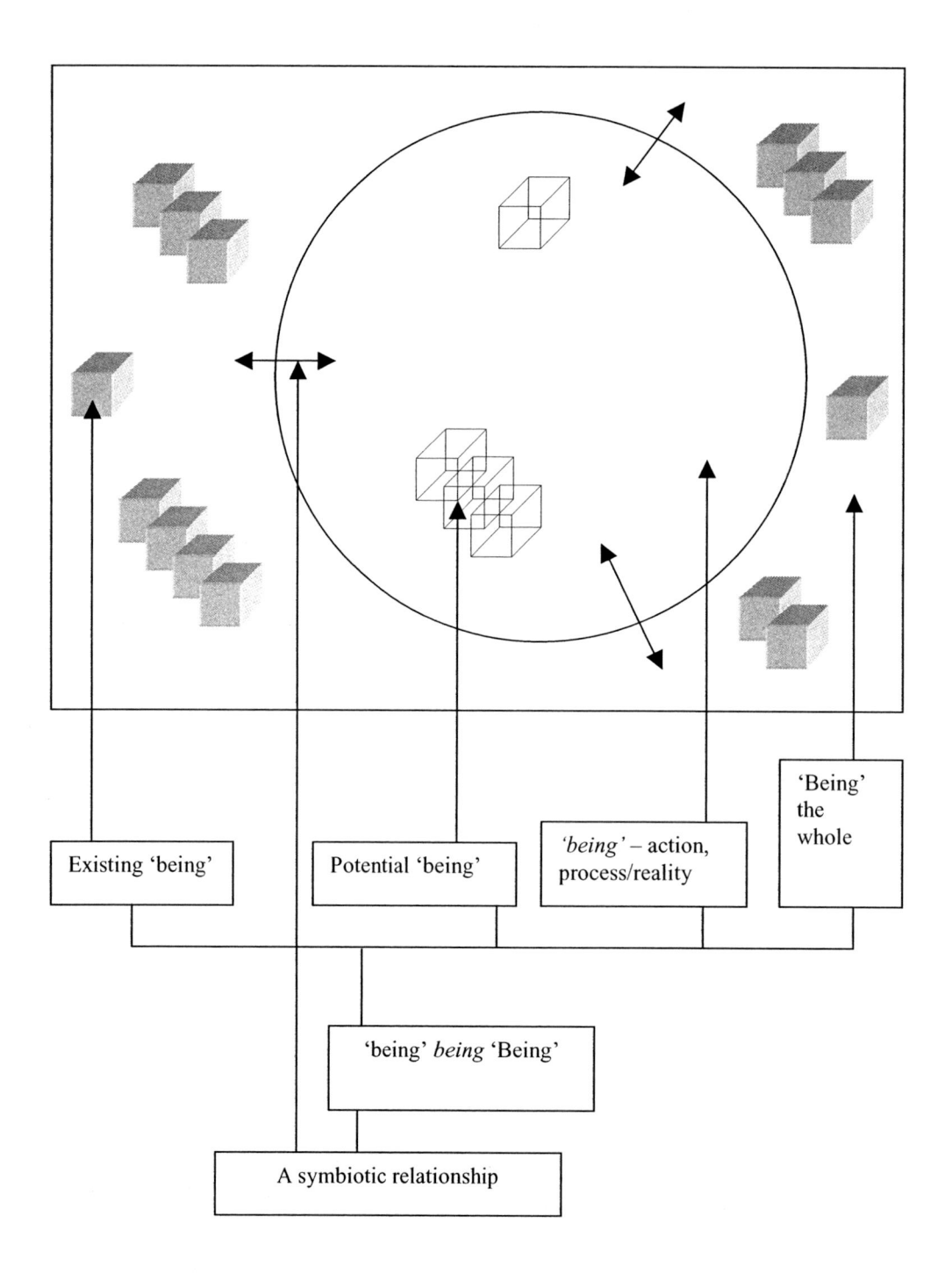

| Existing 'being' | Potential 'being' | *'being'* – action, process/reality | 'Being' the whole |

'being' *being* 'Being'

A symbiotic relationship

In terms of simplicity we simply have:

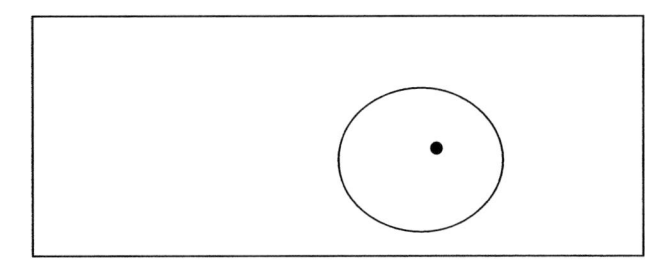

Or simply 'being' *being* 'Being'.

Resolving Kant's four antinomies[20]

Antinomies: a pair of conflicting propositions for which equally cogent proofs can be given on either side.

> Kant believed that antinomies were generated whenever human reason applied itself to any of the following four questions:
>
> 1. Does the world have a beginning in time and a boundary in space, or is it without beginning and without bound?
> 2. Are composite substances made up of simple substances, or do they contain parts within parts *ad infinitum*?
> 3. Are there any actions that are free, in the sense of being caused by volitions that are themselves uncaused, or are all actions caused by causes that have their own causes and so on *ad infinitum*?
> 4. Is there an absolutely necessary being to serve as ground of the rest of what exists, or are all beings contingent?[21]

Philosophers have addressed fragments of these four antinomies in one form or another since the emergence of philosophy. Granted the four antinomies may have been collated and summarized as a group of four by Kant but the issues they identify have been around well before Kant himself.

There are several means to approach the issue of these four antinomies.

1. One can demonstrate one aspect of each statement being correct and the other aspect of each statement being incorrect
2. One can demonstrate both aspects of each statement being incorrect
3. One can demonstrate both aspects of each statement being correct

Means one: One can demonstrate that one aspect of each antinomy is correct while the other aspect of each antinomy is incorrect

This is the process philosophy, in particular metaphysicians, have been attempting to move for the last twenty-five hundred years with no success. The process of demonstrating that one part of the statement is correct and thus the other aspect of the statement is incorrect is the process, which has been unsuccessfully employed by metaphysicians since the time of Zeno. The result: Philosophers

The War & Peace of a New Metaphysical Perception

and in particular metaphysicians are no closer to bringing the four antinomies to a close than they were since the emergence of philosophy itself.

Means two: One can demonstrate both aspects of each antinomy is incorrect.

To proceed in the direction of 'proving' both aspects of each antinomy to be incorrect is to begin with the assumption that our existence is but a 'figment of the imagination of something other than ourselves'. Such a scenario is not to be discarded lightly but for the intents and purposes of this tractate it is much too complex a scenario to attempt to prove or disprove at this time.

Means three: One can demonstrate both aspects of each antinomy is correct

Means three is a new approach to the resolutions of Kant's four antinomies. This approach has never been considered before the time of Kant. Kant, using 'means one', believing he resolved the four antinomies but was never able to demonstrate his solution in a clear and concise fashion let alone demonstrate his solution in a manner so clear and concise it could be demonstrated to everyone including the general public.

Up to and through the time of Kant, the answer would have been: No, there is no metaphysical system, which accounts for all eight scenarios (two for each antinomy)

Through the work of the two giants, Aristotle and Kant, and the assistance of many philosophers working between and after, the answer now becomes: There is a metaphysical system, which accounts for all eight cogent proofs (two for each antinomy) in such a manner as to demonstrate that all eight cogent proofs are simultaneously correct and thus do not contradict one another

The new metaphysical model of 'being' *being* 'Being', symbiotic panentheism, not only accounts for all eight scenarios but incorporates all eight scenarios into its systematic model. In fact, the new metaphysical model, a non-Cartesian system powered by a Cartesian system located 'within' the non-Cartesian system, not only incorporates all eight scenarios within the dynamics of its system but elevates each of the eight scenarios to a level of equal prominence and significance one to the other.

Having said this, let's no move on to demonstrating how it is the model does what it professes to do.

The four antinomies:

1. Does the world have a beginning in time and a boundary in space, or is it without beginning and without bound?
2. Are composite substances made up of simple substances, or do they contain parts within parts *ad infinitum*?
3. Are there any actions that are free, in the sense of being caused by volitions that are themselves uncaused, or are all actions caused by causes that have their own causes and so on *ad infinitum*?
4. Is there an absolutely necessary being to serve as ground of the rest of what exists, or are all beings contingent?

become eight positions of perceptual argument, cogent proofs:

1. The world has a beginning in time and a boundary in space.
2. The world has no beginning in time and no boundary in space.
3. Composite substances are made up of simple substances.

The Error of Kant

4. Composite substances contain parts within parts *ad infinitum*.
5. There are actions that are free, in the sense of being caused by volitions that are themselves uncaused.
6. There are actions that are caused by causes that have their own causes and so on *ad infinitum*.
7. There is an absolutely necessary being which serves as the ground of the rest of what exists.
8. The absolute necessary being is like all beings, contingent.

It is one thing to address the eight issues in words; it is another to address the eight issues graphically. If Kant is correct in believing a system is critical to the issue of metaphysics then theoretical metaphysicians should, if the system is 'clearly understood', be able to put the system into the form of a simplistic metaphysical model. The simplest form of model is one, which can be drawn as opposed to just discussed in a form of a Wittgenstein dialogue of 'words'. Words are the only means of discussing a metaphysical system when the metaphysical system is still too confusing to philosophers for them to demonstrate the system in the more demonstrative form of graphics or models.

Kant believed his metaphysical system addressed the eight issues listed above. Kant, however, could not address the eight statements, let alone model his system in a fashion, which would directly incorporate the eight issues, as equals one to the other. As such, Kant had not yet fully fashioned his metaphysical system into the form of being a fully understood system, which could adequately explain how it is all eight cogent proofs are just that: cogent proofs.

The reason Kant had such a difficult time explaining let alone demonstrating how his system resolved the eight cogent proofs was because Kant himself did not have a complete grasp regarding just 'how' his system functioned.

The War & Peace of a New Metaphysical Perception

Kant's metaphysical system was caught up in the same parameters of limits, which confronted Zeno. Like Zeno, Kant found himself confined by Aristotle. This becomes clear if we reexamine page two of this tractate and examine where it is Kant moved metaphysical perceptions.

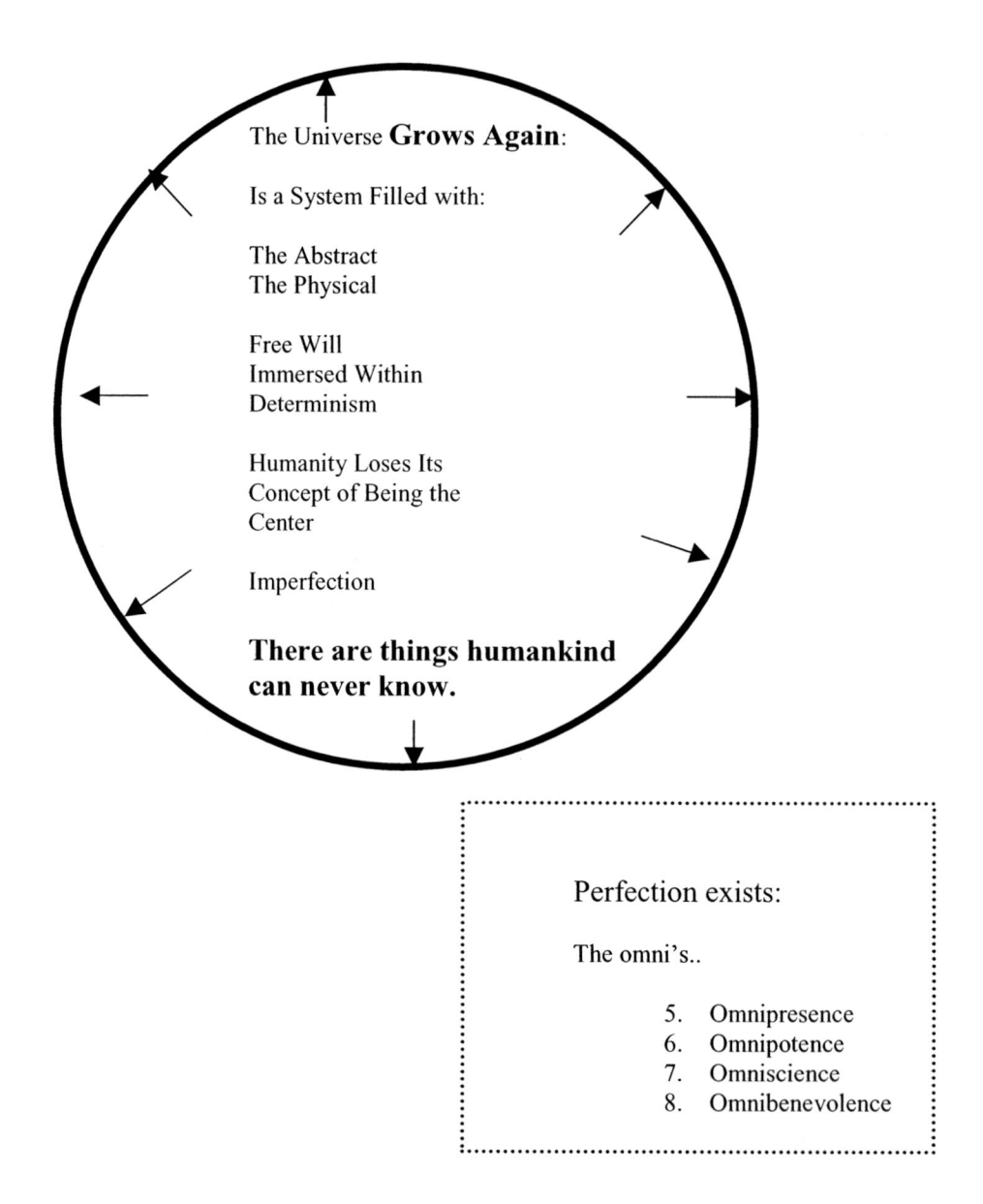

The Universe **Grows Again**:

Is a System Filled with:

The Abstract
The Physical

Free Will
Immersed Within
Determinism

Humanity Loses Its
Concept of Being the
Center

Imperfection

There are things humankind can never know.

Perfection exists:

The omni's..

5. Omnipresence
6. Omnipotence
7. Omniscience
8. Omnibenevolence

The Error of Kant

If we extract from the graphic the concepts superfluous to Kant's most fundamental perception regarding 'location' of the phenomenal and noumenal found 'within' his metaphysical system, we obtain:

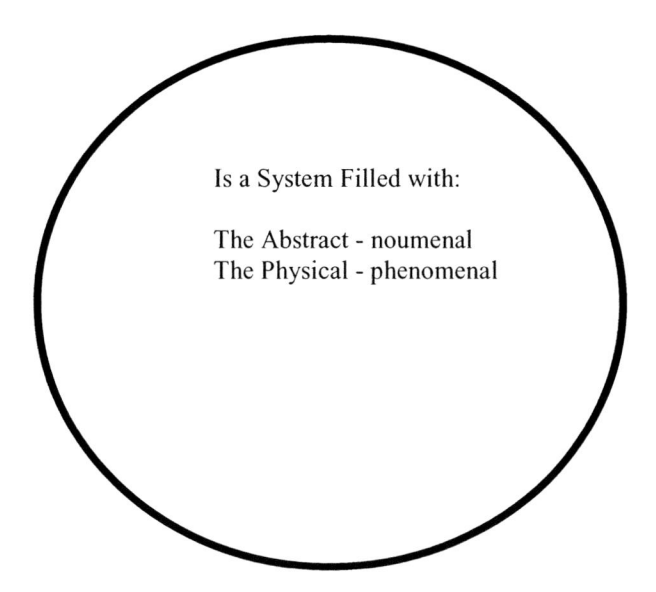

Is a System Filled with:

The Abstract - noumenal
The Physical - phenomenal

The process simply brings us back to Aristotle. This is not to say Kant had nothing new to add to the concept regarding the existence of 'a' metaphysical system. Quite the contrary. What is being said is that Kant, like Zeno (see Tractate 1: Zeno and Seamlessness), could not fully understand how his system worked. Like Zeno, Kant was subconsciously caught up in the perception of 'a' location of singularity versus 'a' location of multiplicity, a location consisting of two distinct locations existing through a process of 'separation through inclusion' versus 'separation through exclusion'.

The examination regarding 'separation through inclusion' versus 'separation through exclusion' will take place in 'Tractate 8: Russell. For now, however we must return to the task at hand, which is to examine the four antinomies with respect to the new metaphysical system of 'being' *being* 'Being'.

Having stated the reason for Kant's problem in understanding his own system, let's examine a system, which would resolve Kant's difficulties. This process will require several steps:

1. Diagram the new system
2. Demonstrate how it is all eight cogent proofs could be 'a' proof of what is without contradicting one another.

Logic is a subject in and of itself. As such we will leave the formality of logical proofs to others and instead examine the base foundation from which such logic should begin: The system itself. Thus when we speak of proofs we are referring to the most fundamental generalization of the proof versus the formal proof itself.

The War & Peace of a New Metaphysical Perception

Part 1: The diagram:

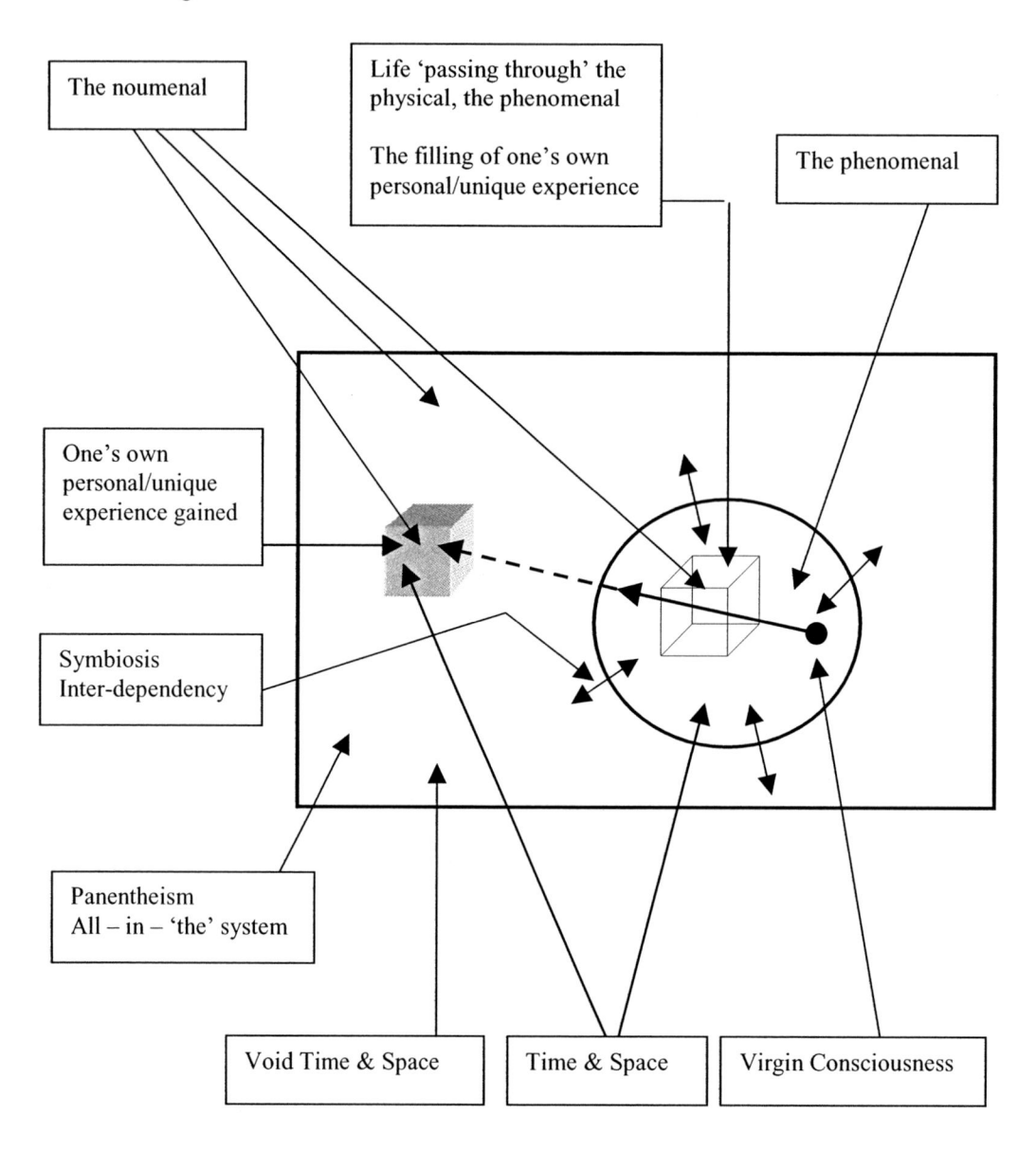

[Diagram with the following labeled elements:
- The noumenal
- Life 'passing through' the physical, the phenomenal / The filling of one's own personal/unique experience
- The phenomenal
- One's own personal/unique experience gained
- Symbiosis Inter-dependency
- Panentheism All – in – 'the' system
- Void Time & Space
- Time & Space
- Virgin Consciousness]

But isn't this exactly what Kant's system suggests. No, it isn't. Kant's system does not explain:

1. The 'growth' component involved with the whole
2. The interaction of the abstract and the physical – noumenal and the phenomenal as Kant would say
3. The region 'existing' beyond the physical (meta-physics)
4. The significance of individual 'being'
5. The significance of *being*
6. The significance of 'Being'
7. The significance of 'being *being*'
8. The significance of 'being' *being* 'Being'

9. Relativistic 1st truth versus 1st truth
10. What 'powers' the whole
11. The dynamics of the whole interrelationship of the noumenal and the phenomenal
12. Etc.
13. Etc.
14. And finally, yet most importantly to Kant: What 'the' 'categorical imperative' is.

Kant's system would be diagramed as:

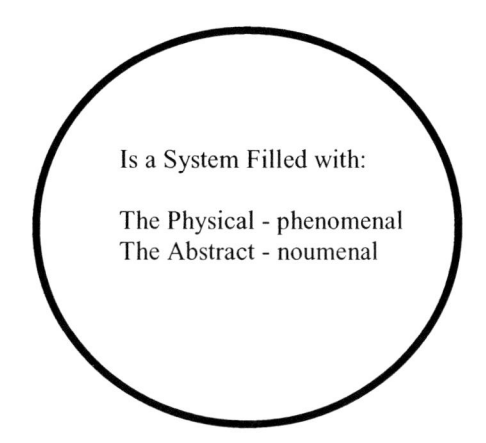

Is a System Filled with:

The Physical - phenomenal
The Abstract - noumenal

The model of the complete system demonstrates that the model is composed essentially of 'one' part.

The War & Peace of a New Metaphysical Perception

The new metaphysical system being proposed, 'being' *being* 'Being', creates a model subdivided into 'distinct' sub-elements, which in essence gives us two parts: the phenomenal and the noumenal. This model can also be reduced to its most fundamental of elements. If we reduce this model to its fundamentals as we previously did to Kant's perceptions, we obtain:

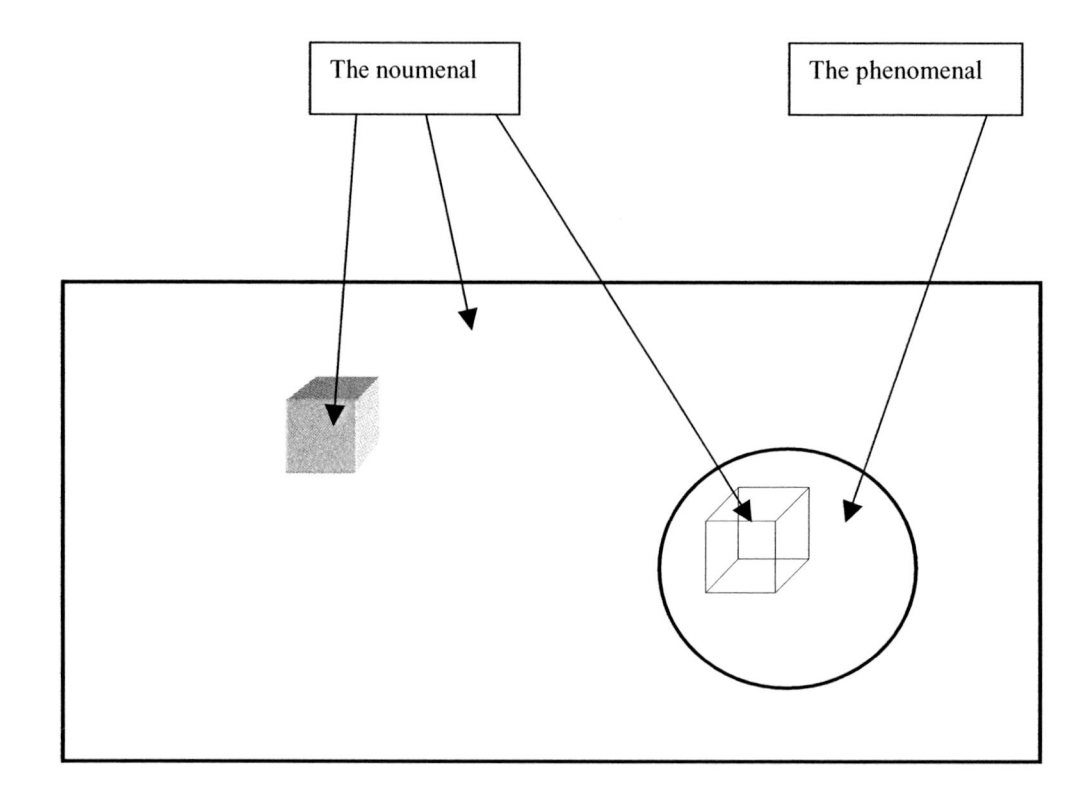

Having reduced 'the' system to its fundamentals, we can now proceed to Part 2.

Part 2: Demonstrating how it is all eight cogent proofs could be 'a' proof of what is without contradicting one another

It is perhaps best to take the eight statements and place them in groups of two, representing each antinomy.

The four antinomies:

1. Does the world have a beginning in time and a boundary in space, or is it without beginning and without bound?
2. Are composite substances made up of simple substances, or do they contain parts within parts *ad infinitum*?
3. Are there any actions that are free, in the sense of being caused by volitions that are themselves uncaused, or are all actions caused by causes that have their own causes and so on *ad infinitum*?
4. Is there an absolutely necessary being to serve as ground of the rest of what exists, or are all beings contingent?

Eight positions of perceptual argument placed into groups of two:

1. The world has a beginning in time and a boundary in space.
2. The world has no beginning in time and no boundary in space.

3. Composite substances are made up of simple substances.
4. Composite substances contain parts within parts *ad infinitum*.

5. There are actions that are free, in the sense of being caused by volitions that are themselves uncaused.
6. There are actions that are caused by causes that have their own causes and so on *ad infinitum*.

7. There is an absolutely necessary being which serves as the ground of the rest of what exists.
8. The absolute necessary being is like all beings, contingent.

Antinomy #1:

Does the world have a beginning in time and a boundary in space, or is it without beginning and without bound?

1. The world has a beginning in time and a boundary in space.

❖

2. The world has no beginning in time and no boundary in space.

The War & Peace of a New Metaphysical Perception

If we examine the new metaphysical model in terms of the two arguments, we obtain:

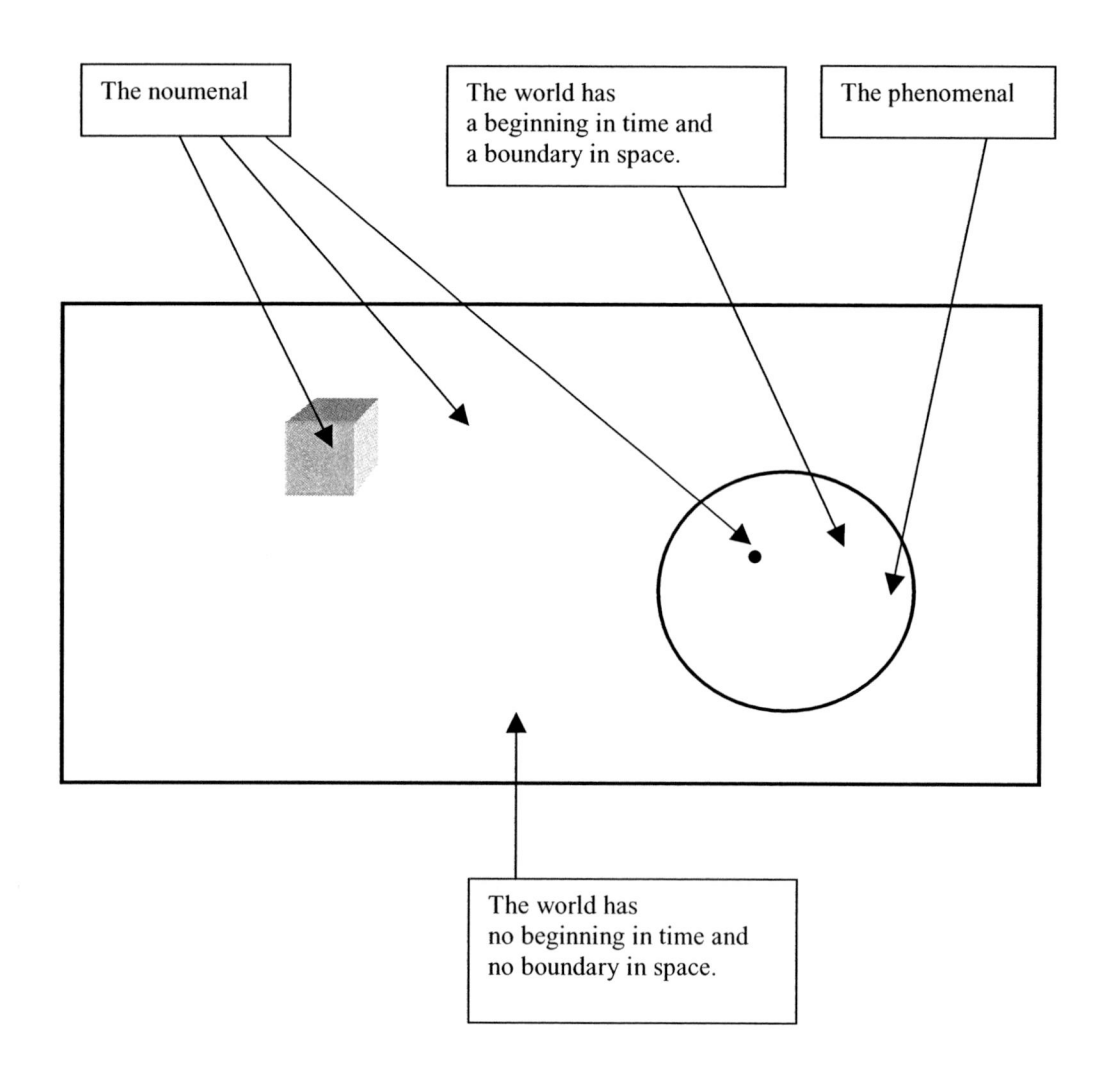

| The noumenal | The world has a beginning in time and a boundary in space. | The phenomenal |

The world has no beginning in time and no boundary in space.

The Error of Kant

The term, 'the world', refers to the whole. In ontological, cosmological and metaphysical terms this has historically referred to the universe, to our reality, to what lies within the boundaries of the physical which Zeno left open yet closed (see Tractate 1: Zeno)

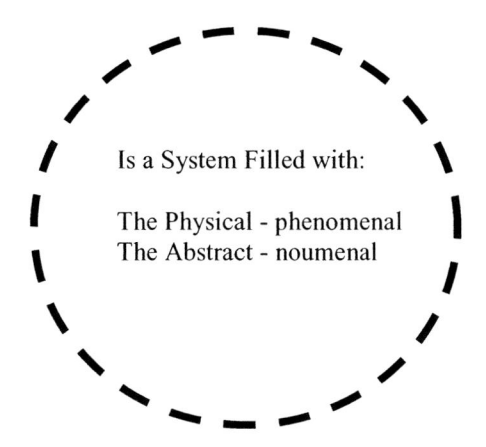

(dashed circle)

Is a System Filled with:

The Physical - phenomenal
The Abstract - noumenal

Aristotle tightly closed Zeno's metaphysical system (see Tractate 2: Aristotle).

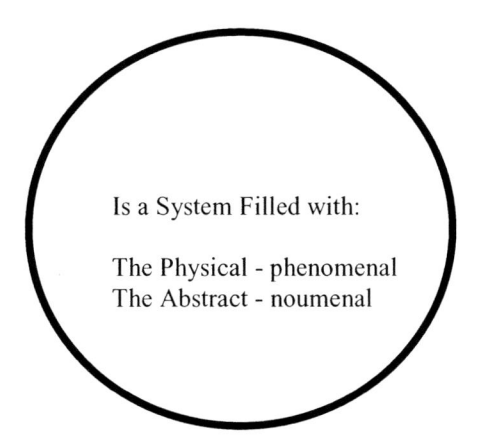

(solid circle)

Is a System Filled with:

The Physical - phenomenal
The Abstract - noumenal

It is this system, which we reopen to obtain the system we suggested. If we then examine the concept of 'world' we see the two seemingly contradictory statements are only contradictory because the opposing sides are defining the word 'world' differently. In argument one: The word world refers to the physical universe, the phenomenal. In argument two: The word world refers to the whole of the system within which the physical world resides.

If we examine the two seemingly contradictory statements in light of the new metaphysical perception, we realize how it can be that the two arguments are not contradictory but rather each are correct and each reinforces the argument of the other.

The War & Peace of a New Metaphysical Perception

Antinomy #1:

Does the world have a beginning in time and a boundary in space, or is it without beginning and without bound?

> 1. The world has a beginning in time and a boundary in space.
>
> ❖
>
> 2. The world has no beginning in time and no boundary in space.

The answer is yes to both. The answer is both states of existence are needed to operate an active form of metaphysical system. The answer is that a non-Cartesian system powered by a Cartesian system located 'within' the non-Cartesian system, cannot exist without the two forms of existence, #1 and #2, themselves existing simultaneously independent one from the other yet simultaneously dependent one upon the other.

Antinomy #2:

Are composite substances made up of simple substances, or do they contain parts within parts *ad infinitum*?

> 3. Composite substances are made up of simple substances.
>
> ❖
>
> 4. Composite substances contain parts within parts *ad infinitum*.

The Error of Kant

If we examine the new metaphysical model in terms of the two arguments, we obtain:

There are two issues to consider in terms of this antinomy. There is the physical and the abstract, the phenomenal and the noumenal.

The physical/the phenomenal:

The physical is found 'within' the universe. The universe is a region we call our reality. This in no way implies that the physical is found only 'within' our universe for there may well be multiple universes within such a metaphysical system.

The physical is found 'within' the universe. The universe is a region we call our reality. This in no way implies that the physical of which we are familiar, is the only set of physical laws to be found within universes for there may well be universes which are 'ruled' by entirely different 'laws of nature' than the 'laws of nature' we find to exist within 'our' universe.

The physical is found 'within the universe. The universe is a region we call our reality. This in no way implies that 'awareness'/'knowing' regarding the physical remains 'within' the physical for within the metaphysical system suggested, awareness/knowing regarding the universe is a form of abstraction and thus permeates abstraction itself. The regions of abstraction permeated with awareness of the physical is found not only in the entities capable of 'knowing' found within the physical but found within entities of 'knowing' found 'outside' the physical as well as found perhaps within 'the whole' of abstraction itself.

Understanding these three statements leads to understanding the finiteness of the physical but what of the infiniteness, what of composite substances contained as parts within parts *ad infinitum*

If Kant is correct in his perception regarding the system of 'critical philosophy', than what is observed changes by the very fact that it is observed. Such a perception allows for an infinite creation of parts within parts *ad infinitum*. The reason being that as we observe smaller and smaller parts, the parts continually become divisible through the active state of physical existence as opposes the Aristotelian passive state of physical existence.

Within the metaphysical system of 'being' *being* 'Being' infinite sub-division occurs not only in terms of the microscopic but in terms of macroscopic observations. The reason the principle applies to the macroscopic as well as the microscopic is that within such a system, the universe becomes 'a' part of the whole and as such is subject to the same infinite active process of division as the microscopic is to our observation for the universe simply becomes 'a' 'part' of the whole just as any object 'within' the universe becomes 'a' 'part' of the whole universe.

The abstract/The noumenal:

What of the noumenal/the abstract? From the model of the metaphysical system proposed, it becomes evident that the addition of entities of knowing, sub-units of the whole, is a continual process only terminated with the termination of time itself which is found in only two locations: within the entity of knowing known as awareness and within the universe itself which imparts the concepts of time and space through experiencing into the entity of knowing.

Such a means of establishing original knowing is not necessarily the only means of the whole establishing knowing but rather is simply 'a' means of establishing knowing which is available to the whole provided by our peculiar form of universe which itself incorporates the concept of time. Within such a metaphysical system, it is conceivable that other universes with universal fabrics other than that incorporating the concept of time may well exist as sources of new and unique forms of knowing.

The Error of Kant

As such:

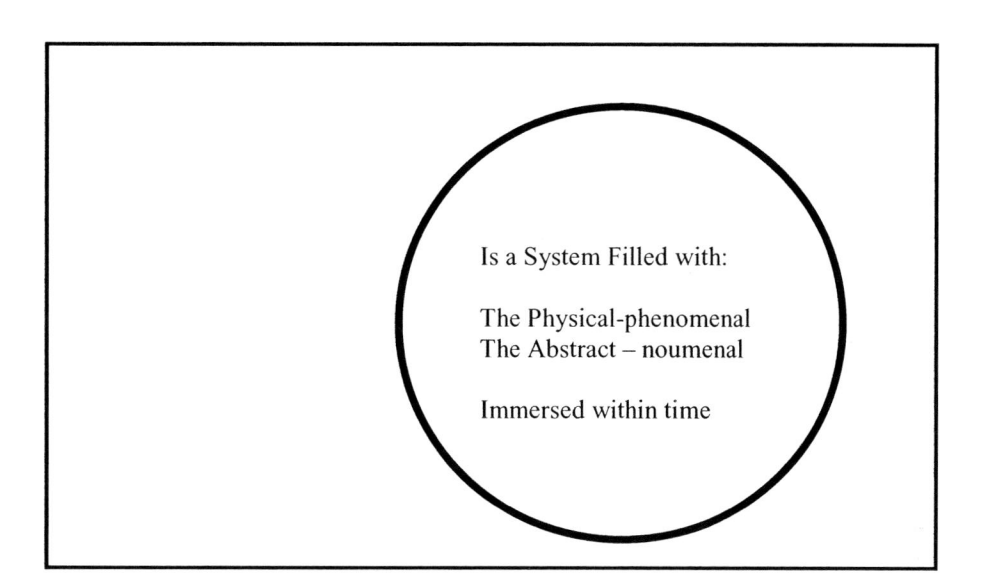

> Is a System Filled with:
>
> The Physical-phenomenal
> The Abstract – noumenal
>
> Immersed within time

becomes:

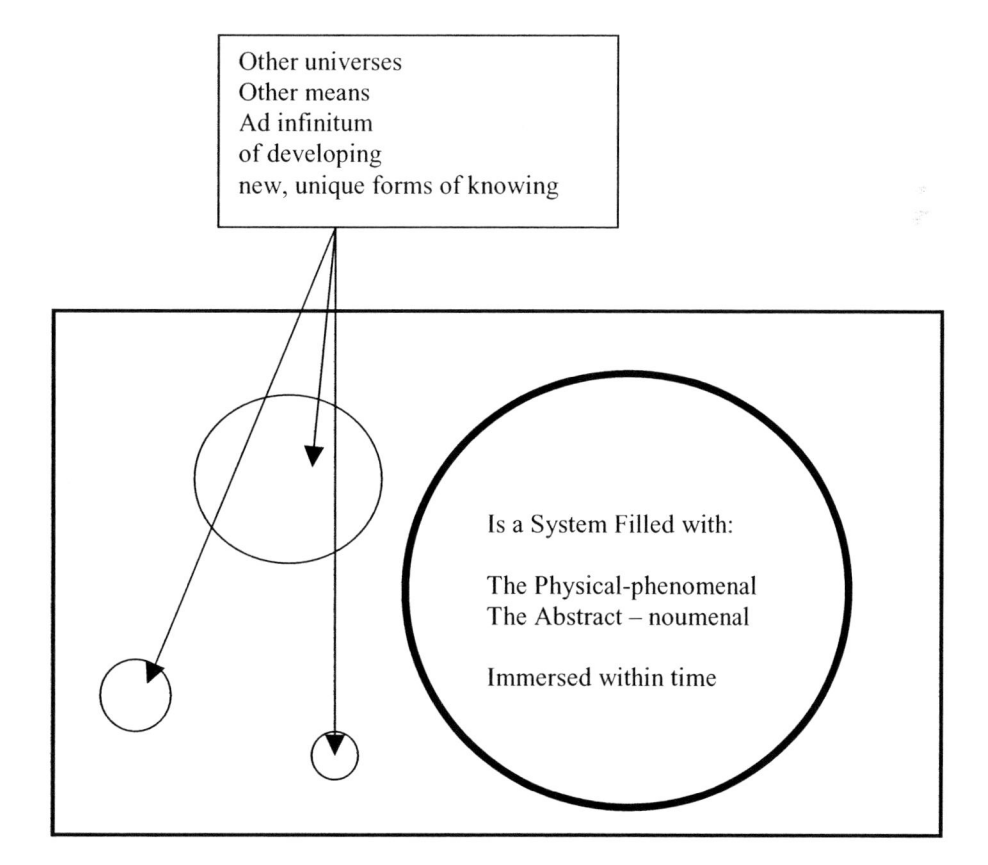

> Other universes
> Other means
> Ad infinitum
> of developing
> new, unique forms of knowing

> Is a System Filled with:
>
> The Physical-phenomenal
> The Abstract – noumenal
>
> Immersed within time

The War & Peace of a New Metaphysical Perception

Thus if we examine the two seemingly contradictory statements in light of the new metaphysical perception, we realize how it can be that the two arguments are not contradictory but rather each are correct and each reinforces the argument of the other.

Are composite substances made up of simple substances, or do they contain parts within parts *ad infinitum*?

>3. Composite substances made up of simple substances.
>
>❖
>
>4. Composite substances contain parts within parts *ad infinitum*.

The answer is yes to both. The answer is both states of existence are needed to operate an active form of metaphysical system. The answer is that a non-Cartesian system powered by a Cartesian system located 'within' the non-Cartesian system cannot exist without the two forms of existence, #3 and #4, themselves existing simultaneously independent one from the other yet simultaneously dependent one upon the other.

Antinomy #3:

Are there any actions that are free, in the sense of being caused by volitions that are themselves uncaused, or are all actions caused by causes that have their own causes and so on *ad infinitum*?

>5. There are actions that are free, in the sense of being caused by volitions that are themselves uncaused.
>
>❖
>
>6. There are actions that are caused by causes that have their own causes and so on *ad infinitum*.

The Error of Kant

If we examine the new metaphysical model in terms of the two arguments, we obtain:

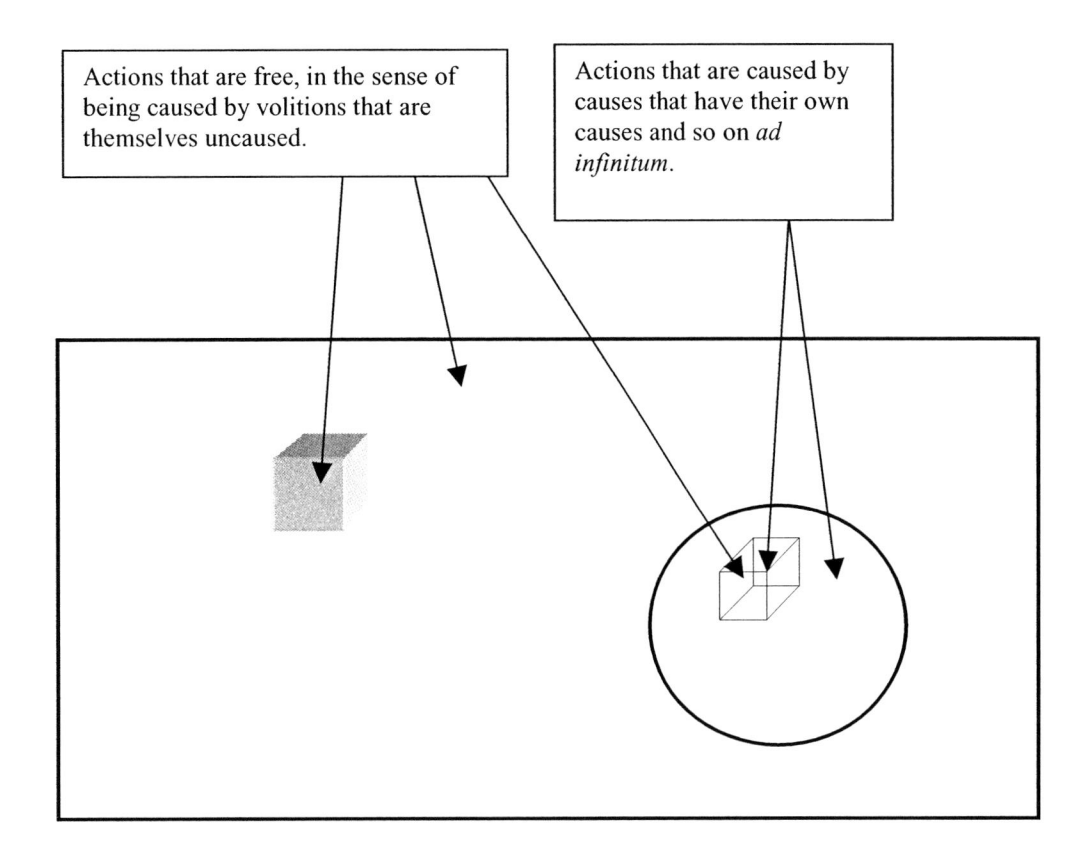

> Actions that are free, in the sense of being caused by volitions that are themselves uncaused.

> Actions that are caused by causes that have their own causes and so on *ad infinitum*.

If we examine the two seemingly contradictory statements in light of the new metaphysical perception, we realize how it can be that the two arguments are not contradictory but rather each are correct and each reinforces the argument of the other.

The details of such an argument are complex and require a complete tractate to address. Tractate 3: Boethius and Free Will addressed this issue in detail. As such, rather than reiterate the concepts of such an argument, the reader will be referred back to Tractate 3.

However it must be emphasized here, regarding the question:

Are there any actions that are free, in the sense of being caused by volitions that are themselves uncaused, or are all actions caused by causes that have their own causes and so on *ad infinitum*?

     5. There are actions that are free, in the sense of being caused by volitions that are themselves uncaused.

❖

     6. There are actions that are caused by causes that have their own causes and so on *ad infinitum*.

The answer is yes to both. The answer is both states of existence are needed to operate an active form of metaphysical system. The answer is that a non-Cartesian system powered by a Cartesian

The War & Peace of a New Metaphysical Perception

system located 'within' the non-Cartesian system cannot exist without the two forms of existence, #5 and #6, themselves existing simultaneously independent one from the other yet simultaneously dependent one upon the other.

Antimony #4:

Is there an absolutely necessary being to serve as ground of the rest of what exists, or are all beings contingent?

       7. There is an absolutely necessary being which serves as the ground of the rest of what exists.

❖

       8. The absolute necessary being is like all beings, contingent.

If we examine the new metaphysical model in terms of the two arguments, we obtain:

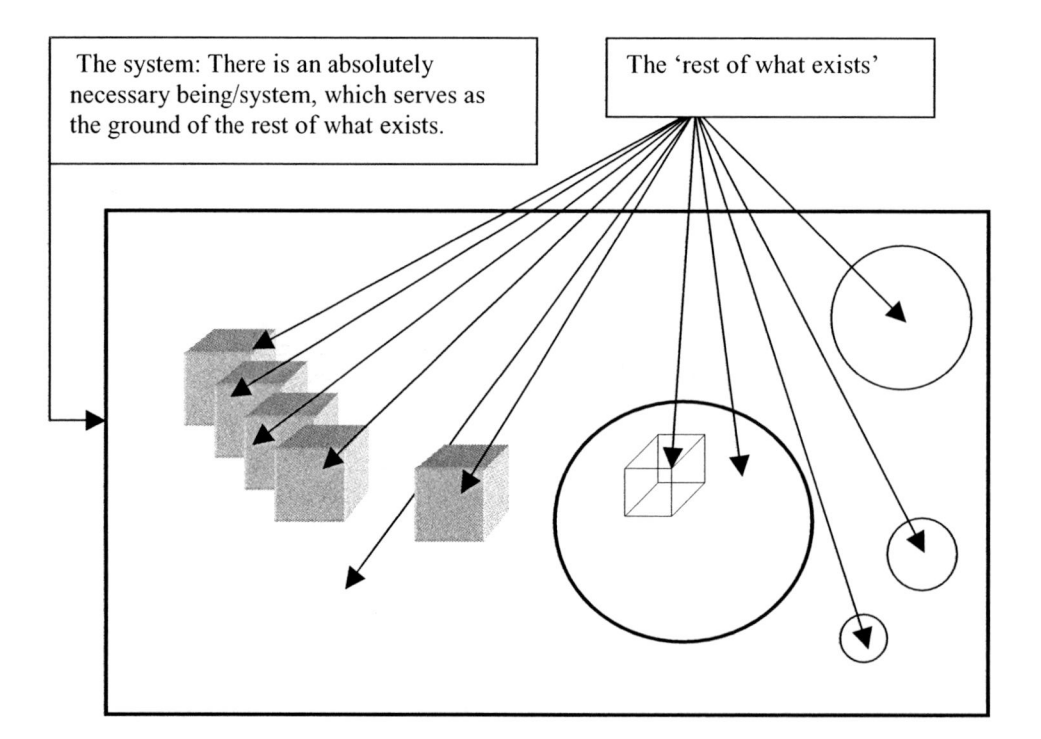

| The system: There is an absolutely necessary being/system, which serves as the ground of the rest of what exists. | The 'rest of what exists' |

The concept of:

> The 'rest of what exists'

Within the metaphysical system of 'being' *being* 'Being', symbiotic panentheism implies the system is the summation of all the parts of the system. Therefore if all the parts but one are removed than the one remaining part is the 'rest of what exists'.

The metaphysical system also suggests that removing any combination of multiple parts results in the same scenario in that what remains is the 'rest of what exists'

In addition the metaphysical system suggest therefore that the sum of all the parts is greater than the sum of its parts for the sum of the parts is an entity in and of itself.

The emergence of paradoxes generated from a metaphysical system of the whole being our universe is nothing short of an indication that we are continually learning. If the whole is an active entity then 'newness' is constantly being generated as opposed to simply existing just beyond our reach awaiting our discovery.

If newness were simply existing just beyond our reach awaiting our discovery, then given enough time it is conceivable we could eventually know everything there is to know. This is what is referred to as a passive form of existence.

On the other hand:

If newness is constantly being generated then given enough time it is inconceivable we could eventually know everything there is to know for the more we observe and learn the more that is created. This is what is referred to as an active form of existence.

Thus if we examine the two seemingly contradictory statements in light of the new metaphysical perception, we realize how it can be that the two arguments are not contradictory but rather each are correct and each reinforces the argument of the other.

Is there an absolutely necessary being to serve as ground of the rest of what exists, or are all beings contingent?

    9. There is an absolutely necessary being which serves as the ground of the rest of what exists.

❖

    10. The absolute necessary being is like all beings, contingent.

The War & Peace of a New Metaphysical Perception

The answer is yes to both. The answer is both states of existence are needed to operate an active form of metaphysical system. The answer is that a non-Cartesian system powered by a Cartesian system located 'within' the non-Cartesian system cannot exist without the two forms of existence, #9 and #10, themselves existing simultaneously independent one from the other yet simultaneously dependent one upon the other.

The suggestion that we have resolved Kant's four antinomies through the development of a new metaphysical perception leads us to examining a possible resolution regarding Kant's 'categorical imperatives'.

Could Kant accept such a metaphysical system as 'being' *being* 'Being'? The system resolves Kant's four antinomies. But what of Kant's concept of the requirements he placed upon the concept of a system?

There were two fundamentals Kant felt should be accomplished with a metaphysical system that approached a significant advancement of metaphysical systems themselves:

1. A categorical imperative should emerge naturally and obviously from such a system.
2. The system should explain Kant's belief:

> 'According to Leibniz the physical world of cause and effect proved the inner harmony of the world's moral purpose. Reading Leibniz led Kant to see humanity as not only participating in nature, but over and above this participating in the ultimate purpose of the universe.'[22]

Due to the unique concept of a categorical imperative to Kant's work and due to the fact Kant was unable to find his categorical imperative, which should have emerged from his system, we will provide the concept of categorical imperative its own unique section within this tractate.

As to the second fundamental:

The system of 'being' *being* 'Being' fully addresses the issue of the ultimate purpose of the universe and humanity's participation in nature.

The understanding of such functions found within the metaphysical system of 'being' *being* 'Being' can better be understood if we use the generic name for the system, symbiotic panentheism. This metaphysical system assigns the task of producing 'new knowledge', new knowing, to the universe. In such a system it is entities of knowing emerging from virgin consciousness and experiencing isolated from the whole and through the application of free will that new untainted knowing emerges. and grows the whole. Thus the universe becomes the location and the virgin entity becomes the means for such growth. The universe gains purpose, a function, and humanity as well as all forms of knowing 'knowing', move through time and space, the universe composed of matter and energy, in order to develop and expand upon their virgin consciousness, in order to expand omniscience itself. Thus symbioses:

The parts to the whole and the whole to the parts become active action itself in terms of the whole and its sub elements of emerging knowing. Thus panentheism: The universe becomes an element of the whole.

The prioritized natural emergence of the first two categorical imperatives

Kant's categorical imperative' calls for a consensus regarding ethics, 'acceptable' behavior

With the concept of 'being' *being* 'Being' what does/do the 'categorical imperative' or 'categorical imperative/s' become?

The principles regarding the 'categorical imperatives' of the metaphysical system of 'being' *being* 'Being' are:

1. Every journey of awareness of 'abstractual knowing' has the right to journey unimpeded by the desires of others
2. We have an obligation to prevent other's from interfering with the creative journey's of awareness of 'abstractual knowing'

The War & Peace of a New Metaphysical Perception

Are these statements simply reiterations of the various forms of what the West calls the 'Golden Rule'?

Confucianism

    What you don't want done to yourself, don't do to others.
                                                         - Sixth Century B.C.

Buddhism

    Hurt not others with that which pains thyself.
                                                         - Fifth Century B.C.

Jainism

    In happiness and suffering, in joy and grief, we should regard all creatures as we regard our own self, and should therefore refrain from inflicting upon others such injury as would appear undesirable to us if inflicted upon ourselves.
                                                         - Fifth Century B.C.

Zoroastrianism

    Do not do unto others all that which is not well for oneself.
                                                         - Fifth Century B.C.

Classical Paganism

    May I do to others as I would that they should do unto me.
                                                   - Plato-Fourth Cen6tury B.C.

Hinduism

    Do naught to others, which if done to thee would cause thee pain.
                                                 - Mahabharata-Third Century B.C.

Judaism

    What is hateful to yourself, don't do to your fellow man.
                                                   - Rabbi Hillel-First Century B.C.

Christianity

    Whatsoever ye would that men should do to you, do ye even so to them.
                                                 - Jesus of Nazareth-First Century A.D.

Sikhism

    Treat others as thou wouldst be treated thyself.
                                                 - Sixteenth Century A.D.

> Perhaps the oldest ethical proposition of distinctly universal character

Such an example of slightly altering 'a universal statement' is exactly what Kant had in mind when referring to a 'categorical imperative', however this is not 'the' 'Categorical Imperative Kant was implying should be established as 'the' universal statement. As exemplary as this universal imperative may have been and may be today, it is fraught with hidden charades.

A charade applied as a 'Categorical Imperative' is no categorical imperative at all but only 'appears' to be a categorical imperative and is accepted as a categorical imperative because there is no better alternative to replace it.

The various statements of the 'Golden Rule' would imply a person who enjoyed being 'hurt' should perform hurtful acts upon another because they themselves enjoy being hurt and enjoy experiencing pain. i.e. the masochist

The various statements of the 'Golden Rule' would imply a culture embracing the metaphysical system of 'survival of the fittest', would be justified in subjugating the weak just as they would 'wish' to be subjugated if they should ever grow 'soft' and fall victim to what they would perceive as the unforgivable sin of 'idleness': i.e. The Zulu's.

The various statements of the 'Golden Rule' would imply a religion, not only 'should' but had 'the moral obligation to' convert non-believers should 'their God require it' in order to 'save' the soul itself from the eternal flames of hell. i.e. Christianity, Islam, etc.

The various statements of the 'Golden Rule' would imply a race was obligated to excise what they perceived to be 'weak' gene in the attempt to hone their own race into a being 'perfection' itself. i.e. Nazi Germany

What then can be said of history and our potential encounter with other intelligence's throughout the realm of the universe/physical reality? History itself is littered with messages vividly illustrating what a lack of a 'complete' metaphysical system suggests will occur again and again in our future as we further explore our own planet and as we begin our travels throughout our solar system, our galaxy, and the far reaches of our universe.

The list is by no means complete. The list initiates an understanding regarding the application of various forms of the 'golden rule' as a form of Categorical Imperative.

Kant could find no Categorical Imperative emerging from his proposed metaphysical system. This is not surprising when perhaps the most universally accepted form of Categorical Imperative, variations of the Golden Rule, itself is fraught with so many pitfalls.

What caused Kant's failure to find a 'Categorical Imperative'? Kant did not look far enough 'outward' to find his holy grail, the categorical imperative. Kant looked in the only place he understood to exist. Kant looked 'within' 'reality', looked 'within' the physical, looked 'within' the Aristotelian metaphysical parameters of the universe and its infinite reach limited by the parameters of infinite time and infinite space.

But space and time appear to be innate characteristics of matter and energy or vice versa. Whichever the case, space and time are 'bound' by the limits of their very selves be it finite or infinite.

The War & Peace of a New Metaphysical Perception

Kant forgot the meaning of 'meta-' (beyond) 'physics' (the physical). As such Kant looked 'within' the physical to understand how his concept of 'active' verses 'passive' observation operated. The understanding of the 'critical philosophy' was not to be found by examining the physical, the phenomenal, alone. Nor was it to be found by examining the abstract, the noumenal, alone. The emergence of the first and second Categorical Imperative lay in understanding the interrelationship that existed between the abstract and the physical.

Had Kant understood a rational metaphysical system incorporating two separate and distinct 'inter' and 'intra' dependent locations of abstractual existence and physical existence, seamlessness and multiplicity, the physical and the non-physical, free will and determinism, Centricism and non-Centricism, …, Kant may have been able to find his dearly beloved categorical imperative.

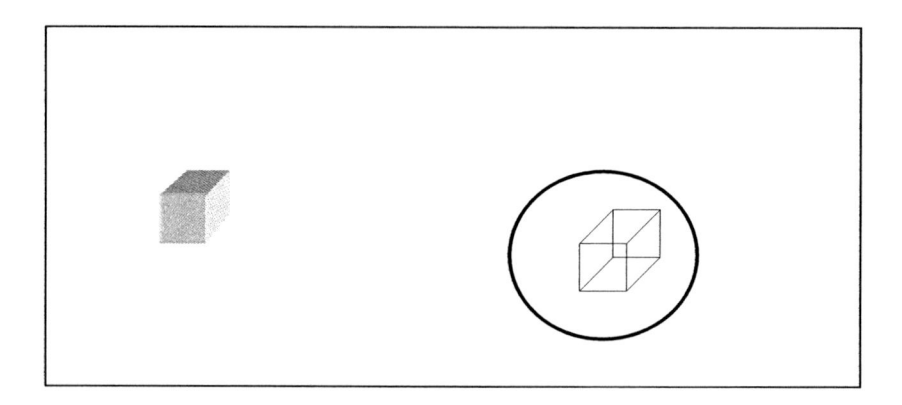

The categorical imperatives, #1 and #2, listed imply an elevation of the journey of 'knowing' entities to the level of being 'divine' and thus sacred in and of themselves. The masochist should be allowed to be masochistic without fear of being rejected for what one is. Should counseling and assistance be available for them should they desire to change? Of course for that is what emerges naturally from this new metaphysical system, which fuses the Aristotelian, and Kantian systems into one system.

The pedophile, the homophobe, the bigot, the paranoid, the schizophrenic, the religious extremist, the 'beautiful', the prostitute, the disfigured, the handicapped, the genius, the rich, the protégés, the strong, the mentally challenged, the happy, the religious, the quadriplegic, the lonely, the strange, the unique thinker, the conformist, the atheist, the individual of color, the individual of the lack of color, should be allowed to be who they are without fear of being rejected.

This metaphysical system of 'being' *being* 'Being', in fact, finds its foundation built upon the very concept of diversity and individuality should it be the case that it is the individual, through its own free will, which desires the diversity.

Should counseling and assistance be available for them should they desire to change? Yes, but again it must be stated that the counseling should not be 'forced' nor interjected to the extent that the unique form of knowing becomes psychologically programmed into conforming to society's perception of normality.

Does such a metaphysical system reject the concept of the possible existence of 'life forms' existing as 'a' unit with awareness of abstractual knowing 'contained' within the social colony versus the individual? Absolutely not, for that in itself is diversity.

Hegel's restatement of the Golden rule as seen by Kant is inappropriate as a categorical imperative. Hegel rephrased the Golden Rule in terms of Kant's categorical imperative as:

> Hegel's game attempt to emulate Kant ended up with Christ saying, 'What you can will to be a universal law among men, and also hold as a law for yourself, according to that maxim you should act."[23]

This is not a 'universal law' but rather this is a law of individual desire. This is not a law protecting the uniqueness of individuality but rather a law suppressing the very concept of 'unique' individuality, suppressing the very concept of the value of the individual being the individual itself. This is a law reinforcing the concept of conformity for then it becomes the majority, which sets the acceptable behavior of the minority.

What then should the categorical imperative be if not the metaphysical transformation of the Golden Rule?

The understanding of the categorical imperative, which Kant could not find, emerged in Tractate 2: Aristotle and Cartesianism. If we refer back to this tractate we find:

> The result:
>
> Responsibilities emerge:
>
> 1. The first responsibility: to universally protect the 'right' of virgin consciousness (one's self and others equally) to journey unimpeded
> 2. The second responsibility: to journey unimpeded

So how is this any different than that of Hegel's Kantian version of the Golden Rule?

These two categorical imperatives (listed in priority of importance) protects the rights of

> The pedophile, the homophobe, the bigot, the paranoid, the schizophrenic, the religious extremist, the 'beautiful', prostitute, the disfigured, the handicapped, genius, the rich, the protégés, the strong, the mentally challenged, the happy, the religious, the quadriplegic, the lonely, the strange, the unique thinker, the conformist, the atheist, the individual of color, the individual of the lack of color, ...

But how can this be without throwing society into a quagmire of unique expressions constantly infringing upon the rights of others through the desire of the first party to superimpose its wishes upon the second party.

That is exactly why the order of the two categorical imperatives are listed in the order they are. The first categorical imperative supercedes one's longing to impose one's personal desires upon a second party and the second categorical imperative expresses your 'right' to be who you are as long as you don't interfere with the rights of others to be who they are.

As an example, a rapist may have the desire to dominate another in a violent physical fashion but they should not be allowed to do so with anyone not wishing to have such action imposed upon them. Likewise they should not be allowed to do so in a fashion, which pollutes any sensual environment of another who does not wish to be exposed to such actions. The sensual environment includes any form of sounds, visuals, etc introduced into the environment known as the public domain: parks, airwaves, written medium, electromagnetic wave media, ...

Categorical imperative number one would emphatically state that telling someone to: Turn off the TV if they don't like what they see', would now become, 'You have no 'right' to infringe upon my journey by putting me in the position of having to monitor what I might see, hear, taste, smell, or feel coming into my home.'

What then of polluters of the public air, water, and lands. Such polluters would need to clean up their act. Pollution would become an act against the first categorical imperative. Granted, the absolute elimination of pollution is a utopian idea but the concept of working towards such a level of cleanliness found within the home, the environment, within which we live, is not. Pragmatism would need to be balanced against both categorical imperatives.

Kant's presumed categorical imperative in essence was not the first categorical imperative but rather a description of categorical imperatives. With the development of the first and second categorical imperatives we can make an interesting application to what is perhaps one of the most significant historical documents regarding the significance of individual units of knowing:

> When, in the course of events of 'beings', it becomes necessary for one group of 'beings' to dissolve the political bands which have connected them with another, and to assume, among the powers of the universe, the separate and equal station to which the laws of nature and of nature's God entitle them, a decent respect to the opinions of 'beings' requires that they should declare the causes which impel them to the separation.
>
> We hold these truths to be self-evident, that all 'beings' are created equal: that they are endowed by their Creator with certain unalienable rights; that among these are life, liberty, and the pursuit of happiness. That, to secure these rights, governments are instituted among 'beings', deriving their just powers from the consent of the governed: that, whenever any form of government becomes destructive of these ends, it is the right of the' beings' to alter or to abolish it, and to institute a new government, laying its foundation on such principles, and organizing its powers in such form, as to them shall seem most likely to effect their safety and happiness. Prudence, indeed, will dictate that governments long established should not be changed for light and transient causes; and, accordingly, all experience hath shown, that 'beings' are more disposed to suffer, while evils are sufferable, than to right themselves by abolishing the forms to which they are accustomed...'

The Declaration of Independence,
Thomas Jefferson

A Declaration
by
the Representatives
of
the United States of America
in
Congress
Assembled.
July 4, 1776

The concept of 'men' was not replaced with the term 'being' for the purpose of present day 'political correctness'. The term 'men' was replaced with the term 'being' because it is Kant with whom we are dealing in this tractate. It is metaphysics and categorical imperatives with which we are dealing. As such:

> Categorical imperatives reach to the very ends of the universe itself and as such categorical imperatives must apply not only to humanity but to all unique units capable of abstractual knowing found throughout the entire universe as opposed to unique units capable of abstractual knowing found within our solar system.

In fact the last sentence must be restated to read:

> Categorical imperatives reach to the very ends of all universes and as such categorical imperatives must apply not only to humanity but to all unique units capable of abstractual knowing found throughout all universes as opposed to unique units capable of abstractual knowing found within our solar system.

And so it is, under a metaphysical system of 'symbiotic panentheism', a document from 1776 becomes a statement of 'inalienable right's for all 'beings' not just men. And so it is we are better prepared for the future than we had ever anticipated we could possibly become. So it is we but need look to 'basic truths', look to a basic system of metaphysics, to find a foundation we can place beneath our perceptions regarding the significance of the individual we have already established within society.

And who will benefit from the action of establishing a universal understanding based initially upon the individual first and society second as opposed to a system of society first and the individual second. The beneficiary of such a metaphysical system would be either mankind or the first beings we encounter as we spread our influence into the near and eventually far reaches of space. But which of the two will it be? Why, it will be the 'weaker' of the two. If for no other reason than pure selfishness, we need to prepare for just such an event for we may find ourselves to be the 'weaker' of the two.

Let us never forget, it is, probability speaking, inevitable that we shall someday be the 'weaker of the two'. Therefore, it is inevitable that we would one day be the beneficiaries of having established just such an unselfish metaphysical system.

We can now begin to understand 'why' the two categorical imperatives are listed as they are:

1. The first responsibility:

    > To universally protect the 'right' of virgin consciousness (one's self and others equally) to journey unimpeded

2. The second responsibility:

    > To journey unimpeded

The War & Peace of a New Metaphysical Perception

Morality versus categorical imperatives

The issue of categorical imperatives is neither a direct issue of ethics nor a direct issue of morality. Rather the issue of categorical imperatives is an indirect issue of ethics and morality.

Categorical imperatives lay the foundation upon which guidelines for ethics and morality emerge. Concepts of 'good' and 'evil', 'bad' and 'good', 'socially acceptable' and 'socially unacceptable' emerge from ontological perceptions, which in turn emerge from metaphysical perceptions, which in turn emerge from metaphysical systems.

Presently western society has simultaneously in place two metaphysical systems: an Aristotelian metaphysical system and a Kantian metaphysical system.

The two contradicting models create complex contradicting social paradoxes as opposed to creating simple social paradoxes. The result: The creation of the Gordian Knot of social dilemmas.

The two systems are different in that the Aristotelian system is a Cartesian/closed system filled with passive action – the observer does not change the event being observed simply through the act of observation itself:

○ Observation is passive

And the Kantian system is a Cartesian/closed system filled with active action – the observer changes the event being observed simply through the act of observation itself:

○ Observation is active

Both systems are the same in that action is 'contained' within a Cartesian/closed system. The system is reality/the universe.

Hegel suggested the Kantian system is non-Cartesian/open:

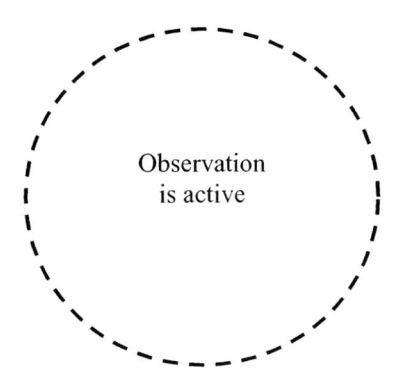

Observation is active (dashed circle)

Which brings us back to Zeno's perception of the metaphysical system. Even so the system is the system and the universe is the system be it open, closed, active, passive...

The new system being suggested as the basis of this work suggests that the more accurate metaphysical system is a combination of all of the above and as such becomes a Cartesian/closed system of active action contained within a non-Cartesian/open system of passive action:

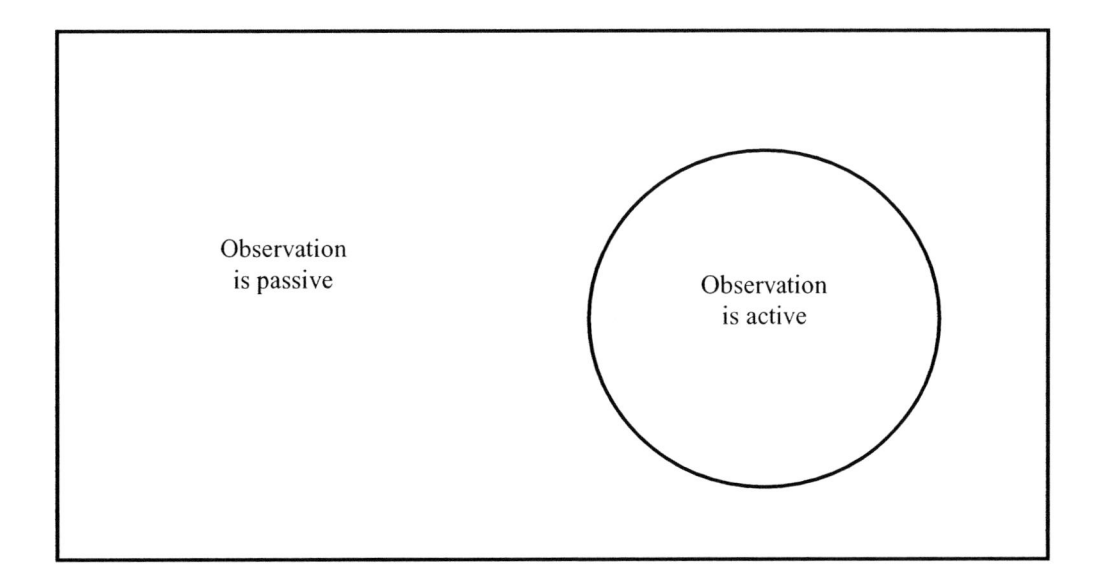

Observation is passive (rectangle) containing *Observation is active* (circle)

The new metaphysical system suggests that we are the observers:

The War & Peace of a New Metaphysical Perception

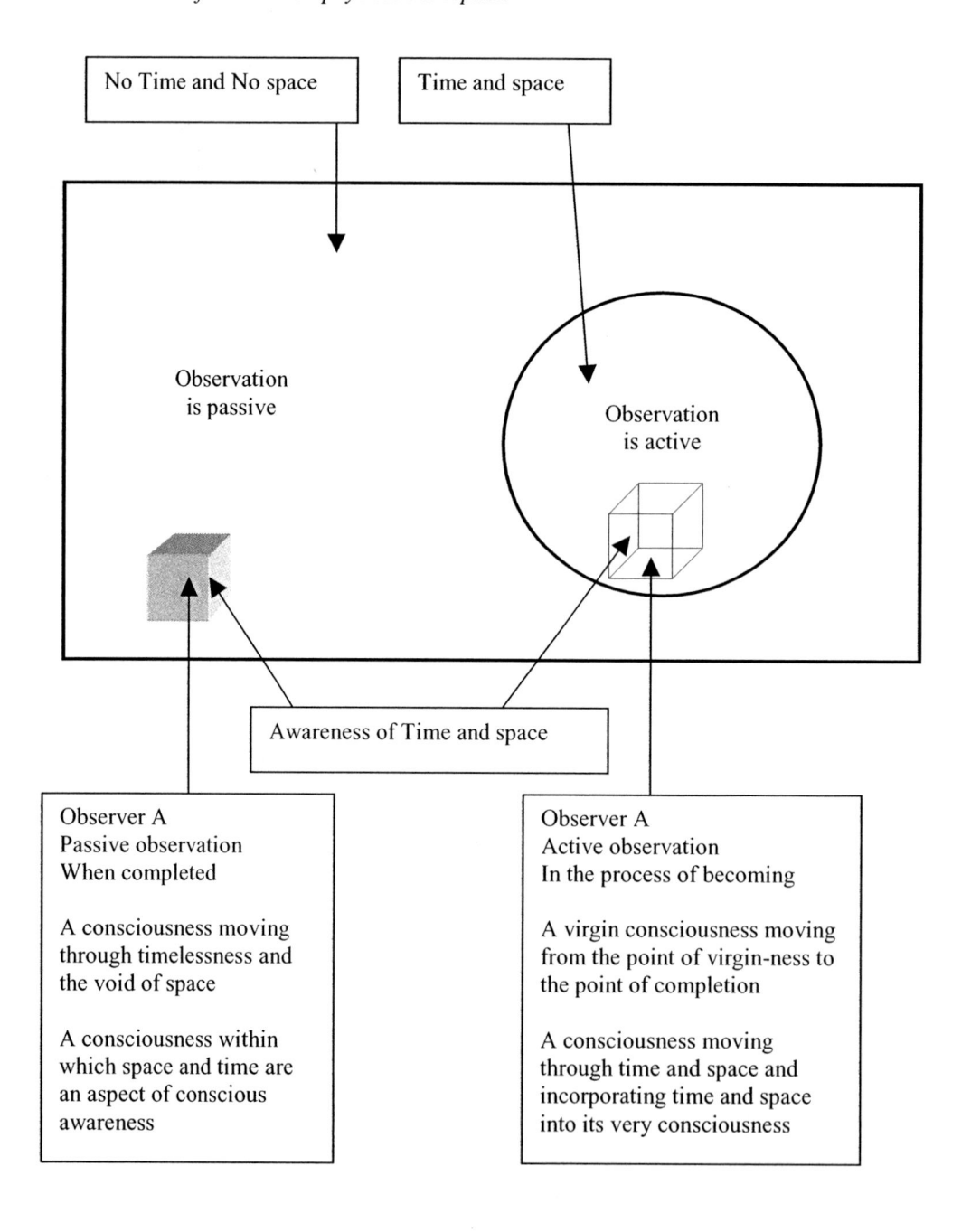

```
┌─────────────────────┐    ┌─────────────────┐
│ No Time and No space│    │  Time and space │
└──────────┬──────────┘    └────────┬────────┘
           │                         │
           ▼                         ▼
┌──────────────────────────────────────────────┐
│                                              │
│                         ╭──────────╮         │
│                        │            │        │
│   Observation          │ Observation│        │
│   is passive           │  is active │        │
│                        │            │        │
│                         ╰──────────╯         │
│      ▲                       ▲               │
│    [cube]                  [cube]            │
└──────────────────────────────────────────────┘
              ▲                ▲
              │                │
        ┌─────┴────────────────┴────┐
        │ Awareness of Time and space│
        └────────────────────────────┘
```

Observer A Passive observation When completed	Observer A Active observation In the process of becoming
A consciousness moving through timelessness and the void of space	A virgin consciousness moving from the point of virgin-ness to the point of completion
A consciousness within which space and time are an aspect of conscious awareness	A consciousness moving through time and space and incorporating time and space into its very consciousness

But what does this have to do with ethics and morality. It has nothing to do with ethics and morality and that is just the point. Categorical imperatives pertain to this metaphysical system and the concept of morality and ethics has nothing to do with this system since the system deals only with 'what was', 'what is', and 'what will be'. 'What was', 'what is', and 'what will be' 'is' the system and 'what could be' becomes the process of action within the system. 'What could be' is the means by which the system becomes active verses 'what was', 'what is', and 'what will be' being the passive aspect of the system.

Thus the passive and the active exist within the system and are separate aspects of the system. But wouldn't this imply the passive is more significant to the system since it involves three, the past, the present, and the unavoidable future, versus one, the potential future, form of action?

The present does not exist. The term 'exist' implies passivity for the term implies fulfillment and completion of the entity, which is a form of passivity, a form of the past. Yet one cannot say the present 'will exist' for that implies a form of the active, a form of the future, a form of continual grow within the framework of future time and time is not a universal fabric found equally distributed throughout 'whole' the system.

The present is of such short duration it is simply 'a' point fusing the past and the future together as an entity of wholeness, allowing a means of distinguishing the past from the future and just as 'a' point in geometry has no dimensions, no length, no width, no height no time elements and thus does not exist, so the present not only has no element of time but has no passive and no active forms of action.

So it is that in the metaphysical system of 'being' *being* 'Being', the present becomes 'the' system since it is the system of 'being' *being* 'Being' wherein the past and the future exist as separate elements of the system completely separate and independent yet dependent one upon the other. So it is the system of the present becomes the means whereby our present day perception of separation through exclusion becomes a new tool of social interaction versus our present day tool of separation through exclusion.

Present day social, perceptual tool
•
Separation through exclusion

Passive action

Omniscience
Omnipresence
Omnipotence

Active action

The War & Peace of a New Metaphysical Perception

As such we see the diagram becomes:

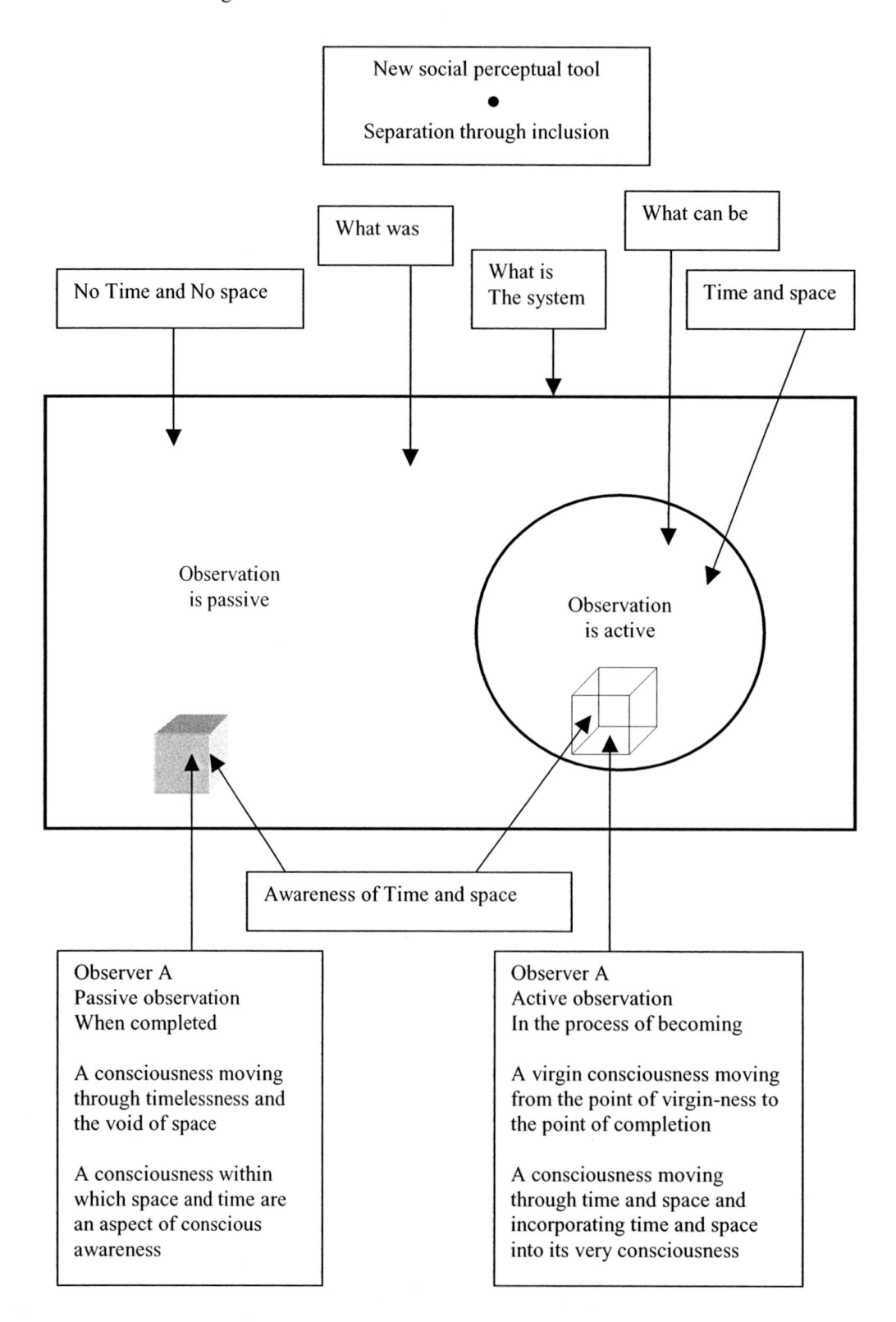

```
                    ┌─────────────────────────────┐
                    │  New social perceptual tool │
                    │             •               │
                    │  Separation through inclusion│
                    └─────────────────────────────┘
```

| No Time and No space | What was | What is / The system | What can be | Time and space |

Observation is passive

Observation is active

Awareness of Time and space

Observer A
Passive observation
When completed

A consciousness moving through timelessness and the void of space

A consciousness within which space and time are an aspect of conscious awareness

Observer A
Active observation
In the process of becoming

A virgin consciousness moving from the point of virgin-ness to the point of completion

A consciousness moving through time and space and incorporating time and space into its very consciousness

The Error of Kant

In terms of metaphysics, there is nothing ethical or moral regarding the past for the past is passive. The past cannot be changed. Morality and ethics apply to action, active action, action one is in the process of taking. Since the present does not exist, morality and ethics apply to future actions.

There is no doubt one can look to the past and 'judge' the action but regardless of how closely one examines the past one cannot change the past. Thus the past finds no morality or ethics to apply to it. Where then do ethics and morality apply and where do categorical imperatives apply?

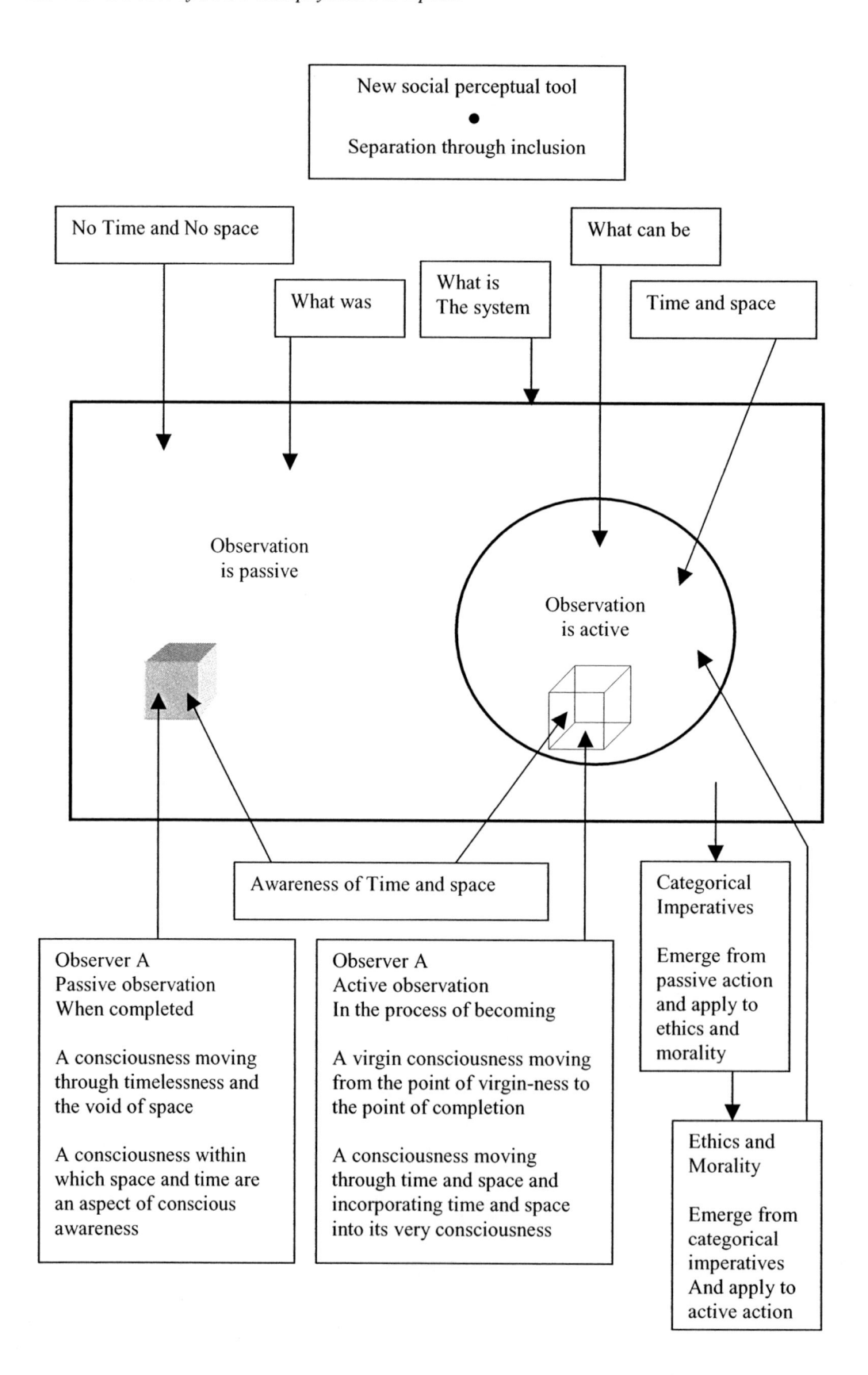

The War & Peace of a New Metaphysical Perception

```
                    ┌─────────────────────────┐
                    │ New social perceptual tool│
                    │            •             │
                    │ Separation through inclusion│
                    └─────────────────────────┘
```

- No Time and No space
- What was
- What is / The system
- What can be
- Time and space

Observation is passive

Observation is active

Awareness of Time and space

Categorical Imperatives

Emerge from passive action and apply to ethics and morality

Observer A
Passive observation
When completed

A consciousness moving through timelessness and the void of space

A consciousness within which space and time are an aspect of conscious awareness

Observer A
Active observation
In the process of becoming

A virgin consciousness moving from the point of virgin-ness to the point of completion

A consciousness moving through time and space and incorporating time and space into its very consciousness

Ethics and Morality

Emerge from categorical imperatives
And apply to active action

Where then does 'what will be' come into this scenario? "What 'will' be" 'will' be and as such there is no preventing "what 'will' be". As such 'what will be' simply falls into the category of 'what was' since it is a form of passive action versus active action.

Such being the case it would appear that ethics and morality do not face off against categorical imperatives but rather work in conjunction with categorical imperatives.

In terms of the new metaphysical system of 'being' *being* 'Being', in terms of an open/non-Cartesian system powered by a closed/Cartesian system located 'within' the open/non-Cartesian system that is correct. In such a system there is a harmony of cooperativeness. In such a system metaphysics lays the groundwork, establishes the system from which ontology emerges to establish morality and ethics.

We now understand that:

> Kant is a vital link in moving our perceptual understanding forward regarding the 'system' being filled with the 'knowable' into that of being 'the' system filled with both the 'knowable' and the 'unknowable'. As such, the 'knowable' and the 'knowable', with the help of Kant, now have a location within which they can be found. And now, the understanding regarding the role of both the 'knowable' and the 'unknowable' as well as the understanding regarding the interrelationship between the 'knowable' and the 'unknowable' no longer remains in a state of confusion. Even more interestingly, the existence of such an interrelationship is not only recognized, as a significant aspect of the 'larger' system but it is now understood as to how such an interrelationship interacts one with the other.

We now understand that:

> Kant is a vital link in moving our perceptual understanding forward regarding the 'system' being filled with time and space to the 'the' system being filled with 'time and space' as well as the system being filled with 'the void of time and space', active observation, and passive observation. As such, 'time and space', 'the void of time and space', active observation, and passive observation, with the help of Kant, now have a location within which each dominates. And now, the understanding regarding the role of all four 'time and space', 'the void of time and space', active observation, passive observation as well as the understanding regarding the interrelationship between 'time and space', 'the void of time and space', active observation, and passive observation, no longer remain in a state of confusion. Even more interestingly, the existence of such an interrelationship is not only recognized, as a significant aspect of the 'larger' system but it is now understood how the four 'time and space', 'the void of time and space', active observation, and passive observation interact one with the other.

---

[1] U.S. News & World Report, Mysteries of History, Special Edition, 2001, p 33
[2] Paul Strathern, Wittgenstein in 90 Minutes, St. Edmunsbury Press, 1996, p. 7.
[3] Clarify: The system Kant proposed was limited since there are things within the system that are not known and can never be known. As an example, the universe could have developed in a direction which it did not and therefore we will never know what it could have become as opposed to what it was, what it is, what it will become, and what it could become.
[4] Paul Strathern, Wittgenstein in 90 Minutes, St. Edmunsbury Press, 1996, p. ????
[5] Tom Rockmore, Before and After Hegel, University of California Press, 1993, p 6.
[6] Tom Rockmore, Before and After Hegel, University of California Press, 1993, p 6.

The War & Peace of a New Metaphysical Perception

[7] Tom Rockmore, Before and After Hegel, University of California Press, 1993, p 7.
[8] Tom Rockmore, Before and After Hegel, University of California Press, p. 5, 1993
[9] Charles Seife, Zero – The Biography of a Dangerous Idea, Viking, 2000, p 25
[10] Bryan Magee, Confessions of a Philosopher, Random House, 1997, P 151
[11] Tom Rockmore, Before and After Hegel, University of California Press, 1993, p 30.
[12] See chapter 6: "The Social Pact," in Rousseau, The Social Contract, ed. And with an introduction by Lester G. Crocker (New York: Washington Square Books 1971), pp. 17 – 19.
[13] Tom Rockmore, Before and After Hegel, University of California Press, 1993, p 21.
[14] Charles Seife, Zero – The Biography of a Dangerous Idea, Viking, 2000, p 25
[15] Paul Strathern, Kant in 90 Minutes, Ivan I Dee, 1996 P 38
[16] Paul Strathern, Kant in 90 Minutes, Ivan I Dee, 1996, P 18
[17] Tom Rockmore, Before and After Hegel, University of California Press, 1993, p 61.
[18] Stephen Hawking, A Brief History of Time, Bantam Books, 1988, p. 174.
[19] Routledge Encyclopedia of Philosophy, Volume 5, P193, 1995.
[20] Antinomies: a pair of conflicting propositions for which equally cogent proofs can be given on either side.
[21] Kim, Jaegwon & Sosa, Ernest, A Companion To Metaphysics, Blackwell Publishers, p.258, 1995.
[22] Paul Strathern, Wittgenstein in 90 Minutes, St. Edmunsbury Press, 1996, p. 18.
[23] Strathern, Paul, Hegel in 90 Minutes, Ivan R. Dee, Chicago, 1997, p19.

Synopsis

Symbiotic Panentheism

❖

'being' *being* 'Being'

•

A Perceptual Shift for Humankind

Synopsis

Symbiotic Panentheism

- A Perceptual Shift for Humankind -

Introduction

Simply put, "symbiotic panentheism" follows the basic, most widely accepted concepts of present day science, religion, and philosophy. The following is the general flow symbiotic panentheism takes when integrated with the most generally accepted concepts held by today's sciences, religions or philosophies. Some items are embraced as basic components by only one of the three fields, some by two, some by all. The bold face concepts are what symbiotic panentheism adds to the general logic flow to cause a perceptual shift for the future of our species, society, and the individual.

The Whole and Panentheism

1. Reality exists.
2. The initiating force - causative factor - of reality is "The Whole."
3. The Whole is omnipresent; as such, **all things are in The Whole, including our known reality.**
4. The Whole is bigger than reality.
5. The Whole is omnipotent; **It has the power to create new, original knowledge.**
6. The Whole is omniscient; **It knows how to create more knowledge. It cannot create new, creative, untainted knowledge within Itself.**
7. The Whole is omnipresent; **It cannot create outside Itself.**

Symbiotic panentheism fully addresses the paradox of numbers five, six, and seven. Panentheism accepts the concepts of omnipotence, omnipresence, and omniscience while at the same time acknowledging the full significance of omnipotence, omnipresence, and omniscience by recognizing The Whole's ability to become even more so.

The Soul and Symbiosis

1. Humankind exists.
2. Humankind exists in the universe, in "reality."
3. The essence of the individual is not the body nor the brain.
4. The essence of the individual is the soul.
5. **The soul, being within reality, which in turn is within The Whole, is a part of The Whole.**
6. **The individual is not The Whole.**
7. **The individual is a part of The Whole.**
8. Reality separates the individual from The Whole and lies between the individual and The Whole.
9. Humankind, souls, are creative and can experience.
10. Soul separated from direct contact with The Whole can create and experience untainted by The Whole's knowledge.
11. Souls can learn and grow.

12. The Whole **can learn through the journey of souls.**
Under the "symbiotic" portion of symbiotic panentheism, the significance of the human species, the significance of the individual, is placed at the level of The Whole and given an importance to The Whole. Thus emerges the rationality for respect due to the individual. Symbiotic panentheism places the soul in a symbiotic relationship - a mutually beneficial, close association - with The Whole.

Human Significance

1. Humanity's perceptions of itself as a species and as individuals determine its behavior.
2. The higher the level of significance we have of ourselves, the higher the level of our behavior.
3. Predestination relieves us of responsibility.
4. Free will raises our level of responsibility.
5. **The level of perception we can assign to ourselves is to be able to have the free will to assist The Whole in the one thing The Whole cannot do as The Whole - grow.**
6. **The soul being The Whole but separated from The Whole (being non-omnipresent, non-omniscient, non-omnipotent) has the ability to learn, experience, and create isolated from The Whole.**
7. **The highest level of significance we can assign to ourselves is to help The Whole, ourselves, become even more omnipotent, omniscient, and omnipresent.**

Human significance now becomes something it has never before been. Human significance now becomes defined. Not only does it become defined, it now becomes defined as significant for it becomes significant beyond human needs. Human significance now becomes significant to The Whole Itself.

Social Ramifications

1. **The** essence of all individuals is the soul.
2. **The essence of all individuals is a part of The Whole, a piece of The Whole.**
3. All individuals are important to The Whole and deserve to be treated as such.
4. **The soul, a piece of The Whole, is important to and needed by The Whole.**
5. The individual, a piece of The Whole, deserves to be treated with the respect due to The Whole.
6. All individuals are equally important.
7. **The individual, The Whole, is not in a hierarchical relationship to itself.**

Symbiotic panentheism provides the logic needed to dismantle all hierarchical systems and perceptions of relative worth. Symbiotic panentheism eliminates the most fundamental hierarchical system created by humankind for humankind - the hierarchy system created between The Whole and humans. It eliminates the status levels between beings. Symbiotic panentheism does not destroy what humanity has; it adds to what humanity has. Symbiotic panentheism accepts the significance of The Whole to the individual and to the species. It also adds the significance of the individual and of the species to this one way concept of The Whole.

Through the fusion of panentheism and symbiosis, we form symbiotic panentheism, a philosophical, perceptual shift for the new millennium that actually defines a purpose for humanity, for the individual, for the environment, and for our relationship to The Whole. Under symbiotic panentheism, it is our job to see that The Whole grows. We have the free will to determine the direction The Whole grows. This is truly an awesome responsibility, an awesome task for humankind and for the individual.

However, just as children rise to the level of expectations we place upon them, humanity will rise to the level of expectations it places upon itself. There is little doubt that society, families, and individuals could use more human, humane, The Wholely compassion in their journeys. To begin to understand this logic, one must examine the four forms of theism and their treatment of the three most universally accepted characteristics of The Whole: omnipresence, omniscience, and omnipotence.

Omniscience

Atheism assigns the least knowledgeable form to The Whole. According to atheism, The Whole does not exist and The Whole as an entity has no knowledge. Pantheism enlarges The Whole's knowledge base over atheism. Under pantheism, The Whole and reality are one and the same size. The Whole has size and The Whole has knowledge. However, the knowledge has limits. The Whole is limited to the knowledge found within the universe, whatever that size may be. Classical or traditional theism enlarges The Whole's knowledge base over pantheism. Classical and traditional theism, however, hold that The Whole knows everything that has been known, is known or could be known. This places limits on The Whole. Since The Whole knows everything, it closes the door on the possibility of knowing what could be, but isn't, for all things.

Panentheism is in sync with classical or traditional theism in terms of what The Whole knows. But whereas classical and traditional theism puts an end to the concept of omniscience and leaves The Whole in a state of permanent equilibrium, panentheism goes on to expand The Whole's possible knowledge base through accepting the scientific principle that permanent equilibrium is an unnatural state - even for The Whole. Panentheism applies the concept of the growth of knowledge to The Whole. Of the four theisms, only panentheism assigns the complete characteristic of omniscience to The Whole, for it is the only theism to assign the knowledge of how The Whole gains more knowledge to grow.

Omnipotence

Atheism basically purports the concept that there is no The Whole. Since The Whole has no size, It has no power. The Whole is powerless. Pantheism magnifies The Whole's power over the perception of atheism. Within pantheism, The Whole and reality are one. The Whole has all the power of our universe and no more, for that is all there is. With the concept that The Whole is greater in size than reality, it follows that The Whole's power is greater than in the case of pantheism. Classical or traditional theism again increases The Whole's power by stating that The Whole is all-powerful; however, it limits The Whole's power to that of Its total power. Under classical and traditional theism, The Whole is all-powerful but is limited, for It is not powerful enough to become more so.

Panentheism magnifies The Whole's power above all theistic perceptions through incorporating the concept that if The Whole is truly all powerful, then The Whole has the power to use Its knowledge to become even more so. This is not a factor tied to a location in time, for time most probably is a factor of universes and realities - not The Whole. Time is the factor allowing the existence of the beginning-end concepts built into universes. On the other hand, The Whole, by definition, has no characteristic concept of beginning-end. Of the four theisms, only panentheism assigns the complete characteristic of omnipotence to The Whole, for it assigns the ability and power of The Whole to gain more knowledge.

Omnipresence

Again, atheism basically purports the concepts that there is no The Whole, The Whole is omnipresent, The Whole is infinitely small, and its nothingness can be found everywhere. The Whole's absence is everywhere. This is clearly the smallest form of The Whole. Pantheism enlarges The Whole over atheism by believing there is one The Whole and that The Whole and reality are one and the same size. The Whole has size and is limited to the size of reality, whatever that size may turn out to be. Classical or traditional theism enlarges The Whole over pantheism by stating that there is one The Whole and The Whole is greater in size than reality. Classical and traditional theism imply, however, that The Whole and reality are separate items from each other. The Whole transcends reality. The Whole is everything except reality.

Panentheism enlarges The Whole over classical or traditional theism. Panentheism purports that The Whole is omnipresent. The Whole incorporates everything; therefore, The Whole is everything and thus, there is no place for reality to be other than within The Whole Itself. Of the four theisms, only panentheism assigns the complete characteristic of omnipresence to The Whole, for it assigns not only an omnipresence incorporating all of our universe, our reality, but all realities that may exist and what lies beyond and between them.

Even more significantly, only symbiotic panentheism proceeds to allow for the expansion of the very characteristics of omnipotence and omniscience of The Whole that, in turn, through increased awareness, expands omnipresence itself by definition.

Omnipresence, omnipotence, and omniscience are three characteristics humanity, in general, wants or appears to want to affix to The Whole. Of the four theisms, only panentheism manages to do so in total. Panentheism is the foundation for symbiotic panentheism, for without the "panentheism" the "symbiosis" becomes illogical. Symbiotic panentheism establishes a metaphysical model that accepts, while at the same time dismantles, the paradoxes of omnipresence, omniscience, and omnipotence. In addition, it is a model that circumvents the state of permanent equilibrium we have assigned to The Whole, a state we often refer to as stagnation.

Panentheism, defined as the location of reality in terms of The Whole's location, is seemingly insignificant, but the subtlety leads to the initiation of enormous perceptual and behavioral shifts for our species, society, the environment, and the individual. Understanding the differences between the four basic perceptions of a causative force (atheism, pantheism, classical or traditional theism, and panentheism) allows us to move forward and begin the examination of symbiotic panentheism in particular.

The Whole

Whatever one professes, humans have always oriented their philosophical discussions around The Whole or The Whole. Whatever one's belief, the fact remains that humans have, to our knowledge, always conceptualized The Whole or a form of The Whole in some sense and, therefore, perhaps this small seed, this nugget of the universality of humans, is true. Is The Whole the originator of reality? The original force? The source of the beginning? Whatever one's belief, there are only two premises with which to identify: either there is the whole, an originator, an original force, a source of a beginning, or there is not. In all of our observations within reality, there is only one observation a this point in time that we cannot directly tie to having a beginning, an origination, and that is reality.

There are two options to consider. The first option is the premise that if all things, except reality, appear to have an identifiable beginning, then reality must also have an identifiable beginning and thus, an originator, Creator, The Whole. Another way of saying this is that all things in reality appear to be affected by time and thus, it is most probable that reality itself is affected by time or, in essence, most probably has a beginning and an end.

The other option is to reject the logic of option one and embrace option two. The second option is the premise that reality itself is different from everything within it and has no origination; in other words, it has no beginning. Thus, one would accept the concept that The Whole, an originator, is illogical. This thought process would allow one to reject the inference to which all of our observations point. It would allow one to conclude and embrace the direct opposite inference that there is no The Whole or originator of reality. Reality has always existed.

The premise that reality had a beginning, that there is a creative originating force, that there is the whole to reality is supported by an almost infinite amount of direct observations and logic. The premise that reality had no beginning, that there is no creative originating force, that there is no The Whole, is supported by nothing we have observed before - no observations and no logic. Is the concept of reality having no beginning possible? Certainly anything we conjure up in our minds is "possible" but not probable.

Assuming we accept the premise of the existence of an originator of reality, an original force, a source of the beginning, we can then move on to examine the concept of reality, where reality fits into consciousness, and where humanity, as well as other forms of consciously aware beings, fit into all of this. In other words, where you and where I fit into the grand scheme of "it all." The picture we have of The Whole is still out of focus. As time passes and our knowledge expands, we will gain greater resolution regarding our observations. In the meantime, keep in mind that the Creator of reality is the Creator of reality and will remain so regardless of what we do or wish to believe.

We cannot create a creator. We cannot insist that a creator is whom we have, through time and custom, drawn it to be, but rather, we must understand that whom we have drawn the Creator to be, through time and custom, was what we needed It to be in order to define our niche in reality. The Creator is what the Creator is to ourselves because we needed It to be such in order to find comfort in our lack of knowledge and to assuage our fears of what we perceive to be mortality.

Religion and science orient around one universe. Science and religion still have not fully accepted the concept of other life forms and have not done so because they do not know how to fuse them into their doctrines of classical or traditional theism. Symbiotic panentheism can help them with that very problem without destroying their essence, identity or uniqueness. It is only under classical or traditional theism that we could assign a greater significance to ourselves, to our home, and to our planet over other entities and their homes or planets.

With increased knowledge (omniscience) comes increased power (omnipotence) and as knowledge grows, so grows awareness (omnipresence). Growth, equilibrium, decline - three choices we can comprehend for the state of The Whole. Scientifically speaking, permanent equilibrium appears to be an unnatural state of being. Religiously speaking, an omnipotent, omniscient, omnipresent The Whole appears to be a contradiction unless it is omnipotent, omniscient, and omnipresent enough to become even more so. Therefore, permanent equilibrium is not an option. Being tied to the whole that exists in a state of decline is not a preferable or advantageous choice to bestow upon our Creator. The only state of being we can comprehend for The Whole is that of a growing The Whole.

Thus develops the symbiotic relationship aspect - a mutually beneficial relationship between us and our Creator. We hope it is mutually beneficial, for it could just as well be a mutually destructive relationship depending upon the actions we take under free will. This is precisely where our responsibility lies. We, along with others, have the responsibility to develop the type of The Whole that exists.

In a symbiotic relationship, beneficial or detrimental contributions are two possibilities that could exist between two identities. Understanding our significance in reality and to its Creator would definitely help us understand what actions we, humans with freewill, should take while functioning within reality. Our actions affect not only The Whole but, in essence, ourselves. Under the model of symbiotic panentheism, nothing, not even the annihilation of our reality's physical mechanism, can diminish our purpose for existence. Nothing, not even total annihilation of our reality itself, can destroy our accomplishments as souls, for they transcend reality and embrace - fuse - with the very essence of The Whole.

Three Ultimate Paradoxes

1. Being omnipotent - all-powerful - but not having the power to become more so.
2. Being omnipresent - everywhere - but limited within the confines that already exist.
3. Being omniscient - knowing everything - but not knowing how to learn more.

The Creator of reality did not create these paradoxes. We, humanity, defined these paradoxes ourselves.

We, humanity, give them a life of their own. And then, we, humanity, perpetuate our irrationality into absolutisms. Eliminating the paradoxes of omnipotence, omnipresence, and omniscience does not alter or call for the elimination of our rich history of traditions or beliefs. Eliminating these three paradoxes expands our view of our pl ace in the universe, our purpose in the scheme of things, and our tolerance for uniqueness. Expansion of our pre sent concepts of omnipotence, omnipresence, and omniscience into a concept that can become even more so does not bring down the foundations of our society; rather, it provides a foundation to our foundation. Omnipotence, omnipresence, and omniscience are paradoxes only because we have made them so and continue to perpetuate these concepts.

Panentheism, the picture grows:

> A-theism: Our universe, reality, is alone.
>
> Pan-theism: Our universe, reality, is not alone; something else exists within it.
>
> Pan-en-theism: Our universe, reality, is part of a greater Reality.

Are classical and traditional theisms complete theisms? No, they are just theisms waiting for a prefix.

"Symbiotic" is the portion that provides the significance. It provides the other half to, "The Whole is significant to humanity." The other half is, "Intelligences within realities, humanity, the individual, is significant to The Whole."

We have the free will to recognize our power - our significance - and dismantle the hierarchical and, therefore, oppressive systems we have created. We are all a part of The Whole and continually contribute to The Whole's knowledge and awareness. We create what we choose to create. Indeed, we all have an awesome responsibility.

Index

V – Volume
T – Tractate

Books

0500 BC – 1804 AD: The Distant Past V1
1831 AD – 1998 AD: The Recent Past V2
2003 AD –   The Future V3

Terms & Contents

- A -

A 'New Metaphysical Perception' regarding Zeno's paradox: V1, T1
A Foundation V1, T6
A misconception of determinism V1, T4
A new meaning of the term 'everything' V1, T6
Absolute Zero Point of Abstraction V1, T6
Absolute Zero point of abstraction, The V1, T6
Abstract Functionality V1, T1
Abstract Functionality V2, T9
Abstract V1, T1
Abstract V2, T9
Abstraction and the void V2, T10
Abstractual hedonism V1, T2
Active Observation within Passive Observation V3
Active observing V1, T6
Adjacent actions of multiplicity V1, T3
Advantage of diversity, The V2, T11
An alternative solution to Russell's Paradox V2, T9
Analytic versus Synthetic 'a priori' V1, T6
Anti-energy V2, T10
Antinomies Active Observation V1, T6
Anti-something V2, T10
Anti-void V2, T10
Aristotelian Points V1, T4
Atheism V2, T12

- B -

Being a Part of 'Being' is not a new idea V1, T1
Being right V2, T11

The War & Peace of a New Metaphysical Perception

Boethius' metaphysical system and perpetual historical acceptance V1, T4
Boethius' metaphysical system and social acceptance V1, T4
Boethius' metaphysical system and why it is we have not presently discarded such a system metaphysical perception V2, T8
Boethius' metaphysical systemV1, T4
Book of Divine Foreknowledge, The V1, T3
Boredom and knowledge V1, T6
Boundary separating the causal and the non-causal, The V1, T6

- C -

Calculus is but a tool – it does not eliminate what is V1, T1
Cardinal Sequencing V1, T3
Cartesian
Cartesian system V1, T2
Cartesian system V1, T6
Cartesian Systems V1, T2
Cartesian V1, T2
Cartesian V1, T6
Causal V1, T6
Causal, The V1, T6
Caution #1: This section is intended only for the mathematically and scientifically inclined V2, T9
Caution #2: This section is intended only for the religiously inclined V2, T9
Caution #3: This section is intended only for the philosophically inclined V2, T9
Centricism V1, T4
Change V1, T6
Changing changeless system V2, T7
Classical and traditional theism V1, V2, T12
Coherency of time V2, T8
Conclusion: The Peer Review V3, T19
Concrete Functionality V1, T1
Concrete Functionality V2, T9
Concrete V1, T1
Concrete V2, T9
Concrete/Physical Functionality V1, T1
Confinement is confinement / the concept of Cartesian V1, T2
Constancy of consistency V2, T8
Constancy of sequentiality V2, T8
Constancy of time V2, T8
Constancy of time verses the Variability of time, The V2, T8
Constant (k) variable, The V2, T8
Constant factor of variability, The V2, T8
Constant of physicality V2, T7
Constant of physicality V2, T8
Constant variable of physicality, The V2, T8
Core: Omniscience, The V1, T5
Creating the paradox of a Physical System V2, T10
Creator V2, T12

- D -

Dance of the angels, The V1, T2
Death of God leads to the death of Metaphysics, The V2, T7
Death of God, The V1, T6
Defining theodicy V1, T5
Desire for Homogeneity, The V2, T11
Determinism V1, T3
Distance equals time V2, T8
Diversity and the disadvantaged V2, T12
Diversity and the right to be who you are – freedom V2, T11
Divine Foreknowledge V1, T3
Divine foreknowledge, predestination, pre-destination, and determinism versus free will V1, T4
Doppler affects of time V2, T8
Dualist is right but the dualist is wrong, The V2, T11

- E -

Einstein introduces the second mirror: The 'i' inversion   V2, T8
Einstein's mirror revisited V2, T8
Einstein's mirror V2, T8
Either/Or V2, T11
Endless Repetition V1, T6
Energy V2, T10
Equality of 'relativistic 1st principle,' The V1, T2
Equality of principle V1, T2
Error through the active process of extrapolation as opposed to the passive process of definition V1, T5
Errors created through the passive process of definition V1, T5
Everything V1, T6
Examination of Contemporary thought V2, T12
Expanding knowing revisited V2, T8
Expanding knowing V2, T7
Experiential permutations V2, T8

- F -

Finite finites V1, T2
Finite infinities V1, T2
First cause becomes a redundancy, The V2, T7
First cause V2, T7
First Shell V1, T5
First shell: Omnipotence and Omnipresence, The V1, T5
Formulation V1, T3
Foundation V1, T6
Foundationless V1, T6
Four forms of action, The V1, T4
Free will V1, T3

The War & Peace of a New Metaphysical Perception

Function of 'nothing,' The V2, T10
Function of something, The V2, T10
Functionality of action V1, T4
Fundamental building block of the abstract V1, T4
Fundamental building block of the physical V1, T4
Fusion of: 0 / ∞ and ∞ / 0, The V1, T6
Future does not exist, The V1, T6

- **G** -

God does not change V1, T6
God: Nietzsche is dead and for that matter Hegel is also dead V2, T7
Goodbye concrete, Hello abstract V2, T8
Greek concept of increments, The V1, T1
Growth V2, T12

- **H** -

Hegel introduces the first mirror: Inverse physicality V2, T8
Hegel, Nietzsche and God are all wrong V2, T7
Hegel: Metaphysics is dead V2, T7
Hegel's 'open' dynamic non-Cartesian system V1, T4
Hegel's mirror V2, T8
Hierarchal systems V2, T12
Historical conflict expanded, The V2, T11
History's Vector V3, T18
Homogeneity V2, T11
How something, which is unchangeable, can change and remain unchangeable V1, T6
Human Significance V2, T12

- **I** -

Idea leads to the concept that 'first cause' is not necessary but the whole is necessary, The V2, T7
Illusion V1, T1
Illusion V2, T8
Illusion V2, T9
Imaginary Numbers V2, T8
Incoherency of individuality V2, T8
Incoherency of time V2, T8
Incremental concentric circles V1, T2
Incrementalism and the Individual V1, T1
Incrementalism V1, T1
Incrementalism V2, T9
Independent dependency V2, T7
Individuality V1, T3
Infinite finites V1, T2
Infinite infinities V3, T17

516

Infinite infinities V1, T2
Infinity
Infinity divided by one V2, T8
Infinity V2, T10
InfinityV2, T8
Influence of fear, The V2, T10
Internationality: the need 'for' a location of determinismV1, T4
Intricacies of concentric circles, The V1, T2
Introduction / Cartesian V1, T6
Introduction / Dimensions V2, T8
Introduction /Relativistic 1st Principles V1, T2
Introduction V1, T1 Zeno's paradoxes V1, T1
Introduction V1, T2
Introduction V1, T5
Introduction V2, T7
Introduction to ∞ / 1 and 1 V2, T8
Introduction: 'Nothingness' is an integral part of it all V2, T9
Introduction V1, T4
Inverse proportionality V1, T4

- K -

Kant's 'closed' dynamic Cartesian system V1, T4
Knowledge V2, T8
Knowledge: The universal building block V2, T8

- L -

Lack of a Foundation, The V2, T7
Land of Limited Abstracts: Infinite Finites, The V1, T2
Land of Unlimited Abstracts: Finite Infinities, The V1, T2
Land without the concepts 'before' and 'after', The V2, T7
Leibniz and the error of addition V1, T5
Let me buy you a beer V2, T12
Letting go V1, T3
Limited abstracts V1, T2
Linear V2, T7
Location of 'imperfection, The' V1, T5
Location of 'perfection', The V1, T5
Location of Determinism, The V1, T4
Location of Free Will, The V1, T4
Locations for actionsV1, T4

- M -

Matter V2, T10
Matter/energy V2, T10

Metaphysical Engineering V3, T13
Metaphysical mirror V2, T8
Metaphysical model V2, T12
Metaphysical perception V2, T12
Metaphysics and Cartesianism revisited V1, T6
Metaphysics V2, T12
Mimesis V1, T2
Minimal extreme of knowing V1, T5
Misnomer of 'free will', The V1, T4
Missing foundation, The V1, T6
Monist is wrong but the monist is right, The V2, T11
Morality versus categorical imperatives V1, T6
Multi-dimensional Combinations of Tessellations V1, T6
Multiplicity of abstraction V2, T10
Multiplicity of individuality, The V1, T1
Multiplicity of individuality, The V2, T10
Multiplicity V1, T1
Multiplicity V2, T7
Multiplicity V2, T9

- N -

Need for 'a' whole remains, The V2, T7
Need for 'a' whole, The V1, T6
Newtonian 'i' - Velocity Equals Distance Divided by Time / Introduction, The V2, T8
Nietzsche: God is dead V2, T7
Non-Cartesainism V2, T7
Non-Cartesian system V1, T6
Non-Cartesian V1, T6
Non-Cartesian V2, T7
Non-Causal V1, T6
Non-causal, The V1, T6
Non-centricism V1, T4
Nothing V2, T10
Nothing: the need 'for' a location of nothing V1, T4
Nothing' is not a 'thing V2, T10
Nothingness V2, T10

- O -

Oil and WaterV1, T4
Omni-benevolence V1, T5
Omnipotence V2, T12
Omnipotence V1, T5
Omnipresence V2, T12
Omnipresence V1, T5
Omniscience V1, V2, T12
Omniscience V1, T5
On 'being' *being* 'Being': Cartesianism 'within' Non-Cartesianism V3

On 'being' *being:* Non-Cartesianism - Active Observation V2
On 'being': Cartesianism - Passive Observation V1
One divided by infinity V2, T8
One equals infinity divided by infinity V2, T8
One equals zero divided by zero V2, T8
One V2, T8
Our point of departure lays in the heart of metaphysics itself V2, T12

- P -

Panentheism V2, T12
Pantheism V2, T12
Paradox of 'i', The V2, T8
Paradox of Cartesian Systems and non-Cartesian Systems, The V1, T2
Paradox of Cartesian Systems, The V1, T2
Paradox of Either/Or, The V2, T11
Paradox of free will and divine foreknowledge, The V1, T4
Paradox of nothing having no function, The V2, T10
Paradox of omni benevolence, The V1, T5
Paradox of seamlessness and multiplicity, The V1, T1
Paradox of seamlessness and multiplicity, The V2, T9
Paradox of the 'unknowable', The V1, T6
Paradox of the death of 'knowing', The V2, T7
Passive observing V1, T6
Past does not exist, The V1, T6
Perceptual confinement V1, T2
Perceptual knowing V1, T5
Permanent equilibrium V2, T12
Physical hedonism V1, T2
Point – individuality, The V1, T1
Point – Individuality, The V2, T12
Potentiality: the need 'for' a location of free will V1, T4
Predestination V1, T3
Preface: An Alien Conversation V1
Preface: How to regain the love of wisdom V3
Preface: There is a little philosopher in all of us V1
Prioritized natural emergence of the first two categorical imperatives, The V1, T6
Puristic non-relativistic values of abstraction V1, T5
Purpose V3, T16

- Q -

Quagmire of diversity, The V2, T11

- R -

Raising metaphysics up from the dead V1, T6
Random Sequencing/factorial V1, T3
Rationalizing the irrational V1, T4
The limits of language V1, T4
'real' and the 'real illusion' illustrated, The V1, T1
'real' and the 'real' illusion, The V2, T8
Real Illusion V1, T1
Real illusion V2, T8
Real Illusion V2, T9
'real' illusion, The V2, T8
Real Numbers / The Tunnel of Abstraction V2, T8
Real numbers V2, T8
Real V1, T1
Real V2, T9
'real', The V2, T8
Reality V1, T2
Relativistic 1st principles V1, T2
Removing a piece of Randomness V1, T3
Removing the physical while leaving the abstract intact V1, T1
Reopening the walls of confinement V1, T2
Resolving Kant's four antinomies V1, T6
Resolving the issue of 'a' cartesian system composed of Infinite Finites V1, T2
Resolving the issue of a categorical imperative with a new metaphysical perception V1, T6
Resolving the issue of a void with a new metaphysical perception V2, T10
Resolving the issue of active observation with a new metaphysical perception V2, T7
Resolving the issue of free will with a new metaphysical perception V1, T4
Resolving the issue of passive observation with a new metaphysical perception V1, T2
Resolving the issue of separation through exclusion with a new metaphysical perception V2, T9
Resolving the issue of the abstract with a new metaphysical perception V1, T1
Resolving the issue of the conflict between homogeneity and diversity V2, T12
Resolving the issue of the square root of the distance divided by the square root of the time with a new metaphysical perception V2, T8
Resolving the issue of theodicy with a new metaphysical perception V1, T5
Resolving the issue of velocity equals distance divided by time with a new metaphysical perception V2, T8
Responsibility V1, V3, T14
Reversing perceptions – counter view V1, T1
Reversing perceptions – counter view V2, T12
Right 'to be' versus submission, The V2, T11
Role of guilt, The V2, T11

- S -

Scholarly confusion regarding Zeon's Paradoxes, The V1, T1
Seamlessness V1, T1
Seamlessness V2, T9
Second Shell V1, T5
Second Shell: Answers to three questions, The V1, T5

Index

Significance of Russell's paradox as discussed in a simulated conversation between Russell and Wittgenstein V2, T9
Significance V2, T12
Silent conspiracy of collusion V1, T1
Silent conspiracy of collusion V2, T9
Simplicity itself: The end of the beginning V2, T9
Singularity of location V1, T1
Singularity of location V2, T9
Singularity of Multiplicity V2, T11
Singularity V2, T7
Sins of the father in regards to the son, The V2, T11
Size of an infinite void, The V2, T10
Size V2, T12
So, do we need a 'system'? V1, T6
Social Ramifications V2, T12
Some thoughts expounded by Boethius V1, T4
Something reducing to a void V2, T10
Soul and Symbiosis, The V2, T12
Soul V2, T12
Space and time V2, T10
Square root of Einstein's equations: 'i', The V2, T8
Stagnation V2, T12
Sub unit of knowing V1, T5
Symbiosis V2, T12
Symmetry emerges out of a void V2, T10

- T -

Taser, The V2, T8
Wittgensteining of Russell, The V2, T9
Theodicy V1, T5
Theoretical metaphysics now evolves into: 'Being' *being* 'being' versus 'being' being 'Being' V2, T10
Thesis, antithesis, synthesis V2, T7
Third Shell V1, T5
Three forms of action V1, T4 Limits placed upon Boethius V1, T4
Three Ultimate Paradoxes V2, T12
Time and distance both divided by 1 V2, T8
Timeless sequencing V2, T10
Total annihilation V2, T12
Totality/Whole V1, T1
Totality/Whole V2, T9
Tractate 1: 500 BC The Error of Zeno: Resolving the problem of Abstraction V1, T1
Tractate 10: 1976 AD The Error of Heidegger: Resolving the problem of The Void of the Void V2, T10
Tractate 11: The Error of Philosophy: Resolving the problem of Monism and Dualism V2, T11
Tractate 12: 1998 AD: Resolving the problem of Cartesianism and non-Cartesianism V2, T12
Tractate 13: Metaphysical System #28: Introducing the problem of Metaphysical Systems 7 & 9 V3, T13
Tractate 14: Principle Three: Introducing the problem of Principles One and Two V3, T14

Tractate 15: Ockham's Razor: Introducing the problem of Reductionism V3, T15
Tractate 16:Wrong Again: Introducing the problem of Being Right V3, T16
Tractate 17: The Beginning: Introducing the problem of The End V3, T17
Tractate 18: Why Now: Introducing the problem of History's Vector V3, T18
Tractate 2: 322 BC The Error of Aristotle: Resolving the problem of Cartesian Systems V1, T2
Tractate 3: 525 AD The Error of Boethius: Resolving the problem of Free Will V1, T3
Tractate 4: 1543 AD The Error of Copernicus: Resolving the problem of Centricism V1, T4
Tractate 5: 1716 AD The Error of Leibniz: Resolving the problem of Theodicy V1, T5
Tractate 6: 1804 AD The Error of Kant: Resolving the problem of Universal Ethics V1, T6
Tractate 7: 1831 AD The Error of Hegel: Resolving the problem of Non-Cartesian Systems V2, T7
Tractate 8: 1955 AD The Error of Einstein – Resolving the problem of Physical Time V2, T8
Tractate 9: 1970 AD The Error of Russell: Resolving the problem of Separation Through Exclusion V2, T9
Tri-linear V2, T7
Truth 'I exist.' vs. the truth 'You exist', The V1, T1
Tunnel of abstraction V2, T8
Tunnel of perception, The V2, T8

- U -

Understanding how 'a' 'whole' can be greater than the sum of its parts V1, T2
Understanding Russell's paradox V2, T9
Understanding V3, T15
Understanding V3, T15
Universal building block V2, T8
Unlimited abstracts V1, T2

- V -

Variability of time V2, T8
Virgin consciousness V1, T2
Virgin physical life V1, T4
Virgin physicality V1, T1
Void of infinity, The V2, T10
Void V2, T10

- W -

Wall of perception, The V1, T4
What 'has been': Divine foreknowledge - A location for 'Being' – the whole V1, T4
What 'is being': Determinism - A location for *being* – action, process/reality – the universe V1, T4
What 'is':Pre-destination/predestination - A location for being – existence of existence V1, T4
What 'will be': Free will - A location for 'being' – individuality V1, T4
What does it mean V2, T8
What happens to nothingness? V2, T7

What happens to potentiality? V2, T7
What is a lack of a void V2, T10
What is a void V2, T10
What is exists V1, T6
What it all means to humanity/all forms of virgin consciousness universally V1, T2
What society 'owes' entities of knowing V2, T12
What the void of space 'means' V2, T10
What the void of time 'means' V2, T10
Where a void cannot be found (and why it cannot be found there) V2, T10
Where one can find a void of a void V2, T10
Where one can find a void of space V2, T10
Where one can find a void of time V2, T10
Where one can find a void V2, T10
Who owns the body V2, T12
Whole and Panentheism, The V2, T12
Whole does change, The V2, T7
Whole does not change, The V1, T6
Whole V2, T12
Whole versus the sub-element/the individual, The V2, T7
Whole, The V2, T12
Whole, The V2, T12
Whole, The V2, T7
Working backward to Zeno V1, T1

- Y -

You are that of which you are a part V2, T7

- Z -

Zeno Himself Says It V1, T1
Zeno: The appearance of the 'real' and the 'real illusion' V1, T1
Zeno's paradox of Motion revisited V1, T1
Zeno's paradox of space/distance V1, T1
Zero divided by infinity versus infinity divided by zero V2, T8
Zero equals zero V2, T8
Zero V2, T10
Zero V2, T8